KU-598-478

Croatia

the Bradt Travel Guide

Piers Letcher

Updated by Rudolph Abraham

edition
4

www.bradtguides.com

Bradt Travel Guides Ltd, UK
The Globe Pequot Press Inc, USA

SERBIA

HUNGARY

Vukovar

Daij

Beli Manastir
Darda

OSIJEK

Vinkovci

Eastern Slavonia

Valpovo

Našice
Gorjani
Dakovo

Slavonski Brod

Sava

Visit the restored town of Vukovar, which was caught up in the 1991 Croatia–Serbia war
page 177

Slatina

Orahovica

Nova Gradiška

Superb bird-watching opportunities in the Lonjsko Polje swamplands
page 164

Virovitica

Daruvar

Novska

B i l o G o r a

Virje

Take a boat tour of UNESCO-listed Plitvice Lakes National Park
page 158

Koprivnica

Bjelovaro

Kutina

Ivanić-Grad

The remote North Velebit National Park is home to bears, wild boar & lynx
page 226

Varaždin

Ivanec

Dugo Selo

Sisak

Una

Trek or climb among Paklenica National Park's limestone gorges
page 254

Zelina

CROATIA

Petrinja

Glina

Soak up summer life on Zagreb's pavement cafés
page 73

ZAGREB

Karlovac

Slunj

Titova Korenica

Kulen Vakuf

Gračac

Knin

LJUBLJANA

Ogulin

Otočac

M a l a K a p e l a

Perušić

Udbina

Benkovac

Hike through fields of wild flowers to the peak of Veliki Risnjak, Risnjak National Park
page 223

SLOVENIA

Ravna Gora

Senj

Gospić

Karlobag

Gračac

Nin

Zadar

Crikvenica

Pag

Olib

Wander the steep cobbled streets of picture-perfect Rovinj
page 187

RIJEKA

Krk

Baška

Rab

Molat

Dugi Otok

Opatija

I s t r a

Pazin

Labin

Cres

Unije

Lošinj

Poreč

Vodnjan

Pula

Rovinj

Visit one of the world's best-preserved Roman amphitheatres at Pula
page 196

SARAJEVO

MONTENEGRO

PODGORICA

Visit Diocletian's Roman Palace at Split
page 286

Stay inside the extraordinary walled city of Dubrovnik
page 309

Marvel at Trogir's UNESCO-listed Renaissance & Gothic palaces
page 277

Find your own secluded beach on the island of Korčula or explore Korčula Old Town
pages 358 & 361

See Mljet National Park's azure-blue saltwater lakes
page 349

Dinara Planina

Imotski

Drvenik

Ploče

Ston

Slano

Dubrovnik

Cavtat

Orebić

Pelješac

Mljet

Sinj

SPLIT

Trogir

Šibenik

Vodice

Supetar

Brač

Bol

Stari grad

Hvar

Blato

Korčula

Korčula

Lastovo

Vis

A d r i a t i c   S e a

Bradt

N

0   50km

0   50 miles

KEY

■ Capital city
● Other city
○ Main town
○ Other town
✈ Airport
━━ Main road
━━ Other road
━━ Railway
─·─ International boundary

Croatia
Don't
miss...

Zagreb
St Mark's Church and its
unmistakable gaudy roof
(CNTB) page 106

National Parks
Hiking in North Velebit
National Park
(RA/Alamy) page 226

Ancient ruins
Split's Palace of
Diocletian
(H/SS) page 286

Medieval cities
Korčula
(SV/SS) page 358

**Stunning
coastline**
Kornati
Archipelago
(H/SS) page 273

Zagreb's twin-spire cathedral
(CNTB) page 110

top   Botanical Gardens, Zagreb (DA) page 108

above   Pick up supplies for a picnic at Dolac, Zagreb's huge daily market (DA) page 81

right   The funicular provides a handy shortcut to Zagreb's *Gornji Grad* (Old Town) (CNTB) page 103

below   Street entertainers on Jelačić Square, Zagreb (SV/SS) page 102 *above* Onofrio's Great Fountain in Dubrovnik dates from the 15th-century (CNTB) page 331

below Šibenik's 16th-century St Jacob's Cathedral (CNTB) page 264

AUTHOR

Born and educated in the UK, **Piers Letcher** has lived in France for close to 30 years. He has had 17 books, more than a thousand newspaper and magazine articles and hundreds of photographs published. From the mid nineties, he spent several years as a speechwriter at the United Nations in Geneva, before returning to his freelance career in 2002. He is the author of *Eccentric France* and *Dubrovnik: The Bradt City Guide*, co-author of *Zagreb: The Bradt City Guide* and contributes irregularly to the *Guardian Unlimited*.

UPDATER

Rudolf Abraham (*www.rudolfabraham.co.uk*) is an award-winning writer and photographer whose work and love of travel have taken him from the Balkans to eastern Turkey, Central Asia and Patagonia. He first visited Croatia in 1998, lived in Zagreb from 1999 to 2001, and continues to make several trips a year to his favourite country in Europe. His books include hiking guides to Croatia, Montenegro and Torres del Paine national park in Chile.

AUTHOR'S STORY

I was enormously fortunate to meet Hilary Bradt in 1986, as it gave me the excuse to spend a year writing the Bradt guide to Yugoslavia. Back in those days, Hilary still marked up all the proofs herself, and it was a red-faced moment for a young writer to have to deal with comments in the margin such as 'Purple prose!'. It was a learning experience, and one I've been very grateful for over the past two million words or so: thank you, Hilary.

After a long interval – paying rent, that kind of thing – I returned to the Bradt stable in 2002 and have spent much of my time since researching, writing about, and travelling in Croatia. It's a highly addictive place, not just for tourism but for what makes any country worth visiting: the people, the unexpected details, the moments of pure wonder.

As a guidebook author, of course, it's never as much fun as people imagine. Which is why – in the name of research – I've done things in Croatia such as breaking a tooth trying to eat a decorative gingerbread heart; being escorted around an all-naturist hotel; or bursting into a family's front room, on the assumption that their simple dwelling was part of an anthropological museum village.

On one occasion I was trying to get back into Croatia – having somehow slipped into Slovenia on a back road – when I was caught at an illegal border crossing. It didn't help that excessive heat had caused a bottle of home-distilled spirits to explode in the boot of the car. Fortunately, every guidebook writer's most useful local language phrase – 'I am writing a book about your wonderful country' – did the trick and got me off the hook.

Whilst none of these things should happen to you, I hope you'll get as much pleasure from Croatia as it's given me over the years.

PUBLISHER'S FOREWORD   *Adrian Phillips, Publishing Director*

Croatia has come a long way since Piers Letcher wrote the Bradt guide to Yugoslavia back in 1989. A country as popular as Croatia needs an expert author – or in our case two. Piers is one of our most-praised writers: travellers love his informal style combined with meticulous research and insider observations. Rudolf Abraham knows Croatia equally well, so we were delighted he could team up with Piers to update this fourth edition.

Fourth edition May 2010
First published 2003

Bradt Travel Guides Ltd, 23 High Street, Chalfont St Peter, Bucks SL9 9QE, England
www.bradtguides.com
Published in the USA by The Globe Pequot Press Inc, 246 Goose Lane,
PO Box 480, Guilford, Connecticut 06475-0480

Text copyright © 2010 Piers Letcher
Maps copyright © 2010 Bradt Travel Guides Ltd
Photographs copyright © 2010 Individual photographers
Editorial Project Manager: Emma Thomson

British Library Cataloguing in Publication Data
A catalogue record for this book is available from the British Library
ISBN-13: 978 1 84162 319 1

Photographs AgeFotostock/Superstock (AF/SS), Croatian National Tourist Board (CNTB), Daniel Austin (DA), Hemis.fr/Superstock (H/SS), ImageBroker/FLPA (I/FLPA), Jon Smith (JS), Jurgen & Christine Sohns/FLPA (J&CS/FLPA), Mike Lane/ FLPA (ML/FLPA), Paul Hobson/FLPA (PH/FLPA), Photononstop/Superstock (P/SS), Pictures Colour Library/Alamy (PCL/Alamy), Rudolf Abraham (RA/Alamy), Steve Vidler/Superstock (SV/SS), Stuart Black/The Travel Library (SB/TTL), Travel Library Limited/Superstock (TLL/SS)
Front cover Island view with wild flowers, Primosten, Dalmatia (SB/TTL)
Back cover Diocletian's Palace, Split (JS); Pag Island (CNTB)
Title page Woman in doorway (CNTB), Aerial view of Dubrovnik (JS), Plitvice Lakes National Park (AF/SS)

Maps Greg Best, Malcolm Barnes (colour map)

Typeset from the author's disc by Wakewing, High Wycombe
Production managed by Jellyfish Print Solutions and manufactured in Italy

Acknowledgements

For this fourth edition, first and sincerest thanks must go to Rudolf Abraham, whose unrivalled knowledge of the country and tremendous efforts on the ground ensured that this edition of the guide is as up to date as it can possibly be. Rudolf would like to thank the Croatian National Tourist Board and Charisma PR for making one of his visits to Croatia in 2009 possible; and as always his wife Ivana, who read through and commented on the language section.

For their help in Croatia, thanks must go to Dubravka Mičić, Amelia Tomašević and Iva Čaleta at the Zagreb Tourist Board; Lidija Mišćin and Vlatka Marić at the Zagreb County Tourist Board; and Ingrid Lovrić and Krešo Jakubak at the Medvednica Nature Park. For their assistance, I'd also like to thank Silvija Berković, Vladimir Crnković, Ivana Čukvina Nikolić, David Frayer, Vladimir Fumić, Gary Jarvis and Renata, Edo Kletečki, Deana Kovačec, Sanjin Mihelić, Mario Mirković, Stuart Panes, Borivoj Popovčak, Jakov Radovčić, Mirjana Randić, Ivana Rončević, Darinka Širola, Sanda Sokol, Petra Tramišćak and Vesna Vrabec in Zagreb; Duda Dravica Modriča in Velika Gorica; Krešimir Režek and Želko Škiljan in Plešivica; Dina Begić, Anđd-đelka Mađd-đar and Dubravka Lapčić in Karlovac; Branka Tropp, Tanja Bunjevac and Elizabeta Dolenc in Varaždin; Sandra Bojić in Krapina; and Kristijan Kovačić and Rudi Gruba in the Med-đimurje.

For their feedback and input, I'm grateful to Zeljka Jelavić (Etnografski Muzej Zagreb), Vlasta Krklec (Museum of Krapina Neanderthal Man), Emilio Mendušić (Sokolarski Centar Dubrava), Rudi Grula (Međimurje County Tourist Board), Aleksandra Kolić Puškarić (Turistička Zajednica Grada Ogulina), Turistička Zajednica Grad Karlovac, Joško Matušan, Richard Ellis, Fritz Frigan, Judy Johnson and Katherine Ljubojević.

A heartfelt thank you, too, to all the people whose names I never caught, who offered help, hospitality and kindness along the way.

I'd also like to thank Hamadoun Touré and Doreen Bogdan at ITU for having me back; and of course Brice and Alec.

Finally, as always, I am indebted to Sarah Parkes (my sun and moon) for her kindness and thoughtfulness, her company and help in researching this new edition, and her generous spirit.

Contents

FEEDBACK REQUEST

At Bradt Travel Guides, we're well aware that guidebooks start to go out of date on the day they're published – and that you, our readers, are out there in the field, doing research of your own. You'll find out before us when a fine new family-run hotel opens or a favourite restaurant changes hands and goes downhill. So why not write to us and tell us about your experiences? We'll happily include you in the acknowledgements of the next edition of the guide if we use your feedback – so write to us: we'll look forward to hearing from you!

Piers Letcher e bradtcroatia@yahoo.co.uk

LIST OF MAPS

NOTE ABOUT MAPS

A couple of maps use grid lines to allow easy location of sites. Map grid references are listed in square brackets after listings in the text, with page number followed by grid number, eg: [104–5 C3].

UPDATES WEBSITE

For the latest travel news about Croatia, please visit the new interactive Bradt update website: www.updates.bradtguides.com. It provides a forum whereby the latest travel news can be publicised online with immediate effect.

Introduction

I've had a love affair with Croatia for over 25 years, ever since I first inter-railed around Europe in 1982 and got stranded in Split for four days, waiting for someone to show up who never showed. It wasn't difficult to find my way out to the islands of Brač and Hvar, and from there to Korčula and on to Dubrovnik, by which time I was off the inter-rail map, and into a different place altogether.

Next time out I got diverted in Trieste and ended up in Pula instead of Athens, and worked my way down the coast as far as Split again, stopping in at Rab, and then for a week at the lovely Paklenica National Park (still a Croatian favourite). To get back to where I was going, I went up through the country to Zagreb, and saw the Plitvice Lakes for the first time. I travelled inland and visited the pretty, Baroque town of Vukovar, then wandered up through Osijek into Hungary.

It wasn't long before I was hammering at Bradt's door and clamouring to write about (what was then) Yugoslavia. That book came out in 1989, just in time to be washed away by the war – I spent 1991 glued to the television set, watching in horror as Vukovar fell and Dubrovnik was shelled, and had to wait a decade for my second chance.

My guide to Croatia was published in 2003, with a second edition in 2005, a third in 2007, and now this fourth edition – the most comprehensive and (I hope) useful guide to the country, and the only one that covers all the national parks and nature reserves.

Part One

GENERAL INFORMATION

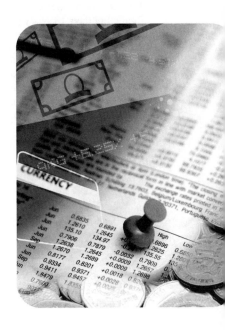

Country name Republic of Croatia
Croatian name Republika Hrvatska
Border countries Slovenia, Hungary, Serbia, Bosnia & Herzegovina, Montenegro
Size 56,542km^2
Islands, reefs and islets 1,185
Inhabited islands 67
Coastline 5,835km (1,777km mainland and 4,058km islands)
High point Mount Dinara, 1,831m
National parks Eight
Nature parks Eleven
Protected species 380 (fauna), 44 (flora)
Population 4.49 million (2009 estimate)
Capital Zagreb (population 786,000, 2007 estimate)
Other major cities and towns Split, Rijeka, Osijek, Zadar, Slavonski Brod, Karlovac, Pula, Sisak, Varaždin, Dubrovnik
Language Croatian
Religion Roman Catholic (87.8%), Orthodox Christian (4.4%), Muslim (1.3%) (2001)
Currency Kuna (kn). €1 = 7.26kn, £1 = 8.24kn, US$1 = 5.40kn (April 2010)
President Stjepan (Stipe) Mesić
International telephone code +385
Time CET (GMT + 1 hour)
Tourist board website www.croatia.hr
Public holidays 1 January (New Year's Day); 3 February (St Blaise's Day); Easter (24 April 2011, 8 April 2012, 31 March 2013); 1 May (Labour Day); Corpus Christi (60 days after Easter Sunday, and taken seriously in Croatia, with processions and lots of first communions. Corpus Christi falls on Thursday 23 June 2011, Thursday 7 June 2012 and Thursday 30 March 2013); 22 June (Day of Antifascist Struggle); 25 June, (Statehood Day); 5 August (Homeland Thanksgiving Day); 15 August (Assumption of the Virgin Mary); 8 October (Independence Day); 1 November (All Saints' Day); 25 and 26 December (Christmas).

Background Information

FACTS AND FIGURES

Croatia's curious shape – wishbone, boomerang, croissant, or what you will – tells you immediately about its historical past. Between the Austro-Hungarian Empire to the north and the Ottoman Empire to the southeast, Byzantium to the east and Rome and Venice to the west, Croatia sits at the crossroads of Europe.

NAME It's one of those countries like Finland or Albania whose name appears quite differently to foreigners from the way it appears to locals. For us, it's the Republic of Croatia – for them, it's Republika Hrvatska. That is why the top-level domain name (TLD) for Croatia on the internet is .hr.

AREA The country covers 56,542km² of southeastern Europe. It also claims 31,067km² of territorial waters in the Adriatic Sea.

LOCATION Southeastern Europe bordered by the Adriatic Sea and Italy to the west and southwest, Slovenia and Hungary to the north, Serbia to the east, Bosnia & Herzegovina along Croatia's inside arc, and the newly independent Montenegro for all of 25km in the far south.

A Bosnian corridor to the sea cuts Dubrovnik and the south coast off from the rest of the country – though now Bosnia has harmonised its visa requirements with Croatia, this shouldn't cause you any problems (see box on page 309 for further details).

The westernmost point of Croatia is the settlement of Bašanija near Umag, at 13°30'E; the easternmost point is Ilok, in Slavonia, at 19°27'E. Croatia also stretches from Žabnik in the Međimurje in the north (46°33'N) to Lastovo in the south (42°23'N).

POPULATION The 2001 census measured a population of 4.44 million people, down from the Croatian Central Bureau of Statistics' mid-year estimate for 1999 of 4.55 million – partly due to the displacements of people during the turbulent 1990s, but also partly due to changes in the census methodology. The next census is due in 2011.

CITIES Croatia's administrative, cultural, academic and communications centre is the city of Zagreb, with 780,000 inhabitants in town – though over a million people live in and around the capital.

The next largest city, Split, is only a quarter of the size of Zagreb, with 189,000 inhabitants. This is followed (2001 census) by Rijeka (144,000), Osijek (115,000), Zadar (75,000), Slavonski Brod (65,000), Karlovac (60,000), Pula (59,000), Sisak (52,000), Varaždin (49,000) and Dubrovnik (44,000).

COAST AND ISLANDS Croatia has 5,835km of coastline, including 4,058km on the 1,185 islands, islets and reefs. There are 67 inhabited islands, the largest of which are

Krk (the largest island in the Adriatic, at 409km², population 16,400) and Cres (404km², population 3,200).

MOUNTAIN HIGHS Croatia starts at sea level and peaks at Dinara (1,831m, near the Bosnian border, inland from Šibenik), the highest point on the eponymous Dinara range, which runs down almost the whole length of the coast.

Some of the other peaks over 1,500m are: Kamešnica (1,809m), Sv Jure (Biokovo, 1,762m), Vaganski vrh (Paklenica, Velebit, 1,758m), Sveto brdo (Paklenica, Velebit, 1,753m), Mali Rajinac (northern Velebit, 1,699m), Lička Plješevica (Ozeblin, 1,657m), Bjelolasica (Velika Kapela, 1,534m), Risnjak (Gorski Kotar, 1,528m), Svilaja (Dalmatia, 1,508m) and Snježnik (Gorski Kotar, 1,505m).

GEOGRAPHY

The country is perhaps most famous for its enormous – relative to the country's size – coastline and wealth of islands, but it's also geographically diverse away from the beaches. A long ridge of mountains – or rather series of ridges, peaking at Dinara – stretches from the northwest to the southeast of the country, while the plains of Pannonia dominate the Hungarian border to the north. Rolling hills dominate much of the rest of the country from behind the Dinara mountains to the Pannonian plain, while the Adriatic islands can be surprisingly mountainous, with peaks up to 778m (Brač), and Cres, Hvar, Lošinj, Vis, Krk, Korčula and Mljet all rising to over 500m.

The coast and islands are Croatia's natural selling point (especially when it comes to tourism), and they provide the country with an astonishing 5,835km coastline. Although it's only about 500km in a straight line from Trieste, the last town in Italy, to Herceg Novi, the first town in Montenegro, the Croatian coast itself is 1,777km long, with the remaining 4,058km accounted for by 1,185 islands, islets and reefs. See *Coast and islands*, page 3.

CLIMATE

If you're seeking an escape from a wet winter, then Croatia's probably not for you – most of the rain here falls in the cooler months, making it chilly and damp in the interior and mild but drippy along the coast. Outside the long, dry summers, Croatia is wetter than you might think, with an average annual countrywide precipitation of close to 1,100mm (compared to about 600mm on average for London and 1,400mm for Scotland as a whole), but the humid winters are more than compensated for by warm, early springs, hot, dry summers and prolonged autumns.

Croatia's climate falls into three distinct patterns, varying from northern to central Croatia, and different again for the coast and islands.

The north has a moderate continental climate, equating to hot, dry summers and cold, damp winters. Average daily winter temperatures vary from around −1 to +3°C, while in summer they range from 22 to 26°C. The capital, Zagreb, is coldest in January, when the daily average barely creeps above freezing, and warmest in August, when it's 21°C, and often much higher. You can expect about 24mm of rainfall in the capital in August, but closer to 100mm a month from September through to November.

Central Croatia has a semi-highland and highland climate, making for cool summers and hard winters, with plenty of snow. Average daily winter temperatures run from −5 to 0°C, while in summer they bounce up to 15–20°C.

Up in the mountains, you need to be well equipped for the weather. In Risnjak National Park, at around 1,500m, you can expect precipitation in the sort of quantities you'd be unlucky to find even in the wettest parts of England's Lake District – though here much of the annual 3,579mm falls as snow. At the mountain lodge in the park,

The geological term 'karst' came from the rock formations of neighbouring Slovenia (Kras), and the term karst is now used to describe any similar terrain – very useful as that includes most of the limestone mountains along Croatia's coast and on its islands.

Karst is grey, wild and very dry. It is formed by the absorption of water into porous limestone, which then corrodes and finally erodes the harder limestone underneath – this, combined with a history of earthquakes, is the geological reason for the shape of the Adriatic and its islands.

Young karst is typically characterised by small fissures in the rock, while more developed areas contain long underground caves, rivers that appear from the rock and then disappear again almost immediately, and highly porous limestone that is completely dry only a few minutes after rain has fallen. Karst is irregularly sculptured into sharp and wild shapes, and is extremely abrasive.

Croatia's karst was once almost entirely covered in vegetation, but large parts, particularly along the coast and on the islands, were deforested (the Venetians, in particular, needed a lot of wood) and then lost their soil from wind, erosion and over-grazing. This is known as naked karst, and can be seen at its most spectacular and barren on the island of Pag and on some of the islands of the Kornati archipelago. It's incredibly poor land, on which it seems unlikely that anything could survive – but people do live here, and somehow eke out a living from the wilderness.

When an underground cave collapses, the surface is flattened, and soil gradually accumulates. Usually, this is then cleared of rocks, walled in, and cultivated. One of the hazards of this type of field (known as polje) is that they don't always drain as quickly as they fill up, creating lakes of a few days' or weeks' duration. Every so often, you'll be surprised by a boat at the edge of a field or pasture, even in the mountains. It's also the reason why you'll never see houses built on the polje itself, but always to one side.

at 1,418m, snow stays on the ground for an average of 157 days a year, and can be up to 4m deep.

Weather in the mountains is unpredictable all year round, so plan accordingly. Snow can fall in every month of the year at 1,700m, and I've been caught in terrible hail in June on the Velebit massif at 1,200m, just a few kilometres inland from the coast. It has even been known to snow in coastal resorts like Trogir.

Down at sea level, of course, the coast and islands have a Mediterranean climate, with wet, mild winters, and long, hot and very dry summers. Daily averages range from 5 to 10°C in winter and from 25 to 30°C in summer, though almost never exceed 35°C – and daily maximums in Dubrovnik never fall below 12°C. The coast gets most of its precipitation in the autumn months, with 508mm falling in Rijeka and 377mm falling in Dubrovnik from October to December, but only 10mm of rainfall expected in Split in July.

The sea is for many the main attraction, so you should remember that it cools down to a chilly 8°C at Pula in winter, although from mid-June to early September it stays above 20°C, making for pleasant swimming (especially in August, when the water reaches its maximum temperature of 26°C).

There's also no shortage of sunshine on the Adriatic – Pula's pleased with its 2,480 hours annually, while Brač brags about its 2,700 sunny hours per year, and Hvar claims to have more hours of sunshine than anywhere else on the coast. Bring plenty of suncream.

NATURAL HISTORY AND CONSERVATION

Croatia is blessed with unpolluted lakes, spectacular limestone scenery, and the cleanest coastline on the Mediterranean. During Tito's days, Yugoslavia embarked on a progressive programme of tourist development, and although some of the resorts along the coast might be considered overdeveloped, there's also a wealth of national parks and other protected areas.

NATURAL HISTORY In the remoter forests of the interior and in the inland national parks, there are still bears and wolves at large, though you're unlikely to see them – bears are notoriously cautious, while wolves only come down from the mountains to raid villages for scraps during the depths of winter. Wild boar, however, are still common in the northern and eastern forests (and you can go on a photo safari to see them on Klek, near Ogulin – see page 225), along with red, fallow and roe deer. You might also be lucky enough to see chamois and mouflon in the mountains along the Slovenian border and through Dalmatia. But you're more likely to see eagles than griffon vultures or lynxes – lynx being almost shyer than bears, and griffon vultures now being confined to a small colony on the island of Cres.

Snakes are reasonably common, but there are very few that are poisonous (admittedly one of these, the nose-horned viper or *poskok* is very poisonous), and the old saying is worth repeating: they're much more frightened of you than you are of them. Snakes will mostly avoid regularly walked paths or roads, but if you're heading across country, it's as well to wear sensible shoes or boots. In accumulated months of walking in Croatia, I've seen several dozen snakes of four or five species, but never anything dangerous, so please don't kill them out of ignorance or fear.

You'll see a number of charming species of lizard if you're out walking, or even sightseeing – they love to bask on warm stone the moment the sun's shining. Look out, too, for frogs if you're near water, and several varieties of toad that are peculiar to the woods which grow on limestone mountains. Martens, wild cats and squirrels also live in these forests, but they're pretty shy.

From early summer onwards, Croatia features several species of butterfly you won't see often in the UK – look out for swallowtails in the mountains, white admirals on the islands, and hosts of butterflies of all species if you're here in late spring or early summer.

A total of 44 species of vegetation and 380 species of animal are protected in Croatia. Most endangered of all is the fast-disappearing Mediterranean monk seal, with a Croatian population of 25 or less according to the IUCN (International Union for the Conservation of Nature). The seals can only be found on the small island of Šćedro, off the south coast of Hvar, and on the uninhabited islands of Brusnik and Svetac in the Vis archipelago. These elegant dark brown seals grow to around 2.4m in length and weigh up to 300kg or more. There are also a surprising number of dolphins along the coast, and notably around the island of Cres, as well as further south.

Croatia's flora is also delightful. Along the coast and on the islands, you'll find aromatic herbs and abundant bougainvillea. In the woods and forests, there's a wide variety of plants and trees ranging from orchids to holm oak to pine and beech woods, while higher up in the mountains, you'll find beautiful summer pastures, home to tiny flowers and fragrant herbs.

As the summer wears on, the colours fade and everything dries out, leaving an arid impression across much of the country, which doesn't really wear off until the leaves change to their superb autumnal colours.

ENVIRONMENTAL ISSUES In spite of the long-standing promotion of ecotourism, the creation and maintenance of a whole crop of national parks and protected areas (see below), and its pride in having the cleanest waters of the Mediterranean, Croatia hasn't entirely escaped the blights of the modern world. Metal works, refineries and other factories have damaged some forests with acid rain, while coastal pollution from industrial and domestic waste has been experienced in some areas, and new roads continue to chew a path through forests on mountains such as Velebit.

Much more significant, in environmental terms, however, has been the destruction of both infrastructure and natural resources by the civil strife of the early 1990s. In spite of the quick repairs in tourist centres like Dubrovnik, it will take some time before the damage is entirely fixed countrywide, and longer still before the countryside returns to its natural state – there are still a handful of minefields that haven't yet been fully cleared.

Fire is another environmental hazard – a landscape that quickly absorbs what little water there is and a hot dry summer is a recipe for accidental combustion. The starting of any kind of fire in Croatia in summer is strongly discouraged in most areas, and is forbidden in the national parks. If you're going to be barbecuing, do so carefully, and be sure you have what it takes to put the flames out if things get out of control.

Croatia is also strongly exposed to one other environmental risk: earthquakes. A major and active earthquake fault network runs through Italy and the Balkans, and it was an earthquake in 1667 that killed more than 5,000 people in Dubrovnik and levelled most of the public buildings. In 1880, another major earthquake destroyed much of Zagreb, and most of what you see in the capital today dates from the post-1880 reconstruction of the city.

The most recent serious earthquake in Croatia occurred in 1996, with its epicentre in the area of Slano and Ston, 50km up the coast from Dubrovnik. The historical town of Ston – now famous for its excellent oysters – was almost completely destroyed. Although there were no fatalities, around 2,000 people in the area lost their homes to the earthquake damage.

NATIONAL PARKS, NATURE PARKS AND OTHER PROTECTED AREAS Croatia has an impressive range of national parks, nature parks and other protected areas. Below, you'll find a summary of what's on offer – more detail can be found in the relevant chapters.

National parks Croatia has eight national parks covering a total of 98,697ha (987km^2).

The Brijuni Islands (see page 193) Often written 'Brioni' in English, these islands were the government's (ie: Tito's) private retreat for decades, off limits to the general public and used for entertaining heads of state and the like. The group of two larger and 12 smaller islands lies off the west coast of Istria, and was once a fashionable holiday destination for the upper classes. Now it's a pretty national park featuring ruins from antiquity and a large open-air zoo – many of the animals are the descendants of gifts to the former Yugoslavia. Be warned, however, that it's on the package-tour circuit – it's the closest and most accessible park to Croatia's busiest stretch of coast.

The Kornati archipelago (see page 274) This is a scattered group of 147 uninhabited islands, islets and reefs south of Zadar; 89 of the islands were declared a national park in 1980. Popular with the yachting community, it's relatively difficult to access for other visitors to Croatia, but is nonetheless one of the most striking national parks I've ever seen, with sheer cliffs, unusually indented coastlines, clear seas and no water sources at all.

The Krka River and waterfalls (see page 265) The Krka River runs from Knin to Skradin, just inland from Šibenik. The park – which is mainly visited by boat – features stunning karst scenery of lakes, waterfalls, canyons and deep forests. At the river's widest point, you'll find a lovely Franciscan monastery on an island.

NATIONAL PARKS

HUNGARY

VARAŽDIN

Drava

KOPRIVNICA

SLOVENIA

BJELOVAR

ZAGREB

Risnjak NP

KARLOVAC

SISAK

POŽEGA

RIJEKA

Sava

Krk

Cres

Plitvice NP

Rab

Otočac

N. Velebit NP

BOSNIA &
HERZEGOVINA

Pag

Paklenica NP

ZADAR

Ancona

Telašćica NP

Krka NP

Kornati NP

SPLIT

Brač

Makarska

ADRIATIC SEA

Hvar

Drvenik

Dubrovnik

Vis

Ploče

Korčula

Pelješac

Mljet NP

Mljet

0   50km

0   30 miles

Mljet The western part of the island of Mljet (see page 349), between Korčula and Dubrovnik, has been designated a national park with good reason. Home to Europe's only wild mongooses, lush vegetation, and a former monastery on an island on one of two saltwater lakes, Mljet is a delight.

Paklenica National Park (see page 254) This pair of fabulous limestone gorges runs up from the sea into the Velebit massif not far from Zadar. Popular with Croatian climbers and walkers, it's one of my personal favourites and offers hiking from the merely gentle to the seriously strenuous.

The Plitvice Lakes (see page 158) These are one of Croatia's best-known and biggest draws. Situated inland, halfway between Zagreb and Zadar, the national park contains 16 lakes at different levels, inter-connected by waterfalls. Excellent walking trails keep you away from the crowds, but fun can be had too on the mini-train and organised boat rides.

Risnjak (see page 223) Situated north of Rijeka, where the Alps and the Dinara meet, Risnjak is the perfect national park for mountaineers and naturalists alike, featuring as it does Croatia's biggest diversity of flora and fauna. The beautiful forests and magnificent views here are understandably popular with locals, but you're surprisingly unlikely to bump into foreign visitors.

North Velebit Between Senj and Karlobag, where the Kvarner Bay turns into northern Dalmatia, lies the forbidding ridge of North Velebit National Park (see page 226). Here, you'll find some of the remotest hiking in Croatia just inland from one of the most deserted parts of the coast. There's a good reason for that, of course – there's little room along the narrow coast for development, while the massif behind it can be a wild, unwelcoming place, cold in spring and autumn and baking hot in summer. It's not for the faint-hearted, but it is your best chance of seeing a bear in the wild – around 500 live up here.

Nature parks Croatia also boasts eleven designated nature parks covering a further 424,285ha (4,242km²) of the country.

Biokovo (see page 291) This is the name of the massif overhanging the Makarska Riviera, between Split and Dubrovnik, and although it's a hard walk to the summit, it offers the most breathtaking views out over the islands of Brač and Hvar.

Kopački Rit (see page 174) On Croatia's eastern border, where the river Drava flows into the Danube, this area of swampland features superb bird and plant life, along with plenty of deer and wild boar. It's a birdwatchers' paradise, but take serious mosquito repellent.

Lonjsko Polje (see page 164) Running along the river Sava in Slavonia, this is one of the biggest swamps in Europe, featuring huge oak forests and excellent birdlife (some 240 species) – and, in particular, storks. It's still well off the tourist trail.

Medvednica (see page 124) Just north of Zagreb, this low-key mountainous area provides the capital's nearest refuge from city life for the locals. Pleasant beech and fir forests, steep-sided valleys, and well-maintained walking paths make this a lovely and quiet alternative to some of the more strenuous parks, and it's very easy to get to.

Papuk (see page 168) At under 1,000m high, this is eastern Slavonia's biggest mountain and its forested slopes make for some lovely summer walking, with well-marked and well-maintained trails, burbling brooks, and even thermal baths to swim in.

Telašćica (see page 274) Bordering on the northern end of the Kornati archipelago, and hogging the cleft-stick inlet at the southern end of Dugi Otok (Long Island), Telašćica has Croatia's biggest cliffs, rising a dramatic 180m out of the sea. It's naturally popular with anyone lucky enough to be on a sailing holiday.

Učka (see page 208) This is the name given to the massif above Opatija, in Istria. Rising to 1,400m, the park provides excellent views out over Rijeka and the islands of the Kvarner Bay, and a welcome relief from the crowds along the shore. Well-marked trails and pleasant oak and beech forests make this an excellent day trip from the coast.

Velebit (see page 226) Stretching for more than 100km, from Senj to Zadar, the 2,000km² Velebit Park includes both the Paklenica and North Velebit National Parks, the latter being home to the **Velebitski Botanički Vrt** botanical gardens and the strictly protected Hajdučki Kukovi nature reserve. The gardens, established in 1967, are some of the remotest in Croatia, being situated at around 1,500m in the most inaccessible part of the Velebit, and featuring flora unique to the region.

Vransko Jezero (see page 254) Between Zadar and Šibenik, in northern Dalmatia, lies Croatia's largest natural lake, famous for its mix of sea and freshwater fish, and an ornithological reserve, which is home to a wide variety of wading birds and a colony of rare purple herons.

Žumberak-Samoborsko Gorje (see page 150) West of Zagreb, across the Sava River and nestled up against the Slovenian border, lies this protected area of pretty villages connected by well-marked trails, and popular with weekend hikers from the capital.

Lastovsko otočje (see page 367) Croatia's newest nature park comprises the islands of the Lastovo archipelago.

Other protected areas This section wouldn't be complete without a brief mention of some of Croatia's other protected areas.

Probably the most famous – and the one you may have seen photographed from the air – is **Zlatni Rat** (Golden Cape), at Bol, on the island of Brač, one of the prettiest beaches on the Adriatic. The 600m spit of fine gravel, backed by pine forests, changes shape according to the sea currents and seasonal winds.

Hajdučki Kukovi nature reserve shelters one of the dozen deepest caves in the world, **Lukina Jama**, which was only discovered in 1993, and has now been explored to a depth of nearly 1,400m. In the same cave complex, you'll find **Patkov Gust**, the second deepest vertical shaft in the world, dropping a dizzying 553m. Take a torch – and a rope.

Apart from the famous Krka (see above), six other rivers in Croatia deserve a mention here. The **Danube** (called the Dunav here) roughly delineates the eastern border, with Serbia, while the great **Sava** runs past Zagreb, the capital, and then through Lonjsko Polje before marking the long border with Bosnia & Herzegovina. The **Drava**, for its part, starts in Slovenia and runs along the border between Croatia and Hungary, and is one of Europe's best-protected large rivers (it's a candidate for being nominated as a world biosphere). The fast-flowing **Dobra**, near Karlovac (50km west of Zagreb), is popular for rafting, kayaking and canoeing, while the **Mrežnica**, nearby – a tributary of the Kupa River – is all the rage with bathers. Finally, the 30km-long **Gacka**, near Otočac, inland from Senj, is a trout-fisher's paradise, with clear waters flowing past picturesque old water mills.

On the west coast of Istria is the fjord-like 10km inlet of **Limski Zaljev**. A nature reserve since 1979, it's an important haven for fish overwintering or spawning. The low salinity and high plankton count make it popular too with mussel and oyster farmers – and eaters.

Down at the other end of the coast, between Makarska and Dubrovnik, is the **Neretva Delta**, one of the Adriatic's most important waterfowl reserves, featuring swampy salt marshes, lagoons, reeds and meadows. Inland from Makarska, near Imotski, are the Red and Blue Lakes (**Crveno Jezero** and **Modro Jezero**), a pair of unusually deep water-filled holes in the karst. The bottom of Red Lake is only 19m above sea level, with a depth varying from 280 to 320m, and Blue Lake really is blue. As indeed is the Blue Cave (**Modra Špilja**), of course, on the island of Biševo, off the western end of Vis. The cave – like the Blue Grotto on Capri – is visitable only by boat, and many rate it as highly as its Capri counterpart.

Finally, a mention should be given to **Gorski Kotar**, the strictly protected nature reserve east of Rijeka, which contains Risnjak National Park (see page 221). In the forests here, which are among Europe's most unspoiled, wolves, brown bear, lynx and wild boar can still be found in the wild, along with a wide variety of bird species and plant life. Gorski Kotar also features such striking natural phenomena as the extraordinary karst rock formations at Bijele and Samarske Stijene, or Vražji Prolaz (the Devil's Pass) near Skrad, a narrow canyon with a perilous footpath running through it.

HISTORY

Croatia is at once a very old country and a very young one. Inhabited since the early Stone Age, and a linchpin of the Roman Empire, it only became a modern nation in 1991, and parts of the country were still under UN control – following the war – until 1998. And whilst it was a respectable kingdom of its own in medieval times, Croatia has spent most of the past millennium attached to (or subjugated by) its near neighbours. As a result, the country's history is unbelievably turbulent; fraught with foreign intervention, plagued by constant strife from pre-Roman times on, and richly textured with assassinations, intrigues, piracy and treachery.

Over the past 2,500 years, a succession of empires invaded, annexed or occupied Croatia, and each left its mark. For example, islands along the Adriatic coast that were deforested by the Venetians in the 18th century are still barren, yet the coastal towns and cities wouldn't be half as lovely if it weren't for the Venetian Gothic architecture.

Croatian independence today is remarkable given the sheer numbers of land grabs it's been subjected to, with Greeks, Romans, Ostrogoths, Avars, Slavs, Franks, Byzantines, Venetians, Hungarians, Tartars, Austrians, French, Italians, Turks, Germans and Serbs all having had their eye on a piece of the Croatian action.

Which is hardly surprising: the Adriatic has been the most practical trade route between Europe and the East since trade began there, around 3,000 years ago. Croatia has also been a buffer zone between east and west and between north and south for centuries.

ILLYRIANS, GREEKS AND ROMANS In spite of lots of early Stone Age finds, recorded history in Croatia starts with the Illyrians, a group of tribes that shared techniques for building and burying their dead, but not much else, it seems. By the 7th century BC, they were trading with the ancient Greeks, and, within two centuries, the Greeks had established colonies in the area, notably at Pharos (now Stari Grad, on the island of Hvar) and Salona, and on the island of Vis.

By 229BC, the Greeks were calling on Rome to help them in their quest to dominate the Illyrians, and the Romans pitched in with enthusiasm – though it took them more than two centuries to complete the job. In AD9, five years before becoming emperor, Tiberius finally annexed the area for Rome, thereby becoming the first (and last, until 1918) person to unify this bit of the Balkans.

Under Roman rule, the Balkans – and Dalmatia in particular – prospered, providing the empire with troops and provisions and receiving the protection of a major world power in return, setting something of a pattern for the region. The Romans built (or reinforced) many of the existing settlements, with their principal cities being Pola (Pula), Jadera (Zadar) and Salona (Solin). As was their wont, they also constructed summer palaces along the coast and on the islands, and reinforced trade links all the way from Pula to Cavtat.

The most famous Dalmatians to make it big at this time were the three who went on to become Roman emperors, most notably Diocletian, who ruled from AD284 to 305 – an astonishingly long period given that more than a dozen emperors had come and gone in the generation before he came to power. Diocletian ruled from Nicomedia (now Izmít, in Turkey), but started building himself a fabulously swanky retirement home just along the coast from his native Salona within months of taking the purple. Diocletian's palace in Split remains one of Croatia's most impressive monuments, with its corridors today being streets and its rooms entire houses.

In AD293, Diocletian partitioned the empire into the western and eastern parts, with the river Drina being the boundary, thus sealing Croatia's fate forever as a province on the frontline. Diocletian's frontier ran through the cities of Budva and Belgrade, and a rough approximation of this can still be seen on maps today, marking the eastern border of Slavonia in Croatia, and running down the eastern side of Bosnia & Herzegovina and Albania. Everything east of this line ultimately became Byzantium, and Orthodox, while everything west became part of Rome (and the eventual Holy Roman Empire), and Catholic. The division is also clearly visible today in the use of the Latin alphabet to the west and Cyrillic to the east.

Diocletian abdicated in AD305 and retired to Split, spending the last 11 years of his life in palatial splendour, rousing himself only to have Christians thrown to the lions; having tolerated the religion for most of his reign, he spent the rest of his life in relentless persecution of it.

ARRIVAL OF THE SLAVS The Roman Empire imploded in the 5th century, leaving the way clear for invasions by Huns, Goths, Vlachs, Avars, Bulgars and – most importantly for this guide – Slavs.

One group of Slavs, coming from what is now Poland, was the Croats. They conquered Roman Pannonia (now roughly the area known as Slavonia) and much of Dalmatia, and drove the inhabitants from the Dalmatian capital, Salona, to the nearby islands of Šolta, Brač, Hvar, Vis and Korčula.

During the same period, other Slavic ethnic groups, the Slovenes and the Serbs, settled the areas roughly corresponding to Slovenia and Serbia.

After a series of tussles with the Franks, Avars and Byzantines, the Croats finally managed to unite Dalmatian and Pannonian Croatia in AD925, under the crown of King Tomislav. For more than a century, the kingdom prospered, with the greatest Croatian king being Petar Krešimir IV, who ruled over Bosnia, Slavonia and the Dalmatian towns and islands from 1058 to 1074.

Byzantium and Venice were already encroaching on the southern and northern coastlands, however, and Hungary soon captured most of the interior, driving a corridor through to the sea by 1089. After the death of King Stjepan II in 1091, it all fell apart. A decade later, in 1102, the Hungarian King Kalman knocked together the heads of the 12 most powerful Croatian clans, persuading them to sign up to the Pacta Conventa, under which they would accept the Hungarian monarch's rule, but were able to maintain Croatia's traditions and customs. Amazingly, the treaty held until 1918.

VENETIANS, AUSTRO-HUNGARIANS AND THE ILLYRIAN PROVINCES Over the next 700 years, Croatian history largely depended on which of its neighbours was the most powerful at the time, with Hungary/Austria driving down from the north, the Ottoman Empire steaming in from the southeast, and Venice ever expansive from its corner of the Adriatic. Much of the architectural heritage of the country dates from this period, with the coast and islands still looking remarkably Venetian, and the interior retaining a monumental Habsburg feel.

During the 16th century, Austria created the Krajina (literally 'zone'), as a buffer against the advance of the Ottoman Turks, and Serbs who had escaped Ottoman rule were given land in the Krajina in exchange for military service.

In 1558, the Croatian and Slavonian diets were united, and Zagreb became Croatia's capital. Just 15 years later, the peasants revolted and – as you'd expect – were ruthlessly suppressed. Their leader, Matija Gubec, was executed in Zagreb (see page 106).

A century later, in 1671, another rebellion was set in motion against the Habsburgs, this time led by the aristocratic Petar Zrinski and Fran Krsto Frankopan. Expecting help from abroad that never materialised, they were swiftly brought to task, and they too were executed (see page 76).

USKOKS For much of the 16th century, the regional balance of power along the coast had been in the hands of a small third party, the Uskoks, who were pirates, based in the port of Senj from the 1530s until the Uskok War of 1615–17.

The Uskoks (from the Croatian word *uskočiti*, to 'jump in' or 'to board') were refugees who had been driven north by the advancing Ottoman Turks, but as their swashbuckling exploits grew, they attracted rebels from all quarters. When a party of Uskoks was hanged in Venice in 1618, nine of them turned out to be English – of whom six were apparently of noble birth.

At first, until the mid-1560s, the Uskoks attacked the Ottoman Turks on land and sea, but after this anyone appears to have been fair game, especially the Venetians, who were accused by the Uskoks of being un-Christian. This suited the Habsburgs just fine. Even though they paid lip service to condemning piratical exploits (they were after all the nominal rulers of Senj at the time) anyone that was harassing their enemies was a friend rather than a foe.

The Uskoks, however, appear to have been reluctant pirates, and pleas for tillable land in the interior fell on deaf ears for more than 50 years. They also had an honourable reputation amongst their immediate neighbours, the Kvarner Bay islanders of Krk, Cres, Rab and Pag, redistributing their booty whenever possible and paying for provisions when they had the money to do so.

The unwilling pirates were finally crushed during the eponymously named Uskok War in 1615–17, after which the Habsburgs agreed to a military occupation of Senj. The surviving Uskoks were impelled 30km inland to Otočac, which they had wanted all along. They disappeared without trace.

RAGUSA At the same time, another city, Ragusa, was at the height of its fame and powers. Ragusa was one of the most important – and independent – of the Dalmatian cities, fending off unwanted interference by successfully paying off the Ottoman Turks and the Hungarians. Ragusa, in fact, remains one of Croatia's most fashionable tourist attractions today … under its Croatian name, Dubrovnik.

THE ILLYRIAN PROVINCES Venice and Ragusa alike were swept aside by Napoleon, who created the Illyrian Provinces, a region running all the way from Trieste and Slovenia in the north to Dubrovnik in the south. The region was administered by Marshal Marmont, and for a few brief years benefited from the French passion for building roads, fortifying towns and encouraging the local south Slav culture – in a bid to create a buffer against undue Russian and Austro-Hungarian ambitions. 'Though Marmont was a self-satisfied prig, he was an extremely competent and honourable man, and he loved Dalmatia,' as Rebecca West so succinctly put it when she came through in 1937.

AUSTRO-HUNGARIANS It was for nought; Napoleon fell, and Habsburg rule was restored in 1815, albeit within a separate Kingdom of Croatia and Slavonia. By the middle of the 19th century, an educated elite, led by Ljudevit Gaj, started defending Croatian nationality and sovereignty and worked towards a national revival, under the moniker of the Illyrian Movement. Count Janko Drašković helped the movement along in 1832 by publishing the first political pamphlet in Croatian.

In 1848, the viceroy of Croatia, Ban Josip Jelačić, led an army of 50,000 soldiers towards Hungary, but, instead of winning independence for his country, he unfortunately allowed Austria to take over both countries. Nonetheless, he was a great hero, having abolished feudalism and brought in reforms allowing elected officials to join the nobility in parliament (the Sabor). After his death in 1859, a great statue of him on horseback was raised in Zagreb's central square. A year later, a new constitution allowed Croatian to become the national language.

The Kingdom of Croatia and Slavonia continued under Austro-Hungarian rule until the 525th anniversary of the Ottoman defeat of Lazar, last of the independent Serbian rulers, at the battle of Kosovo Polje in 1389.

On that day (28 June 1914), Archduke Franz Ferdinand, heir to the Austro-Hungarian Empire – in a remarkable display of hubris, given that it was a day of

KARAĐORĐEVIĆ ROYALTY

Having been born in the Royal Palace in Belgrade in September 1923 and been pronounced king at the age of 11 after his father's assassination, it must have been a shock for the 17-year-old monarch, King Petar II, to find himself sitting out the war in London.

Fortunately for the Karađorđević dynasty, Petar married Princess Aleksandra of Greece (the daughter of King Alexander) at the Yugoslav Embassy in London in 1944, and on 17 July the following year she bore him a son, Crown Prince Aleksandar II of Yugoslavia.

Parliament, under the orders of Winston Churchill, stepped in quickly and proclaimed Suite 212 of Claridges as Yugoslav territory, so that the putative heir would have the right to be king some day, and the child was baptised in Westminster Abbey by the Patriarch of Serbia. No prizes for guessing the godparents: King George VI and his daughter Princess Elizabeth (QE II, to you).

An auspicious start to Aleksandar's life, perhaps, but, in November 1945, the Yugoslav monarchy was abolished by the communists, under the leadership of Tito, and although King Petar II never abdicated, he never saw Yugoslavia again, either.

He died after a long illness at the Colorado General Hospital, in Denver, in 1970, only a year older than his father had been when he was assassinated in Marseille in 1934.

Since the summer of 2001, post-Milošević, Crown Prince Aleksandar, for his part, has been living in the Royal Palace in Belgrade, with his family, returned from lifelong exile. As the great-great-grandson of Queen Victoria and the cousin of King Juan Carlos of Spain, he half expects to see the monarchy restored – on constitutional lines, of course – but he has one major disadvantage: he apparently speaks very poor Serbian.

national mourning – ignored all warnings and paid an official visit to Sarajevo. And with his wife, Sophie Chotek, was shot dead by a 19-year-old student called Gavrilo Princip, thus kicking off World War I. Austria had long been looking to declare war on Serbia, and this provided the perfect excuse. Russia took offence; Germany supported Austria; Britain and France piled in with Russia; and the world's bloodiest war to date was underway.

THE KINGDOM OF THE SERBS, CROATS AND SLOVENES
Aware that the Austro-Hungarian Empire was going to come out of the war at best badly diminished, Slovenia and Croatia threw in their lot with Serbia in 1918, resulting in the creation of the Kingdom of Serbs, Croats and Slovenes, under the Crown of King Petar I from the dynastic Karađorđević family (see box opposite).

Petar was succeeded on his death, three years later, by his son, King Aleksandar I, in the face of increasing irritation, on the part of the Croats, that they had so little power in Belgrade. The Croatian Republican Peasant Party, led by firebrand Stjepan Radić, had won local elections in 1920, but this wasn't of any use to the party in the capital.

Tension remained high through the 1920s, until, on 20 June 1928, Radić was shot in Belgrade's parliamentary chamber by a Montenegrin deputy. Six weeks later, Radić died and more than 100,000 turned up to his funeral in Zagreb. The king suspended parliament 'reluctantly' at the beginning of 1929 and established a dictatorship in its place, promising to restore democracy once unity had been achieved. In October that year, however, he did finally manage to put diplomats and letter-writers out of their misery by changing the country's name to the much more manageable Yugoslavia – Land of the South Slavs.

So much for the good news: 1929 also saw the founding of the Ustaše by Ante Pavelić, a party dedicated to the violent overthrow of the Yugoslav state, and one that would later have a dramatic effect on Croatia's future.

Croatian national sentiment continued to run high, and, in 1934, King Aleksandar, aged 46, was assassinated in Marseille, in a plot sponsored by the Ustaše, but executed by a Macedonian with Italian support. Aleksandar's death left the ill-equipped Prince Petar to run the country – aged only 11. His uncle, Prince Pavle, was drafted in to help, but Yugoslavia was in no state to prosper. And war was once again on the horizon.

WORLD WAR II
By the time World War II broke out – not the Balkans' fault this time around – the country was in a mess. The Ustaše fascists wanted complete independence for Croatia, Macedonia was trying to secede, and only the Yugoslav Communist Party, founded in 1919 and outlawed nine years later, had any kind of countrywide support.

Yugoslavia managed to remain neutral for the first year and a half of the war, but increasing axis pressure resulted in Prince Pavle signing a pact on 25 March 1941, aligning Yugoslavia with fascist Germany and Italy, in spite of his personal pro-British sentiments. Two days later, a group of air force officers, backed by both the communists and the Orthodox Church, staged a coup d'état, deposed Prince Pavle and installed King Petar II, now aged 17½, in his place.

The pact was annulled and Yugoslavia reaffirmed its neutrality; Hitler responded by bombing Belgrade on 6 April. On the same day, massive German and Italian armies entered the country, and Yugoslavia capitulated ten days later. King Petar II escaped to London with the Yugoslav government and set up house in Claridges, never to return to his former kingdom.

THE USTAŠE
Once Yugoslavia had thrown in the towel in 1941, the Ustaše declared the Independent State of Croatia (Nezavisna Država Hrvatska, NDH), leaving the rest of Yugoslavia to be carved up between Germany, Hungary, Bulgaria and Italy –

something for which the Ustaše has never really been forgiven by many. Contrary to what has been claimed by some, resistance to the Ustaše was strong across Croatia throughout the war, but it was often the subject of ruthless suppression.

From the start, the Ustaše tried to clear the Serbs out of Croatia. When this proved impossible, they set up a number of concentration camps, the most notorious being the Jasenovac complex, a string of five camps on the bank of the Sava River, about 100km south of Zagreb. The camps were used from 1942 to 1945 to eliminate not just Serbs, but also religious minorities (including thousands of Jews) and political opponents of the Ustaše, and reports are that they were just as bad as the more notorious German camps at Auschwitz, Belsen or Treblinka. Scenes of unbelievable barbarism were reported at the Jasenovac 'death factory', including contests to see who could kill the most people in a single night.

Nobody will ever know for sure how many people were killed by the Ustaše, but it's now thought that between 300,000 and 400,000 Serbs were killed in total, with 40,000–50,000 being murdered at Jasenovac alone. One of the unfortunate reasons for the confusion over the numbers is that Jasenovac has long been used by both sides in a propaganda war between Serbia and Croatia, with some Croatians calling the Serbian numbers (up to a million) inflated, while many Serbs feel that Croats have tried to whitewash the past.

THE RESISTANCE After the fall of Yugoslavia, in April 1941, resistance was immediately organised, but divided into two fiercely opposed groups, the Četniks and the partisans. The royalist, pro-Serbian, Četniks supported the government in exile in London, and hated just about everybody else – Croats (both Ustaše and resistance), Germans, Italians, communists, and a host of non-Serb minorities.

As anti-Germans, the Četniks were aided at first by the allies, but they were regarded with distrust by many Yugoslavs. The partisans, on the other hand, led by Josip Broz 'Tito', were the army of the communist party, and although only 42,000 strong at the outset, their effective resistance and daring attacks earned them wide support from communists and non-communists alike.

Unfortunately, however, the desire of the two resistance groups to rid Yugoslavia of invaders – and indeed the Ustaše – was at times exceeded by their determination to kill each other, resulting in a long and bloody civil war being run in parallel with the greater conflict. The partisans themselves are thought to have murdered up to 100,000 of their opponents at the end of the war, interring them in caves, never to be mentioned again.

When the end of the war was close, Ustaše-founder Ante Pavelić mobilised large numbers of Croat reservists and civilians and persuaded them to go to Bleiburg, in Austria (the British HQ), to surrender to the allies. The British, to whom they surrendered, immediately handed them back (against American orders) to Tito's troops, who had some shot and buried in mass graves on the spot and marched the rest to the other end of Yugoslavia along what Croats now call the Križni Put (Way of the Cross). Contemporary Croat history tells us that at least 50,000 died along the way. Ante Pavelić wasn't one of them: he escaped to South America (Pavelić and many of his closest allies were helped by Argentina's leader, Juan Peron, who offered them blank passports) and then on to Franco's Spain, where he died in 1959.

Yugoslavia paid a terrible price during World War II, with more than a tenth of its citizens being killed. Among them were at least 300,000 Croats, 300,000 partisans and nearly 400,000 Bosnians. But the resistance had successfully tied up enormous numbers of axis soldiers, and it's quite possible that the allies couldn't have won the war without Yugoslavia.

With the help of the British (aid was transferred from the Četniks to the partisans in 1943), and the Red Army, Belgrade was finally liberated in 1944, and by 1945 a provisional government, in temporary accord with the government in exile, was in force.

TITO AND A NON-ALIGNED YUGOSLAVIA Post-war elections not surprisingly gave the communists 90% of the vote – with separate ballot boxes provided for those who cared to vote against Tito. That gave the government the freedom to set up on the lines adopted by Stalinist Russia, and to embark on a disastrous experiment with collectivisation.

Stalin, however, was wary of Yugoslavia, as it was the only country in the Eastern Bloc to have made its way entirely independently. And indeed, in 1948, Tito broke with the Cominform, the economic ground base for the countries allied to the Soviet Union. This declaration of non-alignment was arguably the greatest political act of Tito's career, allowing Yugoslavia to develop its own brand of communism. And it's the main reason why Serbs, Croats, Slovenes, Montenegrins and Macedonians get huffy even today if you lump them in with the Eastern Bloc.

Tito's was a brave political move, for sure, but it brought hard times for Yugoslavia in the 1950s, starting with an economic blockade by the Soviet Union. Credits from the West and the launch of mass tourism in the 1960s saved the country, however. Tito introduced the idea of workers' self-management, putting the country's hospitals, schools and factories in the hands of those who staffed them, and despite leading to sometimes excessive decentralisation, it allowed competition within the framework of communism, proving reasonably effective during the 1960s and 1970s.

In an attempt to solve Yugoslavia's nationalist problems, Tito had also decentralised the state itself, giving each of the six republics complete control over its internal affairs. While Tito lived, this was a remarkably effective strategy, mainly because he was ruthless in suppressing opposition. Croatian writers and intellectuals had issued a declaration in 1967 stating that Croatian was a different language from Serbian, and Croatian Serbs had quickly counter-declared their right to be taught in Serbian, but Tito would have none of it, and was quick to quash the so-called 'Croatian Spring' in 1971.

After being declared President for Life in 1974, Tito died in 1980, three days before his 88th birthday. He made one more trip around the country in funeral state, in the Blue Train made famous during the early post-war days when he toured the country tirelessly promoting his programme of Brotherhood and Unity. This time it was mourners who lined the tracks in their thousands, and it's difficult now to conjure up just how important Tito's funeral was. It still stands as one of the best attended ever, from an international perspective, with official mourners coming from more than 120 countries, including four kings, 32 presidents and other heads of state, 22 prime ministers, and more than 100 representatives or secretaries of communist and workers' parties.

POST-TITO Like so many singularly powerful men, Tito left his country with a weak succession. Each of the republics would, in theory, get a year as head man, but without Tito's personal charisma and unifying strength it was never going to work. It wasn't long before the old problems of nationalism, unfair distribution of wealth between the republics, and corruption in government resurfaced.

Onto this scene arrived Slobodan Milošević, who rapidly gained popularity in Serbia after defending Serb protestors against mostly ethnic Albanian police in Kosovo in 1987. Two years later, on 28 June 1989 – that date, again (see page 14) – Milošević addressed a million Serbs at Kosovo Polje and was elected president of Serbia in the autumn.

This was the beginning of the end for a united Yugoslavia. Milošević's talk of an ethnically pure Greater Serbia was never going to sit well with Slovenes, Croats, Bosnians, Macedonians – or indeed most Kosovars.

WAR – AND CROATIAN INDEPENDENCE The fall of the Berlin Wall in 1989 and the collapse of communist governments across Europe encouraged several republics, led by Slovenia and Croatia, to try and change the political structure of Yugoslavia.

In 1990, led by former army general and dissident (some would prefer revisionist) historian Franjo Tuđman (see box below), the Croatian Democratic Union (HDZ), won elections. Once in power, the HDZ pushed parliament to drop the word 'Socialist' from the Croatian republic's name, and the red star was quietly removed from public symbols. The HDZ also put Croatia's 600,000 Serbs on the defensive by changing their status from 'constituent nation' in Croatia to 'national minority', and many Serbs in government lost their jobs. The HDZ didn't improve matters by making itself an easy target for Serb propaganda, party members playing straight into Serb hands by attempting to rehabilitate the Ustaše or by saying that the numbers of people killed at Jasenovac were inflated (whether or not that was true).

At the same time, most of the republics tried to negotiate a transition to a confederation, on the Swiss model, but this went completely against the Milošević view of a Greater Serbia, with money and power concentrated in Belgrade. As a result, the rebellious republics raised their sights, aiming for independent statehood instead. Trouble was inevitable.

During the summer of 1990, encouraged by Belgrade into fearing real danger, Croatia's Serbs (armed by the Yugoslav People's Army, the JNA) declared an

FRANJO TUĐMAN – CROATIA'S FIRST PRESIDENT

Franjo Tuđman was born in 1922 and, at the age of 19, joined Tito's partisans, becoming a decorated hero by the end of World War II. His youngest brother was killed as a partisan in 1943, and his depressed father is said to have shot himself and his second wife in 1946 – though Tuđman himself claimed first that they were victims of the Ustaše and, later, that they had been killed by the communists. (As a curious parallel, both of Milošević's parents committed suicide; his mother when Milošević was a child; his father when he was 18.)

After the war, Tuđman was sent to the advanced military academy in Belgrade, and he stayed in the army until 1961, when he retired at the age of 38, with the rank of Major-General. During the 1960s, as a historian, Tuđman gradually began to fall out of favour with the communists, and in 1971, following the suppression of the 'Croatian Spring', he was jailed for a short time, escaping a longer sentence only through the intervention with Tito of the respected Croatian writer Miroslav Krleža. He served nine months in prison in 1972.

A decade later and more strongly nationalist than ever, Tuđman was sentenced in 1981 to a three-year sentence and banned from all public activity for his dissident/revisionist views on history and for advocating a pluralist democracy. He served about half of this before being released because of failing health.

In 1987, having finally got his passport back after 17 years, he travelled widely in the West, promoting the cause of Croatian independence, and in 1989 he founded the Croatian Democratic Union (HDZ), which became the dominant political force in the first multi-party parliamentary election in the spring of 1990. The tenor of the campaign can be measured by Tuđman's reportedly having said 'Thank God my wife is neither a Serb nor a Jew'.

In spite of the strong words, Tuđman nonetheless found time for a secret meeting with Milošević in March 1991, to discuss how Croatia and Serbia might best carve up Bosnia & Herzegovina for themselves. Nonetheless, Tuđman was hugely popular, as the first person since the Middle Ages to gain international recognition for Croatia as an independent state. At his funeral, in December 1999, thousands filed past his coffin – but only his death may have saved him from being indicted, like Milošević, by the Tribunal in The Hague.

Most men dressing for work in the morning don't spare a thought for Croatia – which is a pity, as the ubiquitous necktie they put on not just originated there, but is named after the country.

The origins of one of fashion's most durable accessories date back to the Thirty Years War in Europe, which ran from 1618 to 1648. The story goes that Croatian mercenaries of the period wore a colourful silk scarf tied around the neck. Some of their number were stationed in Paris, and were presented to the court (whether that of Louis XIII, who died in 1643, or Louis XIV, who succeeded him, is debatable), triggering off a copycat craze for cravates – the word coming from dressing *à la Croat* (or Hrvat, in Croatian).

During the dandyish reign of Louis XIV, the wearing of cravates by French men became widespread, and the new fashion soon spread right across Europe – indeed the French word '*cravate*' exists in one form or another in almost every European language, from '*gravata*' in Greek to '*krawatte*' in German.

Today, businessmen across the whole world consider the tie as a basic part of their wardrobe, though for the most part they probably aren't wearing the enormously expensive long and floppy silk scarves favoured by Croatian soldiers, but the rather more sober ties launched in England at the end of the 19th century.

autonomous region around Knin, 50km inland from Šibenik. Croatian police helicopters, sent in to sort out the trouble, were soon scuttled by Yugoslav air force MIGs. Tension continued to mount until March 1991, when Knin paramilitaries took control of the Plitvice Lakes, resulting in the first casualties of the conflict.

Slovenia, meanwhile, had unilaterally decided to declare independence on 25 June 1991, so Croatia declared independence on the same day – after a referendum held in May had delivered a 94% verdict in favour of a sovereign and independent Croatian state. Milošević immediately sent tanks into Ljubljana, in Slovenia (and I'll never forget the phone call I had from a friend in the Slovene Mountain Association, who had a tank outside his office), and to the Italian and Austrian borders. The world sat up and took notice, and the EU introduced sanctions; within a week, Serbia realised it didn't stand a chance (with Italy and Austria so close) and the war in Slovenia was over. Within a month, the army had left the country – though it only retreated as far as Croatia, and later distributed many weapons to the local Serb population.

Croatia, with a significant Serb minority, wasn't as fortunate as Slovenia. As soon as it proclaimed independence, the Serbs countered by proclaiming the independent state of Republika Srpska Krajina (RSK) within Croatia, declaring loyalty to Belgrade and Milošević (the commander of the army), and choosing Knin as its capital.

In six months at the end of 1991 – with the help of the JNA, and heavy fighting, bombardments and air strikes – the Serbs ethnically 'cleansed' nearly a third of Croatia, reawakening memories of the brutality of the 1940s. Thousands of Croats were forced to leave their homes and many were killed by the JNA or loosely associated paramilitary forces.

Many towns were besieged and bombarded for months, with wholesale destruction and local suffering involved. Worst of all was the siege of Vukovar, which ended with appalling atrocities being carried out on the local Croatian population. Dubrovnik was also besieged, suffering huge damage and considerable loss of life.

Local industry across the country was effectively destroyed, and Croatia was paralysed by the RSK, which controlled most of the country's oil resources, the land routes to the Dalmatian coastal cities, and the main access road from Zagreb into

Slavonia. The tourist trade – one of Croatia's main sources of foreign earnings – came to a complete halt.

By the time the UN was able to broker a ceasefire in January 1992, thousands of people had died, tens of thousands of homes had been destroyed, and Croatia had hundreds of thousands of local refugees, placing a huge burden on the main cities. Only then did the European Union (in spite of French and British reluctance) recognise Slovenian and Croatian independence. In May, after amending its constitution to protect minority groups and human rights, Croatia joined the United Nations.

It was not a happy country, however. Croatia was all but impossible to administrate with its newly fragmented borders, and from 1994 it lobbied hard, against intense European opposition, to end the UN policing of the ceasefire line. Failing on that front, it took matters into its own hands. From June 1995, Croatia 'liberated' the Krajina in a series of lightning assaults, first reclaiming the main road into Slavonia, and then focusing on the main part of the RSK in August.

In just three days, fuelled both by fear and by propaganda from Belgrade, most of the civilian Serb population fled the land they had lived on for centuries, in perhaps the biggest example of ethnic cleansing in the war so far. The leaders of the RSK launched rocket attacks on Zagreb and Sisak as a parting shot, before retreating to Serbia. In the vacuum left in the Krajina, however, Serb houses across the RSK were looted and destroyed, while the authorities turned a blind eye.

The December 1995 Dayton Peace Agreement finally helped to restore stability to the region, reinforced at the end of 1996 by the signing of a peace treaty between Croatia and Yugoslavia, although the last bit of eastern Slavonia that was still in Serb hands was only returned to Croatia, under UN supervision, in January 1998.

A vast reconstruction programme has meant that most houses have now been rebuilt, and Serbs have been encouraged to return – though nobody's sure quite how many have actually done so. What is clear is that with so much bloodshed, anguish and suffering across the region, reconciliation is a painful process, and it's not surprising that some people are still bitter about the failure – of Britain in particular – to support Croatia early on during the conflict.

POLITICS

Independence brought Croatia a new constitution (online in English at *www.constitution.org/cons/croatia.htm* if you're interested) and a new political system that – as the Ministry of Foreign Affairs says on its website (*www.mvp.hr*) – is now 'democratic and based on a respect for human rights, law, national equality, social justice and multiple political parties'. The last part is certainly true enough, with a bewildering array of three- and four-letter acronyms to deal with. At the elections in the year 2000, following the death of Franjo Tuđman (see box on page 18), more than 4,000 candidates from 55 political parties stood for office. As Rebecca West said witheringly, when she was here in 1937, 'There is no end to political disputation in Croatia. None.'

Croatia's independence also brought it a new flag, known locally, irreverently, as the 'zoo' – above the chequerboard of the main flag are the old coats of arms from the regions, featuring Dalmatia's three crowned leopards, Istria's goat, and Slavonia's marten.

Croatia's legislature consists of a parliament, the Sabor, with 151 MPs elected for a four-year period. The popular centrist president (re-elected for a second five-year term in 2005) is the colourful Stjepan (Stipe) Mesić – a former Secretary of the HDZ, who was also Croatia's first prime minister. See www.president.hr for more information.

Like Tuđman, Mesić had also been condemned in the repression of the 'Croatian Spring' in 1971, and he served a one-year jail sentence at the notorious Stara Gradiska prison. Later, however, he went on to be elected to the Sabor, the body from which Yugoslav presidents were appointed in rotation, following Tito's death in 1980. As a result, Mesić also became the last president of a united Yugoslavia, until his resignation in December 1991.

In 1994, disagreeing with the HDZ policy on Bosnia & Herzegovina – Tuđman still appearing to be keen to carve it up between Serbia and Croatia – Mesić left the party and set up the rival Croatian Independent Democrats (HND). Three years later, he joined the Croatian People's Party (HNS) and became the HNS executive vice president.

In the parliamentary elections of 2003, the HDZ saw a return to form, winning 66 of the 151 seats available in the Sabor (parliament), and forming a government via an informal coalition with other smaller parties, with Ivo Sanader as prime minister. Quite suddenly in July 2009, Ivo Sanader resigned, and Jadranka Kosor, Croatia's first female prime minister, was elected in his place.

Croatia is keen to join NATO and the EU – it has been a candidate for EU membership since 2004, and hopes to join by 2011, though whether or not this will happen is not entirely certain.

ECONOMY

Progress towards economic reform after the war in the 1990s was hampered by coalition politics and resistance on the street, mainly from trade unions, but the government is now keen to achieve EU membership, and the economy is looking in better shape than it has for years.

Inflation was 6% in 2009 (up from 3.3% in 2005), and GDP per capita in 2008 was estimated at US$15,632 – still under half that in the UK or France. Average net salary had risen to 5,178kn per month (around € 707), however, and unemployment was down to 13.2% in 2008 and just 10.6% in Zagreb county – though these figures were up slightly due to the global downturn in 2009.

Vital to the economy – especially along the coast – is tourism. In the year 2000, revenue from tourism finally exceeded the 1990 figures for the first time, and in 2005 was worth something like US$8 billion annually to Croatia's economy. The government expects this figure to reach US$20 billion within ten years.

TOURISM

In 1990, more than 16 million tourist nights were spent in Istria alone, and 3.5 million nights were spent in Dubrovnik – more than 814,000 of them by the British. The following year, people stayed away in droves. In Istria – one of the parts of the country least affected by the war – tourist nights plummeted by more than three-quarters, to below 4 million.

Since 1998, however, the recovery has been rapid and continuous, and the number of tourist nights in Croatia as a whole grew from 47.8 million in 2004 to just over 57 million in 2008. The number of foreign visitors to the country over the same period grew from 7.9 million to more than 9.4 million, staying in over 968,000 beds. Visitor figures have now overtaken their 1990 peak, when just over 5 million foreign tourists and almost 3.5 million domestic tourists visited Croatia.

Istria is Croatia's undisputed tourist capital, registering a staggering 18.6 million tourist nights from 2.8 million visitors in 2008. In the same year, Dubrovnik county, one of the next busiest places on the tourist map, registered 910,000 visitors.

The vast majority of visitors (around 90%) to Croatia are foreigners, with the majority coming in search of sea and sunshine. The most numerous among them in

2008 were Germans (1.5 million) and Italians (1.2 million), with the UK some way down the list, with 261,000 – down slightly on the previous couple of years, though still roughly 70% more than came in 2003. The number of UK visitors is set to keep rising with the rash of direct budget airline routes that began operating in 2006.

PEOPLE

In spite of the large displacement of people – both Serbs and Croats – during the war of the 1990s, Croatia's total population has remained fairly stable (at around 4.4 million) over the past 20 years. Ethnic demographics have changed, however.

In the 1991 census, around three-quarters of people considered themselves Croats, while 12.2% said they were Serbs. A decade later, the 2001 census showed that almost 90% of people thought of themselves as Croats, while Serbs only accounted for 4.5% of the population. There are a number of reasons for the decline in Serb numbers, including the introduction of a new category, 'ethnically uncommitted' (which attracted 2% of the population in 2001), changes in the census methodology, especially relating to Croatians living abroad (ethnic Croats were counted; ethnic Serbs weren't), and the exodus of Serbs from Croatia during 1995. It will be interesting indeed to see the results in 2011.

Croatia also has a whole host of other tiny national minority populations, as follows (2001 census): Bosnians 0.5%, Hungarians 0.4%, Italians 0.4%, Slovenians 0.3%, Albanians 0.3%, Czechs 0.2%, Montenegrins 0.1%, Macedonians 0.1% and Slovaks 0.1%.

However they describe themselves, I've always found the people of Croatia to be warm, hospitable and generous, though inevitably this varies from place to place and person to person. In the interior, and especially in the national parks and nature reserves, people tend to have more time for you, whereas along the coast you might sometimes find a certain brusqueness, especially at the height of the season. But in Croatia, as everywhere, you'll find that if you treat them right, people on the whole will treat you right too.

LANGUAGE

The official language is Croatian, written using a Latin alphabet. Though comparatively unfamiliar to most, it is not as difficult as it might seem – it's a phonetic language, for a start, so letters are always pronounced in the same way (unlike English) – and it's well worth making the effort to learn a few words and phrases. English is widely spoken in Zagreb, on the coast and in major tourist centres – less so off the beaten track. See Appendix 1 for more details and vocabulary.

RELIGION

In the 2001 census, some 87.8% of the population labelled themselves as Roman Catholics (up from three-quarters in 1991), and Catholicism has long been tied to national identity here – it's as much a statement against Tito's brand of socialism or Serbia's Orthodox Church as it's a credo in itself. As a result, church attendance was hugely popular in the first years of Croatian independence, though has tailed off somewhat in recent years.

Outside of church service times, there are often people worshipping privately at the bigger churches and cathedrals, and their quiet and privacy should of course be respected. Smaller churches – and even some of the bigger ones – may well be closed outside of the periods immediately before and after mass.

Beyond Catholicism, 4.4% of the population say they're Orthodox Christians, while Muslims account for 1.3% of the population.

EDUCATION

Children in Croatia begin school at the age of six or seven, attending primary school (*osnovna škola*) and then from age 14, secondary school (*srednja škola*). Secondary schools can take the form of *gimnazija* (similar to grammar school), vocational or art schools. Zagreb also has an American and a German international school (*www.aisz.hr, www.deutscheschule.hr*). As of 2008/9 the secondary school leaving examination (*matura*) has started to replace entrance exams at some universities. Zagreb's university is the oldest in Croatia (first founded in 1669); other universities include Zadar, Split, Osijek and Dubrovnik, and there are also a fair number of polytechnics and other accredited schools of higher education. The standard is high, and the syllabus demanding – as anyone who has worked their way through the reading lists for literature courses will happily tell you.

CULTURE

Millennia of foreign occupation have left Croatia with an impressive architectural heritage, ranging from Greek and Roman ruins to a wealth of Venetian Gothic to the Habsburg splendour of the cities in the north. See the individual chapters for specific sights (and sites).

By contrast, there are very few Croatian artists, writers or composers who are well known outside the country, the most famous probably being the sculptor Ivan Meštrović. Which is not to say the Croats are an uncultured lot; on the contrary, it's simply that most of the country's culture hasn't been exported.

What you can see – and hear – is Croatia's abundant folk music, often as *klapa*, the quite beautiful Dalmatian a cappella singing, or sometimes as the somewhat eclectic mix known as 'turbofolk'. Tito's communist government was unusual in encouraging people to retain their folk tradition, and as a result most of the popular tourist destinations – notably Dubrovnik and Split, and many of the islands – have summer music festivals that highlight the best in folk songs and dancing, along with jazz and classical music too.

Practical Information

WHEN TO VISIT

High summer is a great time to be in the higher parks, such as Risnjak, in the north, or to visit the capital and other towns away from the coast, as lots of locals are themselves on holiday then. But bear in mind that inland Croatia can get pretty hot and sweaty in the absence of sea breezes – and you'll need to book tickets on public transport in advance.

If you have a choice, September is the best month to be on the coast or visit the islands. The weather is fine, the school holidays are over and the sea is still easily warm enough for swimming. October is also fine, but by November the sunshine hours are down and the rainfall hours up. May and early June, too, are absolutely gorgeous along the coast, though there's an increasing tendency for accommodation and ferries to fill up as June progresses.

September and June are the best months for walkers and hikers, closely followed by October and May, and autumn in the inland parks provides stunning visuals as the leaves change colour. Earlier than May and you may find it damp in the lowlands and freezing higher up; later than October and you run the risk of being caught by the first snows.

Yachting, sailing and motor-cruising have a season running from the beginning of May to the first week of October. Outside this period, charters won't be possible and you'll find the weather in any case less pleasant, with a more frequent gale-force *bura* blowing between September and May.

July and August are easily the most popular months with all types of visitor, so you may want to leave well alone, unless you're absolutely set on clubbing, or that deep suntan. These are the months when you'll be competing for rooms with up to six million others, and, if you're travelling by car, you'll find parking a hassle, and queues for the car ferries measured in hours. That said, July and August are easily the best months for being on the beach, and Croatia's coastal nightlife only really comes alive in summer.

If you're not bothered by the damp and cold, winter is a great time for cultural exploration – the coast and islands are deserted and you'll have museums and churches to yourself. Waiters and hoteliers will be delighted you're there rather than hassled by the next customer, and while you may have to wait a day for the next ferry, you won't have to queue to get on it. If you're in inland Croatia in winter, however, do wrap up warm. Finally, if you're planning winter trips to any of the islands, especially the smaller and remoter ones, bear in mind that from November until Easter they're simply not expecting you. That means accommodation can be hard or impossible to find and restaurants may be closed for the duration – check ahead before you catch the ferry.

SUGGESTED ITINERARIES

THE WEEKEND For a weekend trip, the top of your list should really be the Croatian capital, Zagreb, which you'll find has more than enough to keep you busy for at least two to three days – if not longer. Alternatively, you could take advantage of budget fares to Dubrovnik, Split or Pula – or Osijek, which might just give you enough time to visit Kopački Rit as well.

ONE WEEK A one week visit would give you enough time to base yourself on the coast, visiting some of the islands, or to start from Zagreb and explore some of inland Croatia. Budget flights make it easy to fly into one city and out of another, with two single tickets not necessarily costing any more than a return – so you can potentially cover a lot more new ground.

TWO-THREE WEEKS If you have two or three weeks, you can see quite a bit of Croatia without having to rush – although there's always the temptation to rent an apartment and spend a whole week in one place. In either case, you can work your way up or down the coast making the most of the excellent ferry network, visit Istria, and head inland to Zagreb and Slavonia. A two- or three-week stay also gives you plenty of scope to include a decent hiking trip on Velebit or Gorski kotar.

A MONTH Those with a month in Croatia should count themselves lucky indeed, and as with a two or three week visit can divide their time between travelling along the coast and visiting Istria, Zagreb and inland Croatia.

HIGHLIGHTS

SCENIC INTEREST For wild karst scenery right on the seashore, you can't beat the Velebit massif, at its most accessible in Paklenica National Park, which has well-marked trails for all grades of walking. Less rugged scenery, punctuated by falling water, is provided by the rightly famous Plitvice Lakes National Park and the Krka River and Falls, both of which easily outshine the crowds.

Offshore, the island of Mljet is a personal favourite, with its saltwater lake and roaming mongooses, while if you have no time to do anything at all, you'll still have time to take the ten-minute ride from Dubrovnik to the island of Lokrum. The country's most famous beach is Zlatni Rat, near Bol, on the island of Brač, though if it's sand not shingle you're after then head to Šunj on the island of Lopud, and if you have your own boat then you'll find the exquisite Kornati archipelago irresistible.

Inland, there's little to match the rugged beauty of the Istrian interior, with its hilltop villages, or the Zagorje and Žumberak regions to the north and southwest of Zagreb, where rolling hills are home to vineyards and dozens of castles from the late Middle Ages onwards.

WILDLIFE AND BOTANY Gorski Kotar, the strictly protected nature reserve to the east of Rijeka, has the country's rarest fauna, with bear, lynx, wild boar and wolves on the hoof, and various species of eagle and vulture in the air. In the Velebit, you'll also find chamois and mouflon, along with red, fallow and roe deer.

Ornithologists really are spoiled for choice, from the waterfowl and wading birds on the Neretva Delta, south of Split, and Vransko Jezero, near Zadar, to the storks at Lonjsko Polje and the abundant birdlife at Kopački Rit, in Slavonia.

Botanists, for their part, can head up to the remote Velebitski Botanički Vrt gardens and their unique mountain flora.

BY BOAT Croatia's section of the Adriatic is a sailor's paradise, with more than a thousand islands to choose from, and spectacular scenery all along the way. Remote, uninhabited islands compete with the charm of old towns like Hvar, Korčula and Rab on the islands and Rovinj and Zadar along the coast. With a boat, you can sail alongside Croatia's most spectacular cliffs at Telašćica (on the island of Dugi Otok), or lose yourself amongst the thousands of inlets and harbours of the islands of the Kvarner Bay. And there are few greater pleasures than being thrown a mooring line from a private jetty belonging to a tiny restaurant, with an evening of eating, drinking and music ahead of you.

ART AND ARCHITECTURE From the Austro-Hungarian magnificence of the northern cities like Zagreb and Osijek, to the Venetian Gothic of towns along the coast and islands, visitors to Croatia are spoiled for choice. Add one-offs like Roman Pula, medieval Dubrovnik, palatial Split, Renaissance Šibenik and Baroque Varaždin, and you'll find yourself having to pick and choose – or come back again next year. Croatia's place at the crossroads of Europe means you can find anything here, from Habsburg palaces to Greek and Roman ruins, from fortified churches to Venetian loggias and from Byzantine mosaics to medieval frescoes.

PUBLIC TRANSPORT Almost everything in this guide can be reached on public transport, which in Croatia mostly means by the regular and inexpensive buses. A good train network also connects the main cities together, but doesn't go as far as Dubrovnik. Some parts of the mountains, obviously, are a whole lot easier to reach by car than by bus, but having a car won't solve all your problems, as driving in Croatia can be pretty hard going – though it's improving every year as the road network gets upgraded. If you can't easily reach something on public transport, we'll tell you in the text.

FIFTEEN OF THE BEST This list isn't in any particular order, but represents the places I've been most taken with in Croatia.

Plitvice lakes Much-hyped, these 16 lakes interconnected by waterfalls never fail to impress, and deserve their UNESCO classification as a World Heritage Site. See page 158.

Diocletian's Palace, Split Spreading out from the peristyle, the streets of the old town of Split were once palatial corridors and the houses huge reception rooms for the former Roman emperor in retirement. It's difficult not to be captivated. See page 281.

Risnjak National Park Situated within the confines of Gorski Kotar, and featuring Croatia's biggest diversity of flora and fauna, this is the perfect park for mountaineers and naturalists alike. See page 223.

Šibenik Cathedral Šibenik itself is lovely, but the 15th-/16th-century cathedral here – Croatia's most important Renaissance monument – is terrific. See page 264.

Biokovo Overhanging the Makarska Riviera, Biokovo is Croatia's answer to Cape Town's Table Mountain, offering fabulous views out over the islands of Brač and Hvar. See page 291.

Lokrum This is a haven, just a short boat ride away from the bustle of Dubrovnik, offering rocks to swim from, woods to picnic in, and a small café set in a ruined Benedictine monastery. See page 341.

Roman amphitheatre, Pula It may look like a cliché on a postcard, but the world's sixth biggest extant Roman amphitheatre is a wonderful monument all the same. See page 203.

Zagreb My number one European capital city; a happening mix of bars and alfresco terraces, lovely architecture and excellent museums and galleries. See page 73.

Practical Information HIGHLIGHTS

2

Lonjsko Polje One of Europe's largest concentrations of storks – more than 500 pairs – makes this wetland park a stunning place to visit. Go by boat, when it floods in spring. See page 164.

Krka River and Falls Several sets of travertine waterfalls you can walk over, across and around, a monastery on an island in the river, and boat trips up and down, along with the chance to swim at the base of the falls, make Krka a delight. See page 265.

Trogir The traffic-free old town of Trogir is one of the most charming on the whole Adriatic coast. A medieval island settlement, it's astonishingly well preserved and well deserving of its classification as a UNESCO World Heritage Site. See page 277.

Paklenica National Park Twin karst canyons running up from the sea into the Velebit massif offer some of the best and most accessible walking and hiking in Croatia. See page 254.

Dubrovnik Clichéd, over-busy and over-priced (relatively speaking, anyway), there's still nowhere else on earth like Dubrovnik, and I keep going back, and miss it when I'm away. See page 309.

Rovinj The site that has graced a million postcards is Istria's jewel. The organically medieval historic centre of Croatia's most Italian town stands on a former island, with red-tiled roofs crowned by a Venetian campanile. See page 187.

Mljet Lush vegetation, an abandoned monastery on an island on a lake on an island, Europe's only wild mongooses and relatively few visitors make Mljet a treasure not to be missed. See page 349.

TOUR OPERATORS

IN THE UK There's a long history of package tourism as well as independent travel from the UK to Croatia, and there are plenty of operators to choose from – beyond those listed below, it's worth seeing what your local travel agent has to offer, as well as visiting www.visit-croatia.co.uk/touroperators and www.tourist-offices.org.uk.

Activities Abroad ☏ 01670 789 991; www.activitiesabroad.com. Offering family & adult activity holidays in Croatia, & perfect for those wanting to get close to Croatia's nature; activities include sea kayaking in Dubrovnik.
Activity Yachting ☏ 01243 641 304; www.activityyachting.com. Small company offering sailing holidays in Croatia, mainly based on the flotilla concept.
Adriatic Holidays ☏ 01865 516 577; www.adriaticholidaysonline.com. Specialises in sailing in the Croatian Adriatic with boats out of every major port in the country – sailing boats or motor boats. Based in Britain, the company is staffed primarily by Croatians & prides itself on its unrivalled local knowledge.
Balkan Holidays ☏ 0845 130 1114; www.balkanholidays.co.uk. Has a wide variety of package destinations on offer along the coast & on the

islands. You can order brochures & book online, or through your local travel agent.
Bond Tours ☏ 01372 745 300; f 01372 749 111; www.bondtours.com. An excellent variety of packages as well as city breaks. Highly recommended.
Bosmere Travel ☏ 01473 834 094; www.bosmeretravel.co.uk. Specialist operator with a whole variety of themed holidays, from old-timer sailing to naturist, with accommodation usually in small hotels.
Cosmos Holidays (Monarch Holidays) ☏ 0871 4238 422; www.cosmos.co.uk. Claims to be the UK's largest independent tour operator; flights from London, Manchester, Birmingham & Glasgow.
Croatia For Travellers ☏ 020 7226 4460; f 020 7226 7906; www.croatiafortravellers.co.uk. Aimed squarely at independent travellers, they can tailor a holiday to your precise requirements, or just book flights & hotels.

Croatian Villas ✆ 020 8888 6655; www.croatianvillas.com. Offering a wide selection of villas & apartments in good locations, & specialists in multi-centre holidays within Croatia & the neighbouring Balkans.

First Choice ✆ 0871 200 7799; www.firstchoice.co.uk. Specialises in southern Dalmatia, with packages to Koločep & Cavtat as well as Dubrovnik. Also offers 'Exclusive top Dubrovnik Hotels' under its Sovereign Holidays brand. Flights from London & Manchester.

Headwater Holidays ✆ 01606 720 033; f 01606 720034; www.headwater.com. Specialises in walking & sightseeing tours in Dalmatia.

Hidden Croatia ✆ 0800 021 7771; www.hiddencroatia.com. Offers flights-only as well as tailor-made trips. Flights from London & Manchester.

Holiday Options ✆ 0844 477 0451; www.holidayoptions.co.uk. One of the biggest & best-known operators, with flights from London, Manchester, Birmingham, Norwich & Glasgow.

My Croatia ✆ 0118 961 1554; www.mycroatia.co.uk. Small operator specialising in private gourmet and discovery holidays to Croatia.

Nautilus Yachting ✆ 01732 867 445; f 01732 867 446; www.nautilus-yachting.com. Well-established company offering good learning-to-sail & flotilla holidays.

Saga Holidays ✆ 0800 096 0074; www.saga.co.uk. Aimed at the over-50s, Saga has a fair range of Croatian destinations on offer along the coast & a loyal following, though their website's a navigational nightmare.

Sailing Holidays ✆ 020 8459 8787; f 020 8459 8798; www.sailingholidays.com. Specialists in flotilla sailing in central & southern Dalmatia.

Simply Travel ✆ 0871 231 4050; www.simplytravel.co.uk. Offers individual packages to villas, small hotels etc. Flights from London & Manchester.

Thomson Lakes and Mountains ✆ 0871 230 8181; www.thomsonlakesandmountains.co.uk. A subsidiary of the UK's biggest tour operator, with flights from London & Manchester.

Vamos Travel ✆ 0845 299 7807; f 0870 762 1016; www.vamostravel.com. A central & eastern Europe specialist offering a wide range of city breaks, opera & ballet holidays, stag weekends, adventure holidays, active family break holiday packages, etc, with flights from London.

IN NORTH AMERICA A growing number of North American operators now include Croatia in package tours. You can contact the New York office of the Croatia National Tourist Board (✆ +1 212 279 8672; f +1 212 279 8683) though a quicker route to a Croatian holiday is often to simply contact one of the UK operators listed above. It's also a good idea to check what's available at your local travel agent, since new tour itineraries are being developed all the time to meet evolving demand. With Croatia voted *National Geographic Adventure* 'Destination of the Year 2006', expect plenty more US operators to start including the country in their European packages.

Friendly Planet Travel ✆ +1 800 555 5765; f +1 215 572 9803; www.friendlyplanet.com. Efficient family-run Philadelphia-based operator with an emphasis on upper-end hotels & luxury coach touring.

Homeric Tours ✆ +1 800 223 5570 (within US), +1 212 753 1100 (outside US); f +1 212 753 0319; www.homerictours.com. A Mediterranean-focused operator founded in 1969.

Picasso Tours ✆ +1 800 995 7997/+1 310 645 7527; www.picassotours.com. A Washington DC-based boutique operator that includes a comprehensive itinerary covering the coast, the Plitvice Lakes & Zagreb.

Trafalgar Tours ✆ + 1 866 544 4434; www.trafalgartours.com. One of the world's largest & best-known tour operators. Croatia features in its extensive Treasures of Europe coach tour spanning 9 European countries from Italy & Germany to Hungary, Austria & the Czech Republic.

IN CROATIA There are a number of well-established tour operators and travel agents within Croatia who can organise holidays from abroad, including the travel to and from your home country. Unless you're coming from the particularly well-served UK, you may want to try one of the following:

Atlas ✆ 020 442 222, 020 442 900; f 020 411 100; www.atlas-croatia.com. The Dubrovnik-based company has been around since 1923, & offers everything from tailor-made holidays to coach tours.

2

Generalturist ☎ 01 480 5652; www.generalturist.com. Also founded in 1923, Generalturist has been owned by Diners Club since 1999, & offers a full range of holidays, usually booked through travel agents rather than direct.

Marcopolo ☎ 052 816 955; f 052 816 616; www.marcopolo.hr. Rovinj-based operator, specialising in individual & activity-based holidays in the northern Adriatic.

For details of tour operators in Zagreb see page 84.

RED TAPE

PASSPORTS/VISAS Nationals of most English-speaking and EU countries only need a valid passport to visit Croatia for up to three months; if you want to stay for longer, it's far easier to leave the country and come back in again than it is to get an extension. If you don't need a visa for Croatia, you shouldn't need one for hops across the border to neighbouring Bosnia & Herzegovina and Montenegro, which now apply the same three-month visa exemption for tourists as Croatia.

Full details of who does and doesn't need a visa for Croatia, as well as up-to-date addresses and phone numbers of all the Croatian diplomatic missions worldwide – and foreign diplomatic missions in Croatia – can be found on the Ministry of Foreign Affairs' website (*www.mvp.hr*).

CROATIAN DIPLOMATIC MISSIONS ABROAD
UK and Ireland
UK Embassy of the Republic of Croatia in the United Kingdom of Great Britain & Northern Ireland, 21 Conway St, London W1T 6BN; ☎ +44 207 387 1144/ 2022; f +44 207 387 0936/0310; e croemb.london@ mvp.hr/consular-dept@croatianembassy.co.uk. (Embassy also covers Croatian representation for Gambia, Ghana, Liberia, Nigeria, Uganda, Sierra Leone.) ⊕ Mon–Thu 11.00–14.00, Fri 10.00–12.00.
Ireland Embassy of the Republic of Croatia, Adelaide Chambers, Peter St, Dublin 8; ☎ +353 1 476 7181; f +353 1 476 7183; e dublin@mvpei.hr

Australia and New Zealand
Canberra Embassy of the Republic of Croatia (also covers New Zealand), 14 Jindalee Crescent, O'Malley, ACT, 2606, Canberra; ☎ +61 2 6286 6988; f +61 2 6286 3544; e croemb@bigpond.com
Melbourne Consulate General of the Republic of Croatia, 9/24 Albert Rd, South Melbourne, 3205, Victoria; ☎ +61 3 9699 2633; f +61 3 9696 8271; e croconmel@mvpei.hr/concro@labyrinth.net.au
Perth Consulate General of the Republic of Croatia in Australia, St George's Terrace, Perth, 6831, Western Australia; PO Box Z5366; ☎ +61 8 9321 6044; f +61 8 9321 6240; e croconpe@mvpei.hr/ crocons.perth@mvpei.hr
Sydney Consulate General of the Republic of Croatia, 4/379 Kent St, Sydney, 2001, New South Wales 1230; ☎ +61 2 9299 8899; f +61 2 9299 8855; e crocons.sydney@mvpei.hr/ cro_con_Sydney@speednet.com.au
New Zealand Consulate General of the Republic of Croatia, 291 Lincoln Rd, Henderson/PO Box 83200, Edmonton, Auckland; ☎ +64 9 836 5581; f +64 9 836 5481; e cro-consulate@xtra.co.nz

USA and Canada
Chicago Consulate General of the Republic of Croatia, 737 North Michigan Av, Suite 1030, Chicago, IL 60611; ☎ +1 312 482 9902; f +1 312 482 9987; e chicago@mvpei.hr/croatia@chicagonet.net
Los Angeles Consulate General of the Republic of Croatia, 11766 Wilshire Bd, Suite 1250, Los Angeles, CA 90025; ☎ +1 310 477 1009; f +1 310 477 1866; e crocons.los-angeles@mvpei.hr/croconla@aol.com
Mississauga Embassy of the Republic of Croatia in Canada, 918 Dundas St E, Suite 302, Mississauga, Ontario L4Y 2B8; ☎ +1 905 277 9051; f +1 905 277 5432; e genmiss@mvpei.hr
New York Consulate General of the Republic of Croatia, 369 Lexington Av, New York, NY 10017; ☎ +1 212 599 3066; f +1 212 599 3106; e newcons@ mvpei.hr/croatian.consulate@verizon.net

Ottawa Embassy of the Republic of Croatia, 229 Chapel St, Ottawa, Ontario K1N 7Y6; ☎ +1 613 562 7820; f +1 613 562 7821; e croemb.ottawa@mvpei.hr; www.croatiaemb.net

Washington DC Embassy of the Republic of Croatia, 2343 Massachusetts Av, NW, Washington DC, 20008; ☎ +1 202 588 5899; f +1 202 588 8937; e washton@ mvpei.hr/public@croatiaemb.org

There are also consulates in New Orleans (☎ +1 504 586 8300, ext. 316); Pittsburgh (☎ +1 412 843 0380); Seattle (☎ +1 206 772 2968); and Kansas City (☎ +1 816 333 3317).

FOREIGN DIPLOMATIC MISSIONS IN CROATIA
Most English-speaking countries have embassies or consulates in the capital, Zagreb, while the UK also has consulates in Dubrovnik and Split.

UK and Ireland

UK (Zagreb) Ivana Lučića 4, 10000 Zagreb; ☎ 01 600 9100; f 01 600 9111; http://ukincroatia.fco.gov.uk/en/. Note that since 2009 all UK passport applications in Croatia have been handled by the British Passport Processing Centre in Düsseldorf.
UK (Dubrovnik) The British Consulate, Vukovarska 22/1, Mercante centar, 20000 Dubrovnik; ☎/f 020 324 597

UK (Split) The British Consulate, Obala Hrvatskog narodnog preporoda 10/III, 21000 Split; ☎ 021 346 007; f 021 362 905
Ireland (Zagreb) Miramarska 23, 10000 Zagreb; ☎ 01 631 0025. At time of writing (April 2010) the Irish Consulate in Split was temporarily closed; no reopening date was available.

Australia and New Zealand

Australia (Zagreb) Nova Ves 11/III (Kaptol Centar); 10000 Zagreb; ☎ 01 489 1200; f 01 489 1216. Visa section ☎ 01 489 1209; f 01 489 1230; www.croatia.embassy.gov.au; www.auembassy.hr

New Zealand (Zagreb) (c/o the Croatian Homeland Foundation) Trg Stjepana Radića 3, 10000 Zagreb; ☎ 01 615 1382; f 01 611 5116

USA and Canada

USA (Zagreb) Thomasa Jeffersona 2, 10010 Zagreb; ☎ 01 661 2200; f 01 661 2373, www.usembassy.hr. Out of town, towards the airport; good directions available on the embassy website.

Canada (Zagreb) Prilaz Đure Deželića 4, 10000 Zagreb; ☎ 01 488 1200; f 01 488 1230

For a comprehensive click-through list of all embassies and consulates in the Croatian capital, go to www.zagreb-touristinfo.hr, and select Diplomatic Institutions from Useful Information in the sidebar menu.

POLICE REGISTRATION
All visitors to Croatia are expected to register with the police within 24 hours of arrival. If you're staying in a hotel, hostel or campsite, or in a private room arranged through an agency, don't worry – this will be done for you automatically.

If you're staying in a private room or with friends, they're supposed to register you. This doesn't always happen – but unless you're picked up by the police, it shouldn't be a problem. Even if you are questioned, if it's clear you're just a tourist, the police will generally just tick you off and make sure they know where you're staying. But if you've been unregistered for a long while, you could be in more serious trouble.

CUSTOMS
There are no restrictions on the personal belongings you can bring into Croatia, though the government recommends you declare big-ticket items (boats, laptop computers, expensive camera or movie equipment etc) to be sure of being able to re-export them hassle-free. Crossing into or out of Croatia in your own non-Balkan registered vehicle, it's incredibly rare to be stopped or seriously questioned for any length of time, however.

Standard customs allowances apply for duty-free – 200 cigarettes, one litre of spirits, two litres of table wine and 250ml of perfume per person – and large amounts of some products, such as coffee and non-alcoholic drinks, also attract a special tax and should be declared. If you're taking your pets, then make sure they have an international veterinary certificate showing that it's been at least two weeks, but not more than six months, since they've had their rabies shot.

You can take as much foreign currency as you want in and out of the country (though you're expected to declare amounts larger than 40,000kn), but you can't export more than 15,000kn worth of local currency. For goods purchased in Croatia costing over 500kn, you can claim a VAT refund on the way out of the country on presentation of the PDV-P 'tax cheque' the merchant will have given you for this purpose – but it can be a giddyingly long procedure. Any questions you have can be answered by the helpful staff at the Customs Administration in Zagreb, ✆ 0800 1222 (general information) or ✆ 01 610 2333 (main office), www.carina.hr.

GETTING THERE AND AWAY

There are five main ways of travelling to Croatia: plane, train, bus, car or boat. You could also arrive on foot, by bicycle or by hitching a lift (but see page 50).

✈ **BY AIR** Flying to Croatia is easily the quickest way of arriving – Zagreb is just two hours from London, and Dubrovnik is only half an hour further. Both British Airways (*www.britishairways.com*) and Croatia Airlines (*www.croatiaairlines.hr*) fly to Croatia, though not always direct or every day – summer flights tend to be both direct and a good deal more frequent. Expect to pay anything between £100 and £500 for a scheduled return flight, including taxes.

In 2006, a whole slew of budget airlines started flying to Croatia from the UK:

easyJet www.easyjet.com. From Bristol & London Luton to Rijeka (the airport there is actually on the island of Krk) & from London Gatwick and Bristol to Split & from London Gatwick & Liverpool to Dubrovnik (easyJet also operates flights to Ljubljana, which is a possibility for Zagreb).
Flybe www.flybe.com. From Birmingham, Exeter & Southampton to Dubrovnik, & Birmingham & Southampton to Split (summer only).
Jet2 www.jet2.com. Belfast & Leeds Bradford to Dubrovnik, & Newcastle to Split (summer only).

Ryanair www.ryanair.com. From London Stansted to Pula & London Stansted, Edinburgh & Dublin to Zadar. Ryanair also operates flights from Osijek to Frankfurt, which then has plenty of onward connections to the UK.
Thomsonfly www.thomsonfly.com. From London Gatwick & Manchester to Dubrovnik, & London Gatwick, Birmingham & Manchester to Pula (summer only).
Wizz Air www.wizzair.com. From London Luton to Zagreb.

Routes and timetables tend to change, so check the websites.

There are also charter flights available, with Airtours (*www.airtours.co.uk*) offering flights from London Gatwick and Manchester to Pula; First Choice (*www.firstchoice.co.uk*) from London Gatwick and Manchester to Dubrovnik; Hidden Croatia (*www.hiddencroatia.com*) from London Stansted and Manchester to Pula, Rijeka, Split or Dubrovnik; Holiday Options (*www.holidayoptions.co.uk*) from London Gatwick, Birmingham, Bristol, Manchester, Norwich and Glasgow to Split or Dubrovnik; Newmarket Holidays (*www.newmarket-group.co.uk*) from London Gatwick, Belfast, Exeter, Newcastle, Glasgow, Cardiff, Manchester, Edinburgh and Liverpool to Dubrovnik (but not in July and August, bizarrely); Palmair (*www.palmair.co.uk*) from Bournemouth to Split and Dubrovnik; Sunsail Holidays (*www.sunsailflights.co.uk*) from London Gatwick to Dubrovnik; Thomas Cook (*www.thomascook.com*) from London

Gatwick and Manchester to Split and Dubrovnik; and Thomson Holidays (*www.thomson.co.uk*) from London Gatwick and Manchester to Pula.

There are no direct flights from the USA, Canada, Australia or New Zealand, but most airlines will be able to route you through a European hub, usually in conjunction with Croatia Airlines. Prices from New York to Zagreb start at around US$1,000, but can rise to over US$2,000 depending on the time of year and your choice of airline. From Australia and New Zealand, standard tickets are US$2,500+, but with some judicious searching you can usually get a much better deal by choosing to route your Europe-bound flight through one of the hubs served by low-cost carriers, such as German Wings (*www.germanwings.com*) or Wizz.

If you're having trouble finding a reasonably priced flight through the usual channels (newspapers, travel agents etc), there are a number of alternatives. One is to take a package tour – see the list of tour operators on page 28. Even if you want to sort out your own accommodation, some operators will be happy to arrange a 'flights-only' package for you. Even if this isn't the case, it can sometimes still work out cheaper to book yourself on a package and then not use the entire accommodation segment – though if you do this, you should check the conditions very carefully to ensure you still have a return flight home. Charter operators flying to Croatia from the UK are listed above.

You should also surf the internet, as it can be a great place to shop around for flights. If you're looking for the cheapest route, try www.whichbudget.com, as well as UK sites such as www.cheapflights.co.uk, www.lastminute.co.uk, www.opodo.co.uk, www.skyscanner.net or www.travelocity.co.uk, or US sites like www.expedia.com or www.farebeater.com. But don't imagine that just because it's on the internet it's necessarily the cheapest – you may find the fare in your local travel agent's window is still better. Note, too, that the sites listed immediately above don't include fares from low-cost carriers or charter operators.

BY RAIL The train is a slow and difficult way of getting to Croatia, and not significantly cheaper than the plane. The journey from London to Zagreb or Rijeka takes over 24 hours non-stop, and involves at least three or four changes – and there's no railway to Dubrovnik. But if you're a train lover, have access to a cheap ticket or are planning on stopping off at various places on the way, it's nonetheless a great way of travelling.

If you're roving round Europe, Croatia can be included on an Interrail (*www.raileurope.co.uk*) or a Eurail pass (bought outside Europe – see *www.eurail.com*).

International connections come in to Zagreb from Ljubljana (five daily, 2½ hours), Belgrade (four daily, 6–7 hours), Budapest (three daily, 5–7 hours), Munich (two daily, 9 hours), Trieste (four connecting trains daily, one direct, 5½ hours), Venice (two daily, one direct, 7–8 hours), Innsbruck, Salzburg and Vienna (one daily, 9, 8½ and 6½ hours), Sarajevo (one daily, 9 hours) and Skopje (one daily, 9 hours).

BY BUS Luxury coaches cruise between most cities in Europe, but it's a long journey (London to Zagreb takes between 30 and 40 hours) and buses aren't as cheap as they used to be (sample fares, without student discount, range from £120 upwards). That said, if you can get a discount, this may be a viable way to go. A vast range of bus-related websites are available from www.budgettravel.com, while from the UK, National Express (*www.nationalexpress.com*) is the principal operator.

In the old days, the cheapest way of getting to Croatia was to get on one of the many Athens-bound buses and ask the driver to let you off in Zagreb. It's still an option of sorts, though a risky one. It may be cheap, but there's a very real risk of never seeing your luggage again – not to mention being dumped miles out of town in the middle of the night.

BY CAR In spite of the long drive (London to Zagreb is 1,640km by road; London to Dubrovnik 2,175km) and the expense (tolls and fuel in Europe are pricey), having your own car in Croatia can certainly be an advantage, especially if you're travelling as a family, or planning on moving around a great deal and wanting to visit remote places. Unless you're wedded to the idea of touring in your own vehicle, it can be much more cost effective to rent a car once you get there rather than take your own, and all the big companies have agencies in the main cities and airports. If you're doing this, make sure you book the car before you arrive in Croatia, as it's much more expensive once you get there if you haven't reserved ahead. Note that traffic on the coast can be extremely busy in the summer.

If you do decide to drive all the way, you'll find life greatly improved with a new fast road from Ljubljana to Zagreb (though the tolls in Slovenia are surprisingly expensive), and a new motorway from Zagreb to Split, making Dalmatia a whole lot easier to get to than it used to be. The motorway is planned to run all the way to Dubrovnik, although at the time of writing (2009) it hadn't got that far south yet.

An alternative – slower, but with its merits – is to drive down through Italy and then take the car ferry across. At around € 90 for the passage (car + driver), it's more pricey than coming through Slovenia and Croatia – especially if you take a cabin – but it does mean you can take a break in Italy on the way. Ferries run from Ancona, Pescara and Bari, in Italy, direct to Zadar, Split and Dubrovnik, as well as to some of the larger islands. There are also services from Venice to Pula, Poreč and Rovinj. If you're doing this in summer (and some of these lines only run in the summer), it's essential to have a ferry booking – Italians simply love Croatia, and tend to bring their cars with them. The five main companies plying the Adriatic are Azzurra Line (*www.azzurraline.com*), Jadrolinija (*www.jadrolinija.hr*), SNAV (*www.snav.it*), Split Tours (*www.splittours.hr*) and Venezia Lines (*www.venezialines.com*). There's also a new fast catamaran that runs from Pescara to Split, via Hvar, in just five hours – check out www.sanmar.it.

In truth, however, if you're only going to main tourist centres – especially in high season, when coastal traffic can be terrible – why not just forget about driving altogether and stick to public transport?

 BY BOAT You can travel across and up and down the Adriatic on one of the many ferries that ply the Croatian coast all the way from Pula and Rijeka in the north to Split and Dubrovnik in the south. The ferries are a slow but very attractive way of getting around, and a reminder of the only way people travelled any distance here as recently as the 1930s.

International ferries aren't especially cheap, with a typical passenger fare across the Adriatic in summer starting at € 40 – see the previous section for details of the various ferry companies operating between Italy and Croatia. If you're travelling down through Italy by train and planning to cross the Adriatic from Ancona, also make sure you get off at the Ancona Maritime stop rather than the main train station. And if you're coming via Bari airport, bear in mind that the seaport is a long way distant, and you'll need to factor in moderately expensive taxi rides (or inconvenient buses).

Ferry travel is the only way to get between the coast and islands, and the main centres are well connected all year round, though ferries are generally more frequent in summer. If you're on foot, there's no need to book (on the whole), and the short-hop ferries are inexpensive.

One of the most attractive ways of seeing the Adriatic and the Croatian coast and islands of course is from your own – or a chartered – boat. There is an extensive network of around 50 marinas offering around 12,500 berths, while a whole raft of companies offers charters, from skippered motor launches to self-sail yachts. Prices vary enormously depending on what you're looking for (see page 52 for more details), and you should book well ahead, as it's becoming increasingly popular.

TOURIST INFORMATION AND MAPS

Croatia has an active national tourist board and dozens of tourist organisations locally, so there's usually no shortage of information available. Maps, while often great at the town or regional level, are less satisfactory when it comes to providing for hikers – for these, search out the local hiking maps published by SMAND (see below).

TOURIST INFORMATION The Croatian National Tourist Board is an excellent source of information and can provide you with maps, brochures and accommodation details. The www.croatia.hr website is a great place to start, but if you don't have easy access to the internet you may want to contact one of the following offices for information:

Head office Croatian National Tourist Board, Iblerov trg 10/IV, 10000 Zagreb; ☏ +385 1 469 9333; f +385 1 455 7827; e info@htz.hr
UK office Croatian National Tourist Office, The Lanchesters, 162–164 Fulham Palace Rd, London W6

9ER; ☏ +44 20 8563 7979; f +44 20 8563 2616; e info@croatia-london.co.uk
USA office Croatian National Tourist Office Inc, 350 Fifth Av, Suite 4003, New York 10118; ☏ +1 212 279 8672/8674; f +1 212 279 8683; e cntony@earthlink.net

(These are the only English-language offices. For other European regional offices, see *www.croatia.hr*.)

Once in Croatia, you're likely to find that most tourist or information offices – in reality and on the map – are actually closer to travel agents; they'll be keen to help you find accommodation and arrange excursions, but may not be so useful when it comes to maps or finding local information. Official tourist information offices, where they exist, are listed throughout this guide.

MAPS The national tourist board can provide you with a useful reversible 1:1,000,000 (1cm = 10km) road map/tourist map that is good for situating yourself and planning an itinerary, and is perfectly acceptable for most users. This can be complemented with Michelin map #736 (the same scale), which covers all the countries formerly in Yugoslavia – some drivers prefer it over the tourist office's map, though there's frankly not that much to choose between them.

More detail – at a higher price – is provided by Freytag and Berndt's 1:250,000 Croatia/Slovenia road atlases, or the separate maps covering the various parts of the country, available from the Austrian publisher in 1:250,000, 1:500,000 and 1:600,000 sections. Two chunks of the Dalmatian coast are even covered at 1:100,000.

Kümmerly and Frey, the Swiss publisher, also does a reasonable 1:500,000 map covering Slovenia, Croatia and Bosnia and Herzegovina; Belletti Editore has a similar offering, but only covering Croatia and Slovenia; and Nelles has a good driving map of the Croatian Adriatic Coast with Istria at 1:225,000 and the rest of the coast at 1:525,000, and includes town plans for the main centres. You may also see the Hungarian Cartographia (1:850,000) on offer, but it's not great, to be honest.

Far and away the best map for drivers is the 1:300,000 two-sided map of 'Bosnia Erzegovina', which is published by Studio FMB Bologna – it covers all of Croatia except eastern Slavonia, and is a good deal more accurate than any of the others, though unfolding it and turning it over on the move is no joke, as it's enormous.

Finally, there's a pretty good 1:100,000 scale map of Istria published by Bruno Fachin Editore in Trieste, which also includes the only accurate map of the island of Krk I've ever seen.

None of these of course is much use for walkers or hikers looking to stretch their legs in the national parks or nature reserves. The best hiking maps by far are the detailed local (usually 1:25,000) series published by SMAND (*www.smand.hr*). These cover most of the main hiking areas (Velebit, Gorski Kotar, Bjelolasica, Biokovo, Učka,

Medvednica, etc) as well as some (though not all) of the islands. They are available through some of the larger bookshops in Zagreb (try Mladost on Ilica) and other main cities, and usually sell for about 55kn.

There is also an excellent series of maps published under the Trsat Polo imprint of the Geodetski zavod Slovinje (Slovenian Institute of Surveyors), which covers the whole coast at 1:100,000, with separate maps for Istria, Kvarner and Dalmatia 1–4. They're available in most Croatian bookshops, and at around 30kn a pop they're a bargain. The series is aimed at sailors, hikers and drivers, and includes plans of the marinas as well as sea and mooring guidance, along with contours and clearly marked footpaths – although the latter are *not* always accurate, and for hiking you really are far better off sticking with the SMAND maps. If you're planning a walking holiday, it's also well worth getting hold of Rudolf Abraham's book *Walking in Croatia*, or Sandra Bardwell's *Croatia: Car Tours and Walks*, both of which cover a range of walks on the coast and islands.

Town and city plans are generally available cheaply or for free at local tourist offices, and will get you round the main sights, though they may not be all that much help if it's a particular street address you're looking for.

✚ HEALTH *with Dr Felicity Nicholson*

The chances are you'll never need them, but here are three phone numbers worth knowing: ➊ **92** for the police, ➊ **93** for fire and ➊ **94** for an ambulance.

There is no reciprocal healthcare agreement with EU countries, so make sure you have proper health insurance for major emergencies. Normally hospital treatment and some other medical and dental treatments are free. If you are travelling from the UK then you will need to show your passport, but if you are a UK resident but not a UK national then you will need a certificate of insurance from HM Customs Centre for Non-Residents. Prescribed medicines are not free and are often no cheaper than they would be at home. In practice, you may well be told that the service you need (and that should be free) isn't available, and that you can only obtain it privately. Another reason for that all-important health insurance!

If you have a pre-existing medical condition, are pregnant or are travelling with children then you would be wise to establish healthcare facilities before arriving in Croatia. Larger hotels and tour company representatives are often able to assist, but failing that then contact the nearest British embassy or consulate for advice. A list of clinics is also provided by the International Society of Travel Medicine and can be found on their website (*www.istm.org*).

For minor treatment, a visit to one of the ubiquitous pharmacies (*ljekarna*) should sort you out, and there's very often someone who speaks some English. For more serious problems, get yourself to a clinic or hospital (*klinika* or *bolnica*).

There are no legal requirements for vaccinations for Croatia, but most doctors would advise immunisation against diphtheria, tetanus and polio (given as an all-in-one ten-yearly vaccine – Revaxis), and hepatitis A (Havrix Monodose or Avaxim). For longer trips (four weeks or more), or for those working in the medical field or with children, vaccination against hepatitis B is advised. Ideally, a course of three injections is required, the minimum time for which is over 21 days.

Similarly, a course of rabies injections (three doses over a minimum of three weeks) is advisable for those working with animals, or spending a longer time in Croatia (see page 39). Tuberculosis (TB) is spread through close respiratory contact in crowded conditions and may occasionally be spread through infected milk and milk products. Experts differ over whether a BCG vaccination against tuberculosis is useful in adults: discuss with your travel clinic.

Travellers planning to go rambling or trekking in the countryside during the spring–autumn period are at risk of tick-borne encephalitis. The ticks that transmit this potentially fatal disease live in long grass and overhanging tree branches. Precautions include wearing long trousers tucked into boots, and a hat. Using tick repellents and checking for ticks at the end of the day can also help. Remove the ticks (see box below). If you do find ticks, remove them as soon as possible (see below) and go to a doctor for treatment. Pre-exposure vaccine is in short supply in the UK, but, if you do manage to track some down, it's worth having. Three doses can be given over two weeks if time is short. However, it's still important to seek medical help in the event of a tick bite.

If you use needles for any reason, you should bring a doctor's note explaining why, and if you wear contact lenses or glasses, bring spares; repairs and replacements aren't a problem, but can take time. It also does no harm at all to have a doctor's and dentist's check-up before you go – far easier at home than abroad.

You can drink the water if it's from a public supply; however, the mineral content may well be different so could cause stomach upsets. It is always safer to drink bottled water.

TRAVEL CLINICS AND HEALTH INFORMATION A full list of current travel clinic websites worldwide is available on www.istm.org. For other journey preparation information, consult www.nathnac.org/ds/map_world.aspx. Information about various medications may be found on www.netdoctor.co.uk/travel.

FITNESS Many a walking, hiking or cycling holiday has been ruined by a lack of form, so if you're planning one, try to get fit before you go. The best exercises are cycling and hill walking – far preferable to running or jogging. If you're surrounded by a dearth of hills to practise on, ordinary stairs make for easily the best substitute.

COMMON PROBLEMS You're less resistant to disease during your first weeks abroad, so make sure your diet contains enough vitamins – take supplements if you're not sure. Drink bottled water if the source is suspect – publicly supplied water is fine, but in the mountains, rivers and streams should be treated with caution; use chlorine-based water purification tablets if you're a long way off the beaten track. You may also want to bring with you a mild laxative and something for diarrhoea, although both problems can normally be fixed with a change in diet (soft fruit for the first; dry-skinned fruits for the second). If you're afflicted with diarrhoea, your biggest danger is dehydration, so make sure you drink plenty – soft drinks are good.

Even if you're not heading into the wilds, it's a good idea to bring along a small supply of sticking plasters (band-aids), antiseptic cream and mild painkillers (aspirin or paracetamol) – you can top up your supplies of these at any pharmacy.

TICK REMOVAL

Ticks should ideally be removed as soon as possible, as leaving ticks on the body increases the chance of infection. They should be removed with special tick tweezers that can be bought in good travel shops. Failing that you can use your finger nails by grasping the tick as close to your body as possible and pulling steadily and firmly away at right angles to your skin. The tick will then come away complete as long as you do not jerk or twist. If possible douse the wound with alcohol (any spirit will do) or iodine. Irritants (eg: Olbas oil) or lit cigarettes are to be discouraged since they can cause the ticks to regurgitate and therefore increase the risk of disease. It is best to get a travelling companion to check you for ticks and if you are travelling with small children remember to check their heads, and particularly behind the ears. An area of spreading redness around the bite site, or a rash or fever coming on a few days or more after the bite, should stimulate a trip to the doctor.

From May onwards, you should think about protecting yourself against mosquitoes. Along the coast and on the islands all you'll need is a gizmo that plugs into a wall socket at night (with the screw-in bottle of fluid; the ones that take tablets aren't effective) and you can buy these anywhere where mosquitoes are present. It is also wise to use insect repellents whenever you are outside of your accommodation. This is even more important in other parts of the country – and notably in the wetlands of the Lonjsko Polje and Kopački Rit – where you'll be confronted with evil, savage beasts, which will attack you day or night, and are perfectly capable of puncturing light clothing. Use the gizmo at night, but double up with an effective spray-on repellent during the day.

Finally, don't hesitate to see a pharmacist or doctor if you're even slightly unsure about a diagnosis or cure. But know your source if you need a blood transfusion – HIV/AIDS is less prevalent in Croatia than in many countries, but you can't be too careful. Occasionally immigrants or long-term expatriates may be asked for proof that they are free from HIV infection. Check if you need this when applying for visas or work permits.

MOUNTAIN HEALTH Prevention being far better than cure, walkers and hikers should be conversant with first aid – or at the very least carry a booklet covering the basics. It's especially important to know how to deal with injuries and hypothermia. If you're in real trouble, call the police or alert the mountain rescue service (see *Mountain safety*, page 51).

Hypothermia This is responsible for the deaths of more walkers, hikers and climbers than any other cause. It occurs when the body loses heat faster than it can be generated, and the commonest cause is a combination of wet or inadequate clothing, and cold wind. It's easily avoided by making sure you always have a waterproof, a sweater or fleece, and a survival bag with you – even if you're hiking with only a daypack.

If one of your party shows signs of hypothermia – uncomfortable shivering, followed by drowsiness or confusion – it's essential that he or she is warmed up immediately. Exercise is not the way to do this. Wrap the victim in warm clothing, or even better a sleeping bag, then increase blood-sugar levels with food, and hot, sweet drinks.

Injury Again, prevention is much better than cure. Try to avoid walking or climbing beyond your limits – the majority of accidents happen when you're tired. If scrambling or bouldering, avoid using your knees or elbows, and keep at least three points of contact with the rock (two hands and a foot, or vice versa). In the event of being injured, use surgical tape for cuts that would normally be stitched, and then bind the wound laterally with zinc-oxide tape. If you're going a long way off the trail, take an inflatable splint.

Altitude sickness Croatia's lack of very high mountains means this is one problem you're unlikely to face, but if you've trekked up from sea level to 1,500m and feel dizzy or confused you should stop and rest. If this doesn't work, return to a lower altitude. And remember, altitude sickness doesn't discriminate – youth and fitness don't help at all.

SNAKES In the extremely unlikely event of being bitten by a snake, try not to panic, as a racing heart speeds up the spread of venom – much easier said than done, of course. Most first-aid techniques do more harm than good. If possible, splint the bitten limb and keep below the height of the heart, then get the victim to hospital immediately.

RABIES Rabies is present throughout the country and is spread by the saliva of any warm-blooded mammal – most commonly dogs. If you are bitten, scratched or licked over an open wound then wash the wound with soap and running water and apply an antiseptic – even alcohol will do. Go as soon as possible to a doctor for treatment. You should still go for treatment even if you have had the pre-exposure course, but it does make treatment easier and less expensive than if you have not. This helps stop the rabies virus entering the body and will guard against wound infections, including tetanus. Pre-exposure vaccinations for rabies is particularly important if you intend to have contact with animals and/or are likely to be more than 24 hours away from medical help. Ideally three doses should be taken over a minimum of 21 days,. Contrary to popular belief these vaccinations are relatively painless.

If you think you have been exposed, then post-exposure prophylaxis should be given as soon as possible, though it is never too late to seek help, as the incubation period for rabies can be very long. Those who have not been immunised will need a full course of injections. The vast majority of travel health advisors including WHO recommend rabies immunoglobulin (RIG), but this product is expensive and may be hard to come by – another reason why pre-exposure vaccination should be encouraged.

Tell the doctor if you have had a pre-exposure vaccine, as this should change the treatment you receive. And remember that, if you do contract rabies, mortality is 100% and death from rabies is probably one of the worst ways to go.

INSURANCE A good idea – it's reassuring to know you can be flown home if necessary. Read the fine print and make sure it covers what you'll be doing (walking in the mountains, for example). A general policy, covering health, theft and third party insurance, is usually cheaper and less hassle than multiple policies, though you may find you're already covered for some or all of the risks by existing insurance, such as private healthcare (which sometimes includes foreign travel) or that provided to holders of credit cards.

If you need to claim, you'll have to provide supporting evidence in the form of medical bills, in the case of health, or a police statement, in the case of theft. Obtaining the latter can be very hard work, but essential if you're hoping for reimbursement.

Travel policies are issued by banks, travel agents and others, and it's worth shopping around amongst reputable providers, as the price varies considerably. Arrange for the insurance to cover your full journey time, and keep the policy safe with your other travel documents.

SAFETY

Croatia is safer and freer of crime than most EU countries, though the normal precautions you'd apply at home apply here, too – don't be showy with money, jewellery or flashy possessions, and avoid the seedier or ill-lit parts of cities at night. You're more likely to be robbed by fellow travellers than by Croats, so be especially careful in hostels, campsites and overnight trains or buses, and keep your valuables close to you and separate from the rest of your luggage.

Car theft, however, is increasingly prevalent, and foreign-registered cars – and especially expensive foreign-registered cars, such as Audis, BMWs and Mercedes – are attractive to thieves. Generally speaking, you wouldn't expect problems along the coast, though be careful where you leave your car in any big city, and don't leave your vehicle unattended for more than a day anywhere – it's tantamount to painting a 'Steal Me' notice on it.

You'll see lots of police around, and they have rather fearsome powers – freedom of dissension shouldn't be taken for granted. The police carry out occasional spot checks on locals and foreigners alike for identification, so make sure you have your passport or identity card with you at all times. Otherwise, you'll find the police friendly and helpful, though, apart from along the coast and in the capital, few speak any English.

If you're driving, keep to the speed limits. There are an astonishing number of speed traps – especially along the Magistrala, the coast road running all the way from Opatija to Dubrovnik – and foreigners attract police attention. If you're stopped for a traffic violation, you may find the police negotiate a lower penalty with you – the heavier fine for speeding, for example, may be traded down to the lower fine (payable in cash) for not wearing your seat-belt.

Turning into a one-way street the wrong way in Dubrovnik, I was immediately stopped by the police, and told to park the car in a spot reserved for the disabled. I was then given a choice of having my licence taken away and a 1,500kn fine (for driving the wrong way down a one-way street – unmarked as such, I might add), or paying the 150kn fine for parking in a disabled spot. I'll leave you to guess which I chose (clue: I still have my licence).

If you do get closely involved with the police, stay courteous, even (especially) when it's difficult to do so. Stand, rather than sit, if you can (it puts you on an even footing), and establish eye contact – if you can do so without being brazen or offensive about it. Some people recommend shaking hands with officialdom, but it depends very much on the circumstances. Wait until an interpreter arrives (or anyone who understands you clearly) rather than be misunderstood, though this may not happen on the same day. And remember that you can be held at a police station for up to 24 hours without being charged. Your consulate will be informed of your arrest, normally within the first day.

MINEFIELDS Along the frontlines of the war of the early 1990s – and that means in about a third of the country – minefields were laid down, and a handful still haven't been completely cleared. Most are plainly marked off with barbed wire and skull-and-crossbones signs saying 'Mine', and it would be plainly stupid to explore further.

Not every minefield is labelled, however. If you see villages that seem to have been abandoned for ten years or more, or fields that haven't been cultivated for a long while, there's a real risk of uncleared mines, and it's best to leave well alone – I was going to say 'tread carefully', but that hardly seems appropriate.

There are uncleared mines in parts of southern Velebit and Paklenica – all the more reason to carry a decent map.

Finally, if you're travelling in the former war zone – most of Slavonia, and pretty much anywhere inland between Karlovac and Split – it's wise to stick to roads and tracks that carry regular traffic, or to marked footpaths in the national parks and nature reserves.

SMOKING Non-smokers beware: with more than a million smokers (and one of Europe's highest rates of lung cancer), Croatia is one of the last bastions of the 40-a-day habit, and – until very recently – very few places offered non-smoking facilities, and bars and cafés were often thick with smoke.

However, in May 2009, Croatia introduced a ban on smoking in indoor public spaces – including cafés, bars and restaurants. Needless to say, this was a vast improvement, but it caused such an uproar among smokers that whether the ban actually stays in place is now open to question – it was due to be reviewed in October 2009. Restaurants at least seem destined to remain smoke-free.

Regardless of the outcome, most of the upper-end hotels have offered non-smoking rooms, and even non-smoking floors, for some time, so it's worth asking when you make your booking. Likewise, the bars and restaurants in these hotels – and some of the more upmarket establishments – have smoke-free sections, though you're still inevitably going to get some exposure to the smoke drifting over from the main area. In such cases, with smoking very much the norm, it may still be difficult to ask local people to refrain.

WOMEN TRAVELLERS Croatia is a safe country for women travellers, though, like anywhere with a big influx of holidaymakers, it has its fair share of local men on the make. This tends to come in the form of courteous persistence rather than aggression, and is usually easily rebuffed. Speaking firmly – in any language – should make your intentions clear.

People dress here the same way as they do anywhere in Europe, so there's nothing to worry about as far as dressing modestly is concerned – though wandering around churches in beachwear is likely to offend. If you want to get your kit off, head for the nearest naturist beach (usually marked FKK) – you won't be pestered.

GAY AND LESBIAN TRAVELLERS Homosexuality may have been legalised a generation ago in Croatia, but you won't find people particularly tolerant or open about it. Zagreb's first-ever gay parade wasn't held until June 2002, and only a few hundred people took part – heavily protected from hecklers by a slew of riot police.

Most activity is still very much underground, and even in Dubrovnik, one of Croatia's most tolerant and liberal cities, there is only a small gay/lesbian scene – though Zagreb does now finally have some good gay clubs, bars, video stores and saunas, and some hotels in the city have earned a reputation for being gay-friendly.

Elsewhere, same-sex couples (men in particular) can still raise eyebrows (or even hackles) when checking into hotels, though, as everywhere, younger people tend to be more tolerant than their elders. How you handle it will be up to you – some may be happy with a plausible cover story; others might find this too hypocritical.

For further information on gay-friendly places in Croatia, see www.croatia-gay.com.

TRAVELLING WITH KIDS Though perhaps not as children-friendly as the UK in terms of facilities, Croatia is nevertheless a great place to travel with kids, who will love the endless coastline, warm sea, ferry-hopping and mountainous ice creams. Many of the larger resorts cater for families with children, and with the new smoking ban (at least, if it stays in place – see opposite), cafés and restaurants are no longer as smoke-ridden as they once were. See Will Gray's excellent *Travel with Kids* for inspiration.

DISABLED TRAVEL Croatia has done a great deal to introduce active programmes and legislation to support the disabled. The country's main airports, train stations and bus stations are disabled-friendly, with ramps and lifts where needed, and good disabled toilets.

There are also ramps and lifts in all buildings with public access across the country, and most of the better hotels and restaurants are also equipped for the disabled.

In the capital, Zagreb, you'll find lowered public phones, and an ongoing curb-lowering initiative which makes the pavements more wheelchair-friendly. Most street crossings are equipped with pedestrian tracks and sound signals for the visually-impaired. City public transport is free for the disabled, and a good number of the city's trams and buses, as well as the funicular up to the old town, are wheelchair-friendly too. Trams are equipped with displays for the deaf and spoken announcements for the blind – though these are in Croatian only.

In Dubrovnik, there's no disabled access onto the famous city walls, but you can get in and around most of the old town with no major problems – though the crowds at particularly busy times of year (or day) can be oppressive if you're wheelchair-bound.

Access for the disabled in other cities and tourist destinations is generally pretty good, but obviously less easy where there are cobbled streets in old towns or through the narrow streets and lanes of hilltop villages.

There are disabled parking spaces across the country, and these are generally well-respected, particularly following a campaign based around the immediate towing away of improperly parked vehicles combined with signs carrying the message 'if you take my place, take my disability'.

WHAT TO TAKE

The best way for packing for anywhere – and Croatia's no exception – is to set out all the things you think you'll need and then take only about a third of it. How much you eventually end up taking will depend to a large extent on whether you have your own transport (everyone takes more in their own car) and whether or not you're planning on camping (camping comes with a list of irreducibles – see opposite). But be realistic, especially if you're going to have to carry all your own stuff – what feels like an easy 15kg pack in your living room can be more like a sack of rocks halfway up a mountainside.

If you're coming to Croatia for a beach holiday, it's worth remembering that the majority of the beaches are rocks or pebbles, so bring appropriate beach footwear – along with the usual hat, sunglasses, suncream etc. Summer evenings along the coast can be cool, but are rarely cold, so a light sweater should be sufficient; but if you're coming here in winter, bring warm clothes, especially if you're going inland or into the mountains.

Don't forget the usual range of documents you'll need – passport, tickets, travellers' cheques, cash, insurance papers, credit card, driving licence – and something to carry them in. A belt-bag or pouch is practical, but also draws attention to where you're keeping your valuables; I prefer a zipped pocket for the essentials, whether that's in a daypack or trousers, but it's a personal choice. And bring any books you want to read – except in the major cities and tourist centres, you'll have trouble finding much more than yesterday's papers.

Also, bring spare glasses if you wear them, along with any special medicines you need. You may also find it handy to have a tube of travel detergent with you for rinsing out your smalls, and a travel alarm for those early starts. And last but not least, if you're bringing any electrical appliances – even just a hairdryer or a phone charger – remember an adaptor. Croatian sockets are the same round two-pinned variety you find all across Europe.

WALKERS AND HIKERS Walkers and hikers need adequate clothes from the ground up, so make sure you have decent footwear – light, waterproof boots with good ankle support and a strong sole can make the difference between comfort and misery. But bring another pair of lighter, more flexible shoes, too, as you can get seriously fed up with wearing boots night and day. Proper hiking socks, whilst expensive, are worth every penny, but, again, make sure you have alternatives, not just for washing, but for those evenings out or for travelling to and from your hiking destination.

For hiking in the mountains, you'll need hard-wearing trousers, especially if you come into contact with karst. Jeans are tough, but useless in the mountains, as they're heavy and uncomfortable when wet and take ages to dry. Unless you're travelling in winter, you'll also need shorts, as it can warm up quickly during the day.

Take a variety of tops, so you can wear more thin layers rather than fewer thicker ones, and don't forget the all-important fleece and waterproof jacket. It's definitely worth spending more on these last items – breathable, workable clothes are the difference between being warm and dry and cold and wet.

If you're using a rucksack as your main luggage you might prefer to go for tall and narrow rather than short and wide – not only is this easier for walking but it's also a whole lot more manageable for going through doorways and along narrow corridors.

Whatever your luggage, make sure you also have a good daypack, with adequate space for everything you might need on a full day's walk – extra clothing, survival bag, water bottle(s), food, camera, maps, compass, penknife, medical kit, sunglasses, etc (see also *Mountain health*, page 38). If you're going high into the steeper national parks (notably Paklenica), you should definitely have walking poles or a stick with you, as the paths can be slippery. The best sort are retractable poles, which can fit into your bag.

CAMPING It sounds obvious, but if you're camping, take a tent that's easy to pitch (and practise at home before you leave) – trying to assemble an unfamiliar model on a windy and rainy night is suffering itself. I know: I've been there. Bring tent sealant and repair material; both are hard to find outside rare specialist shops.

What you have in the way of a sleeping bag and sleeping mat will define the shape of your nights – and, again, it's worth testing these before you leave home. Buy a down-filled bag if you can afford it, as they're warmer and more comfortable in use, and more compact when rolled, although care should be taken to keep them dry, as they lose their insulating properties when wet and take a long time to dry.

It can be worth dispensing with cooking materials, eating utensils and pre-packed food altogether. Given that freelance camping is illegal, you're generally going to be close to both restaurants and supermarkets, and in summer three hot meals a day aren't essential. Again, it's a personal choice, but the business of finding fuel, the weight and bulk, and the overriding cheapness and cheerfulness of cafés and restaurants, has always put me off doing my own cooking while camping in Croatia.

$ MONEY

Since May 1994, Croatia's currency has been the kuna – literally a marten, named after the trade in marten skins in Roman times, and first struck as a Croatian coin in AD1256. It's one of the few currencies in the world still officially named after an animal (the American buck was never legal tender, even if the word's still in fashion an awful long time since trading in deer skins was a measure of anything in the USA).

The kuna (HRK is the international three-letter code) is divided up into 100 lipa (literally lime tree, or linden). There are 1, 2, 5, 10, 20 and 50 lipa coins, 1, 2 and 5 kuna coins and 5, 10, 20, 50, 100, 200, 500 and 1,000 kuna banknotes. There's also a 25-kuna coin, but the chances are you'll never see one. On the whole, people aren't comfortable with the two largest notes, and you may have trouble breaking them – ask for 100s and 200s when you're changing money.

The euro has also increasingly been used as a semi-parallel currency – the vast majority of Zagreb's visitors switched to the euro in 2002. Most people are comfortable with euro pricing, and you can usually pay with euros if you need to – but don't necessarily expect the right (or complete) change. You're much better off changing enough money for a couple of days at a time and getting used to the kuna. The kuna is pretty stable, averaging around 7.30 to the euro and 8.4 to the pound.

Finding a place to buy kuna is a doddle – all banks, exchange offices and post offices, and most travel agencies and hotels will happily let you turn in your money, though you're better off with euros or sterling than US dollars, as there are so many dollar forgeries in circulation. Exchange rates are (remarkably) almost the same wherever you choose to change your money – fractionally worse at hotels, perhaps, but the difference is minimal. The black market for currency exchange – which thrived in the former Yugoslavia in spite of being one of the least efficient known to man – was mercifully put out of its misery.

Banks – unusually for Europe – are often open from seven in the morning to seven in the evening on weekdays and until one o'clock on Saturdays, though many close for lunch. At major train stations and airports, and in the bigger cities, some banks even open on Sundays.

Major credit cards (notably Visa, Eurocard/MasterCard and American Express) are accepted by most big hotels, restaurants and shops, though away from the coast their use isn't ubiquitous – and if you're staying in private rooms (see page 55), you'll find cash is king. Credit and debit cards can also be used for raiding cash dispensers (widespread on the mainland, less so on the islands), though most take either Visa or Eurocard, but not both.

Money is safest brought in the form of travellers' cheques, which are worth the small commission you pay for the peace of mind. You lose about the same percentage of your money if you use a credit card, but it's easier to keep track of cheques. American Express cheques are still the most widely used, easily recognised and most quickly refunded in case of loss or theft, and your local bank will issue them to you (though you may have to insist).

Finally, have enough money/resources with you – having money wired to you from home is an expensive hassle.

BUDGETING

How much you'll spend will depend mostly on what level of luxury you're looking for, and to some extent on the season and where you're going.

Camping and using public transport is going to cost a lot less, obviously, than staying in swanky hotels and cabbing it around town. That said, Croatia is neither particularly cheap nor expensive – broadly speaking you should expect to pay about the same as in western Europe. Hotel accommodation and restaurants are on average slightly cheaper than in the UK, but about the same as in France – though house wine can be considerably cheaper than in either. Supermarket prices are slightly higher than they would be in the UK.

After the cost of getting to Croatia, your biggest single expense will be accommodation. Expect to pay € 40–100 per night for a double room in private accommodation in summer, while doubles in hotels start at around € 40 and rise beyond € 500 (room prices are always quoted in euros though paid in kuna). Single rooms are relatively scarce, but when available go for about 70% of the cost of a double. Off season along the coast those establishments (both hotels and private rooms) that don't close up altogether will discount by up to 20% in spring and autumn, and as much as 50% in winter. And in Zagreb, you can expect to pay a bit less at most hotels at weekends.

For a couple, daily food and drink costs from around 250kn for picnic food bought in supermarkets and maybe one meal a day in a cheap restaurant or pizzeria, to 600kn for breakfast in a café and lunch and dinner with wine in more upmarket restaurants. An average grill-type restaurant meal for two, with salad, skewers of meat and wine, averages around 100kn a head. A nice fish dinner on the Adriatic, on the other hand, can easily set two of you back 750kn or more.

Public transport is fairly inexpensive by EU standards, with a single-zone Zagreb bus ticket costing 10kn. Typical bus fares in autumn 2009 were 110–125kn for the 285km from Zagreb to Zadar, and 200–235kn for the 565km from Zagreb to Dubrovnik.

If you're really eking out the kuna (camping, picnic food) you could get away with a budget of 150kn per person per day. Twice that would get you into private rooms and cheap restaurants, while 500kn would buy you a nice holiday, but not fish every day. For that, and upper-end hotels, you'd need to count on 1,000kn or more per person per day.

For two weeks in the shoulder season (May and October) using public transport and staying in private rooms, expect to spend around 560–600kn a day for two people.

Travelling 4,000km in a fortnight in June with your own car and staying in a mix of small hotels and private rooms, will cost 900–1,000kn a day – in both cases this doesn't include the cost of getting to Croatia.

Entry fees for attractions are reasonably inexpensive, but in a constant state of flux, so haven't been specifically included with each sight here – in 2009, however, you could expect to pay 7kn to see the treasury in Dubrovnik Cathedral, 30kn to visit the Meštrović Atelier in Zagreb or 50kn to walk around the walls of Dubrovnik. Entry to the national parks ranges from 30kn (North Velebit) to 110kn (Plitvice).

TIPPING A service charge isn't included in your restaurant bill, so – assuming the service has been good – it's appropriate to round up the bill to the nearest 10kn or so (although waiting staff in places like Dubrovnik increasingly expect 10%). Don't be afraid not to tip if you think the service has been terrible, but equally don't be too stingy or extravagant – people appreciate a little extra, since they're generally less well off than their customers, but leaving a huge tip can tend to rub it in (as well as spoiling things for future diners). Taxi drivers the world over expect fares to be rounded up, and Croatia's no exception.

OPENING TIMES

Croats are industrious and hard working, but like to knock off early and enjoy the evening. So you'll find people up at dawn, and many offices and shops open from 07.30 or even 07.00, but you may well find businesses shut after 16.00. Supermarkets and pharmacies have fairly long hours, and tend to be open all day, while smaller shops may take an extended lunch hour.

Generally speaking, things tend to be open when they're needed – if there's a real demand, then it'll be met. So you'll find tourist agencies in the main resorts open from early in the morning until late at night, seven days a week, in summer, but probably only open in the morning and on weekdays for the rest of the year. To be sure of finding a tourist office open, the 08.00–11.00 slot is far and away the most reliable time, all year round.

If everything's closed and you're looking for accommodation, you can almost always find something by asking at the nearest bar or café – there's usually someone who knows somebody with a spare room.

Museums are almost always closed at least one day a week – Monday, more often than not, but see individual listings for details – and many close for the day at 13.00 or 14.00.

Restaurants generally serve lunch from 12.00 to 15.00, and dinner from 18.00 to 22.00, though cheaper places like pizzerias, and almost everywhere on the coast in summer, will have more extended hours.

Many churches – even some of the bigger ones – are only opened for church services, and the periods just before and after them. The tourist office can sometimes help you find the person with the key, however, if there's something you absolutely must see.

GETTING AROUND

You can get around Croatia by plane, train, bus, car, bicycle and hitchhiking – or on foot – and around the Adriatic by ferry, or on your own (or a rented) boat. The train network is good to points connected to Zagreb, but poor (non-existent) along the coast, where you'll find yourself on the ubiquitous buses or ferries. Public transport is regular, effective and good value for money, but can be slow and is sometimes overcrowded – notably in summer.

✈ **BY AIR** Croatia Airlines' (*www.croatiaairlines.hr*) domestic flights are pretty good value, and a great way of getting from one end of the country to the other, especially if you've already seen it all from the bus. A one way, online fare from Zagreb to Dubrovnik went for as little as 219kn (€ 30) in autumn 2009; the flight takes around 55 minutes, compared with the 12- to 14-hour, 230kn bus ride. Buy tickets from any travel agent or online at the website, but if you're planning on flying in summer make sure you book well ahead and bear in mind that if you do so from a travel agent outside Croatia, the price could be considerably higher.

🚅 **BY RAIL** Trains have greatly improved in the past decade, and cover the north and east of the country fairly comprehensively. They're about the same price as buses, for any given distance, but can be faster (inter-city, *brzi*) or slower (local trains, *putnički*). Trains can get very crowded, especially in summer, but they tend to be reasonably punctual. Local trains (the ones not marked in red on timetables) are usually much less crowded, and much less punctual. The high-speed line between Zagreb and Split has been dogged with problems (including a major accident in 2009), but has reduced the journey time between the two cities to around 5½ hours.

For all trains, buy tickets in advance (unless there's no ticket office); you'll pay a surcharge if you wait until you're on board. *Dolazak* means arrivals, while both *odlazak* and *polazak* mean departures. *Blagajna* is where you buy your tickets.

Major railway stations all have left-luggage facilities, normally costing around 10kn a day per piece of luggage. Don't lose your receipts or you'll have a terrible time recovering your bags.

If you have access to the internet, you'll find all the timetables at the most excellent Croatia Railways website (*www.hznet.hr*).

🚌 **BY BUS** The bus network is wide-ranging, reliable and regular, and operated – as in Switzerland – by a well-organised federated system of inter-connected small companies. Buses offer the best way of coming into contact with local people, and are the only way of travelling on public transport along the coast and on the islands. The hourly average speed clocks in at about 45km/h, and costs around 40–50kn per 100km, though prices and speeds vary quite a bit depending on the route. Buses that go on ferries to the islands include the ferry fare in the cost of the ticket.

On major routes – such as Zagreb to Rijeka or Zadar, for example – buses leave every hour or even more frequently; in remoter areas, they may only run once or twice a day, or even once or twice a week, to coincide with local needs.

If a bus originates in the town you're leaving from, then you can buy tickets and make reservations at the bus station, and you should do this a day or more ahead if you can. Otherwise, wait for the bus to arrive and either pay the conductor as you get on or pay once you're underway. If you can't get a reservation, don't buy a ticket – with several companies often plying each route, it's sensible not to lock yourself in to any particular one until you're sure of being able to travel.

Luggage is stored in the holds under the bus, and you'll pay a small supplement (often around 10kn) for this. The price seems to be entirely arbitrary and provides you with paltry insurance, but it's an amount sufficiently large for the bus company not to want to lose, however, so your luggage should be guarded safely.

If your bus breaks down – it happens – the chances are it will be taken away and repaired enough for your journey to be completed. Your luggage won't be returned to you until repairs are complete, so keep with you anything you might conceivably need in the next few hours, even on short journeys.

Buses stop every two hours or so for a *pausa*, and the conductor shouts out the duration of this above the din: *pet, deset, petnaest* and *dvadeset minuta* are the commonest break lengths (5, 10, 15 and 20 minutes). These invariably occur where you can grab a quick drink/snack/meal. Watch the driver and you won't go far wrong, but be warned that the bus will go without you if you've made a mistake. Buses sometimes change drivers at these stops – this would have caught me out on a couple of occasions, were it not for the helpfulness of fellow passengers.

It's sometimes difficult – particularly inland – to obtain reliable information on bus departures. Sometimes this is out of helpful ignorance, sometimes from a willingness to please. If it's known you want a bus at 11.00, you may be told there is one, just to make you feel better. Ask several sources open rather than closed questions (ie: 'What time is the bus to Koprivnica?' as opposed to 'Is there a bus to Koprivnica early tomorrow morning?') and you may find a consensus building up.

Another problem you may encounter is localised information, meaning that if you have to change buses to get to your destination, you may not be able to find out the timings for the second part of the journey before you get there. There's not much you can do about this.

BY CAR The most comfortable and often quickest way of travelling is by car, and sometimes it's the only way to get somewhere really remote. Road quality has improved enormously in the 20-odd years since I first drove in Croatia, and there are now several good sections of motorway open – you'll pay tolls on these, though they're not excessive. The most expensive stretch, the 380km from Zagreb to Split, costs 161kn, while the 40km bit of motorway from Karlovac to Zagreb is 16kn. The toll bridge across to the island of Krk costs 30kn, while the Učka tunnel, above Opatija, is 28kn. Fuel costs around 8kn per litre.

Inland, the roads are less well maintained than you'd expect in western Europe (and often unpaved in really remote areas), while along the coast the single-lane Magistrala, running from Rijeka to Dubrovnik, inevitably clogs up in summer with holiday traffic – though the opening of the new motorway from Zagreb to Zadar and Split has alleviated the problem to some extent, and within the next couple of years (it was still incomplete in autumn 2009) the fast road should extend all the way to Dubrovnik.

Street parking in cities is a non-starter (pay instead for public parking) and parking anywhere along the coast can be a major hassle in high season.

You may find Croatian drivers rather ambitious – to the extent that blind corners and oncoming traffic aren't seen as a natural impediment to overtaking – but don't be competitive; the omnipresent (and omnipotent) traffic police are quick to keep drivers in line with steep fines and worse. Speed limits – 50km/h in built-up areas; 90km/h out of town (locally variable; keep your eyes peeled) and 130km/h on the motorway – are strictly enforced.

In the event of an accident or breakdown, you can call the Croatian Automobile Club's hotline (\ 987; *www.hak.hr*). If you see someone else in need of assistance, you're legally obliged to stop and help. And remember: it's illegal for drunks or children under 12 to sit in the front of the car; the blood alcohol limit is 0.05%, or zero for drivers under the age of 24 (it was zero for all drivers until recently); all passengers must wear seat belts; it's illegal to drive whilst using a mobile phone; and headlights must be on at all times.

To source car parts or fix problems, your first port of call should be a petrol station – these are usually open from dawn until dusk, though on some main roads and in big cities there are 24-hour outlets. Try to ensure your car's roadworthy and insured against fatal breakdown, however. Although parts are in better supply and repairs more quickly effected than they used to be, it can still be an expensive and time-consuming business.

Car hire Car hire in Croatia isn't especially expensive, as long as you book ahead, from outside the country – count on spending from €300 a week with full insurance and unlimited mileage. The major companies are represented in all the main population

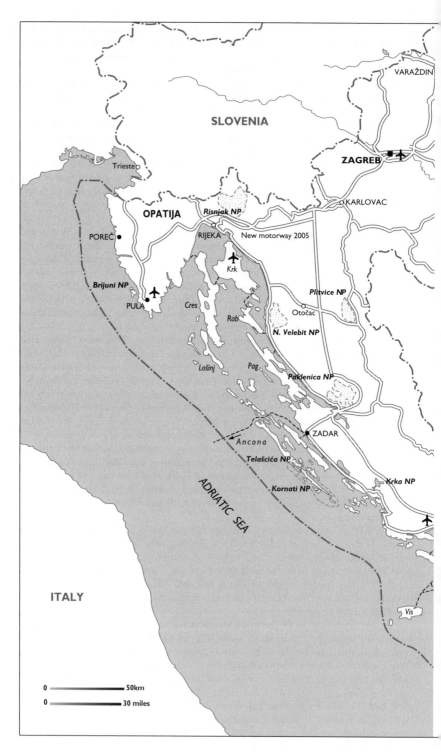

VARAŽDIN

SLOVENIA

ZAGREB

Trieste

OPATIJA   *Risnjak NP*   ○KARLOVAC

POREČ●   RIJEKA   New motorway 2005

Brijuni NP   *Krk*

PULA   *Cres*   *Plitvice NP*

Rab   Otočac

N. Velebit NP

Lošinj   *Pag*   *Paklenica NP*

Ancona   ●ZADAR

Telašcića NP   *Krka NP*

Kornati NP

ADRIATIC SEA

ITALY

Vis

0 ▬▬▬▬ 50km

0 ▬▬▬▬ 30 miles

HUNGARY

KOPRIVNICA

BJELOVAR

Drava

SISAK

Sava

POŽEGA

ĐAKOVO

OSIJEK

VUKOVAR

SLAVONSKI BROD

BOSNIA & HERZEGOVINA

SPLIT

Brač

Makarska

Hvar

Drvenik

Ploče

Korčula

Pelješac

MLJET NP

Mljet

DUBROVNIK

Bari

SERBIA

MONTENEGRO

centres and the most popular tourist destinations, as well as at airports, and increasingly don't hit you for a huge penalty if you pick up and drop off at different places. For details of car hire companies in Zagreb see page 80.

BY BICYCLE Sadly, as a keen cyclist, I have to report that main-road mainland Croatia's really not very cycle-friendly. Courtesy is in short supply, traffic density is too high for comfort, and along the coast there isn't even the alternative of small roads or cycle paths to choose from. You should do anything you possibly can to avoid the Magistrala – it's not just busy, but downright dangerous, particularly in summer.

One way of doing this is to be clever with ferries and the islands, which are absolutely superb for cyclists. Central Dalmatia, in particular, has taken an excellent initiative in publishing a great series of maps entitled 'Central Dalmatia by Bike', which covers the islands of Šolta, Brač, Hvar and Vis, with suggested routes and route-profiles provided. Zagreb County has also published a fine series of cycle routes/maps – see page 127 for details – and there's a fine 'Bike and Bed' initiative (*www.bike-bed.com*) from the Croatian Cycling Association (*www.bicikl.hr*), which lists cycle-friendly places that aren't too far apart from one another.

Cycle touring can also be a great way of visiting the interior, and remains an excellent way of getting to meet local people. There are innumerable little Croatian villages connected by roads that aren't even on the map because they don't carry any traffic, but you do need to be good at navigating, and well provisioned, as road signs are in short supply. Make sure you have decent off-road tyres, too, as surfaces are highly variable (and often gravel rather than tar).

HITCHHIKING Definitely not a recommended option. Tourists are unlikely to pick you up and locals tend to be travelling very short distances.

🚶 WALKING AND HIKING Walking is the slowest but most interesting way of getting around – you could follow in the footsteps of Patrick Leigh Fermor, who walked from the Hook of Holland to Constantinople in 18 months in 1933 and 1934. Plan on taking more money than he did though – he survived on a pound a week.

Croatia is a country ideally suited to the walker, with lots of national parks and nature reserves, and marked trails that range from the gentle stroll to the strenuous hike. A network of local and national walking, climbing and mountain associations keeps the paths in good repair, and staffs and maintains the mountain huts and lodges.

Hiking in the Velebit karst is a lot like walking in the Alps or the Dolomites. Even though the Velebit is considerably lower, it shares the fairly hard climate and there's generally not much surface water around, winter or summer. You need to be well equipped and have plenty of food and water with you if you're hiking here, but it is some of the most rewarding walking I've ever done.

North of Velebit, the mountains are lower and less harsh (in Gorski Kotar, for example), while the mountains of Slavonia, between the Drava and Sava rivers are different altogether. Here, you can find rich vegetation and plenty of water, and the softer, older mountains make for excellent hill walking.

If you're going to focus on walking, consider getting hold of Rudolf Abraham's *Walking in Croatia* or Sandra Bardwell's *Croatia: car tours and walks*, which have a whole range of hikes from the easy to the demanding, covering most of the coast and islands.

Mountain safety Up in the mountains, in regions where the regular emergency services don't operate, you can call on the help of Croatia's mountain rescue service, the GSS (*Gorska Služba Spašavanja, www.gss.hr*), if you're in real trouble. Like mountain rescue people anywhere, the volunteers who staff the service won't be amused if you call them out for no good reason, but will willingly risk life and limb to bring you to safety if needed.

You can reach the GSS through the nearest information point or via a police station (*call* ❏ 92), or by calling ❏ 112. You can also contact the GSS through one of their local offices, which are listed on their website (*Gospić* ❏ 091 721 0007; *Split* ❏ 091 721 0001; *Rijeka* ❏ 091 721 0000; *Delnice* ❏ 091 721 0004), or through the head office of the Croatian Mountaineering Association (*Hrvatski Planinarski Savez or HPS;* ❏ 01 482 4142; www.plsavez.hr). If you're well equipped with enough clothing, food, water, maps and a compass, the chances are you won't need to make that call.

Marked trails Most of the trails in the national parks and nature reserves are well marked using a painted red circle with a white dot in the middle, or two red lines separated by a white line. The markings are maintained by local hiking and mountaineering associations, and are usually very clear, but if you're in a remote or rarely accessed part of the mountains, then you may find markings worn or damaged, especially if there's no mountain lodge nearby. Occasionally, you'll find trails where trees have been cut down, leaving the way ahead uncertain – try to make sure you have a local map (see page 35) and a compass with you in any case.

🛳 BY FERRY There are few experiences more pleasant than a ferry ride on the Adriatic, and in Croatia they're plentiful, economical, regular and reliable. Most domestic services are run by state-owned Jadrolinija (*www.jadrolinija.hr*), though in summer other local operators provide supplementary services.

Services vary from the roll-on, roll-off ferries used for very short hops between the coast and the nearest islands, to fast hydrofoils and catamarans, to the huge ships that ply the whole length of the coast from Pula and Rijeka to Split and Dubrovnik, once a day in each direction.

2

Local ferries are inexpensive – typical passenger fares are rarely more than 20 or 30kn – while the main coastline service, which involves a night on board, can be pricey or not depending on what accommodation option you've taken. The fare for the whole length of the coast (Rijeka to Dubrovnik) was around 250kn in the summer of 2009, dropping 20% in low season, for a place on deck or in one of the bars; a couchette was nearly twice as much; while a cabin cost up to three times the price per head.

Taking your car to the islands needn't break the bank. Short hops are charged at under 100kn, while medium-length journeys cost from 200–300kn. On the main coastal service, you'll pay a supplement of around 600kn to bring your car on the 20-hour journey.

BY BOAT: SAILING, YACHTING AND MOTOR-CRUISING

Whether you have your own boat or whether you've chartered one, and whether you're travelling by steam or by sail, there's really no better way of seeing Croatia's wealth of islands. Once you've swallowed the costs associated with the boat itself (and here the sky really is the limit), a sailing or boating holiday is (or can be) quite reasonable, with the only significant outlays being food, drink and marina expenses.

The coast and islands between Split and Dubrovnik are on the whole less crowded than the north, and are most popular with English speakers – though English is widely spoken among the whole sailing community. The Kvarner Bay is understandably preferred by Germans and Austrians, being much closer to home, while the Italians love it all, from north to south. Friends who sailed here recently have compared it to sailing in Greece 15 years ago, with uncrowded waters, hospitable marinas and local restaurants, and wonderfully picturesque villages and fortified historical towns.

Sailing and yachting experience

The type of sailing or yachting holiday you embark on will depend at least to some extent on your level of experience. Beginners can be catered for either by a pre-arranged package (see page 28) or by having more experienced friends, but bear in mind that a week on board in a confined space can strain even close friendships, so choose carefully. Once you're on board, the captain's word really is final – if he or she says jump, you jump.

Learning-to-sail holidays cost from around £450–650 per person for a week, or £700–900 for a fortnight, including flights from London.

If you're at an intermediate level, and at least one member of your crew is reasonably experienced, then sailing in a flotilla is an excellent way of improving your sailing skills, while not having to worry too much about navigation or the *bura* (gusty northeasterly wind) around the corner. Boats can be chartered by between two and eight people, with the cost decreasing as the numbers go up. Expect to pay close to £1,000 per person for a week at the height of the season if there are just two of you, but under £500 per person if you're a party of eight in May or September, both including flights from London.

Take the experience requirements for renting a boat seriously, even if not all the charter companies are as diligent about checking as they might be. Sailing is a tremendous activity, but it's also potentially hazardous and even life-threatening, so make sure you – or people in your party – have the necessary skills. Most charter companies won't need to see certificates (not all countries issue them anyway), but you may be asked to demonstrate your ability before heading out into open waters unaccompanied.

An alternative is to hire a local skipper with your boat – a good idea if no one in your group has the requisite experience, and a great way of finding hidden nooks and crannies in the islands. Expect to pay £350–500 a week for the services of a skipper.

Charters

Most people will end up chartering a boat, and there's an excellent (and comprehensive) list of charter companies – over 150 at the time of writing – complete with full contact details and type and size of boats for hire on the tourist board's website. Around 14,000 vessels are available in total, with 10,000 of these being sailing boats and the rest motorboats. Go to www.croatia.hr then select Accommodation, and then Marinas, and then look for Charters under Tourism Plus. People I know have recommended Ecker Yachting for their well-maintained boats – Ecker is based in Zadar (✆ +385 23 881 999), and has a range of sailing boats from 11 to 16 metres. Also highly recommended are Gardelin Charters (m 098 378 082; www.gardelin.hr).

During the war of the early 1990s, many boats left Croatia for havens in Italy and Greece, and some have yet to return, so there's a greater demand than supply for charters. Even if you do book early, you may find boats in less good condition than you were expecting, with the charter business still somewhat in recovery mode.

Price depends on model, size, capacity and season, starting from around £500 a week for a three- to four-berth boat in low season and escalating rapidly up to the thousands for an eight-berth yacht in August. In the summer of 2009, you could expect to pay £1,800–2,000 per week for a six-berth, 12.48m Bavaria 40 sailing boat.

Mooring Croatia's Association of Nautical Tourism, based in Rijeka, has a total of 48 marinas with some 12,500 sea moorings. The full list, along with all their facilities and individual websites (where available), can be found on the tourist board's website. Go to www.croatia.hr, then select Accommodation, and Marinas. The Adriatic Croatia International Club (known everywhere as ACI), based in Opatija, runs 21 of these (17 all year around) and has an excellent website (www.aci-club.hr) listing fees, locations and facilities.

Marinas tend to be well equipped, with restaurants, bars and shops either on-site or nearby, and good technical services. Be aware that not all charter boats have shore power installations, even though electricity is usually available. Many marinas also have hot showers and some have laundry facilities. ACI day rates run from around € 37 for small craft to € 70 for boats up to 15m.

An alternative to marinas is mooring 'stern-to' in the smaller ports. You can also find mooring lines in some harbours, while remoter restaurants seeking sea-trade will put out mooring lines to encourage you in. Ports and bays are sometimes free, but can charge variable fees depending on the length of the boat and how much jetty you're occupying – they're meant to provide services (such as rubbish collection, and the supply of groceries), and a receipt, in return.

Provisions/restaurants Keeping yourself in food and drink shouldn't be a problem. You can stock up on speciality items in supermarkets in towns, but you'll also find plenty of street markets and small shops in the villages on the islands. If there's been a prolonged spell of bad weather and there isn't a ferry service you may find it hard to get bread or fresh fruit, but it's very unlikely to affect you during the summer sailing season.

Restaurants, especially on the smaller islands, tend to be good value, with local wines and cheeses recommended, and you're more likely to find the homely *konoba* here than on the mainland.

Water and fuel Watering and fuelling isn't usually a problem, with all marinas and most ports having abundant supplies of both, though you may have to scout around to find the right person responsible for supplying water to boats. Some islands, however, have no water supply of their own, so don't expect to fill up here.

Charts and guides Croatian waters are very well charted, and Croatian, English, German and Italian charts are available. The Croatian sea charts come well recommended, and can be bought in most marinas and harbours once you're there. If you want to do some advance reconnoitring, you should be able to order charts from

Kelvin Hughes Charts & Maritime Supplies (*New North Road, Hainault, Essex, UK IG6 2UR;* ✆ *+44 208 502 6887,* f *+44 208 500 0837; www.kelvinhughes.com*).

If that doesn't work out (or you're not based in the UK), you can go direct to the publisher (*Hrvatski Hidrografski Institut, Zrinsko-Frankopanska 161, 21000 Split;* ✆ *021 308 800;* f *021 347 242;* e *office@hhi.hr; www.hhi.hr*), or Plovput, the government agency that looks after all the lighthouses, beacons etc (*Plovput, Obala Lazareta 1, 21000 Split;* ✆ *021 390 666;* f *021 390 630;* e *plovput@plovput.hr; www.plovput.hr*).

Also highly recommended comes the *Adriatic Pilot*, which is now in its fifth edition. This 440-page nautical guide to the Adriatic comes in at £32.50, and is well worth the expense. Another useful book is *777 Harbours and Anchorages: Croatia, Slovenia & Montenegro*. Both are available through Imray, Laurie, Norie & Wilson(✆ *+44 1480 462 114; www.imray.com*).

Winds If you're sailing outside the summer months, you'll need to keep a weather-eye out for the *bura* (the gusty northeasterly that can blow at gale-force from September to May for anything from four days to a fortnight), and the *jugo* (a warm, humid, east-southeasterly, accompanied by heavy clouds and rain).

Once winter's over, you can expect lighter winds and better weather, though during July and August storms are more frequent, and during September winds strengthen again.

Summer is characterised by the prevailing *mistral* (*maestral*), which is no relation of the Provençal horror. The *mistral* here is a sailor's dream, a fair-weather wind that springs up locally mid morning, strengthens until the early afternoon and then dies down at sunset.

The summer *bura* is more localised and much less persistent than the winter version, springing up in sudden squalls and capable of gale-force strength, particularly in the Gulf of Trieste and the Velebit Channel. Fortunately, it's very reliably forecast, so listen carefully to the weather bulletins on the radio and head for a well-sheltered port if a *bura's* on the way.

The summer *jugo* is also mostly a local wind, and is more frequent in the south than the north. Be warned it can switch quickly to a *bura* – something to be borne in mind if you're in a mooring exposed to the northeast.

Weather forecasts/safety Marinas always have the latest forecasts available, but Croatia also has three coastal radio stations that broadcast excellent weather reports – particularly for the *bura* – and warning announcements in both Croatian and English, several times a day. They receive radio-telephone messages round the clock and re-broadcast these, so stay tuned to whichever station is nearest. All three operate on VHF channel 16. They also operate on the following channels, with weather updates at the following times:

Rijeka Radio VHF channel 24 – at 05.35, 14.35 & 19.35
Split Radio VHF channels 07, 21, 28 – at 05.45, 12.45 & 19.45

Dubrovnik Radio VHF channels 04, 07 – at 06.25, 13.20 & 21.20

After the weather, the coastal radio stations broadcast nautical warning messages, with information on obstacles to navigation, lighthouse failures, prohibited areas etc. Continuous weather forecasts are also issued by harbour offices in Pula (VHF 73), Rijeka (VHF 69), Split (VHF 67) and Dubrovnik (VHF 73).

During the day, you can usually contact marinas on VHF channel 17, while harbourmasters' offices are on channel 10. Harbourmasters tend to have their own patrol boats, which can be used to help boats in distress, and (as elsewhere) they can also call on the help of any suitable ship in the vicinity, including foreign boats.

If you run into trouble, it's worth knowing that the radio-telephone is more likely to get you help than a CB-radio distress signal, as the authorities aren't usually tuned into CB channels.

⌂ ACCOMMODATION

Thanks to its popularity with tourists in the 1970s and 1980s, Croatia has a good supply of accommodation, coming in five flavours – private rooms, hotels, campsites, hostels and mountain lodges.

Private rooms offer the best value for money, but if you're in the mood to splash out there's little to beat the old-fashioned luxury of the grand hotels of the Austro-Hungarian era in the capital and in old resorts like Opatija. Most hotels on the coast and islands were built in the tourist boom of the 1970s, though the great majority have been upgraded and well restored since the war of the early 1990s, and there's a whole wealth of smaller, smarter hotels opening up around the country.

Hotel accommodation and campsites in the main resorts fill up fast in summer, so you need to reserve well ahead of time (phone ahead – weekdays 08.00–14.00 are your best bet – and confirm by fax). Turning up on the fly in high season in Poreč can be a disappointing experience.

In a category all of its own, you could also choose to holiday in a lighthouse, of which 11 are available. Pictures and descriptions are available at www.croatia.hr or www.lighthouses-croatia.com – for further information and bookings, you should contact Hrvoje Mandekić at Plovput (☎ *021 390 609;* e *turizam@plovput.hr; www.lighthouses-croatia.com*) or Adriatica.Net (☎ *01 241 5611 in Croatia; 020 718 304 37 in the UK;* e *info@adriatica.net; www.adriatica.net*).

PRIVATE ROOMS/APARTMENTS Anywhere that sees regular tourists has a supply of private rooms (*privatne sobe*) available, and for most independent travellers these represent the best-value accommodation option. They are the equivalent of B&Bs in the UK (though usually breakfastless), and are generally clean, comfortable and friendly. Their big advantage over hotels – other than reduced cost (many private rooms go for under €50 a night) – is that they offer you a chance to meet local people, though in the most popular places families are showing a tendency to insulate themselves from their lodgers.

Rooms can be sourced through local travel agencies (or through the tourist office, where there aren't agencies), but you can often save money by stopping anywhere you see signs saying *sobe/zimmer/chambres/camere/rooms/privat*.

Where buses, trains and ferries arrive in the main destinations – and notably in Split and Dubrovnik – gaggles of touts will be on hand to offer you rooms. Check both the price and location carefully, but these can be a good bargain, especially if you're staying for only a couple of nights. Through official channels, a 30–50% surcharge is usually applied for stays of only one or two nights, but if you're negotiating direct with the owner a lot will depend on the time of year and how busy a place is. Singles in theory get a double room for around 70% of the full price, but in a seller's market you may end up paying the full whack.

> **NOTE ON PRICES**
>
> Accommodation prices throughout the guide are given in euros, as this is the currency used in pre-negotiations, reservations and official accommodation quotations – although your final bill usually will be in kuna. All prices were correct as of autumn 2009.

Private rooms are classified by the local tourist office and come in three categories, I, II and III. Category I rooms will be clean and functional, but you'll almost certainly be sharing a bathroom. In Category II, you'll be bathing en suite and may even have a TV, while in Category III you'll be in some luxury.

Private accommodation also includes apartments, which can be great value for families or small groups, but check how many beds have been crammed into each room before you buy. More expensive apartments tend to be better located rather than roomier.

Inland, there's also a healthy move towards eco- or agro-tourism, with rooms being available in farmhouses and small villages. This is a nascent trend and not yet well established, but look out for signs if you're in the countryside.

Finally, with both private rooms and apartments don't be afraid to say no if you don't like the look of the place – staying somewhere that doesn't suit you can really spoil your holiday.

HOTELS

HOTELS Croatia's numerous hotels are classified by the standard international one- to five-star system, though at the lower end they don't represent very good value for money when compared with the better private rooms, which generally cost around half the price of the worst hotel in any particular town (though notably not in Zagreb and Dubrovnik).

Many establishments are still of the large, modern and functional variety, though there is a groundswell of smaller, family-run hotels appearing. Assuming you can't afford the Habsburg opulence of one of the few pre-World War I hotels still in operation, the smaller hotels are often the nicest places to stay, though rooms need to be booked well in advance. Most of the bigger hotels – which is where you're likely to be if you're on a package – have been substantially upgraded since 1995, so you're unlikely to experience the cracked plaster, 70s light fittings and intermittent hot water that made Croatian accommodation such an unlucky dip in the 1980s.

Breakfast is almost invariably included in the room price, and ranges from rolls, butter and jam to a full buffet, with a strong correlation between the quality of the food and the number of stars. You can save a fair amount of money by opting for half or full board – the supplement is usually only small – but bear in mind you'll also be condemning yourself to eating largely unexciting meals in the hotel, rather than getting out and about.

CAMPING

CAMPING In a country with fine weather and beautiful countryside, camping ought to be the ideal option. It ought to be, but it isn't always. Campsites are not especially cheap, and sites are often huge and far removed from easy access by public transport. Some of the places you're most likely to visit – notably Split – don't have campsites at all.

The explanation is a simple one – camping is mainly aimed at northern Europeans with their own transport, who come for a week or two and set up a temporary base on the beach. And if that's what you want to do, then you'll find Croatia's campsites friendly, clean and very well equipped. Expect to pay around € 20 a night for two people, a pitch and a parking space at an *autokamp*.

Freelance camping in Croatia is illegal and, if you're caught, you'll be subject to an immediate and fairly hefty fine. If you're off the beaten track and camping freelance, however, then please, please don't let it be you that starts off the forest fire. Many areas of the country, especially in the mountains and on the islands, have no free water supply, and fires are a major hazard – so much so that in some areas even smoking is forbidden (in a country that is smoking-mad). Huge areas of forest – and more than one mountain lodge – have been devastated by fire.

YOUTH HOSTELS AND STUDENT DORMITORIES

YOUTH HOSTELS AND STUDENT DORMITORIES Croatia has only a handful of officially recognised youth hostels (*www.hfhs.hr*), but with summer prices averaging under € 15 a head it can be easily the most economical option for single travellers (if you're in Zagreb, Pula, Rijeka, Zadar, Dubrovnik, Veli Lošinj, Krk or Punat). For two or more people travelling together, private accommodation tends to be both more convenient – no daytime lockout, for example – and competitive on price.

At Zagreb University, there's some access to student accommodation in summer, but, again, it's not especially good value unless you're travelling alone. Rooms go for around € 20 a head, and can be organised via the tourist office.

A new generation of hostels has sprung up over the past few years, which have added considerably to the previously rather restricted range of budget accommodation available in places like Zagreb.

MOUNTAIN LODGES Croatia has over 100 mountain huts and lodges, with facilities ranging from the basic (roof and walls) to the positively hotel-like. They're excellent value for money and are usually run by the local mountain associations under the auspices of the Croatian Mountaineering Association (*Hrvatski Planinarski Savez, HPS, Kozarčeva 22, Zagreb;* ᐱf *01 482 4142 or* ᐱ *01 482 3624;* e *hps@plsavez.hr; http://en.plsavez.hr/hps*) where you'll find a full list of the accommodation available, along with altitudes and contact numbers. You can also ask at the various park offices around the country.

Huts usually fall into the following three categories: *planinarski dom* (staffed mountain hut), *planinarska kuća* (hut open only by prior arrangement), and *sklonište* (unstaffed shelter, usually open all year).

✖ EATING AND DRINKING

What you eat and drink in Croatia will depend on where you are – in Slavonia, along the Hungarian border, you can expect to find spicy sausages and heavy, meaty soups, while along the coast you'll find an Italian flavour to the food, with plentiful pizza, pasta and fish dishes, followed by lashings of ice cream. What you're unlikely to find these days, sadly, is Hoppel Poppel on the menu. According to my trusty 1966 Gateway Guide, 'Hoppel Poppel, which the visitor feels inclined to tackle straight away because the name sounds so amusing and exotic, turns out to be a well-known international dish – hash.' Each region has its own wines and beers to be proud of, and across the country you'll find a range of fearsome spirits, designed to warm the cockles and cement friendships.

FOOD The day starts for most of us with breakfast, though it practically doesn't exist as a meal per se in Croatia. If you're in a hotel, however, then breakfast of some sort will invariably be included in the price – usually in the form of a self-service buffet, with the quality and variety of fare on offer closely correlating to the number of stars.

If you're in a private room, you can rely on cafés and *slastičarnice* (cake shops) to sell you pastries and cakes for breakfast, and if you're outside the most touristed areas you may still find *burek*, a pastry filled with cheese (*sa sirom*), meat (*sa mesom*) and just occasionally spinach (*špinat*). *Burek* is cheap, filling and usually delicious – if occasionally too greasy for comfort – but a good deal harder to find than it was a decade or so ago.

You'll also find cheap restaurants and snack bars everywhere – often billed as *bife* (bar) or *roštilj* (grill bar) – serving up lunch or dinner of *ćevapi* or *ćevapčići* (spiced meatballs or small sausages, usually accompanied by spring onions and spicy green peppers), *pljeskavica* (a wad of minced meat often served in pitta bread – the Croatian hamburger), or *ražnjići* (kebab). Try any of these dishes with fiery *ajvar*, a sauce made from tomatoes, peppers and aubergines, with a dash of chilli.

Bakeries (*pekarnica*) sell a wide variety of breads (though occasionally only powdery white rolls and plain loaves) and sometimes offer ready-made sandwiches (*sendviči*) available with cheese (*sir*) or ham (*šunka*) fillings. Street markets (*tržnica*) will provide you with the usual fare for picnics etc, and you can ask for sandwiches to be made up to order at any deli counter in a supermarket (*samospluga*) – just point at the type of bread you want filled, say '*sendvić*' and point at your choice of filling.

Pizzerias are the next step up the food chain, and represent great value for money. Pizza here is close to what you get in Italy, with a thin crust and a variety of toppings – including excellent chilli peppers. Pizzerias also tend to do good (and keenly priced) pasta dishes – though personally, I tend to find Croatian pasta cooked closer to soggy than al dente.

Restaurants (*restoran, konoba* or *gostiona*) tend to focus on meat and/or fish dishes. Meat isn't especially exciting, leaning towards pork and lamb chops and cutlets, pan-fried veal, or steak, but it's generally tasty enough. Fish for its part is ubiquitous and delicious – but can turn out to be pricey. For most white fish, you'll pay by the raw weight, and a decent-sized fish for two can come in at as much as 400kn on its own. Whitebait, blue fish (sardines, mackerel, etc) and squid are, on the other hand, a lot cheaper.

Shellfish is especially popular on the coast, with steamed mussels on many menus and cockles appearing in pasta dishes and starters, and in winter (through to mid-May) you can get great oysters in the south (from Ston) priced at 10–15kn apiece. You may also see crab and lobster on the menu – but mind the price tag (and watch out for mis-translations; crayfish is often billed as lobster). Finally, you'll see plenty of *škampi* (grilled or cooked in a tomato '*buzzara*' sauce) and *crni rižot* (literally black risotto) on offer; it's a pungent dish, made with squid ink, and though it's popular it's not to everyone's taste.

You'll also see lots of *pršut*, Croatia's answer to Italy's *prosciutto*, and pronounced (and produced) in almost exactly the same way. The air-dried ham is an Istrian and Dalmatian speciality and practically melts in the mouth when sliced thinly enough – which generally it isn't.

Of course if you're vegetarian, *pršut*, like much else on the menu, is a non-starter – indeed it's a non-main and a non-dessert, too. Vegetarianism is no longer off the menu altogether, however, and even where restaurants don't offer specific vegetarian options, you can always get a cheese omelette (*omlet sa sirom*), a meat-free pasta dish, or a pizza, along with a range of salads. There are also a number of homemade cheeses (*sir*), often kept in oil, which vary from the tastily pungent to the surprisingly bland. A must-try is the slightly salty, hard sheep cheese from the island of Pag, *Paški sir*.

For basic restaurant vocabulary, see *Appendix 1, Language*, from page 369.

DRINK The most important thing you need to know is that you can drink the water – all publicly supplied water is safe unless it explicitly says otherwise. The next piece of good news for drinkers is that alcohol is pretty inexpensive when compared to northern Europe, with a half-litre of draught beer (*pivo*) costing anything from 10 to 20kn, depending on the establishment. Premium brands go for a little more, but local beers are just great, my personal favourite being *Karlovačko pivo*, from Karlovac.

Wine Croatia makes lots of wine (*vino*), and the quality – drinkable at worst – continues to improve. Almost the entire production is guzzled down domestically, however, so you're very unlikely to see it on the supermarket shelves at home. Equally, you won't see much in the way of non-local wine on menus or in the shops, so you're pretty much obliged to go the Croatian way.

In shops, you can pay anything from 30 to 300kn for a bottle, while in most pizzerias and restaurants a litre of the house red or white goes for 50–100kn and bottled wines start at around 80kn and head rapidly up from there. Swankier establishments don't always sell house wine (it's always worth asking, however, even if it's not on the menu), and you can easily find yourself spending upwards of 200kn a bottle.

Increasingly, Graševina (a white grape variety) is coming to dominate local restaurant tables – a disappointing development given the country's many better wines. The reason, as usual, is economic – the Graševina grape is easy to grow and make into cheap but acceptable wine that offers restaurants a better sales margin. While that's not to say there's not some good (and even excellent) Graševina wines, if given a choice it's worth making the effort to try some of the local Rieslings or Chardonnays too – or the excellent Vrbnička Zlahtina from the island of Krk. If you like your reds, try the sublime Dingač, which is made from *plavac mali* grapes (without fertilisers) grown on the Pelješac peninsula – but prepare to pay upwards of 150kn a bottle in a supermarket or 250kn in a restaurant.

Spirits (Rakija) Spirits are common, dangerous, and fairly cheap. In supermarkets you'll find brandies and other spirits at around 70–100kn a bottle, but you can also buy fiery and frequently excellent home-distilled spirits – especially *travarica*, a drink featuring a lot of alcohol and a few herbs – in the markets for anything from 50 to 100kn a bottle. The quality of spirits varies enormously and can't usually be determined from the label – price is a reasonable (but far from infallible) indicator. A personal favourite is Velebitska Travarica, which is made by monks up in the mountains and comes in an especially attractive bottle. On the other hand do anything you can to avoid a drink called Pelinkovac. I once had three in a row in Zagreb, convinced that at some point the apparently re-bottled wood-stain would become palatable – but it never did. It brings a bad taste to the mouth even now, just writing about it.

Friendships, business deals and meetings are all cemented with *rakija*, and it's surprising how often you'll find yourself expected to down lethal drinks. If you don't drink at all, then it's not a bad idea to come up with a plausible reason why not (health is always a reliable standby), as Croatians tend to be suspicious of anyone who won't join in.

Soft drinks In marked contrast to the abundance of alcoholic choice, there are surprisingly few soft drinks available. Cola is of course mind-numbingly popular and bottles of sweet fizzy orange are ubiquitous. In the most popular tourist spots along the coast there's a better range of drinks now available – largely due to the presence of Italians here – but otherwise the most exotic thing you'll find will be the delicious homemade lemonade sometimes available with your morning *burek*.

Coffee and tea Coffee is as popular here as everywhere, and in cafés tends to be excellent – though what you'll be served with breakfast in the lower-end hotels can be frankly disgusting. Tea is most often of the fruit variety or comes in dodgy-looking bags that tend to work better with lemon than milk. Ordinary 'English' tea is known as black tea (*crni čaj*), but don't expect to find anything you'll be able to stand a spoon in unless you bring your own. Tea and coffee will cost anything from 7 to 20kn in a café, depending on the upmarketness (or otherwise) of the establishment. If you want a latte-style coffee ask for a *bijela kava*; for decaff – increasingly available – ask *bez kofeina*.

PUBLIC HOLIDAYS AND FESTIVALS

Croatia has the usual mix of religious and secular public holidays, as well as innumerable feast days, folk festivals and annual cultural events. Specifics are covered in the relevant sections, but the national holidays and a few of the festivals are included here.

NATIONAL HOLIDAYS You should expect banks and shops to be closed on Croatia's national holidays, which fall as follows:

1 January	New Year's Day
3 February	St Blaise's Day
Easter	Sunday 24 April 2011, 8 April 2012, 31 March 2013
1 May	Labour Day
Corpus Christi	60 days after Easter Sunday, and taken seriously in Croatia, with processions and lots of first communions. Corpus Christi falls on Thursday 23 June 2011, Thursday 7 June 2012 and Thursday 30 May 2013
22 June	Day of Antifascist Struggle
25 June	Statehood Day
5 August	Homeland Thanksgiving Day
15 August	Assumption of the Virgin Mary
8 October	Independence Day
1 November	All Saints' Day
25 & 26 December	Christmas

FESTIVALS Croatia's robust Catholic heritage was built on the back of a strong pagan culture, and you'll find lots of the festivals and celebrations here owing more than a little to each. The calendar of festivities is based around both Christian (**Easter, Corpus Christi, Saints' Days**) and seasonal (**spring, solstices, harvest**) events, with Croats ready and willing to celebrate them all.

On religious holidays and feast days – not to mention the local patron saint's day – villagers and townspeople will hold processions, masses and major celebrations, and they're a great thing to be a part of if you're in the neighbourhood.

There are also innumerable festivals relating to the business of survival on the land or sea. Most seaside towns, villages and ports have at least one annual fisherman's festival (where the sea is treated with the usual mix of fear and due respect, and blessed by the local priest), while inland you can still find people casting away bad luck after the winter (using bells or branches as talismans against misfortune).

Pretty much every island and town along the coast now has a 'cultural summer' and 'musical nights' which keep things lively once the sun's gone down, with Dubrovnik's summer festival being the largest and most famous. Concerts and theatre productions are held most evenings in the old town, through six weeks of July and August, and the festival culminates in spectacular fireworks.

You'll also find two main types of folk music on show. First off are the big festivals that bring together hundreds – or even thousands – of performers. The most celebrated of these is the **Zagreb Folk Festival** in July, a five-day extravaganza drawing huge crowds and mirrored on a smaller scale across much of Slavonia. The second is the lower-key folk entertainments put on wherever tourists are to be found. Whilst these certainly shouldn't be scorned, neither do they have the originality or the authenticity of the big festivals inland. You may be better off keeping your ears pricked for a wedding party, almost invariably featuring vibrant local costumes and music.

The festival year kicks off (or closes, depending on your viewpoint) with the **New Year's Regatta** on the island of Hvar, held annually and running from 28 to 31 December, and featuring seriously competitive dinghy racing.

Things are reasonably quiet from then until the wildly popular carnival season gets under way in February, culminating on **Shrove Tuesday** – or sometimes on the weekend before. Masked parades and gaudy floats can be found in many Croatian towns, but Rijeka takes the biscuit for the biggest and most showy event. Rijeka's carnival is now second only in Europe to the one in Venice, attracting more than 10,000 active participants and 100,000 spectators. At the same time men wearing sheepskins drive evil spirits away from Rijeka's hinterland villages, using bells.

In April, in odd-numbered years, Zagreb holds its *biennale*, the International Festival of Contemporary Music. This draws the biggest names in contemporary classical music (past stars have included Stravinsky, Stockhausen, Cage and Shostakovich) and is an absolute must for those trailing music's leading edge. Check out www.biennale-zagreb.hr for more information.

Film festivals kick off in July, in Pula and Motovun. By the end of July, bikers across the continent will be revving up and heading towards Pula for the annual Istria Bikers' Rally, which draws not just rock musicians and heavy-metal bands but also more than 10,000 leathered motorcyclists. Barely a week later, on the first Sunday in August, 18th-century-uniformed cavalrymen charge around the town of Sinj, inland from Split, on horseback with lances, in the colourful *Sinjska Alka* festival which celebrates the town's 1715 victory over an army of Turks.

August sees snow as well – or at least the celebration of it – in the village of Kukljica, on the island of Ugljan, where the **Feast of Our Lady of the Snows** features both a parade and a flotilla of fishing boats setting off in honour of the snow said to have fallen there one August centuries ago. Throughout July and August on the islands you'll also have the chance to see one of the festivals of sword dances. The most famous of these is the *moreška* on the island of Korčula, which continues a tradition dating back at least 1,000 years.

In the autumn, once the harvest is in, the biggest festival is **All Saints' Day**, when every graveyard and cemetery in the country becomes a mass of flowers. The year then closes with **Christmas**, which is much as you'd expect, though a big fish rather than a turkey is the thing to have during the main celebration on **Christmas Eve**.

SHOPPING

Croatia's not a great place for bargain hunters, with prices for most goods pretty much in line with those across the EU, though you'll find an unbelievable number of shoe shops and people selling beachwear, both at prices a wee bit lower than in London or Milan. If you've forgotten to bring something with you, it'll be fairly easy to replace, but you're probably not going to need to buy extra suitcases for all the things you bought here on the cheap.

PDV (VAT) Purchase tax (PDV, or VAT) is set at a flat rate of 22% on all goods except essentials and books. In theory foreigners can get this reimbursed on single-ticket items costing over 500kn, but you have to really want the money. Fill in the PDV-P form at the point of sale and get it stamped, so that when you leave Croatia, you can have the goods, receipts and forms certified by the Croatian Customs Service – not a process for the impatient.

And that's the easy part. You then post back the certified receipts etc to the shop, along with your bank account details. Within a year or so, bingo: the money reappears. It's worth the hassle, of course, on really big-ticket items, but bear in mind when you're bringing goods back into your home country you may in any case be subject to import duties or asked to prove you've actually paid the VAT.

BOOKS If you run out of holiday reading along the coast or in the capital, you shouldn't have too much trouble finding something to read, though expect to pay about 20% over the cover price. Inland, and especially in eastern Slavonia, it's a different matter, with school textbooks often being the only English-language reading material available.

MUSIC If you get hooked on the local music – and it happens – make sure you buy before you leave the country. There's a whole Croatian pop and rock music scene, as well as traditional folk music and the curiously popular 'turbofolk', but even in an online world, Croatian music is pretty hard to come by once you're out of the country. CDs are about the same price as in most of the EU.

HANDICRAFTS When Rebecca West travelled round Croatia in 1937, she spent a good part of her trip buying up antique peasant costumes, while noting that fewer and fewer people were wearing them. This trend has continued unabated to the present day, meaning you're unlikely to see traditional dress at anything other than folk festivals or weddings. The beautifully embroidered waistcoats and skirts are still being made, but only really to fill a tourist need. Genuinely old costumes are now sufficiently hard to find – and precious – that you'd have to treat anything 'original' for sale with more than a dash of scepticism.

ARTS AND ENTERTAINMENT

With more than a nod to Austria in the north and Italy to the west, Croats love going to the theatre, and there are excellent productions to be seen at the professional theatres in Zagreb, Osijek, Rijeka, Split and Dubrovnik.

The **Croatian National Theatre** in Zagreb isn't just a theatre, it's an entire experience (see page 99). The fabulous building sees more than 200 performances annually, in a season that runs all year except August, and includes excellent **ballet**, **opera** and **theatre** productions in a mix of premieres and revivals. Theatre productions tend to be in Croatian, but all opera is put on in the original language, and of course ballet is universal. Tickets can be hard to get (though some tickets are kept aside for sale on the day), partly because – by the standards of most countries, and especially for opera – they're inexpensive, costing 30–200kn apiece. The current programme can be found in English at the theatre's website at www.hnk.hr.

Croats are also great **cinema**-goers. Fortunately for English-speakers, most of the films are subtitled rather than dubbed, straight from Hollywood. This makes going to the cinema easy enough, and tickets are cheap, but you'll be lucky to find films made outside the USA/UK that you'll be able to understand without good language skills. I once sat through the full six hours of Bertolucci's *Novocento* in Italian, with Croatian subtitles, but it's not something I'd necessarily recommend.

Croatia has more than its fair share of **concerts** and **festivals**, too. See *Festivals*, page 60, as well as individual entries throughout the guide for more information.

Most towns of any size have at least one **museum** or **gallery**, though the quality of these varies greatly – there are few modern art galleries, for example (though Zagreb's and Dubrovnik's are excellent). Mostly, too, galleries and museums reflect Croatia's long history of attachment to one empire or another, so you'll see a lot of Austro-Hungarian and Venetian influences in the art and architecture. The most notable exception is the sculptor Ivan Meštrović, whose work you'll see everywhere, and in particular at eponymous collections in both Zagreb and Split.

PHOTOGRAPHY Croatia has some of the best photo opportunities you'll find anywhere, with great weather, good light, and a wide variety of photogenic subjects. While there are lots of opportunities to shoot wild flowers and the like, wildlife photography itself can be difficult, since the most interesting animals (bear, wolves, lynx, eagles etc) tend to shy well clear of people (though you can easily become a wild boar bore, by going on the photo safari above Ogulin – see page 224).

With a long history of tourism, you're unlikely to run into people-problems with photography in Croatia – they're used to it – but that doesn't mean you shouldn't apply the usual ethical standards. Respect people's privacy, don't take pictures you know will offend, and especially don't take pictures when you're asked not to. The one thing you should be aware of, however, is that with war memories still fresh, don't even think of photographing places that might have military significance. Spending the rest of your holiday being questioned by the authorities is no fun at all.

Digital photography is ever more popular – but bear in mind the usual limitations of memory size, battery life etc, and know your camera well. If you're using a film camera it's worth noting that while print film is easily available (if a bit more expensive than at home), slide film is relatively hard to find. If you are buying film, check the use-by date; some rolls for sale are way past their prime. Finally, take film home for processing, unless you absolutely have to have the prints or slides while you're away.

ℓ MEDIA AND COMMUNICATIONS

For a country of under 4.5 million people, Croatia has a surprisingly vigorous and wide-ranging press, though it's only very recently that the main newspapers, TV and radio stations have been anything other than a mouthpiece for the state.

Communications also suffered from the heritage of state communism, but the rapid uptake of mobile telephony and the internet in the new millennium, and the increased integration of Croatia with the rest of Europe, means Croatia now has services worthy of its status as an EU supplicant. Electricity comes in the European standard size and shape, at 220V and 50Hz, and twin round-pinned plugs are used.

MEDIA Croatian independence in 1991 did little to bring freedom to the media, and it's only since the election of Stipe Mesić (in 2000) that any real efforts have been made to liberate editors and journalists from half a century of government puppet-hood. Since then the president himself has spoken out in favour of keeping the media free from politics, and has encouraged journalists to practise their profession independently, as public servants rather than government acolytes.

The dominant media provider is Croatian Radio and Television, HRT, which attracts an audience in excess of two million a day to its three TV channels and its national and local radio stations. HRT 1 and 2 produce the usual mix of news, documentaries, entertainment and game shows, while HRT 3 is dedicated almost exclusively to sport. The website, at www.hrt.hr, has an English-language site-map that will help you find the various web-streamed audio services on offer.

The most important daily newspaper is *Vjesnik* (*online at www.vjesnik.com*), which until recently was about as dry and unbiased as TASS in pre-Gorbachev days. With a change of management after the 2000 elections, the paper has found some independence – though it can still be a heavy read.

Right at the other end of the publishing spectrum is the weekly *Feral Tribune*, which even uses a fake *Herald Tribune* masthead (*see www.feral.hr*). Originally a satirical supplement to Dalmatia's largest daily, *Slobodna Dalmacija*, before the mother paper was closed down by the government in 1992, Feral Tribune gradually became more serious, and was a regular thorn in the side of the Tuđman government.

For news in English, your options are fairly limited. You can tune in to the BBC World Service on a short-wave radio, or – if you're lucky – catch one of the intermittent English-language news bulletins on HRT radio. In the bigger centres, you can pick up the main English papers a day or two (or more) out of date. Otherwise, the internet's easily your best bet, either by going through paper-specific websites like www.guardian.co.uk, the Croatian news portal www.hic.hr, or by tuning in directly to the BBC or another English-language news provider (http://news.bbc.co.uk, www.cnn.com, www.abcnews.go.com, etc).

POST Mail out of the former Yugoslavia used to take anything from two weeks to three months, and frankly post out of 21st-century Croatia isn't all that much better

– postcards within Europe tend to drift home in around two to three weeks, while airmail letters are quicker, but not enormously so. Just occasionally, something slips through a hole in the space-time continuum – a letter once arrived home in three days, and a card sent to Australia got there in eight – but you should reckon on post being fairly slow unless you pay for a premium, guaranteed-delivery service.

Post offices (*pošta*, or HPT) have long opening hours, usually from 07.00 to 19.00 (or 08.00 to 20.00), and until 13.00 on Saturdays, and parcels are reasonably cheap to send, but don't seal them until you've given the cashier time to check you're not posting bombs or contraband. If you send anything valuable you may have to pay duty on it when you get home.

If you want mail sent to you, have it addressed to Poste Restante, Pošta, postcode, Town Name. It will be delivered to the town's main post office if there's more than one – and remember you'll need photo ID, such as a passport, to recover your mail. If your family name is underlined and/or in capitals your mail is more likely to be filed correctly – but if there's nothing for you it's always worth asking them to look under your first name as well. Incoming post takes around ten days from most European destinations, and about two weeks from North America – but can be quicker, or indeed slower.

Stamps (*marke*) are also sold at news stands, tobacconists and anywhere you can buy postcards, which can save you queuing at the post office. Expect to pay around 3.50kn to send a postcard or 5kn to send a letter to Europe, and 7.50kn to send a postcard to the USA, Australia or New Zealand.

PHONE Croatia's phone network has vastly improved in the last 15 years, and you'll no longer be faced with multiple attempts to get access to the outside world. The international access code is 00, so for international calls simply dial 00 (or +) followed by your country code (+44 for the UK, +1 for the USA and Canada, +61 for Australia and +64 for New Zealand) followed by the local phone number (without the leading zero in most cases, but not in Italy or Russia, for example).

The international code for calls into Croatia is +385. Area codes within Croatia are for the most part refreshingly simple, covering large geographical areas (the whole of central Dalmatia is within the 021 area code, for example), though there are one or two anomalies, with the island of Pag being cut in two (served by 023 in the south and 053 in the north), and a whole clutch of codes used in the north. The map here shows the regional codes across the country; they're also included at the beginning of each chapter.

Partial privatisation of the former state-owned operator Hrvatski Telekom (HT) has seen the company rebranded as T-Com/T-Mobile by majority shareholder Deustche Telekom (*www.t-com.hr*). Phone boxes are plentiful, and operated by 25- to 500-unit phone cards, with the 25-unit card costing 15kn and the 100-unit card costing 40kn. Local calls normally cost one unit, with long distance calls being quite a bit more expensive, especially at peak time (*07.00–19.00 Mon–Sat*). International calls can also be made from main post offices. International calls mostly aren't exorbitant, but it does depend on the destination.

Croats, like most other Europeans, have gone mobile-mad, and almost everyone has a mobile phone – at least one. There are three mobile operators: T-Mobile, Tele-2, and VIP – though with limited geographical coverage and obscure international charges, Tele-2 isn't yet really a viable option for visitors. The network is comprehensive and the local operators have roaming agreements with their foreign counterparts, so you should find your own phone works – as long as you're on GSM.

If you're using your own mobile, however, remember that international calls will be expensive. Remember if you're calling your travelling companions that you need to make an international call: to dial a UK registered mobile being used in Croatia for example you need to dial 0044 or +44 first. And remember too that this will cost a packet, as you'll be calling from Croatia to home and back again, and paying for both segments.

If you're going to be glued to the phone, one option is to buy a local pre-paid subscription and then top up your SIM card as needed – if you do this, keep the SIM card for your home subscription in a safe place. Not only is a local pre-paid number convenient for your outgoing calls, but it also means you can easily be called from

WRONG NUMBER?

There's nothing worse than buying a guidebook and then finding out some of the phone numbers are wrong – but the sad truth is that (even though every single number is checked before going to print) numbers do change. So what to do? Your best option when we fail you (my apologies) is to log on to www.tportal.hr/imenik/default.asp?lang=en, Croatia's outstanding online phone directory. It's fast, efficient and up to date, and there are even links to other online directories worldwide. Another option is to call the tourist office – assuming their number hasn't changed in the meantime...

home. Prepaid vouchers last six months, and the subscription remains valid (and able to accept incoming calls) for a further six months. Mobile calls to other European countries cost 5–10kn per minute.

A T-Mobile pre-paid subscription in 2009 cost 148kn, including 100kn worth of calls. VIP had pre-paid subscriptions costing 159kn, including 150kn worth of calls – but their international rates were more opaque than T-Mobile's.

One final word about phones – like everywhere else in the world, you should aim to avoid calling long distance or international from your hotel room. Tariffs for fixed and mobile calls may have fallen, but hotel rates certainly haven't. The cost of a 15-minute call home from a decent hotel room can spoil your entire trip.

Some useful phone numbers:

Emergencies
Police ☏ 92
Fire ☏ 93
Ambulance ☏ 94

Public emergency centre ☏ 985
Roadside assistance ☏ 987

General
Croatian Airlines ☏ 060 300 300
Weather forecast ☏ 060 520 520

Speaking clock ☏ 95
Exchange rates ☏ 9864

Telecoms
International operator ☏ 901
International directory enquiries ☏ 902
General information ☏ 981

Local operator ☏ 988
Long-distance operator ☏ 989

INTERNET Internet uptake has been rapid in Croatia, and there's an enormous amount of information now available online (see page 378). You'll also find that most towns and resorts have an internet café of some sort, with hourly online fees coming in at anything from 20–40kn. The public access points haven't all been listed here, as they change every few months, but the nearest internet café du jour should be easy to find (ask at the tourist office or hotels).

Where Croatia has been slower on the uptake is in the regular use of email. While some people are instantly responsive, there's unfortunately barely a hotel or tourist board in the country that will reply to an initial email. During the research for this book, many hundreds of emails were sent, the vast majority into the void. The frustrating thing is that when you do follow up with a phone call, the first response is all too often: 'Ah, yes, we saw your email!'.

BUSINESS/TIME

Most Croatian businesses operate from 08.30 to 16.30, Monday to Friday. If you're calling ahead of your journey – or having people call you in Croatia – it's useful to know that Croatia's on Central European Time (CET). That's an hour ahead of GMT, six hours ahead of New York and Washington, nine hours ahead of California, and eight hours behind Sydney and Melbourne (ten in the European winter). Summer time dates in Croatia are the same as in most other European countries, with the clocks going forward an hour in spring and back an hour in autumn.

The working environment – dress, culture etc – is similar to that in most European countries, but if you're doing business don't be surprised if you're expected to cement deals or friendships with a shot (or several) of *rakija*. If you don't drink out of choice, you need to invent a good reason why – the culture isn't particularly tolerant of non-drinkers.

BUYING PROPERTY

Although prices have risen sharply over the past few years (particularly in Dubrovnik), Croatia still represents good value when it comes to buying property, whether an old stone house or a new apartment. Rules for foreigners buying property as an individual eased up in 2009, with EU buyers no longer requiring government approval. However, there is still a certain amount of red tape – and it is particularly important that land registry and other documentation is in order – so make sure you choose a reputable estate agent, and keep up to date with the current value for the area you are interested in (calculated in euros per square metre). Try the following companies: Ozana Real Estate (*www.ozana.hr*), Trinity Croatia (*www.trinitycroatia.com*), Milenka Real Estate (*www.milenkarealestate.com*).

INTERACTING WITH LOCAL PEOPLE

Croatia has been affected hugely by tourism, which has brought an improved standard of living to the country as a whole and to hundreds of thousands of individuals along the coast and on the islands. Tourism has also destroyed a way of life that was poorer and harsher and yet, paradoxically, is often fondly remembered. Your surly, inattentive waiter at the dog-end of the summer season is probably dreaming of being the fisherman his father was – even though he knows how hard a fisherman's life really is. Don't expect to be able to unravel this contradiction.

Away from the tourist spots – and especially in the mountains, and in smaller communities inland – there are plenty of opportunities to build bridges between foreigners and local people. Take the time to talk to those you meet, show people what life's like back home (photographs and postcards say more than words ever can, even if you do speak the language) and share in a cup of coffee, or a drink and a cigarette, if invited. Off the beaten track in Croatia I've been asked into the homes of people who have virtually nothing, only to be offered the little they do. Bring pictures to show, perhaps a frisbee or sketchbook to share with the children, and Western cigarettes for the adults – most Croatians smoke and, whatever your feelings, cigarettes are appreciated everywhere. There are good arguments against giving gifts to kids on the street, or handing out largesse to beggars – both encourage dependence – but in people's homes, there's very little else you can do to return hospitality.

In Croatia as a whole – and especially in the parts of the country directly affected – it's a good idea not to discuss the recent war. It's a conversational minefield, and the last thing you want is to step on a conversational landmine. Even with a population that's now 90% Croat, you won't always know immediately whether you're talking to a Croat or a Serb and, even if you are sure, opinions are sufficiently divergent to be dangerous. The only really safe thing you can say, if you're asked directly, is that you're pleased it's all over, and that peace is clearly bringing prosperity.

CULTURAL ETIQUETTE

All visitors have an effect not just on a country but on its people too. There are numerous arguments for and against this that don't need to be enumerated here – suffice to say that it's worth considering both the environmental and sociological effects of your visit.

ENVIRONMENT Croatia's environment is in good shape (see *Environmental issues*, page 6), so don't spoil it – preserving it is in everyone's interests.

The biggest impact you personally can have on the environment is to start a fire. There's almost nothing that can be done once a fire's out of control in Croatia's drier areas, so be especially careful here. Unless there's a plentiful supply of water nearby, in fact, it's advisable to avoid fires, or even naked flames, altogether.

Litter, by comparison, is a simple question of ugliness. Paper tissues take months to deteriorate, orange peel positively glows, and tin cans always look horrible. Take your litter with you – and if you collect any you find along the way you can feel suitably saintly about yourself. If you're in the wilds, and you can't find a toilet, do at least bury your doings – there are few sights (or sensations) more unpleasant than coming across someone else's.

DRESS/NATURISM In summer you won't look out of place in shorts and a T-shirt, but you won't be able to visit churches if you're too skimpily dressed – there are signs outside churches along the coast and islands giving you a pretty good idea of the dress code. Seaside topless sunbathing won't offend, but you shouldn't really be anywhere off the beach in your swimsuit (or indeed out of it).

Inland, you'll find local people more modestly dressed, though things have changed a lot in the last 15 years – you'll no longer look or feel out of place dressing the way you do back home (well, it depends on how outrageous you are back home, of course), or attract unwanted attention if you don't make an effort to conform. Quite the opposite is true these days – as a visitor you'll probably get strange looks if you're a woman in your fifties dressed all in black, or decked out entirely in retro denim if you're a man.

Back on the coast, Croatia is the main homing ground for the great European naturist – hundreds of thousands come here every year just to get their kit off. There are entire naturist resorts (the most popular are in Istria), campsites and apartment complexes, and most towns have a dedicated beach. Just look out for the FKK signs if you're interested. Croatia's also the only place I've been where you can go on a naturist sailing holiday. Mind your tackle.

DRUGS Illegal drugs are best avoided in Croatia. They're available, but the penalties are stiff, and harsher still for smuggling – don't be tempted or tricked into carrying anything across borders. Slavonia in particular has something of a reputation with the authorities for being part of a drugs corridor from Asia to the West, so be especially vigilant, and – without excessive paranoia – make sure you know exactly what's in your bags.

TRAVELLING POSITIVELY

After travelling in Croatia (and possibly even before you go) you may want to do something for the country – the two obvious ways you can help are through voluntary work or through supporting a Croatian charity.

VOLUNTARY WORK There are a number of well-established voluntary programmes operating in Croatia, though happily they're all popular and you need to book well ahead if you want to participate. Below are a few, but you can find many more if you do your own research.

A well-established organisation is **Volunteers Centre Zagreb** (*Volonterski Centar Zagreb, VCZ; Ilica 29, 10000 Zagreb;* ↘ *01 301 33829;* e *info@vcz.hr; www.vcz.hr*), which was started in 1996, and has been working to promote peace and human rights since the war ended. VCZ organises working camps in Croatia.

It's also worth getting in touch with the **Croatian Red Cross** (*Hrvatski Crveni Kriz; Ulica Crvenog Križa 14/1; 10000 Zagreb;* ↘ *01 465 5814;* f *465 5365;* e *redcross@hck.hr; www.hck.hr*), which is not just active in its own right but also works with many other partners.

The **Croatian Heritage Foundation** (*Hrvatska Matica Iseljenika; Trg Stjepana Radića 3, 10000 Zagreb;* \ *01 611 5116;* f *01 611 1522;* e *hmi-info@matis.hr; www.matis.hr/eng (in English)*), for its part, caters mainly for the Croatian diaspora of 3.5 million people around the world. The foundation organises a summer 'Task Force', which focuses on a different project each year, such as restoring medieval town walls, replanting damaged botanical gardens, or rebuilding paths in the national parks.

The **ECCIB** at Beli on the island of Cres, established to help protect Griffon Vultures, runs volunteer programmes – see page 231.

CHARITIES The single most important thing you can do to improve life in Croatia is to support any of the many organisations involved in mine clearance. In the UK, Heather Mills has done a lot in getting prosthetic limbs and financial aid to mine victims in Croatia, and has also been instrumental in setting up the **Adopt-A-Minefield** programme. Visit the website at www.landmines.org.uk, which co-ordinates anti-landmine activity and fundraising, and is directly involved in Croatia, raising money for mine clearance and for the survivors of landmine accidents. The **Croatian Mine Action Centre** or 'CROMAC' for short (Hrvatski Centar za Razminiranje, HCR) does a huge amount of work on the ground and keeps up-to-date statistics and maps on mine clearance at its website at www.hcr.hr.

Another active organisation is the **American Chamber of Commerce in Croatia** (*AmCham Croatia; www.amcham.hr*). Founded in 1998, and based in Zagreb, AmCham Croatia stresses its independence from the US Government, and has various fundraising programmes for Croatian charities, in addition to its main mandate of promoting mutual co-operation and friendship between Croatia and the USA.

Part Two

THE GUIDE

Part Two

3

Zagreb

Telephone code 01 (+3851 from abroad)

Rebecca West sized up Croatia's capital nicely when she was here in 1937: 'Zagreb makes from its featureless handsomeness something that pleases like a Schubert song, a delight that begins quietly and never definitely ends. It has the endearing characteristic noticeable in many French towns of remaining a small town when it is in fact quite large.' Indeed, today, with a population of a million, Zagreb is easily Croatia's largest and most cosmopolitan city, though the centre is still agreeably manageable on foot.

Zagreb's heart is a fine, clean example of solid Habsburg architecture, tending towards palatial elegance, and large squares from which to view it – though if you move away from the city centre you'll find sprawling suburbs and high rises, thrown up to accommodate waves of incoming workers over the past 60 years.

For more than six months of the year Zagreb is a lively outdoor city, with café tables spilling out across the pavements and flowers everywhere. In winter it can be cold and a bit oppressive, with snow on the ground for an average of over 50 days annually and the streets of the lower town seeming too large for their occupants – but with a big university and heaps of bars, clubs and nightlife on offer, the locals certainly know how to have a good time. The city is also particularly strong on classical culture, with regular opera, ballet, theatre and musical performances of international standard.

WHAT'S IN A NAME?

There are several conflicting theories about why Zagreb should be so-called, but everyone agrees that the name was first recorded in 1094, when Hungary's King Ladislav founded the bishopric here.

The most logical hypothesis is that 'Zagreb' means 'in the ditch', because of its geographic situation – a theory backed up by the old German name for the city being Agram, a contraction of '*am Graben*', meaning the same thing. Another supposition is that the city was named after efforts to scrape and dig away the soil in search of water here – though I'm sceptical about how much water that theory can hold, with the great river Sava a stone's throw away.

The name could also – if the word is Slavonian, which is itself doubtful – come from '*za grebom*', meaning 'behind the tomb', though which tomb also seems to be a well-shrouded mystery.

My favourite explanation, however, is that 'Zagreb' is a corruption of '*za breg*', meaning 'behind the hill'. Quite apart from anything else, it reflects an elegantly Austro-Hungarian-centric view of the world; anyone else would describe Zagreb as being 'in front of the hill'.

ZAGREB
Overview

↑ *Varaždin*

A   **B**   **C**   **D**

I

✕ Puntijarka

Cable car 🏠   1030m ▲ *Sljeme*

Pansion Medvednica 🏠 ☐

Tomislav Dom

MEDVEDNICA

● Zrinski Mine

2

Nature Park office ●

✕ Kraljičin Zdenac

✕ Šestinski Lagvić

Medvedgrad Fortress 🏛 ☐

Kulmerovi Dvori Mansion 🏚

3

Kod Pavela ✕

Glavica Mountain Hut ⬆

✝ Šestine

G PREKRIŽJE

Veternica Cave 🔘

Mihaljevac tram station ☐

MIHALJEVAC

4

see Zagreb Attractions n

TUŠKANAC

GRADEC

5

ALEJA BOLOGNE

Dubravkin Put 🏠

ILICA

Four Points by Sheraton 🏠

DONJI

SELSKA CESTA

TREŠNJEVKA

Zlatni Medo ✕

AVENIJA International ☐

SAL SKA

☐ Gaj

SPUNK ☆

6

Mex Cantina ✕

Fala 🏠

Movie Hotel & Pub 🏠

Močvara ☆

Ljubljana →

Sava

Best ☆

OBILAZNICA

Gallery ☆

Jarun Lake

☆ Aquarius

AVENIJA

LJUBLJANSKA AVENIJA

Remetinec Hostel 🏠

7

⛺ Motel Plitvice

Karlovac, Rijeku →

JADRANSKA AVENIJA

A   **B**   **C**   **D**

Judging by the remains found in the Veternica Cave (see page 125) on Medvednica, people have been living in the Zagreb area for at least 35,000 years. Modern history here doesn't begin until much, much more recently, however – around the 4th century BC – when Celtic tribes poured in from the north, only to be swiftly mopped up by Romans arriving from the south.

The Romans created several settlements in the area, which was important then, as now, as a crossroads on east-west and north-south trade routes. After the decline of the empire, the region faded back into obscurity, however, until the year 879, when it became part of the first Croatian state, which reached its apotheosis in 925 under King Tomislav – the guy on the big horse in front of Zagreb's main train station.

At the end of the 11th century, a lack of heirs saw the Croatian crown pass to Hungary, paving the way for the creation of the Zagreb diocese in 1094. It was nonetheless the rival communities of Kaptol (with the cathedral) and Gradec (today's old town) that made the running for several centuries thereafter.

The first cathedral was built in 1217, only to be trashed – along with everything else – by rampaging Tartars 25 years later. As a consequence, Bela IV, the Hungarian king, authorised the construction of fortifications for Gradec (it was home to the Hungarian garrison, after all) in 1242, and gave the settlement 'Free City' status for its part in hiding him from the enemy.

Solid ramparts and walls were built around Gradec by 1266, though today the only signs you'll see are the Lotrščak Tower (where the noonday cannon is fired from – see page 103) and the Stone Gate (Porta Lapidea, see page 107), one of the original entrances to the old town, though the current version is 18th century. Up above the city, on Medvednica, meanwhile, work started in 1254 on what would eventually become the imposing Medvedgrad Fortress – though from the 16th century to its pricey restoration in the 1990s, there wasn't much more to it than a few ruins.

Kaptol, for its part, was only allowed to fortify in the 15th century, with the Turks practically on the doorstep. In 1469, the Sultan's army got as far as the Sava river, where they were miraculously scared off by a single cannon shot from the Lotrščak Tower. No, of course they weren't – but that's the legend behind the cannon still fired towards the Sava every day at noon. What actually repulsed the Turks was the Sava conveniently and spectacularly bursting its banks (something that would happen regularly, and catastrophically, until the current dykes were built in 1971).

The Ottomans went on being uppity for another century, though even their great victory of 1525, which led Croatia to seek Habsburg protection, didn't see Zagreb directly invaded, and the Turks were finally routed definitively in 1593 at Sisak, 50km southeast of the city.

With no common enemy to divert them, Gradec and Kaptol were now free to continue their rivalrous relationship across the Medveščak creek dividing them (now Tkalčićeva). The painted wooden bridge across the brook was the scene of frequent and violent conflicts – most famously in 1667, when drunken soldiers loyal to the powerful Zrinski family were persuaded by Kaptol to attack Gradec, with bloody results on both sides. Although today neither creek nor bridge remains, the short street where the bridge once stood still bears the name 'Krvavi Most' – literally 'Blood Bridge'.

It was only in the 19th century that the ancient rivalry between Gradec and Kaptol began to ease, with common interests finally prevailing – Zagreb was, after all, an important regional staging post on the routes from Vienna and Budapest to the sea. They were also brought together by the resurgence of Croatian nationalism, driven in large part by Ljudevit Gaj, who oversaw the publication of the first Croatian newspapers in 1835. New institutions flourished, with the founding of the Music Society in 1826, Croatian (originally Illyrian) Heritage in 1839, the Academy of Arts and Sciences in 1866, and the University in 1874. Key to this burgeoning scene was Josip Jelačić, the guy on the big horse in Zagreb's eponymously named main square. Jelačić was made 'ban' (viceroy) of Croatia in 1848.

Two years later, Franz Josef I, the Habsburg emperor, proclaimed Zagreb as a single city, and ushered in a whole new architectural era – particularly after 1857, when new building regulations came in stipulating streets at least 13m wide intersecting at right angles, and prescribing the heights and shapes of all new buildings (Habsburg, basically).

Everything was going swimmingly for Zagreb until 9 November 1880, when a devastating earthquake almost totally destroyed the city. The massive rebuilding programme that followed explains the uniform late 19th-century architecture that characterises Zagreb today, and was particularly noteworthy for the achievements of two men, the architect Hermann Bollé, and the urban planner Milan Lenuci. Bollé was responsible for the new neo-Gothic façade on the cathedral, the lovely Mirogoj cemetery north of the city and the solid elegance of the Arts and Crafts Museum, while Lenuci designed the so-called 'Green Horseshoe', a series of grand, green squares that dominate the lower town between the train station and the central square.

During the 20th century, Zagreb's history closely followed Croatia's (see pages 11–20), though the city was fortunate during the homeland war in largely avoiding direct conflict. The ban's palace (the official president's residence) was successfully targeted by a rogue rocket attack (you can see a reconstruction in the City Museum of what happened – see page 112) in 1991, and seven people lost their lives during the last shellings of the city in 1995, but compared to what happened elsewhere, the damage was minimal.

The city was spared, but the people of Zagreb were scarred, and from 1993 a touching raw brick monument to lost and missing soldiers and civilians was built by their mothers and relatives around the UN Peace Mission headquarters (on the corner of Ilica and Selska) – with each brick representing a dead or missing person. The monument is being replaced by a new formal memorial in Mirogoj cemetery, though relatives are upset that the original bricks won't be visible.

In 1994, while the war was still on, Pope John Paul II visited Zagreb as part of the city's 900th anniversary celebrations, and a million people turned out to see him.

Zagreb people are proud of their city and those of its natives who go on to achieve world fame; so expect at least to be able to name local sporting celebrities if you're

PENKALA THE INVENTOR

Largely forgotten now, but enormously influential at the time, was a man called Eduard Slavoljub Penkala (1871–1922). An inveterate inventor, he was forever looking for ways to improve day-to-day life. In 1906, he patented the world's first 'mechanical pencil', the pioneer in a whole range of writing devices that actually worked, and from 1914 to 1926, as a direct result, Zagreb became the European capital for the production of writing instruments.

Penkala himself never gave up his job at the Ministry of Finance (where he was Royal Technical Controller), but seems to have had plenty of time to work on his inventions, leaving him free to become Croatia's first aviator, in 1909, and the inventor of its first two-seater aircraft the following year. He also patented a hovercraft design in 1908, half a century ahead of Christopher Cockerell's antics on the Isle of Wight, and a rotating toothbrush the same year, when dental hygiene was still barely a blip on the horizon.

In a short life – he died of pneumonia, aged only 50 – Penkala came up with hundreds of inventions and registered over 70 patents.

here. Clue: former AC Milan player Zvonimir Boban owns a restaurant in town, and skiing star Janica Kostelić, who came home with three golds and a silver from the 2002 Winter Olympics, is fêted wherever she goes.

GETTING THERE AND AWAY

As the capital, Zagreb is well served by both international and domestic transport routes, and has an international airport, as well and major rail and bus terminals.

BY AIR Zagreb's diminutive Pleso Airport is 17km southeast of the city centre. As soon as you come out of International Arrivals you'll see the airport bus stop – shuttles to the main bus station in Zagreb run hourly or half-hourly (depending on the time of day) from 07.00 to 20.00, seven days a week. Outside the standard times, buses will also run whenever new flights arrive.

The trip takes about 25 minutes, and costs 30kn. If you're going to need to make frequent trips to the airport, it might be worth investing in a monthly ticket for 300kn, or a book of 20 tickets for 350kn. For full schedule information, check with Pleso Transport Company – they have an easy-to-follow English language website at www.plesoprijevoz.hr, and you can also get ticket and schedule information over the phone at ☎ 633 1999.

Airport shuttles from the main bus station back to the airport run from 05.00 to 20.30 (or from 04.00 to 20.00, depending on the day), seven days a week, as well as two hours before any international flight and 90 minutes before domestic departures. Buses leave from their own small terminal (rather than main long-distance bus departure gates), which is located on the ground floor level on the north side of the bus station. Buses are marked Zračna Luka Zagreb/Zagreb Airport, seating is first come, first served, and you buy your ticket on board. Don't worry if the driver isn't around when you get on – you can get your ticket when he or she does a round of the bus, just before departing.

With such an efficient bus service you're unlikely to need a taxi, but if you do, the stand's right next to the airport bus stop. Zagreb taxi drivers have a good reputation, but it does no harm to make sure the meter's switched on when you set off. Expect to pay upwards of 150–200kn to the main Zagreb hotels, bearing in mind you'll also pay a few kuna extra per piece of luggage, and that there's a 20% surcharge at night, as well as on Sundays and public holidays.

More information on the airport, including real-time flight arrival and departure times (look under *Timetable* on the home page), can be found at www.zagreb-airport.hr.

BY RAIL The railway originally linked Zagreb to its Habsburg rulers to the north, before assuming a more glamorous international role as one of the stops on the Simplon Orient Express line from Paris to Istanbul in the 1920s.

When you arrive, make sure you get off at the central station, Zagreb Glavni Kolodvor; there are two other stations at which trains may stop (but which you don't want): Zagreb Klara and Zagreb Zapadni Kolodvor.

The station itself – Glavni Kolodvor – is an imposing neo-classical edifice completed in 1891 by the Hungarian architect Ferenc Pfaff (who presumably had to endure a lifetime of wags telling him to stop faffing about). It's also known as Željeznički Kolodvor, just meaning 'railway station', but as it's a bit of a mouthful you're safer sticking with 'Glavni', meaning 'main'. It's located at the southern end of the city, a straight kilometre down from Zagreb's main square, Jelačić Square – trams #6 and #13 connect the two, or it's a ten-minute walk. From the train station it's a rather dreary 1.5km east to the main bus station, which can be comfortably shortened by four stops on tram #2 or #6.

The station has good facilities, including large Arrival (*Dolazak*) and Departure (*Odlazak*) boards in the main hall, and a terrific new website in English providing comprehensive information on timetables, ticket prices, journey duration, train types and configuration and more – see www.hznet.hr. For trains to and from Zagreb, select Zagreb Gl. kol as your departure or arrival station from the drop-down menu.

Lockers are available at 15kn per 24 hours, with extra-large ones for 20kn per 24 hours, making this a cheaper and more convenient place to store your stuff than the main bus station (see below). Coins for the lockers and information on timetables are available at the Croatia Express office (✆ *457 3253*), which also has a foreign exchange service.

The kiosks in the central hall offer a limited selection of foreign-language newspapers and magazines, as well as selling stamps and postcards. A radical makeover has meanwhile turned the station bistro – once a fairly dismal place to hang out pending departure – into a pleasant, cheery venue with its own outdoor terrace; it's conveniently open for drinks, snacks and more substantial meals from 05.00 to 23.00. Public toilets (3kn) and shower facilities (45kn including towel, shampoo and hairdryer) are available at the west end of the main platform, beyond the bistro.

BY BUS Zagreb's main bus station – Autobusni Kolodvor – is the largest and busiest in the country, as you'd expect, with around 200 arrivals a day, from destinations both domestic and international. Like bus stations everywhere, it's a bit shabby, but has good facilities, including a small supermarket, several cafés, various fast food outlets and newsagents. Up on the second floor there's also a post office and a bank, while down on the ground floor (at platforms 1 and 6) you'll find 24-hour left-luggage facilities – though at 5kn per hour per bag up to 4 hours and 2.50kn per hour thereafter, it's quite a bit more expensive than those at the train station (see above).

If you're planning on leaving by bus (not counting the airport transfer; see above), you should try and buy your ticket as early as possible – from the main ticket office on the first floor – as long-distance buses tend to be booked out ahead of time, especially in summer.

The bus station is 1.5km east of the main train station, which makes for a dull 15-minute walk (cross the railway lines, then walk west along Branimirova) or a four-stop ride on the #2 or #6 tram. Tram #6 also continues on past the station two stops to Jelačić Square, Zagreb's central square.

Like the train station, the bus station also has a spanking new website in English, at www.akz.hr. Be warned, however, that if your computer doesn't support Croatian accents, the database won't always find your requested destination – the best way to avoid frustration is simply to type in the first two or three letters, and then use the drop-down menu of possibilities, from which you can quickly select your destination (though this doesn't work for places that start with accented letters, like Šibenik).

BY CAR If you can find a way of avoiding driving in town, then do so. Zagreb is compact enough to manage easily on foot or using public transport, and having your own car with you is, frankly, a bit of a liability – I speak as one who knows. A government credit on new cars, while good for the economy, has helped to further clog up Zagreb's arteries, while negotiating your way around the busy centre or the old town is made even harder by a tricky one-way system. Many streets are also car-free, designated for pedestrians or trams only.

If driving is a nightmare, parking is worse. Legitimate street parking spaces are a good deal scarcer than hen's teeth, but if you park illegally it's likely that the infamous 'spider' (*pauk*) will take your car away. If your car does disappear, try calling the spider on ✆ 631 1888, ✆ 631 1884, or ✆ 631 1881, before you panic and report its disappearance to the police – it might save you a lot of time and hassle. The pound – where you can pay the hefty fine and recover your car – is at Strojarska 14, just west of the bus station (it's the first right on Branimira heading east from the train station, after about 1km).

Street parking (I hardly know why I'm bothering to tell you this – but I suppose you might find a space) is divided into three zones – red, yellow and green – corresponding to one-, two- and three-hour maximum stay respectively. You pay 14kn per hour in the red zone, 7kn per hour in the yellow zone and 3kn per hour in the green zone. Payment is easy as pie; either by getting vouchers (*Parkirna Karta*) at kiosks, paying in cash at automatic ticket dispensers, or – best by far – sending an SMS with your registration number (no spaces) from your mobile phone. Send it to 101 for the red zone, 102 for the yellow zone and 103 for the green zone. One SMS equals an hour's worth of parking, and you get a return SMS to confirm you've paid, and another SMS 5–10 minutes before your parking time expires.

There are also a growing number of underground car parks, which are safe and secure, though even here, at 5kn per hour, you can end up with a hefty bill if you're in the city for any length of time. The best-located are at the Sheraton Hotel, the Branimir Centre, the Kaptol Centre (at Nova Ves), a block and a half east of Jelačić Square (on the corner of Vlaška), and at the Importanne shopping centre near the train station – though the entrances can be hard to find and easy to miss, what with the one-way system and heavy traffic.

You could also consider leaving your car in the suburbs, where there's ample daytime parking, and catching a tram or bus into town – but, with car theft a real possibility, this may not be a great decision if you plan on leaving your vehicle unattended for days at a time. A safer option – though not a cheaper one; prices vary from 60–120kn per day – is to choose a hotel with its own parking, where you'll have the peace of mind of knowing your car will be secure for the duration of your stay. It's also worth considering staying somewhere out of town for the Zagreb part of your trip if you have a car with you (Samobor, for example) and making the short journey into the city on the regular bus service – another advantage being that out-of-town hotels can offer excellent value for money.

Car hire Car hire is easy to organise direct through any of the main agencies, which can all be found at the airport.

🚗 **Avis** Pleso Airport; ☎ 626 5190; www.avis.com; ⏱ Mon–Fri 07.00–23.00, Sat 08.00–23.00, Sun 08.00–23.00. Also an office at the Sheraton Hotel, Kneza Borne 2; ☎ 467 6111; ⏱ 08.00–20.00 Mon–Sat, 08.00–12.00 Sun

🚗 **Budget** Pleso Airport; ☎ 626 5854; www.budget.hr/Rent-A-Car; ⏱ 07.00–20.00 Mon–Sat, 08.00–12.00 Sun

🚗 **Dollar** & Thrifty Pleso Airport; ☎ 626 5333; f 626 5444; www.subrosa.hr; ⏱ Mon–Sun 07.00–21.00. Also downtown at Sub Rosa, Radićeva 13; ☎ 483 6466

🚗 **Hertz** Pleso Airport; ☎ 456 2635; www.hertz.hr; ⏱ Mon–Sun 08.00–21.00, & Vukotinovićeva 4; ☎ 484 6777; ⏱ 08.00–20.00 Mon–Sat, 08.00–15.00 Sat, 08.00–12.00 Sun

🚗 **National** Pleso Airport; ☎ 621 5924; f 456 2550; www.nationalcar.hr/Europcar; Mon–Sun 07.00–21.00, & at the Westin Hotel, Kršnjavoga 1; ☎ 481 1764; ⏱ 07.30–20.00 Mon–Sat, 08.00–12.00 Sun

🚗 **Sixt** Pleso Airport; ☎ 621 9900; www.e-sixt.com; ⏱ 06.00–22.00 Mon–Sun, & Sheraton Four Points Hotel, Sportova Trg 9; ☎ 301 5303; ⏱ 08.00–19.00 Mon–Fri, 08.00–18.00 Sat, 08.00–12.00 Sun, & also Regent Esplanade Hotel, Mihanovićeva 1; ☎ 639 6020; ⏱ 08.00–11.00 & 17.00–19.00 Mon–Sat

ORIENTATION

Zagreb is 'pleasantly situated between the north bank of the Sava and the mountains which culminate in Sljeme' (according to my trusty 1911 *Encyclopaedia Britannica*) –

and the mountain and the river are the two principal landmarks you'll still find on the larger city maps today, along with the railway line that separates the main city centre and old town to the north from the suburbs to the south.

The vast main square, **Jelačić Square** (Trg Bana Jelačića), sits on the northern side of the city centre, and is the main rendezvous point in town – for decades the exact spot was under the tail of Jelačić's horse, but people now seem to prefer meeting under the modern clock, about 50m away.

A series of great leafy squares run south to the main **train station**, and these form the eastern arm of the so-called 'green horseshoe' – which then continues west from the station to the Esplanade Hotel and the Botanical Gardens, before turning north for another three blocks.

North of Jelačić Square you'll find **Dolac**, the city's huge daily market, with fruit, vegetables, fish and flowers upstairs, and meat, cheese and all the rest downstairs. To the northeast stands the twin-spired, partly scaffolding-clad cathedral, at the heart of **Kaptol**, which was formerly a separate religious centre, while to the northwest is the old town, **Gradec**, home to the president's palace and the parliament building (Sabor), along with several of the city's museums. Kaptol and Gradec are separated by **Tkalčićeva**, a café- and restaurant-filled pedestrian street running north, and **Radićeva**, a cobbled street parallel to and above it.

Running west from Jelačić Square is **Ilica**, Zagreb's main shopping area (along with the streets running off it), while to the south and southwest are the regular blocks and streets of **Donji Grad**, the lower town, where you'll find most of the remaining museums and other sights, and which was made possible by the construction of the railway embankment in 1860.

South of the railway are the suburbs built between the two World Wars, while across the river Sava is **Novi Zagreb**, the residential area that sprang up in the 1950s and 1960s to house incoming labour. Just south of the railway line, a kilometre or so east of the main train station is the main **bus station**; which is where the shuttle comes in from **Pleso Airport**, itself 15km further southeast.

The bus station, train station and Jelačić Square – and indeed the whole city centre – are well connected by a regular and efficient tram network (see next section).

Zagreb's weekend playgrounds – beyond the obvious bulk of Mount Medvednica to the north – are the **Jarun Lake**, to the southwest, with its summer beaches, and the enormous forested **Maksimir Park** (where you'll also find the zoo) to the northeast.

GETTING AROUND

PUBLIC TRANSPORT Zagreb has excellent public transport, based around trams (and a tiny funicular) in the city centre, and a wide-ranging network of buses running to the inner and outer suburbs, all managed by ZET, Zagrebački Električni Tramvaj (*www.zet.hr* – *in Croatian only*) and all running from 05.00 to 24.00 – with a selection of night trams and buses as well. Maps of the network are published at most tram stops, making the system easy to navigate.

There's a flat fare ticket that costs 8kn from news stands or 10kn on board (you'll be expected to have the right money) and which is valid for 90 minutes from the time you punch it on board. Trips far into the suburbs cost two, three or even four tickets apiece, but everything in the city itself is within the central zone; though all night trams and buses cost two tickets each. The on-the-spot fine for travelling without a ticket is 150kn. Recently, travel on trams within central Zagreb (between Britanski Square, Jelačić Square, Glavni Kolodvor and Kvaternikov Square) became free, so you no longer need to buy a ticket to ride on these sections.

A great-value day pass is available at 25kn, which is valid until 04.00 the following morning. And if you're here for three days or more, consider the 90kn Zagreb Card (see page 84), which covers not just all the public transport for 72 hours but also the cable car ride up to Sljeme on Mount Medvednica – and gives numerous discounts to boot.

Trams Trams have been part of the very fabric of Zagreb since the first horse-drawn variety was introduced in 1892, and particularly since the electric tram started up in 1910. Today there are 15 day routes, and another four night routes, which run from 24.00 to 04.00. It's a good gag to get people to meet you at a #10 or #16 tram stop, as these routes don't exist.

The network is extremely efficient, though trams can get pretty crowded, particularly around the rush hour. All day routes run at least six times an hour, though as routes run in parallel you'll rarely find yourself waiting even five minutes for a ride. Night routes (#31, #32, #33, #34) go from the same stops as the day routes and are serviced about every 45 minutes, but take routes that even locals consider abstruse. When the tracks are being repaired, night trams are substituted by buses.

For quick reference, these are the stops you're most likely to use, and the trams that service them:

Jelačić Square #1, #6, #11, #12, #13, #14, #17
Glavni Kolodvor (train station) #2, #4, #6, #9, #13
Autobusni Kolodvor (bus station) #2, #5, #6, #7, #8
Westin #12, #13, #14, #17
Sheraton #4, #8, #9, #13
Bukovačka (Maksimir Park, zoo) #4, #7, #11, #12

Local buses Anywhere there isn't a tram you'll find a bus, with ZET operating some 120 routes in total (70 within the city and 50 to the outer suburbs); almost all of them connect neatly into the tram network. Frequency varies enormously, with some routes running up to eight times an hour and others operating every half hour or hour; a few routes only run during the rush hour. Where specific buses will be useful to you I've provided details in the text.

Funicular There's a charming little funicular that runs from the main shopping street, Ilica, up to Gradec, the old town. Originally opened in 1891, as a steam-powered affair, the funicular was electrified in the 1930s. It's said to be the shortest in Europe, and at just 66m in length it's certainly a plausible claim; it's also one of the steepest funiculars in the world, with a vertical gain of 30m (which makes you wonder, though, at what degree of steepness a railway becomes a funicular, and a funicular becomes a plain old-fashioned lift). Anyway, it's a bit of fun, and well worth the 4kn fare, and it takes the legwork out of schlepping up to the Lotršcak Tower.

Cable car If the funicular isn't enough of a thrill for you, then try the cable car that climbs up towards the highest peak on Mount Medvednica, Sljeme (1,030m), covering a horizontal distance of 4km and a vertical one of nearly 700m. Built in the early 1960s, it's currently (2009) closed for upgrading. Until it stopped running it cost 11kn one-way/17kn return, ran every hour on the hour (but not at all if windy), and the journey took about 25 minutes. For more details on both the cable car and Medvednica, see page 124.

Taxis By local standards, taxis are a very expensive way indeed of getting around, though if you don't get stuck in traffic (which is, however, a real risk), it's a reasonable option, especially if there are three or four of you. Fares for radio taxis start at 19kn, and they charge 7kn per km on top of that, 50kn per hour for waiting time, and 3kn per bag, with a 20% surcharge at night and on holidays. You can pick up a taxi fairly easily in a number of public locations, including Trg Maršala Tita, by the theatre, or near the cathedral at Kaptol, as well as at any of the bigger hotels. If you're calling a taxi yourself, the central number to ring is ☏ 970; you can also try ☏ 668 2505, 660 0671, or ☏ 660 1235.

Bicycles As a keen cyclist myself, I'd love to rave about what a fabulously cycle-friendly city Zagreb is, but the truth is that even though it ought to be perfect (mostly flat terrain, wide streets, large leafy squares, and 135km of cycle paths), it just isn't. City drivers aren't used to sharing their roads with cyclists, and can be somewhat aggressive, if not downright dangerous, so you're pretty much forced to use the pavements – which you then have to share not just with pedestrian traffic but also illegally parked cars.

That said, continuous efforts are being made to make Zagreb a better place for cyclists, and, ironically, cycling on some the city's biggest thoroughfares, especially south of the railway line, is great, as the dedicated cycle paths there are kept well away from the traffic – notably along Vukovarska and Slavonska/Ljubljanska, and across both the central and eastern bridges over the Sava to Bundek and Novi Zagreb.

For the more athletic, there's fantastic cycling up on Mount Medvednica, and good cycle maps available which cover the trails through the woods, while a more leisurely spin can be had down on Lake Jarun or at Bundek – though both can get very busy on a summer Sunday afternoon. There's also excellent cycling available in Zagreb County, and you can pick up a whole raft of first-rate maps from the county tourist office (see page 84), which detail not just the routes along with profiles etc, but also places to stay and eat, and useful stuff like the locations of the nearest bike repair shops. Be warned, though, that you'll need a sturdy bike as quite a few trails take advantage of traffic-free gravel roads.

There aren't that many places you can rent bikes, but I can wholeheartedly recommend Vladimir Fumić, former pro and Croatian champion, who has a shop in town as well as a bigger hire place on Jarun Lake, which is open mainly at weekends and in summer. All bike rentals come with a lock and a helmet included, and prices (as of 2009) were one hour = 20kn, two hours = 30kn, half-day = 50kn, one day = 80kn, one week = 480kn. If you're renting for more than a couple of days, bike delivery to your hotel can be arranged. The shop is at Vlaška 81a (go into the courtyard), ☏ 466 4233; f 466 4247; www.fumic-bicikli.hr.

There's also a busy cycling association in Zagreb, which sponsors activities across Croatia, and is working notably on the major Danube cycle path project, as well as the popular 'Bike and Bed' initiative, which promotes cycle-tourism (*www.bike-bed.com*). Alternatively, you can hire a **Segway** from Segway City Tour Zagreb (*www.segway.hr*).

TOURIST INFORMATION AND MAPS

Zagreb has excellent tourist information, with a number of good free guides and maps available along with an information-packed website (*www.zagreb-touristinfo.hr*).

Heading north from the railway station towards the town centre, the first tourist office you'll come to is on the left-hand side, just past the Strossmayer Gallery, at Zrinjevac 14 (✆ *492 1645*; ⊕ *09.00–17.00 Mon–Fri*). The main **Tourist Information Office** [104–5 D4] (✆ *481 4051/2/4*; e *info@zagreb-touristinfo.hr*; ⊕ *08.30–20.00 Mon–Fri, 09.00–17.00 Sat, 10.00–14.00 Sun*) is on at Jelačić Square, less than ten minutes' walk from the railway station heading towards the town centre. You can also get information by email.

Ask the friendly staff for a city map, and the City Walks and monthly Events and Performances brochures. They'll also be able to give you advice on (but not – officially, anyway – help in) finding accommodation, and can sell you the 72-hour Zagreb Card. This is tremendous value at 90kn, with unlimited city transport for the duration, half-price entry to the city's museums, 20% off most theatre tickets, and discounts on a huge range of goods and services, from restaurants and hotels to medical, dental and beauty treatments – ask for the Zagreb Card Guide for full details, or visit www.zagrebcard.fivestars.hr. The tourist office also has a good walking map of Mount Medvednica for sale, and, if you're here for more than half a day, the bi-monthly *Zagreb: In Your Pocket* guide is a superb resource easily worth the 20kn cover charge.

For information on sights immediately outside the Zagreb metropolitan area, you'll need to contact the **Zagreb County Tourist Office** [104–5 C5] (*Turistička Zajednica Zagrebačke Županije, which is at Preradovićeva 42;* ✆ *487 3665;* f *487 3670; www.tzzz.hr;* ⊕ *08.00–16.00 Mon–Fri*). The office has friendly, English-speaking staff, as well as everything you need to know about local attractions such as the picturesque town of Samobor, local wineries, rural accommodation and country restaurants, as well as a free cycling and walking maps for those keen to enjoy the great outdoors.

MAPS There are about half a dozen different Zagreb maps in circulation, mostly with the old town on one side and the surrounding city on the other. Given the modest size and scale of the place, any of these should be more than adequate – despite the frequent lack of helpful information like scale, footpaths, bike tracks and so on.

If you're into cycling or walking, and planning to take a trip out of town, get hold of the Zagreb County Tourist Board's excellent maps, which show biking and walking trails along with suggested touring itineraries that take you through some of the county's prettiest countryside on smaller, mostly traffic-free roads.

LOCAL TOUR OPERATORS AND TRAVEL AGENCIES

There's a host of local tour operators and travel agencies in Zagreb; of these the following are the best known and longest established. Most can organise entire holidays for you, including travel to and from your home country, as well as excursions and accommodation. You can also book air tickets by phone through the Croatia Airlines office, listed below.

Atlas [104–5 D5] Zrinjevac 17; ✆ 480 7300; f 487 3049; www.atlas-croatia.com. Zagreb office of the Dubrovnik-based company established in 1923 offering a wide range of coast-focused services, from flights & coach tours to accommodation, & also the Croatian representative for American Express. ⊕ 08.00–20.00 Mon–Fri, 08.00–14.00 Sat.

Croatia Airlines [104–5 D5] Zrinjevac 17; ✆ 481 9633. Online booking at www.croatiaairlines.hr. Croatia's national airline, offering great-value domestic flights if you reserve & pay for them within Croatia – the catch being that you need to do so a long way ahead. Now a Star Alliance regional member. ⊕ 08.00–20.00 Mon–Fri, 09.00–12.00 Sat.

Croatia Express [104–5 D4] Teslina 4; ☎ 481 1842/1836; f 481 1920, and Tomislav Trg 17; ☎ 492 2237; f 492 2230; www.zug.hr. Specialising in rail, bus, ferry & airline bookings; also luxury coach charter & excursions.

Croatian Youth Hostel Association (HFHS) [104–5 B3] Dežmanova 9; ☎ 484 7474; f 484 7472; www.hfhs.hr. Advance bookings for Croatia's (few) youth hostels. You can also get an ISIC student card here (proof of student status required).

Dalmacijaturist [104–5 D5] Zrinjevac 16; ☎ 487 3073; f 487 3075. Focuses, as you'd expect, on accommodation & holidays on the Dalmatian coast. ⊕ 08.00–20.00 Mon–Fri, 08.00–12.00 Sat.

Generalturist [104–5 D4] Praška 5; ☎ 480 7660, Ilica 1; ☎ 481 2993 and Bogovićeva 6; ☎ 4873 121; www.generalturist.com. A Croatian specialist of 80 years' standing, now owned by Diners Club, offering boat tours, charters & sailing schools, accommodation, coach tours & charters, skiing holidays & wellness programmes, along with Budget Rent-a-Car bookings. ⊕ 08.00–20.00 Mon–Fri, 09.00–14.00 Sat.

Jadrolinija [104–5 C4] Marko Polo Travel, Masarykova 24; ☎ 481 5216; f 483 0473; www.jadrolinija.hr. Croatia's national ferry operator, operating more than 400 departures a day to coastal destinations during the summer months.

Kompas [104–5 D4] Gajeva 6; ☎ 481 1536; f 481 1938 and Zrinjevac 14; ☎ 487 8750; f 487 8759; www.kompas.hr. Day excursions, bus tours, accommodation in Zagreb & on the coast, & a range of outdoor activities. ⊕ 08.00–20.00 Mon–Fri, 09.00–13.30 Sat.

Plitvice Lakes National Park [104–5 D6] Tomislava 19; ☎ 461 3586/492 2274/487 0111; f 492 2270; www.np-plitvicka-jezera.hr. The park office can arrange excursions & accommodation to the national park. ⊕ 8.00–16.00 Mon–Fri.

STA Zagreb [104–5 D3] Krvavi Most 3 (1st floor); ☎ 488 6340; f 488 6345; www.sta-zagreb.com. Part of the STA Travel group; specialises in student & discount travel. ⊕ 09.00–13.00 & 14.00–17.00 Mon–Fri.

⌂ WHERE TO STAY

As a bustling, business-oriented capital city, Zagreb presents a problem if you're looking for true budget accommodation. Private rooms are in short supply (and twice the price of anywhere else in the country, with the exception of Dubrovnik), hostels fill up quickly, and there isn't a campsite I can honestly recommend.

Zagreb does have plenty of hotels, but they don't come especially cheap; there's nowhere within easy reach where you'll find a room for under € 60 a night, and the most luxurious establishments charge a fairly breathtaking € 250-plus per night for a double, all year round.

Of course, the nicest places fill up fast at any time of year, so it's recommended that you reserve well ahead of time, and confirm by fax (emails tend to go astray).

HOTELS While Zagreb hotels are classified by the standard international star system, quality is a little bit hit and miss, so I've done my best to let you know what places are really like.

Hotels are detailed below in three categories – luxury. mid-range/upmarket, and affordable – and are listed within each section in alphabetical order.

Luxury Zagreb has three five-star hotels, which are almost exclusively used by business people on expenses, the jet set, or celebrities, most travellers lacking the wherewithal to fork out upwards of € 250 a night on accommodation.

⌂ **Regent Esplanade** [104–5 D6] (209 rooms) Mihanovićeva 1; ☎ 456 6666; f 456 6050; www.regenthotels.com. Built in 1925 as a swanky stopover for Orient Express passengers en route to Istanbul, the Esplanade has now been restored to its former glory. The public areas reek of 1920s European opulence, the rooms are ultra-stylish & spacious, & the staff combine 5-star professionalism with unfailing friendliness. Check-in is a sit-down affair with complimentary fizz while the formalities are completed. There are even discounts at w/ends. Check out the fabulous Emerald Ballroom & the set of clocks inside the main entrance that tell the time in New York, Buenos Aires, London, Zagreb, Moscow, Tokyo & Sydney. B/fast is simply wonderful – but then so it should be, at 200kn a head. *Room from €140.*

🛏 **Sheraton Zagreb** (300 rooms) Kneza Borne 2; ☏ 455 3535; f 455 3035; www.sheraton.com/zagreb. Located 2 blocks up & 3 blocks east of the station, the Sheraton is a glass-fronted city block that offers as much luxury & all the facilities anyone's going to need, including a gym & an indoor pool – though you have to ask yourself which humorist was responsible for putting the fitness centre on the smokers' floor. *Dbl from €130, discounts w/end.*

🛏 **Westin Zagreb** [93 A7] Krsnjavoga 1; ☏ 489 2000; f 489 2001; www.westin.com. Formerly known as the Opera (the National Theatre is just up the road), the hotel might be a bit of an architectural monstrosity, but inside it's all tasteful opulence & impeccable service. Rooms are spacious & comfortable, with a special emphasis on luxurious bed & bath facilities (though personally I still think the bathrooms at the Esplanade are nicer). For fitness fans there's a gym & an indoor pool, & the b/fast is terrific – unlimited *pršut, paški sir*, smoked salmon & the like, & dishes cooked to order. B/fast is an additional 140kn pp & secure parking an extra 60kn a day; but the hotel does offer 20% discount on room rates at w/ends. *Dbl from €130.*

Mid-range/upmarket

🛏 **Arcotel Allegra** [93 D6] (150 rooms) Branimirova 29, Branimir Centar; ☏ 469 6000; f 469 6027; www.arcotel.at/allegra. Very modern, very chic, with spacious, minimalist rooms. Part of an Austrian chain, the Arcotel has earned a reputation for gay-friendliness in a town that's still a bit uneasy about same-sex couples. If you plan to partake of the copious b/fast buffet, count an extra €15 per person. *Sgl & dbl €66–180, suite €190–400. Count on substantial discounts at w/ends.*

🛏 **AS** [104–5 A1] Zelengaj 2; ☏ 460 9111; f 460 9303; www.hotel-as.hr. Excellent hotel with clean, spacious rooms and good service hidden out amid the greenery of Zelengaj, north of Britanski Square. *Sgl €120, dbl €134.*

🛏 **Astoria (Best Western)** [93 D7] (102 rooms) Petrinjska 71; ☏ 480 8900; f 480 8908; www.bestwestern.com. With many rooms & a very handy location in the town centre, this 4-star hotel has recently benefited from a major makeover from the American chain. Very comfortable rooms. The hotel also boasts a fairly upmarket Croatian restaurant, the Ragusa. *Sgl from €77, dbl from €100.*

🛏 **Central** [93 D7] Branimirova 3; ☏ 484 1122; f 484 1304; www.hotel-central.hr. An affordable 3-star hotel, the recently renovated Central is extremely well located just across from the railway station, & has straightforward AC. If the building's façade is rather characterless, the friendly, helpful staff will do their best to make you feel at home. *Dbl from €100–110.*

🛏 **Dubrovnik** [93 C4] Gajeva 1; ☏ 486 3555; f 481 3506; www.hotel-dubrovnik.hr. If the exterior is a tribute to 1970s socialist architecture, the refurbished interior is starting to look a bit tired, & the staff can be a bit surly – the Dubrovnik's location overlooking Jelačić Square is unbeatable if you want to be right in the thick of things. Rooms are comfortable & have AC, & those overlooking the square are also noise-proofed against the coming & going of Zagreb's trams. *Small sgl from €105, dbl €140, twin €160.*

🛏 **Four Points by Sheraton** [74–5 D5] Trg Sportova 9; ☏ 365 8333; f 309 2657; www.starwoodhotels.com. A smart, business-oriented hotel about 3km southwest of the city centre. The very comfortable dbls have all the facilities you'd expect. Special offers usually available at w/ends. *Dbl €82–120.*

🛏 **International** [74–5 D6] (207 rooms) Miramarska 24; ☏ 610 8800; f 610 8700; www.hup-zagreb.hr. Completely restored & refitted in 2006, this modern 4-star business hotel is a 10min walk south of the railway & features elegantly appointed rooms. *Dbl €135–165 (20% discount at w/ends).*

🛏 **Palace Hotel** [93 C6] (125 rooms) Strossmayerov 10; ☏ 489 9600; f 481 1358; www.palace.hr. A Zagreb institution, the Palace was built in 1891 & has been a hotel since 1907. While it retains much of its old-fashioned Secession-era charm, its rooms have all been thoroughly modernised. *Dbl €145–170, suite €230–315.*

🛏 **President** [104–5 A3] Pantovčak 52; ☏ 488 1480; f 482 3475; www.president-zagreb.com. Very nice, stylish boutique hotel, newly opened, and only a short distance up Pantovčak from Britanski Square. *Sgl €89–225, dbl €109–240.*

🛏 **Vila Tina** [74–5 E4] (24 rooms) Bukovačka Cesta 213; ☏ 244 5204; f 244 5138; www.vilatina.com.hr. A modern Italianate villa set in the pleasant hills near Maksimir Park, this is a stylish option. A small outdoor swimming pool is complemented by a jacuzzi, solarium & sauna, & there's also a nice restaurant. To get there on public transport, take tram #1, #9 or #17 to Svetice (the stop before Borongaj, the terminus), & then bus #203, & look for the small stone lions flanking the hotel's gate on the left-hand side of Bukovačka, heading up the hill. *Sgl €80–90, dbl €90–100, trpl €125.*

Affordable

🏠 **Dora** (24 rooms) Trnjanska 11e; ☎ 631 1900; 📠 631 1909; www.zug.hr. A 10min walk south of the station, just off Vukovarska, & 20min south of Jelačić Square. A simple, good-value hotel. *Dbl €95.*

🏠 **Fala** [74–5 D6] Trnjanske Ledine 18; ☎ 611 1062; 📠 619 4498; www.hotel-fala-zg.hr. Another pleasant affordable choice, spotless, newly furnished – if a bit spartan. To get there, take bus # 219, 220, 221 or 268 from the main train or bus stations & head a couple of stops south towards Novi Zagreb. *Sgl €50, dbl €70.*

🏠 **Gaj** [74–5 C6] Jezerska 24a; ☎ 381 7222; 📠 381 7225; www.hotelgaj.hr. A quiet, modern 3-star hotel offering AC dbls, trpls and suites, as well as shared internet facilities, free access to the solarium & fitness centre. An excellent option if you're arriving by car, as it's easy to drive to & has plenty of secure parking. While it looks to be well to the west of town, it's only 3min walk from the terminus of the #118 bus, which sets off every 10mins from Trg Mažuranić. If you're arriving by bus from town, walk back to the first street on the right, & cross the stream over the footbridge at the end, & you'll see the hotel on your left. *Sgl €61, dbl €82 & suite €98.*

🏠 **Ilica** [104–5 A4] (23 rooms, 1 apartment) Ilica 102, ☎ 377 7522; 📠 377 7722; www.hotel-ilica.hr. Set in a courtyard just 2 tram stops (or 10–15min walk) west of Jelačić Square (& 100m west of Britanski Square), this cosy hotel has a rather mercurial owner. Rooms are a bargain & get booked up very fast indeed. *Sgl €54 dbl €68.*

🏠 **Jadran** [93 D4] (48 rooms) Vlaška 50; ☎ 455 3777; 📠 461 2151; www.hup-zagreb.hr. Although extremely well located on Vlaška, just a few mins east of Trg Jelačića & round the corner from the cathedral, the Jadran has definitely seen better days – but the staff are friendly & the prices are very reasonable for a place this central. Most of the rooms have been recently (if modestly) refurbished. If you mind the smell of smoke, definitely ask for a non-smoking room. *Dbl €100.*

🏠 **Jaegerhorn** [93 B4] Ilica 14; ☎ 483 3877; 📠 483 3573; www.hotel-pansion-jaegerhorn.hr. Perfectly located, but tucked away from the hustle & bustle of Ilica itself, at the end of a narrow shopping arcade, this family-run hotel has simple, pleasant sgl, dbl & trpl rooms. There's also a decent restaurant & leafy, tranquil

garden terrace with a waterfall, backing onto the steep park that leads up to the old town. *Sgl €67 dbl €95.*

🏠 **Maksimir** [74–5 E5] Maksimirska 57a; ☎ 666 6160; 📠 666 6178; www.hotel-maksimir.hr. Brand new, clean and well-priced little hotel just a few stops out towards Maksimir (tram #11 or #12 from Jelačić Square). Very good value. *Sgl €50, dbl €70.*

🏠 **Meridijan16** [74–5 E5] (25 rooms) Vukovarska 241; ☎ 606 5200; 📠 606 5201; www.meridijan16.com. Located bang on the 16th meridian, just 500m south of the main bus station, this new hotel's rooms are all tastefully furnished & have AC. The situation, on most of Zagreb's main tram routes, makes getting in & out of town a breeze (#2 & #6 run direct to the bus & train stations, #6 & #13 direct to Jelačić Square). *Sgl €60, dbl €80 and trpl €100.*

🏠 **Movie Hotel** [74–5 D6] (20 rooms) Savska 141; ☎ 600 3600; 📠 600 3601; www.the-movie-pub.com. Newly opened above the Movie Pub (see page 97), guests can choose from themed rooms named after stars like Sharon Stone, Harrison Ford, Catherine Zeta-Jones & Al Pacino. With private car parking & a tram stop (#13, #14) just outside, the place is easy to get to – but you can't help feeling that most of the guests might be patrons from downstairs who've either been 'over-served' or struck it lucky. *Sgl €40, dbl €75.*

🏠 **Sliško** [74–5 E5/6] Supilova 13; ☎ 619 4210; 📠 619 4223; www.slisko.hr. A clean, well-run establishment located just 300m southeast of the main bus station in a quiet street with a couple of useful grocery stores nearby. Bright, airy rooms in pastel tones, & its own bar & café/restaurant. Very good value. *Sgl €52, dbl €70, trpl €87, quad €102.*

🏠 **Zagreb** [74–5 E6] Bundek; ☎ 663 7333; 📠 663 7229; www.hup-zagreb.hr. While the lake & park opposite have been newly restored, the same can't be said for this 2-star hotel, which manages to retain all its 1970s socialist-era functional feel. The rooms are pretty basic, but clean, & with ample free parking, it's a great choice if you're on a tight budget, & don't mind a bit of a schlep into town (bus #219, #220 or #221 will take you straight to the train station, however). *Sgl €48, dbl €55.*

PRIVATE ROOMS/APARTMENTS For a big city, Zagreb has a surprisingly limited supply of private rooms, so count yourself lucky if you manage to secure one of the few rooms in the city centre – more likely you'll find yourself out in the suburbs, using public transport to get into town.

In terms of cost, Zagreb's cheapest single private rooms (shared bathroom) start at about €30 per night, with doubles for around €45. If you're looking for a double room with its own bathroom, expect to pay anything from €50 to €80. A studio sleeping up to six people goes for €70–100 or so, depending on the size and location.

Your best bet is the Zagreb Tourist Office, which maintains a list of private accommodation options on its website (*www.zagreb-touristinfo.hr*) – you can find them by clicking on the Accommodation option on the home page.

Evistas also handles private room bookings (☏ *483 9554;* f *483 9543*), Šenoina 28, a block north of Branimirova (the main road running east–west in front of the train station). The agency is open Monday to Friday 09.00 to 20.00, and Saturday 09.30 to 17.00, but rooms go quickly, so try to arrive early. Private room rates are usually quoted per person per night for a minimum of two nights; add 20% to the standard per-night rate if you're only planning an overnight stay.

YOUTH HOSTELS AND STUDENT ACCOMMODATION Zagreb has two official hostels that are part of the Croatian Youth Hostel Association (HFHS), one in the centre of town, and the other in the suburb of Remetinec, southwest of the city, across the river from the Jarun Lake. There's also an excellent private hostel in the suburb of Ravnice, east of the city centre and easily reachable on the tram.

In summer, it's also sometimes possible to get a bed in the university student dorms (ask at the Tourist Office on Jelačić Square), though prices aren't always as low as you might expect. A handful of other budget possibilities is posted on the Zagreb Tourist Office website (*www.zagreb-touristinfo.hr*); click on the Accommodation section and follow the link 'For students and youth'.

🏠 **Fulir Hostel** [93 C4] Radićeva 3a ☏ 483 0882; www.fulir-hostel.com. Newly opened in 2006 & a mere stone's throw from Jelačić Square, this is perhaps the best of the bunch as far as hostels go in Zagreb – clean, central, well priced & friendly. *Dorm beds €19pp per night.*

🏠 **Buzz Backpackers** [74–5 E5] Babukićeva 1b; ☏ 232 0267; www.buzzbackpackers.com. Another good new place, near Maksimir. *Dorm beds from €17pp per night, dbl €55.*

🏠 **Ravnice Youth Hostel** [74–5 F5] (30 beds) Ravnice 38d; ☏ 233 2325; f 234 5607; e ravnice-youth-hostel@zg.hinet.hr; www.ravnice-youth-hostel.hr. Located past the Dinamo Stadium & Maksimir Park, on the right-hand side, by the tennis courts (follow the wonderful smell emanating from the Kraš Chocolate Factory). From town, take tram #4, #7, #11 or #12 (direction Dubrava or Dubec) to the Ravnice stop, walk south for about 3mins, & look for the large hostel sign on the building itself. Opened in 2000, this bright, friendly family-run place sleeps guests in spotless rooms that accommodate 2–12 beds. ⊕ 24hrs (reception is staffed 09.00–22.00), & there are no curfew or age restrictions. Book directly over the internet, or by phone. *Beds from €15pp per night.*

🏠 **Youth Hostel** [93 D7] (210 beds) Petrinjska 77; ☏ 484 1261; f 484 1269; e zagreb@hfhs.hr; www.hfhs.hr. Centrally located near the train station and recently renovated, but despite having over 200 beds, it's almost invariably full, & (at least in the past) had a reputation for being a bit rough, especially if you're travelling alone. *€17pp for a bed in a 6-bed room & €18 for a place in a 3-bed room. There are also some sgl rooms available at €29 (shared bathroom) or €37 (private bathroom), & a few dbls at €40 (shared bathroom) or €50 (private bathroom).*

CAMPING At the time of writing, Zagreb really wasn't set up for campers at all, and you're pretty much limited to a couple of options.

Å **Carpe Diem Hostel** [104–5 F1] Milana Šufflaya 3; ☏ 468 0199; www.hfhs.hr. Hostel in the Šalata area which allows camping.

Å **Motel Plitvice** [74–5 A7] ☏ 653 0444; f 653 0445; e motel@motel-plitvice.hr; www.motel-plitvice.hr. Rather dismally situated on the Plitvice road, southwest of the city, near the motorway junction, this motel has camp sites. A bridge over the highway brings you to the service station, where you can at least take advantage of the shops and self-service restaurants.

✖ WHERE TO EAT AND DRINK

Food and drink are easy to find in Zagreb, with restaurants, bars and cafés for all tastes – and budgets – and a wonderful seven-day-a-week open market in Dolac, just north of Jelačić Square (see page 81).

As you'd expect in a fast-moving city, there are plenty of places where you can get a bite on the hoof, fast food coming in traditional (sausages etc) or contemporary (burgers and the like) formats, and the city having quite a few sandwich bars, both local and US-style, as well as plentiful ice cream shops.

You can also go for Zagreb's big speciality (and it is big), *štrukli*, which is something of a death by cream, doughy-pasta and cottage-cheese experience. It's somewhere between a giant cream-soaked ravioli and a cheese-stuffed dumpling. The dish technically comes from outside Zagreb, but the locals consume it here by the plate-load (boiled or baked; sweet or savoury; as a starter, main or dessert), and argue fiercely over where the best *štrukli* can be found (at the Regent Esplanade, in this food-taster's opinion).

Zagreb also has its very own chocolate factory, Kraš, beyond Maksimir Park, which smells absolutely mouth-watering from anywhere in the vicinity (notably the Ravnice Youth Hostel), and churns out a good wide range of tasty sweetmeats.

RESTAURANTS At places marked as inexpensive in the (alphabetical) listings below, expect to pay around 200kn for two, including wine; mid-range places will set you back 250–500kn for a couple; while at expensive restaurants two can easily pay 600kn and up – though there's nothing to stop you having a soup, a salad and a glass of wine at a ritzy place and coming away with change from 300kn for two.

Most restaurants catering to tourists stay open from around 11.00 to 23.00, though some (especially top-end establishments) will close for a period during the afternoon. Reservations are not normally expected (or accepted) except at the very upper end; where they are recommended, I've included the phone number with the listing.

I've listed restaurants here in four groupings for convenience: the upper town (everything from Gradec to Kaptol and along Tkalčićeva); Jelačić Square and the area west, south and east of it; the rest of the lower town (as far as the railway station); and restaurants a bit further afield (not including Mount Medvednica, which is covered separately in the Surrounds section).

Upper town
Expensive
✗ **Lopud** [93 C2] Kaptol 10; ☎ 481 8775. A short stroll north from the cathedral. The menu here is limited to whatever fish has come in that day, & the wine list is positively spartan, but the Lopud's reputation as one of the best seafood places in town means reservations are highly advisable.

✗ **Takenoko** [93 C1] Nova Ves 17 (in the Kaptol Centar); ☎ 486 0530; www.takenoko.hr. On the Tkalčićeva side of the Kaptol Centar, this very chic Japanese restaurant is a welcome addition to Zagreb's rather Euro-centric restaurant scene, serving traditional sushi & sashimi along with more adventurous Japanese fusion cooking. Reservations recommended.

Mid-range
✗ **Agava** [93 C3] Tkalčićeva 39; ☎ 482 9826; www.restaurant-agava.hr. The situation & setting – spread over several small terraces cascading down onto bustling Tkalčićeva – is just about unbeatable, & the food isn't bad either. Informal atmosphere, large range of salads, & an extensive choice of well-cooked pasta dishes (though they curiously only had one sort of pasta, fusilli, in stock, on the day I ate there).

✗ **Atlanta** [93 C2] Tkalčićeva 65; ☎ 481 3848. Upscale place offering a wide choice of pasta, fish &

seafood, steak & traditional Croatian dishes in a cosy, romantic atmosphere. Reservations recommended.

✗ **Baltazar** [93 C1] Nova Ves 4; ☎ 466 6999; www.restoran-baltazar.hr. A traditional, upper-end restaurant just up from the cathedral, popular with business people & large groups, with an extensive menu featuring mainly meat dishes (for fish from the same kitchen, see Gašpar, below). Chef Tomislav Špiček carried off Croatia's coveted Chef of the Year award in 2003 & 2004. Reservations recommended.

✖ **Gašpar** [93 C1] Nova Ves 4; ☎ 466 6999; www.restoran-baltazar.hr. Shares a kitchen with its neighbour Baltazar (see above), but specialises in seafood. A good choice of freshly prepared dishes, served in a polished-wood setting styled to resemble the interior of an ocean cruiser. Reservations recommended.

✖ **Ivica i Marica** [93 C2] Tkalčićeva 70; ☎ 481 7321, 482 8999. Taking its name from the Croatian for 'Hansel & Gretel' – look out for the gingerbread motifs – this upmarket option takes its food seriously. The emphasis is on organic, locally grown fresh produce, there's a good wine list, & manageable portion sizes mean you might even find room to indulge in one of their sumptuous desserts. If you're in the mood for something local, try the top-notch baked *štrukli* – one of the finest in town, & certainly the only serious rival in Zagreb to Le Bistro at the Regent Esplanade (see page 92). Reservations recommended. Closed Sun.

✖ **Kerempuh** [93 C3] Kaptol 3; ☎ 481 9000; www.kerempuh.hr. Right on the corner of the Dolac market square is my favourite restaurant in all of Zagreb. Run by the ever-cheerful Nikica Vuksan, it's

Budget

✖ **Capuciner** [93 C3] Kaptol 6; www.capuciner.hr. Next door to Kaptolska Klet, this place is popular with independent travellers in spite of (or perhaps because of) its simple, unpretentious décor. Efficient service, cheap prices & great pizza & pasta dishes with a view of the cathedral from the side terrace.

✖ **Kaptolska Klet** [93 C3] Kaptol 5. Right opposite the cathedral, with a large, rustic internal courtyard, this large restaurant is popular with tour groups & invariably busy. Service can be slow & rather offhand, but the food – traditional country-style Croatian cooking – is good for the price.

✖ **Katedralis** [93 C3] Tome Bakača 9; ☎ 481 4938; www.katedralis.hr. A conveniently located place in a pleasant setting facing the cathedral. You'll find most of the local staples at good prices, along with a tourist menu offering 4 courses for 90kn. 10% discount for cash.

✖ **Maharadža** [93 C3] Opatovina 19. If you're in the mood for a curry, this welcoming place on the pedestrian street running north out of the Dolac market serves up a good range of classic favourites, authentically prepared – though don't expect it to compete with what you'd find in the UK.

✖ **Mangiare** [93 C3] Tkalčićeva 29. A tiny, cosy place serving pizzas like they make them in Italy – wood-fired oven, thin crust & a good range of toppings. Large, appetising salads are also a speciality.

only open at lunchtime & at least half the tables seem to be permanently reserved by an eclectic bunch of retired university professors, former footballers & journalists. The menu is made fresh daily, & varies according to whatever's best in the market that morning. Chic, stylish interior, brisk, friendly service, & the view out over the market square from the newly extended terrace is wonderful. Reservations recommended.

✖ **Peperoncino** [93 B3] Kamenita 5. Fashionable, modern & informal Italian-style bistro just up from the Stone Gate, where grazers can choose from a range of *bruschette* or a keenly priced full brunch menu. Pasta dishes, including Istrian *fuži*, are also a speciality, & they do a good b/fast for 30kn.

✖ **Pod Gričkim Topom** [93 B3/4] Zakmardijeve Stube 5; ☎ 483 3607. Tucked away from the crowds just under Strossmayerovo Šetalište, with a fine view out over the lower town from the garden terrace, this friendly, professional place serves up well-cooked Croatian favourites in a homey setting. It's located at the top of the steps leading down to Ilica, or easily reachable on the path up from the bottom of Radićeva, or from the Lotrščak Tower. Closed Sun.

✖ **Mikina Klet** [93 C2] Tkalčićeva 59. With its vine-covered terrace & folksy, homespun interior (a *klet* is a small wooden house amongst the vineyards), this is a good place to enjoy traditional Croatian meat dishes like *ćevapčići* & *ražnjiči*, along with pizza & *štrukli*.

✖ **Nažigač** [93 C3] Kaptol 6 (in the alley, opposite Kapuciner's terrace). Named after the informal word for 'lamplighter', this tiny place specialises in earthy local dishes served in hearty portions at great prices. One caveat – while the *grah* (hearty bean stew) is particularly good, traditional fare like horseburgers may not be to everyone's taste. Confusingly, the restaurant also seems to trade under the name 'National Fast Food'.

✖ **Nokturno** [93 C3] Skalinska 4. The ever-popular Nokturno, on the steep street running down from Kaptol to Tkalčićeva, serves up good pizzas & a wide range of pasta dishes in a simple, cheerful setting. There's a terrace, & their crisp Đakovo Riesling is among the most keenly priced in town.

✖ **Tkalčina Vura** [93 C2] Tkalčićeva 57. A simple, friendly place right in the heart of bustling Tkalčićeva, with a pretty terrace & a good choice of well-priced standard fare – grilled meats, risotto, calamari & the like.

On and off Jelačić Square
Expensive
✗ **Rossini** [93 D4] Vlaška 55; ☎ 455 1060; www.korum.hr. Very upscale Italian opposite the Jadran Hotel, complete with chic interior & an extensive menu of timeless favourites covering everything from antipasti to risotto, pasta & classic Italian meat & fish dishes. Reservations recommended.

Mid-range
✗ **Boban** [93 C5] Gajeva 3; ☎ 481 1549; www.boban.hr. This enduringly popular & well-located establishment (just down from Jelačić Square) is owned by Croatian national team & AC Milan football superstar Zvonimir Boban. Underneath the café you'll find a busy Italian-themed restaurant in a brick-vaulted cellar, with excellent pasta dishes.

✗ **Jaegerhorn** [93 B4] Ilica 14. Part of the Jaegerhorn Pansion, the restaurant is located at the end of a narrow arcade off Ilica, with a lovely summer terrace (though the fountain really is noisy) & a large indoor seating area for colder weather. Traditional Croatian fare.

✗ **Korčula** [93 B5] Teslina 17; ☎ 487 2159. Excellent, long-established and unpretentious seafood restaurant. Closed Sun.

✗ **Lady Šram** [93 A3] Mesnička 12; ☎ 485 1122; www.ladysram.hr. A 5min walk west along Ilica from Jelačić Square, and up the hill a few steps, this place is named after a famous Croatian actress & beauty of the 1920s. The stylish Edwardian interior, soft lighting & upmarket ambience make this a great venue for a romantic evening out. With a chef who's passionate about keeping traditional recipes alive, expect a menu heavily slanted towards game, homemade pâtés & meat stews; & the homemade *štrukli* is also highly rated. Reservations recommended. Closed Mon.

✗ **Piccolo Mondo** [93 C4] Gajeva 1 (in the Hotel Dubrovnik). Don't be fooled by the rather middle-of-the-road décor; this place does some of the best al dente pasta in Croatia, along with pizzas & good international-style fish & meat dishes. Service is efficient & friendly, & the location (right on Jelačić Square) couldn't be more central.

✗ **Stari Fijaker** [93 A4] Mesnička 6; ☎ 483 3829 www.starifijaker.hr. Just down from Lady Šram (see above). The name means 'old coach', & the emphasis is very much on old-fashioned country cooking from the Zagorje region north of Zagreb. The menu can be a little earthy for some – specialities include blood sausage, offal, turkey & *grah* (hearty bean stew), accompanied by an extensive selection of local & international beers.

Budget
✗ **Mimice** [93 D4] Jurišićeva 21. Genuine, no-frills local seafood eatery with barstool type seats – fried squid or sardines served with French fries, a wedge of bread, and a glass of red wine.

✗ **Pizzeria Lav** [93 D4] Vlaška 23. A basic place (the name means 'lion') just east of Jelačić Square with vaulted interior & a wee terrace tucked into an alleyway, serving decent pizzas from a wood-fired oven.

✗ **Pizzicato** [93 A4] Gundulićeva 4. Another very simple pizzeria with a tiny courtyard terrace, but this time a block west of the flower market. Its location under a music academy means you'll munch your margherita to the background strains of aspiring local musicians – talented or otherwise.

✗ **Purger** [93 D5] Petrinjska 33. A wholesome Croatian place on the street running southeast out of Jelačić Square, named after the local word for 'citizen' (a variant on burgher). It's modestly priced, popular with local politicians, & has a terrace at the back in summer. Closed Sun.

✗ **Vallis Aurea** [93 B4] Tomićeva 4. A wonderful, rustic, down-to-earth place on the short pedestrian street off Ilica that leads up to the funicular, specialising in Slavonian & traditional Croatian dishes, served simply & in generous portions. Menu changes daily. Has a miniature terrace in summer on the street. Closed Sun.

Lower town
Expensive
✗ **Fontana** [93 D6] Kneza Borne 2 (at the Sheraton). With swanky surroundings, a renowned buffet, & a fairly traditional à-la-carte menu, this restaurant is mainly favoured by the hotel's own business travellers & upmarket package tour groups.

✗ **Gallo** [93 B6] Hebrangova 34; ☎ 481 4014; www.gallo.hr. Located 1 block west of Preradovićeva in the atrium of the Castellum Centre, Gallo is 1 of Zagreb's most upmarket eateries. The décor & menu have a Mediterranean flavour, with lots of terracotta, wrought iron, Tuscan tones & a pleasant garden terrace complementing the seafood specialities. I have heard that it may be resting on its laurels a little – so let me know if I'm wrong. Reservations recommended.

✗ **Opium** [93 D7] Branimirova 29 (Branimir Centar); ☎ 461 5679; www.opium.hr. A stylish new place serving upmarket southeast Asian & Japanese cuisine. Reservations recommended.

✗ **Sorriso** [93 D6] Boškovićeva 11; ☎ 487 6392; www.sorriso.hr. A very stylish Mediterranean-inspired place, half a floor below street level in an old brick cellar, midway between Jelačić Square & the Sheraton Hotel. Modern Italian & French cuisine, beautifully presented, make this a popular choice for a special night out. Reservations recommended. Closed Sun.

✗ **Zinfandel's** [104–5 D6] Mihanovićeva 1 (in the Regent Esplanade); ☎ 456 6666. Belgian chef Marc Fontenelle heads up the Regent Esplanade's flagship restaurant, offering Mediterranean-inspired fare with an Asian twist. Named after the celebrated wine grape believed to have originated on the Adriatic coast, the restaurant's emphasis on using the very best Croatian produce means prices reflect quality. Modern, sumptuous interior, or eat out on the lovely Oleander Terrace in warm weather. Reservations recommended.

Mid-range

✗ **Asia** [93 D7] Šenoina 1. With a new location overlooking Tomislav Square (it used to be at the Astoria Hotel), Asia is one of the very few places serving upmarket Asian food. Good range of traditional Chinese dishes, though if you're used to takeaway prices back home, you'll find it on the expensive side.

✗ **Le Bistro** [93 B7] Mihanovićeva 1 (in the Regent Esplanade); ☎ 456 6666. Lovely French-style glass-roofed balcony & outdoor terrace, with pretty good value lunch options, excellent homemade pastries, & the very best *štrukli* in town. Reservations recommended.

✗ **Hrvatski Kulturni Klub** [93 A6] Trg Maršala Tita 10; ☎ 482 8084. Tucked away in the basement of the Arts & Crafts Museum with a lovely terrace at the back, this traditional restaurant is popular with intellectuals & arty types, & serves up solid Croatian fare. Reservations recommended.

✗ **Kaptol** [93 A7] Krsnjavoga 1. The Westin Zagreb's large, airy restaurant is surprisingly good value (steady on the extensive & expensive wine list, however), mixing international dishes with good Croatian staples.

✗ **Mašklin i Lata** [93 B6] Hebrangova 11a; ☎ 481 82 73. Located in the basement underneath the Old Pharmacy Pub (see page 96), this small family-run restaurant serves up Šibenik-style food with an emphasis – as you'd expect – on fish dishes. Closed Sun.

✗ **Palace** [93 C6] Strossmayerov Trg 10; ☎ 481 4611, 489 9600. A favourite venue for the city's better-heeled residents during the socialist era, the Palace's dining room retains a good deal of its old-world charm, even if the food lacks sparkle for a place of this calibre. Reservations recommended.

✗ **Paviljon** [93 D7] Trg Kralja Tomislava 22; ☎ 481 3066; www.restaurant-paviljon.com. In an old glass & wrought-iron exhibition pavilion set in pleasant parkland opposite the station, the Paviljon is one of Zagreb's oldest upper-end restaurants. The spacious dining room & outdoor terrace attract diners with a decent expense account – which you'll certainly need if you're going for the vintage champagnes. Happily, those with more modest tastes can still get a 1st-rate plate of pasta here or a dish of *štrukli* without breaking the bank. Reservations recommended. Closed Sun.

✗ **Radicchio** [93 D6] Branimirova 29 (Branimir Centar). Part of the Arcotel Allegra hotel complex, this is modern, Mediterranean-inspired cuisine at its Croatian best. Good value for lunch, when they do a fixed-price menu including wine.

Budget

✗ **Huatian** [93 D7] Kneza Mislava 1. Located opposite the Sheraton, a Chinese restaurant (signed Kineski Restoran) serving up unpretentious dishes at a reasonable price. Don't on any account be tempted by a shot of Pelinkovac as your after-dinner treat.

✗ **Pivnica Tomislav** [93 C7] Trg Kralja Tomsilava 18 (almost opposite the Paviljon, see above). Excellent hearty fixed-price lunch menus comprising soup plus main plus salad for 25–35kn, as well as an à-la-carte range of simple, home-cooked dishes. Very popular with locals, there's a small street-side café, with the main restaurant halfway underground indoors.

Further afield
Expensive

✗ **Dubravkin Put** [93 B1] Dubravkin Put 2; ☎ 483 4970. Northwest of the old town, tucked into in the woods, this very fashionable restaurant serves up excellent fish, shellfish & meat dishes – all specialities of

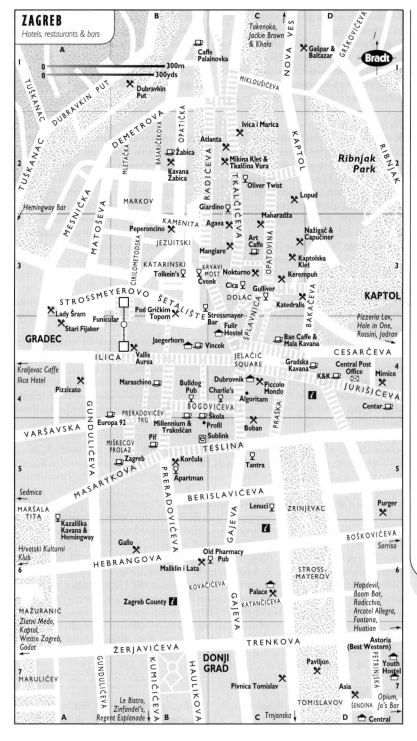

ZAGREB

Hotels, restaurants & bars

0 _____ 300m
0 _____ 300yds

TUSKANAC

DUBRAVKIN PUT

Caffe Palainovka

Dubravkin Put

Takenoko, Jackie Brown & Khala

NOVA VES

Gašpar & Baltazar

GREŠKOVIČEVA

MIKLOUŠIČEVA

RIBNJAK

Bradt

DEMETROVA

MLETAČKA

BASARIČEKOVA

OPATIČKA

Atlanta

RADIČEVA

Ivica i Marica

Mikina Klet & Tkalčina Vura

Žabica

Kavana Žabica

Oliver Twist

TKALČIĆEVA

KAPTOL

Ribnjak Park

Lopud

MARKOV

MESNIČKA

MATOŠEVA

Hemingway Bar

KAMENITA

Peperoncino

JEZUITSKI

KATARINSKI

Giardino

Agava

Mangiare

Maharadža

Art Caffe

OPATOVINA

Nažigač & Capuciner

Kaptolska Klet

Tolkein's

ČIRILOMETODSKA

KRVAVI MOST

Čvenk

Cica

Nokturno

DOLAC

Gulliver

Kerempuh

STROSSMEYEROVO ŠETALIŠTE

Lady Šram

Funicular

Stari Fijaker

GRADEC

Pod Gričkim Topom

Strossmayer Bar

SPLAVNICA

Katedralis

BAKAČEVA

KAPTOL

Pizzeria Lav, Hole in One, Rossini, Jadran

Fulir Hostel

Jaegerhorn

ILICA

Vallis Aurea

Vincek

Ban Caffe & Mala Kavana

JELAČIĆ SQUARE

CESARČEVA

Kraljevac Caffe Ilica Hotel

Pizzicato

GUNDULIČEVA

Maraschino

Bulldog Pub

Dubrovnik

Charlie's

BOGOVIČEVA

Algoritam

Piccolo Mondo

PRAŠKA

Gradska Kavana

K&K

Central Post Office

JURIŠIČEVA

Mimice

Centar

VARŠAVSKA

PRERADOVIČEV TRG

Europa 92

Millennium & Trakošćan

Profil

Škola

Sublink

Boban

MIŠKECOV PROLAZ

Pif

TESLINA

MASARYKOVA

Zagreb

Korčula

Apartman

PRERADOVIĆEVA

Tantra

Sedmica

BERISLAVIĆEVA

GAJEVA

Lenuci

ZRINJEVAC

Purger

MARŠALA TITA

Kazališka Kavana & Hemingway

BOŠKOVIĆEVA

Sorriso

Hrvatski Kulturni Klub

Gallo

HEBRANGOVA

Old Pharmacy Pub

Mašklin i Lata

STROSS-MAYEROV

Hopdevil, Boom Bar, Radicchio, Arcotel Allegra, Fontana, Huatian

KOVAČIĆEVA

Palace

KATANČIĆEVA

GAJEVA

Zagreb County

MAŽURANIĆ

Zlatni Medo, Kaptol, Westin Zagreb, Godot

ŽERJAVIĆEVA

GUNDULIĆEVA

KUMIĆIĆEVA

HAULIKOVA

DONJI GRAD

TRENKOVA

Paviljon

PETRINJSKA

Astoria (Best Western)

Youth Hostel

MARULIĆEV

Le Bistro, Zinfandel's, Regent Esplanade

Pivnica Tomislav

TOMISLAV

Asia

ŠENOINA

Opium, Jo's Bar

Trnjanska

Central

the Dubrovnik area. Reservations are essential, & prices are on the steep side.

✘ **Kod Pavela** Gračanska Cesta 46; ☎ 467 5036. Out of the way, but sumptuous Istrian cuisine in a charming garden setting, accompanied by a great selection of the region's best wines & liqueurs makes the journey worthwhile (take tram #8 or #14 to the terminus, then walk up the hill, signed Sljeme, for 10 mins; the restaurant is on the right). Black & white truffles, homemade pasta & gnocchi, fresh sea fish, & gorgeous Italian-inspired desserts make this a great choice for a special lunch or evening out. It's much-frequented by Zagreb's well-heeled set, so be sure to book ahead.

Budget

✘ **Mex Cantina** [74–5 D6] Savska Cesta 154; ☎ 619 2156; www.mex-cantina.hr. As Zagreb's most authentic Mexican diner, the slightly out-of-town location is worth the journey if you're in the mood for spicy home-cooked Tex-Mex treats in a cosy cantina-style atmosphere – take tram #13, #14 or #17 down Savska Cesta. Its popularity with students makes it worth booking ahead on busy nights.

✘ **Zlatni Medo** [74–5 D6] Savska Cesta 56 (formerly Pivnica Medvedgrad); ☎ 617 7119; www.pivnica.hr. On Savska Cesta about 10 mins south of the Westin Zagreb (on the corner of Vukovarska; take tram #13, #14 or #17), this cavernous, noisy boutique brewery serves up its own range of beers & vast, wholesome platefuls of local food. In addition to the fabulous *weiss* beer, try the *zlatno* (lager), *trenk* (brown) or *ban* (dark) varieties, along with homemade dishes including various types of sausage & *čvarkuša*, a flavoursome cross between a Yorkshire pudding & a scone. While individual dishes aren't especially cheap, serving sizes are huge, making it exceptionally good value for money.

WHERE TO DRINK With great summer weather and lots of visitors, there's no shortage of cafés, bars and pubs in Zagreb. Most restaurants with terraces will also be happy to serve you drinks between meals.

Café society is firmly centred in the area around Jelačić Square – the pedestrianised streets and squares to the southwest become one vast terrace in summer, and the ambience is wonderful, with frequent more or less impromptu live music in the area.

North of the main square, Tkalčićeva, a long, winding, pedestrianised street, is very much the humming heart of Zagreb nightlife. The charming old-style houses along here are now almost all cafés, bars and cheap restaurants – there's a great relaxed vibe just about any time of the day or night, and it's absolutely the place to kick off an evening out.

On Sunday mornings, Jelačić Square plays host to one of the most unusual spectacles in the world, when the Croatian political elite – from the president down – comes out to sit at the café terraces and chew the fat. Blasé locals have been known to criticise this overt populism, but it's a refreshing change from the aloof remoteness of most of the world's leaders.

Saturdays are even busier, with the weekly *špica*, a Zagreb tradition that is a bit like a sit-down version of Italy's *passeggiata*. It basically involves dolling yourself up to the nines and meeting friends for a leisurely coffee/brunch at a favourite watering hole – for preference, one of the high-profile ones off to the southwest of Jelačić Square. The aim is to see and be seen, while catching up on the week's news and gossip in a relaxed, unhurried atmosphere. Again, don't be surprised if you see President Mesić at one of his favourite cafés; he used Charlie's, opposite the Hotel Dubrovnik, as the stump from which he launched his election – and subsequent re-election – campaigns.

We've grouped cafés, bars and pubs – like restaurants, above – into four sections for convenience: the upper town (everything from Gradec to Kaptol and along Tkalčićeva); Jelačić Square and the area nearby to the west, south and east; the rest of the lower town (as far as the railway station); and places further afield (not including Mount Medvednica, which is covered separately, see page 124).

Upper town

▭ **Art Caffe** [93 C3] Tkalčićeva 18. Groovy place with a fashionably grungy interior.

▭ **Caffe Palainovka** [93 B1] Ilirski Trg. In a picturesque part of the old town, right next to the

Priest's Tower, this old-fashioned café boasts a lovely garden terrace & a 19th-century-inspired interior decorated with old photographs & even a penny-farthing bicycle. If you're planning to take part in the lamplighting tour of old Zagreb (see page 110), this is where you'll meet up with your friendly lamplighters.

Y **Cica** [93 C3] Tkalčićeva 8. Groovy place decorated with bohemian bric-a-brac & specialising in exotically flavoured artisan *rakijas*. Honey & rose, blueberry, fig & pear took my fancy; a little research to find your own favourites will set you back 10kn a pop. If the bar staff are to believed (I had had a few), the bar's name means 'tits'.

Y **Čvenk** [93 B3] Radićeva 23. Popular with locals for its long opening hours, keen bar prices & appealing brick-vaulted interior. Has a leaning towards grungy rock music.

Y **Tolkien's** [93 B3] Katarina Trg 3. Hobbits will feel right at home in this homage to Dungeons & Dragons & all things Middle Earth up in a nice quiet part of the old town. Nice terrace. ⌚ till late.

Y **Giardino** [93 C2] Tkalčićeva 37. Comfy wicker sofas on the pavement for summer, & a post-modern interior for winter, marred only slightly by the presence of a large-screen TV. The terrace is one of the best places on the street for watching the world go by.

Y **Gulliver** [93 C3] Tržnica Dolac. One of several down-to-earth cafés along the mezzanine level on the steps leading up from Jelačić Square to Dolac market, & catering largely to traders & local customers. Large terrace, cheap beer.

On and off Jelačić Square

Y **Apartman** [93 B5] Preradovićeva 7/1. Retro beanbags, old school desks, tatty green felt, dark smoky ambience & live DJs, all combining to create a shabby, trendy atmosphere that attracts a hip young crowd. Like so many such places, it's rather souless in the daytime.

⎌ **Ban Caffe** [93 C4] Jelačić Square. Like Mala Kavana next door, what you're paying for here is the location right on the main square. It's a great place to unwind after a tough morning's shopping in nearby Dolac market. Gradska Kavana, at the end of the square, is marginally less expensive, & if anything, swankier.

Y **Bulldog Pub** [93 B4] Bogovićeva 6. Extremely popular place in this café-filled, pedestrianised street off the Flower Square.

Y **Charlie's** [93 C4] Gajeva 4. A popular Zagreb institution & 1 of the president's favourite watering holes. Founded by former Zagreb Dinamo player Mirko 'Charlie' Braun (who died in 2004), & easy to recognise by the black wicker chairs.

Y **Jackie Brown** [93 C1] Nova Ves 17 (in the Kaptol Centar, but downstairs, actually on Tkalčićeva). A trendy lounge bar with a retro-70s feel, attracting an affluent, older set. Large selection of upmarket whiskies & cognacs.

Y **Khala Bar** [93 C1] Nova Ves 11. Also located in the Kaptol Centar at the very top of Tkalčićeva, another groovy lounge bar, but this time with a Persian/Central Asian vibe. Serves up appetising nibbles & upmarket wines by the glass.

Y **Oliver Twist** [93 C2] Tkalčićeva 60. Snuggled into a cutting about halfway along Tkalčićeva, the large green Tuborg umbrellas & vast terrace make it hard to miss. Or indeed pass up, with friendly service, a welcoming wood & brass interior for colder weather, & an extensive menu of foreign beers.

Y **Strossmayer Bar** [93 B3] Strossmayerovo Šetalište bb. Perched at the top of the steep climb up to the old town from Radićeva, serving keenly priced drinks on a quiet, shady terrace overlooking the Zagreb rooftops (also accessible by walking along from the bottom of the Lotrščak Tower, or down from the corner of St Catherine's Square). If you're game, you can venture indoors & shoot pool in a cavernous inside hall.

⎌ **Žabica** [93 B2] Opatička 5. A traditional, refined, genuinely old haunt up in the old town, with lots of authentic detail & fabulous hot chocolate. Also doubles as a sometime internet café.

⎌ **Dubrovnik Hotel Café** [93 C4] Gajeva 1 (next to Charlie's). With an ample terrace & an excellent location bordering on Jelačić Square, this place is a little pricey, but wonderfully convenient if you've been trawling around the city's shops.

⎌ **Europa 92** [93 B5] Varšavska 3. Part of the cinema complex. A nice enough terrace on a pedestrianised street, but be warned that it's probably named after the last year when the toilets were properly cleaned.

⎌ **Gradska Kavana** [93 D4] Jelačić Square. With an outdoor terrace & huge Art-Deco-inspired interior on 3 levels, it's reputedly the favourite Sunday morning coffee spot for the president & the political elite. The usual selection of cakes, coffee, soft drinks, wine & beer, at prices marginally more modest than at the Ban Caffe & Mala Kavana along the square. There's an adjoining restaurant serving traditional dishes at moderate prices.

Y **Hole in One** [93 D4] Vlaška 42. Polished dark wood & brass railings make for a homely pub-like atmosphere, though prices are also scarily reminiscent of London.

The smoky little pizzeria next door is part of the same establishment; for reasons unexplained, the day I was there it claimed to have no house wine, & wanted 180kn for a very ordinary-looking bottle of white – which I was easily able to resist.

K&K (Knjiga & Kava) [93 D4] Jurišićeva 5. Cosy café on 2 levels just east of Jelačić Square, with an old-world, bookish feel & walls crammed with vintage photos of Zagreb (the name means 'books & coffee'). Ensconce yourself at 1 of the marble tables, or on the small outdoor terrace if the smoky atmosphere gets too much, & settle into a traditional *sachertorte* accompanied by coffee, beer or a glass of wine, all without blowing the budget. Owner Miličić is a popular local writer & a close friend of the great & the good.

Kraljevac Caffe [93 A4] Britanski Trg 9. This café 2 tram stops west of Jelačić Square comes into its own on Sun, when the lively flea market at Britanski Square gets into full swing. Take time out from perusing the bric-a-brac & haggling with the stall owners to enjoy a coffee, beer or a *spricer* on the green love seats.

Mala Kavana [93 C4] On the north side of Jelačić Square, next door to the Ban Caffe, the central location has made the Mala Kavana a long-standing favourite. Serves light snacks, cakes, ice cream sundaes & the usual selection of drinks, with prices at the upper end.

Lower town

Boom Bar [93 D6] Branimirova 29 (Branimir Centar). 1970s retro décor, groovy ambience, & surprisingly expensive. Popular as a pre- & post-cinema hang-out.

Hemingway [93 A5] Trg Maršala Tita 1 (opposite the Croatian National Theatre). Spacious terrace, large cushioned benches & trendy but uncomfortable oriental glass & wicker stools. The interior is a spartan all-white affair with large photos of Papa. Extensive (& expensive) selection of cocktails, foreign beers & wines. Young, affluent crowd, but service can be on the surly side – & heaven only knows what the old man himself would have made of it.

Hopdevil [93 D6] Branimirova 29 (Branimir Centar). Newly opened pub offering 101 types of beer & seating for 300.

Jo's Bar [93 D7] Branimirova 29 (Branimir Centar, at the Arcotel Allegra). Modern, minimalist & gay-friendly; they also do light food, & sometimes have live jazz.

Kazališka Kavana [93 A5/6] Trg Maršala Tita 1. Next door to Hemingway (see above), but with an altogether less affected, friendlier atmosphere, cheaper prices, & the same great view of the National

Maraschino [93 B4] Margaretska 1. Trendy place just off Ilica, a very popular hang-out that takes its name from Zadar's world-famous cherry liqueur, known to locals as *maraska*. Good hot chocolate – their own version, infused with the aforementioned liqueur, is a special treat – & a selection of cocktails & Croatian wines.

Pif [93 B5] Preradovićeva 4. Excellent little café just off the Flower Square, with tables spilling outside in the summer.

Škola [93 B4/5] Bogovićeva 7 (3rd flr). A renovated school that's now one of the city's trendiest bars, with prices & snooty staff to match. A slick pure-white interior houses chic drinking & eating areas ranged over 2 levels; it's also one of the first places to offer a snack menu featuring a selection of Italian-inspired goodies. Very busy on Fri/Sat after 9pm, but otherwise a quiet haven for an afternoon drink. Email & blog addicts will revel in Škola's T-Mobile wi-fi hotspot, safe in the knowledge that their MacBooks will blend perfectly with the all-white décor.

Tantra [93 C5] Gajeva 2 (2nd flr). Very groovy lounge bar with wooden floors, indoor plants, & capacious armchairs & sofas that are particularly popular with snogging youths. Great views out over Jelačić Square, young, friendly staff, & reasonable prices. Their salsa nights on Thu & Sat are all the rage – for details ☎ 539 9551.

Theatre across the road; the location of choice for pre-theatre drinks.

Lenuci [93 C5] Zrinjevac 15. Just up from the Palace Hotel, this stylish, unpretentious wine bar is named after the man who designed Zagreb's 'green horseshoe'. Bold design & a spacious, airy interior spread over 1½ floors, with subdued lighting & music to match. Popular with smart professionals.

Old Pharmacy Pub [93 C6] Hebrangova 11. On the south side of the street just east of Preradovićeva, this charming venue is a firm favourite with locals, who like to relax on the banquettes & sofas & partake of a coffee, beer or glass of wine in an authentic, turn-of-the-century atmosphere.

Sedmica [93 A5] Kačićeva 7a. Look out for the Guinness sign that marks the entrance to this fashionable, unpretentious place that remains popular with Zagreb's boho crowd (it's not far from the National Theatre). Marble bar tables flanked by tall bar stools, a retro, grungy look & a back room that's practically a semi-terrace.

Further afield

♀ **Dublin Pub** [74–5 E5] Maksimirska 75. With walls clad in photos of old Dublin, décor featuring the humble potato, & comfy brown leather sofas, this is as Irish an atmosphere as you're going to find in the heart of Croatia. Get there on tram #4, #11 or #12 towards the zoo & the Dinamo Stadium.

♀ **Godot** [93 A7] Savska 23. Authentic pub feel & cheap *travarica* at 7kn a shot, just south of the railway line. The youngish crowd reflects the bar's location in the student district.

♀ **Hemingway Bar** [93 A2] Tuškanec 21/23 (behind the Kino Tuškanec cinema). Zagreb's original Hemingway's, west of the old town, has evolved from a swanky cocktail bar to an upmarket eatery/nightclub, mainly used for hosting functions. Smart, with prices to match.

♀ **Movie Pub** [74–5 D6] Savska Cesta 141. Take tram #13, #14 or #17. Enormously popular place out of the city centre, with seating for 350 & an authentic pub feel – though a little too faux-British (& pricey) for my taste. If the crowd inside gets noisy, there's also a small but pleasant outdoor terrace. And if you've really overdone it, then there's always the Movie Hotel upstairs (see page 87).

♀ **SPUNK** [74–5 D6] Hrvatske Bratske Zajednice bb. On the main road south to the Sava & Novi Zagreb, on the right-hand side, between Vukovarska & Slavonska, & part of the giant University Library complex. This small, modern bar is a favourite with students, not least because of its cheap beer & regular live music. Also makes for a handy freshener on your way out to the Močvara Club (see page 100).

ICE CREAM Zagreb's first ice cream is believed to have been served up on 2 May 1847 by local restaurateur Mato Pallain in the coffee shop he'd opened on the city's North Promenade a decade earlier. Since then, it has firmly entrenched itself as a national staple whose enormous popularity is attested to by the large numbers of ice cream parlours – *slastičarnica* – dotting the city.

Croatians favour Italian-style gelati, though the local version tends to be somewhat heavier. Note that, as in Italy, the cost of your cone or cup depends on the number of flavours you choose – be warned, however, that unless you speak Croatian, you'll have to 'fly by sight' when ordering, as English translations of the wealth of flavours available are rare.

🍦 **Centar** [93 D4] On Jurišićeva, on the right-hand side heading away from Jelačić Square towards Palmotićeva. Our absolute number one favourite in Zagreb, &, by the look of the queues, plenty of other people's too.

🍦 **Hotel Dubrovnik** [93 C4] Gajeva 1 (though the shop is actually on Jelačić Square). Mountains of luridly presented flavours; very popular with the locals.

🍦 **Millennium** [93 B4/5] Bogovićeva 7. Heavier & creamier than Centar's more Italian-style fare. Zagreb's most extensive & exotic choice of flavours. Nice outdoor seating in this pedestrianised street.

🍦 **Orient** [74–5 E5] Maksimirska 34 (close to the tram stop). Run by 2 sisters who serve up the usual classic favourites along with more imaginative options

like 'Ginger & Fred'. The homemade cakes are also much prized by sweet-toothed locals. A bit hard to find – look for the yellow & red cake sign outside.

🍦 **Trakošćan** [93 B4/5] Bogovićeva 7. Next door to Millennium, & longer established & less flashy than its newer rival. Has a very loyal old-school following.

🍦 **Vincek** [93 B4] Ilica 18 (& various other locations around the city). A Zagreb institution offering excellent quality & a wide variety of flavours. Also makes an outrageous all-cream torta that goes for a very reasonable 10kn.

🍦 **Zagreb** [93 B5] Masarykova (at the corner of Preradovićeva). Another excellent choice, & also selling a wicked range of popular cakes.

MARKETS, SUPERMARKETS AND BAKERIES Seven mornings a week, **Dolac** market does its wonderful, bustling thing, with all kinds of fresh produce available, from seasonal fruit and vegetables on the upper level to meat, cheese and dairy goods, fresh pasta and delicatessen items in the basement, and the catch of the day in a separate fish section upstairs.

Locals still come here daily to sell their own vegetables and other produce, and most people in Zagreb are loyal to their preferred *kumica* (literally 'godmother') – usually an older woman who serves as their trusted source for the best home-grown produce.

A bronze statue of a *kumica* has been placed in honour of the tradition at the top of the stairs up from Jelačić Square.

The action generally kicks off at about 07.00 – earlier for the fish market, where you'll be jostling for the choicest items with buyers from Zagreb's best restaurants – and winds up before 14.00, when the big clean-up begins, ready for the next day's trading. At the foot of the steps leading up to the market there's also a daily flower market, dominated, again, by local women selling their own cuttings.

If you're near the bus station, it's worth knowing that there's also a smaller daily market at the eastern end of Branimira, just north of the railway line. And if you're west of the city centre, there's also a daily market on Britanski Square, two tram stops along Ilica from Jelačić Square; on Sundays, bric-a-brac replaces the fruit and veg – see page 101 for details.

There are also plenty of **supermarkets** large and small in Zagreb, where you can stock up on essentials. The local Konzum chain is the most widespread, with branches throughout the city, but there are also quite a few independent shops as well. Prices are generally competitive, and there's usually a good selection of local produce as well as wholesale food. You can ask for sandwiches to be made up to order at the deli-counter in most supermarkets – just point at the type of bread you want filled, say '*sendvič*' and indicate your choice of filling(s); you're just charged for the ingredients by weight.

Bakeries (*pekarnica*) are also widespread and sell a good variety of breads and sometimes also offer ready-made sandwiches (*sendviči*) with cheese (*sir*), ham (*šunka*) tuna (*tuna*), egg (*jaja*) and occasionally more exotic fillings, as well as various pies, sausage rolls and the like.

Finally, if you find yourself craving American-style snacks, there's a donut shop two blocks east of Jelačić Square opposite the main post office, and a Subway sandwich outlet on Gajeva, right by the Hotel Dubrovnik, where you can sate your appetite with a foot-long sandwich or US-style muffins and cookies.

ENTERTAINMENT AND NIGHTLIFE

As the capital, Zagreb gets more than its fair share of cultural happenings, ranging from excellent ballet, opera and theatre (notably at the national theatre), to an entire summer schedule chock-full of local and international performances – everything from classical to jazz to rock and beyond. In summer, you'll often find free street concerts taking place in and around the city, in addition to more organised happenings, and the capital is also endowed with a good number of clubs and venues large enough to attract big-name stars. It's worth checking the Zagreb Tourist Information Centre website (*www.zagreb-touristinfo.hr*), the monthly 'Events and Performances' guide, and street hoardings, for details of events as they come up.

As in Dubrovnik, there's also a major summer festival, which runs for two weeks from the end of July. This features some of Croatia's best folk performances, and remains one of your best opportunities to see genuine folk dancing with the traditional costumes being worn. Zagreb also hosts several other festivals, one of the biggest being Animafest (*www.animafest.hr*), the world festival of animated films, which has a week of short films in even-numbered years (usually June) and full-length features in odd-numbered years (usually October). Odd-numbered years also see modern music celebrated at the Music Biennial.

MUSIC, OPERA, BALLET AND THEATRE
Lisinski Concert Hall (*just south of the railway station, off Vukovarska; Trg Stjepana Radića 4; box office* ☎ *612 1166; www.lisinski.hr*) There's a regular programme of concerts at the Lisinski Concert Hall by the Zagreb Philharmonic Orchestra, visiting artists, and

the city's many other classical ensembles. The venue offers a rich and varied programme featuring classical, jazz, contemporary world music and even popular rock acts, and you can choose, book and pay for your seats online in English. Collect your tickets from the box office 60 minutes before the performance begins.

Croatian National Theatre [104–5 B5] (*Trg Maršala Tita 15; box office* ✆ *482 8532; www.hnk.hr*) For opera, ballet and theatre, the Croatian National Theatre dominates, with an impressive year-round programme of new productions and revivals, featuring plenty of popular favourites mixed with more eclectic pieces. Unless you're fluent in Croatian, the theatre programme is hard work. Instead, head along to the opera or ballet, where you'll see and hear top local and visiting performers for just a fraction of the price you'd pay in the larger European capitals. The theatre has a useful online booking facility (in Croatian and English), which shows seat availability and pricing.

Live gigs Keep your eyes peeled for posters around town advertising upcoming events, which mostly take place at one of the venues listed under Nightlife, below, or, for the biggest names, at sports stadiums and open-air festivals. Big names aside, Croatia has a thriving local music scene, of which Zagreb is the natural hub. There's plenty of talent about, and if you're relaxed about the fact that you won't usually understand the lyrics (though some artists do perform in English), it won't be long before you find yourself carried away by local bands' energy and enthusiasm.

NIGHTLIFE Zagreb has plenty of late evening lounge bars and cafés, and in summer popular haunts like Tkalčićeva stay humming until the wee hours. There's also a fair sprinkling of dance clubs, though the current fad for 'turbofolk' – an electronic take on the traditional Balkan theme – is unlikely to strike a chord with most visitors. In summer, the mainstream dance music scene – like much of the city's population – moves out to the Adriatic coast, and things stay pretty quiet in the capital until September. The inverse is true of live music, which consistently draws crowds large enough to ensure Zagreb remains a fixture on major European tours. The summer months welcome plenty of visiting bands, who play open-air festivals as well as the various live venues around town.

☆ **Aquarius** [74–5 C7] Aleja Matije Ljubeka; ✆ 364 0231; www.aquarius.hr; tram #17 to Horvati. Situated lakeside at Jarun, Zagreb's longest-established dance club is still the most popular, with dance floors thumping to commercial hip-hop, R&B & some of Europe's best celebrity DJs. The club has a massively popular offshoot in summer on the island of Pag, at Zrče beach.

☆ **Best** [74–5 C6] Jarunski Cesta 5; ✆ 301 1943; www.thebest.hr; tram #14 or #17 to Savski Most. Huge, glitzy venue specialising in commercial techno, disco, house & hip-hop, along with special theme nights featuring soul, trance & the like.

☆ **Boogaloo** Vukovarska 68; ✆ 631 3022; www.boogaloo.hr; tram #13 to Miramarska. A vast place accommodating 1,000+, located in the OTV Dom building, a venue with a long history of breaking new ground in the Zagreb music scene. Features DJs & live bands.

☆ **BP Club** [104–5 D4] Teslina 7; ✆ 481 4444; www.bpclub.hr. Local jazz celebrity Boško Petrović

manages this prestigious basement jazz venue, with graffiti on the walls attesting to the presence of big names like Ronnie Scott & Joe Pass. Cosy & intimate, there's also a good selection of international wines, beers & spirits.

☆ **Brazil** Veslačka; 091 200 2481; tram #14 or #17 to Veslačka, then head to the riverbank. This dilapidated barge on the Sava stays open very late, making it a popular end-of-evening stopover for those on their way back from other venues like Močvara (see below). Reggae & world music, mostly.

☆ **Gallery** [74–5 C6] Aleja Matije Ljubeka; ✆ 099 444 2444; www.gallery.hr; tram #17 to Horvati. Another of Jarun Lake's popular nightspots, Gallery is the capital's most exclusive dance venue, with a very strict dress code (yep, no trainers) & a wealthy young crowd. The focus in the chic interior is on the latest celebrity DJs. At the time of writing, one of the only clubs to accept credit cards – & you'll quickly see why, if they deign to let you in.

3

☆ **KSET** Unska 3; ☎ 612 9758; www.kset.org. A small venue that's actually part of the University of Electrotechnical Science, KSET has a long tradition of pioneering new bands & hosting stylistically diverse genres, from punk & underground to avant-garde jazz. Friendly atmosphere, & prices way cheaper than at the glitzier clubs.

☆ **Močvara** ('Swamp') [74–5 D6] Trnjanski nasip; ☎ 615 9668; www.mochvara.hr; tram #13 to Lisinski, then walk south towards the river; the club's down behind the Sava dyke. Set up in an old factory, this legendary venue is popular with an alternative crowd interested in punk, thrash, grunge & indie sounds, & puts on all manner of gigs & special events. Occasional DJ nights, & cheap drinks. If you're aiming to get home by taxi, you need to head across to the restaurant nearby, just 100m north of the venue.

☆ **Route 66** Paromlinska 47; ☎ 611 8737. Behind the University Library complex (see SPUNK, opposite), on a parallel road heading down to the river. Classic rock & blues dive with a grungy feel & cheap beer, & popular with musicians. Also features country & western cover bands & demos from local new contenders.

☆ **Saloon** Tuškanac 1; ☎ 483 4903. Smart, minimalist venue playing a mainstream disco sound; popular with the young & affluent.

☆ **Sax!** Palmotićeva 22; ☎ 487 2836; www.sax-zg.hr. A block or so east of Jelačić Square, & owned by the Croatian Musicians' Union. Informal venue hosting good jazz sessions & album promotions Tue–Sat.

☆ **Shamballa** Savska 30; ☎ 099 721 7777; www.shamballa.hr. Enormous new café/club on Savska, near the Westin.

☆ **SPUNK** [74–5 D6] Hrvatske bratske zajednice; ☎ 615 1528; tram #13 to Lisinski & then walk south towards the river; the bar's on the right, & part of the University Library complex. While technically a bar, this exceedingly popular student venue is also 1 of Zagreb's top spots for garage & underground music – & has the cheapest beer in town.

☆ **Tvornica** Šubićeva 2; ☎ 777 8673; www.tvornica-kulture.hr; tram #1 or #17 to Šubićeva station. A large (1,500+) live venue hosting names like David Byrne, Faithless, Madradeus & John Cale; also does big club nights.

GAY AND LESBIAN After decades of being very firmly in the closet, Zagreb's burgeoning gay scene is beginning to come out with confidence, with a couple of good venues, its own annual Gay Pride march, and the Queer Zagreb festival. All too predictably, old Croatia's Catholic/macho culture means male gays are still better served than lesbians both for venues and cultural acceptance.

The city's Gay Pride march (*www.zagreb-pride.net*) takes place in June. While the event still seems to need vigorous policing, it's gradually gaining acceptance as part of the city's mainstream festival calendar. Queer Zagreb (*www.queerzagreb.org*), a cultural festival focusing on art, theory and activism, with an extensive film programme, takes place in April, and is the largest event of its kind in eastern and central Europe.

☆ **Bumerang** Mažuranićev Trg 2; ☎ 485 4754; www.bumerang.hr. Sauna between Trg Maršala Tita and the Botanical Gardens. ⊕ 17.00–24.00 daily.

☆ **Global** Pavla Hatza 14; ☎ 481 4878; www.globalclubzg.hr. 2 blocks north of the train station, on a street running east from the 'green horseshoe'. Zagreb's only dedicated gay club, with 3 bars, a VIP lounge, a dance floor, a darkroom & a weekly programme of strippers & gay films. A happening spot at night; doubles as a sex shop & café by day.

See the Zagreb listings on www.croatia-gay.com for more information.

SHOPPING CENTRES AND CINEMAS

Avenue Mall Avenija Dubrovnik 16; www.avenuemall.com.hr. Zagreb's newest shopping mall, with some 130 shops including Zara, Marks & Spencer, Esprit, Benetton, Calvin Klein, Tommy Hilfiger, Lacoste and Mango, as well as cafés & restaurants & a cinema complex. In Novi Zagreb, south of the river Sava.

Branimir Centar [104–5 F6] Branimirova 29, just east of the railway station. Offers a good mix of fashion, beauty, bars, restaurants, the 13-screen Cinestar cinema

multiplex (films often shown in English), the Wettpunkt 24hr casino, & the Arcotel Allegra Hotel.

Kaptol Centar [104–5 D1] Nova Ves 17; www.centarkaptol.hr. (just up from Kaptol, & connecting the top of Tkalčićeva with Nova Ves). One of Zagreb's newest (& most glamorous) shopping temple, housing big-name brands like Hugo Boss, Joop, Lacoste, Mandarina Duck, Max & Co, Paul & Shark & Tommy Hilfiger, along with Marks & Spencer (clothing only). The centre also boasts the Broadway 5 cinema multiplex & a few plush bars & restaurants – & is expanding next door. **Importanne Centar** [104–5 D6] Starčevićev Trg, located underground between the railway station & the Regent Esplanade. Considerably more downmarket, but has a good selection of shops including fashion & jewellery, photo processing, shoes, stationery & so on. There's also a good number of takeaway sandwich & hot fast-food stalls, a biggish supermarket, a couple of newsagents & a branch of DM (for toiletries etc).

Importanne Galleria [104–5 F4] Iblerov Trg (on Vlaška, between Draškovićeva & Smičiklasova). Just east of the Jadran hotel, this modern complex covers everything from electronics, music, photo processing, jewellery, clothes & the inevitable shoe emporia, to pets, eyeglasses, perfume, toys & children's wear. There's a fast food hall downstairs, along with a good supermarket & a large DM outlet. The centre also has a clothes alterations & repair service in the basement, for unexpected emergencies.

If you want to go to a good old-fashioned cinema rather than a multiplex in a shopping mall, head for **Europa** on the Flower Square (Cvjetni Trg).

Secondhand goods For secondhand bargain hunters, there's an excellent Sunday crafts and bric-a-brac market at Britanski Square, two tram stops west along Ilica from Jelačić Square. There's everything here from bayonets to wagon wheels, old china, music scores, clothing and wooden farming implements. If prices seem high at first, remember that bargaining is virtually obligatory, so expect to be able to knock 20–40% – depending on your negotiating skills – off. Loads of fun, though you might have a job getting that 19th-century scythe through customs.

Bookshops The two best English language bookshops in Zagreb are **Profil Megastore** (*Bogovićeva 7; www.profil.hr*) and **Algoritam** (*Gajeva 1; www.algoritam.hr*).

OTHER PRACTICALITIES

BANKS AND POST OFFICES Zagreb has dozens of different banks, and ATMs abound – locally based Zagrebačka Banka has more than 150 dotted around the city, including 11 on Ilica alone, accepting MasterCard, Maestro, Visa, Visa Electron and Diners.

There are two vast main post offices – one right next to the train station, and the other a block east of Jelačić Square on Jurišićeva.

24hr Post Office [104–5 E6] Branimirova 4, 10000, Zagreb; ☎ 498 1300. Send letters weighing less than 5g from lines 9–11, packages less than 3kg from the parcel area on the east side of the building, & heavier items from the HPT office 50m further east of the main entrance. Local & international phone calls can be made from the 1st floor – get a phonecard from reception, & pay for the time used after you've made your call. ⏰ 24/7.

Central Post Office [104–5 E4] Jurišićeva 13, 10101, Zagreb; ☎ 481 1090. ⏰ 07.00–21.00 Mon–Fri, 07.30–14.00 Sat

If you're based south of the railway line or arriving or departing by bus, there's also a convenient post office at the main bus station (*Autobusni Kolodvor, Marina Držića 4;* ☎ 611 9077; f 611 8977; ⏰ 08.00–19.30 Mon–Fri, 07.30–14.00 Sat).

PHONE AND INTERNET The main mobile operators have a big local presence:

T-Mobile Shops dotted throughout the city, the most convenient of which is the one next to the church at Preradovićeva 3, near the corner with Bogovićeva.

VIP Centar Located right opposite the Dubrovnik Hotel, at Gajeva 2b, near the corner with Jelačić Square.

There are also several conveniently located internet cafés, with hourly fees coming in at anything from 15 to 40kn.

Charlie's [93 C4] Gajeva 4; ✆ 488 0233. Conveniently situated just a few metres south of the Dubrovnik hotel, across the street. ⏱ 08.00–22.00 Mon–Sat, 11.00–21.00 Sun.

Net Kulturni Klub Mama Preradovićeva 18 (in courtyard); ✆ 485 6400; www.mi2.hr. ⏱ noon–midnight daily.

Sublink [93 B5] Teslina 12; ✆ 4819993; www.sublink.hr. Excellent, fast, friendly and convenient. Hidden away at the back of a courtyard, this was

Croatia's first internet café, opened in 1996. ⏱ 09.00–22.00 Mon–Sat, 15.00–22.00 Sun.

VIP Centar Iblerov Trg 10; ✆ 091 209 1091. Located on the upper floor of the Importanne Galleria shopping centre; fast, pay-as-you-go coin-operated access – but eye-wateringly smoky at times. ⏱ 08.00–23.00 Mon–Sat, 09.00–23.00 Sun.

VIP Preradovićeva 5; ✆ 483 0089, www.vipnet.hr. ⏱ 08.00–23.00 Mon–Sat, 09.00–23.00 Sun.

If you're travelling with your laptop, you'll also be able to take advantage of the city's growing number of wi-fi hotspots with a fast wireless connection, courtesy of T-Com or VIP. Payment can be made via pre-paid voucher or online via credit card.

HOSPITAL AND PHARMACIES Zagreb's main hospital (*opća bolnica*) is located at Draškovićeva 19, on the corner with Boškovićeva near the Sheraton Hotel, and as you'd expect the accident and emergency service works 24/7. ✆ 461 0011; for emergencies, call ✆ 94.

There are dozens of pharmacies (*ljekarne*) spread around Zagreb. Opening hours are usually from 07.00 to 20.00 Monday to Friday, 07.00 to 14.00 Saturday, but those listed below operate 24/7.

Gradska Ljekarna Zagreb Trg Jelačića 3; ✆ 481 6159

Gradska Ljekarna Zagreb Ilica 301; ✆ 375 0321
Gradska Ljekarna Zagreb Ozaljska 1; ✆ 309 7586

WHAT TO SEE AND DO

To see all of Zagreb's sights would take several intense weeks, with an astonishing 57 varieties of museum and gallery open to the public, not counting monuments, public sculptures or even churches. If you want to see the top-rated attractions, you'll need to allow three or four days – partly because opening hours don't always mesh as well as they might.

There's a lot to see, but don't be too obsessive. Not everything needs a visit (or is open), and in the end the main sight is the city itself, along with the wealth of café terraces, bars and restaurants that make Zagreb such an agreeable place. A trip up to the top of Sljeme on the cable car followed by an alfresco dinner might turn out to be much more rewarding than religiously ticking off some of the more arcane subjects in the following pages.

Outdoor attractions such as the zoo or Mount Medvednica, and more out-of-the-way sights, such as the monastery church in Remete, are covered in the next section, Surrounds. In this section, within each sub-section, the sights are listed – very roughly speaking – in order of merit.

A WALKING TOUR OF THE CITY The route suggested here is a figure of eight, starting and ending on the city's central square, Jelačić Square covering the old, upper town first and the lower town second. It would make for a leisurely two- to four-hour tour, depending on how much you choose to visit on the way.

Jelačić Square and the Lotrščak Tower The main attraction in Jelačić Square [104–5 D3/4] is the terrific equestrian statue of Ban Josip Jelačić himself. As the viceroy of Croatia in the middle of the 19th century, Jelačić was a natural reformer, and did a great deal to advance the causes of Croatian statehood. After he died, the heroic statue (by the Austrian sculptor, Fernkorn) was erected in 1866, with Jelačić's drawn sword facing Budapest as a sign of defiance – by this time Croatia was already losing what little independence it had.

After World War II, the statue was torn down because it was considered unpatriotic within Tito's Yugoslavia, and the square was renamed Trg Republike. For more than 40 years, Jelačić languished in pieces, in a cellar. However, when the statue was restored to its former glory, on Croatian independence in 1991, it was put up facing the other way – towards Belgrade rather than Budapest – and today the drawn sword points uncompromisingly towards Knin, the short-lived capital of the erstwhile Republika Srpska Krajina (RSK). (For more Croatian history, see pages 11–20.) Old photographs – such as those on the ground floor corridor of the Hotel Dubrovnik, connecting the restaurant to reception – show the statue on the other side of the square, facing north.

Head west out of the square on Ilica, Zagreb's longest street. After 250m you'll come to Tomislava, a short dead-end street which leads up to the diminutive **funicular** [104–5 C3] (see page 82), the easiest route up to the upper town (Gornji Grad, also known as Gradec).

The funicular leads straight up to **Strossmayerovo Šetalište**, a lovely west-east promenade giving magnificent views south out over the city, and the **Lotrščak Tower** [104–5 C3], one of the few vestiges of the original 13th-century city fortifications. The climb up to the tower's tiny rooftop terrace (⊕ *May–Oct, 11.00–19.00 Tue–Sun; 10kn*) gives even finer panoramic views.

For centuries a bell was rung from the tower every evening to announce the closing of the city's four gates (only one survives – see page 107), but now it's the midday cannon which is the main attraction. The tradition started on New Year's Eve 1877, and has continued every day since. They're on the fourth cannon now (the other three are in the City Museum), with the current version being an American 76mm model from World War II; a gift from the Yugoslav army for the 1987 University Games in Zagreb.

If you climb the tower shortly before noon you can see the cannon being fired by Stjepan Možar, who's practically become a Zagreb institution since taking on the job more than thirty-five years ago (he started work on 12 April 1974). For the first twenty years, he didn't take a single day off, though now he has the occasional holiday, with the army ensuring the cannon still goes off at noon – but he has no plans to retire, and he'll continue for as long as he's able. Get close enough, and you can see that Stjepan has three separate watches to make sure he gets the timing right – though he's sure he could do it no problem using his finely tuned internal clock, and after a third of a century you have to believe him.

To St Mark's Square From the tower, head east along the promenade, and then up at the end, via the lovely café terrace here, onto St Catherine's Square (Katarina Trg). The northern side of the square is taken up with the Kulmer Palace, formerly the Museum of Contemporary Art (which is moving to Novi Zagreb), while on the southern side you'll find the Dverce Mansion and the Jesuit College, the 1607 Gymnasium, which is still a grammar school today.

The Jesuits were also responsible for the square's main attraction, and Zagreb's finest Baroque church, **St Catherine's** [104–5 C3]. Built between 1620 and 1632, it features some highly superior 18th-century stucco work and an amazing *trompe l'oeil* altarpiece (those aren't real pillars), an extraordinary work from 1762, by the Slovene painter Kristof Andrej Jelovšek.

Before leaving the square, check out what's on at the **Klovićevi Dvori** gallery [104–5 C3], a lovely space that is used for major temporary exhibitions. Opposite, there's a small but dramatic sculpture of a fisherman wrestling with a vicious-looking snake, by Simeon Roksandić. Trivia fans will be pleased to know that there's a much larger version of the same statue in Belgrade's main park, up above the confluence of the Sava and Danube rivers.

ZAGREB
Attractions

A   B   C   D

AS (hotels)

↑ Medvednica

Mirogoj
Cemetery

1

KOZARČEVA

TUŠKANAC

JURJEVSKA

NOVA VES

KAPTOL

Kaptol
Centar
(shopping
centre)

Bela & Miroslav
Krleža House

Museum of the
City of Zagreb

2

KUKULJEVIĆEVA

DUBRAVKIN PUT

DEMETROVA

OPATIČKA

RADIĆEVA

TKALČIĆEVA

OPATOVINA

Natural
History
Museum

Golden Hall

Collection of
Anka Gvozdanović

Ban's Palace

MARKOV

Stone
Gate

Croatia
Historical
Museum

MATOŠEVA

Klovićevi
Dvori

STA
Travel

St Mary's
Church

3

President
(hotels)

ROCKOVA

DEŽMANOVA

Church of Sts
Cyril & Methodius

JEZUITSKI

KATARINA
TRG

KRVAVI
MOST

SPLAVNICA

BAKAČEVA

Lotrščak Tower

St Catherine's

>>> Walk 1 >>>

DOLAC
MARKET

Croatian YHA

STROSSMEYEROVO

ŠETALIŠTE

GRADEC

Funicular

ILICA

<<< Walk 1 <<<

JELAČIĆ
SQUARE

i

Ilica

BRITANSKI
TRG

Kraljevac
Caffe

ILICA

FRANKOPANSKA

GUNDULIĆEVA

Holy
Transfiguration

PRAŠKA

Generalturist

4

VARŠAVSKA

BOGOVIĆEVA

Croatia Express

CVJETNI
TRG

Meteorological
Station

St Blaise's

MIŠEĆOV
PROLAZ

TESLINA

Archaeological
Museum

Ljubljana

Marko Polo
(Jadrolinija)

MASARYKOVA

>>> Walk 2 >>>

BP Club

PRERADOVIĆEVA

BERISLAVIĆEVA

GAJEVA

ZRINJEVAC

i

Strossmayer
Gallery of
Old Masters

PRILAZ GJURE DEŽELIĆA

MARŠALA
TITA

Viktor
Kovačić
Apartment

5

KLAIĆEVA

Arts & Crafts Museum

Croatian
National
Theatre

HEBRANGOVA

Modern Gallery

STROSS-
MAYEROV

KAČIĆEVA

Mimara
Museum

Ethnographic
Museum

Zagreb County

i

**DONJI
GRAD**

GAJEVA

KRŠNJAVOGA

MAŽURANIĆA

<<< Walk 2 <<<

ŽERJAVIĆEVA

TRENKOVA

6

MARULIĆA

GUNDULIĆEVA

KUMIČIĆEVA

HAULIKOVA

Plitvice Lakes
NP office

TOMISLAVA

Croatian
State
Archives

King Tomislav

STARČEVIĆEV
TRG

SAVSKA

JUKIĆEVA

CMATKOVA

MIHANOVIĆEVA

MIRAMARSKI

Regent
Esplanade

Importanne
Centar
(shopping centre)

PAROMLINSKA

Technical
Museum

SAVSKA

Botanical Gardens

7

Pivnica,
Medvedgrad,
Jarun Lake

KOTURAŠKA

Novi Zagreb

A   B   C   D

KEY
1 Meštrović Atelier
2 St Mark's Church
3 Croatian Parliament (Sabor)
4 Zagreb City Hall
5 Croatian Museum of Naïve Art
6 Croatia Airlines, Atlas,
  Dalmacijaturist and
  Kompas Agencieh

Pedestrian roads

Walk 1
Walk 2

Mirogoj Cemetery,
Carpe Diem
Hostel (hotel)

Ribnjak
Park

GRŠKOVIĆEVA

RIBNJAK

VOĆARSKA

Maksimir
Park, Zoo

PETROVA

VLAŠKA

Cathedral
KAPTOL

VLAŠKA

VLAŠKA

CESARČEVA
Central Post Office
JURIŠIĆEVA

Importanne
Galleria
(shopping centre)

MARTIĆEVA

Stock Exchange

RAČKOGA

BAUEROVA

VOJNOVIĆEVA

ŠUBIĆEVA

ĐORĐIĆEVA

Croation Artist's
Centre

ZVONIMIROVA

BOŠKOVIĆEVA

PALMOTIĆEVA

DRAŠKOVIĆEVA

Hospital

MISLAVOVA

ŽRTAVA
FAŠIZMA

VIŠESLAVOVA

STNČIĆEVA

PETRINJSKA

HATZOVA

BORNINA

DOMAGOJEVA

KRALJICE JELENE

Sheraton
Zagreb

ŠENOINA

Branimir
Centar
(shopping
centre)

Arcotel
Allegra

Evistas

BRANIMIROVA
24-hour Post Office

GRGUROVA

Train station

STROJARSKA

DRŽIĆEVA

Bus
station

Bradt

'Spider' Pound
(illegally parked cars)

TRNJANSKA

0   400m
0   400yds

Pleso,
Aerodrom Zagreb

Zagreb WHAT TO SEE AND DO

3

The street running north from the corner of St Catherine's Square is Ćirilometodska, which leads along to St Mark's Square, Zagreb's political heart. On the way up the street notice the Greek Orthodox **Church of Sts Cyril and Methodius** [104–5 C3], boxed rather uncomfortably between two small town houses. Cyril and Method were the men responsible for the Glagolitic script (the best example of which is in the cathedral, see page 110), and ultimately, the Cyrillic alphabet. To see inside – typical orthodox layout with an iconostasis separating the clergy from the congregation, and not much in the way of furniture – you normally need to ask at the Greek Catholic seminary next door.

Next door again is the **Croatian Museum of Naïve Art** (see page 121), which is well worth a visit, while at the end of the street, as you come onto **St Mark's Square** (Markov Trg), is the **Zagreb City Hall**, which was originally built as a theatre in 1835 by a man called Stanković who had won a huge lottery the year before. It was used for various historic parliament meetings in the 19th century, and is today a place for ceremonial gatherings – and weddings, upstairs in the registry office. On the opposite (right-hand) corner you'll notice a sculpted stone head depicting the unfortunate Matija Gubec, doomed leader of a 16th-century peasant uprising. Gubec was supposedly dramatically put to death right in front of the church here by the Austro-Hungarians, who held a mock coronation for him with a crown of red-hot iron.

Today the square is dominated by swanky German cars and lots of police – which is hardly surprising, as it's the seat of the Croatian government. On the left-hand side of the square is the original **Ban's Palace** [104–5 C2] (Jelačić himself lived and died here), which was the target of a Serb rocket attack on Zagreb in 1991 – Tuđman, Mesić and the Croatian prime minister were all inside when it happened, so it's lucky there were no casualties (see page 77 for more historical detail). On the other side of the square is the **Croatian Parliament** [104–5 C2], the Sabor.

Between the two stands **St Mark's Church** [104–5 C2], its distinctive roof (which finally emerged from scaffolding in 2009) gaudily tiled in the fashion of seaside resorts with clock flowerbeds. The left-hand coat of arms is that of the Kingdom of Croatia (the chequerboard you still see on the national team's football shirts today), Slavonia (a *kuna* running between two rivers, the Sava and the Drava) and Dalmatia (three lions); on the right-hand side is the city of Zagreb's.

The original church here was built in the 13th century, with 14th- and 15th-century additions. Most of the church of this era has long since disappeared, though the southern portal, with 15 beautifully carved statues by the Parler family, from Prague, dates from 1420; if they ever finish restoring it, it's well worth a look.

Most of the rest of the church is a late 19th-century Gothic reconstruction. Like so much of post-1880 earthquake Zagreb, it's by Hermann Bollé, though the bell tower is an 1841 original. The interior was refurbished in the late 1930s by the painter Kljaković and the sculptor Meštrović; the former's frescoes are closer to socialist realism than Gothic masterpieces, but the latter's crucifix is suitably imposing and dramatic.

From the top of Gradec to the Stone Gate
Head out of the far left corner of the square and up Mletačka, where you'll find the excellent Meštrović Atelier (see page 119) on the right-hand side, housed in the famous sculptor's house and studio. At the top of the street it's worth taking a detour down to the left, where you'll find the charmingly old-fashioned Natural History Museum (see page 117), and the elegant dead-end street of Visoka. Heading back up Demetrova, check out the classic façade of the Jelačić Mansion at number 7, home to the famous Ban's brother, and the Balbi Mansion at number 11, with the old town's last original wooden well in the courtyard.

At the top of Demetrova turn left and then round the corner to the right, where you'll find the **Priest's Tower** (Popov Toranj), which was originally the only defence allowed to be used by neighbouring Kaptol, which had no defences of its own. It's now part of the tremendous **Museum of the City of Zagreb** (see page 112), which has its entrance on Opatička.

Continue down Opatička and then turn left into Kamenita, which leads to the Stone Gate. Before you get there, note two curiosities. On the left is a section of heavy black chain, which is supposed to have come from Nelson's ship, HMS *Victory*, though nobody seems to have the faintest idea how or why. On the other side of the street is a **pharmacy**, which has been in business since 1355, apparently, when it was opened by one of Dante's family – making it the second oldest in Europe, after Dubrovnik's.

The **Stone Gate** (Porta Lapidea) [104–5 D3] is the only one of the four original 13th-century city gates, which were closed at nightfall and reopened at dawn the following day, to protect the old settlement of Gradec from outsiders, and notably from their neighbours in Kaptol.

The gate owes its present appearance to a fire that ravaged the town in 1731. Amongst the ashes in a first-floor flat were found a perfectly preserved icon of the Virgin Mary (provenance unknown), so in 1760 a church was built into the fabric of the gate, and the icon given pride of place (the gold gem-studded crowns were added in 1931, to celebrate the bicentennial of the miracle).

A protective iron grille was added in 1778, presumably to keep grubby fingers away from the miraculous icon, and – in spite of curiously persistent calls for the gate's demolition over the centuries – it's still a major place of pilgrimage today. The walls are cluttered with votive plaques thanking the Virgin for her intercession in answering prayers, and a multitude of candles sends flickering shadows over the faces of the faithful in the semi-darkness. It's an atmospheric place, whatever your religious beliefs (or lack thereof).

Head through the Stone Gate and down the ramp, where you'll find a fine statue of St George and the (curiously catfish-faced, in this version) Dragon, with St George looking remarkably contrite. The road leads out onto Radićeva (originally called Duga Ulica, meaning 'long street' – and if you're heading uphill with a lot of shopping it certainly is), which continues downhill until it meets **Krvavi Most** (Blood Bridge) [104–5 D3], named for the bloody feuds between Gradec and Kaptol long ago (see page 76).

To Kaptol Krvavi Most connects the bottom of Radićeva with the bottom of Tkalčićeva, which is more or less one continuous café. It was originally a creek (hence the bridge), but it was diverted and the street paved over in 1899, as the stench from the tanneries upstream had become intolerable. Take a detour up the street – even if it's only for a coffee or a beer – and check out the statue on the left-hand side of Marija Zagorka, Croatia's first female journalist and something of a proto-feminist (she died in 1957) as well as a popular novelist.

Returning to the bottom of Tkalčićeva, take the steps up to **St Mary's Church** [104–5 D3], the last remnant of the Cistercian abbey that was pulled down to make room for Dolac, the main market square. Although the foundations of St Mary's are 13th century or so, the current model is mostly 18th century, including a fine fresco behind the altar by Jelovšek, the man also responsible for the great frescoes in St Catherine's (see page 103).

Heading across **Dolac** [104–5 D3] (see page 81) brings you to the unmistakable twin spires of the **cathedral** (see page 110). On the square in front of the cathedral stands a gilt Madonna, surrounded by four angels, by Fernkorn, the Austrian sculptor also responsible for the statue of Jelačić on his horse in the main square. The cathedral is flanked by the vast 18th-century Archbishop's Palace, and the canons' distinctive houses; all that's now left of the great fortress that once dominated Kaptol. After visiting the cathedral, it's a short drop back down to Jelačić Square.

The lower town After the winding streets and old houses of the upper town comes the planned munificence of the lower town (Donji Grad), which was made possible by the draining of the swamp below Kaptol and Gradec and the building of the railway embankment in the second half of the 19th century.

Head south out of Jelačić Square on Praška to the first of the three great, green leafy park-squares, which eventually bring you down to the railway station. The squares – Zrinjevac, Strossmayerov and Tomislava – are lined with sober, imposing buildings, and closed off at the southern end with the formal elegance of the railway station. They form the eastern wing of Lenuci's 'Green Horseshoe', which was designed by Milan Lenuci after the catastrophic 1880 earthquake, and is completed by the Botanical Gardens at the bottom, and the western arm heading up through three more leafy spacious squares culminating in the national theatre.

Zrinjevac, Strossmayerov and Tomislava The first attraction you come to on Zrinjevac, on the northern side of the square, is a rather charming 19th-century meteorological station, where you can check out the weather for your walk. Over on the right-hand side, if you're looking south, is the huge Archaeological Museum (see page 113), which is well worth a visit, if you have the time – and there's a very pleasant courtyard café behind it, if you're ready for a break.

Further down towards the station, on the same side of the road as the Archaeological Museum, on the corner, is Zagreb's excellent and recently refurbished **Modern Gallery** (see page 119).

Centre stage in the square itself is the **Croatian Academy of Arts and Sciences** building, which you should pop into even if you don't want to visit the **Strossmayer Gallery of Old Masters** (see page 120), upstairs. The reason to check it out is that in the foyer are two particularly important bits of Croatian art/history: the first is the 11th-century Baška Tablet, which was found on the island of Krk, and records the gratitude of the local monastery to the king for his donation of a block of land. Originally part of a rood screen, the tablet was once coloured blue, yellow and green, and you can still see vestiges of paint in the upper left-hand corner. The Baška Tablet in Baška itself, since you're asking, is a good copy; this is the original.

Also in the atrium of the Academy is the magnificent Sarcophagus of St Simeon, supported by four angels. Although this time it's the one here that's the copy (the original is in Zadar), the benefit is that here you can see all the way round and admire the fabulous 15th-century gold-plated silverwork by Francesco da Milano. Check out the central panel on the front, which is directly inspired by one of Giotto's frescoes in the Scrovegni Chapel in Padua, and the panel to the left, which depicts the burial scene (even if it looks more like the poor chap's actually being chopped up). Round at the back, note the excellent medieval scene of a woman fainting melodramatically at the sight of the dead body.

Behind the Academy, looking pensively down towards the station, is Bishop Strossmayer himself, as portrayed by Ivan Meštrović ('What time is the last train to Đakovo, Ivan?' he muses, consulting an imaginary timetable).

At the top of the next square, Tomislava, is the charming **Art Pavilion**, which mainly does service these days as a good restaurant, Pavilijon (see page 92). It's actually a pre-fabricated iron-framed structure, which was the brainchild of Vlaho Bukovac (see page 343), who had it built for the Millennium Exhibition in Budapest in 1896, and then shipped back to Zagreb afterwards (which, when you consider its size, is probably why it's not very far from the train station, even now). Indeed, the only thing separating it from the railway is enough of an expanse of lawn to set off the grand equestrian statue of **King Tomislav** [104–5 D6], who was crowned in AD925 as medieval Croatia's first king.

From here, turn right, and head west from the station past the Esplanade Hotel to the **Botanical Gardens** [104–5 C6], which have been providing an oasis of calm to

Nominated as archbishop of Zagreb in 1937, Alojzije Stepinac courted controversy during World War II by not being quick enough to denounce the Ustaše fascists or the Independent State of Croatia (NDH) – though he subsequently not only criticised the regime but also helped Jews escape from it, and spoke out in favour of persecuted minorities, much to the ire of the NDH, and later the Germans.

He was no friend of Tito's communists, either, refusing to separate the Croatian Catholic Church from Rome, and after the war he was arrested. After a disgraceful show trial in 1948, he was condemned to 16 years' hard labour. He served five years of the sentence, in total isolation, and was then released, only to spend the rest of his life under house arrest in Krašić (see page 152).

In spite of being forbidden from pursuing his religious duties by the state, Stepinac was made a cardinal by the Pope in 1953, though he never went to Rome to receive the crimson, as he was certain he'd never be allowed home to his beloved Croatia. He died in 1960 (quite possibly of poisoning), and in 1998 was beatified by the Pope.

generations of visitors since being opened to the public in 1894. It's a low-key affair, and the glasshouses are for botany enthusiasts only, but it's a pleasant place for a break.

Marulića, Mažuranića and Maršala Tita Running north from here are the other three big squares that complete the horseshoe, Marulića, Mažuranića and Maršala Tita. The first big building you'll see here is the **Croatian State Archives** (see page 116), which seems sober and formal enough until you notice the giant owls perched on the roof. In the square beyond, there's a statue of Marko Marulić, the father of Croatian literature, who was from Split.

On the west side of the next square north, you'll find the undeservedly under-visited **Ethnographic Museum** (see page 115), where you can admire a comprehensive collection of Croatia's myriad national costumes. Round the corner, a block further west, and unmissable on Roosevelt Square, is the palatial neo-classical building (formerly a school) which houses the extraordinary **Mimara Museum** (see page 111), which is probably the one museum to visit in Zagreb even if you see no other.

Up from here, you come onto Maršala Tita, which is pretty much the last place in Zagreb to publicly acknowledge the man who created – and sowed the seeds of destruction of – modern Yugoslavia. On the left-hand side is the **Arts and Crafts Museum** (see page 117), in yet another huge, late-19th-century building (by Hermann Bollé). In the greenery, as you come out of the museum, look out for another Fernkorn sculpture, this time of St George slaying the dragon.

Across the square is the **Croatian National Theatre**, which was designed by the Viennese architects Ferdinand Fellner and Hermann Helmer, who made something of a career of theatre design, being responsible for over 40 across central Europe, from Switzerland to the Ukraine. An opportunity to see one of the frequent performances here (opera, ballet, theatre) shouldn't be missed (see page 99).

In front of the theatre is Meštrović's sculpture, the *Well of Life* (*Zdenac Života*), dating from 1905, and one of the clearest indicators that his early work was influenced by Rodin, whom he'd met and studied with – in this case the source of inspiration is clearly *The Burghers of Calais*, though the *Well of Life* itself couldn't be mistaken for a Rodin. Across the road, in front of the university's elegant Faculty of Law, is another Meštrović masterpiece, the *History of the Croats*, a simple composition of a single, seated woman, serene but stern, holding a stone tablet.

From the theatre, a few hundred metres up Masarykova brings you to the beginning of the pedestrian zone heading up into Cvjetni Trg, the old flower market, and a wealth of places to sit and have a drink along Bogovićeva. At the top of the square is the **Orthodox Church** (actually the **Church of the Holy Transfiguration**) [104–5 C4], with a rather drab 19th-century exterior hiding quite an imposing iconostasis and a dramatic deep-blue fresco across the apse depicting an unusually benign-looking Jesus with outspread arms. It's a particularly atmospheric place when there's a service on, with lots of smoke and incense on the go.

At the end of Bogovićeva you'll see the 70s plate-glass windows of the Hotel Dubrovnik, which brings you right back out onto Jelačić Square.

The cathedral [104–5 E3] The unmistakable twin spires of Zagreb's cathedral can be seen from all over town, which makes it a pity that they've been undergoing restoration for as long as I can remember, with no sign of the scaffolding ever coming down. Up close you can see just why the façade needs restoring: the sculpture is astonishingly worn and damaged after a mere century of existence; cheap sandstone is to blame.

The cathedral was built from the 13th to the 15th centuries on the site of an earlier Romanesque church, but what you see today is mostly the work of the Viennese architect Hermann Bollé, following the 1880 earthquake, including the neo-Gothic façade, and the 104m and 105m spires (don't ask). Inside, the cathedral's a light, spacious building, with an uncluttered feel to it. A touch of drama is added by the enormous 1941 Glagolitic Memorial, commemorating the 1,300th anniversary of the first contacts with the Holy See, during the reign of Pope John IV (AD640–642). It takes up most of the wall behind you as you come into the cathedral, and it really is a strange script, even to eyes used to Cyrillic.

(Just in case your Glagolitic's got a bit rusty, the inscription reads: 'Glory to God in the highest! In memory of the 1,300th anniversary of the conversion of the Croatian people, who promised an eternal allegiance to Peter the Rock, having received from him the promised protection in every trial. Placed by The Society of the Brotherhood of the Croatian Dragon – conserving the relics of our ancestors and commending the Croatian homeland to the Mother of God – 641–1941.')

There isn't a great deal in the cathedral that pre-dates the earthquake, though the inlaid choir stalls are early 16th-century, and several of the altars and the pulpit are Baroque, from the beginning of the 18th century. There are also a few faded medieval fresco fragments in the sacristy, which date from the 13th century, along with an interesting triptych featuring the *Crucifixion of Golgotha* by Albrecht Dürer.

The biggest draws, however, are the monument and tomb of Alojzije Stepinac (see box page 109); the monument is a great casket, with a life-size effigy of the cardinal, behind

THE LAMPLIGHTERS' TOUR

On the first and third Friday of every month, 'Bring light to the upper town' and join Zagreb's lamplighters as they wend their way through the maze of cobbled streets lighting the 270 original gas lanterns which still illuminate this part of the capital.

You'll pick up all sorts of bits and pieces of history and trivia on the way, and may even get the chance to light some of the lamps yourself. It's tremendous fun, with the tour starting at dusk, and lasting for about an hour. For details, contact Globtour (℡ 488 1100; www.globtour.hr). The place to meet for a drink before the tour is at Caffe Palainovka, on Ilirski Trg, next to the Priest's Tower, right at the top of the upper town.

the altar, while his tomb is over on the north wall, with a touching Meštrović sculpture. Until 1991, and Croatia's independence, you'd have been unwise to spend much time near either; these days you'll only be one of many people paying your respects.

On your way out of the cathedral, check out the enormous organ, made by Walcker of Ludwigsburg, which was first installed in 1855, and expanded and renewed in 1912, 1939 and 1987. It's reckoned to be among the ten most valuable in the world.

MUSEUMS

Mimara Museum (Muzej Mimara) [104–5 B5] (🕐 10.00–17.00 *Tue, Wed, Fri & Sat, 10.00–19.00 Thu, 10.00–14.00 Sun; 40kn*) Without question, Zagreb's most interesting and intriguing museum is the Mimara. Housed in a palatial neo-classical building (formerly a school) on Roosevelt Square, it covers everything from Egyptian glassware to old masters, and medieval sculpture to French Impressionists. Altogether there are more than 1,500 items on display, so allow plenty of time.

The entire collection was given to the state in 1985 by Ante Topić Mimara and his wife Wiltrud. But how on earth did the ebullient, bon vivant Mimara manage to accumulate such a wealth of treasures? One answer may be his having lived in Berlin between the wars; a period of exceptionally ripe pickings for canny art collectors. Nonetheless, it's never been clear how Mimara came by either his money or the great majority of his artefacts, and many may well be… well, not quite the real thing. (Authenticity, of course, is especially troublesome to establish when the provenance is unknown.) Mimara himself was said not to be that bothered; he cared more about an object's beauty than its being 'genuine'.

The collection is broadly chronological in arrangement, but unless you have a particular speciality you want to start with, it's most easily handled from the top floor down, giving you time to appreciate the most famous and obvious works before succumbing to museum-fatigue.

Second floor: Western art At the top of the stairs on the second floor pop into the donor's room, where you'll find a bronze death mask of Mimara himself, looking positively beatific after a full and hedonistic existence.

Turn right out of here and head round the floor anti-clockwise for a chronological tour through Western art, starting with icons in rooms 29 and 30 and sticking with solid religious themes through to room 35. The big draw here is Raphael's St Luke the Evangelist, which is almost certainly not by Raphael, though very much of the period/style.

Other attractions in the same room – which is the heart of the old masters' collection – include a disputed Rembrandt of a noble lady with a neck ruff the size of a wheel of brie, and van den Eekhout's *Ruth and Boaz*, which is very fine and almost certainly the real McCoy. Still staying in room 35, check out Rubens' vast *Virgin with the Innocents*, which brims over with more fleshy pink infant bottoms per square metre than was surely strictly necessary (or indeed tasteful), and an unusual Hoppner portrait of Wellington and his family, all oddly disassociated from one another, as if they'd been Photoshopped in later.

Moving on, there's a fleshy *Venus* in room 36 by Jordaens, notable mainly for the poor cupid doing his level best to hold up the goddess's extra chins, but it's the last room (#40) which is most popular, with a disputed double-sided Renoir in the middle, and a couple of lovely Manet still lifes, with succulent oysters, and shiny, organic-looking apples.

First floor: archaeology, sculpture, arts and crafts Downstairs, on the first floor, start in room 13 (under the donor's room), which has some excellent and rare archaeological artefacts, including a fine lion's head which was probably the central boss of a shield and dates back to the 7th century BC, and a Persian pin and disc from the same period, with a lion/goddess in the centre, and pomegranates for fertility around the outside (picked up by Mimara in a market in Tehran in the 1930s, apparently).

Among Greek theatrical masks, Roman artefacts and Mesopotamian figures you'll also see a Hellenistic sculpture of an *ephebe* (young boy), claiming to be 3rd century BC, though the curator is pretty sure it's actually 16th-century German – not just because the hair and the base seem odd for the period, but because the statue has a distinctly slack Renaissance bum.

Rooms 14 to 28 cover a huge range of European sculpture and arts and crafts from the early Christian era right through to the beginning of the 20th century. There are hundreds of things to see, but look out for fishy lamps (room 14), an intricate English hunting horn carved from a walrus tusk (room 17), and a wooden monk carrying a cross and looking decidedly unsteady on his feet (room 19).

In room 20, there's an excellent wasp-waisted ballet dancer of a St George (Jacques de Baerze, 14th century), and a feisty 15th-century Flemish Archangel Gabriel, apparently in the act of saying 'up yours!'. Both the archangel and his attendant angels have been modelled on the likes of Felicity Kendall and Zoë Wanamaker.

Moving on, check out a two-foot wooden *Hercules* from 16th-century Florence (room 23), clearly inspired by the Farnese version of the same, and a stunning enamel jewellery box (room 24), dating from 1540 and possibly by Pierre Raymond. Finally, room 26 has some extraordinary ivory, including a Polish ivory-carved pyx (for consecrated communion bread) and a scabbard, both commemorating King Jan III Sobieski's 1683 defeat over the Turks in Vienna. When Poland approached Mimara to acquire them, he's playfully said to have agreed, but only in exchange for one of their better Rembrandts.

Ground floor: glass, carpets and Far Eastern art If your appetite's still unsated, head downstairs to the ground floor, where there's enough glass – ancient Egyptian, Roman, Islamic, Venetian, European – in rooms 1–5 to leave you utterly glassy-eyed, not to mention oriental carpets in room 6, and an extensive collection of Far Eastern art in rooms 7–12. Amongst the bronze, ceramics, jade, and porcelain, the most unusual artefact is an amazing pair of 19th-century 'goblets' in room 10, made from whole carved rhinoceros horns standing on intricately sculpted wooden bases depicting Taoist landscapes. You probably wouldn't want them at home.

Museum of the City of Zagreb (Muzej Grada Zagreba) [104–5 C2] (*www.mgz.hr;* ⊕ *10.00–18.00 Tue, Wed & Fri, 10.00–22.00 Thu, 11.00–19.00 Sat, 10.00–14.00 Sun; 20kn)* It might seem unlikely, but the City Museum is one of Zagreb's most appealing.

The museum was founded in 1907 and originally housed – bizarrely – in the Stone Gate (see page 107), before being transferred in 1925 to the Art Pavilion (see page 108), and finally finding a permanent home in 1947 in a former convent at the top of the old town, abutting onto the Priest's Tower (see page 103). It's a wonderful museum, with good English-language labelling (sadly still something of a rarity in Croatia) and imaginative displays, and well worth a visit; happily, only a small fraction of the total of 75,000 items in the collection are on display.

The visit starts with an excellent archaeological dig within the museum itself, and moves engagingly through Zagreb's history, giving you a real flavour of life at different periods from Neolithic times right up to the damaged furniture from the 1991 rocket attack on the Ban's Palace.

There are some fine bits of sculpture from the portal of the original pre-earthquake cathedral, as well as pennants, charters, Golden Bulls and coats of arms, as well as a genuinely unpleasant 17th-century cast-iron 'mask of shame', used to punish miscreant market traders.

Perhaps most interesting of all, however, are the reconstructions of various shops from the past and the working rooms of several Croatian notables, along with my personal favourite, a fabulous room with a coloured map of the city inlaid into the floor, with scale models of the main buildings on small pedestals.

Archaeological Museum (Arheološki Muzej) [104–5 D4] (*www.amz.hr;* ⊕ *10.00–17.00 Tue, Wed & Fri, 10.00–20.00 Thu, 10.00–13.00 Sat & Sun; 20kn*)

The Archaeological Museum, on the west side of Zrinjevac, is a truly monumental collection ranging from prehistoric times through to the early medieval period.

Most of the four million or so objects here were collected in the 19th century, but thanks to major revamps since 1999, and the very best in modern display techniques, the museum is a light and airy place, and well worth a visit if you have even a glancing interest in archaeology, Egyptology, classical studies or numismatics. Clearly numbered explanations in Croatian and English go a long way to help.

Start at the top floor, where you'll find the recently renovated prehistoric and Egyptian displays. The prehistoric collection is excellent, with highlights including a headless bronze age figurine from Dalj (near Osijek) decorated with geometric patterns, and large collections of Bronze Age and Iron Age pots, axe-heads, jewellery, and cloak pins etc, all well displayed. Also noteworthy is the lapodium collection; the lapods were an ethnic group from the Plitvice Lakes area, and cultural finds on display here (mostly from gravesites) are characterised by unusual head-dresses and the lavish use of chunky amber jewellery.

The star attraction, though, is the so-called Vučedol Dove (which should really be the Vučedol Partridge). The three-footed Copper-Age vessel dates back to the fourth millennium BC, and is one of the best artefacts from the period ever found. It's decorated with the grooved geometrical patterns typical of objects from this era and area (along the Danube, near Vukovar), with the white paste filling the grooves being made from seashells. The partridge became a major symbol for Croatian peace and unity, and a memorial for Vukovar, after the 1990s war, so you'll see it everywhere – including on the 20kn note.

The Egyptian collection is also outstanding, with several hundred artefacts, including painted coffins and treasures from tombs, mainly from the Ptolemaic period (1070BC to AD30). In its own separate room is the real prize of the collection, the Zagreb Mummy, who was the wife of a tailor at the court of the Pharaoh, and still looks frighteningly deathlike today.

The mummy was acquired by Zagreb in 1859, and when unwrapped, it was discovered that the linen bandages were actually an Etruscan manuscript. At around 1,200 words, the 'Linen Book of Zagreb' is the longest text ever found in that obscure, still undeciphered, language. It appears to be an Etruscan liturgical calendar; if you have any clearer notions, or indeed a translation, I'm sure the museum curators would be delighted to hear from you.

Head downstairs to the newly renovated Greek, Roman and medieval displays. Among an impressive collection of Greek vases and Roman artefacts of all kinds, check out one of the more unusual and tranquil works from antiquity, the 2nd-century *Head of a Girl* from Solin.

You may also be able to admire the astonishing *Apoxyomenos* statue, which was found by a Belgian diver off the coast of Lošinj in 1998. The larger than life-size figure of a young Greek athlete is believed to be a Hellenic copy of a classical piece, and was painstakingly restored over many years before finally going on display in 2006. It is due to go on permanent display on the island of Lošinj from 2011. Finally, numismatists will hardly be able to contain themselves in their rush to see the museum's stunning coin collection; one of the world's most comprehensive, with over quarter of a million pieces.

When you've had enough – or even if you just fancy a break during the visit – scope out the café in the courtyard behind the museum, where you can sit outside amongst ancient sculpture (fragments from the 1st to 4th centuries) and enjoy a pleasant drink.

Technical Museum (Tehnički Muzej) [104–5 A7] (*www.mdc.hr/tehnicki/hr;* ⊕ *09.00–17.00 Tue–Fri, 09.00–13.00 Sat & Sun; 15kn*) Zagreb's Technical Museum is a bit out of the way, but well worth the detour – and trams #13, #14 and #17 take you straight there.

If you're in town with kids of almost any age, then it's a must; as a grown-up kid myself, it ranks amongst my favourite diversions in the city. The museum is housed in an industrial-looking barn on the right-hand side of Savska, at #18, not far past the railway bridge.

The collection starts with fire engines, including Zagreb's first, a horse-drawn number that was bought for the city by a public-spirited lottery-winner. It goes on to cover various machines, ancient and modern, which are used to transform energy, from watermills to great steam engines to a whole collection of aircraft engines.

The main central hall houses a wide range of goodies, from a pint-sized 1935 Fiat tank to an Italian submarine abandoned during World War II near the island of Lošinj, to various old cars, including a 1926 Renault NN and a Mercedes sportster from the same period, with a frightening top speed of 170km/h. Even more terrifying is a motor sleigh from 1931, which was powered by a giant propeller on the back and has no visible means of stopping.

Also on display is Dubrovnik's last tram; after derailing and killing two people, it was permanently taken out of service (as anyone who's battled with Dubrovnik's traffic today will still lament); a replica of an old horse-drawn Zagreb tram; and the delightful *Samoborček*, the mini steam train that made the short run over to Samobor from 1930–1960, so the locals could indulge in their weekend *kremšnite* (see page 148).

To one side there are scale models of ships (everything from a 5th-century BC Greek trireme to a 17th-century Venetian galley to modern warships), while hanging from the ceiling are various flying machines, from biplanes to a US Thunderbolt to the tatty-looking helicopter that was pressed back into service during the war of the 1990s.

Two other displays on the ground floor are of particular note. The first deals with early aviation, and in particular the pioneer Otto Lilienthal, who made 2,000 successful glider flights in planes of his own design, but died after falling 17m and breaking his spine on his 2,001st flight. His last words were '*Opfer müssen gebracht werden!*' ('Sacrifices must be made!'). The photos make you realise just how unsuited humans are for winged flight.

There's also a good display on the dirigibles pioneered by Croatian aviator David Schwarz – called Schwarzoplans, naturally. They were commissioned by the German army and tested in 1897 in Berlin, but although successful, one also crashed; Schwarz died of a heart attack soon after, reportedly brought on by the news that the invention had actually been accepted. Schwarz's widow sold the plans to a certain Count Ferdinand von Zeppelin, who of course went on to build his eponymous airships, including the extraordinary *Hindenburg*.

Upstairs there's a rather dry exhibition on the 'basics of agriculture', but the effort is amply rewarded by a fantastic bee exhibit at the far end, consisting of three working beehives with glass sides and tubes giving access to the great outdoors, allowing you to see what the bees are really getting up to. It's an excellent display.

Also upstairs is an optical planetarium, which gives you anatomically correct views of the star-filled night sky at any time of year and from the poles to the equator. It costs an extra 10kn to get in, and is usually only open during the hour before the museum closes.

Back downstairs, there are two more major highlights, both only visitable by guided tour. The first, underneath the museum, is a mine, with some 300m of tunnels, showing what working conditions in mines at different periods were (and indeed are) like – tours usually go at 15.00 daily, 11.00 at weekends, or you can try and hitch onto the back of a group visit. It's a truly excellent experience.

And finally, there's an amazing reconstruction of some of Nikola Tesla's working experiments, including both 3MW and 12MW sparks around a Faraday Cage (lightning is around 20MW, for comparison), along with an interactive exhibition, which has been fully revamped in honour of the 150th anniversary of the inventor's birth in Croatia. Tours happen at 15.30 on weekdays, 11.30 at weekends.

Tesla was an extraordinary man, pretty much defining the way we use electricity even today, and also inventing the radio ahead of Marconi – though this wasn't recognised until after Tesla's death, impoverished and forgotten, in 1943. Tesla demonstrated a radio-controlled boat in Manhattan, almost fifty years earlier, in 1897, though such things didn't become commonplace until the 1960s. and at the time of his death, he was working on a teleforce weapon, or death-ray (intended of course as a peace-ray).

Ethnographic Museum (Etnografski Muzej) [104–5 B5] (*www.emz.hr*; ⊕ *10.00–18.00 Tue–Thu, 10.00–13.00 Fri–Sun; 15kn; free Thu*) The Ethnographic Museum is occasionally invaded by noisy school groups, but usually curiously deserted – which is unfair, as it's a tremendous insight into the way life was lived by most Croatian people until relatively recent times.

The collection is housed in a Jugendstil building which was originally designed at the turn of the 20th century to be a museum of trade and commerce (check out the allegorical figures around the dome). After World War I, it took on its new function as the Ethnographic Museum, focusing on everyday village life, special festive items, and national costumes – and unless you're in Zagreb on the right dates in July (see page 60), this will be the absolute best chance you get to see the huge variety from across the country.

The current exhibition dates back to 1972, and is definitely showing its age. Happily, full renovations are planned, though at the time of writing (2009) financial restrictions still prevented these from being undertaken.

The permanent collection upstairs starts with a simple village house interior. Note the photograph of a large village clan of over 30 people; the abolition of the feudal system by Jelačić (see page 102) in 1848 saw most clans disintegrate, but some persisted through until the 1930s.

Opposite the house interior there's a display of decorative women's headwear from northern Croatia, which tells you a lot about hair-related superstition. Young girls' hair is allowed to be seen, but married women's woven bonnets cover it all up, and bridal bonnets are often highly reflective to ward off the evil eye. The superstition reigned that a woman's strength and goodness lay in her hair, and so this should be reserved for the family; as a result, any hair lost had to be burnt, to prevent witches from getting hold of it. In some of the more remote villages of Croatia, these beliefs still persist today. Even in Zagreb, you'll find people being superstitious about chimney sweeps (you see them in the streets) and nuns, with one for good luck, two for bad, three for good, etc. It can't be a coincidence that nuns and sweeps usually work in pairs.

Looking at the fabrics and costumes, you'll see lots of red, black and white. Red was believed to ward off evil spirits, and was often used during childbirth to divide the room, to separate the women from the rest of the household. Red dresses also symbolise youth and vitality. Black, of course, is usually associated with death – to wrap the body for burial or cover the burial chest. But until around a century ago, white was the traditional colour for mourning across most of Europe, and still is in Croatia, Hungary, and even parts of Spain today. White was the simplest fabric, so the total absence of decoration and colour signifies a lack of interest in personal appearance in the wake of tragedy.

In the main display rooms you'll also see rustic furniture, communal ovens, baking implements, and valuable bridal chests, usually made from wood from the island of Rab. The wood was sold off so enthusiastically to the Italians and French – it was a favourite for cognac casks – that the island eventually became denuded and entirely barren on the east side, and remains so today.

Also noteworthy are hand-operated corn mills, which were once the 'morning music' heard in every village; primitive wooden carnival masks used to chase away the evil winter spirits (local carnivals continue today, and there's a huge one in Rijeka); small wax votives (of limbs in need of repair, or sick animals); and the ubiquitous red-iced gingerbread hearts (*licitarsko srce*) decorated with mirrors, traditionally given by young men to their brides-to-be: 'look who I have in my heart'.

Among the costumes themselves, look out for the grass capes used by shepherds to keep the rain off, and the shaggy (positively hippy) costumes and rugs from the Lika region, which come from vertical looms which can't be used to make linen.

Richer garments reflect wealthier parts of the country, and notably the Slavonian costumes, with silver and gold thread, complex embroidery, and an abundance of fabric, as well as necklaces with coins sewn in to them for unmarried daughters, symbolically representing their dowry.

Downstairs, don't miss the unusual – and quite entertaining – foreign ethnographic collection, with artefacts and costumes from India, Bengal, the Pacific islands, Australia, Africa, Easter Island, Japan, Brazil and Latin America. Most of the material here came from the expeditions led at the turn of the 20th century by Mirko and Stjepan Seljan, an exotic pair of explorer brothers from Karlovac.

And last but not least, see what's happening on the rest of the ground floor; the temporary exhibitions here are generally first-rate.

Croatian State Archives (Hrvatski Državni Arhiv) [104–5 B6] (↘ 480 1981; www.arhiv.hr; guided tours in English, German & Croatian 12.00, 13.00, 14.00 Mon–Fri and 2nd Sat each month, by special arrangement; 20kn) The Croatian State Archives are housed in Zagreb's finest Jugendstil building, down near the Botanical Gardens. If you have the time, it's well worth taking a tour, as the inside is as grand as the exterior.

At first sight, the edifice seems as sober and formal as you'd expect from something that was originally built as a monumental university library in 1913, but wait until you see the four sets of giant green owls supporting globes on the roof – they're fabulous! Before you go inside, also check out the four sets of reliefs above the main entrance, which are allegories of the four collegiate sciences – from left to right as you're looking at them, Medicine, Theology, Philosophy (Socrates confronting the very naked truth indeed) and Law.

The magnificent building is the work of local boy Rudolf Lubynski, who used the knowledge he gained studying architecture in Karlsruhe to create Zagreb's first concrete building. He also took charge of the sumptuous interior decoration, which includes geometric marble inlay floors, Bohemian crystal glass panelling, Slavonian oak wainscoting, and light fittings from Murano, all set off by tasteful touches of gold leaf decoration.

Inside the main hall, notice the mosaic depictions of some of Croatia's most important sites, including Đakovo, Dubrovnik, Senj and of course Zagreb. There are plenty of other owls around too, symbolizing illumination and knowledge.

The tour takes in the lovely Professors' Reading Room, which features comfortable reading desks and fine Art Nouveau lamps, as well as several large allegorical paintings by Ivan Tišov, depicting the natural sciences, the liberal arts and the scholastic arts. Above the entrance hangs Robert Auer's image of Athene Palladia holding a figure of Athene Nike, a pictorial embodiment of the maxim 'through knowledge to victory'.

The other main attraction inside is the aptly named and genuinely enormous Large Reading Room, which is still in use today. Two vast chandeliers (imported from Prague and weighing in at over a tonne apiece) complement the elegant beaded reading lamps and the lovely stained glass in the ceiling.

On the north wall (above the entrance doors) are three imposing paintings by Mirko Rački, depicting Science in Antiquity to the left (note Homer), Science in the Middle Ages to the right (featuring Dante), and Science in the Modern Age in the middle. The huge canvas opposite is the Evolution of Croatian Culture by Vlaho Bukovac (see page 343), and features 27 Croatian luminaries – with a little knowledge and a sharp eye you can spot the playwright Ivan Gundulić, Bishop Strossmayer and Ljudevit Gaj, while that person on the right-hand side peeking out from behind the figure in a green cape may well be Lubynski himself.

Back outside, dizzy from all the accumulated knowledge and wisdom – not to mention the owls – see if the small graffito telling you what it's really all about ('Sex and Money and Guns') has been cleaned off yet. It's on one of the small pillars holding up the chain fence, to the left as you leave – or it was on my last visit, anyway.

Arts and Crafts Museum (Muzej za Umjetnost i Obrt) [104–5 B5] (*www.muo.hr*; ⊕ *10.00–19.00 Tue, Wed, Fri & Sat, 10.00–22.00 Thu, 10.00–14.00 Sun; 30kn*)
Zagreb also has an outstanding Arts and Crafts Museum, housed in yet another huge, late 19th-century building (Bollé, again), just across the square from the National Theatre. The only real disappointment is the almost complete lack of English-language captions and legends.

The great pastel edifice was purpose-built for the museum, and was designed to house a 'collection of samples for masters, crafts and artists' – a remit it certainly manages to fulfil to this day, covering pretty much everything from the 14th to the 20th centuries, and displaying around 3,000 objects from its total collection of over 150,000 artefacts.

What you find most appealing will depend on your own specialist areas of interest; you can choose from furniture; textiles and clothing; ceramics; glass; Gothic and Baroque sculpture; European miniatures from the 17th to 19th centuries; ivory; silverware; musical instruments; religious art and liturgical objects; a magnificent collection of 400 clocks and some 200 pocket and wrist watches; and pretty much all the Secession and Biedermeier you can eat.

If that's not enough to knock the stuffing out of you, there are also sections on printing, graphic and industrial design, and photography – with both old photographic equipment and photographs on display, including early daguerreotypes, documentary photographs from World War I, and pictures from dashing mountaineering expeditions of the 1920s. Finally, there's an interesting collection of European art, with the focus primarily on the 17th century. Rembrandt's student Ferdinand Bol is represented here, along with Charles Le Brun, the painter who (with Poussin) pretty much determined the course of 17th-century French painting.

The museum has a nice, classy shop, where you can buy good reproductions as well as modern ceramics and textiles, and downstairs (with its own courtyard at the back) is the Hrvatski Kulturni Klub – nothing whatsoever to do with a Croatian Boy George, but instead a rather good café and restaurant (see page 92).

Natural History Museum (Hrvatski Prirodoslovni Muzej) [104–5 C2] (*www.hpm.hr*; ⊕ *10.00–17.00 Tue–Fri, 10.00–13.00 Sat & Sun; 20kn*) If you fancy a trip back in time, then Zagreb's Natural History Museum is just the ticket.

Situated up in the old town in a palatial but rather run-down building, the collection comprises around two million specimens, most of them in anachronistic wooden glass-fronted cabinets.

Get past the surly socialist-era ticket sellers, and you can lose yourself in room after room of rocks and fossils, moon dust and meteorites, and bones, skeletons and specimens you'd rather not think about in formaldehyde-filled glass jars.

The top floor is the main attraction, especially if you're travelling with kids. Here you'll find seriously old-fashioned displays of stuffed and preserved animals from throughout Europe, including a large shark in a suitably aquamarine environment, and a long corridor of specimen jars leading through to mammals, birds, insects and some very fine butterflies.

For serious naturalists, the museum also houses a library of some 40,000 volumes that you can consult; the oldest is a natural history encyclopaedia in Latin dating from 1638.

Before you leave, make sure you step into the museum's courtyard, where you can check out the excellent mineralogical map of Croatia, made from a bit of stone from each part of the country, and a geological column stretching from 350 million BC to about 10,000 years ago. One side shows rocks from Mediterranean Croatia; the other stone from the continental interior, including various fossils representative of different eras.

Finally, don't be surprised if you see anthropologists of world renown snooping around the museum, as it's also the repository of the extraordinary Krapina Man find, the world's largest collection of Neanderthal fossils from a single site. This isn't open to the public, but a dedicated museum on the subject has been developed at Krapina itself (see page 142, and box).

Croatia Historical Museum (Hrvatski Povijesni Muzej) [104–5 C3] (*www.hismus.hr;* ⏁ *10.00–18.00 Tue–Fri, 10.00–13.00 Sat & Sun; 10kn*) If you're kicking your heels or it's a rainy day, pop into the Croatia Historical Museum, which has temporary exhibitions focusing on – yep – Croatia's history. The museum is one block west of St Mark's Square in the old town.

There's no permanent exhibition, which is a pity, as they have all sorts of important goodies in stock, from Jelačić's 1848 flag to armour, weapons, stone sculpture, painting,

---

KRAPINA MAN

Krapina Man was discovered in August 1899 by Dragutin Gorjanović-Kramberger – or to be more accurate, a fossilised human molar was found, pointing to the existence of a Neanderthal settlement in the area some 130,000 years ago. Thanks to Gorjanović-Kramberger's enormous diligence, scholarship and plain hard work, the collection grew in size to become the world's largest and most important set of Neanderthal fossils from a single site, comprising 900 pieces from 70 to 80 individuals.

The current curator, Jakov Radovčić, has dedicated a great part of his life to the collection, and is the author of a fascinating biography of the finder, (see page 378). Radovčić is currently setting up a new database with the help of EU funding, which will allow for extensive data sharing, without the need for the priceless original specimens to be handled.

His great personal achievement – after decades of lobbying – is the new, state-of-the-art interactive museum being developed at Krapina (see page 142), which will display replicas of the collection, and recount what we know about Neanderthal man.

clocks, maps and photographs. The temporary exhibitions are usually good, but the amount of information you'll get in English varies.

GALLERIES

Meštrović Atelier (Fondacija Ivana Meštrovića) [104–5 C2] (*www.mdc.hr/mestrovic*; ☉ *10.00–18.00 Tue–Fri, 10.00–14.00 Sat & Sun; 30kn*) Arguably the most interesting, and certainly the most accessible of Zagreb's galleries is the Meštrović Atelier. Ivan Meštrović was Croatia's most famous sculptor, and he lived at this house in the upper town between the two world wars, before emigrating to the USA.

Inside, you'll find an excellent collection of the sculptor's work, in a much more intimate setting than the vast Meštrović Gallery in Split. The house itself is lovely, with the collection spread across three floors and the artist's studio, and demonstrating the diversity of his work. There's more than a nod to Rodin, who Meštrović befriended in Paris before World War I, but the sculpture goes a good deal deeper than that, and also owes a debt to Slavic culture, Christian iconography and the work of Michelangelo.

The collection is a fine introduction to some of the large Meštrović works dotted around Zagreb – Bishop Strossmayer behind the Strossmayer Gallery, Marulić in front of the State Archives, the *Well of Life* in front of the National Theatre, the *History of the Croats* next to the Faculty of Law, or the great *Crucifixion* in St Mark's Church.

Modern Gallery (Moderna Galerija) [104–5 D5] (*www.moderna-galerija.hr*; ☉ *10.00–18.00 Tue–Fri, 10.00–13.00 Sat & Sun; 40kn*) The Modern Gallery on Strossmayerov houses 'Two centuries of Croatian Visual Arts'. In spite of one of the steepest entry fees in Zagreb, and the works being mainly by artists most of us haven't heard of, this is nonetheless one of the best galleries in Zagreb.

It's recently been expensively and beautifully restored, and the rooms are bright, light and airy, running chronologically from around 1800 onwards. For me personally, the show is stolen by Vlaho Bukovac (see box on page 343), and the gallery holds some great works by him – but don't let that stop you enjoying the rest of what's on show here.

The first room you come into sets you up a treat, with a symbolic feast from the 'School of Zagreb' painters, dominated by a vast bacchanalia from Celestin Mato Medović. That leads you into something of a vacuum in the next couple of rooms, but it's worth sparing a moment for Fernkorn's models of the statues of St George and the Dragon, and Ban Jelačić, the full-scale versions of which you'll have seen in the city. There are also four very strange portraits by Vjekoslav Karas, which fall uncomfortably between the naïve and the expressive, and were painted before the young artist drowned himself in Karlovac in 1858 (see page 154).

The next room's more cheerful altogether, with some wonderful Bukovac works, and a couple of excellent hyper-realistic sculptures by Robert Frageš Mihanović; his St Dominic is particularly good.

In the next long room check out the transition from Jugendstil to Symbolism, and a fine picture of water lilies by Croatia's first important female painter, Slava Raškaj; a deaf mute, she died before the age of 30 in an institution. In the same room, there's a fine diptych in a Jugendstil frame by one of Croatia's most influential painters, Emanuel Vidović – it's entitled *Mali Svjet* (Small World); with the house he was born in on the left, and the graveyard where he will be buried on the right.

The main oval room, which comes next, showcases the arrival of German Expressionism, and sees Vidović retreat into his dream world of *The City of the Dead*. Also check out the photographically framed seascapes by Menci Clement Crnčić, and some dramatic portraits by the short-lived Josip Račić (he died when he was just 23), including the *Lady in White*.

Moving on, there are two excellent self-portraits by Miroslav Kraljević, who made it to the ripe old age of 28 before dying of consumption; a great painting of a woman with a gun by Croatia's second great female painter, Nasta Rojc; a fabulous 1923 self-portrait by Milivoj Uzelac – Schiele-influenced and Expressionism at its cruellest; and a 1927 Picasso-feel self-portrait by Ivo Režek.

Head up the stairs and check out the works by the socially committed architect Drago Ibler in the first room – distinguished by the brick wall backgrounds denoting lack of choice. There are also some fantastic photographs in the same room of 1930s workers by Tošo Dabac, and a couple of very late works by Vidović of Split and Trogir cathedrals.

After World War II you get everything from beauty to landscapes to social realism and – post 1951 – geometrical abstractionism. Look out for works by the husband and wife team Frano Šimunović and Ksenija Kantoci; abstract landscapes of fields and dry stone walls from the Dalmatian hinterland from the former, and abstract sculptures from the same landscapes, usually of peasant women, from the latter.

The exhibition ends with art that was banned during the Yugoslav era, including an excellent conceptual work featuring doctored hyper-inflation banknotes and worthless coins being scooped up by a ladle.

Strossmayer Gallery of Old Masters (Strossmayerova Galerija) [104–5 D5]

(*www.mdc.hr/strossmayer;* ⊕ *10.00–13.00 & 17.00–19.00 Tue, 10.00–13.00 Wed–Sun; 10kn*) In the square across the street from the Modern Gallery you'll find the Croatian Academy of Arts and Sciences (see page 108), the top floor of which is given over to the excellent Strossmayer Gallery of Old Masters.

Josip Juraj Strossmayer was the fervently pro-Croat bishop of Đakovo, in eastern Slavonia, and was the founder of the Academy. He was also a serious art collector, and what you get here is his private collection of some 256 works from 1884, supplemented by various donations over the years from the likes of Augustinčić (see page 139) and Mimara (see page 111).

The gallery is at the top of the stairs, and spans religious works from the Renaissance right through to 19th-century France. The lack of English-language captions is a pity, but not a show stopper. Heading clockwise, chronologically around the gallery, the first room is noteworthy for a fine 15th-century work by Fra Angelico depicting St Francis and St Peter, and a *Madonna and Child* by Roselli, featuring dreary-looking angels – even by the standards of the day.

The next room houses Strossmayer's own favourite works, and notably another *Madonna and Child*, this time by a follower of Raphael. Rooms three and four make the small stylistic leap from the Ferrara school to the Venetian school – a bit less detail in the works, but still camp as Christmas. Look out for a dramatic *Resurrection* from Carpaccio, with Jesus positively leaping out of his grave and stepping on the sleeping soldiers on his way out, an inspiringly simple *Ecco Homo* by Filippo Mazzolo, and a suggestive San Sebastian by Andrea del Sarto.

In the next three rooms, check out Ribera's dramatic *Jerome* (clearly inspired by Caravaggio), a wonderful *Mary Magdalene* by El Greco (centuries ahead of his time as usual), and a great treatment of Salome, by Elisabetta Sirani, who managed to churn out more than 170 oils by the time of her death, aged just 27, in 1665.

Rooms eight, nine and ten take you through Croatian, Flemish and French works for the most part, with the likes of Breughel, Poussin, Delacroix and Courbet on show – and a fantastically stodgy portrait of famous beauty and salon-hostess Juliette Récamier by Antoine-Jean Gros.

As you leave, look out for Carpeaux's bust of Eugène-Emmanuel-Ernest d'Halwyn, Marquis de Piennes, who was France's ambassador to Zagreb under Napoleon III – and known here as plain old Etienne. Piennes bequeathed his private art collection to the Strossmayer Gallery on his death in 1911.

Croatian Museum of Naïve Art (Muzej Naivne Umjetnosti) [104–5 C3]

(*www.hmnu.org;* ☉ *10.00–18.00 Tue–Fri, 10.00–13.00 Sat & Sun; 20kn*) One of Zagreb's most interesting galleries is the Croatian Museum of Naïve Art, up in the old town, just south of St Mark's Square.

The gallery was opened in 1952, as the Peasant Art Gallery, making it the oldest museum of naïve art in the world. From 1956 it was called the Gallery of Primitive Art, and in 1994 took its present name. There are around 80 works on show, from a total collection of over 1,600, covering naïve artists who had no professional training and little or no education – but all went on to make a living from their work.

Croatian naïve art developed from the 1930s in Hlebine, near the Hungarian border, with the first important artist being Ivan Generalić, who showed in Paris to great critical and commercial acclaim in 1953. Characteristic of Generalić and his followers was the technique of painting highly stylised rural scenes on glass, which was then reversed for framing. Apart from being valuable in its own right, the movement was particularly important for giving us a record of the terrible hardships of peasant life until quite recent times.

A common motif is the rooster, a symbol of rebirth (as it is in the work of Federico García Lorca); look out for the Godzilla-sized version on the barn roof in one of the paintings in the first room, which is dedicated to Generalić's work, or the particularly colourful cockerel in *The Death of Virius*, a homage to another painter from Hlebine who died during World War II – note the dead trees and concentration camp, with life going on far behind the barbed wire. Finally, check out the striking self-portrait from 1975, with its uniform background and Generalić looking down in contemplation.

In complete contrast is follower Ivan Večenaj's *Evangelists on Calvary*, with blood pouring down the cross, the evangelists present in their animal form (ox, lion, eagle, angel), people strung up in the trees, inscribed parchments everywhere, and a blood-red sky; the stuff of nightmares. If you don't like it, you probably won't much enjoy his portrait of an inbred peasant woman with her cat, either.

More palatable – to this author, anyway – are the winter landscapes by Mijo Kovačić. Reminiscent somewhat of Brueghel, particularly good examples are 1962's *Singeing a Pig* (using burning straw to remove the pig's skin), 1967's *Swineherd*, and 1974's *Frozen in the Snow*, depicting dead partisans in a super-realistic snowdrift.

Moving into the third room, check out the large, accomplished work by Genarlić's son Josip, *Guiana '78*, which deals with the mass suicide of Jim Jones and his 900 followers that year, and marks the start of a general trend towards the depiction of more modern life, rather than simply peasant culture.

Two other artists are particularly worth singling out: Emerik Feješ and Ivan Rabuzin. You can spot a Feješ a mile off, as the scenes are mostly geometric multi-coloured churches, including Vienna and Milan cathedrals, St Mark's in Venice, and Sainte-Chapelle in Paris.

Rabuzin's work is also highly distinctive, and he's arguably the most accessible of all the naïve artists, as he leaves people out of the picture (literally; he believed that the presence of people was a 'blot' on the beauty of the world). His bright, optimistic pastel landscapes feature repetitive geometric forms in the trees and flowers – and I even once saw a reproduction in a French hotel.

Finally, check out the work of naïve sculptor Petar Smajić, and particularly his charming *Adam and Eve*, which is Henry Moore-like in its simplicity.

If you're really serious about naïve art, then it's well worth making the trip up to Hlebine, a couple of hours northeast of Zagreb, where you can visit both a state gallery and the private collection of Generalić father and son. The virgin landscape of the early paintings may no longer exist, but the old way of life persists. In 2009 a series of giant Easter eggs, painted in naïve style, were placed in squares in central Zagreb.

Museum of Contemporary Art (Muzej Suvremene Umjetnosti) [74–5 E7]

(*www.msu.hr;* ⊕ *11.00–19.00 Tue–Sun, 11.00–22.00 Thu; 30kn*) For a long while, the Museum of Contemporary Art was housed in the Kulmer Palace, on the other side of St Catherine's Church, but the space was much too small for comfort. As a result, a large new museum building has been built on Avenija Dubrovnik in Novi Zagreb, which finally opened in December 2009.

OTHER NOTEWORTHY BUILDINGS

The Stock Exchange [104–5 F4] Zagreb's most dramatic neo-classical building is the former stock exchange, now home to the Croatian National Bank. It was designed by the architect Viktor Kovačić, though he didn't live to see its completion; it was finished off in 1927 by his associate Hugo Erlich.

The front of the building is a striking white marble porch, supported by Ionic columns, which dominates the square it's on. If you get a chance to peek inside, do (it's not all that likely, but there's no harm in trying). A tremendous staircase leads up from the entrance hall to the foyer of the original trading floor, a great circular room topped by a huge cupola with a round opening to let in the light.

The Croatian Artists Centre (Dom Hrvatskih Likovnih Umjetnika) All roads in the eastern part of the lower town seem to home in on Zagreb's only large circular building, the white marble Croatian Artists Centre. Supported by a colonnade of fine white marble pillars, the building was designed by Ivan Meštrović (see page 119) to house temporary art exhibitions, a function it still performs to this day (though it's also seen service as a mosque and a socialist museum in the meantime). It's worth popping in, even if the current exhibition's not something you're mad about, just to see the great space, diffusely lit from above by its glass ceiling.

The Golden Hall [104–5 D2] (*Opatička 10*) In the old town (easy to find because of the big wrought-iron gates), is the mansion housing the Croatian History Institute. And inside that, there's an extraordinary Baroque room called the Golden Hall, which is used mainly for swanky functions. If you ever get the chance to see inside, it's well worth it, with the abundant gilding that gives it its name, and major paintings celebrating great Croatian moments in history. Best of the lot is the dramatic depiction by Vlaho Bukovac (see box on page 343) of Emperor Franz Josef arriving in Zagreb, with the back of what's now the Mimara Museum (it was then a school) clearly visible behind the assembled welcome reception.

St Blaise's Church [104–5 A4] Situated a few blocks west of the National Theatre, St Blaise's Church is mainly famous for its reinforced concrete dome. The church was the brainchild of local architect Viktor Kovačić, and was built according to his designs between 1912 and 1915. Sceptics were certain that the 18m-wide dome would collapse the moment the supporting pillars were removed, so Kovačić sat out the night underneath it to confound his critics, and the dome still looks pretty solid today. The church is pretty plain inside, and usually closed (except during services), but you can get into the porch and have a peek through the bars if you're keen.

SURROUNDS

If you just worked your way through everything in the previous sections, you'll clearly be after a breath of fresh air and some outdoor attractions. Happily, Zagreb has plenty to offer here too, from one of the best cemeteries anywhere, Mirogoj, to the huge city park, Maksimir, where you'll also find a great zoo, to a cable-car ride up to the easily accessible Sljeme, the peak of Mount Medvednica. Zagreb even has its own beaches, at Jarun Lake and Bundek – and if that's still not enough, there's also the charming monastery church of Remete to visit in the northern suburbs.

MIROGOJ CEMETERY [74–5 E4] You don't have to be in the least bit morbid to enjoy a trip up to Mirogoj Cemetery, one of the best burial grounds I've ever visited. Just hop on bus #106, which runs up from Kaptol, above the cathedral, and get off ten minutes later when you see the semicircular entrance gate to the cemetery, dominated by the dome of the main chapel.

Mirogoj was opened in 1876 as the city's monumental municipal cemetery, and the main feature is a series of divine, greening cupola-ed arcades running either way along the inside of the walls. They're the work of Hermann Bollé, and in their own way every bit as impressive as the cathedral.

The cemetery is not just non-denominational but a positive Pantheon, housing Jews and Muslims, Orthodox Christians and Catholics, communist partisans and the German dead from World War II. There are literally thousands of touching memorials to individuals, families, and different historical tragedies, with sculpture from pretty much every notable Croatian artist.

The largest and most impressive memorial of all is right at the top of the main avenue, where Croatia's first president, Franjo Tuđman, is honoured by a vast expanse of black marble. It's big, but it's not as poignant as the memorial to Stjepan Radić, who was shot in Belgrade's parliament in 1928 (see page 15), which you'll find to the right of the entrance as you come in, under the arcades. Just before Radić is the memorial to the poet Petar Preradović, which features a wonderfully sculpted mourner laying a single flower on the bier, while four cupolas beyond, check out the lovely monument to Emanuel Prister (whoever he was), with a tremendous depiction of a woman closed in upon herself with grief.

Once you've paid your respects, you can return to the city on the bus, or simply walk down the hill – it takes around half an hour, heading down Mirogojska (head straight out of the cemetery, not left down Hermana Bolléa) until you reach the tram stop at the bottom of the hill, and then make your way across at the lights to the top end of Medvedgradska, which runs down the hill until it becomes Tkalčićeva (it's one street across from the top of Nova Ves, which then becomes Kaptol).

MAKSIMIR PARK AND THE ZOO [74–5 F4] A few kilometres east of the city centre is the sprawling Maksimir Park, easily reached on tram #4, #7, #11 or #12 (get off at the Bukovačka stop, heading towards Dubrava or Dubec), which also plays host to Zagreb's wonderful zoo. It's right across the street from the Dinamo Stadion, home to Zagreb's 'Bad Blue Boys', the local – and enormously popular – football team.

Maksimir itself is a real oasis of calm, feeling far, far away from the noisy city streets. Measuring around 2km by 1.5km, it was landscaped in the manner of a 19th-century English park, and features lakes, woods, hidden paths, meadows, and even the occasional folly to divert you. It's a great place for a stroll, and an even better one for a picnic.

Zagreb's **zoo** (*www.zgzoo.com*; ⏰ *09.00–20.00 daily, last admission 18.30; shorter hours outside summer months; 30kn*) is spread along the southern edge of Maksimir Park, and is absolutely first-rate, putting far bigger cities like London and Paris to shame. From its founding in 1925, when it boasted just three young foxes and a pair of owls, it's grown – and indeed matured – to become one of the nicest zoos I know.

Many of the 2,000 or so animals here, from nearly 300 species, live in modern, airy, outdoor enclosures, rather than cages, and there are some real treats in store for visitors, from a fearsome pack of wolves, to the most charming red panda I've ever seen, to a pygmy hippo (called 'Hypo' after the local mortgage lender), to a comic pool of savvy seals and sea-lions. There are excellently themed didactic exhibitions covering different regions of the world, with the emphasis on ecosystems rather than simply the fauna to be found there.

Two particular exhibits make the zoo stand out even further. The first is a house that shows off domestic fauna in its actual setting, from mice in the cupboards to cockroaches under the floorboards to birds nesting in the roof. The second is even more adventurous, comprising two cages marked 'Homo Sapiens', complete with full species data, such as height, weight, longevity and average number of young. You can go inside, of course, to see what it's like behind the bars, but the trick is: you get to choose whether you want the cage furnished with plastic and non-renewable materials, and junk food on the table, or the cage done out with wooden and cane furniture, and a bowl of fresh fruit.

MOUNT MEDVEDNICA [74–5 D1]

For a real breath of fresh air, look no further than Mount Medvednica, the mountain that provides Zagreb's permanent backdrop and an excellent local resource. As a well-managed Nature Park, there's lots to see and do up here, from pleasant not-too-strenuous walking to cycling, to just taking in the views and the cooler air above the city. The biodiversity here is wonderful, with 1,200 plant species on Medvednica, compared to 1,600 in the whole of Great Britain.

If that's not enough to tempt you, there's also Medvedgrad (a splendid medieval castle), a bat cave to explore, and a small reconstructed mine to visit, as well as places you can stay and eat. In winter you can even ski down the back of the mountain and pretend you're local hero and four-time Olympic winner Janica Kostelić.

Getting there (and skiing)

Getting up the mountain isn't difficult at all, and can be comfortably managed in a half-day trip, using public transport. Take tram #8 or #14 to the Mihaljevac terminus, followed by tram #15 to the end of the line at Dolje. From here it's a pleasant ten-minute walk through a short tunnel and up a forest path to the cable-car station (*Žičara Sljeme*), and a 23-minute ride (hourly, on the hour) up to the 1,035m peak of Sljeme, the highest point on Mount Medvednica. If it's windy, the cable car doesn't operate, and they usefully post a notice at the Mihaljevac terminus saying so (*Žičara ne vozi*). At present (2009) the cable car is closed for a major upgrade (for the possible destruction of forest this upgrade may entail, see www.zelena-akcija.hr). The price of the ride was previously 11kn one-way, 17kn return (free with the Zagreb card).

By road (assuming you have your own wheels), head north from the city and follow signs to Sljeme, turning right at the Mihaljevac tram and bus terminus, and then left a couple of kilometres further on, at Bliznec. The road, which winds up the mountain, along the top, and down again a few kilometres west, is a one-way system (after you've passed the Nature Park's office on the first left-hand hairpin), so when you come down the mountain it's actually into the suburb of Šestine – more or less due north of Britanski Square, on Ilica.

If you're planning on skiing, you can rent kit at the top of the mountain – but be warned that since the Kostelić phenomenon kicked in, Zagreb's gone skiing mad, and it can get pretty busy. Best fun of all is the Snow Queen, a twice-weekly night-slalom that takes place throughout the season (from the end of November to the beginning of April).

There are some lovely walks on Sljeme (see below).

Medvedgrad Fortress [74–5 C2/3]

From the top of the cable car, it's a little under an hour on foot to the 13th-century Medvedgrad Fortress. This was abandoned in the late 16th century and fell into ruin, but was expensively restored in the 1990s, as a patriotic gesture by Franjo Tuđman – it's become something of a nationalist symbol, and as such is mildly controversial: could the money have been better spent on something else, the locals ask, not unreasonably. Whatever the politics, it's an atmospheric place in a great location, all the same, on a bluff with lovely views out over the city, and a fine restaurant in the vaults.

If you're coming by car, Medvedgrad is a bit non-intuitive to find, as it has its own access road. If you're coming down the mountain, pass the Šestinski Lagvić restaurant, then turn right at the attractive, gaudily roofed Šestine church, towards Talane, and then right again at the next junction, which is signed for Medvedgrad; the road takes you straight up to the castle.

The **Šestinski Lagvić** restaurant [74–5 C2] itself is an excellent place to eat, but quite pricey. For something a little more reasonable, there's the **Kraljičin Zdenac** restaurant [74–5 C2] further up the hill (ie before you get to Šestinski Lagvić, if you're driving). If you fancy a stroll, it's a lovely shady walk up to Kraljičin Zdenac along the Kraljevic stream, avoiding the road.

If you're driving (or cycling) down the hill, look out for the huge, newly restored mansion to the right, after you come out of the woods and before you get to Šestine church; it's called **Kulmerovi Dvori** [74–5 C3], and now belongs to the Todorić family, the owners of the successful Konzum supermarket chain.

The Veternica Cave [74–5 B3] (*www.pp-medvednica.hr*) On the southwestern corner of

Medvednica is the Veternica Cave complex (named after the eddies of wind at the entrance which led to its discovery), over 7km of which have been explored. On Sundays from May to August you can visit the first well-lit 400m of the cave as part of an excellent guided tour (call the Nature Park office for more detailed information; see below; 25kn), which covers the cave's geological and natural history, as well as its former use as (probably) a Neanderthal shrine of some kind; over 100 bear skulls were found in the cave, but the original entrance is too small for bears.

You'll also see a date on one wall in an inner cave. This was daubed here by a daring young blood called Fabrici, who came all the way inside in the dark in 1934; unfortunately his mates didn't believe he'd actually done the deed, so he had to climb the cathedral tower instead to prove his worth – happily without unfortunate consequences.

Serious speleologists can go much deeper into the complex (by arrangement with the Nature Park authorities), and squirm their way on hands and knees up the Stairs of Calvary, past the Stinky Lake and through Ramses' Passage (ooh-err).

Outside the summer season, the cave is closed to the public, as it's the natural hibernation place for 14 of Croatia's species of bat, as well as all sorts of other unusual wildlife, including the peculiar *Chthonius jalzici*, a mock scorpion endemic to Veternica that was only classified in 1988.

The easiest route to Veternica is the 20-minute hike downhill from the Glavica mountain hut, itself a three-hour hike from Grafičar hut. The other route to the cave is by taking tram #2, #6 or #11 to the Črnomerec terminus, and then bus #124 to the end of the line, after which it's a kilometre or so uphill (walking trail #3 on the map) to the cave entrance – allow 45 minutes up and 30 minutes back.

The Zrinski Mine [74–5 C2] (*www.pp-medvednica.hr*) More historical nuggets (though

no silver ones, these days) can be gleaned from the Zrinski Mine (also called Rudarski Vrt, especially on maps – meaning 'miners' garden'), which has been excellently and evocatively reconstructed to give you a feel for miners' life in the 16th century.

What that feel is, mostly, is of just how hard a miner's life was (and in many places still is). If mining was your chosen (or designated) career up here, you could expect to start work at age 12, and die of lead poisoning by the time you were 30. In the brief years between, you worked the mine, doing a 12-hour shift, six days a week, plus the hour and a half commute each way from the bottom of the mountain (ironically where you'll now find Zagreb's ritziest real estate). Each day, you would dig out, with the other 15 miners on your watch, around a tonne of rock, which might yield a little silver and a bit more lead.

The mine was abandoned for over 400 years, but has now been restored (by the Nature Park) to show something of its history and workings. Most important of all is the presence in mines everywhere of St Barbara, the patron saint of miners. Why St Barbara should be their protector is a bit of a mystery, as the unfortunate Barbara is best known for having her head cut off by her father, and her father then being killed by lightning by God (so why didn't He throw the lightning bolt before Barbara's untimely decapitation, you have to ask?).

The tour is enlivened by talking wooden statues of Zagorje mining types (whose accents are apparently especially hard for Dalmatians to understand), the first of which is the mine manager – you can tell by the silver buttons on his coat. With low ceilings and narrow corridors, along with drippy-water sound effects, it's an atmospheric experience and especially worthwhile if you're here with kids.

The mine is open on weekends and public holidays (when it's not snow-covered), from 11.00 to 17.00, and also by arrangement (with the park office, see below) for groups; entry is 25kn. The mine is located about 25 minutes' walk west of the top of the cable car, on the main road, just below the Grafičar hut. If you're walking up from Medvedgrad, allow around 40 minutes.

Walking and cycling

Walking and cycling Medvednica is ideal for both walking and cycling, and there are good maps available for both pursuits – available either direct from the park office or at the main tourist office on Jelačić Square. The walking is on the whole rather less demanding than the cycling (walkers can use the cable car to cut out a good deal of the legwork), which requires you to get up the mountain in the first place. The cycling map – available for the time being in Croatian only – details 15 different rides of varying difficulty, and helpfully gives not just distances and routes, but profiles too, as well as the total climb you're in for. For more information on walking on Medvednica see Rudolf Abraham's book *Walking in Croatia*.

Practicalities

Practicalities You can get heaps of information from the cheerful, friendly and helpful staff at the Nature Park (*Park Prirode Medvednica;* ☎ *458 6317;* ☏ *458 6318; www.pp-medvednica.hr*), whose office is situated on the main road into the park, above Bliznec – you can hardly miss it, as there's a fabulous bear trimmed from a large bush on the corner. Just below the park office, criss-crossing the stream, is an excellent nature trail, which – in a world first for the blind – has all the legends in Braille as well as access for the handicapped. From the far end of this, a longer, steeper trail continues up to Tomislav dom on the top of Sljeme.

There are several places to stay on Medvednica, and most notably the **Tomislav Dom** (☎ *456 0400;* ☏ *456 0401; www.hotel-tomislavovdom.com*), which is just a few minutes up from the top of the cable car. Chalet-like doubles go for about € 80 per night, which is a bit expensive for something this far out of town, although there are discounts for longer stays. Another option, Pansion Medvednica, closed in 2009 – but check with the tourist office in case it reopens. Finally, there's the **Pansion Zvonimir** (*Zvonimirov dom, formerly Hunjka;* ☎ *458 0397;* ☏ *455 2185; www.zvonimirov-dom.com*), which has pleasant rooms (€70 *doubles*) in a largish chalet overlooking the Hunjka meadow, about 4km east of Sljeme, on the old road heading down off the back of the mountain.

You're also unlikely to go hungry on top of Medvednica as there are a number of cafés and restaurants at the top of the mountain (as well as the two near Medvedgrad, see above). **Dom Grafičar** (☎ *455 5844*) is an excellent place to stop for hearty, reasonably priced food near the summit of Sljeme. Our personal favourite is **Puntijarka**, in the Ivan Pačkovski mountain lodge. It's out of the way a bit, about 3km east of Sljeme, but serves up lashings of mountain food at unbeatable prices. Fill up on a delicious bowl of *grah* (heavy, meaty bean soup) for just 15kn, or turkey with *mlinci* (thin homemade doughy pasta) for 40kn. Be warned: portion sizes are almost as big as the mountain itself.

JARUN LAKE [74–5 C6/7] About 5km southwest of the city centre, Jarun Lake is an artificial playground tucked into a bend of the river Sava. It was built for the 1987 World University Games, and comprises a great big lake, with a handful of islands, long pebbled swimming (and sunning) beaches, cycle paths, jogging tracks and places you can rent bikes, pedalos, deck-chairs, canoes and even sculls.

As the lake warms up quickly and stays that way throughout the summer months, with average water temperatures of around 24°C, it can get pretty busy with swimmers and strollers on summer weekends. And as you'd expect, there are plenty of bars and cafés as well as snack- and ice cream-type establishments to keep you going. Jarun is also home to a couple of Zagreb's most important nightspots, **Aquarius** (see page 99) and **Gallery** (see page 99).

You can get to Jarun Lake easily enough, either directly on the #113 bus from behind the main railway station (Jarun is the last stop), or almost all the way on tram #5 or #17 to the Jarun stop, which is just a few minutes' walk north from the lake.

BUNDEK [74–5 E6] For years, Bundek, just across the river Sava on the way to Novi Zagreb, and opposite the race course and fair grounds, was an edgy area where you were more likely to tread on a needle or find last night's forgotten undergarments. Happily, that's all changed now, with a major redevelopment of the lake and surrounding park, which reopened in 2006.

As a result, you'll now find lovely flowerbeds and a glistening lake spanned by an elegant bridge at its narrowest point, as well as numerous cycle paths, pebble beaches and lots of lawn space for sitting around on. It's all very pleasant, and very popular at weekends.

REMETE If you're looking for a bit of an excursion, then the monastery Church of St Mary in the northern suburb of Remete is a nice place to visit – but don't go unless you've really covered a lot of ground already, or are particularly passionate about Mary, as it's a little over 5km from the city centre and not that easy to get to without your own transport (take bus #203 or #226).

The church is famous primarily for the wooden sculpted Virgin Mary, which the faithful still come to admire, particularly on the Feast of the Assumption (15 August), though it's also a popular place to get married, or – if you're sufficiently famous – buried. Before you go inside, check out the excellent reliefs outside the front door, with the saint on the left apparently holding a dodo, and the one on the right standing on a wild boar.

Inside, apart from the Holy Virgin herself, the big deal is the wealth of amateurish but powerful frescoes depicting her intervention in a huge range of domestic dramas. On the right-hand side, on the upper wall near the door, there's an endearing gentleman who looks as if he's definitely had one *travarica* too many.

INLAND CROATIA

40km
20 miles

HUNGARY

SLOVENIA

Vojvodina (SERBIA)

BOSNIA & HERZEGOVINA

Budapest

Belgrade

Danube

Beli Manastir

Kopački Rit

OSIJEK

Čepin

VUKOVAR

VINKOVCI

Ilok

Županja

ĐAKOVO

Orahovica

Našice

Slatina

Voćin

Papuk

POŽEGA

SLAVONSKI BROD

Sava

Virovitica

Drava

Velika

Grubišno Polje

Daruvar

Nova Gradiška

Novska

Čakovec

KOPRIVNICA

Hlebine

Đurđevac

BIJELOVAR

Kutina

Lonjsko Polje

JASENOVAC

VARAŽDIN

Zlatar

Križevci

Ivanić Grad

E70

SISAK

Petrinja

Krapina

Zabok

Zagorje

E59

Zaprešić

Mt Medvednica 1030m

ZAGREB

Turopolje

Samobor

Sesvete

Žumberak

Jastrebarsko

Glina

KARLOVAC

Vojnić

Slunj

Plitvice NP & Lakes

Vrelo

Rijeka

Bosanci

Ogulin

Josipdol

Jezerane

Otočac

Split

Bjelolasica 1534m

Klek 1181m

Jasenak

Vrbovsko

Velebit

E65/71

E59

E65

E71

128

4

Inland Croatia

Inland Croatia is in complete contrast to the dramatic karstic landscapes of the coast and the holiday resorts on the islands. With the exception of the famous Plitvice Lakes, Croatia's most popular national park, the area is still largely unvisited – and unjustly so.

North of Zagreb is the delightful Zagorje region, with hundreds of churches and dozens of castles and country houses set amongst wooded hills, while the country's northern provincial capital, Varaždin, is a Baroque masterpiece. Southwest of the capital are the low mountains, remote villages and excellent vineyards of the Žumberak, bracketed by the lovely little town of Samobor on one side and the purpose-built Renaissance fortress town of Karlovac on the other.

South of Karlovac are the Plitvice Lakes, while to the southeast are the marshes and wetlands loved by birdlife – practically anywhere south and east of Zagreb you'll see nesting storks, but most notably in the Lonjsko Polje.

Further east of here you're into Slavonia, where hunting castles and deep forests contrast with the big Pannonian plains. The fine provincial town of Požega is the obvious access point to the Papuk Nature Park, where you'll find burbling streams and shady woods to walk in, while Slavonski Brod and Đakovo offer some of the region's most interesting folk events.

Here, you're in the heart of Slavonia, bordered by the three great rivers, the Sava, the Drava and the Danube. The region's busy capital, Osijek, is the gateway to the huge wetlands of Kopački Rit, one of Europe's most important bird sanctuaries, and the breeding ground for some of the world's most vicious mosquitoes. Make sure you wear repellent, even in the daytime, and use one of those protective wall-socket plug-ins at night – you can buy them anywhere round here, not surprisingly. Finally, at the eastern end of Slavonia is Vukovar, which suffered terribly during the war in 1991, but is now gradually finding its feet once again.

With few tourists, once you're inland you'll find a general lack of accommodation facilities, though in the Zagorje and Žumberak there are more and more agro-tourism offerings available, as well as several hotels in converted country houses. It's well worth contacting the Zagreb County tourist office (✆ *01 487 3665;* f *01 487 3670; www.tzzz.hr*) ahead of time for the latest information.

Further east, there are really only a handful of places to stay (they're listed in the text), with the whole of Slavonia boasting fewer than half the number of hotels you can find in Poreč alone.

Phone codes vary across the region – they're included within each listing.

CYCLING IN ZAGREB COUNTY

Cyclists should jump at the opportunity of taking advantage of an excellent new series of maps entitled 'Biking Routes of Zagreb County' that were published for the first time in 2004 by the Zagreb County tourist board (see details above). These describe a series of routes to the north and west of the capital following low-traffic-density roads across beautiful rolling countryside, and range from the easy to the moderately strenuous. Altitude and distance profiles let you know exactly what you're up for and full details are provided of everything you could possibly need along the way from restaurants and accommodation options to bike repair shops. It's a wonderful initiative – but go for knobbly tyres, as quite a few of the trails go off the tarmac and onto gravel to avoid the traffic. There's another good map of bicycle trails covering the Žumberak Nature Park (see page 150), which you can pick up in Samobor (see page 147).

VARAŽDIN *Telephone code: 042 (+385 42 from abroad)*

Tucked into the northernmost corner of Croatia, about 80km north of Zagreb and just 45km from the Hungarian border, Varaždin is a provincial capital and a Baroque delight. It has great architecture, a fine castle, a wonderful pedestrianised city centre, and enough to see and do without it being anything like hard work. The city is the most cycle-friendly in Croatia (over 20,000 bicycles for a population of just 50,000), and one of the most wealthy – the elegant buildings and spacious streets are the result of centuries of prosperous agriculture and trade, and very little damage from recent wars.

HISTORY Known as Garestin in Roman times, little of importance happened here until Varaždin was recognised by Hungary in AD1181, and then developed first as an administrative and later as a defensive centre – from the 15th century on, the city was on the frontline against the Ottoman Empire.

With the Turkish threat under control by the early 17th century, Varaždin became an affluent and influential city, and in 1756 even became the capital of Croatia. It wasn't to last – after a catastrophic fire in 1776, the Ban (the local governor) moved to Zagreb. Varaždin was still a prosperous city, however, and its wealthy merchants didn't miss the opportunity of rebuilding their houses and palaces according to the latest fashion of the day.

Today, the Baroque centre of town has been beautifully restored, and it deserves to win its bid to be included on UNESCO's World Heritage list. With everything comfortably within walking distance in the centre, and plaques on many of the buildings in Croatian, English and German, it's also an easy place to visit.

GETTING THERE AND AROUND Varaždin is easy to reach, with buses running at least once an hour from Zagreb, and trains making the journey a dozen times a day. Buses take around 1½ hours, while trains rarely achieve the distance in under 2½, though the notoriously slow train ride is a much more picturesque way of making the journey. Varaždin is also a stop on the major international bus and train routes north to Austria and Hungary. By car, it's not much more than half an hour on the motorway from Zagreb, once you've cleared the city. Parking is metered in the city centre, and you can pay in cash or by sending an SMS from your mobile phone.

The bus station is five minutes southwest of the town centre, while the train station is ten minutes away to the east. Most of the old town is pedestrianised, with the curving shopping street Gundulića leading up to the main square Trg Kralja Tomislava. A block northwest, on Padovca, you'll find a friendly and helpful tourist information office. The newly expanded city map is well worth the 25kn, though if you're on a tight budget you can certainly get by with the free materials.

WHERE TO STAY Varaždin's only real shortcoming is a lack of upmarket accommodation. There are plans for boutique hotels, but nothing's materialised yet, so for the time being you'll have to make do with one of the town's existing hotels, which are mostly within five minutes of the bus station, on the southern side of town.

All cater primarily to business people passing through, so reserve ahead if you're coming midweek, particularly at the Maltar and Turist.

🏠 **Istra** (11 rooms) 📞 042 659 659; **f** 042 659 660; www.istra-hotel.hr. The most expensive place in town. *Dbl €117–135.*

🏠 **Maltar** (25 rooms) 📞 042 311 100; **f** 042 211 190; www.maltar.hr. Well appointed, with very friendly staff and en-suite dls. *Dbl €60–64.*

🏠 **Turist** (109 rooms) 📞 042 395 395; **f** 042 215 028; www.hotel-turist.hr. Much bigger & slightly swankier than Maltar; internet access. *Dbl €70–90.*

🏠 **Varaždin** (27 rooms) Kolodvorska 19; 📞 042 290 720; **f** 042 201 915; www.hotelvarazdin.com. Newly opened in 2007, a stone's throw from the bus station. *Dbl €80–100.*

There's one other really lovely option, if you don't mind being out of town, and have your own wheels:

🏠 **Zlatne Gorice** 📞/**f** 042 666 054; www.zlatne-gorice.com. Situated about 4km south of Varaždin, on the main road to Varaždinske Toplice (Varaždin's spa complex), in the locality called Turčin – it's on the left, right at the top of the hill. The establishment is actually an upmarket restaurant, with 4 small, individually furnished dining rooms, owned by the same people who run Zlatne Guska (see below), but upstairs they have 3 brand-new, comfortable dbls, which are good value – they make their own excellent wine too. *Dbl €50.*

Varaždin also has a limited supply of private rooms, though you'd be unlucky not to find one in town or the surrounding countryside. Stop in at T-Tours (📞 *042 210 989;* **f** *042 210 990*) on Gundulića, which is the only agency handling rooms, and expect to pay € 25–30 for a room all year round – for once there's no surcharge for short stays – or have a look at the ones advertised on www.spancirfest.com.

✕ WHERE TO EAT AND DRINK
As a prosperous town, Varaždin has no shortage of places to eat and drink, and some of the restaurants and bars have terraces in pleasant courtyards hidden away behind the Baroque façades, or overlooking the park.

♀ **Aquamarin** Just north of the main square, next to the town hall, & sharing with the cinema (Kino Gaj), this bar is trendy & popular for its cocktails – as well as the sea-themed decoration.

✕ **Domenico** Varaždin's most popular pizzeria, on Trg Slobode.

♀ **Galliano** Nice bar tucked away in a good location along one of the little shop-filled alleys off the main square.

♀ **Green Pub** Just south of the castle, with a biggish terrace & pub-like atmosphere; popular with students. 🕐 until 02.00 on Sat nights.

✕ **Grenadir** Formerly the Šibenik, this friendly eatery serves moderately priced salads, pasta dishes & risotto.

☕ **Kavana Korzo** Right on the main square, the place to hang out with a coffee & be seen.

♀ **Mea Culpa** Groovy lounge bar situated next door to the tourist office.

✕ **Park** A great terrace overlooking the park, & good, standard, Croatian fare.

✕ **Pivnica Raj** A cheerful place on Gundulića, which, as you'd expect (pivnica being a brewery), serves up its own beer & various grills.

✕ **Zlatna Guska** 📞 042 213 393; www.zlatne-gorice.com. Easily the most upmarket restaurant in town, & the only place you'd really need to think about making reservations. Next door to the Park (see above), it benefits from the same location overlooking verdant parkland, & has a medieval-style vaulted interior downstairs, complete with crests, maces, lances & colourful banners. An extensive menu (steak's a speciality, but they do great soups & salads too), & an unusually wide range of desserts.

WHAT TO SEE AND DO
The main sight in Varaždin is the harmonious old town, which you'll likely be approaching from the south, as this is where the hotels and bus station are. Across the bottom of town is a lovely park, with the **National Theatre** on the southwest corner – if you have the chance to look inside, or see a performance here, you'll find it a sumptuous red velvet and gilded treat.

In the park itself, look out for the statue of Vatroslav Jagić, the Slavic languages expert who was born here in 1838. His statue's a bit of an embarrassment for local clothes manufacturer Varteks (Varaždinska Tekstilna), as his coat buttons are on the wrong side for a gentleman's garment.

Moving up into town, stop at the **Church of St Nicholas** on Trg Slobode (Freedom Square). Nicholas is usually the patron of seafaring cities, but got chosen here because of Varaždin's dependence on the Drava river for trade. The church is also dedicated to St Florian, with his red flag – he's the patron saint of firemen – as a reminder of the 1776 fire. Up on the tower there's a stone bear; the legend is that the bear turned to stone on returning to the site of the church to find her cubs gone.

Turn up into Gundulića, which is known locally as Dučanska, as this is the place to shop (*dućan* = shop). Note the casement windows at the corner of Habdelića, which were designed so that wealthy ladies could snoop on what was going on below. At the top of the street, take a detour left to the 17th-century **Franciscan Church**, which was built on the foundations of something much earlier – its tower, at 54m, is the tallest thing in Varaždin.

Outside the church, anyone who's been to Split will recognise the pint-sized version of Ivan Meštrović's most distinctive statue, *Grgur Ninski* – strangely undramatic in its reduced form. As in Split, the erstwhile bishop's big toe has been worn golden by people hoping their wishes will come true.

Almost next door, and an absolute must for entomologists, is Varaždin's wonderful **World of Insects** museum, featuring a thousand species of bugs and more than 4,000 exhibits. It was the work of Franjo Košćec, who spent decades collecting the specimens here, and was personally responsible for the museum's creation in 1954. It's one of the best collections of its kind, demonstrating not only Croatia's endemic species, but also the life-cycle and habitats of various insects, in a modern, stylish setting – and there's even a charming re-creation of Košćec's study. If you're interested, or have kids, the interactive '*Kukci*' CD-Rom for sale here is simply excellent.

Heading back the way you came brings you to Varaždin's 17th-century **cathedral**, on the right, with a plain Baroque façade giving away few secrets about the riotous over-the-top altarpiece inside. Multi-coloured pillars frame dramatic saints in late-medieval garb, overlooked by gesticulating angels and overflown by abundant putti. It's absolutely marvellous – but you wouldn't want one at home. The doors, dating from 2002, celebrate Varaždin's becoming a diocese, with its own bishop.

On the corner of the main square opposite the cathedral stands the Drašković Palace, which was the Ban's residence during Varaždin's (very) brief stint as Croatia's capital in the 18th century. The main square itself – **Trg Kralja Tomislava** – is dominated by the town hall, dating from 1523, with an unlikely spire rising from its centre. Look out for the mermaid sign hanging outside the Bonbonnière Kraš sweet shop on one side of the square – the sign originally denoted a shop selling exotic goods sourced from abroad (the original sign is in the town museum, if you want to see it). You'll also notice the Ritz and Jacomini buildings side by side in the main square; the family plots are also side by side in the cemetery (see page 134). Finally, while you're here, scope out the arcades that lead off the square and the surrounding streets, and hide enticing boutiques, cafés and restaurants.

Heading north from the main square brings you round onto Trg Milijenka Stančića, which faces onto the drawbridge and gatehouse that lead across to the castle and town museum. On the square itself, in a gaudily fronted palace, is the **Municipal Art Gallery**, which mostly comprises old masters by artists you won't have heard of – but it's none the less interesting for that.

From here head through the gate into the park housing Varaždin's trademark whitewashed fortress, the **Stari Grad**. Set amongst defensive earthworks that have pleasantly metamorphosed into lovely gardens, the fortress was originally built in the

14th century, before becoming a major defence against the Turks in the 15th century and evolving into its present shape during the 16th century.

The fortress now houses the **Town Museum** (*Strossmayerovo šetalište 7;* ❁ *042 658 754; www.gmv.hr*), which was established in 1925, and is one of the best municipal collections outside Zagreb. Even if you're not especially into the paintings, weaponry and furnishings on display here, the entry fee is amply repaid by the chance to wander round the rooms and the two three-tiered courtyards – and there are some old and droll hunting targets on display, including one featuring the faces of the hunters' wives. Of particular interest are a series of rooms each furnished in a different period style, from the 17th century through to Biedermeier, with original paintings, furniture and furnishings. Finally, don't miss the chapel and sacristy built into the tower on the first floor – and drop me a line if you have the faintest idea how they got that massive piece of furniture in there.

From the fortress it's a ten-minute stroll west to the town's wonderful cemetery, which has much more in common with a well-tended garden than a traditional resting place, with the plants and shrubs dominating the graves. It's the life-work of Herman Haller, who ran the cemetery from 1905 until 1946, with the intention of creating a 'park of the living' rather than a 'place of the dead'. You'll find all sorts of wonderful memorials here, amongst the avenues and promenades, including 376 red rose bushes commemorating the town's World War I fallen. One of the most interesting graves of all is that of the mountaineer Lucijan Zlatko, which features a piece of rock from every peak he climbed. It seems terribly ironic that as a climber he lived to the age of 93, while his wife Vera succumbed when she was only 48.

If you're still looking for something to do in town, you can also visit the **Art Atelier** of eccentric and bohemian local sculptor, painter and performance artist Darwin Butković, which is next door to the tourist office, in a space converted from the old Franciscan granary – the tourist office will introduce you to him, if you're interested.

If all the sightseeing's left you hot and bothered, and you have your own transport, head a few kilometres east out of town to **Aqua City**, where you'll find a lake to swim in, a shingle beach to sun yourself on, and a restaurant. Without wheels you can still get the shore-side experience by walking 20 minutes northeast of the old town to the **Dravska Park Šuma**, where you'll find jogging paths along the banks of the great, still river Drava.

Varaždin festivals

Varaždin is the perfect venue for many festivals during the year, with the two largest being the **'Špancirfest'** at the end of August and the Festival of Baroque Music in late September. There are also weekly festivals every Saturday from April to October, which feature workshops around the old town highlighting traditional metiers and arts and crafts, along with music and theatre for children.

The Špancirfest (*www.spancirfest.com*) runs for ten days from the last Friday in August and features music from all over the world, as well as comedy performances and street theatre, and draws around 150,000 people a year.

A month later, the **Festival of Baroque Music** features a host of first-rate concerts which take place in the city's churches and old buildings; it's well worth trying to get tickets (ask at the tourist office) if you're going to be in town.

ČAKOVEC AND THE MEĐIMURJE

North of Varaždin is Croatia's smallest but most densely populated county, the Međimurje. Sandwiched between the Mura and Drava rivers, the area has always been seen as something of an island, both geographically and culturally – it was known as Insula Dravanam by the Romans – while benefiting from its position at the trade crossroads between east and west, and north and south. The region only joined Croatia in 1919, after centuries of Austro-Hungarian control, when it proved it was 98% Croatian-speaking.

You're most likely to arrive over the Ban Josip Jelačić bridge, which was used by the Ban himself in 1848 to cross the Drava and boot out the Hungarians (temporarily), and today carries both the road and the railway from Varaždin to Čakovec and on to Budapest. The other access to the region is the motorway from Zagreb to Hungary, which passes just east of both Varaždin and Čakovec.

ČAKOVEC Situated just 13km northeast of Varaždin, Čakovec is the northernmost town in Croatia, and though there's not a whole lot to do or see, it's worth a visit even if only to take in the Museum of the Međimurje. Several buses and trains a day come up from Varaždin, usually heading on to Hungary. The bus station is just north of the town centre, while the train station is just south.

The town's history is dominated by the influential and colourful Zrinski dynasty, who were in charge here from 1546–1691, and whose main role was to use the Međimurje as a buffer zone against the Turks – they manned 23 forts along the Mura river. After the Hungarians made peace with the Turks in 1664, Petar Zrinski and his cousin Fran Krsto Frankopan led an ill-advised campaign against the monarchy; once they realised this had failed, they went to Vienna to apologise, but were imprisoned for a year instead, before finally being executed on 29 April 1671. Their bones were returned to Croatia in 1919, and reburied in Zagreb cathedral.

The Zrinski Castle, west of the town centre, looks a bit shabby these days, but it does house the eclectic **Museum of the Međimurje** (⊕ *10.00–15.00 Tue–Fri, 10.00–13.00 Sat & Sun; 15kn*), a collection ranging from Neolithic finds to an excellent, if small, Roman collection (with labels in English), to period furniture, to arts and crafts, and silverware and glass – all from the Međimurje. The most poignant exhibit is Petar Zrinski's letter to his wife Katarina, written the day before his execution in Vienna. Also check out the reconstructed old-time pharmacy, a 19th-century telescope, and the small art gallery, as well as the interesting ethnographic collection on the first floor, which goes through the seasons of the year, starting with the February carnival and the strange Poklad masks used to chase away the evil spirits of winter.

Heading back into town you'll cross the castle's old moat, which was drained in the 1980s (to extirpate the town's once-serious mosquito problem), and a lovely park, which brings you into the pedestrianised town centre. The first thing you'll notice here is the wonderful Secessionist **Trade Union Hall**, which was built in 1904 and still looks moderately bonkers today, with its frivolous decorative brickwork quite unsuited to the serious business of organised labour.

Across the street is the friendly **tourist office**, which will help you out with local information and give you details of the Međimurje Wine Road, as well as accommodation options in the region. Round the corner from the Trade Union Hall is the town's smartest café, the **Gradska Kavana**, which has a nice terrace – though there's no shortage of alternatives if you can't find a table – with a newly renovated concert hall and art gallery opposite. Further down the same street, towards the market, on the left-hand side, there's a small memorial to the Jewish community, which was strong in Čakovec until World War II, when all the Jews were rounded up and deported to Auschwitz, and the synagogue here was destroyed.

There are plenty of places to eat, but the best is without question the **Katarina**, which is underground in the modern shopping centre on the west side of town, towards the castle (and owned by the same people as Zlatna Guska in Varaždin). The restaurant is in the suitably atmospheric brick cellar of the original building on the site here, and features the famous letter from Petar to Katarina Zrinski, as well as a fine range of soups, salads and pasta dishes – and more expensive fare for those who want it. Definitely worth trying is the local *Turoš* cheese, a spicy, salty, paprika-flavoured tower quite unlike anything else I've ever tasted.

 Where to stay If you want to stay in town, there are two obvious choices:

 Hotel Aurora (10 rooms) Franje Punčeca 2; \f 040 310 700; www.hotelaurora-ck.com. 5mins north of the castle, on the road to Lendava, in Slovenia, with a handful of clean, comfortable dbl rooms upstairs from the Allegro Restaurant. *Dbl €72.*

 Hotel Park (60 rooms) Zrinsko Frankopanska bb; \ 040 311 255; f 040 311 244; www.hotel-park.info. Just west of the castle, on the Varaždin road, a boxy socialist-era place with rooms that are nicer than the building might suggest, with a strange Modernist hunting mural in the bar. *Dbl €60.*

If you have the energy, it's also worth going to have a look at the extraordinary **Feštetić Castle** in the village of Pribislavec, about 3km east of Čakovec. It's an extraordinary neo-Gothic pile with a marvellous tower on one end dating from 1870. You can't go inside, unfortunately, as it's now the village school.

THE MEĐIMURJE The practically unvisited Međimurje region is now working hard to attract visitors, notably to the attractive Međimurje Wine Road, which comprises more than 25 vineyards set amongst the lovely rolling hills which lead up to the Slovenian border to the north and west of the county.

Wine's been a big deal here for a while – back to Roman times, in fact – but recent years have seen a dramatic increase in quantity, variety and most importantly quality. If you have the time, it's well worth picking up information from the tourist office in Čakovec and taking a tour – many properties offer tastings, and some also have restaurants and/or rooms, which adds to the atmosphere. See the 'wine cellars' page of the useful Međimurje tourist office website (*www.tzm.hr*) for details.

Some of the best wine in the region can be found at **Vino Lovrec**, in Sveti Urban, near Štrigova, and they speak English, so give them a call on m 040 830 171 if you fancy a tasting. If you happen to be at this end of the county, it's worth stopping to have a look at the enormous twin-spired **Church of St Jerome** in Štrigova itself, which was built to celebrate the birth of the saint here (although he was actually born, it's thought, in Stridon, in what's now Bosnia & Herzegovina). If the church is open – which it often isn't – check out the fabulous frescoes inside by Ivan Ranger, the best of the local fresco masters.

Another good place to taste wine is **Dvorac Terbotz** (\ *040 857 444;* f *040 857 445; www.terbotz.hr*), in Železna Gora, which is actually a restaurant, and therefore open daily. Upstairs there's a terrific formal dining room, which is where the Zrinski Guard hold their banquets, while downstairs there's a big wine cellar for tastings. They're also planning to open a hotel on the site within the next few years.

For the time being, one place you can stay is at the **Vinska Kuča Obitelji Turk** (\f *040 855 154;* m *098 241 926; http://seoskiturizam-turk.hr*), in Vučetinec, 10km northwest of Čakovec, which is run by the former manager of a Yugoslav band. They have several rooms available at € 35 a night, and great local food to go with their own very palatable wine – though English is very much a second (or third) language.

If you've overdone it on the wine tasting and fancy a spa to recover, then head up to the northern part of Međimurje, near the Slovenian border, where the **Sveti Martin Baths** (\ *040 371 111;* f *040 371 172; www.toplicesvetimartin.hr*) offer indoor and outdoor pools, as well as saunas, massages and the rest. It's a well-developed resort, and very popular in summer. Just east of here, towards the river, you can visit a reconstructed **water mill** on the Mura, at Žabnik – back in the 1920s there were 90 mills like this along the river, but the last original one closed down in the 1980s.

Trains and buses regularly ply the route up from Zagreb through Varaždin and Čakovec to Budapest, and the formalities are minimal as visitors from the EU and most English-speaking countries don't need a visa for a tourist visit of up to three months.

The motorway north from Zagreb goes as far as the border at Goričan, which claims to be Croatia's busiest border crossing. There's a decent restaurant, the Zelengaj, on the river here, with a floating terrace and lots of good Međimurje staples on the menu.

If you're planning to go across the border, grab a copy of the excellent *Hungary: The Bradt Travel Guide* or *Budapest: The Bradt City Guide*.

The Eastern, 'lower' Međimurje is flat as a pancake and dominated by fields of maize and sunflowers. The main centre here is the small industrial town of **Prelog**, which is famous locally as being home to an international speedway centre, if that's your thing. If you're here, however, it's well worth trying to get inside **St Jacob's Church**, whose plain pale grey exterior hides a magnificent Baroque altar, stretching all the way across the end of the church.

Between Prelog and Goričan is the village of **Donji Kraljevec**, which is famous for being the birthplace of the scientist and philosopher **Rudolf Steiner**. Until recently, the house he was born in (at Ludbreška 13) was being used as a stable, but it can now be visited by appointment – contact Sandra Percač (**m** *099 215 578*) or the Međimurje tourist office (**↖** *040 390 191*) for details.

THE ZAGORJE

The northwestern corner of Croatia, known as the Zagorje, is one of the most beautiful parts of the country, with scores of castles, country houses and hilltop churches looking down across rolling wooded hills and vineyards. It's largely neglected by foreigners on their way to the beach, but it's no secret to locals, who come out here at weekends to relax.

Many of the old houses – and especially the little buildings adjoining the vineyards (*klets*) – have been converted into weekenders for people escaping Zagreb, but come here on the right Tuesday in February, and you'll find the local winemakers' wives getting plastered in *klets* on every vineyard, which seems to me to be a splendid tradition.

Many of the castles (the French word châteaux is more appropriate, really) are in ill-repair, empty and abandoned, and could do with fixing up, and of those which have been restored, many are in private hands and can't be visited. As Croatia becomes more prosperous, however, more of this wonderful heritage is being restored and opened to the public, and some places are also in the process of being transformed into upmarket hotels. There's also talk of building a tunnel through Mount Medvednica to make the region easier to get to from Zagreb, but – in this author's humble opinion – it seems easy enough to access already on the motorway round the western end of the mountain.

It is difficult to get the most out of the Zagorje without your own wheels, however: even though many of the sights can be reached on public transport, it may take you all day to see a place worth only an hour of your time. Consider renting a car for a couple of days – but be prepared for some of the roads being narrow and winding.

There aren't that many places to stay, with most of the area's hotels being attached to the various spas in the region, but agro-tourism is on the rise, and there are a number of other options listed within this section (and notably Dvorac Bežanec, Vuglec Breg and Dvorac Gjalski, which are all excellent).

Inland Croatia THE ZAGORJE

4

ZAGORJE

SLOVENIA

HUNGARY

Budapest

MEĐIMURJE

Letenye

Ormož

ČAKOVEC

PODRAVINA

KOPRIVNICA

Hlebine

Vinje

BJELOVAR

Čazma

Ludbreg

Kalnik

KRIŽEVCI

Vrbovec

Ivanić
Grad

Novi Marof

VARAŽDIN

Maruševec
Castle

Klenovik
Castle

IVANEC

Lepoglava

Belec

Zlatar

Marija
Bistrica

DUGO SELO

SESVETE

Trakošćan
Castle

Trakošćan

Krapina

Gornja
Stubica

1030m
Medvednica

ZAGREB

Rogaška Slatina

Veliki
Tabor

Pregrada

Dvorac
Bežanec

Miljana

Kumrovec

Klanjec

Zabok

Vuglec
Breg

Dvorac Gjalski

ZAPREŠIĆ

Samobor

Dvorac Miljana

Zagorska Sela

20km

10 mile s

0

Bradt

Zagorje eating is almost always a treat, whether you stick to the simple standards or try the local dishes, such as *štrukli* (see page 89), which is usually at its finest here. Intended for decoration rather than eating are the *licitarsko srce*, iced gingerbread hearts. As gifts they're keenly priced; as snacks they're expensive (and tooth threatening).

The following attractions are ordered here in an itinerary heading very roughly clockwise from Zagreb towards Varaždin and back again, with those to the east of the main road to Hungary appearing at the end of the section. Covering the whole lot would make for a fairly hectic two- or more relaxed three-day tour.

ZABOK AND KLANJEC Heading northwest out of Zagreb, it's around 20km to Zabok, which is nothing special, but as you come off the motorway you'll see a newly restored mansion up on the hill which is now a nice hotel called **Dvorac Gjalski** (✆ *049 201 100;* f *049 201 135; www.dvorac-gjalski.hr*). It makes a lovely stopover, even though the views to the back of Mount Medvednica are blighted somewhat by the light industrial landscape inbetween – fortunately there's a lovely terrace behind the hotel, and a fine restaurant within. The rooms are impeccable, too, and very good value indeed at € 78 for doubles and € 95 for a suite.

From here, it's under 20km northwest to the small town of **Klanjec**, nestled right up against the Slovenian border. If you're on public transport, buses make the journey two or three times a day and there's also a train – change at Savski Marof. The main reason to stop here is to visit the **Antun Augustinčić Gallery** (✆ *049 550 343; www.mdc.hr/augustincic;* ⊕ *Apr–Sep 09.00–17.00 daily, Oct–Mar 09.00–15.00 Tue–Sun; 20kn*), which maintains a comprehensive collection of the sculptor's work from the 1920s right through to the 1970s.

You may not think you've heard of Augustinčić, but if you've ever seen the monumental horse and rider outside the UN building in New York, or the pick-wielding miner outside the International Labour Organization (ILO) in Geneva, then you'll recognise his work.

Augustinčić was born in Klanjec in 1900, and studied sculpture under Croatia's most famous sculptor, Ivan Meštrović, and in Paris, where he exhibited in the annual salon from 1925. By winning various prestigious public commissions – including those mentioned above – he became Yugoslavia's official state sculptor. In 1970 he donated a wide range of works to his native town, and the museum here was opened in 1976.

The gallery comprises three rooms and a small sculpture garden. The public monuments – including a life-size copy of the UN sculpture, *Peace* – are far and away the most impressive, though if you catch the ILO miner on the right angle it does look exactly like a cricketer hitting a ball for six. Augustinčić and his wife are buried in the garden, watched over by the touching sculpture *The Carrying of the Wounded* – it's only a pity that Augustinčić's *Boy*, an unpleasantly realistic copy of the Manneken Pis in Brussels, wasn't suppressed by the taste police.

On the way out of town there's a monument to Antun Mihanović, the 19th-century polymath who wrote the lyrics to the Croatian national anthem here, clearly inspired by the ravine along the Sutla River.

KUMROVEC Continuing north, another 10km up the road brings you to the ethnographic museum-village of Kumrovec – which you can get to on public transport as for Klanjec, above. The ethnographic museum (✆ *049 225 830; www.mdc.hr/kumrovec;* ⊕ *Apr–Sep 09.00–19.00 daily, Oct–Mar 09.00–16.00 daily; 20kn*) is a 15-minute walk from the train station.

For half a century the Kumrovec name was synonymous with Josip Broz Tito (see box on page 141), as he was born here, but these days that angle's very much downplayed – except on his birthday, 25 May, when rival pro-Tito groups congregate here and get amusingly huffy with one another. Generally, however, although the authorities haven't quite gone as far as removing the marshal's life-sized statue (another work by Augustinčić – see above) from outside his mum and dad's front door, you don't see much mention of Tito anywhere else in Croatia. Which is a pity; whatever your feelings about the man, he was an important player in 20th-century history.

Today the museum part of the village consists of more than 30 houses, each displaying a different feature of life as it would have been lived at the end of the 19th century, when Tito was a boy. Mannequins in period costume, the full range of authentic furnishings, tools and implements, and excellent labelling in English, make this easily the best of Croatia's many ethnographic museums.

In different houses you can imagine what it must have been like (hard work, mostly) to be a wheelwright, a baker, a blacksmith, a linen manufacturer, a toy-maker, a potter or a gingerbread man. One house is given over to a wedding feast, with a shy bride-to-be in her bedroom, doubtless deafened by the jolly music-making going on at the banquet across the hall.

The Broz family house is a low-key testament to Tito's fairly humble origins. The main room is given over to a small collection of Tito memorabilia – a few documents, one of his wartime uniforms, and a handful of photos of Tito with other statesmen from Churchill to Nixon. Without exception, the whole lot look as if they've been amusingly doctored to include Tito after the fact. In 1956, Nasser and Nehru shake hands, but Tito appears to have been pasted in behind; by 1963, it's John and Jackie Kennedy in the frame, with Tito scissored-in on the left-hand side.

The chickens wandering around and the hay drying on the attractive Slovenian-style lattice frames should alert you to the fact that not all the houses are part of the museum – before you wander unannounced into someone else's authentically rustic living room (as I did), check for the tell-tale trainers or gumboots outside.

Within the museum complex there's a nice place to eat, the **Zagorska Klet**, where you'll find a wholesome range of local food at reasonable prices. You can then pick up a *licitar* heart in the gift shop.

Heading up the Slovenian border from Kumrovec, the countryside becomes ever more beautiful, with Austro-Hungarian spires crowning hilltop churches – stop briefly for the photo-op at Zagorskje Sela, where from **St Catherine's Church** you get lovely views across the valley into Slovenia.

Not much further up the road from here, as you come into Miljana, is the turn-off to Desinić, which is the road for Veliki Tabor. If you want to visit the lovely Renaissance manor house here – **Dvorac Miljana** is probably the very finest of the restored châteaux of the Zagorje – think again. The separate coach and car parks are blind alleys for the time being, though there's still talk of opening the place up for public viewing.

Don't miss the turn-off to Veliki Tabor and Desinić – you'll find yourself in Slovenia before you know it, either through the heavily manned border post, or on a mountainous road leading across an unmanned bridge to the spa town of Atomske Toplice. If that's your route into Slovenia, you can forget about trying to argue your way back into Croatia anywhere near here – head all the way back to the Kumrovec border post instead.

VELIKI TABOR, PREGRADA AND DVORAC BEŽANEC

A few kilometres up the road from Miljana, on a 333m hill, is Veliki Tabor (☎ *049 343 963; www.veliki-tabor.hr*), arguably the most picturesque authentic castle in Croatia. Originally dating from the 12th century, the distinctive defensive round towers were added in the 16th century. From the road there's a lovely view – as indeed there is from the excellent and authentically rustic **Grešna Gorica** restaurant, clearly signed off the main road, a few hundred metres beyond the steep track leading up to the castle.

Unfortunately the castle itself doesn't really deliver on its promise. The lovely five-sided, three-tiered courtyard is undergoing much-needed restoration, and it looks as

Josip Broz was born in Kumrovec in 1892, to a Slovene mother and a Croat father. Drafted into the Austro-Hungarian army in 1914, to fight in World War I, he was captured the following year, but escaped early enough to join the Red Army in 1917. In 1920, he returned to Croatia, where he devoted his time to communism and unionism while employed as a metalworker.

With the Communist Party banned in 1928, Broz was frequently in trouble (and jail) but quickly worked his way up through the ranks. On joining the Central Committee in 1934, he took the name Tito. By 1939 he was Secretary-General of Yugoslavia's Communist Party, and when Yugoslavia capitulated in 1941 he was in a good position to rally resistance – not just to the Germans and the Italians, but also to the NDH, and indeed to anyone who wasn't a communist, including other factions of the resistance.

Charismatic, ruthless and utterly determined – though not the military genius he liked to think he was – Tito persuaded the Allies to switch their aid from the Četniks to the Partisans in 1943, and ended the war as the de facto dictator of the new Yugoslavia. His enemies – including large numbers of Croatian reservists and civilians – were brutally purged (notably at Bleiburg).

In 1948, Tito became the first communist leader to break ranks with Stalin, and was the founder of the non-aligned movement, which included India and Egypt. He continued to embrace communism, though a considerably softer version than that espoused by the USSR and the Eastern Bloc – Yugoslavs, notably, were allowed to own private property, and were free to travel, live and work abroad. But neither Tito himself nor the Communist Party ever brooked the slightest dissent, and prison was a real possibility for anyone who tried.

As Marshal and President for life, Tito made a point of trying to hold the country together, and was quick to quash nationalistic sentiment from the divergent republics – notably the Croatian Spring in 1971 – in spite of being half Croatian and half Slovene himself. Nonetheless, he put in place the legislation that would inevitably lead to the break up of Yugoslavia after his death, in particular by guaranteeing the republics' right to secede. Since his death in 1980, the entire country has broken up into its constituent pieces.

if it'll take years. The rooms leading off the galleries house a fairly mundane collection, and the art and pikes don't really warrant the 20kn entrance fee.

Like all good medieval castles, Veliki Tabor has its own romantic fable attached to it. In this case the local landowner's son wouldn't renounce the peasant girl of his desires, and was imprisoned in the castle until his death. The girl, for her part in the sorry story, was bricked up into the castle walls – they say the skull in the chapel here is hers. Count yourself lucky if you live in a time or country where you can choose who you marry.

You could get to Veliki Tabor by taking the bus from Zagreb to Desinić, and then walking 3km, but until they're done with the restoration I wouldn't particularly recommend it – unless your heart's set on lunch at Grešna Gorica.

Eight kilometres east of Veliki Tabor is the village of **Pregrada**, where the local parish church is so big it's known locally as the Zagorje Cathedral. It's 38m long and 19m wide, and its two 45m towers dominate the village. Inside, check out the monumental organ (avoiding 'monumental organ' jokes of course), by Focht, which used to belong to Zagreb Cathedral until they sold it to Pregrada for 600 forints in

1854. Frankly, it's much better value than the 600 forints the church then spent eight years later on the vast altarpiece of *The Adoration*, which looks like it can only have been bought by the square metre – or indeed the rather druggy modern stained glass in some of the church's windows.

Another 4km east leads to **Dvorac Bežanec** (✆ *049 376 800;* f *049 376 810; www.bezanec.hr*), which is in a great setting and has been converted into a swanky hotel and conference centre. Originally built in the 17th century, the château was remodelled in 1830 in the classicist style, and it can be a wonderfully luxurious place to stay, with nice suites at €100–120 a night. Be fussy about your room, however – some of the standard doubles (at €82) could really use a lick of paint, and there's no excuse in a place this nice for thin towels or plastic shower curtains. Call ahead if you want to take advantage of the horseriding or ballooning opportunities; they can also arrange transfers from Zagreb, if you want to get out of the city, for around €100 return, per carload. The hotel's restaurant – which serves up meals in the courtyard or out on the terrace in fine weather – is absolutely first-rate.

KRAPINA AND KRAPINSKE TOPLICE

KRAPINA AND KRAPINSKE TOPLICE A further 12km east brings you to Krapina, which is on the main road running north from Zagreb to Maribor (in Slovenia) and Graz (in Austria). It's a busy, commercial little town, but the main reason for visiting is that in 1899 the site of an important Neanderthal settlement dating back 130,000 years was unearthed here, on the Hušnjakovo hill above town.

Krapina Man was discovered by Dragutin Gorjanović-Kramberger, who went on to collect the world's largest and most important set of Neanderthal fossils from a single site, comprising 900 pieces from 70 to 80 individuals. The original bones are under lock and key in the Natural History Museum in Zagreb (see page 117), but there is also a brand-new museum here in Krapina (*Museum of Evolution;* ✆ *049 371 491; www.mhz.hr;* ☉ *Apr–Sep 09.00–17.00 daily, Oct–Mar 09.00–15.00 Tue–Sun; 20kn*). You can also walk up to the actual site, where you'll find life-sized (and quite life-like) statues of the Neanderthals brandishing clubs. One of them looks alarmingly like the exchange student we had one year at our school.

Krapina is relatively easy to reach by public transport, with weekday buses running every hour or so from Zagreb, and taking an hour. At weekends you're probably better off taking the train – change at Zabok.

Where to stay If you want to stay in town, you're limited to the fairly basic **Hotel Croatia** (✆ *049 370 547;* f *049 300 146*), which has 15 rooms at €50 for a double. You might also try the tourist office (✆/f *049 371 330*), who should be able to find you a private room in the area.

There are also a couple of places to stay in **Krapinske Toplice**, the spa town 14km southwest of Krapina – contact the Krapina County tourist office (✆/f *049 233 653; www.tz-zagorje.hr*) for more information.

For somewhere much nicer, and in a fabulous location up in the hills between Krapina and Krapinske Toplice, you can't beat **Vuglec Breg** (✆ *049 345 015;* f *049 345 032; www.vuglec-breg.hr*), in the locality known as Škarićevo. A handful of old village houses have been beautifully restored and converted into accommodation with all mod cons, and there's a restaurant and vineyard attached, with excellent local wines (especially the whites). A double room goes for €74, while for €38 per person you get a small thatched house that sleeps six.

TRAKOŠĆAN

TRAKOŠĆAN (✆ *042 796 281; www.mdc.hr/trakoscan;* ☉ *Apr–Oct 09.00–18.00 daily, Nov–Mar 09.00–16.00 daily; 30kn*) Northeast from Krapina is the Zagorje's most-visited attraction, Trakošćan. Billed as a 13th-century castle, you don't have to read much of the small print – or use much architectural intelligence – to work out that what you're seeing here isn't medieval at all but mid-19th-century neo-Romantic all over. That doesn't make it any less worth visiting – although it's all a bit shabby and run down, it's still extraordinary inside and out, with a complete collection of the original (19th-century) furniture and fittings.

The castle was given to the powerful Drašković family in 1584, probably as a belated thank-you for its role in putting down the peasants' uprising a decade earlier (see *Gornja Stubica*, page 145). After the first century or so, the family didn't do much with Trakošćan, preferring to live at the better-appointed Klenovik (see below). But with the Romantic revival in full swing, they then spent a fortune – and more than 20 years – building the castle you see today, and damming and flooding the valley below to give themselves a decent lake.

Access is up a lovely spiralling path and through mock-defensive gates, overlooked by imaginatively crenellated walls and ramparts. Inside it's all heavy neo-Gothic. On the ground floor you'll find the Knights' Room, with lots of clumsy-looking armour and the usual hideous array of pikes and swords. There's also a curious fireplace, with wooden dragons supporting the mantelpiece. At the other end of the building there's a Hunting Hall that verges dangerously close to self-parody.

Upstairs there's room after room of heavy furniture and heavier furnishings, hideous to most modern sensibilities, but a real insight into the mid-19th-century mindset of the ruling classes. You'll also see ten generations of smug Drašković portraits, by the famous local painter Nepozanti Slikar, and presumably his eponymous descendants – since they date from 1680 to at least 1823. (No, I'm kidding – '*nepozanti slikar*' just means 'anonymous painter'.)

Far from anonymous, as far as the paintings here go, are those by Julijana Drašković (née Erdödy, 1847–1901). Much of her surviving work is here in the castle and – although most of it doesn't stand extended 21st-century scrutiny – there are several truly excellent impressionistic portraits.

Other things to look out for, amongst the absurdly chunky Baroque furniture, are an unusual three-seater neo-Gothic sofa (inspired no doubt by church architecture), superb stoves in every room (usually fed from behind, to avoid the unpleasantness of intrusive servants), and what must have been a boy's room on the top floor, with wallpaper consisting of tapestries depicting massive armies of tin soldiers on parade.

You can clear your head outside by a promenade around the lake – the whole circuit takes a leisurely hour and a half.

Practicalities You can't get to Trakošćan directly from Zagreb on public transport, but there are buses roughly every hour from Varaždin, taking less than an hour. Once you're here there's a perfectly acceptable accommodation option, the **Hotel Coning** (\ *042 796 224*; f *042 796 205*), right across from the castle, which has around 100 rooms at €60 for good doubles, and there's a sauna and gym too. The dining room tends to cater to large tour buses and noisy school groups, but you can escape onto the terrace easily enough, and enjoy the view across to the castle.

LEPOGLAVA, KLENOVIK AND MARUŠEVAC CASTLE From Trakošćan it's about 10km southeast to Lepoglava, (in)famous mainly for being the site of Croatia's largest prison. There's hardly a big name in 20th-century Croatian politics who didn't do time here, from Tito himself between the wars, to Archbishop Stepinac after World War II, to Franjo Tuđman, who was banged up here during the 1980s for disagreeing with Serbia's take on history – he suffered four heart attacks in jail here before being released.

The prison's still there, but it was moved away from the town centre to a new location in 2001. The main reason for coming here – the town's pleasant enough, but nothing special – is the fine whitewashed Austro-Hungarian church, with saints in

4

niches on the outside. Inside, the church has a curious right-curving nave, colourful frescoes and a big Baroque altar – which you can see even if the church is closed, as there's a grille inside the portico you can peer through.

Northeast 10km from Lepoglava is Croatia's biggest castle, **Klenovik**, which claims to have 90 rooms and 365 windows. Built in the 17th century, it was for a brief time the seat of the Croatian parliament, and is now a sanatorium, dealing mainly with respiratory complaints. You can only visit today if you're a patient.

Halfway between Klenovik and Varaždin is the mysterious and hard-to-find **Maruševec Castle** (*www.dvorac-marusevec.hr*). Originally dating from the 16th century, today's version is a 19th-century neo-Gothic pile, home to a theology school of the Adventist Church.

BELEC Barely 10km southeast of Lepoglava as the crow flies, but on the other side of the 1,100m Ivančićica mountains (you have to skirt round through Zlatar, and then head 8km north), is the village of Belec, and more importantly the **Church of St Mary of the Snow**. Simple enough on the outside, it's profligate Baroque gone mad once you get inside.

There's hardly an unadorned surface in sight. Putti proliferate off every balcony, mantelpiece and archway, extravagantly gestured saints camp it up like drama queens, and the accumulated wealth of gilt, carving and paintwork is completely overwhelming. Restrained simplicity it ain't – it has to be seen to be believed. Although it's usually only open on Sunday mornings, the woman who lives opposite the gate has a key, and will let you see inside. Expect to make a small donation to the restoration fund.

MARIJA BISTRICA Heading south 10km from Zlatar brings you into Marija Bistrica, a pleasant little town dedicated to looking after the more than 600,000 pilgrims who come here every year, making it Croatia's premier pilgrimage site. The reason? A late 15th- or early 16th-century Black Madonna, which already had a huge following, even before a fire in 1880 destroyed almost everything except the statue itself.

With pilgrims on the increase for centuries, the congregation has frequently outgrown the church, and the church has equally frequently had to be expanded. The current incarnation was completed in 1883 by Hermann Bollé, the man behind lots of buildings in Zagreb, including the cathedral – though here he's been more imaginative (or perhaps less constrained).

From the outside, the **Pilgrimage Church of St Mary** is halfway between a castle and a cathedral. An elegant piazza leads through a gate into a half-cloister, lined with thousands of marble plaques of gratitude from pilgrims whose wishes have been granted over the years, and topped with paintings of specific miracles attributable to the Black Madonna.

Inside, the church is a quiet, awed place, with a continuously shifting congregation of the hopeful (mostly older women) saying their prayers, but also seizing the opportunity to photograph and film the famous Madonna behind the altar.

Behind the church, there's an enormous open-air auditorium, which was built for the Pope's visit in 1998 (when he came here to beatify Cardinal Stepinac), and a Way of the Cross, leading up Calvary Hill. The church and town look lovely from the top, even if you haven't climbed up here on your knees.

Practicalities There are buses every hour or so from Zagreb to Marija Bistrica on most days, though fewer on Sundays. The **tourist office** (✆ *049 468 380;* f *049 301 011; www.info-marija-bistrica.hr*) can point you at private rooms nearby, though it's good to have your own wheels if this is your option, as most of them are some way out into the country. Marija Bistrica's also a good place to eat, with pizzerias and grills aplenty.

You may want to steer clear of the town, however – unless of course you're a pilgrim too – on 15 August, when thousands of people come to celebrate the Assumption of the Virgin Mary.

GORNJA STUBICA From Marija Bistrica it's 11km west to Gornja Stubica, home to the radically named **Museum of Peasant Uprisings** (*Muzej Seljačkih Buna;* ↘ *049 587 880; www.mdc.hr/msb;* ⊕ *Apr–Sep 09.00–19.00 daily, Oct–Mar 09.00–17.00 daily; 20kn*), housed in the local Oršić Palace.

Back in the 16th century, peasants were treated appallingly, overloaded with dues to foreign overlords, expected to fight their battles for them, and driven to the brink of starvation by people who mostly lived idle lives in opulent palaces. By 1573, in this area, it was all too much, and the peasants revolted.

The uprising was quickly and ruthlessly put down by the bishop of Zagreb, a Drašković, who spread word that the ringleader, Matija Gubec, had been made king of the peasants. Within weeks he was horribly executed in St Mark's Square, in Zagreb, by being 'crowned' peasant king with a band of red-hot iron.

There's a dramatic communist-era statue of Gubec on the hill above the town, framed by a huge bronze frieze depicting revolting peasants – it's the work of local boy Antun Augustinčić (see page 139). The museum is well-enough signed if you're coming from Donja Stubica or Gornja Stubica, but if you're coming from Marija Bistrica, the sharp turn up to the monument and museum is easy to miss – if you've crossed over the Oršić River or the railway, or got as far as the Grof Bistro, then you've gone too far.

The museum, over the hill behind the monument, is actually a bit of a misnomer, telling you more about the luxurious lifestyle of the oppressors than the beaten-down existence of the oppressed – though maybe that's the point: this is what you're meant to revolt against. (To be fair, however, there are lots of explanatory panels, in Croatian only, which may do the trick.)

The first thing you can visit is the family chapel, dating from 1756, which has a stunningly convincing *trompe l'oeil* altarpiece and fake dome. The chapel and the room next door house some richly embroidered ecclesiastical garments, originally used at Marija Bistrica at the end of the 19th century. Look out for the distinctive hammer and pliers motif, along with a brightly stitched chicken, sheep, ladder and cross, paintbrush, and wicker basket.

The rest of the museum is upstairs. Above the chapel, out of sight of the peasants below, an Oršić countess sits reading her prayer book in haughty isolation. A roomful of furniture and trinkets only confirms the distance between rich and poor, though you can't help admiring the pocket sundial dating from 1755. 'What time is it, your honour?' 'I'm afraid I can't tell you – it's raining.'

From here there's a bridge through to the rest of the collection, with a group of ragged-looking peasants on one side, and a couple of well-shod militia on the other. You can see the peasants wouldn't have stood a chance.

Practicalities You can get here by train from Zagreb half a dozen times a day – change at Zabok on the Varaždin line, and then take the branch line to Gornja Stubica. In the courtyard of the palace there's a small restaurant with an even smaller menu, but the terrace is a nice place to sit. Otherwise, if you have your own wheels, head uphill to Rody, signed 250m north off the road between the town and the museum – you get a great view south to the back of Medvednica from the terrace, and the food and wine are good value.

VRBOVEC Situated just 45km east of Zagreb, the small town of Vrbovec is way off the tourist radar screen. While the town's nothing special in itself, it does make a great base for exploring the practically unvisited local area, and it has an incredible-value place to stay. Given that it's only 40 minutes by rail into Zagreb, with trains running more than once an hour, and with frequent buses too, Vrbovec is also a possible base for seeing the capital – hotel rooms here are far cheaper than even private rooms in the city.

Four kilometres north of Vrbovec, on the road to Križevci, there's the charming 16th-century **Lovrečina Castle**, with distinctive round towers at either end. Today, Lovrečina is run as a Cenacolo rehabilitation centre, mainly for former drug users.

Practicalities The train station is a ten-minute walk north from the town centre, while the bus station is on the southwestern corner of town, just downhill from the church. From the bus station it's a five-minute walk along Zagrebačka (the main road from Zagreb to Bjelovar) to the excellent Motel Marina (❋ *01 279 1502;* f *01 279 1522; www.motel-marina.com*), which has great rooms with all facilities (phone, satellite TV, minibar, air conditioning) at an astonishing € 43 a night for doubles – you even get a 10% discount if you pay cash. If that weren't enough, there's a nice terrace, and the food is excellent – local produce and local recipes dominate the menu.

There's another accommodation option, the Motel Antonio (❋ *01 279 9955;* f *01 279 9956*), which has 15 rooms also at around € 40 for doubles. With surly staff and charmless rooms, it really comes a very poor second to the Marina.

KRIŽEVCI Just 20km northeast of Vrbovec, and roughly equidistant from Zagreb and Varaždin, is the thriving town of Križevci. It's only an hour or so from the capital by rail, on trains that run about once an hour, but it's far enough off the beaten track to be tourist-free. The town, which has been firmly on the map since the middle of the 13th century, has more than its fair share of churches and old buildings, as well as a fine city museum.

The most obvious sight is the **Greek Catholic Cathedral**. Many of the locals here, as well as the majority of the people in the Žumberak, southwest of Zagreb, were originally Orthodox Slavs. In the face of Turkish expansion they were protected by the Austro-Hungarians, as long as they agreed to recognise the Pope – hence Greek Catholics. The church was rebuilt by the ubiquitous Hermann Bollé in his trademark neo-Gothic style, while the iconostasis inside is marvellous, half an acre of gold leaf surrounding colourful icons of the saints and keeping the congregation separate from the priests behind.

Also worth visiting is the **Church of the Holy Cross**, which started life in the 13th and 14th centuries but has been much remodelled and restored since. Inside there's a dramatic painting of the so-called 'Bloody Diet of Križevci' which took place in 1397, when the Hungarian King Sigismund successfully tricked and murdered the cream of Croatia's nobility here.

Back in the centre of town, the 17th-century **Church of St Anne** is also interesting – the niches outside feature painted saints in the absence of statuary, while inside it's simple Romanesque, with a few fresco fragments on the right-hand wall.

Practicalities The **tourist office** (❋/f *048 681 199*) may be able to help you find private accommodation in the area – otherwise there's the **Hotel Kalnik** (❋ *048 681 522;* f *048 681 521*), which has 40 boxy but good-value rooms with balconies, at € 40 for doubles.

KALNIK FORTRESS Heading out of Križevci towards Varaždin, there's a turn-off after about 10km leading up towards Kalnik, 9km off the main road. The road climbs up steeply to stop right underneath a fabulous ruined ridge-top fortress. Originally built in the 13th century, it must once have been magnificent, although it's been abandoned since the 17th century.

It's been restored enough to make it safe, and stop further deterioration, and it's well worth scrambling up to the highest point – there are handrails on the dodgy sections. You're only 500m above sea-level here, but you can see for miles – to Medvednica in the southwest, and on a very clear day all the way to Papuk, over 100km away.

Just below the fortress there's a lodge run by the mountaineering association, **Planinarski Dom Kalnik** (*www.pdkalnik.hr*), which has a great terrace, fine food and a few rooms upstairs, and information on walks in the area – although it was closed for refurbishment in 2009.

THE PODRAVINA AND HLEBINE Further northeast of Zagreb, running up to the Drava River and the Hungarian border, is the **Podravina**, a rich agricultural basin marked by fields of sunflowers and maize. There's not much to bring tourists here, to be honest, though if you're in the region you may be interested in visiting the village of Hlebine, where Croatian naïve art took off in the 1930s and is still going strong today.

The main centre in the region is the busy town of **Koprivnica**, which is on major rail and road routes. The town is nice enough, though there's nothing special to see or do here. It does make a good place for a layover, however, as there are a couple of useful and affordable places to stay. The nicer of the two is the 14-room **Bijela Kuća** (\ *048 240 320;* f *048 240 321; www.hotel-podravina.hr*), which is close to both the bus and train stations, a ten-minute walk from the town centre. Bigger, boxier and right in the town centre is its sister hotel, the Podravina (\ *048 621 025;* f *048 621 178; www.hotel-podravina.hr*). Both places have reasonable (and fairly priced) restaurants, and offer double rooms at €70 a night.

From Koprivnica it's about 15km to **Hlebine**, and you should expect to use your own transport or take a taxi, as buses are rare. Ever since a local artist fortuitously discovered the works of the self-taught Ivan Generalić in the local shop, in 1930, Hlebine has been a centre of naïve art, and today there are more than 100 painters and sculptors in the area, continuing the tradition. The Hlebine Gallery (\ *048 836 075; www.koprivnica.hr/kultura-i-povijest/galerije;* ⊕ *10.00–16.00 Mon–Fri, 10.00–14.00 Sat; 10kn*) features a rotating collection of works from the village, but you can always be sure of catching some of the original and most striking pictures by Ivan Generalić. Also in Hlebine, but you need to arrange a visit ahead of time (*call the tourist office, on* \ *048 836 139*), is the Generalić Gallery, which features work by Ivan's son, Josip, who worked here until his death in December 2004, and his grandson, Goran, who continues in the family tradition. If you're interested in naïve art, it's also well worth checking out the Generalić website, at www.generalic.com.

SAMOBOR

Less than 20km from downtown Zagreb, and just five minutes from the Slovenian border, Samobor is an attractive little town, with a compact heart set on an elegant, elongated square. A shallow, trout-filled stream is spanned by narrow bridges, and it's a lovely place to sit and soak up the atmosphere while you're tucking into Samobor's culinary specialities.

With buses from Zagreb every half hour (hourly on Sundays), it's easy to reach, and even makes a realistic alternative to staying in the capital itself. The friendly tourist office (\ *01 336 0050; www.tz-samobor.hr*), located right on the main square, will set you up with good local information, and maps of the surrounding area, including the lovely Žumberak region, to which Samobor is the natural gateway.

WHERE TO STAY There are two good hotel options, the first of which is among my favourites in all Croatia:

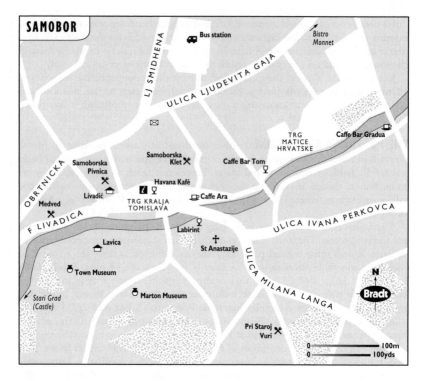

SAMOBOR

LJ SMIDHENA

ULICA LJUDEVITA GAJA

Bus station

Bistro Monnet

OBRTNICKA

TRG MATICE HRVATSKE

Caffe Bar Gradua

Samoborska Pivnica

Samoborska Klet

Caffe Bar Tom

Havana Kafé

Livadić

Caffe Ara

Medved

TRG KRALJA TOMISLAVA

F LIVADICA

ULICA IVANA PERKOVCA

Labirint

Lavica

St Anastazije

ULICA MILANA LANGA

Town Museum

N

Stari Grad (Castle)

Marton Museum

Bradt

Pri Staroj Vuri

0 ————— 100m
0 ————— 100yds

Hotel Livadić (12 rooms) Trg Kralja Tomislava I; 01 336 5850; f 01 332 5588; www.hotel-livadic.hr. On the main square, with a lovely flower-bedecked central courtyard & utterly charming rooms, with old furniture & good-sized bathrooms, at an absolute snip compared to anything in Zagreb. The real treat is a handful of gorgeous, beautifully renovated suites at the top of the building-room: #34 has its bed on a mezzanine, & a sitting room downstairs, while room #35 is spacious & airy &

gives onto the courtyard below. *Dbl from €65, trpl €72.*

Hotel Lavica (22 rooms) Ferde Livadica 5; /f 01 336 8000; www.lavica-hotel.hr. Just across the river from the Livadić, & next door to the town museum, the Lavica has clean, simple rooms at a bargain price, each named after a Croatian intellectual. Its brick-vaulted restaurant – like pretty much everywhere in Samobor – serves up solid local specialities, too. *Dbl €42.*

✗ WHERE TO EAT Samobor – as a long-standing day-treat for Zagreb's workers – is very big on edible treats, and notably its famous *Samoborska kremšnita* – a mountain of cream filling, sandwiched between two slices of flaky pastry. The recipe published by the tourist board makes it sound all too simple: 'Dress lightly. Throw a sweater over your shoulder. Take a vehicle of some kind. Go to main square of Samobor. Take a seat. Order and enjoy.'

The two best places to buy *kremšnite* – we did several tests – are U Prolazu and Gradska Slastičarnica, both on the main square; the latter slightly sweeter, but with lighter pastry than the former. But personally, in the cake department, my money's on the *rudarska greblica*, which is big on walnuts and not quite so creamy. As its name implies, it comes from the village of Rude, just up the valley.

Samobor is also big on sausages, with a **Salami Festival** in April, and produces excellent local *muštarda* to go with them. If you're going the whole hog (insert sausage joke here), also make sure you try the local aperitif, *bermet*, which is red wine flavoured with herbs and spices; it's not to all tastes, but the locals love it.

For sit-down eating and drinking, Samobor is particularly blessed, though – perhaps because it's still focused on visitors from Zagreb, rather than international tourism – there's nothing especially upmarket.

Caffe Ara At the end of the main square, on the north side of the river bridge, a cool place to hang out.

Caffe Bar Gradua On the eastern end of the town centre, with a lovely shady terrace overhanging the river, & a relaxed, trendy clientele.

Havana Kafé Groovy hang-out on the main square, with the usual range of cocktails & drinks, but watch out for the squashy seats.

Labirint On the other side of the stream from Ara (see above), this bar distinguishes itself with attractive flaming torches reflecting off the water.

Medved A block west from the main square, on the right-hand side, this restaurant is just a bit more upmarket than the others, & does especially good sausages.

Bistro Monnet 01 336 7000. 500m northeast of the centre, along Ljudevita Gaja, this is a pub with a good pizzeria at the back & a small terrace in front. Their own homemade Rizling is excellent, at 60kn a litre.

Pri Staroj Vuri 01 336 0548. Nice little restaurant on Giznik, a short walk south of the main square, serving hearty traditional dishes.

Samoborska Klet 01 332 6536. Excellent place, set off the north side of the main square down a short alley, in a shady courtyard adjoining a capacious, simple interior, & offering a regular selection of sensibly priced soups, grilled meats, calamari & side salads, with a 10% discount for cash payment.

Samoborska Pivnica 01 336 1623. You can't go wrong here, even if their terrace is actually part of the car park behind the Hotel Livadić. Serves up all the local specialities, & a particularly generous portion of *štrukli*.

Caffe Bar Tom An unusual, agreeable bar set up next to the river, inside the town's converted bandstand.

WHAT TO SEE AND DO If you can tempt yourself away from the cakes, the most obvious thing to see is Samobor's **Town Museum** (*01 336 1014;* ⊕ *09.00–15.00 Tue–Fri, 09.00–13.00 Sat & Sun; 8kn*), spread out over both floors of local composer Ferdo Livadić's solid town house. Downstairs there are two interesting 1/100 scale models, both by local model-maker Marijan Majdak; one of the castle above the town, as it was in 1776, and the other of the whole of Samobor in 1764 – with the only two things you'll recognise being the church and the Livadić house itself. Also check out the Samobor Chicken (a possible rival to the Vučedol Dove in Zagreb, see page 113), a small local collection of Roman coins, and a well-intentioned palaeontological historical tower, from plastic dinosaurs right up the present day. Upstairs, highlights include an 1877 penny-farthing, a 1920 Puch motorbike, and – if my notes are to be believed – an 1830 portrait of Scooby Doo.

Samobor's other main museum is, if anything, even more eclectic. The **Marton Museum** (*01 332 6426; www.muzej-marton.hr;* ⊕ *10.00–13.00 Sat & Sun; 20kn*) is housed in a fine building from 1841, just above the church, and comprises a private collection of furniture, paintings, glass and china, skilfully put together by local businessman Veljko Marton.

Up to the west of the town is Samobor's 13th-century castle, **Stari Grad**, and the 25-minute walk up to inspect the ruins will do much to get you in shape for the next culinary delight. Follow the path along the stream, then veer left when you see the tennis courts off to the right, and zigzag your way fairly steeply uphill to the overgrown, agreeable ruins of the fortress. Coming back, take the wider, flatter path that leads through the woods to the little Church of St Anne, where you can turn left past a wooden gazebo onto the road which brings you back into Samobor, or uphill through the woods to another chapel, higher up.

More ambitious hiking – but not much more ambitious – is available in the **Samoborsko Gorje** mountains further to the west of town. Increasingly popular at weekends (it's some of the nearest hiking to Zagreb, and not too demanding), you'll find the well-marked trails almost empty out of season, especially if you're here midweek – get a map from the tourist office.

Inland Croatia SAMOBOR

4

The tourist office also has an excellent **cycle route** marked out, and a free map with English instructions on it. The circuit's only 24km long, but the first nine of these are all steeply uphill, gaining 450m – unless you're pretty fit, you may want to do the route in reverse, which makes the climb at a gentler gradient. The only sad thing is that (at the time of writing) there wasn't anywhere to rent a bike in Samobor.

As if the salami thing weren't enough, Samobor also hosts a huge pre-Lent **carnival**. It's one of the most popular in Croatia, attracting hundreds of thousands of visitors, which makes it enormous fun – but no joke at all if you're looking for a room.

Finally, Samobor is a great place to pick up **souvenirs**. On Stražnička, the street heading north out of the main square (to the left of the Hotel Livadić) you can find bead necklaces, *bermet*, and other curiosities at the first shop, and paintings, metalwork and wood next door. At the top of the same street is the Filipec family shop, which is reckoned to be the best place locally for *muštarda*, while on the next street east (to the right of the hotel), you'll find Samoborska Delicije, the most upmarket shop in town, which does nice *licitar* hearts, homemade pâtés, local olive oil, wine and *rakija*, beautifully presented in attractive packaging and gift boxes.

THE ŽUMBERAK

Southwest of Zagreb, and tucked up against the Slovenian border, is the Žumberak region, a sparsely populated expanse of dense forests, steep hills, and sleepy villages, which is a designated Nature Park (*www.pp-zumberak-samoborsko-gorje.hr*). There isn't much to do in the way of specific sightseeing, and you can't get to most places using public transport – indeed, lots of the smaller hamlets and villages don't even have metalled roads to them – but if you do have your own wheels it makes for a lovely region to explore at leisure (especially if you're cycling – see page 50).

The northern part of the Žumberak is mountainous and forested, while further to the south are the beautiful steep vineyards of the Plešivica region (see page 153). The obvious gateway to the region is the pretty town of Samobor, though you can also access it from Karlovac or Jastrebarsko.

There's not much to do or see in the Žumberak itself – beyond enjoying the fine scenery and splendid vistas, and perhaps hiking or biking through the hills – but if you have wheels then there's a good circuit you can do anticlockwise through the region, starting at Samobor, heading round to Karlovac and coming back via Jastrebarsko and the Plešivica vineyards. You need to allow at least two days to see everything, or skip various parts of the itinerary – it's a minimum 200km circuit, with quite long sections on gravel roads. (The circuit works just as well starting in Karlovac, if that's where you're based.)

Start by heading due north to Bregana, but turn left before you get whisked into Slovenia. The road then follows the river (the Slovenian border) for about 10km, until you reach **Divlje Vode**, which becomes something of a minor recreation area at weekends. The restaurant here serves excellent local trout.

ŽUMBERAČKO EKO SELO Shortly after Divlje Vode, the road forks – take the left-hand fork, heading up to Žumberačko Eko Selo (*www.eko-selo.hr*). After a short while the tarmac runs out, and you're on about 8km of gravel all the way up to the camp, a collection of wooden buildings centred on a biggish restaurant in a valley with a pretty stream running through it (it's just off to the right of the main gravel road, when you get as high up as you're going to go).

You can stay up here, in one of the wooden huts (€25 a head) – call Ivana ahead of time (she speaks English) for more detailed information on ☏ 095 905 4198 or ☏ 01 338 7472. You can also book yourself in for horseriding – there's a stable, which only adds to the thoroughly American-cowboy atmosphere; a Stetson wouldn't be

SLOVENIA

ZAGREB

TUROPOLJE

DUGO SELO

KLOŠTAR IVANIĆ

IVANIĆ GRAD

Lonjsko Polje

HRAŠĆELNICA

SISAK

PETRINJA

Zelina

Oborovo

Suša

Odra

Greda

Kupa

Letovanić

Lekenik

Kuče

Buševec

VELIKA GORICA

Velika Mlaka

Sava

Mraclin

D Hrušec

Odranski-Obrež

Lukavec

Šiljakovina

Kravarsko

Pokupsko

ŽUMBERAK

Lučko

Kupinečki-Kraljevec

Pisarovina

Sava

Sv-Nedelja

Horvati

Bratina

Kupa

Sjeničak Lasinjski

SAMOBOR

Beter

Kupja Sela

Ribograd (abandoned)

Crna Mlaka

Donja Kupčina

Rečica

Brezari

Rude

Gonjeva

ZASTREBARSKO

Okičnica

Bukovac

Crna Mlaka

Kupčina

Kamensko

Žumberačko Eko Selo

Noršić Selo

Plešivica

Petrovina

Novaki Petrovina

Vrbanci

Mahično

Samoborska Gorje

Draga Svetojanska

Kupčina

Korana

ILOVAC

KARLOVAC

Budinjak

Kostanjevac

Krašić

Kupa

Jaškovo

Tomašnica

Plitvice Lakes

Duga Resa

Ozalj

0   12km

0   8 miles

entirely out of place. Even if you don't stay, do consider eating here – not only is the restaurant first-rate, it's also the last place for a long time ahead.

There's no question that the easiest way onwards is to head back the way you came, but if you're feeling adventurous then press on – at a number of points the network of gravel roads rejoins the tarred road which winds its way around the northern and western sides of the Žumberak. A good sense of direction and the best maps available will help, but are unlikely to prevent you from getting lost up here. Essentially you want to keep heading west and/or south, and don't be afraid to ask smallholders the way to towns on the main road – Kostanjevac, Pribić and Krašić are all good names to ask for.

Up here life goes on the way it has for centuries, with tiny villages far from the rest of the world, and almost all the work in the small fields still being done by hand.

There's an interesting educational trail up in the northwestern corner of the nature park called the **Trail of the Princes** (Staza Kneževa), which takes in prehistoric tumuli, an early Roman cemetery and ancient rock formations, and takes around 2 hours. The access point is on the main road winding its way west along the Slovenian border (if you'd turned right at the fork after Divlje Vode, rather than left), just before the village of Budinjak – look out for the 'Eko Centar' here.

On your way down towards Pribić and Krašić, it's worth briefly stopping at **Medven Draga**, where you'll find a couple of excellent old water mills. You used to be able to stay at the manor here, but it doesn't look now as if it's still a going concern – if you're interested, contact the Zagreb County tourist office in Zagreb ahead of time (see page 84).

PRIBIĆ The next place you come to after Medven Draga is Pribić – it's easy to overshoot, so look out for a Byzantine-looking church on the right-hand side of the main road, and park here.

You'd certainly never know it now, but Pribić was once an important Greek Catholic centre. Today all there's left to see is the outside of the church and the doomed 'castle' next door, which is gradually losing its battle with the encroaching vegetation.

The church itself sits on a tiny islet, reached over a diminutive bridge. The mosaics on the front are still lovely, kneeling angels flanking a Madonna and child amongst stylised lilies. Over the doorway is a fine carved coat of arms. Look more closely and you'll also see some fine sardonic architectural flourishes, in the form of nightmare gargoyles and a couple of carved eagles – which actually look more like cheesed-off parrots.

KRAŠIĆ From Pribić it's a short, straight run down to Krašić, the home town of Cardinal Stepinac, and the place where he was kept under house arrest during the final years of his life, after being released from Lepoglava. In front of the church there's a statue of the cardinal, while behind it, in the parish priest's house, his two-room flat has been preserved the way he left it. To visit, ring the bell and wait for a nun to let you in. There isn't much to see – the bed he died in, his writing desk, and quite a few photos of the Cardinal (looking worryingly like Vladimir Putin in some shots) – but it's a poignant place all the same. It would be churlish not to make a donation as you leave.

The church itself was rebuilt in 1913, and first impressions of the exterior are misleading – look out for the Jugendstil touches, with stern female friezes built into the walls. Inside, there's not a whole lot to comment on, though the vaulting is attractive, and the altar is positively understated – by Zagorje Baroque standards, anyway.

Practicalities There's nowhere to stay in Krašić, and – in spite of plenty of cafés and a couple of shops – nothing much to eat, either.

OZALJ From Krašić it's a 10km dog-leg west to Ozalj (another turning that's easy to miss – the main road to Karlovac, which you don't want, goes southeast), where you'll find the best of the region's castles.

In a perfect situation, high up above the river Kupa, the medieval settlement here was owned by the Frankopans from 1398, and taken over by the Zrinskis in 1550 – the impressive entrance tower was commissioned by Juraj Zrinski in 1599. During the 18th century, the medieval village was converted into a defensive castle, with the only access being across the drawbridge – the stone bridge you walk across today was built in 1821. It's being restored, but is already a wonder, and has everything you'd want in a castle – towers, solid bastions, ramparts, and great views down to the river.

There's not much else to see in Ozalj, but down in the town, by the bridge across the Kupa, have a look at the neo-Gothic building by the water – it's actually a hydro-electric plant, built in 1908 and still operational today.

From Ozalj it's only about 15km to Karlovac (see page 154), which is a great place to stop and spend the night. And from Karlovac, it's 20km northeast to the one-street town of Jastrebarsko (see page 162), which is the access point for the Plešivica Wine Road, as well as the fish lakes and bird reserve at Crna Mlaka.

PLEŠIVICA WINE ROAD

The 25km road from Jastrebarsko to Samobor is among the most beautiful in Croatia, winding its way up into the hills and then down a long, pretty valley through the village of Rude to complete the circuit of the Žumberak.

The route up brings you through the lovely Plešivica wine-growing region, and it's well worth stopping in at one of the dozen or so vineyards for a tasting if you have time – and if you can persuade your designated driver it's a good thing, or indeed stay over (see listings below). Make a special effort to sample the local speciality, Portugizac Plešivica, a claret-like red, though personally I'm much keener on the crisp white Rajnski Rizling, which is also made here. The Samobor or Karlovac tourist offices should be able to furnish you with a copy of the useful Plešivička Vinska Cesta (Plešivica Wine Road) leaflet, which helps with navigation (though you also need a good road map as well – the best one by far is the map issued by the Jastrebarsko tourist board, if you can find it).

The Plešivica countryside is delightful. Apart from the vineyards, there are lots of fruit trees in the steep fields, and in summer every village has hay drying picturesquely on the charming Slovenian-style latticed hay-ricks – designed surely with aesthetics rather than practicality in mind. Wagons and trailers full of brightly coloured beehives are strategically placed to allow the bees access to the best of the local nectar, and romantic hilltop churches crest every horizon.

 WHERE TO STAY AND EAT

🏠 **Krešimir Režek** Plešivica 39; 🌐 01 629 4836; f 01 629 4387; www.rezek.hr. Down below Ivančić, this winery not only does tastings but has a handful of nice rooms, with the same wonderful views you get from the restaurant. Krešimir himself is very friendly & helpful, but doesn't have much in the way of English; fortunately his excellent Rajnski Rizling does a great job of breaking down the language barrier. *Dbl €47 with b/fast.*

🏠 **Vinska Kuća Jana** Prodin Dol; 🌐 01 628 7372; f 01 628 7337; www.jana.hr. If the setting isn't as picturesque as the places listed, the welcome is just as warm, & you can stay in one of the newly refurbished

rooms upstairs. Wine tasting happens all year round, by appointment, while the restaurant specialises in grilled meat & freshly caught trout. It's a bit hard to find: from Prodin Dol go 2.1km south on a gravel track marked 'Klet Jana', then turn hard right at the tatty wooden sign 'Vinsko Kuća Jana' & continue up a few hundred metres. If you're coming from the south, look for a sign that says 'Klet Jana' to the right, then follow the gravel road uphill for 1.7km to the junction & turn left at the same tatty wooden sign. *Dbl €43 with b/fast.*

✕ **Restoran Ivančić** Plešivica 45; 🌐 01 629 3303; www.restoran-ivancic.hr. Housed in a large green

4

building that's easy to spot from below, & with a view to die for from the terrace, this local favourite has been serving up its own homemade specialities like *pršut*, dried sausage & cheese since 1999. Famous for its goulash, meat stews & hearty soups, it's also vegetarian-friendly, with cheeses, vegetable dishes, gourmet omelettes & the like. Relatively expensive, & extremely popular at w/ends – booking strongly recommended. ✕ **Velimir Korak** Plešivica 34; ☎/f 01 629 3088; www.vino-korak.hr. Above Režek, near the church, this

place also has a stunning view out over the neighbouring vineyards, & is one of the nicest places of all to try wines or their locally made *rakija*, including a fabulous *oskoruša* liqueur, made from the fruit of their service tree (*sorbus domestica*). A tasting area is set out in the garden under the shade of the lime trees, & there's also a family-run restaurant serving up tasty local specialities for groups, but only if you book in advance. ⊕ *12.00–21.00 Fri, 09.00–21.00 Sat.*

KARLOVAC

Most people never see more of Karlovac than the big town suburbs and housing blocks on the outskirts as they speed past on the motorway, but dig a little deeper and you'll find a wonderful provincial old town and somewhere great to stay.

Karlovac (originally Carlstadt) was created from nothing, by the Austro-Hungarians, as a defence against the Turks, with the foundations being laid on 13 July 1579.

A Renaissance six-pointed star defined the limits of the town, and its moats were kept well supplied with water by the citadel's situation, between the Kupa and Korana rivers.

As the Turkish threat receded, Karlovac grew in size and importance – notwithstanding a catastrophic fire in 1692 that razed it to the ground – and became a wealthy and influential provincial capital. Baroque houses and palaces sprang up, and the town walls were pulled down. The shape of the old town is still clearly defined, however, with the moats and earthworks now forming a near-continuous circuit of lovely parks and gardens around the former citadel, or Zvijezda (star).

Karlovac's great claim to fame is its local brewery, one of Croatia's first, which produces the excellent, and deservedly popular beer, Karlovačko Pivo, which you'll see all over the country.

GETTING THERE AND AROUND Getting to Karlovac is easy – it's under an hour from Zagreb, and both buses and trains run pretty much every half hour. There are also good onward connections to Rijeka and Zadar.

The bus station is less than ten minutes southwest of the old town – head up the main north–south axis, Prilaz Vjećeslava Holjevca, and then turn right along Kralja Tomislava, which takes you all the way in. The train station is on the other side of the river Kupa, a kilometre north, also on Prilaz Vjećeslava Holjevca. Just east of the main bridge is the central district where you'll find the Hotel Carlstadt and the tourist office, on Petra Zrinskog, which is also known as Korzo, with the old town just behind it, away from the Kupa, to the southeast.

The **tourist office** (☎ *047 615 115;* f *047 600 602; www.karlovac-touristinfo.hr*) has good maps and can help you find a private room, at around € 25 for doubles. They also have an excellent set of maps aimed at cyclists who want to pedal round Karlovac county, and are keen participants in the 'Bike & Bed' initiative.

WHERE TO STAY Karlovac has three good places to stay, listed in order of (personal) preference. There's also a nice campsite, 15km south of town – see page 158 for details:

🏠 **Hotel Korana-Srakovčić** (15 dbls, 3 suites) Perivoj Josipa Vrbanića 8; ☎ 047 609 090; f 047 609 091; www.hotelkorana.hr. An excellent 4-star establishment in a gracious building on the banks of the River Korana, situated in a lovely park, about 10mins'

walk southeast from the Korzo. The rooms are tastefully furnished; the more expensive ones have balconies, & there's a wonderful suite. There's a nice dining room & a wonderful terrace overlooking the river, & the excellent restaurant serves up specialities

KARLOVAC

Beach

Korana
Srakovčić

Korana

Weir

PRILAZ
KORANI

ŠETALIŠTE
J MAROHNIĆA

Beach

RUSKI PUT

FRANA
KURELCA

STJEPANA RADIĆA

F PREŠERNA
I ŠIMUNIĆA

RADIĆA

I KRAŠA Plaque Column
J KRAŠA
KLAIĆA

Mrežnica
River Beach

M GAMBONA

LJONKEA

DOMOBRANSKA

Franciscan
Monastery

J NINSKOG
STJEPANA

Town
Museum

G

Pod Starim
Krovovi

Zorin
Dom

M VRBANICA

ŠMIČIKLASA

TADIJE

Bus station

Papa's
Bar

Kino
Edison

TRG J

ZRINSKI TRG

KRALJA TOMISLAVA

V NAZORA

RADIĆA

Pivnica
Carlstadt,
Mozart & Otto

J DRAŠKOVIĆA

Kupa

Motorway &
Hotel Europa

BANIJA

TRG A
STEPINCA

Carlstadt

Tiffani

OBALA I

O V MAZURANIĆA

TRNSKOG

PRILAZ V HOLJEVCA

Railway
station

DUBROVAČKA

OBALA V MAZURANIĆA

VLADKA MAČEKA

IVANA MEŠTROVIĆA

LJUDEVITA ŠESTIĆA

MIROSLAVA KRLEŽE

LUŠČIĆ

SUŠAČKA

SPLITSKA

Kupa

DUBOVAC

MARMONTOVA ALEJA

PRIMORSKA

LUŠČIĆ

Dubovac
Castle

Bradt

500m
500yds

0
0

such as quail – though there's plenty for vegetarians too. The hotel also does bike hire – 25kn for 2 hours, 100kn for the day. *Dbl €121–138; suite €185.*

🏠 **Hotel Carlstadt** (40 rooms) ⅋/f 047 611 111; www.carlstadt.hr. Situated handily right across the street from the tourist office, 1st-rate dbls come with full facilities & include a substantial buffet b/fast. It's exceptionally good value, & with such easy transport connections to Zagreb, it's a viable alternative to staying in the capital. *Dbl €62.*

🏠 **Hotel Europa** (33 rooms) Banija 161; ⅋ 047 609 666; f 047 609 667; www.hotel-europa.com.hr. Situated out by the motorway junction, this is a convenient stopover if you have your own car & you're taking a break on your way to or from the coast, but it's not well located if you're relying on public transport & planning on walking round town. It's also a bit pricey for what it is. *Dbl €92–113.*

✗ WHERE TO EAT Karlovac has lots of places to eat and drink, though fewer within the 'star' than you'd expect. That's because when the old town was bombed out in the homeland war, all the action moved up onto the Korzo, and it largely remains there – though there is a sense that things are creeping back into the quieter old town. The three cafés next door to one another opposite the tourist office – **Pivnica Carlstadt, Mozart** and **Otto** – are the busiest and trendiest places, which is a bit of a shame as they're on the main road through town, though there is also a lovely new fountain with a pair of mermaids attractively sitting in it.

The nicest place for a drink in town is **Papa's Bar**, a shameless copy of Hemingway (in Zagreb or Dubrovnik) without the pretension. Formerly the Gradska Kavana, it's in a perfect location with a big terrace and nice teak furniture overlooking the park. It's not cheap, but it's groovy, cheerful, and well worth paying for.

The smartest place to eat is at the **Hotel Korana** (see above), but my absolute favourite is **Tiffany** (which doesn't, curiously, do breakfast), a busy, cheap and cheerful pizzeria (⅋ 047 614 666) with a wood-fired oven that's recently expanded its menu to include grills and barbecue dishes. The *mala* pizza is a good size, the *velika* is what it says (large) and the monster really is a meal for six. Don't be put off by the surroundings – it's located down a slot to the left-hand side of the supermarket, which is itself down the street to the left of the Hotel Carlstadt.

The other place you might try – though the service was a bit sniffy when we were there – is **Pod Starimi Krovovi** (⅋ 047 615 420), which has a nice location in the old town, and a largish, quiet terrace. The food's good value, as it's actually a training establishment for cooks etc (hopefully not for waiters).

Finally, there's Karlovac's annual **beer festival**, which takes place on the last Friday of August (and goes well into Saturday, as you'd expect). This used to happen in the main square, with the central fountain converted into a beer pump for the occasion, which was lots of fun, but the festival is now held on the Korana River, with international folklore performances and – of course – lots of drinking. If you're in the area, it's definitely not to be missed.

WHAT TO SEE AND DO The old town is centred on the big main square, Trg Bana Jelačića, which is still rather forlorn and abandoned, following the damage sustained in the 1991 war. There's talk of one of the big buildings here being turned into a hotel, which would liven the place up – even a café terrace would help – but for the time being it's still only talk.

Check out the **Plague Column** on the west side of the square, dating from 1691, and then move smartly on to the **Franciscan Monastery and Holy Trinity Church**, on the corner. Here you'll find fine Baroque altars and a series of dramatic, neck-cricking, 18th-century frescoes across the ceiling – why they were painted alternately upside down and the right way up is anyone's guess.

Heading north out of the square towards the Kupa river you'll see an old **pharmacy**, called Crnom Orla (the black eagle), which is worth stopping in at as it retains most of its original 1726 fittings. The street leads through to the elegant Trg Strossmayer, where you'll find some vestigial ruins from Karlovac's first ever church, as well as the **Town Museum** (*Gradski Muzej;* ✆ *047 615 980; www.mdc.hr/karlovac;* ⊕ *08.00–15.00 Tue–Fri, 10.00–12.00 Sat & Sun; 10kn*), housed in a former Frankopan summer residence.

The museum is a fascinating collection of everything from fossils to Roman fragments to local art to peasant costumes to civic souvenirs – it's only a pity that the captions are in Croatian only, which can make it a bit hard to follow. In the middle of the collection there's a scale model of how Karlovac used to look, and there are some old pictures of other castles in the Žumberak region. There are also some great photographs of people hauling grain barges along the river, along with the harnesses they used to do it – when the railway came along, Karlovac lost one of its main sources of wealth.

You'll notice a couple of works by the local artist Vjekoslav Karas (1821–58). Recognised for his ready talent with a brush, Karas was sent to Florence in 1838 to study, and spent a decade in Italy perfecting his craft before returning home to his native Karlovac. Unfortunately many of his paintings have been lost, and – given that he rarely signed his work, and experimented with many different styles – there's a big problem of attribution. Some of the works are way ahead of their time, wonderfully insightful portraits that are practically Modernist, while others are embarrassingly amateurish, perhaps reflecting Karas's poor state of mental health. After a failed suicide attempt in Đakovo, where he was the guest of Bishop Strossmayer (a keen art collector), Karas successfully drowned himself in the Korana River at Karlovac, aged just 37. If you're interested in seeing more of his work, there's a whole gallery in an annexe in the new town. Staff at the museum will be happy to point you in the right direction, and may even accompany you there.

The last room of the museum features an excellent collection of peasant costumes and crafts, from pottery and weaving to embroidery and basket-work.

Continuing north, towards the Korzo and the Korana river, it's well worth taking a turn around the parks that were formerly the **walls and moats** of the old citadel – allow a half hour or so for the full circuit.

Heading anticlockwise, the first thing you'll see is a small pink *glorietta*, primarily dedicated to Croatia's fallen in World War I, and the vast neo-classical façade of the Karlovac bank. Heading west, you'll see a large, graffiti-strewn, concrete plinth, which – until its destruction by the locals in the homeland war – was the base of a huge anti-fascist monument. A little further on you'll see **Kino Edison**, which was Croatia's first cinema. It's still operational, though rather damp and run down – the present owner bought it for the well-situated café terrace, rather than cinematographic entertainment.

Beyond the cinema is Karlovac's theatre, the endearing **Zorin Dom**, which was opened in 1892, and has a small version of the Ivan Meštrović masterpiece, the *History of the Croats* (see page 109).

If you have time, it's also well worth visiting **Dubovac Castle** (✆ *047 615 980 or 098 918 1323;* ⊕ *Apr–Sep 14.00–18.00 Mon–Fri, 10.00–18.00 Sat; if visiting Oct–Mar, call the Town Museum at least a day in advance; 10kn*), up on the hill 2km west of town (it's a short drive or a half-hour walk). The castle dates from 1339 (or possibly even earlier), and was a Frankopan and then Zrinski stronghold right through to the beginning of the 19th century, when it was taken over by the French, who added crenellations to make it look more appealingly medieval (there's a picture in the town museum of what this looked like). Fortunately, it recovered its genuinely medieval look in the 20th century, and you get a great view out over the town from the top of the tower – check out the excellent relief map of the whole area, which shows all the different castles and rivers in the area. And if you're here in May, don't miss out on the annual medieval fair that takes place here.

Finally, if you're hot and bothered – and it certainly can be baking here – head down to the Korana River to the wonderful **beach**, just ten minutes from the old town centre; you can bathe in the weir here, which is excellent, or head out to less busy beaches on the Mrežnica river, 3km south of town.

SOUTH OF KARLOVAC

Southwest of Karlovac, on the road to Ogulin and Senj, you pass through **Duga Resa**, which isn't much to write home about, but there is a nice campsite, signed **Autokamp Slapić** (✆ *047 854 754 Apr–Oct;* ✆ *047 854 700 Oct–Apr; www.campslapic.hr*) south of town, just across the river Mrežnica (on an old wooden bridge) from Belavići train station. There's canoeing and safe swimming here, and it's an idyllic spot for families.

Another few kilometres down the main road brings you to **Zvečaj**, which wouldn't necessarily merit a mention here, were it not for the **Zeleni Kut** restaurant (✆ *047 866 100*), which also has a few rooms upstairs as part of the 'Bike & Bed' scheme. On a lovely terrace overlooking the river, the restaurant serves up heaps of freshwater fish, including *pastrva* (trout), *som* (catfish), *smuđ* (zander) and *štuka* (pike), at around 150kn/kg. They can also organise rafting and canoeing trips for you. (For information on Ogulin, Klek and Bjelolasica, further southwest in this direction, turn to page 224.)

Heading south rather than southwest of Karlovac, towards the Plitvice Lakes, brings you (after about 50km, and 20km short of the lakes) to the former Austro-Hungarian garrison town of **Slunj**. Badly damaged during the war of the 1990s, the town's churches at least have now been fully restored, along with the main reason for coming here, the **Rastoke Mills**.

Built to take advantage of the waterfalls where the Slunjčica river drops into the Korana, some of the watermills are now back in working order and a stroll around them is a delight. If you want to swim make sure you choose the Korana, not the Slunjčica – the former warms up to a balmy 28°C in summer, while the latter never rises above a chilly 14°C. If its 'first-class trouts' you're fishing for, however, then the Slunjčica is your man.

If you want to stay in the area, there's the **Mirjana Rastoke Hotel** (✆ *047 787 205; www.mirjana-rastoke.com; dbl €36*), which also arranges excursions in the area, a few kilometres back along the road towards Karlovac.

PLITVICE LAKES NATIONAL PARK

Croatia's best-known and most-visited natural attraction – and a UNESCO World Heritage site since 1979 – is the Plitvice Lakes National Park (✆ *053 751 015;* f *053 751 013; www.np-plitvicka-jezera.hr*). Covering a total of nearly 300km², the prize here is 16 lakes, falling from one to the next in a series of gushing waterfalls. The lakes are set in deep forests still populated by bears, wolves and wild boar, and are all the more unusual for being found in the middle of a typically dry karst region, where surface water is extremely rare.

The national park has been very carefully exploited, and although it can get busy – 600,000 people come annually, averaging around 4,000 people a day in the summer months – the crowds are rarely intolerable. Traffic is encouraged round one-way systems to avoid congestion, and the routes are often carried along attractive wooden walkways serving the dual purpose of avoiding erosion and allowing people to walk over, under, across and alongside the waterfalls, and around the lakes.

The whole park ranges in altitude from 380m to 1,280m, but the lakes are all situated between 502m and 637m, with the largest single waterfall (Veliki Slap) being nearly 70m tall. The combination of running water and altitude makes the park wonderfully refreshing almost all through the summer, although it can be cold and

PLITVICE LAKES NATIONAL PARK

gloomy – not to mention frozen solid – in winter. April and October are the best times to visit – the former with the water flow increased by melting snows, and the latter with the deciduous woods enriched with fabulous autumn colours.

Plitvice was occupied by the Serbs from 1991 to 1995, and the staff and management became refugees. On their return, they found the park mercifully undamaged ecologically, although the park offices and the hotels were totally unusable. Since then, the hotels and other facilities have been entirely rebuilt, and the park today is better than ever.

GETTING THERE AND AWAY Plitvice is situated a little over halfway down the main road from Zagreb to Zadar. Regular buses run from both, and also up from Split. The park has two entrances, wittily called Ulaz 1 and Ulaz 2.

In theory Ulaz 1 (the northern entrance) serves the lower lakes, while Ulaz 2 (the southern entrance) is the access point for the upper ones, but for most people Ulaz 2 is the more useful. It's here that you'll find most of the infrastructure, including the three hotels, the tourist office with access to private accommodation, a post office, a shop and a self-service restaurant – and it's in fact within easy reach of both the upper and lower lakes.

If you don't have your own transport, then leaving the park may be more difficult than arriving. Regular buses pass through on their way to Zadar, Zagreb and Split, but if these are full, or the driver doesn't like the cut of your jib, they have a habit of cruising right on past.

Testimony to this is borne out by the graffiti that builds up over the season in the bus shelter at Ulaz 2, before being removed each winter. In the unlikely event you won't have time to read some for yourself, here's a selection I culled while waiting:

The only natural wonder we saw was the fog and the rain – still waiting at 2.30 for the 1.40 bus.

It takes two hours to get to Plitvice but two days to get out.

So what, no bus, who cares – who wants to leave this paradise? Later … I retract that – a bus, any bus!

and my personal favourite:

Great tourist strategy!

There isn't much you can do to improve this situation, but earlier buses do seem to be better than ones later in the day.

At the tourist office you can buy a map and obtain multi-lingual information on the park. Beside the office there's a small and slightly overpriced supermarket, and nearby there's an open-air grill bar (with trick bitumen on the seats when I was last here, just waiting to stain your clothes). If you have your own car, there's more than adequate parking at both entrances.

Entry to the national park costs a fairly hefty 110kn in summer (80 in winter), though the money is well spent, going towards the park's upkeep and protection. On the ticket is a wonderful series of hieroglyphs explaining the park rules, most of which go without saying: don't pick flowers, make fires, engrave trees, steal nests or break stalactites. Some of the others aren't so obvious: don't leave the paths, sleep rough, go paddling in the lakes or dance wildly around to the sound of your boom-box. The park is open every day of the year, from 08.00 to 16.00 in winter, 08.00 to 18.00 in spring and autumn and 07.00–20.00 in summer. Ticket sales close about four hours before the park closes.

WHERE TO STAY There are three hotels in the park, the **Bellevue**, the **Plitvice** and the **Jezero** (*central reservations for all three, as well as tourist information and private rooms* *on* ✆ *053 751 015;* **f** *053 751 013*), with prices rising slightly and quality rising significantly as you move up the scale. Expect to pay € 75 for the cheapest double at the Bellevue off season, or € 120 for the best double at the Jezero in the middle of summer. Book way, way ahead, if you want to stay here, as even off season all three tend to draw the conference crowd. If you have your own wheels there's also the Grabovac (same contact details as above), 12km up the road towards Zagreb, which has doubles in season for € 70.

Private rooms are widely available, but often far away, which can be a problem if you don't have your own transport. Prices – expect to pay € 30–50 for a double – depend much more on location than quality, which is universally fine. The room I stayed in was at the upper end of the range but only a couple of kilometres from Ulaz 2; cheaper rooms can be anything up to 15km away. Private rooms can also be booked ahead if you're in Zagreb through the national park's office there, just up from the station at Tomislava 19 (✆ *01 461 3586;* **f** *01 492 2270*).

Camping's a problem if you don't have your own wheels – the nearest campsite is **Korana** (✆ *053 751 888*), 8km north of Ulaz 1, which charges € 23 for two adults with a tent and car.

✗ WHERE TO EAT For eating, your options are fairly limited. There's a good-value self-service restaurant at Ulaz 2, though it's not always open in the evening, while at Ulaz 1 there's the capacious Lička Kuća restaurant, serving meaty local specialities (the lamb here is first rate). Otherwise the hotels all have restaurants but they may be full with their own residents. If you do get in at the Jezero's restaurant, downstairs from reception, the tagliatelle with truffles is truly excellent. Otherwise you can pick up picnic food at the mini-market at Ulaz 2.

WHAT TO SEE AND DO The lakes were created and are maintained by their unusual vegetation – the mosses, algae and other freshwater plants absorb the calcium in the water and then deposit it as calciferous mud. This can be seen clearly as a white coating on submerged tree trunks and roots in the smaller lakes. The water flow causes this calciferous mud to be carried to the lips of the lakes, and deposited there, eventually solidifying as travertine (tufa), with the long-term effect that the whole lake system is gradually gaining altitude.

In the short term, the effect is that lots of people are keen to come and see Plitvice, and life has been organised so that this is as easy as possible – to the extent that there's a panoramic train ride, a couple of boats on one of the largest lakes, and a series of itineraries from 1 to 10 hours long that take in the most scenic parts of the park.

After the initial impression of being almost too looked after has worn off, it tends to be replaced by something akin to euphoria – the lakes really are beautiful, after all, and you'd have to be very determined not to be impressed by that much moving water. You can even begin to see why people who live in these conditions start believing in water gods.

Each of the lakes seems to be a different colour, ranging from turquoise to emerald through every blue and green you could imagine. In places the lakes seem as still and reflective as a cathedral, elsewhere they run away fast, frothing through steep gullies and shooting out from fissures in the rock. The magical noise of falling water drowns out even the shrillest of small children. On the less frequented paths it's easy to imagine the bears and wolves, as you walk across a deeply shaded bed of leaves, crunching underfoot.

In a perfect world you'd have at least two full days (ie: three nights) to explore the whole park, but you can get a good impression of it all in a single day. Even if you're on an excursion, up from the coast or down from Zagreb, and you have only a couple of hours here, you won't regret it. Either way, try to start as early as possible, to avoid the worst of the crowds.

Apart from the marked itineraries, which lead you round the best-known sights, there are many other paths open to the public in the national park, though access to them is quietly discouraged by the park management, as there have been incidents of people despoiling nature off the beaten track. If you are wandering away from the marked trails, be ecologically friendly, and stay on the paths.

If you're doing any serious walking – or even if you're just interested – the park publishes an excellent 1:50,000 scale map of the area, including all the footpaths, with a 1:25,000 scale bird's-eye view of the lakes themselves on the reverse, along with all sorts of useful information about the lakes' relative altitudes etc. With the aid of this you can easily find a couple of days' walking in the area, none of which is too strenuous.

It's inadvisable, however, to be in the wilds after nightfall – the bears and wolves avoid the main paths and the crowds, but they do patrol at night. The wolves are normally only seen in winter, but a hungry bear, or one that thinks you're too close to its cubs, may be inquisitive.

There have been no incidents in recent years involving tourists, but it was here, on 16 April 1988 (a few days before my first ever visit to the lakes), that a national park warden was killed by a bear. The poor animal was apparently confused by a storm, and anxious to protect its cub, when it was surprised by the unfortunate warden. Being a Serb, he could probably be counted as the first victim in the Serbo-Croat war, which actually took off here in Plitvice, when the Serbs took over the management offices in March 1991.

Fortunately, the warden is the only recorded human fatality from a Croatian bear in more than 50 years, but local people remain understandably cautious, and discourage the idea of camping out in the woods (which is illegal, anyway). Walk in the daytime and stay on the paths marked on the maps and you'll be quite safe. There are absolutely no wild animals round here that would attack in the daytime unless seriously provoked.

If you're in Plitvice on the last Sunday of May there's a folk wedding held by Veliki Slap. This was once no doubt a highly traditional affair, but now has the air of being staged for the tourists. Nonetheless, even the most cynical visitor should be impressed by the traditional dress, the falling water all but drowning out the songs, and the folk dancing and festivities held afterwards.

JASTREBARSKO AND THE TUROPOLJE

Halfway between Zagreb and Karlovac, the town of Jastrebarsko gives access to the Plešivica vineyards to the north (see page 153), while to the south there's an excellent ornithological reserve, at Crna Mlaka. Further east you'll find the Turopolje, a region characterised by old villages and wooden houses and churches, bordered by the Vukomeričke Gorice hills to the west, the meandering Sava to the east, and bracketed by Zagreb to the northwest and Sisak to the southeast.

Exploring the region's not really possible without your own transport, although you can get to Jastrebarsko easily enough, and Velika Mlaka and Velika Gorica in the Turopolje are both on Zagreb bus route #268.

For a map of the area, see page 151.

JASTREBARSKO AND CRNA MLAKA Jastrebarsko itself is a bit of a commercial one-street town, spread out along the main road from Zagreb to Karlovac. It's worth checking in at the **tourist office** (℣/f *01 627 2940; www.tzgj.hr*), across the street from the bus station, for easily the best map of the area and details of the local vineyards, as well as the particulars of a growing number of agro-tourism offerings.

If you're stuck in town there's a moderately interesting town museum, and there's a pleasant park (walk west down Zrinsko Frankopanska, and across the stream) around the decaying fortress-like Erdödy Castle, built in the 16th century and apparently unmaintained ever since. There's a hotel in town, the **Jaska** (✆ *01 628 1044;* f *01 628 3580*), with functional doubles at around € 60. There are also a few private rooms – check with the tourist office, or see the '*smještaj*' page of their website (Croatian only).

Southeast, across the motorway, is Crna Mlaka (literally Black Marsh). The area was originally conceived as a vast fish farm by the Austro-Hungarians at the end of the 19th century, complete with a narrow-gauge railway running up to join the main line to Zagreb, and a mansion, endearingly named Ribograd ('fish city'). The railway's long disused, and Ribograd's falling apart, but Crna Mlaka lives on as a **bird sanctuary** (✆ *01 628 3453; www.crna-mlaka.htnet.hr*), and it's now home to all sorts of rare and endangered species, including herons in abundance, and highly secretive black storks, who, unlike their white compatriots, prefer to stay in the woods, well away from people. There's talk of the lakes being drained to make way for a golf course, but there's no sign of one yet.

To reach Crna Mlaka, turn left immediately after paying the toll off the motorway (or right immediately before reaching it, if you're coming from Jastrebarsko), and drive 7km down gravel tracks (turn left after 5km, at the sign saying 'IHOR Crna Mlaka'), keeping your eyes peeled for herons. If you're lucky, the restaurant, specializing unsurprisingly in freshwater fish, will be open (it seems unable to make up its mind whether or not it's actually a going concern), but even if it's not, it's great to explore the unmarked gravel tracks which make for pleasant, undisturbed walking around the huge ponds.

THE TUROPOLJE

THE TUROPOLJE The region southeast of Zagreb along the west bank of the Sava is known as the Turopolje, and is worth passing through on your way to Lonjsko Polje (see page 164). Once Zagreb's suburbs have petered out, you'll find old villages and timber churches, and wooden staircases leading up the outside of houses to the upper quarters. If you're planning on exploring the region in any detail, get maps and information ahead of time from the friendly and helpful Zagreb County tourist office in Zagreb (see page 84 for details).

In **Velika Gorica**, the de facto capital of the region, it's well worth stopping in at the **Museum of the Turopolje** (*Muzej Turopolje;* ✆ *01 622 1325; www.muzej-turopolja.hr;* ☉ *Apr–Sep 10.00–18.00 Tue–Fri, 10.00–13.00 Sat & Sun; Oct–Mar 09.00–16.00 Tue–Fri, 10.00–13.00 Sat & Sun; 8kn*). The museum is situated in a nice pastel building on the main street – because of Velika Gorica's one-way system, this is actually the road back towards Zagreb – and contains a small art gallery downstairs and the main museum upstairs. The collection is the usual hotchpotch of everything from ethnographic exhibits to artefacts and images that are historically important to the region. Check out the mammoth tusks and molar, and a small room of naïve art, and in particular the bitter 1977 work by Dragutin Tombetaš, entitled *Gastarbeiter in Öl* (immigrant workers in a sardine can).

If you're into Roman excavations, then you may want to head 9km northeast of Velika Gorica, almost as far as the Sava river, to **Ščitarevo**, which was the former 4th-century Roman town of **Andautonia**. The excavations are quite extensive, but you need to know your stuff to get the most out of the site.

Where to stay If you want to stay in Velika Gorica, there are a couple of options:

🏠 **Hotel Garny** ✆ 01 625 3600; f 01 625 3601; www.hotel-garny.hr. The rooms are perhaps a bit functional for the price, but the swimming pool & sauna compensate. *Dbl €105.*

🏠 **Bijela Ruža** ✆ 01 622 1358; f 01 622 1400; www.hotel-gorica.hr. Business-like place in the middle of town with rather plain dbls. *Dbl €52.*

The Turopolje is most famous for its old **wooden churches**, of which more than a dozen remain – though some of them are spectacularly hard to find. If you see only one, make it **St Barbara's**, which is incongruous amongst the suburban houses of **Velika Mlaka**, off to the left, just before you get to Pleso Airport. The all-wooden church was originally built in 1642, and the decorative work inside covers every available surface. Most interesting of all is the double altarpiece, which folds out to reveal further religious scenes behind. If the church is closed – which it is, usually – ask for Ljubica Lacković, who has a key (and will expect you to make a donation).

Another wooden church that is easy to see is the **Chapel of the Wounded Jesus**, which you'll have noticed if you arrived by plane, as it's right by Pleso Airport. Less accessible altogether, and not really worth the detour unless restoration work has advanced substantially, is the **Chapel of St John the Baptist**, in **Buševec**, 8km southeast of Velika Gorica, on the road to Sisak. If you're in the area, however, it is worth turning off the main road to the village of **Mraclin**, which still has quite a few original Turopolje wooden houses, and retains much more of a 19th-century than 21st-century feel.

Further south, and lost in the hills above the river Kupa, are three more wooden churches worth a look. The first, in a wonderful hilltop location, is the **Chapel of Sts Peter and Paul**, at **Cerje Pokupsko**, about 15km southwest of Buševec. The church looks like it could be centuries old, but the date on the front says 1932. The next, the **Chapel of St George**, at **Lijevi Štefanki**, is one of the oldest churches, which was built at another location in 1677 and then moved here in 1704 – it's quite hard to find, however: turn left down a track about 5km west of Cerje Pokupsko, on a sharp right-hand bend, on the road to Donja Kupčina. The key is held at the farmhouse next door, and it's well worth making the effort as the interior is beautifully painted. Finally, if you've come this far, the **Chapel of St John the Baptist**, at **Lukinić Brdo**, has been well renovated (following damage in the homeland war) and makes a great spot for a picnic, with a table – just below the cemetery containing generation after generation of the same family names – offering fine views out over rolling forested hills.

At the western extremity of the region – on the road to Karlovac, and close to Crna Mlaka (see above), is the small, pretty town of **Donja Kupčina**. It's a favourite nesting spot for storks (see also Lonjsko Polje, below), and there's a small open-air **Ethnographic Museum** (\ 01 629 2157), which gives you a good insight into how village life was lived here until relatively recent times. To visit officially, you need to contact Želka Petrović Osmak at the Ethnographic Museum in Zagreb (\ 01 482 6220; e zpetrovic@emz.hr; www.emz.hr) and make an appointment, but on the day we were there you could wander round happily enough on your own.

The southeastern end of the Turopolje – marked by the first bridge across the Sava since Zagreb – is dominated by the industrial town of **Sisak**. The solid **medieval castle** on the river doesn't entirely compensate for the huge oil refinery here, or the complete absence of road directions. There is, however, an accommodation option, the no-nonsense five-storey **Hotel Panonija** (\ 044 515 600; f 044 515 601; www.hotel-panonija.hr), which is three blocks back from the river and five minutes south of the bus and train stations, with spacious doubles at €94. Make sure you ask for a renovated room, however, as the hotel served as refugee accommodation during the homeland war.

Sisak is also the northern gateway to the Lonjsko Polje.

LONJSKO POLJE

Downstream from Sisak, the river Sava meanders slowly through the great marshy swamplands of the Lonjsko Polje. Prone to frequent flooding (the Sava can rise by up to 10m) and full of fish, the area is hugely popular with migrating birds, and especially with storks. The reedy shores of the ox-bow lakes make for excellent nesting grounds for wading birds such as white egrets, grey herons and spoonbills.

LONJSKO POLJE

Spotted Turopolje pigs root through the flooded oak forests, while dark, chunky Posavina horses – protected, and seen only in this region – graze in the summer pastures. Rustic villages preserve traditional oak houses, with barns on the ground floor and external wooden stairs leading to the living accommodation upstairs. It's a rare chance to see a landscape that was once common across central Europe, and is on the tentative list of UNESCO World Heritge Sites.

On top of many of the houses in the area, and sometimes on platforms on telegraph poles, you'll see big, tatty storks' nests, and (if you're here between April and August) plenty of big, tatty storks, too. They're most endearing. The storks arrive here in spring, and lay three to five eggs per couple, with both parents sharing the month-long incubation duty. The chicks then spend around two months in the nest, and if you're here in May or June you'll see lots of activity going on, with the young growing fast and permanently hungry, and one of the parents always on the move, looking for food.

During August and September, the storks ship out, using the eastern migration path through Turkey and the Middle East, and then along the Nile to central Africa, with some even ending up in South Africa every year.

The Lonjsko Polje (*www.pp-lonjsko-polje.hr*) was declared a nature park in 1990, but you wouldn't necessarily know it – apart from the uninformative sign at the park's border. There's an information centre in the main stork village, Čigoć, at number 26 (\/f *044 715 115*). It's officially open daily from 08.00 to 16.00, but if you find it closed then call Davor Anzil on his mobile (m *098 222 085*). There's also another office in Krapje (m *098 222 086*).

Most visitors will be content enough to drive along the pretty 70km road, most of which is now tarred, which runs through the park from Sisak to Jasenovac – there's a bus from Sisak, but apart from that public transport's not really an option. The villages along here are among the prettiest in the region, and all have storks in greater or fewer numbers, along with yards full of ducks, chickens, bantams and the occasional turkey. Many of the older traditional wooden houses are collapsing in on themselves, but a good number have been restored as weekenders. They're really quite beautiful. Despite the limited accommodation, it would make for the perfect cycle ride.

From Sisak it's 30km to Čigoć, via the single-street villages of Topolovac, Prelošćica, Lukavec Posavski and Gušće. After Čigoć it's another 40km on to Jasenovac, passing through Kratečko, Možilovčica, Suvoj, Lonja, Trebež, Puška, Krapje and Drenov Bok on the way. There are a handful of places where you can sleep or eat (see below).

More serious birdwatchers should contact the park office in advance (if they can – the staff are even more elusive than the black stork), as there are several special ornithological reserves, protecting some 236 species of bird.

⌂ WHERE TO STAY AND EAT

⌂ **Tradicije Čigoć** Čigoć 7a; \ 044 715 124; www.tradicije-cigoc.hr. In Čigoć itself, with a restaurant, and *rooms going for €29 pp B&B.*

⌂ **Usti Lonja** Lonja 8; \ 044 710 621; www.ustilonja.hr. Wonderfully hospitable place in the village of Lonja, between Čigoć and Krapje. Traditional, rustic wooden architecture, & a lovely terrace restaurant with superb food, including delicious grilled carp. *Dbl €50 B&B, FB & HB also available for an additional €9 pp per meal.*

If you're in the area (or driving along the *autocesta* east of Zagreb) it's well worth stopping at the 18th-century church of **Our Lady of the Snows**, in the otherwise unremarkable town of **Kutina** – though there is an adequate hotel, the eponymous Kutina (\ *044 692 400;* f *044 682 729; www.hotel-kutina.hr*), with doubles from €54 to €74.

The plain, simple exterior of the church hides a plain, simple interior. No, of course it doesn't. Inside, it's wildly over-decorated, with stucco, putti, plaster saints, carved pilasters, gilt, medallions, *trompe l'oeil*, the whole bit. The main altar, entirely filling the sanctuary, is almost impossible to look at.

JASENOVAC

Where the Sava joins the Bosnian border, you'll find what must be the saddest town in Croatia. Famous only for having been the site of Croatia's worst concentration camp during World War II, Jasenovac was then fought over by both sides in the 1990s war.

Today the town is still half-abandoned and has a moderately desperate air. Many of the bombed-out buildings have yet to be properly repaired, and it looks as if Jasenovac must be way down on someone's agenda of places to fix up. With the Hotel Sava still in ruins, there's nowhere to stay (not, frankly, that you'd want to) and nothing to do. You could eat at the one Kod Ribica gostionica, however, which seems to attract Bosnians from across the border and does a pretty mean fish stew, *fiš paprikaš*.

The main – let's be honest, the only – reason to visit Jasenovac is to see the site of the former concentration camp. To many visitors it seems as if Croatia would rather forget the camp altogether. In the museum (✆ *044 672 319; www.jusp-jasenovac.hr; ⊕ 09.00–17.00 Tue–Fri, 10.00–16.00 Sat & Sun*), you can see a small collection of photographs and uniforms, but little else.

The main memorial is a dramatic concrete sculpture in the shape of an enormous flower. The path to it is made of old railway sleepers, and on the way you'll find a brass map showing where the huts once stood. There's also a poignant train and cattle wagons (a gift from the Slovenian railway company), like the ones which would have brought prisoners here in the 1940s.

POŽEGA

Set in pretty countryside 175km east of Zagreb (35km from the Nova Gradiska exit off the *autocesta*), the town of Požega makes a great overnight stop if you're heading east, and is within striking distance of the Papuk Nature Park. Under Turkish occupation from 1537 to 1691, it became thoroughly Baroque during the 18th century and still has an attractive old town, centred on the elongated triangular main square, Trg Svetog Trojstva.

On the south side of the square there are two churches, separated by the huge pale-grey wedding-cake frontage of the Franciscan monastery, while the north side is made up of a lovely row of ochre-yellow arcaded houses. In the middle of the square is a Baroque **Plague Column** (being restored at the time of writing) from the middle of the 18th century, which apparently cost – according to the inscription – the princely sum of 300 forints and 2,000 eggs.

A block away to the east is the **Church of St Teresa**, which became the town's cathedral in 1997 on the creation of the diocese. It has a beautiful, freshly restored front, all pale yellow with decorative mustard-icing swirls. The lower Baroque capitals are topped with winged angels, while those higher up are crowned with formalised stone vases, the whole leading up to an elegant clock tower. Inside there's a big Baroque altarpiece and choir, and dark paintings everywhere.

Opposite the church entrance, in the small park, there's a fine, soldierly statue of Fra Luka Ibrišimović Sokol, who apparently single-handedly smote the Turks here in 1689, although he was nearly 70 at the time.

Finally, head north to where the road intersects with **Kamenita Vrata** (literally Stone Gates), and you'll find a new brick-built spiral memorial to the (mostly young) men who lost their lives here during the war of the early '90s. Each of the 102 victims has a plaque at eye-level, and it's heart-rending to read their names and dates.

Like most towns in Slavonia, Požega livens things up with plenty of festivals. Starting the spring off with a bang – literally – is the annual show of cannons and mortars on 12 March, St Gregory's Day, which also features mortar fire in Požega's vineyards, to symbolise the routing of the Turks. In May you can choose between the

4

National Dog Show or the unusual festival of Croatian one-minute films held here, and a month later there are contests to see who can cook up the best fish stews and spicy kulen sausages. In September the town hosts the 'Golden Strings of Slavonia' festival, which brings in crowds from miles around. Contact the tourist office (*Trg Sv Trojstva;* \ *034 274 900;* f *034 274 901; www.pozega-tz.hr*) in the arcades on the main square for more details.

GETTING THERE AND AWAY Požega is on a branch line of the rail network, with eight trains a day coming up from the junction with the main line to Slavonski Brod (change at Nova Kapela-Batrina), and is also well served by buses. The bus and train stations are both northeast of the centre of town – head straight down Stjepan Radića to the main square.

WHERE TO STAY AND EAT There are a number of small pensions in Požega, with the nicest and best located being the **Vila Stanišić** (\ *034 312 168;* f *034 272 608*) on Franje Tuđmana. Head north up the main pedestrian street, which turns into Kamenita Vrata, then turn right and it's on the right, just after the first intersection. The place consists of eight plain but clean rooms above the restaurant; doubles go for around € 40 a night. The other option is the town's only official hotel, the **Grgin Dol** (*Grgin dol 20;* \ *034 273 222;* f *034 272 296*), east of the main square a few hundred metres, and then signed south, just up the hill. It's pretty run-down, to be honest, and they would have done a lot better spending money on fixing up the infrastructure rather than putting satellite TV in every room – in this author's humble opinion. The rooms are spacious enough, however, and many have balconies. Doubles go for € 60 a night, including an astoundingly greasy yet tasty cooked breakfast.

For eating and drinking you'll find heaps of cheap and cheerful places in the pedestrianised streets just north of the main square; the Zrinski pizza bar is a perennial favourite.

PAPUK NATURE PARK

The Papuk Nature Park (*www.pp-papuk.hr*) covers the hills about 15km north of Požega, and rises from the plain up to nearly 1,000m. There's nothing especially dramatic or spectacular about it, but the walking up here is lovely, through deep deciduous woods and along clear, burbling brooks.

The park was only designated in 1999, so there's not much in the way of infrastructure in place yet, though there are two small park offices, one in Velika (*Stjepana Radića 46;* \ *034 313 030;* f *034 313 027*), 12km north of Požega, and the other over the hill, on the northwestern side of the park, in Voćin (\/f *033 565 296*). Whichever one you call first, you're likely to be asked to speak to the other, but they're friendly and helpful when you finally get through.

The park acts as a watershed for numerous refreshing streams that flow down to the Drava to the north and the Sava to the south, and has lots of well-marked trails through the beech and oak woods. None of the hiking is especially challenging, and the fairly dense forest cover means that spectacular views are few and far between, but it's nonetheless one of the pleasantest places in Slavonia. The flora is exceptional (with around 1,500 species) and there's a 33m waterfall hidden deep in the woods. Geological curiosities include rock columns that were thrown up millions of years ago during volcanic disturbances, and there are even three ruined castles you can clamber up to – the ruins of Ružica grad are about 20 minutes up a marked trail from the town of Orahovica, and there's another old fort above Velika.

As you come up through Velika from Požega, the road forks right and leads up to thermal baths, which are extremely popular on hot summer weekends with the locals.

PAPUK NATURE PARK

5km

3 miles

Voćin

Brač

Humljani

Orahovica

D Pištana

Pušina

Slatinski Drenovac

Đuzluk

Ružica Castle ruins

790m
Karpovac

Jankovac

731m

Nevoljaš

820m
Ćeljakovački Vis

743m
Klokočica

Papuk
953m

Ivačka Glava

Velički Grad
ruins

Toplička Glava
(thermal baths)

Velika

Vetovo

Kutjevo

Kaptol

Požega

Stražeman

Ruins of
Kamengrad Castle

Voćin

887m
Toduk

N Zvečevo

Lučinci

Kamenska

Above here, on the last stretch of tarred road, there are some lovely picnic and barbecue spots in the small meadows along the river, and even a couple of small grill restaurants. It's a charming place, though there's no obvious public transport that would get you here.

SLAVONSKI BROD

Heading east into Slavonia, especially on public transport, you're likely to pass through Slavonski Brod, as it's a major transport hub. There's no particular reason to break your journey here, however, unless you've come specially for the Brodsko Kolo, in June, which is arguably Slavonia's (and some would argue Croatia's) best folk festival. On the other hand, if you have a couple of hours between buses or trains, there are things to see.

Until 1891, Slavonski Brod was a military town, but during the 20th century it became an important staging post for trade and industry, both on the Sava, and across the river into Bosnia & Herzegovina. Today, there's still not a great deal of traffic across the bridge to Bosanski Brod (called Srpski Brod by the mainly Serbian population on that side of the Sava), and the remaining shell-scarred Austro-Hungarian buildings on the Croatian side continue to bear witness to the shelling from the Bosnian Serb side during the homeland war.

From the bus or train stations, head south down Vukovarska towards the river, 15 minutes away on foot. On the left you'll pass the large grassy park which was the essence of the town for centuries – there's not a whole lot of the **ruined fortress** (*trvđ ava*) left now, however, but you can get an idea of the size and scale of the place from the earthworks and the crumbling, overgrown brick walls.

Southeast of the fortress, on the other side of Vukovarska is the pedestrianised main square, Trg Mažuranić, which gives on to the river. Here you'll find a number of shops, banks and café terraces but not a whole lot else. Along the river from the main square is Slavonski Brod's only other main attraction, the 18th-century **Franciscan Monastery**, which was the religious and cultural heart of the town when it was a garrison. The church is nothing special, but the Baroque cloisters are lovely, with the monks' cells overlooking the garden in the middle, an oasis of tranquillity.

During June, the town hosts the **Brodsko Kolo**, Croatia's oldest folk dance festival, which also features various horse-drawn cart and carriage contests, lots of traditional costumes, a big folk parade, and plenty of eating and drinking. The tourist office has all the details.

WHERE TO STAY AND EAT The tourist information office (*Trg Pobjede 28/1;* \/f *035 447 721; www.tzgsb.hr*) will be able to help you with accommodation if you want to stay over. There are a couple of hotels in the centre, the Central (\ *035 492 030; www.hotelcentralsb.hr; dbl* €*92*), newly opened in 2008, and the more expensive Savus (\ *035 405 888; www.savus-hotel.com; dbl* €*112*). There are also a number of small (if somewhat functional) pensions available. For eateries, the Zvonimir, just west of the main square and almost on the river, serves up good local fish dishes at a reasonable price, though don't expect anything sophisticated like an English-language menu. For decent pizza, try the cheerful faux-rustic simplicity of Mama Mia, on Ante Starčićeva, heading east out of Trg Mažuranić.

If you have your own wheels, then a quiet, friendly place to stay is **Hotel Vinarija Zdjelarević** (*Vinogradska 102, Brodski Stupnik;* \ *035 427 775;* f *035 427 040; www.zdjelarevic.hr*) west of town, in the wine-growing countryside. They have nice doubles at €80, with half board good value at €105 – featuring hearty local fare and a chance to dip into their wine cellar.

ĐAKOVO

The town of Đakovo lies 50km northeast of Slavonski Brod and 35km south of Osijek. With an inspired, twin-spired cathedral and excellent local food and drink, it makes a near-perfect Slavonian stopover – assuming, of course, you don't crash your car here, like I did (before, not after, the gourmet lunch, I might add).

Whichever way you come into town, the fantastic red-brick neo-Romanesque **Cathedral of St Peter** stands out for miles. Commissioned by Bishop Strossmayer – Đakovo was his see – it was built between 1866 and 1882, and features a wealth of attractive minimalist detail amongst the brickwork. The 84m twin towers are topped with small spires, while from the centre of the church rises a fine 54m cupola.

Inside, it's a glorious, spacious building, with fluted columns, Romanesque arches, and high ceilings. The upper sides of the nave feature almost Pre-Raphaelite biblical frescoes – the first scene on the left shows Adam and Eve, with Adam stolen shamelessly from the roof of the Sistine Chapel, and Eve a passable copy of Botticelli's *Venus*. The ceilings, with gold stars on a deep blue background, wouldn't look out of place in a Tuscan cathedral, while the walls of the apses and sanctuary are decorated with startlingly realistic *trompe l'oeil* curtains. The whole is quite delightful.

Underground there's a large crypt, with Strossmayer's tomb, but it's rarely open. If you're a Strossmayer completist, you'll also want to visit the **Strossmayer Museum**, across the street from the cathedral, on the corner of the pedestrian zone, where you'll find the bishop's letters and other personal items, but it really is for fanatics only.

At the far end of the pedestrian street – full of cafés, bars and ice cream parlours spilling out on to the pavement – is **All Saints Church**, which was the town's main mosque (Đakovo was occupied by the Turks from 1536 to 1678) until the plain Baroque façade was slapped on in the 19th century.

Đakovo's main annual event is the *Đakovački Vezovi* (meaning 'Đakovo embroidery') at the beginning of July, which features lots of traditional costumes (and embroidery), folk singing and dancing, and parades of the traditional wedding wagons, which are a whole lot of fun. Concerts are put on in the cathedral, while at the racecourse you'll also get the chance to see competitive trap-and-wagon driving, with elegant pure-bred Lippizaners strutting their stuff – Lippizaner horses have been bred in and around Đakovo since 1506. Book way, way ahead if you want to be there.

If you want to see **Lippizaners**, there's a stable on the edge of town, 15 minutes due east down Matije Gupica from the cathedral. Ask politely and you may be allowed in to see the horses, or watch them at their morning training sessions.

GETTING THERE AND AWAY Đakovo is well connected with other towns in the region by bus and train. The bus station is two blocks east of the cathedral, while the train station is 20 minutes northeast of the centre – walk down Kralja Tomislava until you reach the pedestrian zone. Buses come in every half hour or so from Osijek and Slavonski Brod, while trains run to both towns six times a day (for Slavonski Brod change at Strizivojna Vrpolje). The **tourist office** (\f *031 812 319; www.tz-djakovo.hr*) is opposite All Saints Church, on Kralja Tomislava.

WHERE TO STAY There's only one hotel actually in town, the **Croatia-Turist** (\ *031 813 391;* f *031 814 063; www.croatiaturist.hr*), five minutes south of the cathedral, on the road out towards Slavonski Brod. It's a great place, with a dozen rooms at around €50 above a fabulous restaurant of many separate dining areas, which makes its own spicy sausage (*kulen*). The establishment is run by the larger-than-life Ivan Balog, who speaks remarkable French. In his company you can enjoy litres of the excellent local white wines – a perennial favourite is the local Đakovačko Rizling. There's also the new **Hotel Đakovo** (\ *031 840 570; www.hotel-djakovo.hr; dbls from €64*) on the edge of town, on the road leading out to Osijek.

OSIJEK

Osijek is the biggest town in Slavonia, and it's a major administrative, economic and cultural centre. Spread along the southern shore of the river Drava, it's a city of wide streets, rumbling trams and attractive parks and gardens, with two city centres, the 18th-century Austro-Hungarian military fortress town of Tvrđa, to the east, and the 19th-century commercial centre of Gornji Grad, upstream to the west. Until 1786, when they were joined together (along with the residential town of Donji Grad, downstream from Tvrđa), they were entirely separate towns.

HISTORY The Romans had a settlement called Mursa here in the 1st century AD, and by 331 it was sufficiently important for the emperor Hadrian to raise its status to that of a colony. Destroyed by rampaging Goths and Huns in the 7th century, its next settlers were Croats, who built a thriving town near the current site in the Middle Ages, until it was destroyed by incoming Turks. The major Turkish town built here was then destroyed in its own turn, when Osijek was finally captured by the Austro-Hungarians in 1687.

From 1712 to 1721, the Austro-Hungarians built a brand new military-urban complex, Tvrđa, on the site of the Turkish town, as a reflection of its strategic importance in the military border zone. What you see here today has escaped more or less intact, though the Tvrđa town walls were pulled down in the 1920s.

In 1779, the building of a new bridge across the Drava connected Osijek not just to Bilje, but to the rest of Europe, and paved the way for the rapid expansion of Gornji Grad and Donji Grad, upstream and downstream from Tvrđa. In 1786 the three towns were joined together, and in 1884 the first tram started operating between them. During the late 19th and early 20th century, Gornji Grad became the administrative and business heart of Osijek, and indeed still is today.

From the middle of 1991 until early 1992, Osijek was bombarded, but never captured, and though restoration has been quick and effective, there are still a few scars to be seen, with shrapnel-pocked buildings in evidence around the town.

GETTING THERE AND AROUND As the biggest regional centre east of Zagreb, Osijek is a major transport hub, and it's easy to get here and easy to get around. Ten buses a day make the four-hour journey from Zagreb, for example, while three a day head up to Pécs (Pečuh in Croatian) in southern Hungary. Every half hour or so there's also a departure for Bizovac, half an hour away, as well as for Slavonski Brod, two hours down the road. Five trains a day head across Slavonia to Zagreb (four–five hours), while there are departures roughly every two hours for Bizovac, only 25 minutes away.

The bus and train stations are 15 minutes' walk southeast of Gornji Grad and 20 minutes southwest of Tvrđa – tram #2 does a loop from the stations up to Gornji Grad, while tram #1 runs between Gornji Grad and Tvrđa. You can also walk between the two centres in 20 minutes or so along Kapucinska and the pretty Europska Avenija, or along the riverside.

The tourist office (*Županijska 2;* \ *031 203 755;* f *031 203 947; www.tzosijek.hr*), opposite the theatre and almost next door to the cathedral, in a grand administrative building, has maps and useful information on the town and region.

WHERE TO STAY

Central (32 rooms) Trg Ante Starčevića 6; \ 031 283 399; f 031 283 891; www.hotel-central-os.hr. Right on the main square near the cathedral, the Central is a good option. The recently renovated 3-star hotel retains some of its original 1899 charm & offers decent dbls – though being on a busy street, it can be a bit noisy. *Dbl €81.*

Mursa (125 rooms) Bartola Kažića 2A; \ 031 224 900; f 031 207 610; www.zug.hr. Owned by the railway company, & appropriately close to the train station, with perfectly adequate dbls. *Dbl €80.*

Osijek (140 rooms) Šamačka 4; \ 031 230 333; f 031 230 444; www.hotelosijek.hr. Of Osijek's hotels,

the smartest option is the eponymous Osijek, a tower-block right on the waterfront, which has been impressively upgraded to a 4-star hotel with stylish, spacious dbl rooms, the best of which have a lovely view of the river – the same view can be enjoyed from the 14th-floor wellness centre. There's also much less noise from the cathedral bells than in many other places. Service here really is first rate, & the breakfast simply outstanding. *Dbl €143–197.*

Silver (16 rooms) M Divaltova 84; \ 031 582 535; f 031 582 536; www.hotel-silver.hr. Nice 3-star, slightly out from the city centre. *Dbl €77.*

WHERE TO EAT

Osijek's a treat for eating out, being good value for money and offering plenty of restaurants and pizzerias. Local specialities tend to be spicy, in sharp contrast with places on the coast, and reflecting Osijek's proximity to paprika-mad Hungary. There's an excellent hot fish stew, made of carp, catfish and pike, fittingly called *fiš paprikaš*, while almost everywhere serves up its own variations on *kulen*, a spicy smoked sausage.

Alas Reisnerova 12a; \ 031 202 311. A great place for fish dishes, near the railway station. The name means fisherman in the local dialect.

Bonus Hrvatske Republike 1; \ 031 202 030. Prize-winning restaurant, though there are reports of late that the service is far from up to scratch.

Galija Gornjodravska Obala; \ 031 283 500. Nice restaurant down by the river, near the Hotel Osijek.

Lav (don't worry, it just means lion) Trg L J Gaja; \ 031 213 375. This place in Gornji Grad serves particularly good fiš.

Mala Kavana Županjska 2. This really is *the* place to go for a coffee on the main square.

Slavonska Kuća Kamila Firinger 26; \ 031 369 955. Slightly kitschy local favourite in Tvrđa. The homemade kulen and fine fiš more than compensate for the somewhat folksy décor.

The best place to sink an Osječko Pivo, proudly brewed in Osijek since 1697, is right in the centre of Tvrđa, where a string of bar and café terraces face the old Military Command across the square.

Inland Croatia OSIJEK

4

WHAT TO SEE AND DO The main sight in Gornji Grad is the neo-Gothic red-brick cathedral. It's actually not a cathedral, but the parish **Church of Saints Peter and Paul**, but being vast, and sporting Croatia's second tallest spire (90m), the cathedral tag is hardly surprising. Built at the end of the 19th century, in the style of the great German cathedrals, complete with flying buttresses, the church has a fine, spacious interior featuring lovely vaulting and plain, simple frescoes on the ceilings and along the nave.

Across and down the street you'll see the freshly restored **Croatian National Theatre**, spoiled somewhat by the garish McDonald's outlet. Inside, it's a beautiful example of classic late 19th-century opulence – the theatre, not McDonald's.

Heading towards Tvrđa, it's worth stopping in at the **art gallery** on Europska Avenija, housed in a luxurious neo-classical villa. The gallery is one of Croatia's best, and you shouldn't be put off by not recognising many of the names on show – the paintings are on the whole excellent. As you head further east on Europska Avenija check out the Jugendstil (German Art Nouveau) houses along here.

Everything in Tvrđa is on or close to the harmonious main square, Trg Svetog Trojstva, which has a distinctive Baroque **Plague Column** at its centre, dating from 1729. The entire north side of the square is taken up with the vast **Austro-Hungarian Military Command**, while the Magistrate building, on the eastern side, now houses the sprawling **Museum of Slavonia** (*Trg Svetog Trojstva 6;* \ *031 250 730; www.mdc.hr/osijek;* ⊕ *09.00–14.00 Mon–Fri, 10.00–13.00 Sat & Sun; 10kn*). The most interesting of the 130,000 bits and pieces in the museum's care are the Roman artefacts from Mursa, though the collection also spans everything from the Stone Age to the 20th century. Nearby is the newly opened Archaeological Museum (*Trg Svetog Trojstva 2;* \ *031 232 280; www.muih.hr/content/view/18/36/;* ⊕ *10.00–15.00 Tue–Fri, 10.00–13.00 Sat & Sun; 20kn*).

A block northeast of here is the Franciscan monastery and the **Church of the Holy Cross**, which was completed in 1732, on the site of a former mosque. The dark, ornate Baroque interior, and women in black praying in hushed voices, lend it some spooky atmosphere, though there's not much to see beyond the big Baroque altar.

On the other side of Tvrđa, also on the site of a former mosque, is the Jesuit **Church of St Michael**, with its pair of distinctive square towers crowned with small onion domes. Built in 1748, inside it's a curious mix of plain, simple Baroque on the one hand, and garish, ornate Rococo on the other. You almost wish they'd gone the whole hog.

When you're done with sightseeing, head across the river on the main bridge or over the elegant suspension bridge to the popular **Copacabana Recreation Centre**, where you'll find a sandy beach on the Drava as well as outdoor swimming pools. Brazil it isn't, but this is still a great place to cool off and have some fun on a hot summer's day.

More watery fun can be had at **Bizovačke Toplice** (*www.bizovacke-toplice.hr*), a big spa resort 20km west of Osijek, easily reached on public transport to Bizovac. The thermal springs here serve a series of different pools, and there's an enormous and terrifying water-slide. Repair your shattered nerves at the **Termia** (*Sunčana 39;* \ *031 685 100;* f *031 685 179; www.bizovacke-toplice.hr*) which has pleasant double rooms at € 78.

KOPAČKI RIT

Just northeast of Osijek is the Kopački Rit Nature Park (\ *031 285 370; www.kopacki-rit.com*), one of Europe's most important wetlands, caused by the confluence of the Drava and the Danube. As a result, it's a birdwatchers' paradise, with 141 species nesting here, and some 285 species recorded (birds, not birdwatchers). About the only downside is that the area's also home to the most vicious mosquitoes I've ever encountered, biting even in broad daylight, and through everything but the thickest clothing. Take effective repellent.

Among the nesting species are geese, grey, white and purple herons, egrets, coots, kingfishers, woodpeckers and storks. There's also the endangered ferruginous duck, several pairs of rare black storks, and a number of white-tailed sea eagles, as well as a cormorant colony. During the spring and autumn migrations, the park is used as a layover by hundreds of thousands of birds, so that's the best time to come, but even in summer it's a wonderful place, even for the most lackadaisical of ornithologists.

For most of the 1990s, the park was closed, being either under Serbian or UN control (it runs along the border with the Serbian province of Vojvodina), and it's been a tough job to clear most of the mines from the area – indeed, some areas are still contaminated by landmines and other ordnance, though de-mining work continues. Stick to marked paths and take any warnings seriously.

With new legislation enacted in 1994, and the park's boundaries being expanded in 1999, there are now ambitious plans on the table to develop Kopački Rit as an eco-tourist destination, with a nature trail, cycle paths, a visitor centre, an ethnological museum, and accommodation in private rooms in the local villages of Kopačevo, Lug and Vardarac.

For the time being, however, most people are still visiting the park on a bus tour (ask at any travel agent in Slavonia or in Zagreb), which takes in the main sights. You can also drive round the park yourself, though the best way of seeing it is from the water, as part of a tour which includes a boat trip to the Special Ornithological Reserve and a visit to Tikveš Dvorec (see below). Tickets are 70kn.

There are also special ornithological tours in small boats, lasting about 6 hours (1,000kn; maximum group size 15 people; book well in advance through the park office). It's one of the best places in Europe for birdwatching, and you can expect to see up to 90 species here in a single day.

It's also possible to adopt a species of bird here – contact the park office or see their website for details (see page 174).

To reach the park, take the Beli Manastir road out of Osijek until you reach Bilje, just 7km out of town (buses run about once an hour). Turn right, passing Prince Eugene of Savoy's splendid hunting lodge (dating from 1707), and continue to the entrance to the park at Kopačevo, 3km further on, where there's an information centre and souvenir shop, and the departure point for the boat tours.

The road into the park goes between the two main lakes, Sakadaško and Kopačko, and then heads up through a reedy area of canals and cultivated fields – a great place to see herons – and home to an excellent konoba at Kozjak.

The road then heads up into the woods around Tikveš, which conceal one of Tito's most-prized hunting lodges, Tikveš Dvorac – he and his pals would come up here for a spot of privacy to blast away at the local game. On the road to the castle there's a sentry box, which would presumably have been used to keep away the hoi polloi, though it's now, like the lodge itself, in a sorry state of repair. There are plans to use the lodge to good effect, however, as a study centre for research scientists, and there are a couple of cafés where you can stop for a drink in the shade. A visit to Tikveš Dvorec is included in the tours on offer at the park entrance.

The Bilje tourist office (℡ *031 751 480;* f *031 751 481; www.tzo-bilje.hr*) can put you in touch with local people with private rooms, if you'd like to stay in the area.

VINKOVCI

In spite of the graffiti announcing Vinkovci as 'Punk City', the reality is somewhat more prosaic, though the town was a centre of stubborn Croatian resistance during the 1990s war. Situated 40km south of Osijek, 35km east of Đakovo and a little under 20km short of Vukovar, the town is Croatia's second-biggest railway junction and a staging post for buses, so it's quite possible you may be breaking your journey here.

Both the bus and train stations are a 15-minute walk just north of the harmonious Baroque town centre, which still sits within the limits of the (mostly long-gone) Roman walls of the Aurelia Cibalae colony which was once here. Vinkovci was the birthplace of two Roman emperors (Valens and Valentinian) and the composer of the music of Croatia's national anthem, Josip Runjanin, but today it's best known for the Vinkovačke Jeseni, the annual autumn folk festival which brings in big crowds from across Slavonia and features a boozy and excellent Plum Brandy Fair.

WHERE TO STAY If you want to stay over, there are two hotels downtown.

Cibalia (24 rooms) Ante Starčevića 51; ☏ 032 339 222; f 032 339 220; www.hotel-cibalia.com. Just two blocks south of the bus & train stations, with clean rooms. *Dbl €70.*

Slavonija (108 rooms) Duga 1; ☏ 032 364 255; f 032 364 260; www.suc.hr. Right in the city centre & towering over the river, with rather functional accommodation. *Dbl €51.*

The **tourist office** (*Trg bana Josipa Šokčevića 3*; ☏ *032 334 653*; f *032 334 658*; *www.tz-vinkovci.hr*) also has a list of other pensions in the area, and can give you more details on the festival.

VUKOVAR

When I first came back to Vukovar after the recent war, in 2002, the reality, after approaching through bucolic fields of maize and sunflowers, was a terrible shock. Gone was the fine Baroque centre and the general air of prosperity delivered by the local shoe and tyre factory at Borovo, which I remembered from the 1980s. In its place was a shambles. The Borovo factory was totally destroyed, and most of the town centre was bombed out, a mess of devastated houses and ruined buildings.

Vukovar suffered more than any other town in Croatia during the war (see box on page 178), and if there's still reconstruction to be done, it's happily now looking incomparably better than the way it was at the end of 1991, when the town finally fell, after the horrifying siege and concomitant massacre, or even at the beginning of 1998, when the UN handed Vukovar back to Croatia. The Franciscan Monastery has been beautifully restored, along with the big school behind it. Shops and banks are open again, while a few apartment blocks – and the Dunav and Lav hotels – have been rebuilt and refurbished, and there's a new film festival in August (*www.vukovarfilmfestival.com*). There's a genuine feeling of optimism, of triumph over adversity, which is hopefully more than simple guidebook-writer naïvety – after all, schooling is still segregated, for example, with separate entrances for Croats and Serbs; and although the children all follow the same curriculum, different languages and alphabets are used for teaching.

Vukovar's history goes back a long, long way – as you'll know if you've ever seen the partridge-shaped vessel, popular all over the country, known as the Vučedol Dove (the original's in Zagreb's archaeological museum, but there are copies everywhere). It dates back nearly 5,000 years, and was found just downriver from Vukovar in 1938. The Vučedol site, after a ten-year gap, is now at last being excavated again, with plans to open it up as a proper heritage site for visitors (there's already a Vučedol Restaurant there, which is a good sign).

Vukovar lies along the southern bank of the river Danube (Dunav), with the little river Vuka flowing lethargically through town to join it. The main street, running parallel to the Danube, changes its name from Strossmayerov west of the Vuka, to Franjo Tuđman across the bridge, where you'll find the old town centre.

GETTING THERE AND AROUND The train station is 2km north along the river, a 25-minute walk upstream towards Borovo. The bus station is closer to town, a block south

of Strossmayerov, next to a big daily market, and is served by buses roughly every hour from Osijek, 36km away. On Strossmayerov itself you'll find the tourist office (℡/f *032 442 889; www.turizamvukovar.hr*), next door to Vukovar's most obvious travel agent, Panturist Plus (℡/f *032 441 790*).

WHERE TO STAY AND EAT

🏠 **Hotel Dunav** (56 rooms) Trg Republike Hrvatske 1; ℡/f 032 441 285. A curious grain-store of a building, the Dunav offers small but spanking-new dbls (accessed via a rather tired lift). Most rooms have some sort of view – either over the town & the Vuka, or across the Danube. Downstairs there's a small souvenir shop, where you can buy Vučedol Doves or reproductions of Vukovar's famously ruined water tower. The Hotel Dunav is also home to a great restaurant, which will serve you a cracking meal at almost any time of day. The grills are great, the *ajvar* sauce is unrivalled, & the Šopska salad (chunks of cheese & flavoursome tomatoes) is lovely. B/fast can be an altogether different experience, however. You can just imagine the fun I had with a lone cold sausage & a wickedly hot under-boiled egg – but neither egg-cup nor spoon. I was able to glean some sardines, however – indeed, whole tins of them were arranged tastefully in a basket on the buffet table. *Dbl €57.*

🏠 **Hotel Lav** J J Strossmayera 18; ℡ 032 445 100; f 032 445 110; www.hotel-lav.hr. Vukovar's citizens are justifiably proud of this newly restored & reopened hotel on the river, which symbolises lasting peace as much as somewhere to stay. Smart, spotless, spanking-new 4-star dbls are the order of the day. There's also a fine, modern, & quite upmarket restaurant, serving up Slavonian specialities. *Dbl €122.*

✕ **Vrške** Parobrodska 3; ℡ 032 441 788. Nice restaurant with a terrace on the Danube, serving up excellent freshwater fish dishes.

VUKOVAR AT WAR

Vukovar's position, right on Croatia's border (that's Serbian Vojvodina you see across the Danube), and its ethnic mix (in the 1991 census, 37% of locals considered themselves as Serbs, while 44% said they were Croats) was at the heart of the disaster in 1991. With Croatian independence on the agenda, barricades were thrown up in Vukovar's Serbian suburbs after a build-up of Serb paramilitaries and provocations instigated from Belgrade. As tensions grew, Croatian policemen were murdered and the Yugoslav army, the JNA, moved in, supposedly to separate the two sides.

By the autumn, Vukovar was surrounded by hundreds of tanks and thousands of soldiers – both regular Yugoslav army forces and Serb irregulars, as well as opportunists. When ground attacks failed, the town was pounded mercilessly by artillery and bombing raids. The residents took shelter in their cellars, living on meagre rations. In the streets above, resistance was fierce, but eventually doomed in the face of the numerically superior and far more heavily armed Serbs.

On 18 November 1991, Vukovar, now completely destroyed, finally fell. With nowhere to run – the ruins of the town were surrounded by enemy forces – the remaining population sought shelter in the hospital. The following day, ahead of the planned Red Cross evacuation, the Serbs cleared the hospital themselves, killing most of the people taking refuge there.

The world – with its attention diverted by the far more photogenic siege of Dubrovnik's beautiful and well-known old town – paid little heed.

Wherever Croats fell into Serb hands, families were separated, and the men were taken away in trucks. Approximately 2,300 soldiers and civilians died in the defence of Vukovar, and another 2,600 people simply disappeared. Many have been found in the mass graves around the town, but others may be buried anonymously in Serbia, unmarked victims of the worst atrocity of the 1990s war in Croatia.

WHAT TO SEE AND DO The badly damaged **Eltz Palace**, from the 18th century, is west of here, also on Strossmayerov, heading out of town. If it seems familiar, flip over a 20kn note, where you'll also find a picture of the Vučedol Dove. The palace used to house the **Municipal Museum**, though the collections were all destroyed or looted during the war. Efforts to recover some of the works from museums in Serbia have proved successful, however, and the building itself is being restored – though given the damage sustained this is likely to take a considerable amount of time, and at the time of writing (2009) it was still closed. Until then, the museum collections are being held in the former house of Lavoslav Ružička, Croatia's first Nobel Prize winner, who was born in Vukovar in 1887.

The bridge across to the old town leads on to one corner of Trg Republike, where you'll find the new town hall, the ruins of the elegant **Workers' Party Building** (home to the second congress of the Communist Party of Yugoslavia in 1920, and formerly the Museum of Modern History, but for the time being an empty shell) and the Hotel Dunav. Behind the hotel, on the riverbank, there's a touching new **memorial**, with stylised gravestones set like falling dominoes, under a couple of poplars, with the broad sweep of the endless Danube behind.

The main street through town (Franjo Tuđman), whose arcaded houses and shops still wear very visible scars, was once Vukovar's Baroque heart. Turn left, uphill, at the brewery (storks nest picturesquely here, on the main chimney), to reach the **Franciscan Monastery**, which has become something of a meeting place for local people since its restoration. The brilliant exterior hides a still partially ruined interior, with bare brickwork where once were pastel plaster and Baroque frescoes. There are good photos showing what the monastery used to look like, and just how badly ruined it got in 1991.

If you've come all the way to Vukovar you should definitely make the effort to get out to the **Vukovar War Cemetery**, one of the most heartbreaking places in the whole of Croatia. This was built on the site of Europe's largest mass grave since World War II, and 938 crosses have been symbolically placed here to commemorate the dead. There are also the black and grey marble tombs of Vukovar's defenders, strewn with flowers, along with the grim sight of unmarked empty graves ready to receive the bodies of the known missing, should they ever be found. It's a terribly moving place, and there's rarely a time when you can come here and not find tearful family members mourning their dead. The images of the all-too-young victims tell their own story.

The cemetery is situated about 3.5km out of town on the road to Ilok, and the easiest way to get there is on the regular Ilok bus. If you're walking (it takes about 45 minutes), head along Stjepan Radić out of town. The street is named after the Croatian firebrand who was shot in the Belgrade parliament in 1928; under Serb occupation in the 1990s the name was changed to that of his assassin, Puniša Račić, but now it's been changed back. The street leads 1km to the war ravaged **water tower**, which has been left unrestored as a permanent memorial to the conflict.

EAST TO ILOK

East of Vukovar, past the war cemetery, Croatia narrows along the Danube's southern bank, into Vojvodina, and ends in a point at the town of Ilok, 35km later.

If you're coming this way under your own steam, the first place to stop is at the **Ovčara Memorial**, where you can pay your respects to the 200 doctors, nurses and patients evacuated from Vukovar's hospital on 19 November 1991 who were found buried in a mass grave here. The grave was found in 1997 after an anonymous tip-off, and 200 small bushes mark the spot, along with memorial plaques. Standing here it's truly awful to think of the tragic end of so many people in such calm, quiet countryside, where today all you can hear is birds singing and crickets chirping. The grave is just past the small farming village of Ovčara – take the right-hand turning (marked with a dove for peace) almost exactly 2.5km after the Vukovar War Cemetery. Follow the road for 5km to Ovčara, then turn left at the end of the road (marked with another dove), and turn left again after 200m or so.

If you're on public transport (ie: the Vukovar to Ilok bus), the first town you come to is **Sotin**, which is not much more than a single street with rebuilt houses, after which you'll pass through **Opatovac**, which has nice vineyards and a shrapnel-pocked church tower. About 10km further on is Šarengrad, which was obviously once quite charming. There are two pretty churches and a fish-rich lake, though the signs of war are still omnipresent.

A final 7km brings you to **Ilok**, Croatia's easternmost town. While the Osijek tourist office's description of the town as 'Dubrovnik on the Danube' is a triumph of optimism over reality, it's still well worth coming here to see the fortified old town, up on the hill above the Danube.

The old town is set within tall, narrow-bricked walls, which were originally built in medieval times but were then beefed up by the Turks, who ran Ilok from 1566 to 1697. The church in the corner is dedicated to **St Ivan Kapistran**, the so-called 'Defender of Belgrade', who died in Ilok in 1456, though the church is mostly much more recent, having been remodelled in 1906 by the busy Hermann Bollé (see Zagreb, etc).

There's an unusual statue of St Francis, right in the middle of the nave, and a couple of 15th- and 16th-century tombs to look at before you get to the dark, sagging altarpiece, depicting St Ivan (senselessly destroyed and left to rot by Serbs) – though without restoration it won't be doing so for much longer.

The Romans were here, nearly 2,000 years ago, and it was they who planted the first vineyards. After being wiped out during the recent war and ensuing occupation, Ilok's vineyards reopened for business in 1997, and fine white wines are once again being produced. Look out for Chardonnay, Graševina, Traminac, White Pinot and Riesling, and head for the **tourist office** (*Trg Nikole Iločkog 2;* ✆ *032 590 020; www.turizamilok.hr*) for information on local wine tours.

WHERE TO STAY AND EAT

🏠 **Hotel Dunav** (14 rooms) J. Benešića 62; ✆ 032 596 500; f 032 590 134; www.hoteldunavilok.com. In a peaceful setting on the Danube, with its own restaurant. *Dbl €70.*

🏠 **Pansion Comfort Masarini** Stjepana Radića 4; ✆ 032 590 050. Good-value pension. *Dbl €40.*

5

Istria

Telephone code for Istria (except Opatija) 052.
Opatija 051

Of Croatia's busy coast, Istria, the northwestern peninsula, is by far the most visited, with holiday accommodation for over a quarter of a million people. What's remarkable, however, is how the region has managed to keep tourist development away from the pretty Venetian old towns along the west coast, or the medieval villages of the hilly, wooded interior. You'll even find picturesque coves and hidden rocky beaches that feel off the beaten track. Roman ruins and Byzantine mosaics are complemented by clear unpolluted waters and a gentle climate, helping to explain why millions of people keep coming back here, year after year. Even if the large socialist-era hotel complexes and mega campsites aren't necessarily for you, Istria has a great deal to offer.

On the west coast, you'll find Byzantine mosaics in **Poreč** and the wonderful Venetian town of **Rovinj**, while on the east lies **Opatija**, the swanky resort of choice for turn-of-the-20th-century Austro-Hungarians. Pazin, inland, is the administrative centre, whereas **Pula**, on the southern tip, with its extraordinary Roman amphitheatre, is the economic heart of the region. Off the west coast stand the **Brijuni Islands**, now a pretty national park, while the **Učka Mountains** in the northeast rise above Opatija, provide a welcome relief from the crowds, even at the season's peak.

Early and late season are great times to visit, with the weather often coming good and the towns empty of tourists. April/May and September/October are especially good – in winter the peninsula gets a fair amount of rain, and though Pula and Rovinj are open all year round, resort towns like Poreč, Novigrad and Rabac pretty much close down altogether.

Istria had five sets of rulers during the 20th century, going from Austro-Hungarian to Italian to German to Yugoslav to Croatian in the space of 70-odd years – prompting anecdotes from tour guides across the region about families with four nationalities in the space of three generations. It makes for an unusually tolerant part of the country, and particularly on the west coast you'll still find many people bilingual in Croatian and Italian.

Warning Croatia's coastal resorts and towns are very busy indeed between late June until early September and you might find that hotels, private rooms and campsites are

ON TO SLOVENIA

Visitors to Istria may well be tempted to nip over the border into Slovenia. This even smaller ex-Yugoslav republic has lots to recommend it, and you'll see excursions offered from Istrian resorts to the famous cave complex of Postojna, along with camera-pleasing Predjama Castle, as well as to the youthful capital, Ljubljana, which mixes abundant cafés, bars and restaurants with numerous museums and galleries. For more information see the excellent *Slovenia: The Bradt Travel Guide* or *Ljubljana: The Bradt City Guide*.

Istria

5

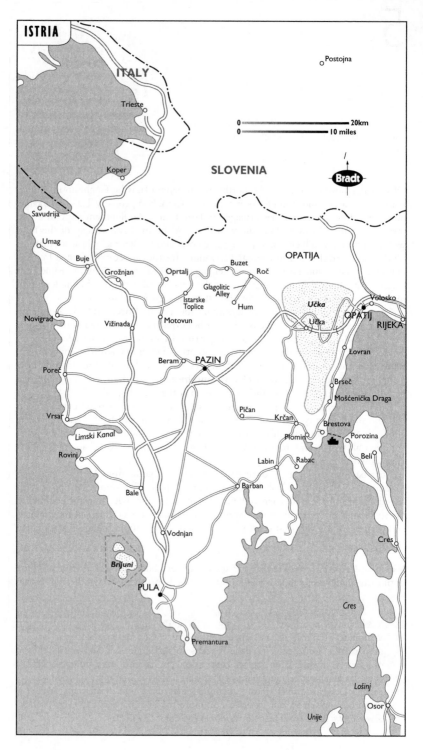

fully booked if you arrive on spec; and even if not, the owners of private rooms and campsites are often simply unwilling to take guests who aren't staying for a minimum of three nights. In high season stays of fewer than three nights in private accommodation usually carry a surcharge. If you want to secure centrally located accommodation, or have a specific hotel in mind, then it pays to book well ahead. If you find yourself struggling to find somewhere to stay then base yourself in Pula, where it's usually easier to find a vacant room, and make day trips out. Another option, if you have your own transport, is to take advantage of the increasing number of farms and villages in the interior offering agro-tourism (bed and breakfast) accommodation – there are now over 120 places, and more are coming on board all the time. Get the brochure from the Pula tourist board (℡ *052 212 987;* f *052 211 855;* e *tz-pula@pu.htnet.hr; www.pulainfo.hr).*

THE WEST COAST TO POREČ

Working anticlockwise round Istria, the first main settlements are **Umag** and **Novigrad**. These were both once Roman towns, on their own mini-peninsulas, but have long been given over unashamedly to the holiday business, with little to show for their historic past. The lack of industry anywhere near here, the clear waters, and the pleasant enough coastal hotels and campsites draw regular crowds. Umag is currently booming and is the host venue for the annual ATP tennis tournament, while Novigrad is emerging as a serious yachting destination with massive investment in a new marina. Big name hotels such as Kempinski are also currently moving into this part of Istria.

Just north of the twin resorts is **Savudrija**, home to a lighthouse with a charming story. Locals insist that it was built by a lovestruck noble in an attempt to win over his unrequited love. Tragically she died before it was finished, but it remains as an eternal tribute to her. Today it's a quiet spot where you can enjoy the sea views or swim off the rocks, with an adjacent campsite (Pineta) for those who want to stay the night. It's also possible to stay at the lighthouse itself (*www.lighthouses-penul.com/penul-eng/index.html*), which is a wonderful treat.

Poreč (Parenzo) itself is the undisputed capital of Croatian tourism. Its resident population may be just under 8,000, but it had over 400,000 visitors (and some 2.7 million tourist nights) in 2008 , spending an impressive 4.6 million nights in the huge resorts spread along the 50km stretch of coast running south from the Mirna River to the Limski Kanal (Lim Fjord). The unashamed devotion to holidaying here means you can find just about anything to divert you (in season), from plain old-fashioned sunbathing and swimming to walking, cycling, riding, water-skiing, diving, jet-skiing, ballooning or paragliding, not to mention tennis, volleyball and the rest. The tourist infrastructure is excellent, with walking and cycling trails (up to 50km circuits), and maps available from the **tourist office** (*at the entrance to the old town, just up from Trg Slobode, at Zagrebačka 9;* ℡ *052 451 293;* f *052 451 665; www.istra.com/poreč),* as well as over 100 restaurants and more than 25,000 beds in the vicinity. Lonely, you won't be.

At the centre of all this is the pretty town itself (more of a village, really), tightly fitting onto a peninsula measuring just 440m long and 200m wide. Here, you'll find stone-paved streets, fine medieval buildings, traces of the Roman colony and arguably the world's best-preserved early Christian cathedral complex, featuring those famous mosaics – enough, in any case, to warrant Poreč being on UNESCO's list of World Heritage Sites.

HISTORY Inhabited for over 6,000 years by the Histrian tribes who gave their name to the Istrian peninsula, Poreč was finally subdued by the Romans in the 2nd century BC and – with the new name of Julia Parentium – was upgraded to the status of colony during the 2nd century AD. There's a small walled garden near the peninsula's tip with lots of Roman bits and pieces from this era, as well as more in the town's museum, but the main thing you'll notice is the street layout – and even the street names, Decumanus and Cardo Maximus – which are still Roman rather than medieval.

Early Christians worshipped in secret here, and Poreč's first bishop, Maurus, was martyred in the 4th century – the town still puts on a good show for his feast day, 21 November, should you still be around that far out of season.

By the 6th century, with Byzantium in charge (from 539 to 751), Bishop Euphrasius reckoned it was time for a major rebuilding programme, tearing down the existing church and putting up a complex consisting of a basilica, an atrium, a baptistery and – naturally – a bishop's palace.

After the usual takeover by Goths and the like, Venice was in power here for more than 500 years (1267–1797), though in charge of not very much, with the plague scything down the local population to just 100 by the 17th century. Venice repopulated the town from southern Dalmatia, before collapsing and leaving the way free for the Austro-Hungarians. With the first guidebook to the area available in 1845 and the first public beach opened in 1895, Poreč was well on the way to its true destiny as a holiday haven.

GETTING THERE AND AWAY Poreč is easily reached by bus – it's just under an hour away from Pula or Koper (in Slovenia), both 55km distant, around two hours from Rijeka, six times a day, or 4½ hours from Zagreb, eight times a day. The nearest train stations are Pazin (on the Trieste/Ljubljana to Pula line) or Koper, while the nearest airport is at Pula. In summer there are also ferries from Pula, Trieste and Venice.

If you're coming in by car, there's a curious dearth of signs to Poreč itself – just follow signs to the main resort of Plava Laguna and you won't go far wrong.

GETTING AROUND In summer, there's a 'tourist train' that plies its way up and down the coast south of Poreč to the main resort areas of Plava Laguna and Zelena Laguna (blue lagoon; green lagoon), with a local boat covering the same turf from the seaward side. Out of season, you'll have to rely on the bus to Vrsar or your own transport. If you're just coming in to see the old town, it's all perfectly manageable on foot from the bus station, at the eastern end of the peninsula, next to the small harbour. The bus station has left-luggage facilities.

 WHERE TO STAY With some 25,000 beds in the vicinity – 5,000 of them in private rooms – accommodation ought to be a doddle in Poreč. Ought to be, but if you're here in season, without a booking, you could well find yourself on the bus back out to Pula in search of shelter.

In the area, you'll find more than 20 agencies handling private rooms, which go for around €35 for a double in summer, but under €25 out of season. From June to September, you'll find agencies open seven days a week until 22.00, but outside these months most close soon after lunch and don't open at all on Sundays. Among the most popular are Di-Tours (✆ 052 432 100; f 052 431 300; www.di-tours.com; at several locations), Atlas (Eufrazijeva 63; ✆ 052 434 933; f 052 451 109; www.atlas-croatia.com), and Generalturist (Aldo Negri 3; ✆ 052 451 839; f 052 451 123; www.generalturist.com).

There are seven main campsites in the vicinity, but four – **Solaris** and **Ulika** (to the north) and Istra and Koversada (to the south) – are reserved for naturists. If you prefer to keep your kit on, then try **Zelena Laguna** (✆ 052 410 700; f 052 401 601; www.plavalaguna.hr) or **Bijela Uvala** (✆ 052 410 551; f 052 401 600; www.plavalaguna.hr), both in Zelena Laguna, or **Lanternacamp** (to the north, reserve ahead; ✆ 052 465 010; f 052 451 440; www.camping-adriatic.com).

The nicest hotels in the town itself are the small Jadran and the Parentino, next door to each other in semi-grand, 19th-century buildings right on the waterfront. Both are run by the much larger three-star Hotel Neptun.

right   **Mosaic from Split's Roman ruins** (JS) page 286

below   **Pula's Roman amphitheatre is a must-see — it's one of the best preserved in the world** (AF/SS) page 203

bottom   **Zadar's Land Gate** (JS) page 254

above **Picture-perfect Rovinj — in the background you can see the spire of the town's Church of St Euphemia** (AF/SS) page 191

below **Rovinj's narrow cobbled streets are wonderful to explore** (CNTB) page 191 *right*   Samobor's quaint, compact town centre (JS) page 147

below   The hilltop town of Motovun is surrounded by vineyards which produce famous red and white wines (TLL/SS) page 211

bottom   The atmospheric ruins of Klis fortress, situated 9km north of Split (JS) page 289 *above* Vis — Croatia's farthest flung island — was colonised by the Greeks in the 4th century BC (JS) page 306

below Trogir is a UNESCO-listed, perfectly preserved, medieval town (CNTB) page 277

St Mary's Island inside the pristine
Mljet National Park (HF/SS) page 353

above left   **Windsurfing off Brač Island**
(P/SS) page 295

above right   **Bungee-jumping in Krka National Park**
(CNTB) page 265

left   **Climbing Paklenica National Park's limestone**
gorges (PCL/Alamy) page 254

below   **Cycling along the Dalmatian coast, near Split**
(HF/SS) page 277

opposite clockwise from

top left   **Lynx are incredibly shy and therefore rarely**
seen (I/FLPA)

top right   **Wild boars are commonly seen in Croatia's**
northern and eastern forests (ML/FLPA)

middle right   **Mouflon and Chamois are often spotted in the**
mountains along the Slovenian border (I/FLPA)

bottom right   **European brown bears are still found in the**
forests of the interior (PH/FLPA)

bottom left   **Griffon vultures are nowadays only found on**
the island of Cres (J&CS/FLPA)

middle left   **Pine marten** (I/FLPA) page 6

Visit the beautiful cascading waterfalls at Plitvice Lakes
National Park (P/SS) page 158

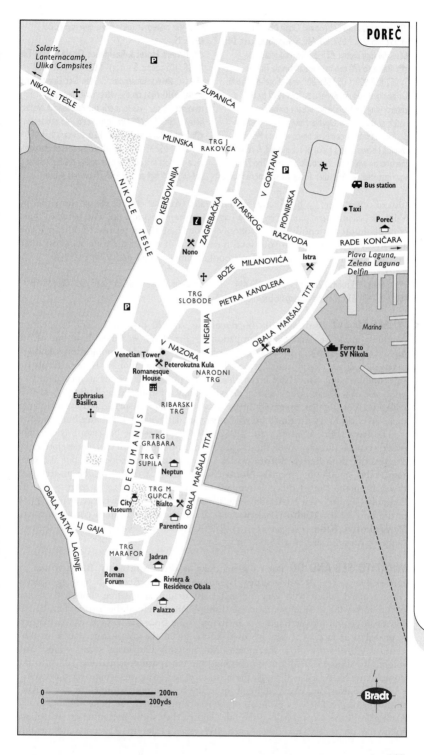

Solaris,
Lanternacamp,
Ulika Campsites

NIKOLE TESLE

ŽUPANIĆA

MLINSKA

TRG J
RAKOVCA

NIKOLE TESLE

O KERŠOVANIJA

ZAGREBAČKA

V GORTANA

ISTARSKOG RAZVODA

PIONIRSKA

Bus station

Taxi

Poreč

RADE KONČARA

Plava Laguna,
Zelena Laguna
Delfin

Nono

BOŽE MILANOVIĆA

Istra

TRG
SLOBODE

PIETRA KANDLERA

A NEGRIJA

OBALA MARŠALA TITA

Marina

V NAZORA

Venetian Tower

Peterokutna Kula

Sofora

Ferry to
SV Nikola

Romanesque
House

NARODNI
TRG

Euphrasius
Basilica

RIBARSKI
TRG

DECUMANUS

TRG
GRABARA

TRG F
SUPILA

OBALA MARŠALA TITA

Neptun

City
Museum

TRG M
GUPCA

Rialto

Parentino

OBALA MATKA LAGINJE

LJ GAJA

TRG
MARAFOR

Jadran

Roman
Forum

Riviera &
Residence Obala

Palazzo

0 ————— 200m
0 ————— 200yds

Bradt

Hotel Jadran (22 rooms) Obala Maršala Tita 24; ☎ 052 465 000; f 052 451 440; www.valamar.com. *Dbl €61–104 high season, €25–57 low–mid season.*

Palazzo (70 rooms) Obala Maršala Tita 24; ☎ 052 858 800; f 052 858 801; www.hotel-palazzo.hr. Originally the Hotel Riviera, built in 1910 by the enterprising Mr Klein, who already owned swanky hotels at the time in Opatija. Failing to get planning permission from a competition-concerned Poreč council, he was sold a piece of sea instead, & reclaimed the land on which he then built his hotel. The Riviera was 'restored' in 1953, then finally given a more recent full 4-star makeover (including a new name). *Dbl €99–299.*

Riviera Hotel & Residence Obala Maršala Tita 15–18 (105 rooms, 8 suites) ☎ 052 465 000; f 052 451 440; www.valamar.com; ⊕ May–Oct. Due to open in May 2010, right on the waterfront, this newly renovated 4-star was formerly the Parentino & Neptun hotels. *Dbl €150–270 high season €86–148 mid season.*

Hotel Poreč (54 rooms) Rade Končara 1; ☎ 052 451 811; f 052 451 811; www.hotelporec.com. Standard-issue comfort in a building overlooking the bus station. *Dbl €80–100 high season, €58–70 low–mid season.*

Out of town, there's a huge range of three- and two-star complexes, all run either by Valamar (*www.valamar.com*) or by Plava Laguna (*www.plavalaguna.hr*), who between them control almost the entire Poreč economy – your best bet in terms of both price and availability is to go through your local travel agent or one of the tour operators listed on page 184, though Valamar has direct booking lines (☎ *052 465 000;* f *052 451 440*).

Delfin (793 rooms) Zelena Laguna; ☎ 052 414 000; f 052 451 658; www.plavalaguna.hr. Enormous place out at Zelena Laguna. Good value. *Dbl €68–98 HB.*

✘ WHERE TO EAT
With around 100 restaurants and 20 pizzerias – not to mention countless snack bars and ice cream parlours – the Poreč area must have one of the highest eatery-densities on the planet relative to its resident population, although practically all are closed out of season. In town itself the emphasis is more firmly on cafés and bars, but you'll have no trouble finding pizza, pasta, or Istrian specialities like *pršut*, *maneštra* (bean soup) and a dizzying array of fish dishes. Lobster (*jastog*) is expensive but popular, especially in pasta (*sa rezancima*). In spring and early summer make an effort to try the fine local wild asparagus, dark and slightly bitter, but delicious.

The **Istra** (*Bože Milanovića 30;* ☎ *052 434 636*), up by the bus station is the right place to splash out on top-of-the-range seafood and other local specialities. Just along the seafront from here is **Sofora**, which not only has a great location but also does remarkably good-value specials. **Nono** (*Zagrebačka 4;* ☎ *052 088*), the pizzeria just down from the tourist office, is reputed to have the best pizzas in town – and it's certainly popular, even off-season – but it wasn't my personal favourite, being pipped at the post by the **Rialto** (*Ljudevita Gaja 3*), on the south western corner of town. **Peterokutna Kula** (*Decumanus 1;* ☎ *052 451 378; www.kula-porec.com.hr*) serves a range of Istrian dishes in a 15th-century tower.

WHAT TO SEE AND DO
Poreč's main draw is the **Euphrasius Basilica** and its remarkable series of 6th-century Byzantine mosaics. Access is via the largely reconstructed (albeit with very old materials) atrium, and is free, though it's worth paying to see the small museum in the Bishop's Palace behind the basilica. This houses lots of stone and mosaic fragments, including some from Maurus's so-called 'oratory' – probably in fact what was his own house, given the clandestine nature of 4th-century Christianity. Note the mosaic fish, the early Christians' secret symbol. You might also want to splash out on climbing the **campanile**, which was added to the complex in 1522 (access through the baptistery) for great views out over the town.

But, like everyone else, you'll end up in the basilica itself, stunned by the mosaics in the main apse. The very plainness of the rest of the church sets these off fantastically. Dating from the second half of the 6th century, they show Byzantine art at its best, following on in the tradition started 100 years earlier in Ravenna, and roughly contemporaneous with the mosaics in Aya Sofya in Istanbul – indeed, craftsmen from Constantinople worked on the wall furnishings here too.

Dominated by the virgin and child, you'll see Euphrasius himself on the left-hand side with a handy-sized model of the basilica. To the left of the main windows is the Annunciation, while on the right a nosy servant gets a rare peek at the Visitation. Over the arch are the first 12 women saints, with Agnus Dei (the lamb of God) as the centrepiece, while across the top are Christ and the apostles. Complemented by coloured stones and fabulous mother-of-pearl – whole scallop and oyster shells have been used – the ensemble is still almost unnaturally vibrant some 1,500 years on.

The stone altar canopy, modelled on the one in St Mark's in Venice, wasn't added until 1277, but blends in surprisingly well with the whole.

On your way out, you can see where excavations have revealed part of the mosaic floor of one of the earlier churches on the site.

The rest of the town is mainly remarkable for its narrow stone streets, pretty squares and occasional architectural one-offs, like the **Venetian Tower** at the top end of Decumanus and the so-called **Romanesque House** further down, with its distinctive 13th-century wooden balcony. Down at the bottom of Decumanus is Trg Marabor, once the Roman Forum. In the low-walled garden behind this you'll find a collection of Roman ruins, mainly coming from a couple of temples that once stood here.

Finally, there's the **City Museum**, housed in the early 18th-century Sinčić Palace on the main drag, with Greek and Roman artefacts and some monumental canvases.

MOVING ON Heading south from Poreč you soon come to **Vrsar**, famous mostly as the access point for Europe's largest naturist resort, at **Koversada** (✆ 052 441 378; f 052 441 761 for the campsite; ✆ 052 441 171; f 052 441 323 for apartments and ✆ 052 441 114; f 052 441 310 for villas; www.maistra.hr). Established in 1960 and catering for the best part of 1,000 people indoors and more than 7,000 campers outside, it's fully booked all season long. Reserve well ahead.

Koversada sits on the northwest corner of the **Limski Kanal** (Lim Channel), a 10km-long flooded valley ideal for cultivating oysters and mussels. There are two ways to get there, either by road or by taking an excursion boat from Poreč, Vrsar or Rovinj. It used to be a secret place, used by pirates and buccaneers as a hiding place between raids on Venetian shipping, but these days, with foodies and tour buses flocking here for the shellfish, there's quite a bustle to it all.

Whether or not Francis Drake's treasure is hidden hereabouts is highly debatable, but it doesn't stop treasure-hunters coming each year to look; what you should be looking for, however, is the dolphins that sometimes come into the channel to play. For the best view of the channel, continue on the road to Vrsar, stopping off at the viewing tower, which opens up a whole swathe of the emerald water and surrounding forest.

✖ Where to eat

✖ **Lim Fjord** ✆ 052 448 222. This place has the best view, but the food isn't always as good as Viking's. All part of the experience, however, is watching the local fishermen landing & sorting the catch of the day by the waterfront.

✖ **Trošt Obala** Maršala Tita 1a; ✆ 052 445 197; www.restoran-trost.hr. Excellent and highly regarded restaurant with a nice terrace.

✖ **Viking Restaurant** ✆ 052 448 223. Of the flurry of eateries, Viking has perhaps the best food, with a wide variety of fish & meat dishes accompanying the range of crustaceans.

ROVINJ

Dominated by its outsize church and campanile, Rovinj (Rovigno) is one of the most attractive places in Croatia, with the steep cobbled streets of the walled old town

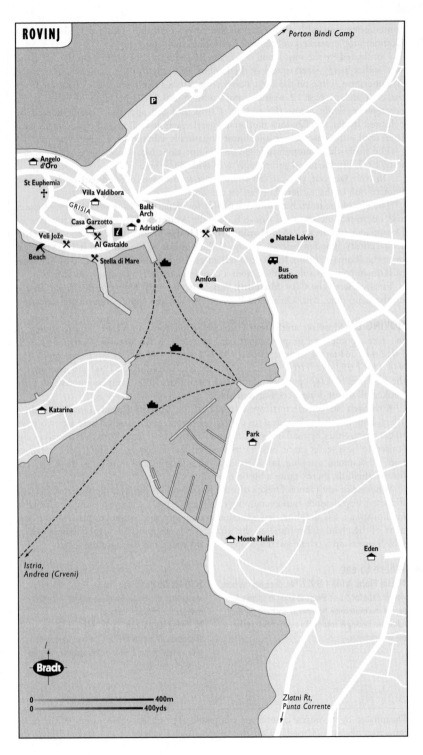

ROVINJ

Porton Bindi Camp

Angelo d'Oro

St Euphemia

Villa Valdibora

GRISIA

Balbi Arch

Casa Garzotto

Adriatic

Amfora

Natale Lokva

Veli Jože

Al Gastaldo

Beach

Stella di Mare

Amfora

Bus station

Katarina

Park

Monte Mulini

Eden

Istria, Andrea (Crveni)

Bradt

0   400m
0   400yds

Zlatni Rt, Punta Corrente

giving way to sunny Venetian quayside cafés and restaurants. Serious tourist development is encroaching on this photogenic, once-upon-a-time island city, but it still manages to accommodate increasing numbers of visitors with ease – mostly away from the old town, along the coast or on one of the nearby islands.

It's also the most Italian place in Croatia, with the people, street signs and menus all being bilingual. A centuries-old fishing tradition is alive and well, though on the wide quaysides you're as likely to witness spontaneous concerts or vibrant café life as fishermen bringing in the catch or mending their nets.

Whilst you're there, check out the curiously flat-bottomed, square-stemmed boats unique to Rovinj – the *batana* probably only survived into the 21st century with UNESCO help, and contrast sharply with the bonanza of visiting super yachts.

HISTORY The island of Rovinj – it wasn't joined to the coast until 1763 – was known in Roman times and was fortified and inhabited through the decline of the Roman Empire and into the Middle Ages. The frequent subject of barbarian attacks, Rovinj's people developed a densely packed, organic urban architecture on the island, and as the population increased and the space ran out, families found themselves living literally on top of one another. Each insisted nonetheless on its own fireplace and chimney, giving Rovinj's old walled town the distinctively jumbled look it has today.

Most of the buildings date from the 13th century on, when the Venetians secured control, retaining it right up to the collapse of the republic at the end of the 18th century. (Quarries near Rovinj furnished the marble you can see today in the lovely church of Santa Maria della Salute, in Venice.)

During the scourge of the bubonic plague, Rovinj remained miraculously unscathed. While Poreč, to the north, and Pula, to the south, saw their populations plunge in the mid 17th century to just 100 and 300 inhabitants respectively, Rovinj could boast 10,000 healthy souls – not far off today's 13,000.

With the isthmus paved over, Rovinj spread across to the mainland from the end of the 18th century, while the introduction of Croatia's first tobacco factory in 1872 brought prosperity to the town – even today the factory makes most of Croatia's cigarettes.

GETTING THERE AND AWAY Rovinj is less than 40km from Pula, and can be reached by bus or car in not much over half an hour from Pula's train station, airport or city-centre bus station – buses run a dozen times a day between the two. If you're coming from the north or east by car you'll see Rovinj clearly signed off the main road. From mid-April to early October the Venezia Line ferry from Venice also stops at Rovinj (*www.venezialines.com*).

GETTING AROUND The bus station (with left-luggage facilities) is halfway between the old town and the marina, a five-minute walk from the main town quay, home to the highly informative if not always especially friendly tourist office (*Pino Budicin 12;* ☎ *052 811 566;* f *052 816 007; www.tzgrovinj.hr*). Once you're there, everything's easily (and only) reachable on foot. If you're coming in by car, you'll almost certainly end up on the northern side of the old town, where you'll find the only large car park, with spectacular views of the ancient walls, crowned by the Venetian campanile.

WHERE TO STAY Popular with well-heeled Croatians, Rovinj has something of a shortage of accommodation in season, and you may find it easier to stay in Pula and make a day trip of it. If you do get seduced by the idea of staying here – and who wouldn't be? – you could do worse than check out the following options.

🏠 **Adriatic** (27 rooms) Pino Budicin; ☎ 052 803 510; f 052 803 520; www.maistra.hr. The smaller, swankier & older Adriatic is right on the old quay. The hotel occupies an ideal spot & offers a dash of character not found in many other hotels. It's popular; reserve in advance if possible. *Dbl €120 in high season.*

🏠 **Angelo d'Oro** (24 rooms) V Švalba 38–42; ☎ 052 840 502; f 052 840 111; www.rovinj.at. This 5-star hotel is in a 17th-century Venetian palazzo on the north side of town; whilst it is expensive, it is in a truly beautiful building. Extras at this sublime accommodation include a leafy garden terrace, a health spa & a raised loggia with views out over Rovinj & the Adriatic. *Dbl €208 in high season.*

🏠 **Casa Garzotto** (4 rooms) Garzotto 8; ☎ 052 8118 884; www.casa-garzotto.com. Nice boutique hotel in the centre of town, a renovated house decorated in period style. *Dbl studio apartment €90–140.*

🏠 **Villa Valdibora** (9 rooms) S Chiurcio 8; ☎ 052 845 040; www.valdibora.com. Beautifully restored old townhouse right in the town centre, with dbls and studio apartments. *Dbl €90–160.*

There are many other hotels south of the old town, on the Zlatni rt/Punta Corrente cape, a 15–20-minute walk from town, or on Katarina or Andrea islands, a short boat-ride away.

🏠 **Eden** (325 rooms) L Adamovića; ☎ 052 800 400; f 052 811 349; www.maistra.hr. The Eden complex is the most luxurious option in these parts. *Dbl €120–200.*

🏠 **Monte Mulini** (119 rooms) A. Smareglia; ☎ 052 636 000; f 052 636 001; www.maistra.hr. Rovinj's most luxurious, newly renovated 5-star. *Dbls from €290.*

🏠 **Istra** (376 rooms) Sv Andrea (also confusingly known as Crveni); ☎ 052 802 500; f 052 813 484; www.maistra.hr. A little further away, the Istria offers 3-star accommodation on an island. *Dbl €108–150.*

🏠 **Katarina** (120 rooms) Sv Katarina; ☎ 052 804 100; f 052 804 111; www.maistra.hr. If you want to be on an island then try the Katarina. *Dbl €144–160.*

🏠 **Park** (202 rooms) I M Ronjgova; ☎ 052 808 000; f 052 808 550; www.maistra.hr. Perhaps the most appealing of the large hotels, the Park has benefited from a recent refurbishment. The nicest rooms have lovely views back across the water to the old town. *Dbl €90–150.*

Rovinj also has plenty of private rooms, though many are outside the old town. Rooms can be booked through any of the more than 20 travel agents in town (*try contacting Dik & Co; ☎/f 052 818 181; www.dik-rovinj.com; or see the tourist office website www.tzgrovinj.hr*), and go for about €25–55 for a double in season, though that's based on a six-night stay. Expect to stump up a supplement of 50% for a one- or two-night stay.

For camping, you can't do better than the pleasantly pine-shaded **Porton Biondi** (*Aleja Porton Biondi 1;* ☎ *052 813 557;* f *052 811 509; www.portonbiondi.hr*), a 15-minute walk north of the old town with its own beach and fabulous views back to Rovinj.

✗ **WHERE TO EAT** Restaurants in Rovinj mainly cater to well-off tourists – often locals – who come here for the excellent fish. Don't expect bargains on the quayside, but consider splashing out while you're here, as the quality is exceptional.

✗ **Al Gastaldo** Iza Kasarne 14; ☎ 052 814 109. The highlight at this Italian-style restaurant is the steak with big slices of fresh black truffle. Abundant soft furnishings, old paintings & hundreds of bottles of wine stored in racks combine to create a cosy interior, with a few tables in the narrow street outside the closest thing the Al Gastaldo has to a summer terrace. The food is much better than in the overpriced photo-menu restaurants on the waterfront a block away. No credit cards.

✗ **Amfora** Obala Aldo Rismondo 23; ☎ 052 816 663. Pricey, but usually very good.

✗ **Stella di Mare** Sv Križa 4; Situated where the quay runs out past the tourist office. If you're on a tighter budget try the Stella di Mare. It's in a great location, right on the seashore, & serves pizzas & spaghetti dishes (you just have to ask for what you want in terms of pasta, as the menu only lists the pizzas).

✗ **Veli Jože** Sv Križa 1; ☎ 052 816 337. Up the steps from the Stella di Mare is this cheerful, cluttered *konoba* oozing atmosphere & specialising in excellent Istrian cuisine. Try dishes with the local *tartufi* (truffles), especially if you're here in spring or autumn.

THE BITINADA AND THE ARIA DA NUOTO

Peculiar to Rovinj are two especially interesting types of folk song, the *bitinada* and the *aria da nuoto*.

The *bitinada* developed, it's said, from music-loving fishermen's inability to play instruments and mend nets at the same time, and depends on an 'orchestra' of human voices. A lead tenor acts as the conductor, singing a phrase that is then echoed by the other 'instruments' in a waltzing rhythm. So convincing is this vocal trickery that there's a popular story told about Mussolini, having commanded a *bitinada* performance in Italy during World War II, insisting on going backstage to find out where the real musicians were hiding.

The *aria da nuoto* (night aria), for its part, echoes the fragments of song that would be passed from boat to boat after dark, with fishermen joining in with new harmonies as the song developed. You can hear both *bitinada* and *arie da nuoto* performed during Rovinj's summer-long festival.

✗ **Villa D'Oro Angelo** V Švalba 38–42; ✆ 052 840 502; www.rovinj.at. Rough hewn stone walls, tables topped with starched white linen cloths, oil paintings & stone floors set the scene for a romantic meal. Polite staff & Istrian specialities that far exceed the quality of that on offer in Rovinj's tourist-orientated eateries make this hotel restaurant a stand-out option.

WHAT TO SEE AND DO Rovinj's main attraction is itself – the charming narrow cobbled streets running up through the warren of the old town, the paved car-free quays, the Venetian palazzi and medieval houses, and the 30-odd churches within the old town walls, some so small you'd never know they were there.

The most obvious access to the old town is from the paved isthmus joining Rovinj to the mainland, home to an elegant Baroque clock tower and the former town hall. Walk through the 17th-century Balbi arch (on the site of one of the original seven town gates) and notice the Turk's head on the outside of the arch; on the inside there's a Venetian.

The arch leads through and up to the main street, Grisia, eventually running right on up to the cathedral. Take time to wander off through the maze of tiny streets on either side, however, and you can begin to imagine how dense and un-private medieval life might have been. Each house still has its own stone water cistern and oil store, and a chimney for every family. High up on some buildings, above the windows, look out for the pairs of protruding carved stones – rods used to be threaded through these, for hanging fishing nets out to dry.

Rovinj is also home to a thriving artists' colony, and if you're here in August you could hardly fail to notice the paintings, watercolours, drawings and prints that festoon the whole length of Grisia – tradition has it that if you're a Rovinj artist you have the right to display here. Most of the shops and stalls are unashamedly geared towards tourists, but this is a great place to pick up artistic souvenirs, as well as some of the more interesting Istrian wines and speciality foods.

Church of St Euphemia At the top of the hill is the improbably large church of St Euphemia. Easily the biggest building in town, on a ground plan of 50m by 30m, with a nave nearly 18m tall, the present structure dates from 1725–36 and is a good example of Venetian Baroque, though the front is a 19th-century add-on.

The enormous campanile from 1680 – Istria's biggest, at over 62m – is a copy of the 98.6m bell tower in St Mark's Square in Venice. Rovinj locals insist of course it's the other way round: that the version in Venice, following the July 1902 collapse of the original, is a copy of the one in Rovinj.

Gloomy and somewhat airless inside, the church retains its fair share of treasures, in spite of much of the original silver having been plundered by Napoleon's troops in 1806. The main attraction is St Euphemia herself; with the original church on the site dedicated to St George (and you can still see a fine sculpture of the dragon-basher on the main altar), Euphemia stole the limelight in the year 800 by improbably washing up on the shores nearby in her stone sarcophagus.

Euphemia was one of a group of early Christians arrested in Chalcedon, near Constantinople, in AD304, and is said to have suffered terrible tortures under Diocletian for failing to recant. Miraculously surviving death by fire, a pit of poisonous snakes and being broken on the wheel, it's likely she was still only a teenager when she was fatally thrown to the lions.

Christians managed to recover her body, and under Constantine, in the 7th century, a church was built in her honour. The iconoclasts threw her remains into the sea in the late 8th century, but sailors recovered them and took her to the Greek island of Lemnos. By 796, she was back in Constantinople, mysteriously disappearing in early 800, only to turn up in Rovinj. Hardly surprising, therefore, that the people here gave her co-patroness status, with St George, and built church after church to house her sarcophagus.

The sarcophagus itself is behind the altar in the right-hand aisle of the church, though there's some confusion about whether it's actually 3rd or 6th century, and it was in any case altered in later centuries. Inside are the saint's relics, wrapped in gold cloth. On the altar is a 16th-century gold-plated stone statue of Euphemia, while by the south door you'll find a 14th-century marble relief of her, incorporating bits of earlier sculpture. Most impressive of all is the 4.7m copper statue of the saint adorning the campanile. Cast in 1758, following the destruction by lightning of an earlier wooden statue (which must have been a dramatic moment), Euphemia also does practical duty as a weather vane, just like the original angel on the Campanile di San Marco used to.

On 16 September – the anniversary of her martyrdom – Rovinj celebrates Euphemia's arrival in Rovinj with processions and the performance of miracle plays in the square in front of the church. It's said that in the year 2000 festivities, on the 1,200th anniversary of her arrival, a cloud formed in the shape of the saint.

Beaches and nature reserves Rovinj itself just has a tiny rocky beach past the end of the main quay, but if you go past the marina onto the Zlatni rt/Punta Corrente peninsula – a protected park/forest covering around 70ha of land – you'll find footpaths leading to any number of bathing spots. The park itself is charming, featuring cypresses, pines, firs and lovely cedar trees, including the unusual Himalayan cedar.

The 22 islands and rocky outcrops off Rovinj also make up a dedicated nature reserve with an unusual biodiversity – on Katerina alone, there are supposedly 456 varieties of flora. Katerina and Andrea (Crveni) islands also have lovely rocky beaches and the clearest water imaginable. Boats motor out from Rovinj harbour every half hour or so in summer.

Back onshore, 10km south of Rovinj is the Palud ornithological reserve. Palud (from the Latin *palud*, meaning 'marsh') now provides shelter to a variety of both migratory and non-migratory bird species, as well as turtles, eels and mullet, though it was once supposedly a Roman fish farm. Off the coast from here are the Dvije Sestrice (two sisters) islands, a major seagull nesting site.

Finally, if you're into diving, you're unlikely to find the remains of Cissa, the legendary city that supposedly sank near Rovinj during earthquakes in 754 and 801, but excursions from the town will help you swim down to the wreck of the *Baron Gautsch*. The ship was the Austro-Hungarians' pride and joy until – after hitting one of its own side's mines in 1914 – it sank, about 10km off Rovinj, with the loss of 284 lives.

BRIJUNI ISLANDS

Just northwest of Pula lie the pretty Brijuni (Brioni) Islands, formerly a holiday retreat for Austro-Hungarians, then the private residence of Marshal Tito for 30 years before becoming a national park in 1983 and opening to visitors in 1984 (*www.brijuni.hr*). Not worth an extensive detour, they're nonetheless well worth a visit if you're in Istria, and can comfortably be managed in a day trip from Pula, Rovinj or Poreč.

Visits remain carefully controlled – the Brijuni is still a state residence as well as a national park – and you can only visit parts of two of the islands, Veliki Brijun and Mali Brijun, on an organised tour or by staying at one of the two hotels or half-dozen villas on the main island. Diving, off-limits for years, is now allowed if you're with a recognised professional operator – check with the national park office (see *Where to stay*, page 195).

HISTORY The Romans made wine and olive oil here, and left behind the remains of a swanky country estate on Veriga bay; Byzantium built an important fortress; and Benedictine monks and Venetian overlords left their mark. But it wasn't until 1893 – when Paul Kupelweiser, an Austrian steel magnate, purchased the islands with a view to starting up a health resort – that Brijuni started featuring on the tour map.

Kupelweiser pursued his dream relentlessly by ridding the islands of malaria (kind of important, that, in a sanatorium), clearing the land, building hotels, villas and heated pools, and providing all the luxury accoutrements demanded by the aristocracy. In the years before World War I, they came in droves. On one day in September 1910 no fewer than 11 archdukes and duchesses were logged, while 31 March 1911 saw 16 princes and princesses and 15 counts and countesses in residence. Franz Ferdinand was here before being shot in Sarajevo, kicking off World War I; so was Kaiser Wilhelm, Thomas Mann, James Joyce, George Bernard Shaw, Richard Strauss and the ubiquitous Marconi, always on hand with a radio experiment to be performed in Europe's best holiday destinations.

On Kupelweiser's death in 1919, his son Karl took over the business, adding a casino and an 18-hole golf course, but ending up bankrupt and suicidal, killing himself here in 1930. The Italians took over, but nothing of much note happened until the islands caught Tito's eye in 1947. From 1949 onwards, for six months of the year or so, he managed the rare trick of effectively running the country from his holiday house, something only the Roman Emperor Tiberius on Capri had previously achieved.

Tito had sub-tropical plants brought in and created a private game reserve on the northwestern end of Veliki Brijun from the animals he was given by fellow heads of state. Their descendants are still here, along with one or two of the originals – notably the elephants, Sony and Lanka, gifts from Indira Gandhi. He also welcomed nearly 100

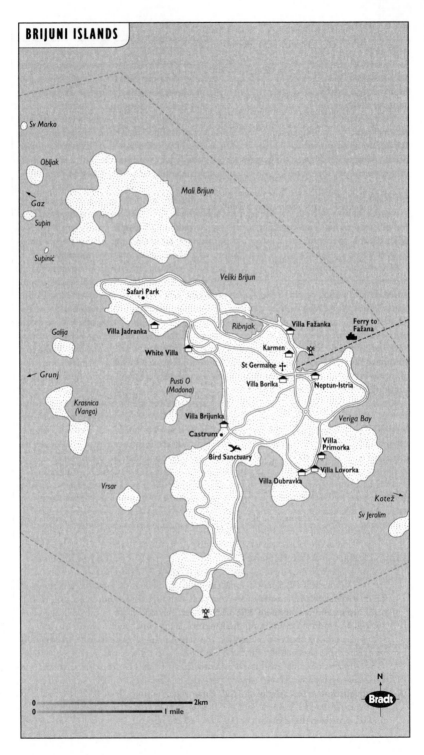

BRIJUNI ISLANDS

Sv Marko

Obljak

Gaz

Supin

Supinić

Mali Brijun

Veliki Brijun

Safari Park

Villa Jadranka

Galija

White Villa

Grunj

Krasnica
(Vanga)

Pusti O
(Madona)

Villa Brijunka

Castrum

Bird Sanctuary

Vrsar

Ribnjak

Villa Fažanka

Ferry to
Fažana

Karmen

St Germaine

Villa Borika

Neptun-Istria

Veriga Bay

Villa
Primorka

Villa Lovorka

Villa Dubravka

Kotež

Sv Jerolim

N

Bradt

0   2km
0   1 mile

heads of state, including Queen Elizabeth II, Ho Chi Minh and the Ethiopian Emperor Haile Selassie, as well as dozens of celebrities, among them Josephine Baker, Sophia Loren, Elizabeth Taylor and Richard Burton.

After Croatia's independence, President Tuđman continued Tito's tradition by summering here, but President Mesić has spent a good deal less time on the islands than his predecessor(s).

GETTING THERE AND AWAY The Brijuni Islands are 20 minutes offshore from the small port of Fažana, 8km northwest of Pula, easily reached on Pula city bus #6. Excursion tickets are available from the Brijuni National Park office on the front in Fažana, and cost 200kn in summer and 170kn in winter. Up to 14 tours a day set off in summer, with just three trips in winter; it's worth reserving ahead at any time of year (✆ 052 525 883; e izleti@brijuni.hr). The national park office will organise your transfer to the island if you're staying over.

Almost any hotel from Poreč to Rovinj to Pula will also be able to put you on an excursion, with the trip (including the bus to Fažana, and – sometimes – lunch) coming in at around 250kn.

In Pula you'll find excursions offered to the islands by private operators for around 200kn a head, but be careful what you're buying, as some of the trips take you round the islands but not onto them, while others are effectively ferries to Mali Brijun for a picnic and a swim. Nice though these trips are, be sure that's what you wanted to do.

Note On the way over to Veliki Brijun keep your eyes peeled for dolphins – small schools are sometimes seen making their way from the Limski Kanal towards the island of Lošinj.

WHERE TO STAY AND EAT Eighty years ago there were five swanky hotels to choose from – not to mention the casino, a horseriding centre, and two polo fields. These days you can either stay at the three-star **Neptun-Istra**, right next to where the boats come in – and the place most of Tito's guests were lodged – or the two-star **Karmen** on the other side of the bay.

Doubles go for €192 at the Neptun-Istra during the priciest three weeks of August but drop right back to €70 from November to April, while rooms at the Karmen are about 10% cheaper. Prices include breakfast and unlimited use of the ferries to and from the mainland, and while they're steep for what you get, they do offer you the only chance you'll get to see the islands outside of a formal excursion.

A choice alternative, if you're in a group, is one of the lovely three- or four-star villas, on the southern end of Veliki Brijun, of which there are half a dozen, sleeping four to eight people. The four-star establishments – **Primorka**, **Lovorka** and **Dubravka**, which are situated right on the beach – come in at around €250 per person per night for bed and breakfast in peak season (€180 in low season), while three-star costs around half that; prices go down around 25% in the off season at the four-star places, but plummet as low as €30 per person per night at the three-star villas in winter.

If you're booked in for accommodation on the island and have driven to Fažana, then you can leave your car in secure parking there for 50kn a day. As for food, unless you brought a picnic with you – a sound idea – you'll almost certainly be eating at one of the hotels; apart from a summer grill (the Plaža) it's all there is.

All accommodation is booked directly through the park office in Fažana (✆ 052 525 888; f 052 521 367; www.brijuni.hr).

WHAT TO SEE AND DO The standard excursion consists of a three-hour miniature-train ride with an English-speaking guide, which takes in the main sights and culminates with an hour or so to explore the museum/exhibitions.

The first thing you'll notice is the herds of deer – there are at least 800 out in the open here, along with mouflon, pheasants and peacocks roaming free. The keener-eyed will also notice the remarkable number of species of flora – at least 600 local and 30 imported.

The northwestern end of the island is fenced-off as a dedicated safari park, featuring zebra, dromedaries, llamas, antelopes, zebu, sheep and the two elephants. The idea of foreign fauna here isn't new – Kupelweiser had the bright idea as far back as 1911 of using the Brijuni Islands to acclimatise tropical animals on their way to European zoos.

You'll also be taken to see the rather tatty ruins of the 1st-century BC Roman country estate at Veriga Bay, which must have been extraordinary at the time but is hard to imagine now. More impressive is the ruined Byzantine fortress on the other side of the island, the heart of the settlement of Castrum, which was inhabited from the 2nd century BC until the early 14th century, when the plague arrived.

The rest of the west coast features the three residential villas of Tito's time, the White Villa, Jadranka and Brijunka. Tito himself had his quarters, along with his exquisite tropical gardens, on the offshore island of Vanga (also called Krasnica), charging between the two and around the other islands by speedboat. The White Villa was used for formal receptions, while Jadranka was where visiting royalty overnighted.

There's no doubt you'll also be shown the Old Lady, an olive tree more than 1,600 years old – carbon-dating says so. In a botanical triumph, and as a vindication of the programme to revitalise the island's olive production, the Old Lady produced enough olives to make oil for the first time in more than 100 years at the end of 2001.

Back at the starting point, the archaeological museum, housed in a small 14th-century Venetian castle, merits a short visit, while the Church of St Germaine, next door, has an interesting collection of copies of Istrian frescoes and Glagolitic inscriptions.

The natural history museum next door is a rather poignant collection of stuffed animals which either died here or on the way here from foreign climes. Upstairs there are two collections, the fascinating photos which make up Josip Broz Tito on Brijuni, and a collection entitled *From the memory of an old Austrian*, dedicated to Paul Kupelweiser.

If you want to see more than is on the tour, you'll probably have to stay over, and hire a guide from the hotel – in-depth freelancing is strongly discouraged. It's a pity, but understandable, given Brijuni's triple function as state residence, national park and tourist destination.

Birdwatchers will most likely want to check out the marshy lakes near the Saline Bay (in the south, unmarked on the maps), which have now been fenced off as a tentative ornithological reservation. Here you'll find excellent nesting grounds for marsh birds including ducks, coots, grebes, quail and noisy pratincoles, as well as warblers, nightingales and other songbirds, while the pine trees provide shelter for goshawks, buzzards and sparrow hawks. Late summer sees the arrival of egrets, storks, herons and bitterns. Contact the national park directly (see *Where to stay*, page 195).

PULA

Strategically situated at Istria's tip, and benefiting from a kind climate and a large, sheltered harbour, Pula (Pola) has been continuously inhabited for the past 3,000 years. What you'll find today, however, is a whole clutch of superb Roman ruins (including one of the world's best-preserved amphitheatres) set in a cheerful, cosmopolitan, street-café city of 65,000 people. Pula lives on the fence, caught halfway between its shipyard, docks and busy commercial port, and the beaches, coves and tourist developments strung out along the indented peninsula a couple of kilometres south of the centre.

Bombarded by both sides during World War II – a rare distinction – the city was quickly restored, and during the Yugoslav era became popular as a holiday destination. The recent war didn't come anywhere near here, but drove away the tourists all the same – though they've now returned in force. Pula's role as a yachting centre, together with the increasing availability of budget flights and the annual Pula Film Festival (see page 202) mean that visitor numbers are likely to rise further still.

HISTORY Mentioned in ancient Greek despatches in connection with Jason and the Argonauts, archaeological findings show that Pula (myths notwithstanding) had already been established as a settlement long before the Histri fortified it in the 1st century BC. Once the Romans had successfully overpowered the Histri, Pula grew rapidly in status and became a colony. Under the first Roman emperor, Augustus, it became an important regional centre, and temples, theatres, a forum and an amphitheatre were built.

At its most prosperous, in the time of Septimius Severus (AD193–211), Pula was an important Roman war harbour, and was by then – according to my 1911 Encyclopaedia Britannica – home to a population of 35,000 to 50,000 inhabitants. Mysteriously, contemporary sources never mention a figure of more than 5,000 to 10,000.

After the decline of Rome, Pula's fortunes were subjected to the usual roller-coaster ride of Goths, Ostrogoths, Byzantium and Venice, and the combination of invasion and plague saw the city shrink to 1,000 inhabitants in the 16th century. By 1631 the population was down to just 300 – hardly surprising therefore that the Venetians considered having the amphitheatre removed from Pula and put up in Venice instead.

Over the centuries Pula was visited by the likes of Dante, Michelangelo, Palladio and Lord Byron, spreading the Pula influence into Italian, French and British architecture – Inigo Jones is said to have used the Sergius Arch (see page 203) as the inspiration for many a loving detail on an English country house.

By 1842, Pula's population had inched up to 1,126, but change was right around the corner. With the collapse of Venice, 50 years earlier, the Austro-Hungarian Empire was seeking major outlets to the Mediterranean, and in 1853 they settled on Pula, rebuilding the town, installing a garrison, starting a shipyard and making it their naval HQ for the empire. By the end of the century Pula's population had exploded to over 45,000.

Badly bombed during World War II, Pula came under Allied administration until 1947, when it passed to Yugoslavia. Today it's the headquarters of the Croatian Navy as well as one of Croatia's three main shipyards, alongside Rijeka and Split.

GETTING THERE AND AWAY Pula airport is 7km northeast of the city, and a regular airport shuttle bus will bring you into town in around 15 minutes or so. If you're on an Istrian package tour of any kind, then you'll probably be transferred straight from the airport to your hotel. An alternative is to fly to Venice and connect with the car ferry, which takes around six hours to make the crossing. From July until the end of August, Venezia Lines (*www.venezialines.com*) makes this journey four times a week.

If you're coming in by train, you'll find the station on the waterfront, ten minutes north of the old town – just head towards the amphitheatre past the Hotel Riviera. There are left-luggage facilities here, but the hours are much shorter than those at the bus station, only being open Monday to Saturday. Three trains a day come in from both Rijeka (2½ hours away) and Zagreb (7 hours). There are also two trains a day from Ljubljana (4 hours).

If you're travelling round by bus, then you'll find the new station a couple of blocks north of the amphitheatre, though most buses do a loop into town via the old bus station as well. Left-luggage facilities are open here 05.00–23.00 seven days a week. A dozen or so buses a day head up to each of Rovinj (40 minutes) and Zagreb (5½ hours), while eight or more go daily to Poreč (1½ hours), two to Split (11 hours) and one to Dubrovnik (15 hours).

PULA

Bradt

CESTA PREKOMORSKIH BRIGADA

ZAGREBAČKA ULICA

MUTILSKA ULICA

ULICA MARSOVOG POLJA

VALTURSKA ULICA

✈ Airport

ULICA

MARULIĆEVA ULICA

P
P
P

DIVKOVIĆEVA ULICA

STANKOVIĆEVA ULICA

RAKOVČEVA

ULICA

MLETAČKA ULICA

Market

RADIĆEVA

Caffe Milan

Galija

DOBRILINA ULICA

Omir
Bounty ✕

KUKULJEVIĆEVA ULICA

New bus station

ULICA 43 ISTARSKE DIVIZIJE

P

Jadran

Hercules Gate ●

LAGINJINA

● Sergius Arch

Uliks

ANTIČOVA ULICA

ARSENALSKA ULICA

Old bus station

Scaletta

●● Amphitheatre

● Historical
Museum of Istria

Twin
Gate

Roman
Theatre

Jupiter ✕

Roman † Mary Formosa
mosaic ●

ULICA
STARIH
STATUTA

Historical
Museum
of Istria

Galerija
Cvajner

FLACIUSOVA ULICA

Riviera

RIVA

RIVA

KANDLEROVA

RIVA

P

TRŠĆANSKA ULICA

□ Railway station

Cathedray of
St Mary

ULICA

☑ The
Forum

Town Hall ⊞

● Temple of
Augustus

RIVA

PARTIZANSKI PUT

0 ————————— 500m
0 ————————— 500yds

Driving round Pula is pretty easy, though in high summer parking in the centre of town can be a problem – not, however, the insurmountable one you'll find in Opatija.

GETTING AROUND The centre of town is all walkable – and mostly pedestrianised – but you might find yourself on bus #21 if you're going up to Fažana to catch a boat to the Brijuni Islands, #2 if you're hostelling, #1 if you're heading towards Stoja, and #2a or #3a for Verudela, where the beaches, the hostel and most of the hotels can be found. See www.pulapromet.hr for bus route map. Bus tickets go for 11kn in town and 15kn or more for longer journeys (eg: Fažana) on the bus, and are valid for two rides each.

WHERE TO STAY Pula has relatively few hotels in town, but many more on the Verudula peninsula, handy for the beaches. Small family-run hotels are opening up all the time, with the encouragement of the tourist board, so check out the **tourist**

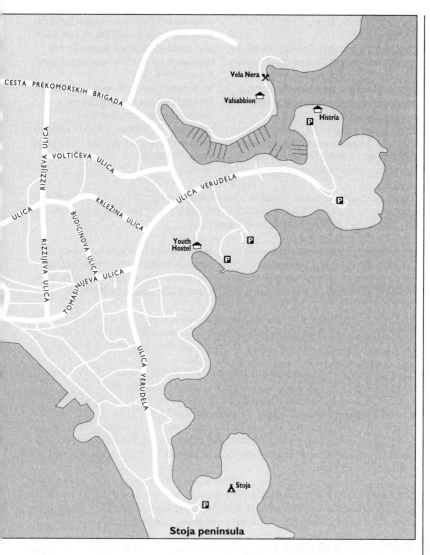

Stoja peninsula

information office (*Fourm 3;* ☎ *052 212 987;* f *052 211 855;* e *tz-pula@pu.htnet.hr;* *www.pulainfo.hr*), which can also give you maps and useful information, as well as providing internet access (if your need is brief). The Histria and another dozen hotels (those in the vicinity are mostly three-star) can also be booked directly through Arenaturist, which manages most of them, during office hours (☎ *052 529 400;* f *052 529 401; www.arenaturist.hr*).

🏠 **Galija** (20 rooms) Epulonova 3; 052 383 802; f 52 383 804; www.hotelgalija.hr. Small, swanky family 3–star in town centre, with its own restaurant. *Dbl* €99 *in season.*

🏠 **Histria** (233 rooms) Verudela bb; ☎ 052 590 000; f 052 214 175; www.arenaturist.hr. Nicest of all is this

palatial 4-star, which has practically an entire promontory to itself, & views out to sea, back to the marina & all conceivable facilities – including nice private balconies, big indoor & outdoor pools, & its own beach. Dbls include a vast buffet b/fast. ⏰ all year round – off-season prices drop as much as 50%.

Take the #7 bus to the last stop, & walk 200m. *Dbl €96–160 in summer.*

🏠 **Omir** (19 rooms) Serglia Dobrića 6; ➚/f 052 213 944; www.hotel-omir.com. The 2-star Omir, just to the east of the old town & close to both the Sergius Arch & the market square, is simple but much better value than the Riviera. Has its own restaurant and long-serving pizzeria. *Dbl €68.*

🏠 **Riviera** (67 rooms) Splitska 1; ➚ 052 211 166; f 052 219 117; www.arenaturist.hr. Most striking from the outside this pre-World War I hotel just down from the train station, a fantastic Austro-Hungarian

edifice that would look more at home in Zagreb than Istria. Once very much luxury class, the hotel is now on its uppers – 1-star, & quite appealing for that, though you're paying a lot for the privilege of former elegance. *Dbl €40–95.*

🏠 **Scaletta** (12 rooms) Flavijenska 26; ➚ 052 541 599; f 052 540 285; www.hotel-scaletta.com. In the middle of town, almost next door to the amphitheatre. The rooms are all delightful, & the food here is also excellent, so consider HB – if you can get a room. *Dbl €80–100.*

The other hotels are out on Verudela, a ten-minute bus ride (#7 or #3) or a half-hour walk away to the south. The peninsula and Stoja, to the west (#1 bus), have all the best beaches, within striking distance of the town itself.

🏠 **Valsabbion** (15 rooms) Pješčana Uvala IX/26; ➚ 052 218 033; f 052 383 333; www.valsabbion.hr. This is a 15min walk round the far side of the marina from the #7 bus route. Due to its low room count it

might be classified 3-star but in most respects it's 4-star. Sea-view dbls, and the restaurant here was voted the best in Istria 5 years running, & the best in Croatia in 1998. Closed in Jan. *Dbl €84–129.*

Pula has its fair share of private rooms, which cost €30–50 for a double, but the locations often leave something to be desired. Book through any of the 20-odd travel agents in town, and expect to pay a 50% surcharge for a one-night stay in summer. There's also a good list of private accommodation on the tourist office website (*www.pulainfo.hr*). **Pula Apartments** (*Flavijevska 2;* ➚ *052 506 217;* m *098 486 109; www.pula-apartments.com*) has apartments close to the amphitheatre.

If you're on a budget you might be better off trying to get in at Pula's excellent **Youth Hostel** (*216 beds; Zaljev Valsaline 4;* ➚ *052 391 133;* f *052 391 106; www.hfhs.hr*), which is basic and simple but in an incredible location, with its own beach and a diving club next door. Bed and breakfast costs €12–16 per person per night. Catch bus #2 or #3 to the Piramida stop, walk back one street, turn left and walk right to the end.

Finally, Pula is great for camping, with an easy-to-reach campground at **Stoja** (➚ *052 387 144;* f *052 387 748; www.arenacamps.com*) – just take the #1 bus to the last stop, about 3km out of town. The Stoja has fairly basic facilities, but an absolutely unbeatable location and some of the best swimming near Pula.

✕ **WHERE TO EAT AND DRINK** The best restaurants in Pula are reckoned by the locals to be south of the town, in Verudela.

✕ **Valsabbion** Pješčana Uvala IX/26; ➚ 052 218 033; f 052 383 333. If you want a touch of class (& have a pretty fat wallet) the Valsabbion is well worth the splurge; you'll be treated like a king & probably eat better than most royals.

✕ **Vela Nera** Pješčana Uvala; ➚ 052 219 209; f 052 215 951; www.velanera.hr. A slightly less expensive option to the nearby Valsabbion, which is unprepossessing enough on arrival but has a lovely seaside terrace, a covered dining room overlooking the marina & excellent food.

In town the emphasis is as much on café life as restaurants, and every district has huge terraces spreading out onto the pavements, packed in summer and surprisingly well attended in spring and autumn. With most of the old town traffic-free, you can take a leaf out of the Puležani's book and take the time to linger over a coffee or an aperitif.

After eloping to Europe in October 1904 with Nora Barnacle, a 20-year-old chambermaid, the 22-year-old James Joyce finally managed to find part-time work teaching English at the Berlitz School in Pula that November.

Moving in with Nora to an unheated apartment in Villa Giulia, just round the corner from the school (in the large yellow building right beside the Sergius Arch – there's a plaque), Jim and Nora spent the winter in Pula half-freezing to death, and spent as much time as they could at the warmer Caffe Miramare delle Specce, down on the waterfront (it's now a furniture shop). In letters to his brother he described Pula as 'Siberia by the sea', but it's clear that Joyce grew to love the city, and he would often be seen on long walks around town and up the coast as far as the fishing village of Fažana.

In February 1905, he was taken to the island of Veliki Brijun for his 23rd birthday by his Berlitz colleagues, and on this trip he broke the news that his first child was on the way. The couple, deciding to settle in Pula, moved to a more comfortable apartment at 1 Medulinska (next door to the university's faculty of philosophy), but following a confusing incident – was Joyce suspected of spying for the Italians or the British? – they packed their bags and hurriedly moved to Trieste, where their son Giorgio was born that July.

Today you'll find little in the way of Joyce memorabilia in town – the Uliks bar, on the ground floor of the apartment building housing the language school, does celebrate the author of *Ulysses* in a modest way with a life-size seated statue of the great artist waiting to be served at one of the terrace tables.

✗ **Bounty** Veronska 8; ☎ 052 218 088. Opposite the market, just up Veronska, this is enormously popular with students & expats. The pub serves up around 2 dozen types of beer & hearty Anglo-style food.

▱ **Galerija Cvajner** Forum 2; ☎ 052 216 502; www.cvajner.com. Down at the bottom of the town in the Forum you'll find the Galerija Cvajner, a café-cum-art-gallery run by the former director of the film festival. It has a lovely terrace (right next door to the tourist office) while inside are great 16th-century ceilings & the remains of old frescoes, uncovered by chance during restoration.

▱ **Jadran** Giardini 3. When the rest of the city's stifling you can't do better than the Jadran, a terrace right at the top end of Giardini, the street leading down along the old town wall from the Hercules Gate to the Sergius Arch. It's 1 of the few places in town with guaranteed shade & a breeze.

✗ **Jupiter** Castropola 42; ☎ 052 214 333. Highly recommended for pizzas, you should try this place on Castropola, the upper street running parallel to

Sergijevaca, though I have to confess to not having eaten there myself; it was full both times I passed.

▱ **Uliks** Trg Portarata 1; ☎ 052 219 158. Up at the other end of the old town, all the way up Sergijevaca, you'll find Uliks, in the building in which James Joyce used to teach (see box on page 200).

▱ **Caffe Milan** On Narodni Trg, 100m further on, alongside the lovely Secessionist cast-iron market building, famous not just for its coffees but also for the underfloor heating on the terrace. It would have suited James Joyce a treat. Inside the market you'll find fresh meat & fish every day, while on the shady square behind there's a vast range of produce on sale, protected from the flies by the chestnut trees – the perfect place to cruise for picnic food.

✗ **Scaletta** Flavijenska 26; ☎ 052 541 599. If you're near the amphitheatre you might eat at the Scaletta hotel's very good restaurant – not inexpensive but well worth the splash. Failing that, you won't go far wrong looking through the windows of busy-looking establishments & choosing for yourself.

Istria PULA

5

WHAT TO SEE AND DO The best way to see Pula is on foot and the best place to start is in the Forum, the large paved square just back from the front, on the southwestern corner of town. Stop in at the tourist office and pick up a free map.

The first thing you'll have seen as you came into the square won't have been tourist information but the **Temple of Augustus**. Built in 2BC, according to most modern sources, the temple is one of the best complete Roman monuments outside Italy, rivalling the Maison Carrée in Nîmes. After suffering a direct hit during World War II, it was pieced lovingly back together in 1947, and you wouldn't know the difference.

Originally this was one of three temples on the Forum, and you can still clearly see the shape and placing of the Temple of Diana, one of the other two (the third has gone without trace), by walking round to the back of the 13th-century **town hall** next door. While you're there don't miss the sculpted Renaissance siren/mermaid on the northernmost corner, warding off evil.

Walking up Kandlerova will take you past the cathedral towards the amphitheatre. The houses along the way are reflective of Pula's mixed past, with Renaissance blending into Venetian Gothic, and Romanesque mixing into Austro-Hungarian solidity.

The **Cathedral of St Mary** itself would doubtless get more attention if it weren't surrounded by so many Roman ruins – indeed the separate (rather chunky) campanile was built in the 17th century entirely from stones from the amphitheatre. Pop into the cathedral for a peek at the altar, actually a 3rd-century sarcophagus, and some fragments of floor mosaics. The cathedral was started in the 5th century as a conversion job on a Roman temple, but didn't reach its present form until the 16th and 17th centuries.

The Amphitheatre
You can't miss Pula's enormous Roman Amphitheatre – it's the sixth biggest in the world (after Rome, Capua, Verona, Syracuse and Arles, since you ask), and has the most complete outer walls of any still standing. Started under Augustus, and continued under Flavian, it was enlarged and completed to its present 130m-by-105m ellipse under Vespasian (whose lover Antonia, it's said, came from Pula) in the second half of the 1st century AD.

Built outside the city walls, the triple-storeyed building originally had seating for over 20,000 people (odd, given the total population at its completion is widely reckoned to be considerably less than this) and had 20 entrances and exits to allow for rapid access to the seats. Most of the seating has long gone of course – used for building as far away as Venice – but once there would have been stone benches up to the second storey and wooden seating (for women and commoners) above that. Seats were a tight 38cm across and season-ticket holders had engraved name-plates.

Four towers gave access to the upper rows – the southwestern tower housed the royal box, while the northwestern one today features a plaque to the Pula-born Venetian Senator Gabriele Emo, who happily persuaded the Senate in 1583 not to take the amphitheatre away.

The arena in the middle would originally have been filled with sand (arena is Latin for sand) and was used for bloody combats until the beginning of the 5th century. Watching a film-screening or taking in a concert here today, it's hard to imagine the awfulness of real gladiator combats – lions and bears were used here against gladiators (mostly luckless prisoners of war), who were also pitted against one another.

After Rome collapsed the arena was used as a marketplace and for medieval jousting tournaments, but the seating was mostly quarried; today's concerts and screenings seat just 5,000–6,000, and even the biggest gigs – your Stings, your Three Tenors – can't pack in many more than 10,000 fans. If you're here in summer, don't miss out on the opera or film festivals.

Back into town Walking back towards the town turn half-left into Carrarina and have a look at the Twin Gate (Porta Gemina), from the 2nd century. This was once part of the aqueduct providing water to the town and one of the town's 12 gates, and was one of the few monuments built with private money. It's now the entrance to the exhaustive Archaeological Museum of Istria, although the exhibits themselves are a bit of a jumble. Re-ordering and re-labelling would work wonders. Even if you don't go inside don't miss the classical sculptures in the garden, or the small Roman theatre here.

The upper road to the right of the museum leads up to the tatty, 17th-century Venetian **fortress**, housing the **Historical Museum of Istria** – only worth seeing if you've done everything else, though the views out over the town and particularly of the amphitheatre are excellent from up here.

Back down at the Twin Gate keep the wall on your right and follow Carrarina down past the **Hercules Gate**. This is Pula's oldest monument, dating from the middle of the 1st century BC; it's now the entrance to the centre for the Italian minority. The gate's unusual oblique angle is a reminder that the road originally leading out wasn't at right-angles to the wall.

Turning into the shady Giardini, follow the walls down to the Sergius Arch (also known as Porta Aurea). This was completed in 27BC as a memorial to three soldiers from the same family, Sergius Lepidus, Gaius Lucius Sergius and Gnaeus Sergius. The arch was originally backed by a gate, so only the inside is decorated – check out the winged victories, imagery which was later co-opted wholesale by Christianity when portraying angels.

The Sergius Arch leads – not surprisingly – into Sergijevaca, the old town's main pedestrian street, running back down to the Forum. Halfway down, cut left to the small, 6th-century Byzantine **Church of Mary Formosa**, once part of a larger basilica, built to a similar plan to the one in Poreč (see page 183). The best mosaics from inside are now in the Archaeological Museum. Just down from here is an impressive 3rd-century mosaic floor, discovered by accident in 1959. Amongst some fine decorative geometrical work the main panel depicts the Punishment of Dirce – Dirce is the woman in the middle, about to be trampled by the bull, in yet another rendition of the story made famous by the Farnese Bull in Naples. Dirce was the classic cruel stepmother, who treated her husband Lycus's daughter Antiope as a slave. Unfortunately for her, Antiope had already borne two children by Zeus, and once they grew up – after the traditional hillside abandonment – the boys returned to kill Dirce by binding her to a mad bull. Not a great way to go.

Out of town Out of town, the main attractions are the Brijuni Islands (see page 193), which are well worth a visit, and the 30km of beaches coves and bays to the south of the city. The nearest of these are just a 20- to 25-minute walk away from the town centre, or a short bus ride away (on #1, #2 or #7).

Further south, right on Istria's point, are the resorts of **Medulin** and **Premantura**. Each has long stretches of beach with fairly shallow waters, making them popular with families. The **Kažela** camp (✆ 052 576 050; f 052 577 460; www.kampkazela.com), on Medulin's sandy beach, has a large (separate) section for naturists. On the other side of the bay, the peninsula's spectacular southernmost spur, Rt Kamenjak, is a dedicated nature park.

THE EAST COAST TO LABIN AND RABAC

From Pula to the resort of Rabac, the Istrian coast is at its least developed and least visited. The new main road barrels up through the centre of Istria to Pazin before cutting through the Učka tunnel to Rijeka, while the old main road stays 5–10km inland from the undeveloped east coast, only returning to the sea after Labin.

There's little or no public transport, and few places to stay, but if you have your own wheels (and some persistence) you can find deserted coves and beaches here at the end of winding footpaths, even though the steep cliffs often make the coast literally inaccessible. It's a great area to explore on day trips from the coastal resorts, or en route to Opatija.

If you're on the bus from Pula to Opatija in the last week of August, it's definitely worth stopping in the village of **Barban**, where the annual Tilting at the Ring (*Trka na prstenac*) festival takes place. The dangerous habit of trying to spear a ring suspended on a rope with a lance from a fast-moving horse used to be commonplace, apparently; today it survives only here and in Sinj (see page 289).

Labin, a charming medieval hilltop town, used to be the centre of a thriving mining industry. You won't see much sign of that now, since the mines closed after subsidence in the 1970s. Today it's a lovely place to visit, with steep and narrow streets, a sprinkling of churches and a handful of Baroque and Renaissance palazzi. The **town museum** features an excellent mining exhibition, complete with a suitably claustrophobic tunnel you can go into, as well as various archaeological bits and pieces from the area. Ask at the museum if Matija Vlačić's birthplace is open – if so you'll find an interesting collection of manuscripts and books by (and about) this 16th-century protestant firebrand, contemporary and colleague of Martin Luther. On the way you can walk up to the fortress (*Fortica*) for a fine view out over Rabac and across the water towards the island of Cres.

Rabac, down on the coast, was once a fishing village but is now unashamedly a tourist resort, with nothing much other than apartments and hotels, though it does have a nice (if busy) pebbly beach.

GETTING THERE AND AWAY Pula–Opatija buses stop in Labin's lower town, a steep 15-minute hike below the old town, and you change here if you're going on to Rabac – buses take ten minutes and run half-hourly down to the resort. Alternatively if you've made it up into Labin's old town you can then walk down to Rabac – it takes about three-quarters of an hour, all downhill, on the old mule path.

WHERE TO STAY There aren't any hotels in Labin, though there are a few private rooms – check at whichever tourist agency is open, or at the **tourist office** (✆/f 052 855 560; www.rabac-labin.com). Rabac, on the other hand, has a dozen or so, though none are open all year round. Expect to pay around € 130–220 at the 4-star **Bellevue** (formerly the Neptun; ✆ 052 465 200; www.valamar.com) for a double in season, or € 72–127 for a double in season with half board at the 2-star **Mediteran** (✆ 052 862 027; www.valamar.com) – in each case for a sea-view double in high season, which can also be booked through Valamar's central reservation system (✆ 052 465 200).

TO OPATIJA AND UČKA Telephone code 051 (+385 51 from abroad)

Istria's northeastern corner has been popular with visitors for over a century, though it's now more nouveau riche than Habsburg chic. If you're here in the middle of August with your own car, expect to have trouble finding anywhere to park, but remember you can get away from it all by climbing up into the Učka mountains behind Opatija.

THE COAST TO OPATIJA Soon after you've left Labin, the road rejoins the steep coast, and you pass the medieval – and abandoned – village of **Plomin**, before turning north on the winding route to the Opatija Riviera, which is technically part of the Kvarner Gulf. If you happen to be driving past Plomin there's a great restaurant on the main road here called **Dorina**, which serves up hearty Istrian staples at very reasonable rates – it's understandably popular with locals. Their asparagus soup is unrivalled, and the *mineštra* (thick bean soup) is excellent. For main courses try the *fuži* (pasta) with truffles or the amazing *gnjoki* (*gnocchi*) which – in a triumph of excess – is served with both squid and truffles together. If that's not enough to convince you, the bargain house white will. The first part of the coast here is undeveloped – it's too steep to build on – though you'll see plenty of summer traffic heading down to **Brestova**, departure-point for ferries to **Cres**. At the height of the season drivers sometimes have to queue for hours to get on board.

From **Brseč** you can take a higher, less busy, parallel road along the coast for 8km or so, offering terrific vertiginous views – keep your eyes on the road and your hands on the wheel if you're driving. Brseč itself is well worth a wander around with some appealing little churches, cute cobbled lanes and stone archways leading you around this hillside town. If you have one too many (ie: one, as the blood alcohol limit is 0.05% for drivers) in the local *konoba*, **Konoba Batelan**, you can stay the night in one of the village's many private rooms. If you're driving to Opatija, just beyond Brseč you'll find a couple of lovely coves blessed with white shingle sand: there are unmarked parking places identified by painted yellow rubbish bins. Just park and follow the steps down through the undergrowth to enjoy a spot of sunbathing or a dip in the Adriatic. The roads meet up again in **Mošćenička Draga**, the first resort in the Opatija Riviera, with the tiny village dwarfed by the **Hotel Marina** (*Aljea Slatina 2;* ↘ *051 737 504;* f *051 737 584; www.liburnia.hr*), which has doubles for € 120–140. Things get more serious 4km later when you reach the pebbles of **Medveja**, the last long concrete-free beach before the far side of Rijeka.

Next up is the Opatija Riviera's prettiest resort, **Lovran**, featuring lots of late Habsburg-era villas and a well-preserved nugget of an old town. Lovran is just 5km south of Opatija and practically merges with it – you can walk along the pedestrianised front between the two in about an hour.

The name Lovran derives from the laurel tree, and you'll see plenty of these in the resort – along with cypresses, palm trees and lovely flowers. You'll also notice the town's obsession with chestnuts, not just as far as trees are concerned, but also in terms of the food. In October, over a two-week period, the *Maranuda* (chestnut festival) is an excuse to binge on every conceivable chestnut-related goodie.

🏠 **Where to stay and eat** There's plenty of private accommodation available, through any of the tourist agencies on the main road, though you may have trouble finding a room if you don't book well ahead. Get the latest list from the Lovran **tourist office** (*Šetalište Maršala Tita 63, 51415 Lovran;* ↘ *051 291 740;* f *051 294 387; www.tz-lovran.hr*). For hotels, the three-star **Lovran** (*Šetalište Maršala Tita 19/2;* ↘ *051 291 222;* f *051 292 467; www.hotel-lovran.hr*) has simple sea-view doubles at € 118 for two in high season, while next door the swankier four-star **Excelsior** (*Šetalište Maršala Tita 15;* ↘ *051 292 233;* f *051 291 989; www.liburnia.hr*), with indoor and outdoor pools, charges € 90–120. Both hotels are just a block from the sea and only a few minutes' walk from the old town. There's also the hugely popular **Delfino** pizzeria (↘ *051 293 293; www.delfino.hr*), owned by the same people as the Delfino in Rijeka.

Lovran makes an ideal base for walking in the Učka massif (see 000), and the tourist office has a good walking map.

North of Lovran, the small towns and little bays (but biggish resorts) of **Ika** and **Ičići** lead seamlessly on to Opatija.

OPATIJA Opatija (originally Abbazia, after the former Benedictine abbey) is astonishingly popular, and has been for over a century. Rooms in the nicest hotels are booked a year or more ahead, and don't even think about trying to find street parking in August.

'Vienna on Sea' is justifiably proud of its Habsburg villas and palaces, its exotic palms and manicured gardens and its 12km-long pedestrianised front, stretching from Lovran in the south to Volosko in the north, but the fashionable winter resort of Opatija never quite made the post-World War II leap from winter to summer tourism. The beaches here are concrete, and netted in (my trusty 1966 *Gateway Guide* explains: 'the visitor should stay within the barriers and never swim far out from the shore since there are sometimes sharks'); the summer crowds can intimidate; and beyond the late 19th-century swank, there's really nothing to see. It's still a great place to come in winter, however, when the town slips quietly back into a nostalgic reverie, and afternoon cakes are picked at with silver forks by retired Austrians.

Until the arrival of the wealthy Rijeka trader, Iginio Scarpa, in 1844, Opatija was the proverbial sleepy fishing village. Scarpa built the **Villa Angiolina** (named after his wife) and created its exotic gardens as a summer retreat, and the high and mighty were soon paying visits.

Given a clean bill of health by doctors to the wealthy – like so many nice places to stay – Opatija soon became a spa town, and *the* place to take a 'cure' (and be seen) in winter. It was helped on its way by the arrival of the railway in Rijeka in 1873 – by 1884 the Kvarner hotel was up and running, and demand was so high that the Imperial was opened only a year later, with the Palace-Bellevue hot on its heels.

Anyone who was anyone in the Austro-Hungarian sphere of influence came here, and it was hugely popular with the aristocracy. Anton Chekhov, Gustav Mahler and Sigmund Freud gave their patronage, while Vladimir Nabokov spent his childhood holidays here (probably up in the hills collecting butterflies).

If you're planning on staying in Opatija in summer it's a good idea to try and book a year in advance – though you may be lucky with private rooms through one of the many tourist agencies in town. It may also be worth writing or calling ahead to the tourist board (*Vladimira Nazora 3, 51410 Opatija;* ☏ *051 271 710;* f *051 271 699; www.opatija-tourism.hr*).

Where to stay If you have the time to plan, and the budget, Opatija is one place where it's really worth splashing out, as the opulent 19th-century hotels are remarkably good value in their class. Opatija is also home, as you'd expect, to three of Istria's big five-star hotels: the Ambassador, the Milenij and the Mozart. The first two have indoor and outdoor pools; the third offers remarkably good-value Viennese-style elegance (see below).

Ambassador (180 rooms) Feliksa Peršića 1; ☏ 051 743 333; f 051 743 444; www.liburnia.hr. Big, swanky & modern, with sea views. *Dbl €188–212 in season.*

Imperial (126 rooms) Šetalište Maršala Tita 124/3; ☏ 051 271 677; f 051 272 848; www.liburnia.hr. Classic hotel with tastefully elegant lobby & bars. *Dbl €80–100 high season, €64–80 winter.*

Kvarner–Amalia (87 rooms) Pave Tomašića 1–4; ☏ 051 271 233; f 051 271 202; www.liburnia.hr. Another classic hotel with an astounding 1913 Crystal Ballroom. *Dbl with sea view €130 in season.*

Milenij (125 rooms) Šetalište Maršala Tita 109; ☏ 051 202 000; f 051 202 020; www.milenijhoteli.hr. Elegant hotel spanning three *fin-de-siècle* villas, with rooms decorated in classic or modern style. *Dbl €170.*

Mozart (30 rooms) Šetalište Maršala Tita 138; ☏ 051 718 260; f 051 271 739; www.hotel-mozart.hr. Much smaller in scale, with very smart dbls with sea view. *Dbl €120–150.*

Palace-Bellevue (210 rooms) Šetalište Maršala Tita 144/146; ☏ 051 271 811; f 051 271 964; www.liburnia.hr. Worth staying at to check out the fabulous reception rooms alone. *Dbl €72–85.*

VOLOSKO If you're in Opatija, make the effort to walk along the shore to Volosko, still a fishing village even though it's barely half an hour on foot from the summer throngs. It's Mediterranean to Opatija's Habsburg, and though it's no secret, it is a pretty place to go for lunch on the shores of the Adriatic looking out towards the islands of the Kvarner Gulf. In recent years it has evolved into something of a gastronomic destination with Le Mandrač (see below), which many Croats rate as the best restaurant in the entire country.

✗ Where to eat and drink

✗ **Amfora** Črnikovica 4; ☎ 051 701 222; www.restaurant-amfora.com. First-rate restaurant serving Adriatic staples & offering fine sea views. The fresh white fish is excellent, but does mean pushing the boat out.

✗ **Kon-tiki** Frana Supila 12; ☎ 051 701 661. Before you break the bank at Le Mandrač (see below), check your bank balance with the Wi-Fi connections at trendy Kon-tiki next door. Alternatively just relax here in their comfy seats, taking in the ambience & watching the local cats weave their way around the harbour side. They do a mean *bijela kava*.

✗ **Le Mandrać** Frana Supila 10; ☎ 051 701 357; www.lemandrac.com. Not for nothing does the *Dobri Hrvatski Restoran* 2005 guide give this stylish eatery, which fuses Istrian & Asian influences, 90/100 (their second highest rating in the fine dining guide). Opened in 2004, it doesn't miss a trick & is well worth the splurge. The design of the restaurant itself is innovative

with the main building topped off with a floor-to-ceiling glass conservatory overlooking the Adriatic. It's in the kitchen, however, that the real creativity's happening, with the likes of sea bass atop an 'octopus burger' & a sauce that manages to successfully marry beurre blanc with a tepanyaki sauce. For lunch try the 4-course mini-degustation menu at 250kn; for dinner splash out on the 'exploring menu', a 490kn 9-course culinary extravaganza that might well be the best meal you ever have in Croatia.

✗ **Plavi Podrum** Frana Supila 4; ☎ 051 701 223; www.restaurant-amfora.com/plavi. As good as it gets seafood restaurant overlooking Volosko's bijou harbour. Compared to Le Mandrač, it's always going to look a little 'old school', but they do the standards such as grilled squid & white fish extremely well, alongside plenty of innovative dishes and a degustation menu. Book early in season if you want a table on the popular terrace.

UČKA Rising up above the Opatija Riviera – and giving it its mild winter/cool summer climate, while cutting it off from the rest of Istria – is the Učka massif, culminating in the 1,396m summit of Vojak, the highest point on Veli Učka (Monte Maggiore). On a clear evening they say you can see the lights of Venice from here; what's sure is that you get a great view of the Kvarner Bay and the island of Cres.

With your own transport you can drive right to the top of the mountain on a tarred road (leading up to the TV transmitter), though parking is limited; walking is a far better way of exploring. Good maps are available from the tourist offices in Rijeka, Opatija and Lovran, with well-marked trails and the chance to really get away from it all.

The most obvious ascent starts off from a junction on the old Rijeka–Pazin road (not the main road, which heads through the Učka tunnel) – this can also be reached from Opatija, or via a dizzying series of hairpins from Ičići.

About 7km after the village of Veprinac, you'll find the **Pansion-Restaurant Učka** (*Vela Učka bb;* ☎ *051 603 340*), with ten rustic rooms at around € 50 for doubles and a terrace with big views. But you'll need your own wheels as the only public transport up here is the #34 bus from Opatija, which operates on Sundays only, once in each direction – unless, of course you've hiked up (see below).

From the Pansion, it's just over 1km to the **Dopolovaro Restaurant** (*Vela Učka 9;* ☎ *051 299 641*), which is usually busy at weekends and generally not open during the week. Just beyond the restaurant you'll find the road on the left which leads up to the summit, almost exactly 6km up the road. On foot it's a pleasant hike up, with great views on the way and even better ones from the top – turn left at the TV and radio mast, and follow the path up to the trig point, on top of a small tower. Avoid sliding down the hang-glider take-off ramp on the way up – unless of course you've brought your hang-glider with you.

Real hikers will of course want to climb the Učka massif from sea-level. To do this the obvious base is Lovran, though there is a path up from Medveja. The Lovran path starts steep and stays that way – it's a fairly tough four hours up to the summit (three hours coming down), so make sure you have plenty of water and food with you (and from Medveja count on an extra hour each way). Most of the walk up is through lovely oak and then beech woods, before you emerge on the grassy shoulder of the mountain itself. By the time you get this far you're less than half an hour from the summit and the TV antenna. See Rudolf Abraham's book *Walking in Croatia* for further details.

If you're in Lovran and keen to walk you should also consider the paths leading to the abandoned village of Sučići, high above Mošćenička Draga, as well as other paths that keep you far from the madding crowds.

INLAND ISTRIA

Head just a few kilometres inland in Istria and the scenery and atmosphere changes completely. The rustic interior, dubbed the 'New Tuscany' by many a travel writer, is characterised by rolling agricultural land, pretty medieval hilltop villages, and a thinner spread of people – in spite of efforts to resettle some villages with artists and the like, the inland population still hasn't fully recovered from the exodus of the Italian population following World War II, and the advent of mass tourism in the 1960s which drew young people away to coastal jobs.

The emerging trend for today is agro-tourism, with the region perfectly suited to it, sharing central Italy's advantages of great food, fine wine, avenues of cypresses and charming villages. Indeed, there's a certain irony about the many Italian gastronomes who flocking here to enjoy great-value, high-quality Istrian cuisine, and notably the prized white truffle (see below). The region is also being opened up through a series of signposted wine routes.

Accommodation options are still quite limited and the lack of public transport makes many villages hard to get to without your own wheels. Nonetheless, be prepared throughout the season to encounter coach-loads of tourists being ferried up on day trips from the coast – especially in Motovun. If you're on a coastal package holiday yourself, however, the Istrian interior makes for an excursion you shouldn't miss.

Istria is famous throughout Croatia and beyond for its truffles (*tartufi*), and you'll find truffle dishes here which are affordable – at least when compared with the prices for those in France and Italy. The world's largest-ever white truffle was found in Istria in November 1999, near Buje, putting the town and its finder, Giancarlo Zigante, into the *Guinness Book of Records*. The monster truffle weighed in at 1.31kg, and measured 19.5cm by 12.4cm by 13.5cm (though it was finally surpassed by a white truffle from Alba, weighing 1.59kg, which was sold in November 2006 for € 125,000, making it considerably more expensive, per gram, than gold). Zigante himself has mushroomed since, and now owns a string of shops in Pula, Buzet, Grožnjan, Livade, Motovun and Umag, specialising in truffle sales (*www.zigantetartufi.com*). Another Istrian speciality is *biska*, or *biskovačka*, a fairly lethal but (at its best) wonderful mistletoe-flavoured spirit.

GETTING THERE AND AROUND In terms of access, public transport is centred on the administrative capital of Istria, Pazin, with buses from all over the region connecting here with trains on the Ljubljana to Pula line. Buses run up to Motovun and Buzet, but you'll find your own transport easier for Oprtalj, Grožnjan, Hum or Roč, though the first two are within a few kilometres' walk of bus routes and the last two within a few kilometres of the train line. The local tourist office has also made a concerted effort to open up local cycle routes in recent years – look out for the Istra Bike leaflets (*www.istra.com/zupan/eng/bike.html*).

WHERE TO STAY If you have your own transport then agro-tourism (*www.istra.com/agroturizam/eng*) is definitely the way to go – check with the Pula tourist office (see the beginning of this chapter for details). Accommodation options for individual towns are listed under their *Practicalities* sections.

It's also worth asking at local bars or cafés whether anyone has a room they're willing to let out – an enquiry at the **Pintur** restaurant in **Grožnjan** (see page 211) delivered a pleasant apartment for two, right in the old town, for € 35.

PAZIN If you're visiting the Istrian interior by public transport you're certain to come through Pazin, and there are worse places to stop. Its status as Istria's capital dates back to the end of World War II, when Yugoslavia was keen to moderate the Italian influence – one in the eye for the much larger and more logical Pula. Pazin has its own attractions, but the main source of interest in the area is the extraordinary 15th-century frescoes at St Mary's Church near Beram (see below).

From the bus and train station walk down towards the town and castle, stopping off at the **tourist office** (see below), which can not only provide you with a map, but also has a list of walks and cycle trails in the area. If you're persuasive they can also ring ahead to arrange for the opening of St Mary's Church.

The main attraction in Pazin itself is **Pazin castle**, a 16th-century pile built on 10th-century remains, right down at the bottom of the town. Inside the monumental building you'll find the **Ethnographic Museum of Istria**, featuring Istrian costumes and handicrafts, along with a curious collection of church bells from Istrian churches through the ages. The castle itself overhangs the dramatic gorge into which the river Fojba disappears, supposedly the inspiration for Dante's entrance to hell (plausible: we know Dante was in Pula) as well as a major scene in Jules Verne's 1885 novel *Mathias Sandorf*; the title character disappears underground here, only to reappear six hours later in the Limski Kanal, near Rovinj, a good 40km away. If you're a Jules Verne fan you should definitely contact Davor Šišiović at the Jules Verne Club in Pazin (\/f *052 622 460; www.ice.hr/ davors/ ejvclub.htm*), who can tell you all about Pazin's annual Jules Verne Days in June.

Pazin's other main attraction is the **Parish Church of St Nicholas**, which has a magnificent free-standing campanile next to it. Inside the church there are some wonderful, if badly faded, 15th-century frescoes – notable are the creation cycle and a battle scene, with baddie angels toughing it out with the good guys.

Practicalities Pazin itself has only one hotel, the two-star **Hotel Lovac** (*Šime Kurelića 4;* \ *052 624 324;* f *052 624 384*), with 27 spartan but clean rooms for around € 60 a double. There's also a sprinkling of private rooms – ask at the **tourist office** (*Franina Jurine 14;* \/f *052 622 460; www.tzpazin.hr*).

BERAM The old village of Beram is 1km off the main road to Poreč, about 5km west of Pazin. Just under 1km west of the village, at the end of a pretty road running into the woods, is the **Church of St Mary**. If you haven't been able to arrange things ahead of time in Pazin, you'll need to go to house #33 or #22 in the village, the home of the Gortan family, as they hold the key (*ključ*) to the church. Usually there's someone available who'll come with you to the church to unlock it and lock it back up again after your visit. It's a good idea to give something in return for their time and trouble – 20kn or so wouldn't be unreasonable.

The little church itself wouldn't be anything to write home about were it not for the Gothic frescoes inside. Dating from 1474 and painted by Master Vincent of Kastav (see the inscription over the south door) and his assistants, they're a triumph of late-Gothic art. That they survived the centuries relatively intact is no doubt due to their having been plastered over; they were only rediscovered in 1913.

Istria INLAND ISTRIA

5

In all there are some 46 panels, most depicting scenes from the lives of Jesus and Mary, but what really catch the eye are the 8m-long *Adoration of the Magi* on the north wall, and the *Dance of Death* (more of a walk, really) over the old main door. Medieval pageantry and Istrian scenery dominate the first, while in the second you'll see all classes heading for the same inevitable fate: death. First come the Pope, a cardinal and a bishop, followed by a king and queen, an innkeeper, a child and a cripple. Bringing up the rear are a knight, and a greedy merchant pointing at his worldly goods. Accompanied by fiendishly lifelike skeletons with musical instruments – and one with the obligatory scythe – the frescoes are a chilling reminder of life's impermanence.

PIĆAN If you're driving round the area, it's also worth stopping at the hilltop village of Pićan, about 10km east of Pazin. There's almost nothing to the place, these days, beyond a fine stone gate into town and a monumental 17th-century church – with an even more monumental campanile beside it – but the views across the Istrian countryside are wonderful.

MOTOVUN Motovun, 15km northwest of Pazin, is the classic medieval hilltop town, and you can see it from miles around. Like many gems of the interior, it can get overwhelmed by visitors – usually on a day trip up from the coast – although there's usually enough charm left to merit a visit. In the last week of July Motovun hosts an increasingly popular international **film festival** (*www.motovunfilmfestival.com*).

The **town walls** have just been restored and offer a lovely promenade – all of ten minutes' walk – with wonderful views out over the surrounding countryside. Otherwise, the town itself is pretty much limited to a single street, cobbled and traffic free in its upper reaches, running up from the valley floor. It works its way up through two ancient city gates, the first of which houses a lapidarium of sorts – Roman fragments on the right and Venetian lions on the left. Note the unusual 1755 face-on attempt at portraying the iconic sculpture – it looks more primitive than its 15th-century counterparts.

Between the two gates there's a lovely sloping terrace, where an ice cream goes down a treat, and an unusual triangular loggia, before the street turns sharply up into the second gate, housing a cheerful restaurant. Through the second gate is the heart of the **old town**, consisting of the ramparts, a main square under which a cistern used to hold the whole town's water supply, the 18th-century church, and the Hotel Kaštel, with its lovely shady terrace out front and gardens at the back. It's an idyllic place to stay (or even eat) – arguably the best in central Istria. But travel light – it's an awfully steep hike up with heavy bags.

The **Church of St Stephen** was designed by Palladio in 1614. Outside it's halfway between Renaissance and Baroque; inside it's plain and airy, with a flat-ceilinged aisle and naves, and some fine portraits of saints high up. Incongruously, the day I was there the church was filled with the strains of a local singing group rehearsing Roberta Flack's *Killing Me Softly*. Next door is the sturdy, crenellated campanile, which looks a good deal older than it is (18th century).

Motovun is famous both for the Malvasija (white) and Teran (red) wines produced locally, as well as the delicious but breathtakingly expensive truffles hidden in the nearby woods. Try both, if you can afford to. Motovun's tourist office is on Trg Jozefa Ressela (✆ *052 617 480; www.tz-motovun.hr*).

Practicalities Motovun also has a solitary hotel, the excellent three-star, 29-roomed **Kaštel** (*Trg Andrea Antico 7;* ✆ *052 681 607;* f *052 681 652; www.hotel-kastel-motovun.hr*), set in a lovely 18th-century building, with spacious high-ceilinged refurbished doubles at € 66–82 (634–684kn) a night. Since 2008 it has included its own spa centre. Contact the **tourist office** (*Trg Josefa Ressela 1;* ✆ *052 617 480; www.istria-motovun.com*) for details of private accommodation.

Pod Voltum (*Šetališta V Nazora;* ℡ *052 681 923*) is a good, down-to-earth place serving Istrian specialities. Alternatively if you want to splash out, try the nearby **Restaurant Zigante** (*Levade 7, Livade;* ℡ *052 664 302, www.zigantetartufi.com*). This fine dining establishment at the heart of the Zigante empire is regarded by many gastromomes as Croatia's best restaurant, and after dining on sheep's cheese infused with black truffle, king scallops and black truffles with a croissant shell and tagliatelle with fresh white truffle, it would be hard to disagree. A menu dominated by truffles, the opulent interior dining room and immaculately turned-out waiters hint at the high prices to come; for truffle connoisseurs, however, the two degustation menus are excellent value for money.

OPRTALJ Six kilometres north of Motovun, up a windy road, is Oprtalj, an almost deserted hilltop village which gives you a good idea of what Motovun and Grožnjan (see below) would have been like had the restorers not moved in. Whilst it's undeniably charming in a run-down sort of way, with a population of barely 100 there's little in the way of life and soul – or indeed much in the way of tourist infrastructure. There is, however, a single *konoba*, and the truffles here are especially good. The tourist office is on Matka Laginje (℡ *052 644 077; www.istria-oprtalj.com*).

GROŽNJAN Halfway between Motovun and Buje, a few kilometres north of the main road, on a spectacular bluff, is yet another hilltop village, Grožnjan. Adopted by artists from the late 1960s on, it's also home to *Jeunesses Musicales Croatia* in the summer, when the strains of classical music echo around the old cobbled streets. It is an increasingly lively place to be during the summer and autumn, with a myriad of art galleries and craft workshops, offering everything from ceramics and installations through to avant-garde art and tourist-orientated oil paintings of the village. You can easily idle away a day here visiting the various small-scale venues, checking out the Venetian-era loggia, relaxing in a café (head to **Café Bar Arta** on Trg Congra 3, ℡ 052 776 405, for a spectacular view), or savouring a lunch of fresh pasta with truffle sauce, before reluctantly leaving one of inland Istria's most attractive towns behind. Mid-September brings the four-day Extempore festival to the town in a celebration of white truffles, red wine and music. Grožnjan's **tourist office** is on U Gorjana (℡ *052 776 131; www.tz-groznjan.hr*).

Practicalities There is a scattering of places offering private accommodation in Grožnjan. Try one of the nice apartments run by the Armani Dešković Mirosav family (℡ *052 776 113; www.villa-olea.com*), which go for € 30–55), or contact the **tourist office** for more options (*U. Gorjana;* ℡ *052 776 131; www.tz-groznjan.hr*).

For meals try either **Konoba Bastia** (*I Svibnja 1, Grožnjan;* ℡ *052 776 370*) where they serve good Istrian fare on a shady terrace, or **Pintur** (*M Gorjana 9;* ℡ *052 776 397*) where you can eat on a. tree-shaded terrace in the centre of town and enjoy Istrian staples like *pršut*, cheese & excellent pasta with truffle sauce and risotto. They also have four rooms.

BUJE The pleasant Italianate town of Buje is famous for producing the world's largest truffle (see page 208). The town has two hotels, both of them casinos – the better of which seems to be the 4-star **Mulino** (*Škrile 75a;* ℡ *052 725 300;* f *052 725 333; www.mulino.hr*), which has doubles at around € 160 in season. Alternatively, the **tourist office** has a list of private accommodation (℡ *052 773 353; www.tzg-buje.hr*).

VIŽINADA The sleepy hill town of Vižinada, south of Grožnjan, is worth a stop off if you want to discover somewhere where you'll feel like you're the only tourist in town. Park your car by the café on the main road and then walk down the hill to the old centre. The Venetian lion proudly overlooks the old Venetian well, with its Latin and Italian inscriptions, and the newer water pump is strictly in Italian only, but the town's

Italian population has been posted missing since World War II. The imposing church and bell tower await restoration patiently, while the real estate agency back up the hill hints at Vižinada's future.

BUZET Backed by the Ćićarija mountains to the northeast, the town of Buzet (self-billed as the 'City of Truffles') is at the heart of what will eventually become the Native Park of Istria. It's a good base for walking, cycling and – of course – eating.

The medieval town on the hill is excellent, in a slightly run-down sort of way, with two well-preserved 16th-century gates, a maze of narrow streets and a couple of marble-paved squares. At the top of the hill, the pale-yellow church has an unusual onion-domed altar canopy inside and some 19th-century paintings – look out for St Mark, on the left-hand side, with St Mark's Basilica, in Venice, as a backdrop.

Below the old town, in the more modern Fontana, you'll find the bus station and the eponymous hotel (see below). Make sure you try a truffle-based dish while you're in Buzet (most commonly with pasta or an omelette) as well as the local beer, even if some visitors do find it unpalatably sweet. Come here on the first Saturday in September to share in the giant truffle-infused omelette that is cooked to celebrate the start of the truffle season.

Practicalities At the bottom of the hill, you'll find the newly renovated **Fontana** (*Trg Fontana 1;* \ *052 662 615;* f *052 662 596*), with doubles for €66 (renovated) and €57 (unrenovated). Contact the **tourist office** about private accommodation (\ *052 662-343; www.tz-buzet.hr*).

In Istarske Toplice ('Istrian Hot Springs'), 10km southwest of Buzet, there's the eponymous **Istarske Toplice** (*Sv Stjepana 60, Livade;* \ *052 603 000;* f *052 603 403; www.istarske-toplice.hr*). It's part of a 100-year-old thermal health resort, which explains why there's a 236-room hotel in a canyon in the middle of nowhere. Check into one of the €75 doubles and enjoy the sulphurous waters, a mineral-mud wrap and a variety of massage treatments.

For eating out, try **Vrh** (*Vrh 2;* \ *052 667 123*) where a shady terrace, the welcoming multi-lingual waitress and the delicate meat, ham, mushroom and truffle-infused Istrian *fuži* combine to make dining the highest point of an inland Istrian tour. The restaurant is well known locally and its owners produce their own wine alongside a range of fiery grappa that finds its way onto many menus in Zagreb. The truffle-flavoured grappa is worth trying for the novelty value alone. Alternatively, 4km southwest of Buzet is **Restaurant Konoba Marino** (*Kremenje 96/B, Momyan;* \ *052 779 047; www.konoba-marino-kremenje.hr*). Gastronomes visit Marino to dine on dishes made with black and white truffles. You can try the aromatic fungi with scrambled eggs, served as an accompaniment to homemade pasta or with tender fillets of beef. The seasonal menu also features wild asparagus and mushrooms.

ROČ AND THE GLAGOLITIC ALLEY When you're boozed-up and truffled-out, head for the tiny 'villages' of Roč and Hum, and the so-called 'Glagolitic Alley' which connects them. Roč, 8km east of Buzet, has an official population of only 17, while Hum, 7km south of Roč, nonetheless steals the tourist limelight with its claim to be the smallest town on earth (with all the basic trappings of a town), even though it has six more residents than the village of Roč.

Buses from Buzet to Rijeka will drop you at the turn-off, a ten-minute walk uphill to Roč, while if you get off the train at the Roč stop you'll find yourself around 2km out of town. Hum is even harder to reach, being more than 5km from the Hum train station, and not on any bus route.

It's hard to believe it now, but **Roč** was an important centre of Glagolitic literature from the 13th century on, and the tiny town, with its low 15th-century walls, is the repository of many treasures of Glagolitic literature from the 16th and 17th centuries. These days there's not a whole lot to see, and the chances are you'll be in and out in half an hour.

Within the main gate there's an interesting collection of Roman stone fragments, and inside, to the right, by the pint-sized concrete playing field, there's a solitary Venetian cannon. On the day I was here, it was Roč and not Hum that was humming, but it turned out just to be a swarm of bees. Within the walls you'll also notice various bits of modern sculpture, all donated by the 'Friends of Roč', and it's worth glancing inside the Church of St Anthony – nice vaulting inside the apse and odd sedan chair-like confessionals. Once a year, in May, Roč really does swing, during the 'Triestina', the annual international knees-up for the harmonica-playing fraternity.

Keen hang-gliders and those with their own transport may want to follow the road past Roč towards **Nugla**. Carefully follow the signs towards Gornji Nugla, then after reaching the village head right for Slum and continue on the sealed road until you reach a crossroads with two hand-written signs for the southern take-off and the northern take-off. Follow the unsealed road (southern take-off) that branches to the left. After a few minutes you'll arrive at a local hang-gliding mecca – worth a trip for the wonderful views over Buzet and the distant hill towns, even if the hang-gliders aren't in evidence.

The 7km road south to Hum is known as '**Glagolitic Alley**' (*Aleja Glagoljaša*), and if you have the time it makes for a pleasant-enough walk – a comfortable 3-hour return trip to Hum and back from Roč. The memorial consists of 11 monuments along the roadside, which were put up in 1977 to celebrate the Glagolitic priests who were among the first people to raise Croatian national consciousness in the 18th and 19th centuries.

The concrete sculptures are variations on representations of letters of the Glagolitic alphabet, which was kept alive in Istria and the islands of the Kvarner Bay long after it had disappeared elsewhere. Invented by St Cyril and St Methodius in the 9th century, the alphabet was adapted by St Clement into the Cyrillic seen today in much of the Balkans and across Russia.

HUM The road ends at Hum, which has all the features you'd expect in a medieval town, though very little in the way of people. An imposing entrance gate (complete with Glagolitic knockers), fortified walls, cobbled alleys, dilapidated stone houses and a small church make up the village. It's in the process of being restored – steeplejacks in harnesses were pulling tufts of grass from between the cracks in the church tower when I was in town – and several of the houses are being done up, but it's still a very, very small place. Commerce exists in the form of a small museum (actually a souvenir shop), and a renowned *konoba* (see below), which serves up excellent Istrian dishes, including *pršut*, and pasta with truffles.

Be warned, however: it may be hard to get to, but Hum can switch from being deserted to being positively overcrowded in the seconds it takes for a tour bus to disgorge its passengers. Trips come up here from the coast, lured by that 'smallest town' tag.

Practicalities Hum's only restaurant is **Konoba Hum** (✆ *052 660 005*), which has a a lovely terrace but is open weekends only.

6

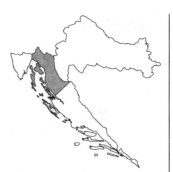

Kvarner Bay and Islands

The Kvarner Bay, with Rijeka at its head and Croatia's largest islands in the middle, has been popular as a holiday destination for over a century. Rijeka itself is a lively port and shipyard, and while it's not somewhere you'd spend your holidays, there's nonetheless plenty to see. Offshore is Cres, home to wonderful griffon vultures, and Lošinj, one of Croatia's busiest and trendiest islands (at least for a fortnight in August). East of Cres and south of Rijeka lies the somewhat lower-key Krk, Croatia's largest island, while the island of Rab sits to the south, blessed by sandy beaches and one of Croatia's prettiest medieval towns.

According to legend the four islands of the Kvarner Bay (Kvarner = Quattro = four) are the limbs of Medea's brother. She enticed the poor lad on board Jason's ship as he fled away with the Golden Fleece, and Jason chopped him up and cast his limbs overboard to slow down the pursuers.

The coast from Rijeka southwards is backed by the steepest part of the Velebit massif and occupied by a string of resort towns and villages centred on Kraljevica, Crikvenica, Selce and Novi Vinodolski, all of which are popular vacation spots in summer with Croatians escaping from the capital, as well as increasingly with independent visitors in search of the low key rather than the high life.

Inland from Rijeka is the wonderfully protected and unspoiled Gorski Kotar region, centred on Risnjak National Park, while further south is the enormous Velebit massif, with North Velebit National Park home to a good proportion of Croatia's remaining brown bear population, and also providing some of the finest hiking in Croatia.

Phone codes vary throughout the region – they're included within each listing.

RIJEKA *Telephone code 051 (+385 51 from abroad)*

Rijeka, Croatia's busiest and most industrial port, with a population rapidly approaching 200,000, isn't really a holiday destination at all – the assumption is that you'll head straight over to Opatija, 14km west, or out onto the islands of the Kvarner Bay. It nonetheless has plenty of sights worth seeing, including the excellent Trsat Castle on its hill, and a number of fine Austro-Hungarian palaces and Secessionist buildings down in the town itself.

A massive investment programme to tart up the waterfront is one sign that Rijeka is on the up, and the sense of returning civic pride is evident in the street sculptures and the recent success of the local football team, whose stadium must have one of the best views in Europe, overlooking the Adriatic and the Opatija Riviera.

Rijeka probably won't be your favourite Croatian city, but if you are passing through – and you may well be, as this is the main transit hub for the entire region – then it is worth at least one night of your time. There's little to beat a relaxing beer or coffee on the central thoroughfare, the stately Korzo, with its lavish Austro-Hungarian buildings.

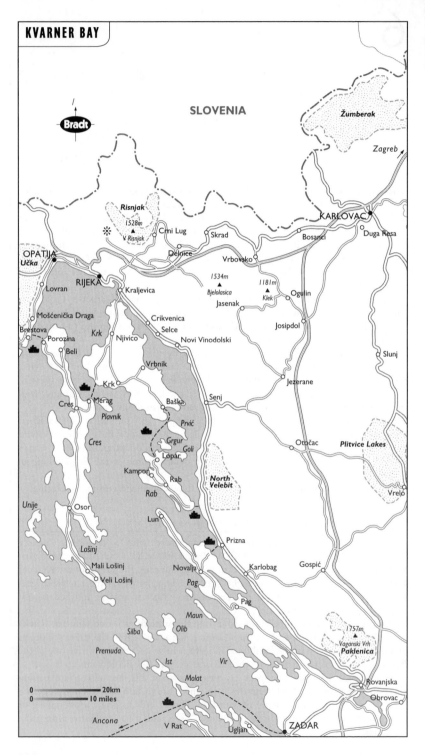

KVARNER BAY

SLOVENIA

Žumberak

Zagreb

Risnjak
1528m
V Risnjak

KARLOVAC

Crni Lug
Skrad
Bosanci
Duga Resa

OPATIJA
Učka
Delnice
Vrbovsko

Lovran
RIJEKA
Kraljevica

1534m
Bjelolasica
1181m
Klek
Ogulin

Jasenak

Mošćenička Draga
Crikvenica
Selce
Novi Vinodolski
Josipdol

Brestova
Porozina
Krk
Njivico

Beli
Slunj

Vrbnik

Krk
Jezerane

Cres
Merag
Krk
Baška
Senj

Plavnik
Prvić

Cres
Grgur
Goli
Otočac
Plitvice Lakes

Lopar
Kampor
Rab
North Velebit

Unije
Osor
Rab

Lun
Vrelo

Lošinj
Prizna

Mali Lošinj
Novalja
Karlobag
Gospić

Veli Lošinj
Pag

Maun
1757m
Vaganski Vrh
Paklenica

Silba
Olib

Premuda
Ist
Vir

Molat
Rovanjska

0   20km
0   10 miles
Obrovac

Ancona
V Rat
Ugljan
ZADAR

HISTORY Like most of the region, the area round Rijeka was home to Liburnian Illyrians until the Romans arrived, and built a port here, on the site of what's now the old town – everything south of the Korzo is on land reclaimed from the sea. Slavs moved in when Rome collapsed, but it wasn't until the 13th century that Rijeka started to grow in importance, though from then until 1947 it was two distinct settlements – Rijeka on the west bank of the river and Trsat (and later Sušak) on the east bank.

Unlike pretty much everywhere else on the Croatian coast, Rijeka never fell under the control of Venice, becoming a key Habsburg possession instead, though it was briefly under Frankopan (see *Krk*, page 237) control. From the early 18th century onwards, Rijeka became a major centre for shipbuilding, and today it's still Croatia's most important shipyard.

During the 19th century, tension increased between Vienna and Budapest, with Hungary insisting it should have its own access to the Adriatic, Austria already having both Trieste and Pula. Rijeka therefore came under the direct control of Hungary, and a railway was built from Budapest via Zagreb to the port (the station, like Zagreb's, is the work of Ferenc Pfaff), dramatically increasing its importance. Under the Hungarians, Rijeka grew wealthy, with its own sugar factory, refinery and paper factory.

In 1915, as a way of persuading the Italians into World War I on the Allied side, Britain promised pretty much the entire post-war Dalmatian coast to Italy. Once the war was won, the Allies reneged on the deal, and the coast fell to the Kingdom of the Serbs, Croats and Slovenes instead – though Italy did get Zadar and some islands as compensation.

This wasn't enough, however, to stop D'Annunzio (see box below) from marching into Rijeka in September 1919, using the pro-Italian census (which cleverly excluded Sušak) as an excuse. D'Annunzio then ruled Rijeka for nearly 18 months – in spite of not even having the Italian government's support. Italy finally pushed D'Annunzio out

GABRIELE D'ANNUNZIO

By 1919, Gabriele D'Annunzio was one of the most fêted men in Italy. Already hugely famous before World War I for his poetry and novels, he signed up for military service, in his fifties, and became a war hero – he even lost an eye in a flying accident.

He was the perfect stooge, then, to lead an officer-backed group of 'volunteers' (discreetly assisted by soldiers whose superiors turned a blind eye) into Rijeka in September 1919, claiming the city for Italy. His troops were the first to wear black shirts, kicking off a hideously popular trend in fascist fashion that would last a whole generation.

But Rome wasn't interested in Rijeka, as it was busy negotiating instead at the Paris Peace Conference for Zadar and some Dalmatian islands. So D'Annunzio, cool as a cucumber, set himself up as *Il Commandante*, at the head of the independent state of Rijeka. For nearly 18 months he got away with it, declaiming manifestos from his balcony every morning.

It couldn't last, of course. At the end of 1920, Italy shelled the town and D'Annunzio gave it up in January 1921. As a successful role model for Mussolini, he was later rewarded by Il Duce with a place in the Italian senate, and was up for even greater honours when he died suddenly in 1938.

Rebecca West, author of the extraordinary *Black Lamb and Grey Falcon* (see page 377), was no fan. 'D'Annunzio marched his volunteers into Fiume, in an adventure which, in mindlessness, violence and futility, exactly matched his deplorable literary works', she wrote, by way of an epitaph to the whole sorry affair.

RIJEKA

LAGINJINA

POMERIO

Maritime & Historical Museum

ŠET V NAZORA

Trsat, Neboder hotel, Tarsa

MUZEJSKI TRG

Capuchin Church of Our Lady of Lourdes

FRANA KURELCA

F SUPILA

River Pub

St Vitus

FIUMERA

Continental

ERAZIMA BARČIĆA

Grand Hotel Bonavia

Municipium

Indigo

TRG GRIVICA

Roman Gate

Pizza Delfino

Jadran Hotel (2km), Youth Hostel

CIOTTINA

Zlatna Školjka

Gelateria Corso

KOBLEROV TRG

TRG

Š KOŽIČIĆA

TRPIMIROVA TRG

Bus station

JADRANSKI TRG

KORZO

City Tower

KORZO

JELAČIĆEV TRG

TRG ŽABICA

Jadrolinija building

TRG REPUBLIKE HRVATSKE

RIVA

RIBARSKA

Railway station (500m)

ULICA IVANA ZAJCA

Ferry terminal

Feral

WENZELOVA

Sušak Panorama point

VERDIJEVA

Market

ZAGREBAČKA

Bradt

0 ——— 400m
0 ——— 400yds

in early 1921, and for three years Rijeka was a free city. But that wasn't stopping Mussolini, who annexed it in 1924.

Rijeka – then called Fiume (both names just mean 'river') – was a divided city once more. The west side was Italian, and fell into decline, while the east side, Sušak, rapidly gained in prosperity as one of Yugoslavia's main shipyards, even though the ships themselves actually had to sail from Rijeka's harbour.

After World War II, Rijeka was returned to Yugoslavia, along with the rest of Dalmatian Italy, and in 1991 the city became part of the new state of Croatia – though it still has a large Italian-speaking population.

GETTING THERE AND AROUND If you're using public transport, you'll sometimes feel there's no way of not getting to Rijeka. Trains come in from Zagreb four or five times a day, while there are ferries and ships constantly on their way in and out of the harbour. The main coastal line to Dubrovnik (daily) starts here, and there are also ferries to various places on the Kvarner Bay islands, though usually that's not the most practical or efficient way of getting there (see the individual sections in this chapter).

Rijeka airport is out on the island of Krk (connected by a big bridge to the mainland), and caters mainly for charter flights bringing in package tours to Opatija and the islands of the Kvarner Bay. There are flights from Zagreb, too, which are met by the Croatia Airlines bus; by the time you've allowed for transfers and check-in time, it's a pretty expensive way of saving a couple of hours on the bus, though if you're coming from outside Croatia the onward leg may already be included in your fare.

A vast array of buses runs frequently to Rijeka from just about everywhere, coming from Pula (2 hours) and Zagreb (four hours – some faster, now that the capital and Rijeka are joined by motorway) roughly every half hour, from Krk (1½ hours), Zadar

(4½ hours) and Split (9 hours) about once an hour, and from a wealth of other destinations besides.

You probably won't need to use local buses much, though it's worth knowing that bus #32 runs from the train station to Opatija twice an hour, and if you want to avoid the walk up to Trsat you can catch bus #1 from Fiumera.

The train station, bus station and ferry terminal are in a line running west–east along less than a kilometre's length of the harbour. The tourist information office (*Užarska 14;* ✆ *051 315 710;* f *051 315 720;* *www.tz-rijeka.hr*) has good maps and brochures, and can be found halfway along the Korzo.

🏠 WHERE TO STAY AND EAT
Rijeka's accommodation – or lack of it – speaks volumes about the city's knowing it's a staging post rather than a destination in its own right. There's no campsite, there are no agencies handling private rooms, and there are only two hotels in the middle of town – though there is a new youth hostel.

🏠 **Grand Hotel Bonavia** (121 rooms) Dolac 4; ✆ 051 357 100, 051 357 985; f 051 335 969; www.bonavia.hr. The lavish 4-star Grand Hotel Bonavia is well located just a block north of the main west–east thoroughfare, Korzo, & is easily the nicest place to stay in the city. It's a modernised old building, & a few of the rooms on the top floors have balconies overlooking the port – rooms 712, 713 & 714 are especially spacious. None of this comes cheap, of course, but the hotel does have all the luxuries you'd expect for the price. It even has that rarest thing of all in downtown Rijeka, its own parking spaces (if you're driving here, you need to get into the one-way system that brings you out on Jadranska Trg, then head up the hill & round behind the back of the hotel). The hotel is also now home to a restaurant worth staying in for. *Dbl €120–190.*

🏠 **Continental** (69 rooms) Šetalište Andrije Kačića – Miošića 1; ✆ 051 372 008; f 051 372 009; www.jadran-hoteli.hr. The only other option right in town is the newly renovated Continental, now 3-star, which is in a Parisian-looking building just across the river, below the Trsat hill. *Dbl €90.*

🏠 **Neboder** (54 rooms) Strossmayerova 1; ✆ 051 373 538; f 051 373 541; www.jadran-hoteli.hr. Further up the hill, this is the place to head for if you're after a reasonably priced option and the Continental is full. It's a rather charmless block of a place, though it was newly renovated in 2008 and most of the rooms have balconies. *Dbl €79–85.*

🏠 **Jadran** (69 rooms) Šetalište XIII Divizije 46; ✆ 051 216 600; f 051 216 458; www.jadran-hoteli.hr. Just 2km along the coast (you can get there on the #2 city bus), & recently upgraded from 2 to 4 stars, with lovely views out over the island of Cres. *Dbl €114–134 (with sea view).*

🏠 **Youth Hostel** (61 beds) Šetalište XIII Divizije 23; ✆/ 051 406 420; f 051 406 421; www.hfhs.hr. Also on the way out of town (& reachable on the #2 bus) is Rijeka's brand-new youth hostel, located in a 19th-century villa – it's only around 15mins away on foot. *Dorm with B&B €19pp, dbl 46 (summer), €44 (winter).*

For a town of its size, Rijeka has surprisingly few restaurants – again a product of the relatively few tourists around to keep business booming. Locals wanting to splash out tend to head over to Opatija, but you can find something to eat easily enough in the streets on either side of the Korzo. There's also a booming café culture, with terraces spilling out on to practically every pavement in the old town, especially along the lifeblood Korzo and the waterfront Riva.

✗ **Feral** Matije Gupca 5B; ✆ 051 212 274. Feral is reckoned to be the best local place to eat seafood, with solid food & decent service, but I prefer Zlatna Školjka (see page 220).

🍨 **Gelateria Corso** Korzo 20. The best & most popular ice cream joint in town. Savour it like a local as you stroll along the Korzo.

✗ **Indigo** Stara Vrata 3; ✆ 051 315 174. Funky bar/restaurant/club, which prides itself on its mantra of 'New York bohemia meets London sophisticates, with a twist of Amsterdam sleaze.' With a stylish interior, oversized sofas on the terrace & live DJs at w/ends it's a great place to spend an evening. Salads, soups & local specialities feature on the menu.

✗ **Municipium** Trg Riječke Rezolucije 5; ✆ 051 213 000. The smartest place in town, where business deals are cemented over good, solid, Croatian fare.

✗ **Pizza Delfino** Vladivoja i Milivoja Lenca 81; ✆ 336 736; www.delfino.hr. Hugely popular and well-priced pizzeria not far from the Korzo, with the same

You won't go far these days without seeing a Moretto (also called Mori, Morči, Morčeki and Morčići, depending on where you're from – and who you ask), as it's become the symbol of Rijeka.

The androgynous turbaned black figure is most commonly seen adorning earrings, but also features on other jewellery, and is prominent during Rijeka's carnival.

Various stories are told of the Moretto's origin – rich women over-fond of black slaves, Turkish invaders slaughtered in answer to local prayers, and others – but it seems the truth is more prosaic, reflecting a 17th- and 18th-century love-affair with the orient. The Moretto first appeared in Venice, and then in Rijeka during the 19th century, in a more modest and affordable form.

A single Moretto earring was frequently worn by men (especially sailors) as a sign of their provenance, though after World War II its production pretty much died out, only being revived with the establishment of an independent Croatia in 1991.

---

ownership as the long-established (and equally popular) Delfino in Lovran.

♀ **River Pub** Frana Supila 12; ☎ 051 213 406. Just up the steps from the Bonavia, with an upturned coxless 4 hanging above the bar, & a grand oil portrait of Winston Churchill upstairs. There's also a rare opportunity here to practise your Croatian karaoke.

✗ **Tarsa** Josip Kulfaneka 10; ☎ 051 452 089. Highly rated locally, this place up near Trsat Castle is an excellent place to try *tartufi* (truffles) if you're not heading into Istria.

✗ **Zlatna Školjka (the Golden Shell)** Kručina 12a; ☎ 051 213 782. My personal favourite, right off the Korzo, with stiff tablecloths, cheerful, semi-formal service & excellent seafood in a cellar-like setting.

WHAT TO SEE AND DO Most of Rijeka was destroyed by a huge earthquake in 1750, and was rebuilt in the monumental Habsburg style, particularly in the reclaimed area south of the Korzo, where you can still be impressed by the sheer grandeur of buildings like the **Jadran** (home of Jadrolinija, the ferry company), or the **Royal Navy Palace**.

Up on the Korzo, one of the few pre-1750 survivors was the **City Tower**, although it was embellished post-earthquake with the Baroque trimmings and the distinctive clock and cupola you see today – not to mention the pompously bewigged reliefs of the Austro-Hungarian Emperors Charles VI and Leopold I over the archway. North of here, through the gate, is a warren of streets and squares marking the site of the original walled city. The town's oldest monument, a plain **Roman Gate** (probably the entrance to a barracks, rather than anything more significant), is up here, on the way to the 17th-century **Church of St Vitus**.

Built on the site of an existing church by the Jesuits, St Vitus is an unusual circular building with a cupola supported by massive marble pillars. The 13th-century crucifix inside (from the original church) supposedly had a rock thrown at it in 1296 by a man called Petar Lončarić. He was swallowed up by the ground, but the body of Christ bled convincingly, and the blood was stored in a vial, starting up a useful counter-cult to Our Lady of Trsat (see below).

Heading west from here it's a few blocks to the splendid **Maritime and Historical Museum**, housed in the former Governor's Palace, home briefly to D'Annunzio during his occupation of the city. The exhibits are interesting enough, but it's the palatial rooms and décor that really make the visit worthwhile.

The other church worth seeing down in the town is the **Capuchin Church of Our Lady of Lourdes**, conveniently located right by the bus station. The neo-

Gothic striped façade stands at the top of a fancy double staircase that wouldn't look out of place in front of one of the palazzi on Lake Como, in Italy. Started in 1904, the lower part was completed by 1908, but the upper part wasn't finished until 1929, in spite of the cash-strapped Capuchins taking advantage of the credulous local people by employing a charlatan calling himself St Johanca, who would raise money by sweating blood on demand (until his arrest for fraud in 1913).

Trsat Up on the hill above Rijeka is the leafy suburb of Trsat, originally the site of an Illyrian hill-fort, and a strategic defence point for people from the Frankopans on. Up here is the **Church of Our Lady of Trsat**, supposedly the site where the Virgin Mary's house stopped and stayed from 10 May 1291 to 10 December 1294, on its way from Nazareth to its present resting place in Loreto, Italy. Fortunately, the loss of the Holy home was compensated for by the gift of a miraculous icon of the Virgin by Pope Urban V in 1367, and the Frankopans built the church to house the icon, as well as the monastery next door. The icon embedded into the gaudy altarpiece here is actually a copy; the original is in the monastery treasury, which is hardly ever open. The copy was originally made for a church in Opatija in the early 20th century, so that people there could see it without having to cross to Rijeka, which was Italian-occupied at the time.

It still draws the pilgrims in good numbers, as you can see from the clutter of offerings in the **Chapel of Votive Gifts**, across the cloisters, and serious pilgrims will climb here from Rijeka on their knees, all the way up the 500-odd stairs leading from the town below. Less serious pilgrims will jump on a #1 bus.

The other big attraction in Trsat is the **castle**, which has been here forever, though in its present form only since Frankopan times. It was bought in 1826 by an Austrian army officer of Irish descent, Count Laval Nugent de Westmeth, and was restored to include the family mausoleum, where the sarcophagi were not just above ground, but upright, too, ready to face their makers. Among the people originally buried here was George Bernard Shaw's Aunt, Jane Shaw, though nobody seems to have the foggiest idea why. On the front of the mausoleum there's an inscription reading 'Mir Yunaka', which means 'Peace to the Heroes' – given the area's turbulent history, it's something of an irony. The castle and mausoleum now serve as a low-key museum, though the whereabouts of the sarcophagi is a mystery; they were still here when Rebecca West came through in 1937, but they're certainly not there now. In their place are maps, drawings and photos showing Rijeka through the ages.

The view from the fort across the sea, and down to the shipyards, is great, and can be enjoyed over a cool drink on the terrace.

The Rijeka Carnival The pre-Lent carnival is easily Croatia's biggest (second only in Europe to the one in Venice, in fact) and Rijeka's most exciting annual event, attracting more than 10,000 active participants and 100,000 spectators. What's most extraordinary about the carnival is its adoption as an instant tradition – it was only revived in 1982, and has grown out of all proportion to expectations, attracting nationwide TV coverage as well as visitors from all over Croatia.

The main events of the week-long carnival are parades and into-the-night festivities, but you should look out especially for the men wearing sheepskins and ringing bells, who hark back to a centuries-old tradition of driving out the evil spirits from villagers' houses at this time of year – and indeed still do so in the Gorski Kotar hinterland.

GORSKI KOTAR *Telephone code 051 (+385 51 from abroad)*

The mountainous area inland from Rijeka is one of the best remaining examples of forested karst, and is home to a wide diversity of flora and fauna. There's a small national park, Risnjak, and there are many other natural attractions, and mountains to

RISNJAK NATIONAL PARK

Delnice

Crni Lug

Gornje Jelenje, Rijeka

Vela Voda

M Selo

Park office

Risnjak

Leska

2km

1 mile

0

0

Bradt

1524m
Veliki Risnjak

Sloserov dom

Risnjak

Gornje Jelenje

Snježnik
1505m

Snježnik

Caltige

Rijeka

Platak

Sušak

Platak

M Platak

hike up, but although the area's reasonably well known to Croatians it's practically unvisited by foreigners. This is starting to change as hotel developers and tourist agencies realise just how attractive this part of the country is and that not every foreign visitor wants to do the coast to death on every visit. Check out www.gorskikotar.hr if you're planning to explore this green oasis.

Buses and trains run through the Gorski Kotar – it's crossed by the main road and railway from Karlovac to Rijeka, but it's a whole lot easier to explore round here if you have your own transport. Accommodation is also scarce across the region (although this is also beginning to change), which makes it more suitable for day trips than extended stays.

RISNJAK NATIONAL PARK Only 15km inland from Rijeka as the crow flies, Risnjak National Park is a wonderful place to come in late spring and summer, with great walking, lovely flowers, spectacular scenery, and a relatively easy peak to scale. The weather can be extreme here, however, with the park affected by four different types of climate – harsh alpine, Dinaric mountain, mild Adriatic and continental Pannonian. In autumn it tends towards the very wet indeed, and in winter there's a good deal of snow – at the Risnjak mountain hut, at 1,418m, there's snow on the ground for an average of 157 days a year, and it can be up to 4m deep – though this can be a beautiful time to hike in the area, for those suitably equipped. For further information on hiking on Gorski Kotar, see Rudolf Abraham's book *Walking in Croatia*.

The local flora includes the protected edelweiss, black vanilla orchids, mountain yarrows, alpine clematis, saxifrage and yellow wood violets, amongst many others, while the fauna includes wild cats, roe deer, red deer, chamois and a small colony of brown bears. After nearly a century away, the lynx has not just reappeared, but is once again well established, and is probably behind the park's name (*ris* meaning lynx). Wolves and wild boar also come through from time to time.

The main entrance to the park is through the village of **Crni Lug**, a narrow and winding 12km west of **Delnice**, itself on the main road and railway line from Karlovac to Rijeka. Buses run twice a day to the village from Delnice, though not at especially convenient times of day – if you're stuck in Delnice itself you could do worse than the Scorpion Pizzeria, which serves up good-value fare.

Just over 1km beyond Crni Lug you'll find the **park office** (\ *051 836 133;* f *051 836 116; www.risnjak.hr*), where you can pick up maps and a good guide, as well as an excellent little leaflet detailing the Leska Nature Trail, which is well worth a couple of hours of anyone's time. The office is also home to a cheerful restaurant, and there are five rooms available (€*30 pp HB*), though you should book well ahead if you want to stay in summer, as the lodge is popular with locals.

From the park office, at around 700m, it's a well-marked 9km walk (count on a little over three hours up) to the main peak, **Veliki Risnjak**, at 1,528m – it's the second highest mountain in Gorski Kotar, being trumped by a mere 6m by Bjelolasica, which is at the heart of the main skiing centre in the area, 25km southeast of here.

A considerably shorter route to the summit, also well-signed, starts from the village of **Gornje Jelenje**, 16km southwest of Crni Lug (21km west of Delnice). Drive up to the head of the gravel road, at around 1,200m, and count on under an hour and a half from here on foot. The summit can also be reached in three hours or so from the small ski station at **Platak**, to the west of the park – this is also the best place to start the climb up the 1,505m summit of **Snježnik**, which can easily be combined with Veliki Risnjak.

Under the peak of Risnjak is a mountain hut, open from May to September – from here it's a rocky 20-minute scramble to the top, and some great views out across Gorski Kotar to the sea. The best views are on clear days in the depths of winter, but if you're climbing at that time of year you need to be a seriously proficient mountaineer, and equipped with an ice-axe and crampons. If you're a winter visitor it's worth knowing there's an unstaffed winter room in the hut, which sleeps six, but make sure you've cleared this with the park office in Crni Lug first.

If you're into the underground rather than the mountain peaks, then you'll love the **Lokvarka Cave** (Špilja Lokvarka), just outside **Lokve**, 6km west of Delnice, on the main road to Rijeka – it's over 1km long, and has truly excellent stalagmites and stalactites. It's open weekdays from mid-June to mid-September (*09.00–17.00; 30kn*), and sometimes at weekends, with guided visits every hour or so; outside these times ask at the Lokve tourist office (*Rudolfa Strohala 118;* ☎/f *051 831 250; www.tz-lokve.hr*) for more details. The tourist office also has access to a handful of attractive, private rooms in the pretty village. If you're here in spring, don't miss out on the Frog Fiesta, which features various froggy frolics and folk music – after all this froggy fun, however, you may want to miss out on the main dish of the day: frogs' legs.

SKRAD AND THE DEVIL'S PASS
About 12km east of Delnice is the small town of Skrad, in itself unremarkable enough. But below the town is a great canyon, nearly 2km long but sometimes as little as 2m wide, known as the **Devil's Pass** (Vražji Prolaz). There's a path, which takes under an hour, down to the top of the canyon from the train station in Skrad, but if you have your own wheels you can drive down a hair-raising 6km to the valley floor (signed Zeleni Vir), and then walk up, which is far more rewarding.

Entrance tickets (7kn) are on sale from the mountain association (HPS) van usually parked at the head of the car park; they also sell drinks. To the left is an old power station (Gorski Kotar's first), beyond which you'll find the **Zeleni Vir** Waterfall, dropping down from the river's source. But it's up the trail to the right you'll want to head, on a narrow path that frequently has to resort to iron bridges and wooden walkways over the gushing torrent beneath. It's a moderately scary trail, but more of a thrill than actually dangerous (though good walking shoes are essential, especially if it's been raining).

It takes around half an hour to walk up through the canyon, after which you'll see a sign to the left to **Muževa Hišica**, a deep cave which was used as a refuge in times of war – you'll need a torch if you want to explore the tunnel, which leads to a biggish chamber containing a good selection of stalactites and stalagmites, and the occasional bat.

Back on the main trail, the path cuts up through the woods to Skrad, some 400m above – count on an hour to reach the station.

There are several trains a day that stop in Skrad on the way from Zagreb to Rijeka and up to 20 buses a day. Skrad's tourist office (*Josipa Blaževića Blaža 8;* ☎/f *051 810 680*) has access to a number of private rooms.

OGULIN, KLEK AND BJELOLASICA
The train line from Karlovac to Rijeka takes a loop southwards away from the main road, before rejoining it near Delnice. On the loop, there's a stop at the small town of Ogulin, which is the access point by public transport to the accessible peak and photo safari opportunities (bears, wild boar, deer) on **Klek** (you can also walk there from Ogulin), and the skiing, hiking and biking at **Bjelolasica**. Ogulin is also easy enough to reach by bus from either Rijeka or Karlovac.

For information on points further north and east, heading up to Karlovac, and across to the Plitvice Lakes, turn back to page 158.

Ogulin
There's not a great deal to do or see in Ogulin, but if you're here you can pick up useful information about the town and the gorgeous mountainous region which surrounds it from the tourist office (*Frankopana 2;* ☎/f *047 532 278; www.tz-grada-ogulina.hr*). At the other end of town – all of 300m north – are Ogulin's main attractions, the solid twin-towered 16th-century **fortress**, which dates back to Frankopan times, and the spectacular gorge from which the Dobra

River emerges. There is a new four-star hotel, the Hotel Frankopan (*21 rooms;* ℡ *047 525 509; www.hotel-frankopan.hr; dbl* €*90–99*), right next to the castle.

The fortress houses the **Town Museum** (🕐 *08.00–14.00 Mon–Fri, 08.00–12.00 Sat; 10kn*), a rather motley collection of ethnographic and archaeological bits and pieces spread over a couple of floors. The most interesting highlight is the prison cell on the top floor, which housed no less celebrated an inmate than Tito, twice, in the 1920s and 1930s. On the same floor, there's a separate mountaineering section, with the usual bearded blokes striking rugged poses. Last but not least, there's lots of stuff about fairy tales in the museum, as Ivana Brlić Mažuranić, Croatia's most famous fairy-tale author, was born in Ogulin – there is a 'fairy-tale route' in town and a visitor's centre (*www.ogfb.hr*), and an annual **fairy-tale festival** in June was inaugurated in 2006.

Outside, you can hardly miss the gorge, which is known as **Đula's Abyss**, after the love-struck princess who is said to have thrown herself to her death here. If you go across to the other side, and look carefully – and the lighting is just so – the more imaginative among you will be able to make out the mournful craggy face of her lover, Milan, looking down into the gorge; you can see his face in profile, with the eyes, nose and a chunky moustache. Maybe.

Klek West of Ogulin is the dramatic peak of Klek, which isn't the highest mountain in the area (it's a fraction under 1,200m), but is one of the most accessible. It can even be walked from Ogulin in three hours or so each way (see Rudolf Abraham's *Walking in Croatia*), though if you have a car or can get to Dom Lovački, 12km out of Ogulin (take the main road west, past the castle, for 2km, then turn left and head up 10km further), at the locality known as Bjelsko, first, then you'll save yourself a good deal of time. From here it's only about a 45-minute walk up through the woods to the Klek mountain hut (which usually serves snacks on summer weekends) and a further half hour to the summit, up a rather vertiginous rocky path above the trees. The panoramic view from the summit is excellent.

The tourist office has information on local cycle routes, photo safaris (with the chance to see to wild boar and deer) and rafting trips on the Dobra. Finally, Klek has long been associated with witches, so look out for the annual **Witches Festival** here, or the **Witches Challenge** cycle race, which charges up the mountain.

Bjelolasica Renowned across Croatia for the best skiing in the country, Bjelolasica also offers good hiking and biking opportunities in summer, and there's an artificial lake, Sabljaci Jezero, which has nice swimming beaches and the Hrvatski Olimpijski Centar restaurant, which is big on trout and the like (though the lake, confusingly, is just south of Ogulin, while the skiing etc is almost 30km west).

On weekends, the morning train from Zagreb to Ogulin is met by a bus that takes you all the way to the (actual) **Olympic Centre** up in the mountains, and in the afternoon there's a return bus and train back.

There's accommodation at the centre, but you need to book well ahead in the winter season, as this is where Croatia's serious skiers train. Call the Olympic Centre (*www.bjelolasica.hr*) on ℡ *047 562 118*, or in Zagreb on ℡ *01 617 7707*. You can also stay at **the Hotel Jastrab** (*42 rooms;* ℡ *051 833 161;* f *051 833 527; www.hoteljastreb.com; B&B dbl* €*94*) in nearby Begovo Razdolje, which claims to be the highest village in Croatia, at over 1,000m. The hotel does bike hire in summer and ski hire in winter, and has maps available.

BIJELE AND SAMARSKE STIJENE Further south, and slightly more difficult to reach unless you have your own wheels (though there are clearly marked hiking trails from Bjelolasica, and you can also walk up from the village of Jasenac on the road between Ogulin and Plitvice Lakes National Park), is the protected nature reserve of Bijele and

Samarske Stijene, which has a wealth of dramatic karstic formations and cliffs rising out of the unspoiled woods. It's a reasonably popular place with local hikers and climbers – some of the cliffs are up to 50m high – but otherwise beautifully untouched by the hand of man, and a great place to find peace, quiet and edelweiss. For more information about hiking in this area and nearby Bjelolasica, see Rudolf Abraham's book *Walking in Croatia*.

NORTH VELEBIT NATIONAL PARK
Telephone code 053 (+385 53 from abroad)

The vast Velebit range – covering 2,000km² and stretching over 100km from Senj to Zadar – contains two national parks, Paklenica, to the south (see page 254), and North Velebit, between Senj and Karlobag, to the north. Of the two, North Velebit is the more remote, and far and away the least visited – it only achieved national park status in 1999, and development of any tourist infrastructure is still in its infancy. You can reach the Zavižan and Alan mountain huts (see below) by minor roads (a 4x4 vehicle is recommended for the former), and there are marked hiking trails to both these and other points from the coast.

Even though the current national park is itself very recent, conservation history in North Velebit goes back a long way – Štirovača park here was one of the country's first, along with Plitvice, back in 1929, and since 1978 it has been part of the UNESCO MAB (Man and Biosphere) programme. There's an inevitable conflict of interest along the park's borders with the highly lucrative local logging industry – most of the jobs in the area are logging-related – but the 1999 legislation promises to keep North Velebit well protected.

Being cool, high up, well forested and very sparsely inhabited, the park is an ideal habitat for brown bears, and there are now reckoned to be around 500 in the area, though they're just as unlikely to be seen here as anywhere else, bears being notoriously people-shy. The park is also home to wild boar, lynx, wild cats, red and roe deer and several species of eagle, along with many other animals – including, deep in one of the caves, *Croatobranhus mestrovi*, a previously unknown (and to this author's eyes, especially revolting) species of leech.

The park also features some of the country's most diverse flora, with a wide range of rare and protected plant species. The **Velebitski Botanički Vrt** botanical gardens – the remotest I've ever visited – were established back in 1967, at 1,480m, to highlight the flora unique to the region, and although the gardens had fallen into disrepair before the creation of the national park, they're now in the process of being restored.

PREMUŽIĆEVA STAZA

Premužićeva staza ('Premužić's path') was built during the early years of the 1930s under the direction of a local forestry engineer, Ante Premužić. Stretching from near Zavižan hut in the north to Baške Oštarije (in the mountains above Karlobag) in the south, and passing through the amazing limestone crags of Rožanski kukovi and below the weird rock fingers of Bačić kuk on the way, it is one of the finest hiking trails in Croatia. The most impressive section, Rožanski kukovi, can be visited as a day trip from the Zavižan hut; to continue to Baške Oštarije you'll need to allow 4 days and be fully equipped.

For detailed information on hiking on Velebit and in other areas of Croatia, see Rudolf Abraham's book *Walking in Croatia*.

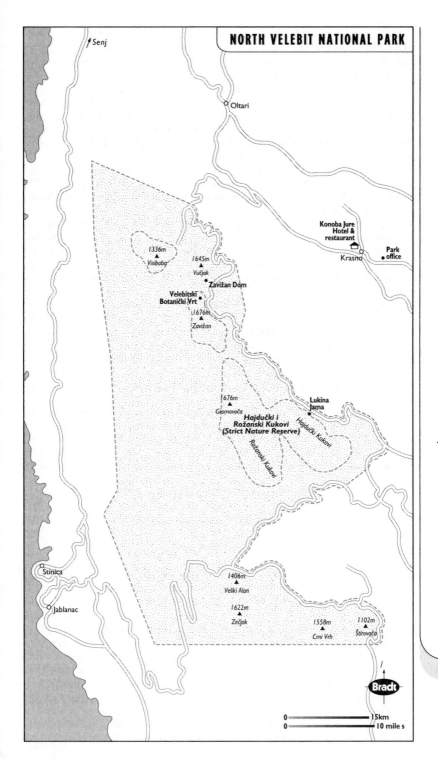

NORTH VELEBIT NATIONAL PARK

Senj

Oltari

Konoba Jure
Hotel &
restaurant

Park
office

Krasno

1336m
Visibaba

1645m
Vučjak

Zavižan Dom

Velebitski
Botanički Vrt

1676m
Zavižan

1676m
Gromovača

Lukina
Jama

Hajdučki i
Rožanski Kukovi
(Strict Nature Reserve)

Hajdučki Kukovi

Rožanski Kukovi

Stinica

Jablanac

1406m
Veliki Alan

1622m
Zečjak

1558m
Crni Vrh

1102m
Štirovača

Bradt

0 — 15km
0 — 10 miles

Deep within the park there's an even more strictly protected nature reserve, **Hajdučki kukovi**, which you'll need special permission (and a very good reason) to visit. Within this reserve is one of the world's dozen deepest caves, Lukina Jama, which was only discovered in 1993. Over the next two years the cave, whose entrance is at 1,436m above sea level, was explored down to a depth of 1,392m, just 44m above the sea (and it's down here that the new leech was found). The cave complex also features Atkov Gust, the second deepest vertical shaft in the world, dropping a giddying 553m. It's for the most serious of speleologists only. Just to the west of this is the breathtaking limestone scenery of **Rožanski kukovi**, and passing through this, Premužićeva staza, arguably Croatia's finest hiking trail (see box on page 226).

North Velebit has two park offices (☎ *053 665 380*; f *053 665 390; www.np-sjeverni-velebit.hr*), with a small branch on the coast, in Senj, and the main office up in the hills, in Krasno, on the minor road from Sveti Juraj (10km south of Senj) to Otočac. Watch out for giant logging vehicles.

There are several access points to the park itself, with the main entrance being off the road from Sveti Juraj to Krasno. There's a well-signed turning off to the right, just after the village of Oltari, 15km uphill from Sveti Juraj, after which you'll need 4×4 if the road hasn't yet been improved. You can also enter the park from the southern end, heading steeply uphill from Jablanac towards Veliki Alan, though you'll need 4×4 to get beyond this. Buy your entrance ticket (30kn for a one- to three-day visit, 50kn for four–seven days) as you come into the park or at Zavižan Dom (see below).

Within the park there are three mountain lodges where hikers can overnight, the best equipped of which is **Zavižan Dom** (☎ *053 614 209*), situated at 1,594m, not far from the botanical gardens. The lodge is also an important weather station, and Ante Vukusić and his family, who live up here, are cut off from the rest of the world for six months of the year. Fortunately they have a homemade fiery spirit from the local mountain herbs (including mint and rosemary) and lovely herbal tea to keep them company.

Zavižan Dom makes an excellent base for hikes through the park, from the ten-minute scramble to the nearby peak of Vučjak, at 1,645m (fabulous views down to the island of Rab), to the 6-hour walk over to the Alan Lodge, at the other end of the park. The trails are mostly well marked, but given the rapid changes in weather here (visibility can drop to nothing in a matter of moments, and there's plenty of rain), make sure you're well equipped and have a good map and compass with you.

In the village of Krasno itself there's the **Konoba Jure** (☎ *053 851 100; B&B €16 pp*), which serves up a reasonable meal and has some accommodation. It's definitely worth checking with the park administration first if you want to stay or visit.

CRES AND LOŠINJ *Telephone code 051 (+385 51 from abroad)*

Until the 11m-wide channel was dug between them, between 2,000 and 3,000 years ago, Cres (try saying something halfway between tsress and trress and you'll be fine) and Lošinj were a single island.

Geographically, they're the spindly, submerged, 80km-long north–south prolongation of the Učka mountain range, with nowhere being more than a couple of kilometres from the sea. Forming the western boundary of the Kvarner Bay, their deciduous forests in the north give way to dense scrub and barren shores further south, though newer pine plantations on Lošinj have softened the landscape there somewhat.

Today tourism accounts for practically all the islands' revenue, and they benefit from more than a century's worth of hospitality and tourist infrastructure. In season you may find Lošinj just a tad too popular for comfort – it attracts a quarter of a million visitors a year (about half as many as Dubrovnik) – but spring and autumn are lovely here. And even in high summer it's easy enough to get away from the crowds by hiking

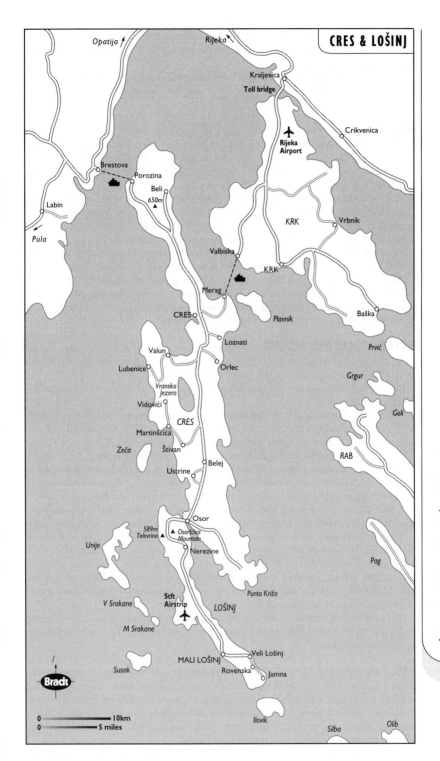

Opatija

Rijeka

Kraljevica

Toll bridge

Crikvenica

✈ **Rijeka Airport**

Brestova

Porozina

Beli
650m ▲

Labin

Pula

KRK

Vrbnik

Valbiška

KRK

Merag

Baška

CRES

Plavnik

Loznati

Prvić

Valun

Orlec

Lubenice

Vransko Jezero

Grgur

Goli

Vidovići

CRES

Martinšćica

Zeča

Štivan

Belej

RAB

Ustrine

Osor

589m Televrina ▲ ▲ *Osorščica Mountain*

Unije

Nerezine

Pag

Stft Airstrip
✈

Punta Križa

V Srakane

LOŠINJ

M Srakane

MALI LOŠINJ

Veli Lošinj

Rovenska

Jamna

Susak

Ilovik

Silba

Olib

0 ▬▬▬▬ 10km
0 ▬▬▬▬ 5 miles

Bradt

or mountain-biking across the islands on one of the numerous trails and paths. Once you're away from the paved roads, there are far more rock beaches and pebbly coves than people looking for them.

Access to both has never been easier with budget flights into Rijeka Airport on the island of Krk from Germany and Norway – and for a while the UK, until Ryanair mysteriously closed this route.

HISTORY Inhabited since the Stone Age, Cres and Lošinj were home to important Iron and Bronze Age hilltop settlements, before being settled by the Liburnians, an Illyrian tribe, around 3,500 years ago. The islands were conquered by the Romans during the 1st century BC, passing to Byzantium on the collapse of the empire, and gradually settled by Slavs from the 7th century on.

Venice took control from 1000 to 1797, with a 50-year break at the end of the 14th century, during which the Croat-Hungarian kings were in charge. Austro-Hungarians stepped in from 1797, after which the islands passed to Italy in 1918, Germany in 1943, and Yugoslavia in 1945, before finally becoming Croatian in 1991.

Under the Venetians, Cres thrived, while under the Austro-Hungarians it was Lošinj that did best, with Mali Lošinj developed as an important dockyard, producing fine sailing ships for the empire. The transition to steam power was disastrous for both the islands, and they declined gradually from then on – notwithstanding Mali Lošinj's status as a winter health resort for wealthy Austrians at the turn of the century – until being saved by the arrival of mass tourism in the 1970s.

GETTING THERE AND AROUND Getting to Cres and Lošinj is easy enough, but be prepared for long queues if you're driving here in summer, and especially during the peak season, running from the last week of July to the third week in August. If you're intending to bring your car, you should factor in a delay of at least several hours at the ferry terminal.

The shortest crossing is from Brestova in Istria to Porozina on Cres, taking just half an hour and running a dozen times a day in winter – and all day and all night in summer. You can also get on to the islands ten times a day from Valbiska on Krk to Merag on Cres's eastern flank – there's a road bridge on to Krk from the mainland.

Jadrolinja runs a ferry service from Mali Lošinj to Zadar, although this is limited to once a week outside of the summer season. In summer there are ferries from Venice to Zadar as well, running up to six times a week in each direction and stopping in at Pula and Mali Lošinj. The journey from Venice by boat takes 11 hours; from Pula it's just a four-hour ride. There's also an airport near Mali Lošinj, which brings in small planes only.

Buses run roughly every hour from Veli Lošinj to Mali Lošinj, then up to Osor on the isthmus and on to Cres town – some then go to Merag and on to Krk, while most head up to Porozina and on to Brestova. There are half a dozen buses a day direct to Rijeka (3½ hours), and two a day to Zagreb (7 hours). If you want to get off the islands' 80km-long main road that connects the main centres then you'll need either your own transport or strong legs.

If you're driving, expect traffic jams at the bottleneck at Osor, especially when the swing-bridge is opened (twice a day, morning and late afternoon) to let boats through the 100m-long channel.

CRES Cres is the less-touristed of the two islands, though don't expect anywhere this attractive, this close to Italy, Austria and Germany, and this warm and sunny, to be entirely visitor-free, especially with Rijeka airport's growing roster of flights. The ratio between locals and tourists in Cres compares favourably to most of the other bigger Adriatic islands, though second-home owners and big tourism developers are greedily eyeing up one of Croatia's least spoilt major islands.

Cres town

Cres town itself (26km south of Porozina) is lovely, almost as Italian-looking as Rovinj, on Istria's west coast, though a good deal smaller. Its *raison d'être* is the well-sheltered harbour, a stopping-off and refreshment point for Venetian convoys, and the source of the island's long-ago prosperity. Today the old stone buildings soak up the summer sun and it's a charming place to while away a few hours, especially now that the main square has been tarted up in a sympathetic style.

Much of the town dates from the 15th and 16th centuries, when Cres was the seat of the Venetian administration for the islands, and there are still lots of well-preserved bits and pieces, including a handful of town gates, a section of the old town walls, and quite a collection of Gothic and Renaissance palazzi. In the main square, Trg Frane Petrića, there's a pretty loggia and clock tower, while through the town gate from here you'll find the sober façade of the 15th-century **Church of St Mary** and its fortified campanile. The church is only usually opened for services – if it is open, however, pop inside to see the fine Gothic (15th-century) wooden carved *pietà* – and a rather sad-looking griffon on the pulpit.

Where to stay Accommodation in the town itself is limited to private rooms, which you can book through the tourist office (*Cons 10;* $\mathcal{V}$f *051 571 535; www.tzg-cres.hr*), right where the bus stops. Expect to pay up to € 35 for doubles in high season, plus a 30% surcharge for stays of under four nights.

Kimen (221 rooms) Melin I/16 ✆ 051 573 305; f 051 573 002; www.hotel-kimen.com. 1km west of Cres, this is the only hotel near town. It's pretty big but it's set in nice grounds a couple of hundred metres back from the pebble beach. The main building was recently renovated, transforming itself into a 3-star establishment, while the two smaller buildings nearby were not, and retain their 'old school' 2-star character. *Dbl in renovated building €52 (out of season), €100 (in season); non-renovated rooms €42–72.*

Kovačine Autocamp Melin I/20 ✆ 051 573 150; f 051 571 086; www.camp-kovacine.com. Another km west, along a pleasant seaside path, on the Kovačine headland, & set amongst pinewoods & olive trees, the Kovačine Autocamp is a small town in itself, with accommodation for up to 2,000 people (including a naturist section), 4 restaurants & bars, a supermarket, a small marina & its own beaches, & offering courses in windsurfing & scuba diving. If you don't have your own tent or camper van then you can book one of the 98 mobile homes, which sleep either 2 or 4–6 people. *Mobile homes €44–115 (4–6 people) and €36–70 (2 people) a night. The campsite beach house has 13 en-suite rooms for €29–44 pp.*

Where to eat Cres boasts an impressive array of local produce with 'organic' food here not being just a modish fashion, but rather a way of life. Look out for the excellent local lamb, great seafood, the award-winning local olive oil and *udič*, the EU directive-defying mutton version of *pršut*. You won't see the latter on many menus but ask the locals for tips and where to try it if you dare.

Belona Blaž Stolnik; ✆ 051 571 203. It may not have the Adriatic views, but the fact that it's so popular with the locals says enough. A solid range of seafood & meat dishes with more marauding cats than fellow tourists in the shoulder seasons – but avoid the house white.

Bukaleta Loznati; ✆ 051 571 606. Cres lamb is right up there in quality with its more famous sibling further down the Adriatic in Pag. Worth the 10-min taxi ride out of town to enjoy lamb in various permutations.

Riva Creskih Kapetana 13; ✆ 051 571 1107. The best place in town for quality seafood. Sit on the terrace overlooking the harbour feasting on langoustines (scampi) & white fish, which you can see being cooked in the open kitchen.

Beli and the Eco-Centre Caput Insulae

(*Beli 4, 51 559 Beli, Cres Island, Croatia;* $\mathcal{V}$f *51 840 525;* e *caput.insulae@ri.htnet.hr; www.supovi.hr; 40kn;* ⊕ *Mar–Oct 09.00–20.00 daily*) Up on Cres's rocky northeastern tip, separated from the dramatic main road along the island's spine by the island's highest peak (650m) is the old hilltop village of Beli, overlooking the western corner of Krk, and sitting high up above a pretty pebble beach.

It's pretty hard to reach without your own transport, as buses only come here twice daily from Cres on weekdays, and not at all at weekends. If you're walking, it's a good hour and a half from the bus stop at the junction on the main road half way between the Cres and Porozina.

The only accommodation options are a handful of private rooms (ask around; there's a tourist office of sorts only in July and August) or the pleasant campsite down in the olive groves towards the shore, which also has a restaurant and a small shop.

Apart from the peace and tranquillity here, the main reason for a visit to Beli is the wonderful Eurasian griffon vulture, one of the largest flying birds. Saved from the jaws of extinction here only in the last few years, the vulture is now protected not just by law but also by the Eco-Centre Caput Insulae Beli (ECCIB), a non-profit, non-governmental organisation established in 1993. Housed in an abandoned school building – depopulation meant there were no more children to teach – the ECCIB works to protect the area's natural, cultural and historical heritage, and is doing a terrific job of protecting one of the world's most magnificent birds.

There are two permanent exhibitions, one on the Biodiversity of the Lošinj Archipelago and the other on the History of Beli and Tramuntana, while behind the building there's a rest hospital for injured or damaged birds, where they're kept until they're ready to go back into the wild. The building also marks the start of a series of eco-routes, guided by a leaflet from the ECCIB, which takes you along trails explaining the culture, flora and fauna of the Tramuntana, the northern part of Cres.

The vultures themselves are truly magnificent, with a wingspan reaching 2.8m, a body weight of up to 15kg and a life expectancy of up to 60 years. They can be super-fast, reaching speeds of up to 120km/h, but usually cruise at 40–50km/h in search of a carcass. Given the relative rarity of dead animals, the vultures cruise in formation, with fewer than one per kilometre, to cover the maximum ground area, signalling a find by circling.

The birds live only on carrion, which was once provided by the abundance of sheep ranging free here – diseased animals would be cleared up by the vultures, keeping the shepherds happy by saving the rest of the flock from contamination. Today, with depopulation, there are fewer shepherds, fewer sheep and fewer vultures, so the ECCIB programme focuses on making sure there are enough dead sheep to go around.

The vultures are also endangered by tourism, particularly by motor boats coming too close to the cliffs and scaring weaklings into flights that can't be sustained, leading to youngsters drowning. With only one egg per couple per year (during the two-month incubation period both parents alternate in keeping it warm and protected), and a five-year delay before sexual maturity, you can see why they're scarce.

Fortunately they're now legally protected, and the fine for killing or disturbing the vultures, or stealing their eggs or chicks, is an off-putting 40,000kn.

From just 24 nesting couples in the mid '80s, the population has now increased to a still precarious 70-odd couples (as of autumn 2009), thanks mostly to the work of the ECCIB, and I can't encourage you enough to support its work.

South of Cres town The hilly main road from Cres town winds 35km south to the village of Osor, on the isthmus. On the way south you'll see the 5km-long and 1.5km-wide Vransko Jezero, the only lake on the Kvarner islands, and the only water supply for the whole of Cres and Lošinj – hence the ban on swimming here.

Before the lake, there's a turn-off to the exquisite village and bay of **Valun**, which isn't easily accessible without your own wheels. Buses only run here three times a week, and although it's barely 1½ hours downhill on foot from the bus stop at the junction on the main road, it's a good 2½-hour slog – all uphill – for the return journey.

Access to the village – even for car drivers – is down a flight of steps leading to the harbour, where you'll find a handful of stone houses and the pretty little church holding Valun's only cultural treasure, the **Valun Tablet**. Housed in the sacristy, this 11th-century engraving was originally a tombstone, and it's one of the oldest pieces of Glagolitic stone-carving in Croatia – with a helpful Latin translation for the Glagolitically challenged.

Accommodation in Valun is limited to a (very) few private rooms, which are tricky to book – there's a tourist office here in July and August, but that's when the rooms are already full of holidaying Italians. Out of season you just need to ask around. Otherwise there's the **Zdovice** campsite (❧ *051 750 604;* f *051 571 163; www.cresanka.hr*), but you should book well ahead to be sure of a space.

On a spur off the road to Valun there's a road leading to the partly abandoned hilltop village of **Lubenice**, though you won't get here (or away) on public transport. The village sits on a bluff at nearly 400m above sea level, and makes for a popular summer evening excursion venue – the views are fantastic – and in season the half dozen local residents do brisk trade selling their own wine and honey and keeping the bar and restaurant going. For the rest of the year it's a deserted and windblown place.

Below the town (far, far below) there's a wonderful bay and beach – the hike back rightly puts most people off, however. If you really want to explore the coast in these parts you're better off doing so by boat.

Back on the main road south, the first turn-off after Vransko Jezero leads 8km or so west to the little holiday village of **Martinšćica**, set on a pretty shingle bay with an attractive half-kilometre beach. At one end there's the large **Slatina** campsite (❧ *051 574 127;* f *051 574 167; www.ac-slatina.hr*), which also has a few apartments. There's also Hotel Zlatni Lav (❧ *51 574 020;* f *51 574 062; www.hotel-zlatni-lav.com; dbl €50–90*). There's a bus service between Martinšćica and Cres – but only one a day, so, getting here may be a matter of having your own wheels.

Osor, on the isthmus, was the capital of Cres and Lošinj until the end of the 15th century, when a combination of plague, epidemic and Venetians shifted the capital up to Cres town, 35km north. Which is why the tiny village of today (population 80) still has a town hall and loggia, a 15th-century cathedral, a bishop's palace and the extant remnants of old stone walls.

It's a lovely stop, in the process of reinventing itself as a museum-village, and for once it's an easy enough place to get to, being on the regular bus route. The cathedral is shut more often than not, but if it's open it's worth popping in to admire the sizeable altarpiece and the somewhat over-the-top chapel to the left – both a good deal more sightly than the ghastly modern stations of the cross adorning the side walls.

Behind the cathedral, in the town square, you'll find a dozen sculptures by the likes of Meštrović and Kršnić, a couple of cafés, and the small town museum. Housed in the old town hall, and open only on weekday mornings, the museum has an interesting collection of 1st- and 2nd-century Roman artefacts from all over the empire, a testimony to Osor's former importance as a maritime trading port.

If you want to stay, there are a couple of good campsites, **Preko Mosta** (℣/f *051 237 350; www.jazon.hr*) and **Bijar** (℣/f *051 237 027; www.camp-bijar.com*), both close to the town and to the beaches, though there's little in the way of private accommodation. In summer Osor puts on excellent classical concerts – check the Cres town or Mali Lošinj tourist offices for details.

Southeast of Osor – off the public transport map altogether – are Cres's best beaches, spread around a crenulated coast, south and east of the village of **Punta Križa**, that's deserted save for the **Baldarin** (℣/f *051 235 680; www.camp-baldarin.com*) naturist campsite. The beaches are no great secret, but you should be able to find yourself a quiet spot, away from an incipient off-roading recreational-vehicle community.

LOŠINJ
Smaller than Cres, but more populous (and more popular) is the island of Lošinj. That has its advantages and disadvantages – the extra tourists mean there are better facilities on hand, while the smaller size makes the island far more manageable on foot. Excellent walking maps are available from the tourist offices in Mali and Veli Lošinj, and the moment you head uphill you'll find you have plenty of space to yourself. Mali Lošinj in the first couple of weeks in August, however, can be seriously busy – seething wouldn't be an exaggeration. The waters around Lošinj are busy too, with playful dolphins that are best visited on organised boat trips from and Veli Lošinj, where there's also a dedicated dolphin research centre.

Nerezine
The first settlement you come to, 4km south of Osor, is Nerezine, a cheerily dispersed village and harbour with a fairly large and well-situated campsite, Rapoča (℡ *051 237 145;* f *051 237 146; www.losinjplov.hr*), in the woods by the beach along the north shore. There are also some private rooms available – contact Lošinjska Plovidba (℡ *051 231 077;* f *051 231 611; www.losinjplov.hr*), or ask at the Marina travel agency (*Obala Nerezinskih Pomoraca;* ℡ *051 237 038;* f *051 604 353; www.marina-nerezine.hr*).

Nerezine lies at the foot of Osorščica Mountain, which culminates in the peak of Televrin (589m), a steep hike up, but one of the best pay-offs in the country, with fabulous views in all directions when you get there – all the way to Triglav (2,864m) in Slovenia, the Velebit massif and Gorski Kotar onshore, Rab and Pag to the east, the length of Lošinj and its offshore islands to the south, and Istria to the northwest. On a clear day you can see as far as the Apennines, in Italy, as well as the smudge of Venice in the distance. Just below the peak is the tiny **Chapel of St Nicholas**, still a place of pilgrimage for the Nerezine locals. A hike up Televrin from Nerezine, descending to Osor on the other side, takes about 4½ hours (see Rudolf Abraham's *Walking in Croatia*).

Mali Lošinj
Mali Lošinj made its reputation in the 19th century as a dockyard, producing great sailing ships for the Austro-Hungarian Empire. When steam came in, the dockyards went out, but tourism of a sort started here around the same time, with the town gaining favour (like Opatija) with well-heeled Austrians as a fine place for a winter rest cure. Many of the elegant villas they built can still be seen above the Čikat Bay and peninsula, home today to the main resort hotels.

The annual influx of visitors – mainly Italian and German – hasn't done much to spoil the old town, spreading along both sides of the v-shaped harbour and meeting in a triangular piazza that leads off into the small but pretty clutter of narrow streets making up the old quarter. The landscaped waterfront with its swaying palms and cacti is the place to head for a relaxing stroll with an ice cream in hand.

There's remarkably little in terms of sights, but the **art collections**, housed a block back from the Riva, are well worth a visit. The gallery comprises two separate private collections, with old masters collected by Guiseppe Piperata on the one hand and more contemporary works collected by Andro Vid Mihičić on the other. Otherwise it's a question of drifting around and soaking up the old town atmosphere before returning to the endless quayside cafés for a well-deserved aperitif.

The main **tourist office** (*Riva Lošinjskih Kapetana 29;* ✆ *051 231 884;* f *051 231 547; www.tz-malilosinj.hr*), halfway along the Riva between the ferry terminal and the main square, has excellent documentation, and you should definitely pick up the *Promenades and Footpaths* map which gives you the walking times between most of the major points on the southern part of the island – an indispensable guide if you're to get away from the crowds in season.

Hotel accommodation is plentiful, but you'd do well to book way ahead in high summer.

Where to stay In the town itself you have the choice of the Apoksiomen or Villa Ana; the others listed here are across the headland on Čikat, and run by Jadranka – see www.jadranka.hr or www.losinj-hotels.com for all five.

Apoksiomen (25 rooms) Riva Lošinjskih Kapetana 1; ✆ 051 520 820; f 051 520 830; www.apoksiomen.com. New 4-star hotel right on the waterfront with its own quayside café. Light & airy rooms feature rattan furniture, Wi-Fi & satellite TV, & the helpful staff go that extra mile for you. *Dbl €160 high season (sea-facing with balcony), €120 (low season).*

Alhambra (41 rooms) Čikat; ✆ 051 232 022; f 051 232 042; www.losinj-hotels.com. Simplest of the Čikat hotels is this 2-star place, which has good-sized rooms. *Dbl €65–105.*

Aurora (393 rooms) Sunčana bb; ✆ 051 667 200; f 051 667 222; www.losinj-hotels.com. Vast place further west on the far side of the Punta Annunziata. *Dbl €130–190 (summer).*

Bellevue (226 rooms) Čikat; ✆ 051 231 222; f 051 231 268; www.losinj-hotels.com. Vast 3-star place. *Dbl €90–135 (summer).*

Helios (128 rooms) Čikat; ✆ 051 232 124; f 051 232 104; www.losinj-hotels.com. More of a guesthouse than a hotel, with plainish rooms. *Dbl €55–90 (summer).*

Vespera (404 rooms) Sunčana bb; ✆ 051 667 300; f 051 667 324; www.losinj-hotels.com. Companion hotel to the Aurora, another huge place on the far side of the Punta Annunziata. *Dbl €120–195 (summer).*

Villa Ana (6 rooms, 5 apartments) Velopin 31; ✆ 051 233 223; f 051 233 224; www.vila-ana.hr. Nice place about 300m from main square, with own restaurant. *Dbl €56–100.*

Private rooms are also in good supply and you shouldn't have any trouble in finding one – ask at any of the dozen or so agencies in town and expect to pay around € 30 for a double, with a 30% surcharge for three-day stays or less. One place well worth trying is the **Ivanka**, just behind the western quayside, right in town, which is a cheerful restaurant with a handful of nice rooms upstairs, which go for € 60 a night for a double in summer and around half that in winter.

The **Čikat** campsite (✆ *051 232 125;* f *051 231 708; www.camp-cikat.com.hr*) is a half-hour walk across the headland, and it's enormous, but well located, right on a good beach.

Where to eat

Baracuda Priko 31; ✆ 051 233 309. Their claim 'we offer you only fresh fish, so we appreciate on understanding if some kind of fish missing momentary' may not win any grammar awards, but the fresh seafood on offer here deserves all the acclaim it gets. Book a seat on the coveted leafy outside terrace. Daily specials tempt from the handwritten board but you can't go wrong with one of Croatia's best fish platters for 2, a snip at 250kn for squid, langoustine, 2 whole sea bass, shark steaks & a tuna kebab.

Konoba Corrado Sv Marije 1; ✆ 051 232 487; www.islandlosinj.com/corrado. The best place on Lošinj to try Cres lamb is worth the 10min walk uphill away from the waterfront. This characterful little *konoba* specialises in cooking the lamb in peka-style (ie: in a bread oven), which must be booked the day before. They also do a good range of meat & fish dishes.

Veli Lošinj In spite of the name (*veli* means large; *mali* means small), Veli Lošinj has under 1,000 residents to Mali Lošinj's 7,000, and although it also has many fewer visitors, there's much less space here, too, so this picture postcard town can get almost as crowded in summer as its larger cousin.

Veli Lošinj is the terminus for the regular bus up to Cres. It's also only about 45 minutes on foot from Mali Lošinj, with the last two-thirds of the route along the coastal path, coming in past the Punta hotel complex. Bring your swimming gear if you fancy a dip in one of the coves en route.

The tiny harbour is dominated by the fortified, barn-like **Church of St Anthony**, built in the 17th century on the ruins of a smaller 15th-century church, and testifying to the former wealth and grandeur of the town. Inside it's stately Baroque, and has a fine collection of paintings from the Titian and Tiepelo schools, though you're only likely to see these during the half hour before or after a service, as the church is usually closed at other times.

Behind the church, stand-offishly distant, is a 15th-century Venetian campanile. Also 15th-century Venetian is the crenellated tower built to protect the town from pirates and now restored to house the municipal museum – a minor triumph of form over content.

Where to stay Everything you need is on or near the harbour front, including a couple of agencies that will find you a private room for anything from € 30 for a double or € 40 for an apartment, with a hefty 50% surcharge for one-night stays. Try the helpful VAL agency (*Zad Bone 16;* \ *051 236 604; www.val-losinj.hr*), which also rents bikes – an excellent way of exploring the island – or Palma (*V Nazora 22;* \ *051 236 179; www.losinj.com*).

Punta (181 sgl & dbl, 53 family rooms) Veli Lošinj bb; \ 051 662 000; f 051 236 301; www.losinj-hotels.com. Up on the northwestern corner of the Veli Lošinj bay, this is a sprawling affair with indoor & outdoor pools & many sports facilities. The buffet b/fast is unique in places I've stayed at in featuring free rum. *Dbl with sea view €110, €55 in winter.*
Pansion Villa Saturn (9 rooms) Obala Maršala Tita bb; \ 051 236 604; www.val-losinj.hr. Good,

bargain-priced place, renovated in 2005 – right on the front, next door to St Anthony's. Nice rooms, though with the terrace below it's not as quiet as it might be. *Dbl with b/fast €40–56.*
Youth Hostel (50 beds) Kaciol 4; \ 051 236 234; f 051 236 239; www.hfhs.hr. Veli Lošinj also has a fine youth hostel with its own small park – book as far ahead as you possibly can, as it's usually full.

Southern Lošinj and islands A 20-minute walk south of Veli Lošinj along the shore or a five-minute hike across the village brings you to the little bay and pretty fishing 'suburb' of Rovenska. There's a cheerful restaurant here, Sirius (\ *051 236 399*) serving up the catch of the day, super-fresh. Ask here about private rooms if you want to stay in the village. If the Sirius is full, try the Mol (\ *051 236 008*) next door, which has excellent daily specials. The Bora Bar Trattoria/Tartufferia (\ *051 867 544; www.borabar.com*), as the name implies, is the place to eat truffles.

The attractive coastal path continues another 75 minutes south past the villages of **Javorna** and **Kriška**, terminating in **Jamna** – there's also a wealth of hiking up to and along the spine of the island, with paths leading down to various settlements, coves and beaches on the pretty west coast. Take plenty to drink, however, as there's not much shade and no water at all.

When you're done with the main island, there are day trips to the offshore ones from Mali Lošinj – you can arrange these through any of the travel agencies, or just negotiate on the harbour front with one of the taxi-boats. There's also a Jadrolinija ferry that makes the circuit of the main offshore islands twice daily.

Most popular is **Susak**, the sandy island off to the west of Lošinj, which is famous for its excellent wines and colourful local costume, featuring orange and yellow pleated dresses and bright-red tights – you're more likely to see this on a local postcard than a local person, however, as most of the population has long since emigrated.

Excursions are also available to the island of **Unije**, the westernmost of the islands in the Kvarner Bay. With only one settlement and fewer visitors than most places it makes for a lovely haven to spend a day or so if it's total quiet you're after. It also has a couple of very well-sheltered moorings if you're sailing.

Finally, to the south of Lošinj there's a handful of islands, the biggest of which is **Ilovik**, famous for its flowers and eucalyptus trees, a testimony to the unusual amount of water here.

There are some private rooms available on all three islands – book these through one of the agencies in Mali Lošinj.

KRK *Telephone code 051 (+385 51 from abroad)*

Croatia's biggest island (410km² to Cres's 405km²) has been connected to the mainland by a 1.4km toll bridge since 1980, and it's been one of the most popular holiday spots on the Adriatic ever since – at the height of the season you should definitely try to book ahead to be sure of a room, when it seems like the bridge is directly connected to Vienna and Munich.

Krk – impossible to pronounce correctly without being Croatian (somewhere between Sean Connery saying 'kirk' and a dog coughing) – is home to industry as well as tourism, with a petrochemical plant near Omišalj, and Rijeka's airport also being on the island. People living in the north commute to Rijeka for work, while in summer Krk is busy and popular with holidaymakers, primarily from Austria and Germany.

The island's infrastructure and local transport are good, making a visit here an easy one, and Krk was fortunate in barely being affected by the war at the beginning of the 1990s – tourism continues to boom and is expected to grow further as the airport sees more budget flights from northern Europe.

The northeastern side of the island is mostly barren, while the main centres and most of the trees are in the softer and milder southern half. Running down the northwestern shore are a string of fully developed package resorts, **Omišalj**, **Njivice** and **Malinska**.

If you're here at the end of July you'll be within easy earshot of the popular **Krk Folk Festival**, which is big on the local bagpipes.

HISTORY People have lived on Krk since time immemorial, but the island was first known to have been settled by the Illyrian Liburnians, who were usurped in due course by the Romans. When Rome fell, Byzantium stepped in, to be followed by Venice, and then Croatia–Hungary.

During the 11th century, Krk became the most important centre of Glagolitic culture in Croatia, and much of the country's valuable Glagolitic heritage comes from the island – the script was used here continuously until the beginning of the 19th century and the arrival of the Austro-Hungarians.

In 1358 Venice granted custody of the island to the Dukes of Krk, who ruled semi-autonomously until 1480. They owed their ascendancy, according to Rebecca West (in *Black Lamb and Grey Falcon*): 'not to virtue nor to superior culture, but to unusual steadfastness in seeing that it was always the other man who was beheaded or tossed from the window or smothered'.

From 1430 onwards, the Dukes successfully re-branded themselves (with the Pope's benediction) as '**Frankopans**', allying themselves to the Frangepan nobility of Roman times. Their new coat of arms gave a nod both to Venice and the Frangepans (which derives, as New Testament scholars will have guessed, from *frangere panem*, the breaking of the bread), and therefore featured lions with loaves.

The return of Krk to Venice in 1480 wasn't good news for the island. The Venetians tore down the oak forests to build their galleys, and then pressed the islanders into service as oarsmen. In spite of a succession of rulers – from the Austro-Hungarians to the French (briefly) to Yugoslavia itself – little else of great note affected Krk until the arrival of mass tourism in the 1970s.

GETTING THERE AND AROUND Being popular, close to Rijeka and connected to the mainland by a road bridge, Krk is pretty well served by public transport. Around 15 buses a day make the 1½-hour journey from Rijeka to Krk town, stopping on the way at Omišalj, Njivice and Malinska, and mostly going on to Punat and then Baška, at the island's southern end. Only a couple of buses a day, however, make the 10km journey across the island from Krk town to Vrbnik.

Four buses a day come direct from Zagreb, five hours away, and direct buses from Lošinj and Cres arrive via the Merag–Valbiska ferry several times a day and pass through Krk town on their way to Rijeka; some, but not all, also stop in Malinska.

By car, the vast majority of people arrive over the bridge, though there's also the ferry connection ten times a day from Merag on the island of Cres, and a new ferry from Lopar, on Rab, to Valbiska.

Rijeka airport is used mainly for charter flights bringing in package tours to Krk, Cres, Lošinj and Opatija, though increasingly budget airlines are also flying in direct from destinations in northern Europe.

KRK TOWN The island's capital is a bit of a suburban (and growing) sprawl, but at its core is a well-preserved old town, with cobbled streets and alleys. The Romans walled the town and built extensive baths here, but the remnants you'll see today are mostly 15th-century Frankopan and onwards.

Krk's most striking sight is arguably the onion-dome on top of the campanile, itself topped by a trumpet-blowing angel. The campanile dates from 1515, though the cupola and angel weren't added until 1765, and the angel you see today (not that you'd know) is a 1975 plastic replica, the original copper-plated wooden version having deteriorated beyond salvation. The **church museum** here is worth a visit, if only for the remarkable silver altarpiece of the Madonna, a gift to the last Duke of Krk in 1477.

The campanile is shared by two churches across a covered alley from one another, the cathedral and the church of St Quirinus.

The Romanesque **cathedral** is usually only open around the time of church services, but it's worth the wait, and you can often peer in from the vestibule anyway. Built on the site of an early basilica founded on the site of the Roman baths, today's cathedral dates from the 12th century on. While much of what you see inside is 15th and 16th century, there are some interesting mosaic fragments, and the columns are mostly Roman – the last capital on the left, by the choir, sports an unusual early Christian Eucharist motif of two birds eating a fish. There are some good 15th- and 16th-century paintings, including the altarpiece, by Pordenone, while the fine 15th-century Gothic chapel on the left-hand side was the Frankopan place of worship, and features their various coats of arms on the ceiling.

St Quirinus, next door, is another fine example of clean, spare Romanesque architecture, also dating mostly from the 12th century. It claims to be the only two-storey church on the eastern Adriatic coast, and it was in the crypt here, dedicated to St Margaret, that condemned men said their final mass before execution in Frankopan days.

Otherwise, there's not a whole lot to see, though the remnants of the medieval walls and the old alleys and streets are suitably atmospheric – as indeed are the summer concerts put on in the old Venetian fortress marking the corner of the old town.

Getting there and around Buses arrive at the southern end of town; it's a short walk past the bustling harbour to the old town. The **tourist office** (*Vela Placa 1/1;* ✆/f *051 221 414; www.tz-krk.hr*) is just inside the main gate, on the left, but was out of maps on the day I came through – fortunately that's not a problem as the old town is tiny, and it's easy to find your way around. More useful is **Autotrans** (*Sv Bernardina 3;* ✆ *051 222 661;* f *051 222 110; www.autotrans-turizam.com*), at the bus station, which can fix you up with a private room (doubles are around € 30, with the usual surcharge for short stays).

Where to stay Most of the town's hotel accommodation is a 15-minute walk east of town, though there's one place, the Marina, right on the waterfront.

🏠 **Marina** (6 rooms, 4 suites) Obala Hrvatske Mornarice bb; ✆ 051 221 128; f 051 221 357; www.hotelikrk.hr. Straightforward rooms in an unbeatable location. Dbl €82.

🏠 **Bor** (20 rooms) Šetalište Dražica 5; ✆/f 051 220 200; www.hotelbor.hr. Just 600m east along the shore from the marina is the newly refurbished & reopened Bor, which offers plain but spacious rooms a stone's throw from the beach. Dbl with sea view € 116 in high season, from €42 in low season.

🏠 **Koralj** (173 rooms) Vlade Tomašića bb; ✆ 051 655 405, 051 221 063; f 051 221 063; www.valamar.com. Best value of the out-of-town package places is the 3-star Koralj, which is on a narrow beach in the woods &

has modern dbls & for a lot less than you'll pay at the equally 3-starred Dražica/Lovorka (see below). Dbl €58–239.

🏠 **Dražica/Villa Lovorka** (137 rooms & 73 rooms) ✆ 051 655 755; f 051 221 022; www.hotelikrk.hr. Both 3-star. Dbl €125–165.

🏠 **Hostel Krk** Dinka Vitezića 32; ✆/f 051 220 212; www.hostel-krk.hr. Krk also has a youth hostel housed in what was originally the island's very first hotel. There's a surcharge for stays of under 3 days; it works out more expensive than private rooms – but the setting is lovely, right in the old town. B&B €18 pp in high season.

Beyond the hotels there's a naturist campsite, **Politin** (℡ *052 465 010, 051 221 351;* f *052 451 440, 051 221 246; www.camping-adriatic.com*); textile campers will prefer **Ježevac** (℡ *051 221 081;* f *051 221 362; www.camping-adriatic.com*), on the other side of town.

AROUND KRK TOWN Krk town is a good base for excursions around the island, both onshore and off. On the quay – or through any of the travel agents – you'll find boats offering the traditional fish picnic, combined with the chance to swim at one of the southern beaches, as well as trips out to the islands between Krk and Rab. There are also a couple of glass-bottomed boats that go out on excellent two-hour trips, giving you a fine view of the marine life.

If you have your own transport, can work out the twice-daily buses, or fancy the walk, then the old stone hilltop village of **Vrbnik**, 10km across Krk on the empty east coast of the island, is a lovely place to visit. The tourist office (*Placa Vrbničkog Statuta 4;* ℡ *051 857 479*) can help with finding you a private room if you want to stay, or there's the 12-room **Argentum** (*Supec 68;* ℡ *051 857 370;* f *051 857 352; www.hotel-argentum.com*), which does simple doubles for € 66–106.

The town was famous in the old days for having been one of the havens of the Glagolitic script, but today its reputation is sealed with a cork – you'll have trouble getting away from Vrbnik without trying the excellent local white wine, Žlahtina, best sampled at one of the several wine cellars. When you're done with wandering and wining, Vrbnik also has a beach below the town.

PUNAT AND KOŠLJUN Eight kilometres southeast of Krk town, facing west into a big sheltered bay, is the former shipbuilding and fishing village of Punat. It still makes a handsome living from the sea, but it's now the yachting trade that keeps the village afloat, with one of the bigger marinas in Croatia attracting a busy passing trade in summer.

The main attraction, however, is the island of Košljun, out in the bay, and its famous 16th-century Franciscan monastery. You can reach the island by taxi-boat from Punat, itself on a regular bus route from Krk town. Unless you're planning on staying in Punat, however, it's more convenient (if more expensive) to take a boat directly from Krk town.

In the airy church on Košljun there are some superb religious paintings from the 16th and 17th centuries, while the monastery also has one of Croatia's finest libraries, home to countless rare volumes, manuscripts, parchments and old maps. As if that weren't enough, the industrious monks have also put together an interesting ethnographic museum, a natural history collection and an assortment of numismatic rarities.

With your head spinning from the surfeit of information absorbed, the perfect cure is a walk around the pretty island before catching the return boat.

Practicalities I wouldn't especially recommend staying in Punat, but if you want to, the tourist office (*Obala 72;* ℡ *051 854 860;* f *051 854 970; www.tzpunat.hr*) can point you at agencies handling private rooms, and also has maps and brochures available. There's plenty of hotel accommodation in the complex south of town, near where the bus stops, run by **Hoteli Punat** (℡ *051 854 024;* f *051 854 101; www.hoteli-punat.hr*), though it may – like everywhere on Krk – be fully booked in summer. Punat also has a **Youth Hostel** (*Novi Put 8;* ℡/f *051 854 037*), right in town, though it too tends to be full through the season.

BAŠKA In a wide bay on the southeastern end of the island is Baška, Krk's most popular resort, with more than 110,000 people visiting the village annually. The reason for its popularity is obvious enough – Baška (population around 1,000) sits at the eastern end of one of what is certainly one of Croatia's best beaches, a 1,800m stretch of sand and pebbles in a wide sweep under the mountains.

The little village dates from the 16th century, and the colourful fishermen's houses and narrow alleys off the small harbour are still very attractive, even amongst the summer crowds. Whilst you won't escape these along the seafront promenade, stretching for a total length of 4km, it's easy enough to get away from it all into the hills behind town, and the tourist office (*Kralja Zvonimira 114;* ✆ *051 856 817;* f *051 856 544; www.tz-baska.hr*) has a great map detailing 15 different marked walks in the vicinity, from 2 to 10km long and taking anything from 30 minutes to four hours. As always, make sure you have decent footwear and plenty of water.

The four-hour walk over to the twin bays and beaches of **Mala Luka** and **Vela Luka** to the east, passing the naturist campsite and beach at **Bunculuka** (✆ *051 856 806;* f *051 856 595*) on the way, is moderately strenuous but well worth the effort, as is the somewhat easier three-hour hike to **Stara Baška**, a tiny village on a bay over the hills to the west.

A kilometre or so north of Baška is the **Church of St Lucy**, in **Jurandvor**, the site of one of Croatia's most important Glagolitic finds, the Baška Tablet, discovered in the floor of the church in 1851 by a local priest. It took over 20 years to decipher the script, which mentions King Zvonimir and dates from around 1100. The original is now in Zagreb (in the atrium of the building that houses the Strossmayer Gallery), but there's a good copy here – and rather less good, smaller, souvenir copies on sale all over town.

Practicalities Baška is easily reached on the bus from Rijeka and Krk town, and with its popularity with tourists, there are also any number of taxi-boats around, which will take you to less busy beaches and hidden coves both on Krk and on the neighbouring islands to the south.

Private rooms can be booked through Primaturist (*Kralja Zvonimira 98;* ✆ *051 856 132;* f *051 856 971; www.primaturist.hr*), with doubles going from € 30, with a surcharge for three days or less (if you can find anyone willing to let you have one) – in summer you should book well ahead. This is even truer if you want hotel accommodation. Call the **Corinthia** (*Emilia Geislicha 34;* ✆ *051 656 111;* f *051 856 880; www.hotelibaska.hr*) far, far in advance for doubles ranging from € 90–100 depending on the facilities.

RAB *Telephone code 051 (+385 51 from abroad)*

Cruising along the old coast road from Rijeka to Zadar you'd have no idea at all that Rab was worth visiting – it's a barren, denuded place, with no settlements and no sign of life.

Go round to the southwestern side of the island, however, and it suddenly becomes clear why Rab posts more than 1.5 million tourist nights a year from around 250,000 visitors. It's a green and pleasant land, with sandy beaches, hidden coves, and a wonderfully preserved medieval old town.

HISTORY Like Cres and Krk, Rab was first settled by Liburnian Illyrians, before the arrival of the Romans, who established an important base here. The Byzantines and Croat-Hungarians followed, before Venice finally imposed itself on the island definitively at the beginning of the 15th century. The rich architectural heritage of the old town of Rab belies the Venetian plunder of the island's timber, resulting in that denuded northeastern coast, or the republic's limiting of essential supplies of salt (fish preservative), generally keeping the population both poor and subdued for the best part of 400 years.

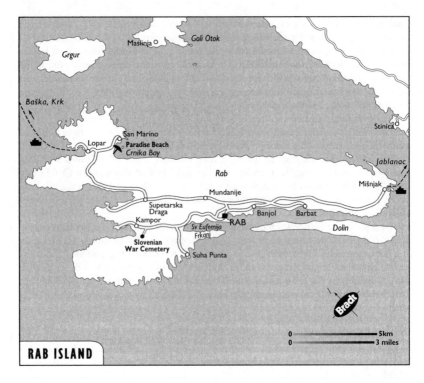

RAB ISLAND

The late 19th century ushered in new hope for the island as a tourist resort. The Austrians and Czechs were the first to invest in hotels – the Praha opened in 1909, a year after the Grand. They were also the first to encourage naturist holidays, heralding in a long tradition on the island – a tradition embraced in August 1936 by Edward VIII, king of England, and his girlfriend Wallis Simpson, it's said (though to an English sensibility it seems implausible that the king would be getting his kit off in public).

During World War II, Rab was occupied by the Italians and then by the Germans, before becoming Yugoslav in 1945. When Tito split with Stalin in 1948 he turned the barren island of **Goli** (Goli Otok), between Rab and the mainland, into an internment camp for Stalinists, and just mentioning it was enough to get you a one-way ticket to the horrors of the local gulag – it wasn't until after Tito's death that the Goli camp's very existence was made public.

Life on Goli Otok was appalling. Apart from the sheer brutality and cruelty, typical tasks for the prisoners would include breaking rocks and hauling them across the island, where they could be used to spell out a giant 'Tito' or other party slogans, only to have to dismantle them and return the rocks to the quarry.

Today, both it and its neighbour, **Grgur** (which used to be a women's prison), have less traumatic potential as offshore day trips.

GETTING THERE AND AROUND Rab ought to be a perfect stop for island-hoppers on their way from Krk to Pag or vice versa, but the idiosyncrasies of local transport make it difficult. The ferry from Valbiska on Krk, to Lopar at Rab's northern end, does run four times daily during summer – but there isn't a ferry to Pag, and only one or two a week to Zadar.

The most reliable way of getting to Rab is therefore the twice-daily direct bus from Rijeka, which takes around three hours, crossing on the ferry from Jablanac to Mišnjak on Rab's southern end before heading into Rab town. In summer, try to book ahead, as the bus fills up quickly. There are also direct buses to and from Zagreb in summer – again, book ahead if you can.

Onward travel south is problematic – you either have to go back to Senj on the Rijeka-bound bus and then retrace your steps on the next bus to Zadar, or get the first bus to drop you on the highway, above Jablanac, and wait (it can be quite a wait, too) for the next southbound bus willing to stop.

On the island itself there are regular buses from Rab town to Lopar, as well as to the other tourist settlements, though there's no local service at all to Mišnjak and the ferry to Jablanac on the mainland. If you miss the Rijeka bus you can get to Barbat easily enough, but it's then a good 1½ hours on foot to the ferry terminal, and an uphill 2km once you get to the mainland, from Jablanac up to the highway plied by the main coastal buses.

It's all a lot easier with your own wheels. Ferries run from Jablanac (100km south of Rijeka) to Mišnjak 13 times daily in winter and 23 times a day at the height of the season, and take just 15 minutes to make the crossing. From Mišnjak it's just 10km to Rab town. That said, the queues for the ferry can be pretty intimidating in July and especially in the first half of August – make sure you have a good book to hand.

RAB TOWN Rab, the town, capital of Rab, the island, is a lovely well-preserved traffic-free medieval city – one of the finest on the coast – stretched along a peninsula, with the town's harbour to one side and the long inlet of St Euphemia bay on the other. It's crowned by a distinctive line of four strikingly beautiful campanili, and is best seen at least once from the sea.

The town has an unusually rich stock of ancient churches, a reminder that there were once many more people living on the island than there are today – in winter, anyway. In high summer you'll find you're not alone admiring Rab's medieval heart, but set an early alarm, walk the streets in the soft morning light, and you'll get quite a different impression of the town, soulful and quiet, settled into its long, long past.

Three roughly parallel streets – Gornja, Srednja, Donja (upper, middle, lower) – run the length of old town, connecting the older **Kaldenac**, at the tip of the peninsula, with **Varoš**, the newer (15th- to 17th-century) part of town, where it widens out. The popular Riva running along the harbour-side makes for a fourth thoroughfare.

As you wander round, prepare to be churched-out – but bear in mind that most of them will only be open just before and after religious services.

The most important church in town is the **Cathedral of St Mary**, a superb Romanesque building consecrated by the Pope himself in 1177, though much altered and rebuilt in the early 16th century – the fine *pietà* above the door dates from 1514. (Observant readers will point out at this stage that it's not technically a cathedral, since Rab lost its bishopric in 1828 – but let's not quibble with the locals.) Inside, harmonious whitewashed Romanesque arches support the triple nave, with each capital subtly different. Dark carved choir stalls, dating from 1445, lead to an elegant grey altar canopy (*baldochino*) from the 11th century. It all goes back much further, even, than this – under the altar floor they're still excavating Roman mosaics.

Behind the cathedral (church, if you must), at the tip of the peninsula, is the small **Church of St Anthony** and a Franciscan convent. Beneath this, in the gardens below, you'll find a brand-new statue of **San Marino**, which was inaugurated here on 9 May 2004, to coincide with the annual crossbow contest (see box on page 246) – San Marino, the founder of the eponymous republic in Italy, was a Rab native.

Heading back along the upper road, the first thing you come to, opposite the cathedral, is the town's tallest **campanile**, an elegant 26m structure from around 1200, topped off with a balustrade with a mini octagonal 15th-century spire rising from

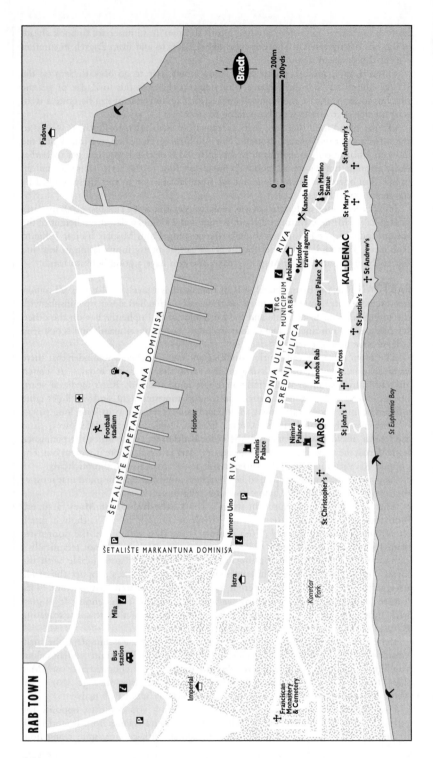

RAB TOWN

Padova

Football stadium

ŠETALIŠTE KAPETANA IVANA DOMINIS A

Harbour

Numero Uno RIVA

Dominis Palace

ŠETALIŠTE MARKANTUNA DOMINISA

Istra

Mila

Bus station

Imperial

Franciscan
Monastery
& Cemetery

Komrčar Park

St Christopher's

Nimira Palace

VAROŠ

St John's

Holy Cross

Kanoba Rab

SREDNJA ULICA

DONJA ULICA MUNICIPIUM ARBA

TRG ARBA

Arbiana

RIVA

Kanoba Riva

Kristofor
travel agency

Cernta Palace

KALDENAC

St Justine's

St Andrew's

St Mary's

San Marino
Statue

St Anthony's

St Euphemia Bay

Bračl

200m
200yds

0
0

244

within it. You can climb up for fine views of the town and harbour, and across the water to the uninhabited island of **Dolin**.

In a line running northwest from here are the town's other three campaniles, interspersed with the churches of **St Andrew**, **St Justine**, the **Holy Cross**, **St John** and **St Christopher**, dating from the 11th to 16th centuries (except St Justine's bell tower, a 17th-century impostor). St Justine's Church now houses the **Museum of Sacred Art**, where you can admire St Christopher's skull in its reliquary, which was used in 1358 to break a siege here (allegedly – see box on page 246). All that's really left of St John's Church is the last of the town's campaniles, which you can climb up – though it's fairly vertiginous – for wonderful views. St Christopher's, a little further along, houses a fairly sparse **lapidarium**, but more importantly gives access to one of the few remaining parts of Rab's **medieval walls**, where you can take the famous pictures of all four campaniles in a row.

Below the row of churches and campanili there are even more churches and any number of palazzi, most notably the impressive 15th-century **Dominis Palace** at the northern end of town, and the **Nimira Palace** not far away. The former has a splendid carved portal, with chubby putti pulling aside curtains to reveal the family crest. Indeed, all over town you should keep an eye out for medieval details, Latin inscriptions, Venetian lions and Gothic windows. In the main square (Trg Municipium Arba) you'll find the **Rector's Palace**, with its 15th-century loggia, which was originally the public court. Leading off this is one of the old city gates, crowned with a 14th-century clock on a 13th-century tower.

When you're ready for a breather (or a picnic) head north to the **Komrčar Park**. The 19th-century landscaped woodland was the work of Pravdoje Belia, who spent years defying the local sheep farmers in his efforts to create a public park – and was rewarded by a small statue in the park itself. It's all agreeably in a slightly run-down state, but the fine mature trees provide welcome shade. At the far end of the park there's a ruined Franciscan monastery and a quiet cemetery.

Paths lead down through the park to the shoreline of **St Euphemia Bay**, and there are places to swim here – though most people prefer to take a taxi-boat across to the **Frkanj Peninsula**, which has lots of coves and inlets, and the famous naturist beaches on the far side (the scene of King Edward VIII's supposed skinny-dipping).

The main **tourist office** (↝ *051 771 111;* f *051 771 110; www.tzg-rab.hr*) is handily by the bus station, on the northern side of the harbour, and they have an information-rich map, with the town on one side and the whole island on the other. There's a second office on the old town's central square. If you fancy a spot of sea kayaking while in Rab, contact Sea Kayak Adventures (↝ *095 9010 109; www.seakayak.hr*).

Where to stay

Arbiana (28 rooms) Obala kralja Krešimira IV; ↝ 051 775 900; www.arbianahotel.com. Set in a lovely old villa in the old town, & renovated to a very high standard in 2006. Most rooms have balcony & sea view. Dbl €140–220 in summer.

Imperial (134 rooms) Plait bb; ↝ 051 724 522; f 051 724 126; www.imperial.hr. One of the nicest hotels in town, in fine shape after nearly a century in business. It's in the woods adjoining the Komrčar Park, close to the bus station & the harbour, & a short walk from the old town. Dbl from €100 plus in season, €74 Oct–Jun.

Istra (100 rooms) Markantuna de Dominisa bb; ↝ 051 724 134; f 051 724 050; www.hotel-istra.hr. Right on the corner of the harbour. Dbl €70–106.

Padova (175 rooms) Banjol bb; ↝ 051 724 544; f 051 724 418; www.imperial.hr. If you're after a beach, a decent pool & a bit of tourist luxury, then head around the harbour & 1km south of town to this big, modern affair, with good-sized dbls with balconies & HB thrown in for not very much extra. Dbl €80–138.

Note that you'll be charged a supplement for stays of three days or fewer at any hotel in town in summer.

MEDIEVAL PAGEANTRY AND THE ART OF THE CROSSBOW

Living in a place like Rab you'd be mad not to dress up in medieval clothes from time to time, so that's what the locals do for the crossbow contests on 9 May and again on 25 June, 27 July and 15 August – and sometimes on other feast days and national holidays too. Amid much pageantry, fanfares of trumpets and formal processions, the tournament is really just an excuse for dressing up and having a good time, and it makes for a great civic occasion. But stay behind the crossbows – they're absolutely lethal.

The tradition dates back to 9 May 1358, when Rab was liberated from a nasty Italo-Norman siege through the intervention of the enterprising bishop of the day, who saw off the besieging army by waving the relics of the head of St Christopher from the city walls. The day has been celebrated ever since, and not only could exiles return for the festivities but husbands also had official permission to beat their wives. Today the wife-beating is mercifully outlawed, but the party does go on for three days, with folk processions, much eating and drinking, and the crossbow contest itself on the final day.

There are plenty of private rooms also available, though very few in the old town itself, and you may find everything already taken if you haven't booked ahead in high season. Use any of the several travel agencies to secure a room, and expect to pay € 30–40 for a double in summer, along with the usual 30% surcharge for short stays. Try the Mila travel agency (*Palit 68;* \f *051 725 499*), a block towards the harbour from the bus station, Numero Uno (*J de Marisa 22;* \f *051 724 688*) on the corner of the harbour or Kristofor (*Poslovni Centar Mali Palit 70;* \ *051 725 543;* f *051 724 811; www.kristofor.hr*).

The nearest campsite, **Padova III** (*Banjol bb;* \ *051 724 355,* f *051 724 539; www.imperial.hr*) is 2km away to the south, past the eponymously named hotel.

✗ Where to eat With its traffic-free streets and open squares, Rab's a good place to eat and drink, with lots of restaurants and even more cafés and bars. Although there's little to choose between many of the establishments, I did have a wonderful mackerel at the **Konoba Riva**, which spills out of its courtyard on to the Riva itself, and the slightly more upmarket **Konoba Rab** (*Kneza Branimira 3;* \ *051 725 666*), set inside heavy medieval walls, serves up excellent squid. Finally, if it's pizza you want in an atmospheric setting, you won't go wrong at the **Cernta Palace**, where you eat in the old palace courtyard.

AROUND RAB The rest of Rab is hedonistically given over pretty much wholeheartedly to holidays, with well-organised resorts catering mostly for sun-seeking Austrians, Czechs and Germans. There are lots of excellent beaches, and excursions available both to Rab town and to the neighbouring islands.

A few kilometres south of Rab town, facing on to the empty island of Dolin, is the rambling village of **Barbat**, which has a few beaches and quite a large number of private rooms and private moorings. With plenty of buses to Rab Town it's a good accommodation alternative in high season. Contact the **Der Barbat** (\f *051 721 716*) travel agency for reservations.

Immediately to the west of the Frkanj peninsula and Rab town is the tourist complex of **Suha Punta**. It's unashamedly package country, but in a very pretty setting, with plenty of rock beaches, pine woods, and sheltered coves in the vicinity. You can walk or cycle over to the less-crowded sandy beaches at **Kampor**, and it's within easy reach of Rab Town. The place to stay in Suha Punta is the newly renovated

Carolina (*Kampor bb;* ☎ *051 667 744;* f *051 724 117; www.imperial.hr*), with doubles overlooking the beach at around €88–126 – the **Eva** (*Kampor bb;* ☎ *051 724 233;* f *051 668 200; www.imperial.hr*) is cheaper (around €66–100) but less well situated.

Around 5km southwest of Rab and 1km short of Kampor, on the left-hand side, is the **Slovenian War Cemetery**, on the site of the 1942–43 concentration camp. It's a sobering place, with rows of graves set out as a memorial to the 1,443 victims of fascism who lost their lives in this quiet spot, where today all you'll hear is the wind in the cypresses and distant dogs barking.

Across the headland from Kampor is **Supertaska Draga**, home to a good marina, as well as quite a few private moorings and private rooms – contact the Rab (☎ *051 771 111;* f *051 771 110; www.tzg-rab.hr*) or Lopar (☎ *051 775 508;* f *051 775 487; www.lopar.com*) tourist offices for more information.

Rab's northern tip is the **Lopar** peninsula, which not only has the ferry terminal hooking up with Baška, on Krk, but also (across the headland, on Crnika Bay, and centred on the settlement of San Marino), the famous **Paradise Beach**, 1.5km-worth of sand and sea. The small, new **Hotel Epario** (☎ *051 777 500;* f *051 777 510; www.epario.net*) is a good bet, with doubles from €88 in season. Otherwise there's the enormous **San Marino** (☎ *051 775 144;* f *051 775 128; www.imperial.hr*) complex, tucked into the woods behind the beach, with nice doubles for €72–116 in season, or the San Marino campsite.

There are at least 20 shallow sandy beaches on the peninsula (including the lovely, primarily naturist **Sahara**, designated FKK), within pretty easy walking distance of Lopar or San Marino, making the area extremely popular with families. It's not too hard to get away from the crowds, however, by using the excellent network of marked paths and trails, leading up onto the plateau overlooking Paradise Beach, and down onto the more remote beaches.

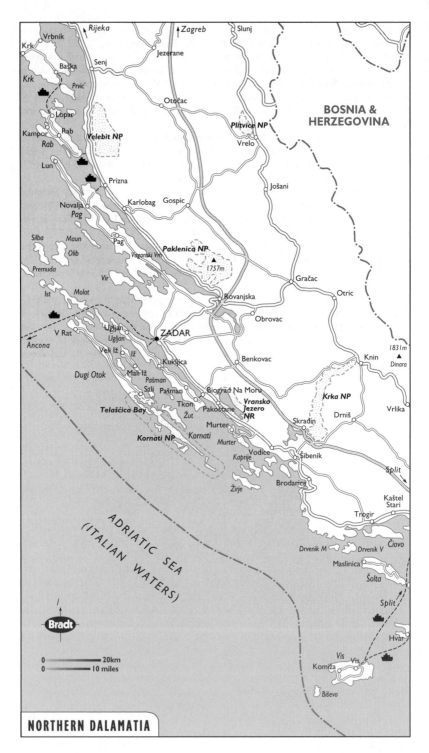

NORTHERN DALAMATIA

7

Northern Dalmatia

Northern Dalmatia is a region of extreme contrasts – you'd never dream, swimming at the foot of the Krka waterfalls, that the most barren islands of the Kornati archipelago were only a few kilometres offshore. Just as you'd never guess, confronted by a wall of heat on dry and dusty **Pag**, that the island of **Pašman** offered such sweet shelter on its wooded southern bays.

Zadar, the region's economic and transport capital, offers a wealth of things to see in a cultured old town, while **Šibenik's** Renaissance cathedral is one of the highlights not just of Dalmatia but of the whole of Croatia. The region is home, too, to three near-perfect national parks and a dedicated nature park: **Paklenica**, where you can hike serious summits and still go swimming in the same day; **Krka**, where you can visit a 14th-century monastery on an island between waterfalls; **Kornati**, where 89 islands, islets and reefs offer the true desert-island experience; and **Vransko Jezero**, privileged home to 100,000 wading birds. Add in the islands of **Ugljan** (Zadar's quiet holiday retreat) and **Dugi Otok** (a sailor's heaven), and you could spend all your holidays here.

Phone codes vary across the region – they're included with each listing.

ZADAR *Telephone code 023 (+385 23 from abroad)*

Zadar, with a population of around 100,000, is the economic and transport centre for northern Dalmatia. While its suburbs sprawl along the coast and inland, at its heart you'll find an unpretentious, partially walled old town on a narrow peninsula, full of fine churches and excellent museums.

HISTORY Zadar was first settled by Liburnian Illyrians the best part of 3,000 years ago, but from as early as the 3rd century BC onwards the Romans had their eye on it, finally making a *Municipium* of it in 59BC and giving Jadera colony status 11 years later.

On the partition of the empire, Zadar became the capital of Byzantine Dalmatia, and had a period of some prosperity until the rise of Venice. Locals today are still proud of the fight Zadar put up against the Venetians, but in spite of four revolts in the 12th century and further uprisings over the next 200 years, Zadar went the same way as the rest of Dalmatia, ceding to Venice in 1409.

The Venetians' endless feuds with the Turks did nothing special for Zadar, though they did leave the city with a fine set of 16th-century defensive walls. Austria picked up the reins on the fall of Venice, with a brief French interlude, and allowed Italian immigrants to take care of the city – something that continued after World War I, with Zadar not joining the nascent Kingdom of the Serbs, Croats and Slovenes, but becoming Italian (Zara) instead. Indeed, some older people still speak Italian, though you'll find the younger generation more switched on to German or English as a first foreign language.

When Italy capitulated in 1943, Germany took over Zadar, and the Allies practically bombed it into oblivion, a fate many feared might happen again during the winter of

1991, when the Serbs laid siege to the city. People went hungry and thirsty during the siege, but the old town remained intact, something that can't be said for the inland suburbs, some of which still show the scars of warfare more than a decade after it ended. What the UN termed 'low-level warfare' continued as late as 1995.

GETTING THERE AND AROUND Zadar is a transport hub, with regular bus arrivals and departures (hourly, for the most part) to and from Zagreb (3½ hours), Rijeka (4–5 hours), Split (3½ hours) and Dubrovnik (6–7 hours), as well as several weekly runs to and from places like Frankfurt and Munich. The best place to buy long-distance bus tickets is at Croatia Express (℄ *023 250 502*), on Široka, right in the middle of the old town.

Trains come in from Zagreb twice a day, but it's a long, long journey, as the route takes a dog-leg via Knin (where you have to change), and works out twice as slow as the bus. Quicker by far is flying, as there's a small airport, about 10km away to the southeast, with daily Zagreb flights being met by the airline bus.

There are lots of ferries out to the islands of the Zadar archipelago (notably Ugljan and Dugi Otok), as well as regular excursions to the Kornati archipelago – see the relevant sections later in this chapter for details. There is a daily ferry up to Lošinj (*www.jadrolinija.hr*), and another which goes to Ancona in Italy. Finally, in summer, there's a fast catamaran that runs daily up to Pula, taking barely longer than the bus (*www.lnp.hr*).

Zadar's bus and train stations are 1km southeast of the old town and port, while most of the hotels and beaches – and the town's marina – are 3km northwest of it, at Borik. There's a bus about three times an hour from the bus station up to Borik, via the harbour.

Everything you want to see in Zadar is in the compact old town, sitting on its own peninsula, separating the harbour from the Zadarski Kanal, the strait running between Zadar and Ugljan. There's a footbridge across the harbour from the old town, leading to the road running north to Borik.

WHERE TO STAY The bulk of Zadar's hotel accommodation is out towards Borik, but a few places are opening up in the old town itself, notably the new Bastion.

The **tourist office** (*Ilije Smiljanića 5;* ℄ *023 316 166;* f *023 211 781; www.tzzadar.hr*), on the southeastern corner of the old town, has good maps and other documentation, and friendly staff. Private rooms, of which only a very few are in or really close to town, are handled by travel agencies, including Jadera Tours (*Poljana Pape Aleksandra III 5/1;* ℄ *023 250 350;* f *023 251 280; www.jaderatours.hr*), off Široka ulica, and Generalturist (*Branimirova 1;* ℄ *023 318 997; www.generalturist.com*), across the footbridge. You'll be lucky to get away with paying under € 40 for a double, plus the usual 30% surcharge for short stays. Most agencies can of course also organise excursions for you, of which there are any number from Zadar, including trips up to the Plitvice Lakes, down to the Krka River and waterfalls, or out to the Kornati archipelago.

⌂ **Bastion** (28 rooms) Bedemi Zadarskih Pobuna 13; ℄ 023 494 950; f 023 494 951; www.hotel-bastion.hr. Plush, efficient new boutique 4-star in the centre of town. Dbl €130–191.

⌂ **Kolovare** (191 rooms) Bože Peričića 14; ℄ 023 203 200; f 023 203 300; www.hotel-kolovare-zadar.htnet.hr. The Kolovare is large, modern & has a small pool & its own beach. ☺ all year round. Rooms have views across to Ugljan. Dbl €112–180.

Borik If you don't stay in Zadar itself, you're almost certain to end up in Borik, which has a campsite and a clutch of mostly package-oriented hotels, many of which could do with a spot of renovation.

ZADAR

Overview

- Railway station
- Bus station
- Kolovare

MAIN MAP

Borik →

OBALA KNEZA BRANIMIRA *i* Atlas

Footbridge

Jazine

Luka

P

OBALA

NARODNOG LISTA

KRALJA TOMISLAVA

BARTULA KAŠIĆA

ŠIME VITASOVIĆA

ANTE KUZMANICA

MEĐU BEDEMIMA

✗ Foša

Foša

Land Gate

TRG PETRA BUNARA

TRG PETRA ZORANIĆA

TRG ŠIME BUDINICA

i St Simeon

✗ Marival

Loggia

TRG NARODNI

E KOTROMANIĆ

SPIRE BRUSINE

RUĐERA BOŠKOVIĆA

P

MIHOVILA PAVLINOVIĆA

OBALA KRALJA PETRA KREŠIMIRA IV

KOVAČKA

VAROŠKA

BORELLI

PLEMIĆA

M KLAIĆA

Clock Tower

Town Hall

FREDERICA GRISOGONA

ZLATARSKA

BEDEMI ZADARSKIH POBUNA

P

UNija BRAKOVICA

Široka ULICA

ZORE DALMATINSKE

BR VANJANIN SABORA

ŠIMUNA KOŽIČIĆA BENJE

MAĐIEVACA

St Mary's

i Archaeological Museum

Church Museum

✗ St

Croatia Express

i

BRNE KRNARUTIĆA

POD BEDEMOM

i Miatours

Roman Arch

JURGA DIVINIĆA

LIBURNSKA OBALA

BEDEMI ZADAR KIH POBUNA

Bastion

TRG 3 BUNARA

BOŽIDARA PETRANOVIĆA

Kornat & ✗ The Garden

I BRČIĆA

LUKE JELICA

I DANILA

ISTARSKA OBALA

MATE KARAMANA

TRG SV STOŠIJE

Cathedral of St Anastasia

Campanile ✗

St Donat's

Roman Forum

P

ZADARSKOG MIRA 1358

ZADARSKOG MIRA IV

OBALA KRALJA PETRA KREŠIMIRA IV

✗ Franciscan Monastery & Church

+ St Grisogonus

Široka ULICA (KALELARGA)

200m
200 yds

0
0

Zadar

Northern Dalmatia ZADAR

7

🏠 **Club Funimation Borik** (306 rooms) Majstora Radovana 7; ☎ 023 206 636; f 023 332 065; www.falkensteiner.com. Large new 4-star. *Dbl €115–230.*
🏠 **President** (15 rooms, 12 suites) Vladana Desnice 16; ☎ 023 333 696; f 023 333 595; www.hotel-president.hr. Unlike some of the other Borek hotels, the President certainly doesn't need refurbishing. It is small but swanky, & priced accordingly. *Dbl €140–207.*

🏠 **Mediteran** (30 rooms) Matije Gupca 19; ☎ 023 337 500; f 023 337 528; www.hotelmediteran-zd.hr. In terms of bang per buck, the best hotel in Borik, with nice dbls with balconies & a view of the sea. *Dbl €80.*
🏠 **Youth Hostel** Obala Kneza Trpimira 76; ☎ 023 331 145; f 023 331 190; www.hfhs.hr. Located between the marina & Borik beach. ⏰ all year round. *Beds €12–16 pp.*

✖ **WHERE TO EAT AND DRINK** The city boasts lively cafés and bars, with terraces spilling out onto the pavements, as well as a handful of good restaurants. This is the place to try Zadar's most famous speciality, Maraskino, the cherry liqueur that has been produced here since the 1820s. It was long Austrian royalty's most popular tipple, and if it's a touch *démodé* now, that shouldn't stop you trying it. Once.

✖ **Foša** Kralja Dmitra Zvonimira 2; ☎ 023 314 421. Dine on fresh seafood on the terrace of the restaurant at the eponymous gate. The grilled squid & Swiss chard (*blitva*) are highly recommended.
✖ **The Garden** Liburnska 6; ☎ 023 364 739; www.thegardenzadar.com. British-owned (by UB40 drummer Jimmy Brown) bar cum lounge cum club is the trendiest place in Northern Dalmatia; to Zadar what Carpe Diem is to Hvar.

✖ **Kornat** Liburnska 6; ☎ 023 254 501. As close to fine dining as Zadar gets, & worth a splurge, serving up Croatian fish & meat mains infused with a Mediterranean twist.
✖ **Marival** Don Ive Prodana 3; ☎ 023 213 239. Atmospheric, great value, old town restaurant serving reliable Dalmatian cuisine. Book ahead.

WHAT TO SEE AND DO All of Zadar's sights are in the old town, within a few hundred metres of each other. They're ordered in the text from the northwestern corner, working back towards the southeast. To get to the start, either walk along the tree-lined, sea-facing promenade (a nice place for a picnic) or walk around the remains of the town walls facing the harbour – these are mostly 16th-century Venetian, though you'll see Roman fragments, particularly near the footbridge across the harbour.

The **Franciscan Monastery and Church** dates back to the 13th century, but it's been much remodelled since and you wouldn't know it wasn't entirely 18th-century Baroque these days. The choir stalls inside are late 14th century, however, and the treasury – rarely open – houses some important works, including a big 12th-century crucifix. The monastery's fine cloisters are mid-16th-century Renaissance.

From here, it's a stone's throw (if they haven't finished tidying up the piles of Roman rubble) to the site of the **Roman Forum** – the single 14m-high **Roman column** standing here is all that's left. Originally 90m by 45m, the forum would have made a decent-sized football pitch. Until the 19th century, criminals were tied to the pillar here, and… well, pilloried, I suppose.

Many of the original bits of Roman stonework ended up in the solid church that dominates what's left of the forum today. The Church of the Holy Trinity was started in the 9th century by Bishop Donat, and has been known as **St Donat's** ever since. It's a 27m-high structure, built on a circular ground-plan, and its tall interior is now used for secular concerts rather than religious worship. Look out for everything from upside-down capitals to gravestones to altars to whole pillars within the structure of the walls – all Roman. Parts of the floor, too, are the original Roman flagstones. You can walk upstairs to the gallery, looking down into the church, but don't lean on the handrails, as they're not very sturdy and it's a long way down.

Round the corner from St Donat's is the triple-naved Romanesque **Cathedral of St Anastasia**, dating from the 12th and 13th centuries. Badly bombed during World War II, it was painstakingly rebuilt afterwards. The façade features an attractive series

When you've run out of things to do in Zadar, an excursion can be made up to the gorgeous little town of Nin, which was important in Roman times, and even more so as a religious centre in the Middle Ages – witness Meštrović's enormous statue of Gregorius of Nin, in Nin and Split (and the far smaller version of the same, in Varaždin).

These days (and for most of the past thousand years, if truth be told), Nin's a quiet town, on its own little island, connected to the mainland by a pair of bridges. There's not a whole lot to see and do, but the Church of the Holy Cross is Croatia's oldest (from around AD800), and you can absorb some more history at the local Archaeological Museum. When you're done, there are a couple of excellent sandy beaches that are popular with surfers, and offer views across to the Velebit massif nearby.

Nin is easily reached on the bus, which runs every hour or so from Zadar and takes around 25 minutes.

of blind arches and two rosette windows. Inside there are some 13th-century frescoes, a 14th-century altar canopy (sheltering an altar containing bits of 9th-century stonework), some 15th-century choir stalls and the marble sarcophagus commissioned by Donat in the 9th century to house the mortal remains of St Anastasia herself.

Behind the cathedral, the bottom half of the lovely **campanile** dates from the 15th century, though it wasn't completed until the 1890s, to a design by the British architect (and sometime writer of ghost stories), Sir Thomas Graham Jackson. Given the centuries-old rivalry between the bishops of Zadar and Rab, and Rab's having lost its bishopric in 1828, it can only have been professional irony that made Jackson model his campanile on Rab's most famous bell tower. Or perhaps simply that he was very good at copying things – his most famous work in England is the Bridge of Sighs, in Oxford. He did get away – for a while – with one amusing prank, however, which was to make the bell tower play God Save The Queen.

Across the forum is **St Mary's Church** – the squat, 16th-century Renaissance front hides a church originally consecrated in the 11th century, along with a few more bits of the Roman forum. Behind it stands yet another Rab-like campanile, though this one's original, dating back to the early 12th century.

Next to this is Zadar's excellent **Church Museum**, which houses a wonderful collection of reliquaries, paintings and sculpture, while nearby, in a modern building, there's the **Archaeological Museum**, a fine collection from Liburnian times on. At both museums the labels are only in Croatian, however.

Heading towards the harbour, the 12th-century Romanesque **Church of St Grisogonus** (also called Chrysogonus – Krševan in Croatian) is all that's left of one of Croatia's oldest monasteries, founded in 908. The outside, with its rows of blind arches and a pretty Tuscan-inspired colonnade on the back of the church, is more endearing than the rather shabby 13th- and 14th-century frescoes inside.

The town gate leading onto the harbour, down from St Grisogonus, contains all that's left of a **Roman triumphal arch** from Trajan's time. Back inside the walls, head towards Narodni Trg, the heart of business life in medieval times, now overlooked by an impressive clock tower. The **town hall** features fine reliefs of Šibenik Cathedral and Diocletian's Palace in Split, while the 16th-century **loggia** across the square, with unusually tall pillars, does service these days as a gallery.

A block east from here is the **Church of St Simeon**. The Baroque building itself can't compete with Zadar's other churches, but **St Simeon's Sarcophagus**, inside, certainly can. Commissioned in 1377, and delivered in 1380, it's an impressively chunky burnished silver and gold coffin, with dramatic reliefs on the front and a life-sized portrait of the saint on the lid, complete with swept-back hair and bushy eyebrows. For more detail, come on the saint's feast day, 8 October, and you'll find even more silverwork and some fine reliquaries on the inside, when the sarcophagus is opened up for its annual inspection. (If you don't see it here, there's a very good copy in Zagreb, in the atrium of the building that houses the Strossmayer Gallery.)

Trg Pet Bunara ('the square of five wells'), nearby, was the town's main water supply for centuries – the Romans of course had proper running water, but from medieval times until the arrival of the businesslike Austrians, the underground cistern here was as good as plumbing got.

From here the easiest way out is through the **Land Gate**. On the outside of this there's a big relief of a no-nonsense Venetian lion – the open bible tells you that Venice was at peace at the time. The miniature harbour here is all that's left of the defensive moat that once protected the city.

The enormous annual dance music festival, **The Garden Festival** (*www.thegardenfestival.eu*), takes place at Petrčane, near Zadar, in July.

SOUTH TO VRANSKO JEZERO South of Zadar are a string of unpretentious resort towns leading to the island of **Murter**, connected to the mainland by a bridge, and the best jumping-off point for the Kornati archipelago (see page 274).

On the way, just past **Biograd** (where you can catch the ferry to Pašman, see page 272), is Croatia's largest natural lake, Vransko Jezero – turn left as you approach Pakoštane, 5km south of Biograd, and then right after just under 2km.

Already an ornithological reserve since 1983, **Vransko Jezero** (Vransko Lake) was declared as a nature park in 1999 in a bid to reinforce the protection of its unique habitat and birdlife. The lake is nearly 14km long and between 1.5 and 3.5km wide, and has a surface area of over 30km^2, but it's never more than 4m deep. A channel that was dug at the end of the 18th century, in an attempt to drain the lake, now provides it with an occasional top-up of salt water at high tide, and it's also partly connected with the sea by underground fissures in the limestone.

A total of 111 bird species have been recorded here, while 41 species over-winter in the park and 49 nest here – including a small colony of rare purple herons. You can also expect to see marsh harriers, ducks, terns and white egrets, and 100,000 coots, which over-winter here.

So far there's very little indeed in the way of infrastructure for the visitor, though there are plans to build a cycle path around the lake – for the time being though you'd need a very rugged mountain bike or a 4×4 vehicle to negotiate the pitted gravel road. There are also plans to build hides, with coin-operated telescopes.

There's a road running behind the hills on the lake's northeastern shore that goes from the village of Vrana to the settlement of Banjevci. If you turn up the gravel road to the right here, it leads steeply up a Križni Put (Way of the Cross) to a small chapel on top of the hills, built as a memorial to the people who were thrown into a deep hole here by the partisans at the end of World War II. It's a moving place, with unrivalled views out west over the lake and the Kornati archipelago.

For more information on the latest state of affairs in the nature park, contact the park office (*Kralja P Svačića 2, Biograd;* ℡ *023 386 455;* f *023 386 453; www.vransko-jezero.hr*) directly.

PAKLENICA NATIONAL PARK

Situated half way between Karlobag and Zadar – an hour from either, by bus – is Paklenica National Park, a pair of wonderful limestone gorges running up from the sea, deep into the Velebit massif. Popular with Croatian walkers and climbers, it's also one of my favourite places in the whole country, offering everything from a gentle stroll to a seriously strenuous trek, and pitches for rock climbers of every level.

The park was opened in 1949, and is unusually interesting for both climatic and physical reasons. Situated under the highest peak of the Velebit massif (Vaganski Vrh, 1,758m), the area experiences three distinct climates – coastal, continental and sub-alpine. The rock is Velebit Karst (see page 5), and walking is possible from sea-level up to the top of the massif.

Most of the lower reaches are heavily forested with deciduous trees, while higher up mountain pastures support sub-alpine flowers and herbs. One of the most attractive features of the park, however, is the more than 80 species of butterfly found here, making it a lepidopterist's paradise.

There are also lots of beetles and several reptiles (you'll see snakes slithering off the path as you approach) and amphibians, and an extraordinary 209 species of bird to watch out for. Sadly, this no longer includes the griffon vulture (see *Cres*, page 231) – the last pair ate poisoned meat, probably intended to kill local wolves. But in the remoter parts of the park you can still scope for peregrine falcons and sparrow hawks, and you're almost certain to see red-backed shrikes.

On the other hand, you're equally certain not to come in contact with the bears and wolves that live in the furthest reaches of the park – they're extremely discreet.

GETTING THERE AND AWAY All buses from Rijeka to Zadar make three Paklenica-related stops. From north to south, the first stop is at Starigrad Paklenica, the second is at the Hotel Alan (the closest stop to the main entrance to the park), and the last is at Seline (closest to the southern gorge, Mala Paklenica). If you're coming from Zagreb then change buses in Zadar.

Although there are lots of buses up and down the coast, leaving in the middle of summer can be harder than arriving, as it depends on the passing buses not being full already. Early mornings are generally better than other times of day, but it's not a guaranteed recipe for success.

WHERE TO STAY The stretch of coast along here is one of the easiest places in Croatia for accommodation, though not one of the most luxurious.

The main campsite is across the road from the entrance to the park, next to the Hotel Alan, and is actually attached to the hotel (see below). There are other smaller campsites along the road north and south of town.

There are any number of private rooms in the area, including some on the trail up into the park. There isn't an agency officially handling these, so your best bet is to wander up and down the road and ask at the numerous places with *sobe* signs – expect to pay €25–45 for a double. The nicest ones, some with lovely balconies and sea views, are in the villages of Seline and Starigrad, but these are only practical if you have your own wheels. If you're really stuck, the tourist office (*Trg Tome Marasovica 1;* \/f 023 369 255) in Starigrad itself, while not having a private-room mandate, will usually help you out. There are also three hotels and a number of smaller pensions.

Hotel Alan (139 rooms) Dr Franje Tuđmana 14; \ 023 209 050; f 023 209 273; www.bluesunhotels.com. Out on the main coast road is this 1970s high-rise hotel, which has a great location on the beach & good views. When I was here in 1988, researching an earlier book, it was my first ever experience of a totally naturist hotel. It gave me something of a shock on arrival to see a family of four loading up their car, totally naked, but presumably they were equally startled by my rude clothed-ness. It's now firmly 'textile' (as the naturist community would have it). *Dbl €90–214*

Pansion Roli (14 rooms) Stipana Bušljete 1; \/f 023 369 018. If it's the seaside you're after, you can't do better than the Pansion Roli, in Starigrad itself & right on the waterfront, where the fishing boats tie up. They serve fabulous mussels & other seafood. *Dbl €50.*

PAKLENICA NATIONAL PARK

1723m
Babin Vrh

1757m
Vaganski Vrh

1709m
Malovan

1201m
Ivinih
Vodica

Borisov Dom

Lugarnica Hut

866m
Vidakov Kuk

Manita Peć

712m
Anića Kuk

Bunker
(underground
tunnel)

VELIKA
PAKLENICA

MALA PAKLENICA

Dokoze

Milovci   Koići

Park entrance

Jukići   Bucići   Kneževici

Kruškovac

Park entrance   Škiljici   Jusupi

Marasovici

Vicko   Punta

Jurline

Starigrad-Paklenica   Rajna

Pansion Roli   Park office

Seline

Alan

Velebitski Kanal

Vinjerac

0 ▭▭▭▭▭▭ 2km

0 ▭▭▭▭▭▭ 1 mile

☖ **Rajna** (10 rooms) Dr Franje Tuđmana 105; ☏ 023 359 121; f 023 369 888; www.hotel-rajna.com. Right by the entrance to the park, it's inevitably full of Croatian climbers – but it's a good place to find out about the best pitches currently being recommended. *Rooms €50.*

☖ **Vicko** (23 rooms) Jose Dokoze 20; ☏/f 023 369 304; www.hotel-vicko.hr. Small, cheerful & family-run, with nice rooms in the main hotel & lovely sea-view rooms. Also has a 4-star apartment annexe, Villa Vicko, just across the street. In addition, the hotel has a good restaurant. *Dbl €60–106.*

You can't camp within the park itself, but there are several mountain huts along the massif. The biggest and best equipped is **Borisov Dom** (*50 beds;* ☏ *023 301 636;* m *095 803 8114*), which is the place to stay if you want to base yourself in the valley and make day trips from there. Check yourself in ahead of time with the park office (☏ *023 369 155;* f *023 359 133; www.paklenica.hr*), and make sure you have a sleeping bag.

✖ **WHERE TO EAT** There are a whole clutch of places where you can eat out, including both the **Vicko** and **Rajna**, along with informal grills and seafood places along the main road and on the shore, and at least one pizzeria. Inside the park, the **Lugarnica** hut, on the way to Borisov Dom, does great sausages and other grilled food. It's open daily through the summer months and on weekends in May and October.

OTHER PRACTICALITIES Everything you need is within easy reach of the park entrance, including a supermarket with good long opening hours and all the makings of a decent picnic, a couple of kiosks, and the park office (see above) itself. Here you'll be given a standard free map which comes with the entrance ticket (*40kn; a five-day climbing pass is 120kn*), but you can buy better ones (essential if you're doing much walking) as well as more detailed climbing and hiking guides. This is also the place to arrange accommodation at one of the mountain huts, or to check about the opening/visiting times of Manita Peć or the Bunkers (see below).

For swimming, there are beaches either side of the Hotel Alan.

THE NATIONAL PARK The national park's geomorphology consists primarily of a horizontal plateau running between the Velebit massif and the sea. Two gorge valleys, Velika and Mala (large and small) Paklenica, with cliffs over 400m high in places, cut through this to the sea, and there are also several networks of subterranean caves. The most famous of these is Manita Peć, which has been explored for nearly 200m of its depth into the mountain and contains two enormous halls.

Because of its triple climate the weather is unusually variable. It's the only place I've ever walked where I've been drenched by rain, then sunburned and finally hailed on, before going for an afternoon swim in the sea. Prepare for all weathers, especially in May and early June, when there's still snow on the north-facing slopes above 1,500m. In high summer the inner parts of the park can be fearsomely hot, but even when the sun's shining on the coast, localised storms can see you hailed on. Be prepared.

There are two official routes into the park, up the two canyons. The main entrance is up a clearly marked road 300m south of the Hotel Alan. A brisk kilometre up here brings you to the park office, where you buy your ticket in, and maps, after which it's a further 2km to the end of the road and the car park. You'll come across the entrance here to what used to be one of Paklenica's greatest secrets, the enormous **bunker complex** built for Tito in the 1950s as a crisis headquarters in times of war. For decades nobody was allowed to even mention its existence, but you can now visit parts of the huge complex, and it's a fascinating glimpse into the paranoia of power. The bunkers are open somewhat irregularly; contact the park administration for more details.

The other entrance to the park is up Mala Paklenica, 4km south, just after and opposite the Church of St Mark. Turn inland and it's nearly 2km to the clearly visible canyon entrance, where you can park.

Anića Kuk This is easily the most-climbed peak in the national park. There are something like 25 routes up the west and north faces, and these are all serious climbs that shouldn't be attempted without ropes and proper climbing equipment. There's also a good walking route to the 712m summit, which makes for a fine six-hour return trip from the Hotel Alan (4½ hours if you have a car).

Anića Kuk is not high, but it's an isolated, exposed peak, and it's the nearest major summit to the sea. The side facing into the gorge is a near-vertical drop of over 400m; don't stray too close to the edge.

The walking route follows Velika Paklenica upstream from the car park, on a well-made erosion-avoiding paved road, until you reach a sharp uphill left-hand bend, hard on the river, after half an hour. Cross the river here at the sign, and follow the faded red and white markers towards the base of the cliff which comes down to a flint-shaped point, and then round the back of the mountain in a wide sweep up through woods and scrub, before emerging onto naked karst.

It's a bit of a scramble, and can be hard on the hands, but another half an hour brings you to the airy, vertiginous summit, which is easily worth it for the fabulous views out across to the barren island of Pag.

Manita Peć and Vidakov Kuk This trail takes in the cave at Manita Peć and the 866m summit above it, Vidakov Kuk. Like Anića Kuk, the summit is close enough to the sea

STAYING ON THE RIGHT TRACK

Within the park, the trails marked on the map in red are marked in reality with red and white flashes on rocks and trees, and it's very rare that you can't easily see from one mark to the next. Some of the least-used paths may have faded markings, but others will impress you with their fresh brightness. There are also lots of paths used by local people that aren't guided on the ground; these are marked with dotted lines on the map. On the steeper paths you may well appreciate the use of a stick or walking-poles, especially if it's been raining, as some of the trails can be pretty slippery.

A word of warning: it's highly inadvisable to leave the marked paths – high up in the park there are still minefields, while lower down you'll have to cross naked karst. And believe me, wild karst is awful stuff to cross – you'll find it extremely wearing, both mentally and on your clothes and hands. The shallowest slopes will confront you with jagged rocks, and even 2m climbs or drops are difficult.

The first time I came here, a marked path up Anića Kuk took me three hours, including a 700m climb. The same descent, across just 4km of shallow karst, took nearly seven hours. I was never in danger of being lost, since everything was clearly visible, but the rocks were nearly impossible to cross, and my fingers were worn to all but the last layer of skin by the end. For a week I couldn't even hold a cup of coffee.

Assistance in case of an emergency depends in the first instance on members of your party, or other walkers and climbers – there is a mountain rescue service (*www.gss.hr; in case of emergency in the mountains call* ☏ *112*), but they need to be alerted. It's a good idea therefore to let people know where you're headed before you set out.

Good, detailed local maps (published by SMAND, *www.smand.hr*) are available through the park office or some of the larger bookshops in Zagreb and other cities. Rudolf Abraham's book *Walking in Croatia* has details of hiking in Paklenica and other mountain areas in Croatia.

to afford wonderful views without an enormous expenditure of effort – though the start of the path from the cave to the summit is very hard to find, and the second part of the walk involves some scrambling and a reasonable sense of balance. As far as Manita Peć, the walk is sometimes steep but never difficult, taking around two hours from the Hotel Alan; allow another 2½ hours from the cave to the summit of Vidakov Kuk, or a total of around seven hours out and back (5½ if you have a car), not counting cave exploration time.

Manita Peć itself can only be visited with a guide, and is usually open three times a week in summer, on Monday, Wednesday and Saturday mornings – check at the park office before you head up here, to avoid disappointment.

From the car park head up the gorge for around 30 minutes until the path levels out (turning from paved to grit). After a short while there's the sign to Anića Kuk to the right, and indicators to Lugarnica (30 minutes) and Planinarski Dom (Borisov Dom, 50 minutes). It's not far from here to the path heading off to the right, which eventually leads to Mala Paklenica (see 000), after which you soon reach the sign saying it's 40 minutes to Manita Peć, and that's about how long you should allow to cover the long zigzags heading uphill to the left, to the cave at 550m.

The cave itself – like most caves – is nothing special outside, but inside it's marvellous. A tunnel-like entrance leads through to two huge chambers, some 40m long and 40–65m wide, with a height of over 30m. The atmospheric artificial lighting shows off the stalactites and stalagmites, and the weird dripstone pillars. Nature's a wonderful thing.

Blinking outside in the daylight, the unmarked (and very hard to find) path up to Vidakov Kuk sets off to the left (with your back to the cave), going down a couple of metres to start with, then traversing a rather steep and insecure scree-like slope, before finally gaining a shallow scrub forest.

The unmarked trail continues consistently upwards and closer to the cliff, drifting right as you look at the ridge. Eventually a way up through a steep split in the cliff is marked, and it's here that you need to be fairly agile, with the terrain rocky and mostly unassisted. As you attain the ridge, the summit is only 50m above you, to your left. There isn't a marked trail to the peak, but there are several fairly easy ways to reach it. But make sure you have secure hand and footholds as the rock's rather friable up here. The view from the top, of course, makes it all worthwhile.

The marked trail continues fairly gently from the Vidakov Kuk peak to the roofless stone ruin at Ramići, where you can either go back down Velika Paklenica, or up towards Velika Golić. There's also an ill-marked route down the back of Vidakov Kuk to the village of Tomići, which takes around three hours – don't take this unless you're absolutely sure of the way down, as it's very easy to get lost.

Velika Golić Some of the more spectacular views in Paklenica can be had from the long ridge of Velika Golić, and an excellent ten-hour walk (8½ if you have a car) takes in this ridge and returns via Borisov Dom.

The walk starts exactly as if you were going to Manita Peć (see above), but heads straight on when the path branches up and left to the cave. After half an hour you'll come to a water trough and a sign saying Borisov Dom 30 minutes. The main path branches up to the left here, and 10 minutes further on you need to take the path branching steeply uphill, away from the river. Follow this up its zigzags for about 40 minutes, after which you'll come to a straighter section, with markings on the dry stone wall leading to the farm at Ramići (not the only place named Ramići in the immediate vicinity, unfortunately).

The main marked trail leading through the farm leads up to Vidakov Kuk – the path you want, to Velika Golić, is a hard right-hand turn, almost behind you as you arrive at the farm. From here, after skirting between a series of dry stone walls, the path rises steadily, and you're soon a long way above the farm. The ground becomes rougher as the path skirts the 903m summit of Čelinka and crosses a rocky wood before surfacing on an open pasture. This leads directly to the corner of the ridge, level with the top of Čelinka. It takes about two hours from the river to this point, from which there are fine views down on to the refuge below, across to the peak of Anića Kuk and over to the sea.

The ridge is an extraordinary formation, consisting of a series of parallel broken limestone ridges at an angle of about 40 degrees. The valley side is nearly a sheer drop, but the side from which you've approached is relatively shallow, as is the line of the ridge itself, which takes the best part of 2km to rise from 900m to 1,285m. There are endless false crests to this, but the summit is superb, with spectacular panoramic views making the four- to five-hour ascent well worthwhile. Make sure you have appropriate clothing, however – this is where I was once caught in a late-May hailstorm.

The best way down is to continue along the ridge, scaling a secondary summit of 1,160m, before the path curves back on itself to bring you down to Borisov Dom. This takes around two hours, after which it's an easy 1½ hours back to the car park.

Mala and Velika Paklenica
This is a terrific circular walk, including both gorges and some very fine views. It runs from the Hotel Alan to Seline, up Mala Paklenica, across the broad ridge between the two canyons and then down Velika Paklenica. It can be done in reverse, but with Mala Paklenica being the tougher walk, you're better off tackling it while you're fresh, and preferably before it gets too hot.

If you take your time, and aren't in a hurry, the walk takes around ten hours, including the hour between the two villages, which you can't avoid unless someone gives you a lift, as you end up where you started. It's a pretty long, tough day out, so be prepared, but it's well worth the effort.

At the entrance to the Mala Paklenica gorge, the dirt road peters out and you're on the trail upstream. It's very rustic and empty compared to Velika Paklenica, and less well marked at first, but the route is clear enough, starting on the left-hand side of the gully before crossing over to the other side. Unless there's been exceptional rain, the gully is dry from May to September.

As you enter the canyon proper the walls steepen and the path becomes clearer and better marked. At the first big boulders on the valley floor the path climbs to the right, crossing the first of three assisted sections, with steel cables and well-secured pitons to help you up.

The next two hours are hard, ascending sharply, but the way the rock's been sculpted by flowing water, the small flowers and trees growing tenaciously from pockets in the cliffs, and the fine views should cheer you up. After a while you'll notice puddles on the valley floor, which gradually become a rivulet and eventually turn into a bubbling, refreshing stream. The path criss-crosses this on well-marked boulders.

When the gorge forks, take the left-hand one, following the stream. Twenty minutes later the path definitively leaves the stream, but only after a couple of false alarms, and then heads steeply uphill, zigzagging until you're at 650m. At the top there's a dry stone wall clearly marked Sv Jakov, though there's no obvious church. This junction is easy to pinpoint on the map.

Take the left-hand of the two paths, marked Starigrad. The path is a bit indistinct here, running across pastures, but there are markers. If you lose these, head west-northwest until you join the marked path coming in from your right. At this point the trail starts down a rocky gully. It divides fairly often, but the correct path is always well marked, eventually coming out at a small farm.

Leave the farm on the leftmost track, and then fork immediately right on the marked path. From here it's easy to find your way to the valley floor – even if there aren't signs, you can follow the donkey droppings, as you're now on the farm's access road. The path comes out suddenly and unexpectedly to the top edge of Velika Paklenica, and it's an ideal picnic spot – it's almost all downhill from here, and the views are great.

The path down is a steep, knee-testing zigzag – you might be grateful of walking-poles here – until you reach the valley floor, after which it's an easy walk back to the entrance of Velika Paklenica.

Other walks The walks described above are only a fraction of what you can do in the area, particularly given that none of them even takes you up onto the spectacular Velebit ridge.

You can also wander happily around at lower altitudes to the west of the park, discovering the abandoned and near-abandoned villages in the hills. One of these, **Bristovac Tomići** (the locals leave off the Bristovac) is the start of a good walk up to Vidakov Kuk, and provides a poignant look at a world where electricity supplies, running water and central heating never quite caught on.

The more ambitious, however, will want to scale the region's highest peak, **Vaganski Vrh**, just 73m lower than Croatia's highest point, Dinara. Bear in mind, however, that the ridge hasn't entirely been de-mined, so discuss your route with the park staff before heading off, and stay on the marked trails.

Whilst an ascent of Vaganski Vrh is possible to complete within a day from the park's entrance, the 14-hour minimum round trip isn't for the faint-hearted, and you need to set off very early in the morning indeed, and be extremely well equipped – friends who've done it reckoned that two litres of water per person was nothing like enough.

Better by far is to stay overnight at Borisov Dom or one of the other mountain huts, and start the five- to six-hour climb to the summit from there. On a clear day they say you can see Italy on one side and a good 100km into Bosnia on the other, but those days do tend to come in winter, when a combination of snow and a vicious *bura* are likely to dissuade you from making the ascent at all.

Best of all is a three-day circuit covering the **Velebit ridge** – again, discuss your route in detail with the park staff before heading out, and remember there are still mines in the ground. On the first day head up Mala Paklenica, going straight on instead of left at Sv Jakov (see previous page), and then right instead of straight on at the junction for Borisov Dom. The route then skirts left of the 999m summit of Martinovo Mirilo, eventually reaching the Ivine Vodice hut at 1,200m, where you can stay the night (check it's open, of course, before you start out).

Day two then starts with the climb up to the ridge, and the chance to reach the summits of Malovan (1,709m, around four hours from the refuge) and Vaganski Vrh (1,758m), among others, before coming down at Borisov Dom for the second night out. Bear in mind that it's a lot further on to Babin Vrh (1,723m) than you might think – count on 14 hours just from the Ivine Vodice hut – and that you don't want to get caught out at this altitude at any time of year.

ŠIBENIK Telephone code 022 (+385 22 if calling from abroad)

Šibenik is something of an odd-man-out on the Dalmatian coast, firstly because it has no classical history – it was founded by the Croats and doesn't show up until the 11th century – and secondly because it's not really a tourist town. Indeed, until the 1990s, and the war with Serbia, it was a light industrial hub with a moderately busy port, and nothing much in the way of either beaches or visitors.

It's well worth stopping here, however, not just for the cathedral – the most important piece of Renaissance architecture in Croatia (and classified by UNESCO as a World Heritage Site in 2000) – but also for its charming medieval old town, and its position as a springboard for trips into the Krka National Park and to the Kornati archipelago (see pages 265 and 274).

ŠIBENIK

Solaris (Hotel)

ANTE ŠUPUKA

FRA JERONIMA MILETE

FRA J MILETE

Railway station

MATIJE GUPCA

29 LISTOPADA 1918

STJEPANA RADIĆA

ANTE STARČEVIĆA

STANKOVAČKA

MACURE

SLOBODNA

Bus station

ZVONIMIRA

FRA STJEPANA ZLATOVIĆA

KRALJA

VLADIMIRA NAZORA

PUT SPLITA

OBALA HRV MORNARICE

TEŽAČKA

MIMINAC

KRALJA ZVONIMIRA

NOVE CRKVE

ZAGREBAČKA

TOMISLAVA

Stari Grad

St Nicholas'

OBALA OSLOBODENJA

Ferry terminal

TEŽAČKA

ZADARSKA

SV LUCE DON KRSTE STOŠIĆA

KRALJA

Jadran

St Barbara

Archaeological Museum

PUT GROBLJA

Gradska Vikećnica

St Jacob's Cathedral

OBALA PALIH OMLADINACA

St Anne Fortress

Bradt

0 150m
0 150yds

By the end of the war in 1995, Šibenik's industrial base was in ruins, and during the second half of the 1990s the town found it hard to recover, with high unemployment and consequently very little money around for spending. The new century seems to have brought with it new optimism, however, and in summer it's hard to find a seat at any of the seafront cafés on a Sunday morning. Recovery isn't complete, but Šibenik's well on the mend.

HISTORY After first being mentioned in 1066, Šibenik was tossed back and forth between Venetians, Hungarians, Byzantines, Croats and Bosnians, before knuckling definitively under Venice (1412–1797) and the Austro-Hungarian Empire (1797–1918). Italy was very briefly in control (only until 1920) before the city became Yugoslav, and finally, in 1991, Croatian.

The Venetians built the defensive walls (best preserved on the north side of town) running all the way up to the three fortresses at the top of the hill, and it was also under Venice that St Jacob's Cathedral was built, in fits and starts, over more than a century.

GETTING THERE AND AROUND Šibenik is easy to reach. A few local ferries come in to the sheltered bay through the narrow Šibenik channel, and dock at the southern end of the old town. The bus station is 200m further south, in the new town, while the train station (only serving local routes inland) is a further 300m to the southeast. Both the bus and train stations have left-luggage facilities.

The old town is entirely pedestrianised, which is excellent, so once you've arrived you'll be on foot – it's all perfectly manageable, though the narrow streets running up to the St Anne Fortress are pretty steep.

The friendly tourist office (*Fausta Vrančića 18;* \ *022 212 075;* f *022 200 183; www.sibenik-tourism.hr*), with town plans etc, is bang in the middle of the old town, just off the main artery of Zagrebačka, across from St John's (Sveti Ivan) Church.

WHERE TO STAY With accommodation in fairly short supply in Šibenik (there are very few private rooms in the old town and only one hotel) you may find it easier to make a day trip from Zadar, Trogir or Split – or indeed go for one of the slew of private rooms in shamelessly touristy **Vodice**, just 12km up the coast, which is enormously popular with Croatians and East Europeans. That said, it's worth persevering – with few visitors spending the night here, you'll find Šibenik evenings pleasant at any time of year.

Most private rooms are out of town, along the coast, though with regular buses this needn't be a problem. If you arrive in summer you'll likely be met off the ferry or bus by women offering rooms – check the location before you agree.

⌂ **Jadran** (57 rooms) Obala Dr Franje Tuđmana 52; \ 022 242 2000; f 022 212 480; www.rivijera.hr. The old town's only hotel is rather boxy and unexciting, but clean, modern and well equipped, and it's right on the harbour. *Dbl €108–116 in summer, €100 off season.*
⌂ **Solaris** (1,300 rooms) \ 022 361 001; f 022 361 800; www.solaris.hr. A huge resort, about 6km south of Šibenik but easy to reach by bus, the Solaris consists of 5 hotels (4 4-star, and 1 3-star), as well as 2 campsites, big beaches and pools complete with pedalos and water-slides, and Šibenik's only disco (though the mass market approach won't suit everyone). *Dbl with half board at Jakov (3-star) €104–150.*

WHERE TO EAT Like most Dalmatian towns, Šibenik's favourite food is fish, but like everywhere else it doesn't come cheap. The restaurant at the **Jadran** (see above) is a good place for fresh fare, while the nicest restaurant in town is unquestionably **Gradska Vijećnica** (*Trg Republike Hrvatske 3;* \ *022 213 605*), set in the ground floor of the loggia, right on the cathedral square.

For more modest fare Šibenik's also well supplied with pizzerias and snack bars, and you shouldn't miss the chance of eating or drinking in **Dolac**, the part of town along the shore that is furthest from the ferry terminal, where the city walls plunge down to meet the sea. Here you'll find dozens of cafés, bars and restaurants, many featuring live music on summer evenings.

WHAT TO SEE AND DO Šibenik's must-see is the wonderful cathedral, though the old town itself is perfectly lovely, from the fluttering flags and cheerful cafés along the seafront to the ruins of the St Anne Fortress on the hill, by way of any number of narrow flagged streets, medieval archways and a mix of Gothic, Renaissance and Baroque buildings.

St Jacob's Cathedral, a triple-aisled basilica with three apses and a cupola, was started in 1431 but not completed until 1536, and reflects the transition from Venetian Gothic to Tuscan Renaissance. What makes it unique, however, is the extraordinary barrel-vaulting, consisting of stones chiselled to fit together snugly using carpentry techniques, and leading to the cathedral's exterior being almost identical to its interior – something you won't see in any other church. It's difficult to get a good look at the roof from outside, as the town crowds up to the cathedral, but postcards – or a hike up to the St Anne Fortress – will give you a good idea. A result of the design is also that the façade is the only one in Europe able to reflect the true shape of the triple-aisled church behind it – all the others are effectively stage-scenery, stuck on for effect.

The cathedral is largely the work of Juraj Dalmatinac (George the Dalmatian), a sculptor who was born in Zadar, but rose to fame in Venice (perhaps under the tutelage of Donatello). He was chief architect here, on and off, from the early 1440s until his death in 1473. The extraordinary frieze on the outside of the cathedral of 74 individual heads running round the apses (a fabulous glimpse of 15th-century life), along with the stunning baptistery inside the big echoing church, are his finest works. In front of the cathedral you'll find a Meštrović statue of him.

The north side of the cathedral makes up one side of the elegant Trg Republika Hrvatske; the other is occupied by a fine loggia, built between 1533 and 1542. Originally the town hall, the version you see today is mostly a post-war reconstruction, following the 1943 bombing of the town – though it's none the less lovely for that.

Otherwise the rest of the old town is really its own attraction, though there are several other churches worth visiting (notably **St Nicholas** and **St Barbara**), as well as a small **archaeological museum**. Up at the top of the town, the **St Anne Fortress** isn't much to look at, but has great views out over the town and across the bay.

About 7km from Šibenik, near the village of Dubrava, there is a **falconry centre** (*Sokolarski Center Dubrava; Škugori bb, Dubrava;* m *091 506 7610; www.sokolarskicentar.com;* ⊕ *10.00–13.00 & 16.00–19.30 daily; 30kn*). As well as informative 45-minute presentations on birds of prey, the centre runs environmental education programmes and one- and five-day falconry courses, and has a small hospital where sick or injured birds are cared for and rehabilitated. Larger groups are asked to call in advance.

NORTH TO KNIN From Šibenik the road runs north along the eastern border of Krka National Park (see below), to Knin, some 60km distant. You're also likely to come through Knin on any other road from central or southern Dalmatia to Zagreb, which is why the town had such significance in the conflict of the 1990s, as the capital of the Serbian RSK (Republika Srpska Krajina) – it effectively cut off southern Croatia from the rest of the country.

Driving up past the unremarkable town of **Drniš**, towards Knin, and on towards Gračac and Zagreb, the scars of the war are still very much in evidence. Many properties along the roadside are devastated, windowless and roofless, and while some of the older Serbs who'd lived here for generations have clearly returned, there are few if any young people around. Houses that weren't destroyed by shells were gutted by fire, and the torched wrecks of cars still stand in their driveways. The farming villages of **Kaldrina** and **Kosovo** in particular are a dreadful reminder of the awfulness of war.

Knin, the short-lived capital of the Serb enclave of Krajina, is an uninspiring place and its population is nothing like what it was 15 years ago. If you stop in Knin (and it's easy, with so many onward buses, and trains to Zagreb and Split), then make the effort to climb up the hill to the terrific **medieval fortress** which dominates the town. It's the way fortresses are meant to be, with great big walls, ramparts, buttresses, towers and a sturdy central keep, and panoramic views out over the surrounding countryside.

KRKA NATIONAL PARK

The 72km Krka River and waterfalls are a popular rival to the Plitvice Lakes further north, and are essentially a result of the same travertine process which formed (and is continuing to form) **Plitvice** (see page 158). Krka makes a great excursion from Šibenik, and is offered as a day trip by any number of tour operators all the way from Zadar to Split, though it's easy enough to visit under your own steam, too.

Krka used to receive many fewer visitors than the more famous Plitvice, but it's catching up now, with close to half a million visitors annually. And it's hardly surprising – there's more to see here, and a far greater water flow. The biggest falls, Skradinsiki Buk (where you can swim in summer), see an average of 55m³ per second all year round, rising to a splashy 350m³ per second after heavy rains inland.

After much wrangling between the proponents of hydro-electricity and conservationists, the middle and lower parts of the Krka River were finally declared a national park in 1985, and the park's recently been extended pretty much all the way to the river's source, near Knin. The two most impressive waterfall systems are Roški Slap to the north and Skradinski Buk to the south, separated by a wide section of river on which you'll find the islet of Visovac and a Franciscan monastery.

For the last 20km downstream from Skradinski Buk, the Krka is at sea level, with a mix of salt and fresh water.

GETTING THERE AND AWAY If you're not on an excursion, you can easily reach Krka National Park on the bus that runs half a dozen times a day from Šibenik to the western entrance at Skradin, stopping on the way at the eastern Lozovac entrance. If you have your own wheels there's plenty of parking at both. Out of season you can usually drive the 4km into the park from the Lozovac entrance, while in summer you have to take the park bus.

Access from Skradin to the waterfalls is by national park boat, included in the 95kn entrance fee, which leaves the quay every hour on the hour and takes around 25 minutes. Both the park bus from Lozovac and the boat from Skradin only run from April to October, so if you're on public transport in winter you need to factor in a good 45-minute walk at either entrance – the entry fee is reduced to 30kn as compensation. You can also sail straight to Skradin from the sea, tying up just downstream from the Skradin bridge.

Inside most of the park itself – from the Skradin bridge upstream – you're restricted, quite properly, to the national park boats and footpaths. And if you want to see the Krka Monastery, towards the northern end of the park, you'll need to arrange this with the national park directly – unless it's been pre-arranged as part of an excursion. For further information, or for reservations on any of the boat-rides upstream of the first waterfalls (see below) – highly recommended in summer – contact the **national park office** in Šibenik (✆ *022 201 777;* f *022 336 836; www.npkrka.hr*) or the **information centre** in Skradin (✆ *022 771 688*).

KRKA NATIONAL PARK

Knin

Krka Monastery

Roški Slap

Visovac
Monastery

Drnis

Knin

SKRADIN

Krka

Watermill
Museum

Luzovac   Skradinski Buk

Šibenik

Bradt

| 0 | 8km |
| 0 | 5 miles |

WHERE TO STAY Skradin – a pretty, leafy town with cafés along the waterfront – is worth visiting in its own right now that it has recovered from being pummelled by both sides during the homeland war. There's a nice place to stay, in the shape of the **Hotel Skradinski Buk** (*Burinovac bb;* ☎ *022 771 771;* f *022 771 770; www.skradinskibuk.hr*), which has simple doubles from € 56–89 depending on the season. In Lozovac there's the **Hotel Vrata Krke** (*Lozovac bb;* ☎ *022 778 091;* f *022 778 092; www.vrata-krke.hr*), with doubles for € 106–144 during summer.

WHAT TO SEE AND DO The national park has a rich variety of plant life (some 860 species and sub-species), as well as 18 different kinds of fish, including 10 species endemic to the Krka River. A diverse range of amphibians and reptiles, more than 200 species of bird, and 18 species of bat – some practically extinct elsewhere in Europe – make the park an important wildlife sanctuary.

In terms of attractions for the visitor, the first and most obvious sight is **Skradinski Buk**, a series of waterfalls dropping down towards Skradin in 17 steps. As at Plitvice, wooden walkways and forest paths lead you from top to bottom and back again, with a full leisurely tour taking a couple of hours. At the bottom there's an excellent opportunity to swim at the base of the falls, so if you're here in summer bring your beachwear.

Back at the top of the falls there's an excellent **watermill museum** – in the past the power of the falls was harnessed for milling, rolling and pounding, and there are demonstrations during the season, included in the park entry fee.

From April to October, you can also take a variety of national park boats/excursions – buy your ticket on arrival if you haven't reserved ahead, and then visit Skradinski Buk while you're waiting. The most popular excursion is the 100kn, two-hour boat ride up to the ridiculously picturesque island of **Visovac**, where you'll be given half an hour to explore the Franciscan church and monastery. Started in the 14th century, it now houses a small museum and a precious library.

A bigger excursion (four hours, 130kn) takes in Visovac and then heads upstream through a gorge to the Roški Slap waterfalls, which may not quite be a match for Skradinski Buk, but make for a delightful hour's wander all the same.

From the upper end of **Roški Slap**, it's a further 100kn, two-hour excursion by boat up to the fine Orthodox **Krka Monastery** (also known as the Archangel Monastery), dating from 1359, though much rebuilt over the succeeding 400 years.

Also within the confines of the national park are some excellent ruined medieval castles; ask for directions and a map when you buy your entry ticket, if you're interested.

PAG

Pag, stretching some 60km alongside the coast north of Zadar, is one of the most barren of the Adriatic's big islands. It supports fewer than 10,000 people (and rather more sheep) in a handful of villages, and it can be a torpid, stifling place in the dog days of August, with the general lack of trees (barring some olive groves in the north, and some stunted figs) being maddening and oppressive.

Nonetheless, it's increasingly popular as a holiday destination, with an interesting old town, some fine sandy beaches and a generally unspoiled air – the lace-makers of Pag town are charming rather than touristy. With tourism Pag's sole source of real prosperity, and the island welcoming over 170,000 overnight tourists a year, with that can only be a good thing. Apart from a few weeks at the end of July and the beginning of August in Novalja – Croatia's answer to Ibiza, with club owners and entire clubs coming down from Zagreb for the season – Pag is still far from crowded.

Pag's reputation in the past was tied to salt, and there are still big salt-pans in the centre of the island, but today its fame rests squarely on Paški Sir, the distinctive hard cheese that is one of the highlights of Croatia's indigenous cuisine. The unique flavour

PAG ISLAND

is a combination of the sheep's diet – mainly salt grasses and sage – and the way it's matured, rubbed with olive oil and ash. Even here, it's relatively expensive, and harder to find than you'd expect, but it's worth making the effort.

HISTORY It's hard to believe now, but Pag was covered with woods when it was first settled by the Illyrian tribes, and was still forested through its Roman occupation, the arrival of the Slavs in the 7th century, and the feuding of the bishops of Zadar and Rab (back when Rab had a bishop) over the island's salt-pans in the late Middle Ages.

It was the Venetians who did the damage, here and all the way around the Kvarner Bay and throughout northern Dalmatia, cutting down the trees wholesale for shipbuilding (it has to be said that the locals were usually quick enough to sell the precious wood). The scrub grasses and roots that were left behind were then over-cropped by sheep, and the *bura* winds blew away whatever topsoil was left. The land has never recovered, even now supporting little more than a few herbs and salt grasses.

Pag fell under Austro-Hungarian control after the fall of Venice, and became Yugoslav after World War I, though neither left much of a mark on the island until the bridge connecting it to the mainland was built in 1968.

GETTING THERE AND AROUND Access to Pag from the south is across the road bridge, while from the north you're better off taking the ferry from Kovači (just down from Prižna) to Žigljen (6km across the island from the main resort of Novalja), which runs hourly in winter and continuously in summer (day and night). Note that when the *bura*'s a-blowing, however, especially in winter, the ferry might not be running at all. There's also a daily catamaran from Rijeka to Novalja via Rab during summer.

Access by public transport is limited to three buses a day from Zagreb and the two daily Rijeka–Zadar buses that run via the island rather than along the coast, stopping at Novalja and Pag town on the way. There's also a daily bus from Novalja and Pag to Split (3½ hours). Most of these routes are run by Antonio Tours (*www.antoniotours.hr*). Pag town is under an hour from Zadar, 3½ hours from Rijeka, and 5½ hours from Zagreb.

The buses from the mainland are also the island's only local transport, effectively providing a connection from Novalja to Pag town five times daily.

PAG TOWN The attractive, partially walled old centre of Pag you see today is in fact the new town – the original Pag was 3km south of here, and you can still see some of the ruins at Stari Grad. The new town was founded in 1443 and built according to designs by Juraj Dalmatinac, the man behind Šibenik's lovely cathedral.

A regular grid of old narrow streets meets at the town's main square (see map), Trg Kralja Krešimira IV, which contains the **Church of St Mary** (meant to be a cathedral), the **Duke's Palace**, and the unfinished **Bishop's Palace** – Pag never quite got its act together on becoming a bishopric.

The church has a fine, simple front, with a carved Gothic portal, four unfinished-looking saints, and a Renaissance rosette window, which is presumably the inspiration for all those lace motifs. Inside, there are lovely Romanesque arches with Corinthian capitals (at the far right-hand end check out the cavorting dolphins), while on the ceiling there's a huge plaster relief of St George and the Dragon. The solid bell tower, behind and to the left, looks firmly rooted in the 16th century.

Given the town's heritage, it would be madness not to pop into the tiny **Lace Museum**, just off the square, which has a small collection of intricate work. Pag has been famous for its lace for centuries, with each piece being unique; after being closed for decades the lace school here was reopened in the late 1990s. If you want to buy lace, your best bet is to purchase directly from the women making it – you'll see them dressed in black in the old town in the mornings, with their hair distinctively braided. The asking price reflects the amount of time it takes to make.

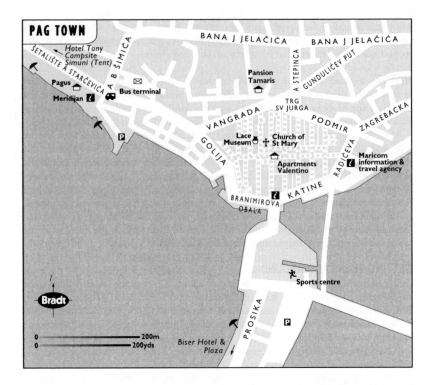

Also revived has been the **Pag Carnival**, in February, a cheerful affair with lots of dressing up, folk music, dancing, parades and processions, and performances of the local play The Slave Girl of Pag. It's so much fun that the carnival is repeated at the end of July – and why not?

Getting there and around The bus stops just west from the old town, near the Pagus Hotel. **Tourist information** (℡ *023 611 301; www.pag-tourism.hr*) is on the southern side of the old town, by the bridge across to the old salt warehouses (one of which has been converted into a disco), and has a good reversible map of the town and the island.

You can book excursions from the usual agencies – the best of these are the day trips out to the Kornati archipelago. Meridijan (see below) also rents out bicycles, a great way of exploring the island, but make sure you have plenty of water and are well protected with sun block – there's no real shade anywhere to speak of.

Where to stay and eat Meridijan (*Ante Starčevića 1;* ℡ *023 612 162;* f *023 612 161; www.meridijan15.hr*), by the bus stop, is a **travel agency** handling a growing supply of private rooms – expect to pay around €35 for a decent double. It's also highly likely you'll be approached by old women when the bus arrives, and given Pag's small size it's worth going and having a look.

The nearest **campsite** is 8km away, at Šimuni (℡ *023 697 441;* f *023 697 442; www.camping-simuni.hr*), on an attractive bay on the western side of the island, half way to Novalja – buses stop here, and there's a popular marina, too.

Biser (20 rooms) A G Matoša 46; ℡ 023 611 333; f 023 611 444; www.hotel-biser.com. Across the bay, a 30min walk from the old town, the 3-star Biser has its own rather nicer beach. *Sea-view dbl at around €60–73.*

Pagus (117 rooms) A Starčevića 1; ☎ 023 611 310; f 023 611 101; www.coning.hr. Unpretentious 3-star place, in a good location right by the bus stop, with its own concrete beach & sea-view dbl, with balconies. *€156 at the top of the season, dropping right back to €78–90 in spring & autumn.*

Pansion Tamaris Križevacka; ☎ 023 611 277; www.tamaris-pag.hr. Central location, with its own restaurant. *Dbl €60–65.*

Plaža (29 rooms) Marka Marulića 14; ☎f 023 600 855; f 023 600 201; www.plaza-croatia.com. Pag's most upmarket accommodation comes in this modern 4-star hotel with an outdoor pool & lovely views back to Pag town. *Dbl in high season for €126.*

Hotel Tony (20 rooms) Dubrovacka 39; ☎f 023 611 370; www.hotel-tony.com. Welcoming, well-priced family hotel, with own restaurant. *Dbl €60–80.*

NOVALJA AND NORTHERN PAG (*Telephone code for northern Pag 053*) Much busier and far more developed than Pag is the resort of Novalja, 20km north. Within reach of a whole load of good beaches (notably **Zrče**, **Časka** and **Straško**), it's understandably popular, and well equipped for visitors, with thousands of private rooms available, and an enormous campsite (*Straško;* ☎ *053 661 226;* f *053 661 225; www.turno.hr*), around a third of which is given over to naturists.

Two kilometres south of Novalja, just off the main road to Pag town, is the beach of **Zrče**, a kilometre or so of shingle that has become one of Croatia's hippest summer night-time playgrounds, with clubbing until dawn. There are three main bars/clubs operational through the summer; the original is **Calypso**, but in recent years offshoots of well-known Zagreb clubs – and notably **Aquarius** – have also taken to setting up camp here. There's a shuttle bus from Novalja if you don't fancy the walk.

Also close to Novalja are the meagre ruins of the Roman town of **Cissa** (now Časka), with the best bits being underwater, as the coast sank here. The main attraction is the underground Roman aqueduct, constructed in the 1st century AD, and visitable for around 150m of its length – further excavations are under way.

For more on Novalja, and accommodation contacts, go directly through the Novalja tourist office (☎f *053 661 404; www.tz-novalja.hr*). Expect to pay around €30 for a double room in summer.

The island of Pag ends in the narrow 20km-long **Lun** peninsula, famous for its olive groves (the few trees not cut down by the Venetians), and ending in the quiet fishing village of **Tovarnele**.

UGLJAN AND PAŠMAN

Just a few kilometres offshore from Zadar are the pretty islands of Ugljan and Pašman. Like Cres and Lošinj in the Kvarner Bay, they were originally a single island, but while Cres and Lošinj have been separate for millennia, the channel between Ugljan and Pašman was only dug during the 19th century, to help sea traffic on its way.

Most visitors are locals, as neither island has yet been developed as a package destination. As a result, Ugljan and Pašman are better geared up for individual visits rather than groups, though they're far from empty, with Ugljan being the most densely populated island in the Adriatic (it's practically a suburb of Zadar).

UGLJAN The island of Ugljan is largely dedicated to the cultivation of olives, and some of Croatia's best olive oil comes from here, although it's rarely commercially available. Many of the rest of the inhabitants work in Zadar, while there are lots of mainlanders' second homes on the island, meaning it can get pretty busy on summer weekends.

Preko Just half an hour away from Zadar, Ugljan's main settlement is Preko, an unpretentious little town focused more on day-to-day life than anything like a tourist industry. Ferries come across every hour, all year round, and alternate ones are met by buses heading north up to the town of Ugljan or south to Pašman, passing through Kali and Kukljica on the way.

The **tourist office** (ʌ/f *023 286 108; www.preko.hr*) is cheerful enough, but not really equipped to help you, though it can point you in the direction of the Rušev agency (*Duga Mocira 12;* ʌ *023 286 266;* f *023 286 085; www.rusev.croadria.com*), which not only handles Preko's plentiful private rooms (around € 25–35 for doubles), but also rents out bicycles and boats, great ways of getting yourself around the island. There's one hotel in town, the pleasant **Preko** (*Mul 14;* ʌ *023 286 041;* f *023 286 040*), with doubles at around € 75 – ask for a sea view if they have one available.

Well worth the hour's uphill hike is the trip up to **St Michael's Fortress**. At 265m it's almost as high as any other point on either island, and the views across to Pag to the north, Dugi Otok to the west, the Kornati archipelago to the south and over to the Velebit massif on the mainland can be absolutely breathtaking. Dating from the early 13th century, the fortress is very much ruined, mostly by time, but also more recently by the Serbs shelling it in 1991.

After your exertions you'll definitely deserve a swim, and Preko has a nice enough town beach, but under 100m offshore is the lovely little wooded island of Galovac, with a 15th-century monastery and the best local beaches. In summer it's easy enough to find a taxi-boat to whisk you across.

Ugljan village

The village of Ugljan, 10km north of Preko, is a forgotten sort of place, though it has a lovely beach and a Franciscan monastery you can visit. Ask at the tourist office (ʌ/f *023 288 011; www.ugljan.hr*) about private rooms, or stay at the **Hotel Ugljan** (*Ugljan 16;* ʌ/f *023 288 024; www.hotelugljan.com*), which has reasonable doubles right on the harbour for € 68. You can also rent bikes and boats at the hotel.

Kali and Kukljica

Heading south from Preko it's not far to the active fishing village of Kali, and a further 5km on to Kukljica, which is a fishing village as well, but also the nearest thing Ugljan has to a holiday resort. The **tourist office** (*Svetog Lovre 2;* ʌ/f *023 282 406; www.kali.hr*) can help you find private accommodation; the Zelena Punta (ʌ *023 373 338;* f *023 373 545; www.coning-turizam.hr; dbl €99–142 in summer*) tourist settlement consists of apartments and bungalows, which tend to be block-booked months in advance. From here it's barely 2km to the bridge leading over to Pašman.

PAŠMAN

Pašman is a smaller, less densely populated, even less developed version of its northern neighbour, and although the number of visitors is growing by 20% a year, that's from a pretty low base.

The island is a popular weekender for locals from Biograd on the mainland, and there are 11 ferries a day all year round (13 in summer) across to **Tkon**, the main settlement in the south of the island, with a couple of reasonable beaches and a naturist campsite, **Sovinje** (ʌ *023 285 541;* f *023 285 304; www.fkksovinje.hr*), 2km to the south, with one of the few sandy naturist beaches in Croatia.

Not far from Tkon, on Mount Ćokovac, is the monastery of **Kuzma i Damjan**. Originally a Venetian fortress, built in 1125, it became an important Glagolitic centre, and is today the only active Benedictine monastery in Croatia. The church here was built from 1369 to 1419, and has a fine 14th-century crucifix.

A few kilometres north, on the way to the village of Pašman, at **Kraj**, there's a solid, defensive Franciscan monastery dating from 1390, though much remodelled in the 16th century. The Renaissance cloisters here are lovely, and there's an interesting little museum housing several valuable religious works.

The village of **Pašman** itself, 6km north of Tkon, is the last place of any significance heading towards Ugljan – after that it's one sleepy fishing hamlet after another. There are a handful of private rooms available – ask at the tourist office (\f *023 260 155*) – and a couple of pleasant beaches from which to swim.

Between Ugljan and Dugi Otok lies the sheltered island of Iž, which is little more than two harbour settlements – **Mali Iž** and **Veli Iž** – connected by what passes for a road in these parts. There's one hotel on the island, in Veli Iž, the **Korinjak** (\ *023 277 064;* f *023 277 248; www.korinjak.hr*), which has 80 fairly simple rooms, and charges € 82–108 full board for doubles in its renovated wing.

In the past Veli Iž was famous for its pottery, supplying large parts of the coast with clay cooking pots. Local lore has it that potters threw unsold goods into the sea on the homeward voyage, rather than face the shame of having failed to sell them. There's a daily ferry to Iž from Zadar – don't bother bringing the car.

DUGI OTOK AND THE KORNATI ARCHIPELAGO

Dugi Otok (literally 'long island') and the Kornati archipelago, stretched in a 75km line marking the outer ridge of the Adriatic's submerged mountains, are among the most dramatic and spectacular places in Croatia.

The endless indentations and extraordinary shapes of the islands are a magnet for sailors in summer, and although there's almost nothing as such to do, the wild scenery alone makes for a remarkable visit.

It's easiest to visit the Kornati archipelago as part of an excursion – these are offered from Zadar and Šibenik, and as far away as Trogir and Split, but are best from Murter (see *Kornati National Park*, page 274), which is home to the park office. Bear in mind that some excursions – from Zadar in particular – only go as far as Dugi Otok and not into the national park itself. Far and away the finest way to see them, however, is from the deck of your own boat, and the archipelago is understandably popular with nautical tourists, although the sheer number of islands means you'll never find them even the least bit crowded.

DUGI OTOK Dugi Otok is nearly 45km long but never as much as 5km wide. All the attention goes to the two lobster-clawed ends of the island. The tiny resort and harbour of **Božava** is in the northwest, while the island's capital, **Sali**, is in the southeast – this is the closest town to the remarkable Telašćica Bay, actually part of the Kornati National Park.

The island has no fresh water supply at all, so it relies on collected rainwater, and in hot summers drinking water has to be ferried over from the mainland; it's not a place to leave taps running. The north is moderately fertile, while the southern end of the island (like most of the Kornati archipelago) is more dramatically barren.

Dugi Otok's settlements are connected by a single road, although if you're here without your own wheels you'll soon discover there's only one bus a week which connects north with south; and if you do bring your own car, remember there's only one petrol station (at Zaglav). With many parts of the island still only reachable by sea, begging, borrowing or renting a boat is still by far the best way of visiting.

There are two different ferry routes to Dugi Otok from Zadar. The car ferry runs three or four times a day, all year round, and takes about 1½ hours to reach **Brbinj**. There's really nothing much here, in spite of the sometimes busy port and surrounding olive groves, so if you're not driving yourself, try not to miss the connecting bus which meets the ferry and makes the 15km run north to Božava.

There's no bus south from Brbinj to Sali, around 20km distant. There is, however, a passenger ferry running three times daily, all year round from Zadar either to **Sali** or **Zaglav**, 3km north – when it goes to Zaglav there's a bus onwards to Sali – and a catamaran running the same route. In summer there are also various privately operated hydrofoil and ferry services from Zadar to the island.

There are a few diving schools on Dugi Otok, including Kornati Diver Diving Center Eric Šešelja in Zaglav (☎ 023 377 167; www.kornati-diver.com) and Diving School Božava (☎ 023 318 891; www.bozava.de) in Božava – see the Dugi Otok tourist office website, www.dugiotok.hr.

Božava The fishing village of Božava, with just 166 residents, is a (very) quiet place most of the time, though it's increasingly popular with Italian yachtsmen and women at the height of the season. There's even a mid-sized hotel complex, the eponymous Božava (☎ 023 291 291; f 023 377 682; www.hoteli-bozava.hr), which has doubles at € 146–170 full board in high summer, and a few private rooms which can be booked through the tourist office (☎ 023 377 607).

A couple of kilometres northwest of Božava is the even smaller village of **Soline**, at the head of **Solišćica Bay**, which has plenty of swimming opportunities on mostly rocky beaches, heading up towards **Veli Rat**, the northernmost settlement on the island. From here it's a few hundred metres north to the lighthouse, and some popular rocks from which to bathe. If you turn left down a gravel road halfway between Soline and Veli Rat, it's a kilometre or so south to **Sakarun**, a half-kilometre stretch of fine shingle on a truly lovely bay, facing south.

Sali Sali, with over 1,000 inhabitants, is Dugi Otok's social and economic hub. It still derives a good deal more of its revenue from fishing than tourism, though that balance is surely set to change, as more people are visiting every year. The town is understandably popular with sailors, who come here on their way to or from Telašćica Bay, the Adriatic's largest and most dramatic natural harbour, and the Kornati islands.

Sali's tourist office (☎/f 023 377 094) will help with finding you private rooms. There's also the **Hotel Sali** (☎ 023 377 049; f 023 377 078; www.hotel-sali.hr), 300m across the headland to the north, set in pine woods, which has double rooms at € 78 in summer and € 50 in winter.

The tourist office will also point you in the right direction for one of the dive centres (see www.dugiotok.hr) here, as well as organising boat trips for you around the island and into the Kornati archipelago – by far the best way of seeing the dramatic scenery. Although you can walk the 3km west to the head of **Telašćica Bay**, you're really missing out by choosing this option.

In the south western pincer, about 7km from Sali, but still within the Telašćica Bay, is **Mir Bay** ('bay of peace'), which harbours a saltwater lake, connected to the sea by underground karstic channels. The rocks around here are popular with naturists.

KORNATI NATIONAL PARK Eighty-nine of the 140-odd islands, islets and reefs of the Kornati archipelago were declared a national park in 1980, with the boundary also including the spectacular Telašćica Bay on Dugi Otok (see above). It's understandably popular with yachting types, and a great place to learn to sail.

The park is managed from the town of **Murter**, on the island of Murter, connected to the mainland by a drawbridge. As it's the closest place to the national park it's also the best starting point for an excursion – you'll see much more if you're not spending most of the day schlepping your way up the coast from Split or down from Zadar.

Murter's also the place to start if you want to stay on one of the Kornati islands and experience so-called 'Robinson Crusoe tourism'. This represents quite an investment, as you can't normally stay for less than a week, you need to pay for transport as well as accommodation, and it doesn't make much sense not to have your own boat while you're out there.

On the other hand, there are few places in Europe that offer you this much isolation or privacy with such a great climate. There's no electricity, let alone shops or restaurants, and the cottages have just the bare essentials, though twice a week a supply boat will come and deliver you staples (food, not office supplies), as well as the gas which powers the fridge, cooker and lights. Catching your own fish, grilling it over an open fire, and watching the sun plunging into the sea on a sultry evening is a sure cure for urban stress.

An interesting alternative to the desert-island week can be had by talking to the locals in Murter and negotiating your way out to one of their own houses on the islands – the archipelago is actually the property of the people of Murter, and there's still a certain amount of fishing and agriculture that goes on. Your chances with this particular strategy will be greatly enhanced if you speak Croatian and can handle your *rakija*.

Even if you're only here on a day trip, you'll see some of the most extraordinary scenery in Europe. Most of the islands are covered in sage and feather grasses, or low scrub, turning the grey karst green, though some also permit the cultivation of figs, grapes and olives.

Where the islands face the open sea, to the southwest, dramatic cliffs plunge into the water. Known locally as 'crowns' (you'll have your wrist slapped if you say 'cliff'), they rise up to around 80m tall, and extend underwater almost as far. The crowns are the most obvious sign of the fault zone running down the Adriatic, the result of sudden tectonic movements in the past.

The highly varied submarine flora and fauna, along with the unusual geomorphology, also make for excellent diving and snorkelling.

MURTER Murter is about 25km up the coast from Šibenik, and is served by half a dozen daily buses – change in Vodice if you're coming from the north. The town itself is nothing special, though there are some pretty good beaches on the island if you have some time to while away.

The **national park office** (*Butina 2;* ☏ *022 435 740;* f *022 435 058;* www.kornati.hr) will sell you entry tickets (per boat, 150kn up to 11m, 250kn 11–18m), a fishing licence (150kn, includes entrance fee), a diving permit (150–300kn, ditto) and good maps, as well as letting you know who's authorised to offer excursions into the park. Note: these are prices for tickets bought outside the park; tickets bought within the park itself cost almost double. There's a list of places selling tickets on the national park website.

There are a number of agencies in town who can arrange both day trips and longer stays on the islands, and costs generally include the park entrance fee. Coronata (*Zrtava ratova 17;* ☏ *022 435 933;* f *022 435 555;* www.coronata.hr) and KornatTurist (*Hrvatskih vladara 2;* ☏ *022 435 854;* f *022 434 853;* www.kornatturist.hr) are both reliable.

7

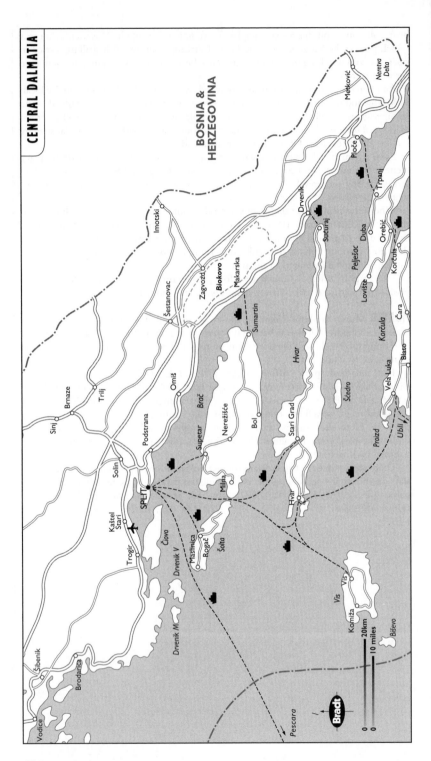

CENTRAL DALMATIA

BOSNIA & HERZEGOVINA

8

Central Dalmatia

Telephone code 021 (+385 21 from abroad)

Central Dalmatia is wonderfully rich both in cultural sights and the great outdoors – whether it be the stark severity of the Biokovo massif above Makarska, or the green islands of Šolta, Brač, Hvar and Vis offshore, with their innumerable beaches, bays, coves and fishing villages. Unmissable are the Emperor Diocletian's palace in Split, the medieval island town of Trogir and the Renaissance elegance of Hvar town – along with the extraordinary shingle spit of Zlatni Rat, at Bol, and the Blue Cave on Biševo, just offshore from the island of Vis, itself only open to tourists since 1989.

TROGIR

UNESCO World Heritage listed Trogir – just 26km up the coast from Split – is one of the most attractive stops in Dalmatia, with the old town being not just excellently preserved but also delightfully car-free. Come here to soak up a pleasantly uncorrupted medieval atmosphere, where stone-carved balconies overhang the narrow streets, and Renaissance and Gothic palaces compete for your attention with the ancient cathedral.

HISTORY Trogir started out in the 3rd century BC as Tragurion, an offshoot of the Greek colony of Issa (on Vis), before being developed as a key port under the Romans. Later overshadowed by Salona (see page 289), Trogir grew in importance once again during the 7th century, when Salona was sacked and its refugees came north to Split.

Relative peace under the Croatians and Hungarians came to a sudden halt in 1123, when the Saracens pretty much demolished the city, but prosperity soon returned, and the 12th–14th centuries were a golden age for the town. From 1420 onwards Venice ruled, while from 1797 to 1918 the Austro-Hungarians were in charge – with a short break for Marshal Marmont and the French, from 1806 to 1814. The rest, as they say, is Yugoslavia – until Croatia won independence in 1991.

GETTING THERE AND AROUND Trogir is on the main coast road, so it's easy to reach by bus from Zadar or Šibenik to the north, or Split to the south. It's also the terminus for the local #37 bus from Split – buy a four-zone ticket on the bus – which runs half-hourly, making Trogir an easily feasible day trip from Split. An even quicker alternative is the regular coach that leaves from the Split ferry terminal. (The reverse is also true – if you can get in at one of the private rooms or small hotels in Trogir itself, it's a really attractive option as a base from which to visit Split.)

Split airport is just 10km east of Trogir, and the #37 bus is again your answer – a taxi from the airport to Trogir is cheaper than one to Split, but will still cost you well upwards of 100kn.

Your only problem might be in leaving, if you're heading north in summer – the coastal buses from Split often arrive here full on their way to Zadar. It's not unheard of to take the #37 back to Split, make an onward reservation, and spend some time sightseeing before heading north again.

TROGIR

Šibenik, Medena

Split

400m
400yds

Market

Bus terminal

St Lovro's Cathedral

Town Hall

Čipiko Palace

Clock Tower & Loggia

_i_

Monika

Fontana

Concordia

Kamerlengo Fortress

Marmont's Pavilion

Vila Sikaa Hotel (100m)

Bradt

Trogir's bus station (more of a bus stop; there are no left-luggage facilities) is right by the stone bridge leading onto the island containing the old town. Just beyond the bridge – and indeed on it – you'll find a colourful local market selling everything from fruit, vegetables and flowers to homemade liquor.

If you're coming in by car out of season then cross the stone bridge and immediately turn right along the quay – there's a certain amount of paid parking along here, and the location's perfect. In summer don't even think about this – traffic snarls up a treat. Instead, stop a few hundred metres west of the bridge on the main road into town, and park in one of the several car parks along here.

Once you're in town you'll find it charmingly small – the whole place, connected to the mainland by the stone bridge and to the island of Čiovo by a drawbridge, is barely 500m long and under half that width.

For all things Trogir, have a look at www.trogir-online.com.

WHERE TO STAY AND EAT The **tourist office** (⌕/f *021 881 412; www.tztrogir.hr*), on the front facing Čiovo, is friendly and has a map for you. For private rooms head for one of the many agencies in town – try Sea Gate (*Bl A Kazotica 5;* ⌕ *021 797 710; www.sea-gate.net*), Kairos (*Obala Bana Berislavica 23;* ⌕ *021 796 290; www.kairos-trogir.com*) or Čipiko (*in the Čipiko Palace, opposite the entrance to the cathedral;* ⌕/f *021 881 554*). Rooms in or very close to the old town get snapped up quickly, with doubles going for around € 40 a night, and there's a 30% surcharge for stays of under five nights here.

Concerning hotels, Trogir seems single-handedly to have implemented Croatia's policy of introducing small, family-run places, and has three excellent establishments to choose from. The only thing you need to do is to book well ahead – Trogir's a lovely place, and the combined capacity for the three hotels in town is just 36 rooms.

Concordia (14 rooms) Bana Berislavića 22; ⌕ 021 885 400; f 021 885 401; www.concordia-hotel.net. On the southwestern corner of the front, the lovely Concordia is near the fortress, & great value. *Dbl €82–100 in season.*

Fontana Obrov 1; ⌕ 021 885 744; f 021 885 755; www.fontana-commerce.htnet.hr. Right by the front in the old town is the reliable Fontana, which boasts nice accommodation; the best room is the top-floor apartment, which is great for families or a couple looking to splash out. *Dbl €95.*

Vila Sikaa (10 rooms) Kralija Zvonimira 13; ⌕ 021 881 223; f 021 855 149; www.vila-sikaa-r.com.

Across the drawbridge on the Čiovo front, facing back towards Trogir (a lovely view) is the Vila Sikaa, with very nice rooms, including superior dbls with spa jets. *Superior dbl €133 in high season; standard dbl €86 Oct–Apr.*

Medena (630 rooms) ⌕ 021 880 588; f 021 880 019; www.hotelmedena.com. If Trogir itself fails you – or if you want to swim – then head 4km west to this resort, where you'll find a rocky beach & hundreds of rooms. To get there catch the Medena bus, which runs about hourly; otherwise it's a dullish 50min walk. *Dbl €120 in summer, around €90 otherwise.*

You can also camp, either at **Rozac** (*Okrug Gornji;* ⌕ *021 806 105;* f *021 882 554; www.camp-rozac.hr*) on the island of Čiovo, or **Seget** (*Hrvatskih zrtava 121;* ⌕/f *021 880 394; www.kamp-seget.hr*), which is a couple of kilometres west of town, and has all the usual facilities, including windsurfing.

Eating in Trogir is as easy as falling off a log. Practically every square has its own terrace set up in summer for alfresco dining, and the only hard thing is to choose which one suits you best – though the **Fontana's** restaurant clearly has the most diverse menu, and **Restoran Monika** (*Budislavićeva 12;* ⌕ *021 884 808*) offers first-rate seafood, with the fish platter for two particularly noteworthy at 240kn. Booking is essential in high season.

WHAT TO SEE AND DO The old town is entered through a 17th-century gate – hook left and right from here and you'll find yourself on the pretty main square, Trg Ivana Pavla II, home to most of the famous sights, including **St Lovro's Cathedral**.

The cathedral's portal, dating from 1240, is the stunning work of truthful but far from bashful local boy Radovan (look for the inscription above the door: '*per raduanum cunctus hac arte praeclarum*' – 'all of this was made most excellently by Radovan'). Adam and Eve stand apparently appalled at their nakedness, atop two superb Venetian lions. The inner pillars, resting on the shoulders of medieval bugbears (Turks and Jews), frame graphic scenes from the calendar year (labours of the summer and winter months), while above it all sits a superb Nativity.

Inside, the cathedral's a cluttered, sombre place, still used by older local women every morning for prayers. The most important thing to see here is the extraordinary **Ursini Chapel**, in the north nave, which is arguably the most beautiful Renaissance monument in Dalmatia. Sculpted by Nikola Firentinac (Nicholas of Florence) at the end of the 15th century, it's here you'll find those torch-bearing cherubs featured in the tourist board's promotional literature.

Other sights within the cathedral include the elaborately carved 15th-century choir stalls, and an octagonal 13th-century pulpit.

Outside, have a good look at the campanile – the first floor's 15th-century early Gothic, the second's pure Venetian Gothic, and the third is late 16th-century Renaissance.

Opposite the entrance to the cathedral is the Venetian **Čipiko Palace** complex, now home to the Čipiko tourist agency. Pop into the hallway and check out the giant wooden cockerel on the wall, a trophy from the prow of some long-forgotten Turkish warship. Across the square is the **town hall** – in the courtyard, you'll see the coats of arms of the ruling families of Trogir.

Completing the square are the town's 15th-century **clock tower** and **loggia**. Both feature more work by Nikola Firentinac, while the loggia also has a large Meštrović bas-relief. Behind the loggia is the oldest surviving pre-Saracen church (**St Barbara's**), dating from the 11th century.

It's a short walk south from here to the Riva and the few remaining preserved parts of the city walls – Marshal Marmont, the Napoleonic administrator in the region from 1806 to 1814, had the rest torn down in an attempt to introduce sea breezes as a cure for malaria. Draining the swampy western end of the island a century later was a far more successful strategy.

Along the lovely Riva you'll find the huge **Kamerlengo Fortress**. Beyond that Trogir peters out with a football pitch and a small car park, but have a look at **Marmont's Pavilion**, if you're up here – it's a small (and sadly graffito-ed) memorial to the man who really did try and do his best for Napoleon's short-lived Illyrian Provinces.

Finally, if you want to visit the nearby islands of **Drvenik Veli** and **Drvenik Mali** (they both have some nice beaches), you should ask at the tourist office on Riva – there are ferries, but the times aren't always convenient for day trips, and there's nowhere to stay. Both islands are emerging as something of a favourite with foreign second-home owners.

SPLIT

Croatia's second biggest city is a brash and captivatingly energetic hub, with a population of over 200,000 – but the old centre is surprisingly compact and easily manageable on foot. The main draw is Diocletian's Roman palace, just along the Riva from the port where you're likely to arrive – still stunning after more than 1,700 years of builders' alterations. Diocletian no doubt had a monster ego (being emperor has that effect), but even he can't have imagined his retirement home would be so well worth visiting in the 3rd millennium.

Split's a lively, friendly city, and although it wasn't the victim of a Dubrovnik-like siege during the 1991–92 war (just one casualty was sustained here), it suffered the effects of large numbers of refugees coming in and a huge drop in tourism, and unemployment is still high. Happily, that doesn't stop people from having a good time, and the café terraces along the front are packed, practically all year round. Split has also long been a voice of political dissension, and is home to the weekly Feral Tribune, a regular thorn in the side of politicians for years, even before Croatia became independent, and continuing through Tuđman's times to the present day.

With the fanatically supported local football team, Hajduk Split, enjoying some recent success, a new motorway that connects the city to Zagreb, and new budget airline connections to the UK, not to mention the massive new Meridien Hotel development to the south of the city, Split is clearly on the up and up.

HISTORY Although previously inhabited, Split only officially came into existence when Diocletian retired here in AD305, after 21 years as Roman emperor. The palace – started half way through Diocletian's reign, in AD295 – was built on a vast 170m-by-190m ground-plan, with walls 2m thick and up to 26m high, making it the largest private residence in antiquity.

Post-Diocletian, the palace continued to be used on and off as a sort of upmarket hotel for the elite, until the Roman Empire finally collapsed. After the Avars burned Salona in 614, refugees moved in permanently, converting chambers into houses, and corridors into streets, using the huge defences to good effect against invading hordes from the north.

Byzantium, the Ottomans, the Austro-Hungarians, the Venetians and Napoleon all left their mark on Split, but it was the Scottish architect, Robert Adam, who practically created it as a tourist destination overnight. Having seen Palladio's drawings, Adam and his team of draughtsmen stopped over in Split for five weeks in 1757, at the tail end of his 'Grand Tour' (tours really were grander then), and made hundreds of drawings and surveys of the palace. Published to huge acclaim in 1764, they came to dominate Georgian architecture, and influenced the future shape of whole tracts of London, Bath, Bristol and Edinburgh.

The name Split is itself relatively recent – the town was probably originally called Aspalatos (after the yellow broom still common round here), before metamorphosing into Spalatum, Spalato and Spljet, and finally settling down as Split.

DIOCLETIAN AND THE PALACE

In its heyday the palace must have been extraordinary. At over 30,000m², it included everything from vast reception chambers to temples, arcaded corridors, baths, huge storerooms, extensive private apartments and an entire barracks. No expense was spared in its construction, with materials shipped in from Egypt and Greece, though it was built in a terrible rush, as it had to be ready for the emperor's retirement.

It's thought that Diocletian's wife and daughter never joined him here, in spite of their having lavish residences within the palace, and it's not clear whether he eventually had them killed – or indeed whether or not he himself committed suicide, was murdered, or died a natural death. What is known is that he passed his retirement years in Split having Christians captured, tortured and put to death – so many were martyred, in fact, that Diocletian holds the individual record for saint creation. Fighting Christianity was a losing battle, however – only two years after his death, in AD316, the Milan edict legitimised the religion. Ironically the site of his former tomb is now the city's Christian cathedral.

GETTING THERE AND AROUND Split's international airport is 20km/half an hour west of town, almost at Trogir, and flights are met by Croatia Airlines buses, which will run you into town for 30kn. Shuttles return to the airport from the air terminal (near the passenger ferry terminal and bus station) 90 minutes before flight departures. If you miss the shuttle, local bus #37 also runs half-hourly from Split to the airport and on to Trogir – buy a four-zone ticket on the bus. A taxi to or from the airport will set you back 250–300kn.

Just to the east of the old town, in a row, you'll find the passenger ferry terminal, the air terminal, the train station, the bus station and the car ferry terminal.

Ferries run frequently from Split not just to the local islands of Šolta, Brač and Hvar, but also to Vis, Korčula and Lastovo, as well as up and down the coast to Rijeka and Dubrovnik, and across the Adriatic to Ancona. If you're planning on taking your car by ferry anywhere in the summer, reserve as far ahead as you can, or expect a long wait. There are good, cheap left-luggage facilities next to the ferry terminal.

The train station is effectively the only coastal railhead south of Rijeka, though the new high speed rail link to Zagreb has been plagued with problems and delays. You may find you're better off on the bus.

Split's incredibly well connected with everywhere by bus – at least a dozen a day go to each of Dubrovnik (5 hours), Rijeka (8 hours) and Zagreb (5 hours). There are also international departures several times a week to destinations in Germany and Holland. Again, book ahead if you can, as buses fill up fast, especially in summer. The bus station has timetables on its website (*www.ak-split.hr*) and a left-luggage office with long hours (🕐 *04.30–22.00 daily*).

If you come in by car you'll discover that Split has its fair share of traffic problems, and parking can be a major hassle in summer. The best-located car park is right on the Riva in front of Diocletian's Palace (10kn an hour), but you'll be lucky to find a spot in season.

Once you've arrived, everything's easily reached on foot, though you may end up taking local bus #12 if you're going to the two galleries west of town, or onto the Marjan peninsula – Split's own nature park, and home to the nearest beaches. Tickets cost 10kn for two trips, and should be bought in advance from a kiosk.

Split's main tourist information office is located on the Riva (*Obala Hrvatskog Narodnog Preporoda 7;* ☏ *021 348 600;* f *021 348 604; www.visitsplit.com*). Nearby, the Turist Biro (*Obala Hrvatskog Narodnog Preporoda 12;* ☏ *021 347 100;* f *021 347 271*) is just one of the many travel agencies that organises private rooms. They can also give you more detailed information on excursions etc. Both offices will sell you the Split Card for 40kn – and it's free if you're staying in town for four days or more. This gives you 72 hours' worth of free access to some of the city's museums, half-price access to others, 20% off selected car hire, 10% off your bill at the Park Hotel, 5% off at the Bellevue, Consul, Marjan and Split hotels, and 5% off at a number of restaurants. There's also a tourist information kiosk inside Diocletian's Palace, by the cathedral (*Peristil;* ☏ *021 345 606*).

Last but not least, Split has Dalmatia's only coin-operated laundrette, in the shape of Modrulj Laundrette, at Šperun 1, just beyond the western end of the marina next to the Šperun restaurant.

🏠 WHERE TO STAY

Hotels As far as hotels are concerned, Split still doesn't exactly overflow with options, but things have improved markedly in recent years. The most notable trend has been for boutique style hotels within the walls of the palace, while the largest development has been the Meridien, which opened late in 2006.

🏠 **Adriana** (14 rooms) Obala Hrvatscog Narodnog Preporoda 8 ☏ 021 340 000; f 021 340 008; www.hotel-adriana.com. 3-star with central, waterfront location. *Dbl €103–130.*

🏠 **Bellevue** (50 rooms) Bana Jospia Jelačića 2; 📞 021 345 644; f 021 362 383; www.hotel-bellevue-split.hr. On the western side of the elegant Trg Republike (a minor copy of St Mark's Square in Venice) & a stone's throw from the old town, is a hotel in serious need of a revamp. It was here that President Mitterrand stayed in 1992, during peace talks. *Dbl at €115.*

🏠 **Consul** (15 rooms) Tršćanska 34; 📞 021 340 130; f 021 340 133; www.hotel-consul.net. 10mins walk north of the old town & palace, with spacious dbls. *Dbl around €130.*

🏠 **Globo** (33 rooms) Lovretska 18; 📞 021 481 111; f 021 481 118; www.hotelglobo.com. Smart 4-star near the Consul, renovated in 2007. *Dbl €155–177.*

🏠 **Jupiter** Grabovčeva Širina 1; 📞/f 021 344 801; www.hotel-jupiter.info. Cheapie within the palace. Beds €34 pp.

🏠 **Le Meridien Lav** (381 rooms) Grljevačka 2A; 📞 021 500 500; f 021 500 705; www.lemeridienlavsplit.com. Down the coast, 8km south of the city, this 5-star resort hotel immediately became Split's swankiest on opening at the end of 2006, though it seems to be aimed as much at the convention & business crowd as holidaymakers. Pools, a spa, & a casino are just some of the hotel's facilities. *Dbl from €135 up.*

🏠 **Park** (54 rooms) Hatzeov perivoj 3; 📞 021 406 400; f 021 406 401; www.hotelpark-split.hr. If your budget stretches that far, the renovated 4-star Park is probably the nicest & best located of the town's hotels, just round the headland from the ferry terminal, & set

above Bačvice beach, a 10min walk from the old town. Noisy summer Sat night festivities can go on until dawn. *Dbl with sea view €180.*

🏠 **Peristil** (12 rooms) Poljana Kraljice Jelene 5; 📞/f 021 329 070; www.hotelperistil.com. A great option tucked within the walls of Diocletian's Palace right by the Peristyle. The staff are genuinely welcoming & will go out of their way to help you. *Dbl €120–162.*

🏠 **Slavija** (25 rooms) Buvinina 2; 📞 021 323 840; f 021 323 868; www.hotelslavija.com. Once the sole preserve of backpackers & students, the Slavija has been reborn with a flash new lobby & cleaned up façade, though the admittedly clean rooms are still relatively basic. A good palace option. *Dbl €108–137.*

🏠 **Simoni** (7 rooms) 📞/f 021 488 780; m 098 974 7439; www.sobesimoni.com. First-rate place, conveniently located just behind the railway station – clean, efficient, friendly and an absolute bargain at 150kn pp in summer. They can even drive you to the airport for the same or slightly less than a taxi. Technically this is 3-star private accommodation, but it's run as well as any hotel, and deserves to be listed as such. *Dbl €42 in summer.*

🏠 **Vestibul Palace** (7 rooms) Iza Vestibula 4; 📞 021 329 329; f 021 329 333; www.vestibulpalace.com. Smart 4-star boutique hotel just up the stairs from the Peristil. Spend the night in the shadows of a Roman emperor on the 2nd tier of Dicoletian's Palace. High on atmosphere, with stylish, modern, tastefully furnished rooms. *Dbl €210–260*

Private rooms There's a good supply of private rooms, and these can most easily be arranged through the Turist Biro (see opposite) on the Riva, just west of the palace. You'll pay the usual surcharge of 30% for three nights or fewer.

If you come in by boat, train or bus you'll also be offered rooms on arrival – these can be a great deal (bargain assiduously), but bear in mind that Split's a big city and some rooms can be far, far away. Even as seasoned a traveller as Dervla Murphy was caught out here, when she was researching her book *Through the Embers of Chaos* – perhaps ripped off by the same woman who did for me a decade earlier when I was researching *Yugoslavia: The Bradt Travel Guide* back at the end of the 1980s. Check the location carefully, and for a realistic idea of where the place actually is, double the time or distance you're told. If you leave your bag at left luggage, you'll have the freedom to reject a room that's too far away, too expensive, or not up to scratch – you'll be back down in this area soon enough anyway. Or just go the simple route and use the Turist Biro.

There are no campsites near Split – the closest is 26km southeast, at Omiš.

❌ **WHERE TO EAT** There are relatively few really good restaurants in Split's tourist-oriented old town, though this is compensated for by some excellent eateries elsewhere. If you're looking for your own ingredients there's an excellent daily market just to the east of the palace, while on the west side of town you'll find the famous fish market. The smell here has more to do with the sulphur spa next door than the fish itself, which is guaranteed super-fresh.

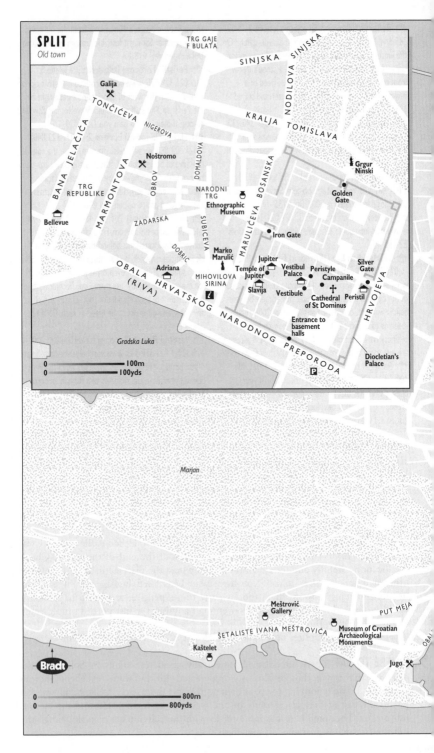

SPLIT
Old town

TRG GAJE
F BULATA

SINJSKA SINJSKA

NODILOVA

KRALJA TOMISLAVA

TONČIĆEVA

NIGEROVA

Galija
✕

Noštromo
✕

DOMALDOVA

OBROV

BOSANSKA

Grgur
Ninski

Golden
Gate

BANA JELAČIĆA

MARMONTOVA

TRG
REPUBLIKE

NARODNI
TRG

Ethnographic
Museum

Iron Gate

Bellevue

ZADARSKA

SUBIĆEVA

MARULIĆEVA

DOBRIC

Marko
Marulić

Silver
Gate

Adriana

MIHOVILOVA
SIRINA

Jupiter

Temple of
Jupiter

Vestibul
Palace

Peristyle

Campanile

Peristil

OBALA HRVATSKOG

(RIVA)

Slavija

Vestibule

Cathedral
of St Dominus

HRVOJEVA

Entrance to
basement
halls

NARODNOG PREPORODA

Diocletian's
Palace

Gradska Luka

0 ———— 100m
0 ———— 100yds

P

Marjan

Meštrović
Gallery

PUT MEJA

ŠETALIŠTE IVANA MEŠTROVIĆA

Museum of Croatian
Archaeological
Monuments

Kaštelet

Bradt

Jugo ✕

0 ———— 800m
0 ———— 800yds

SPLIT

Rijeka, Zagreb
Sinj & Klis
→

KASTELANSKA

⚐ Poljud
Stadium

KASTELANSKA

Archaeological
Museum

Split Art
Gallery

Globo

Consul

DOMOVINSKOG RATA

SLOBODE

DUBROVACKA

VELEBITSKA

LOVRETSKA

NIKOLE TESLE

ZRINSKO FRANKOPANSKA

GUNDULICEVA

MAZURANICEVO

SETALISTE

DUBROVACKA

MATOSEVA

VUKOVARSKA

VUKOVARSKA

PRILAZ

PLINACSKA

Kod Joze

Koteks
Shopping
Centre

NAZOROV

Šperun &
Modrulj
Launderette

VELI VAROŠ

see Split Old Town inset map

SLOBODE

DUBROVACKA

Ferry terminal

Air terminal

Simoni

Dubrovnik &
Le Meridien Lav →

KNEZA BRANIMIRA

Railway
station

Enoteka Terra

POLIČKA CESTA

SPINČIČEVA

Port
ferry terminal
(vehicle)

Bus
station

Park

VIŠKA

PUT FIRVLA

Firule
Bay

Central Dalmatia SPLIT

8

✕ **Enoteka Terra** Braće Kaliterne 6; ☎ 021 314 800; www.vinoteka.hr. A cosy option, set below street level in a candlelit cellar just back from Bačvice. Feast on tapas-style Croatian dishes, such as spicy *kulen* sausage from Slavonia, *pršut* from the Dalmatian hinterland & truffle-infused mushroom *bruschetta*, before moving on to more substantial dishes. A highlight is the excellent English explanations of the various wines on offer.

✕ **Jugo** ☎ 021 398 900. Located near the ACI marina, Jugo has surely the best view of any restaurant in the city, with floor to ceiling windows in the main restaurant & a terrace space outside for sunny days & balmy evenings. Generous portions of *paški sir* & *pršut* are followed by excellent *buzzara* (both mussels & langoustines), as well as a range of pasta dishes. Photos

on the wall depict various famous diners including footballers Mark Viduka & Ronaldinho.

✕ **Kod Jože** Sredmanuška 4; ☎ 021 347 397. A block north of the palace walls, this is one of the best places in Split for seafood – though I have had reader reports of poor service.

✕ **Noštromo** Kraj Sv Marije 10; ☎ 091 405 6666. Upscale restaurant adjacent to the fish market, with dependable grilled fish & generous fish platters (320kn for two).

✕ **Šperun** Šperun 3; ☎ 021 346 999. Bags of character just off the Riva in Varoš. Choose between the tiny outdoor terrace or descend into the main body of the restaurant, which is awash with bric-a-brac & Croatian flags. Mainstays include fresh fish simply grilled, seafood risotto & some hearty meat dishes.

WHAT TO SEE AND DO The main draw is clearly the former palace, on Riva, though what you see now, inside the old walls, is an entire town, centred on Diocletian's peristyle. Around 3,000 local people still live within the walls – barely fewer than in Dubrovnik's much bigger old town – so you'll find the cafés and bars catering to a healthy mix of both visitors and residents.

Enter the old town from the Riva, which is actually reclaimed land – the gate you go through (known as the Brass Gate) was originally on the sea. It was built to be used as an emergency escape route for Diocletian in case of trouble, but may also have seen service as a delivery entrance. The gate leads through a semi-underground chamber, now a small crafts market, flanked by chambers you can visit (see below) before climbing some worn steps up into the peristyle.

The peristyle The peristyle, an open, colonnaded square, was the public heart of Diocletian's Palace, and is still an extraordinary place to sit and wonder. Everything off to the south (towards the sea, behind you) was originally Diocletian's imperial quarters, while to the north were servants' lodgings and soldiers' barracks.

The pink granite columns are Egyptian, while their capitals are Corinthian. You can see that even originally there were four antique columns too few, with local marble pillars making up the difference. The cracked black sphinx dates back to the reign of Thutmosis III, who ruled Egypt from 1504 to 1450BC (though how anyone knows these things for certain beats me), and was originally one of ten imported for Diocletian from the land of the Pharaohs. Another four survive, in varying states of repair – one in the underground chambers, one in the Temple of Jupiter and two in the Archaeological Museum.

The streets out of the peristyle lead to the palace's other three gates – north, to the Golden Gate (the main entrance, coming in from Salona), east, to the Silver Gate, and west, to the Iron Gate. On the peristyle itself you'll find the **vestibule** (above the podrum – see below), the **cathedral** (actually Diocletian's mausoleum), and off down an alley to the other side the **Baptistery of St John** (the Temple of Jupiter – Diocletian reckoned he was Jupiter's son). Inside the barrel-vaulted temple (also known as the Temple of Aesculapius) you should be able to see a couple of classical statues, an interesting 11th-century baptismal font, and a statue of John the Baptist by Meštrović.

The vestibule was the main entrance hall to the imperial quarters. The domed roof has long gone, along with the ornate mosaics that would have lined it, but it's worth walking through here and circling round to the left, back to the cathedral, for some idea of where Diocletian lived – this was originally the dining halls and Roman baths. There are some mosaics here, hidden under protective sand, awaiting restoration.

The Cathedral of St Domnius In a move that must have had Diocletian whirling in his sarcophagus, the emperor's mausoleum was long ago converted into one of Christianity's smallest cathedrals, honouring one of his own victims, St Domnius.

The main structure, including the dome, is original, dating from AD300, but the choir is a 17th-century addition. The entrance doors, with 28 excellent carved wooden panels describing the life of Christ, date from 1214 – the lower four panels have been damaged by centuries' worth of being pushed open by booted feet.

At the base of the dome there's a pagan-looking frieze, and what are said to be medallions of the heads of Diocletian and his wife. Diocletian's ahead of you as you come in, while his wife is two medallions to the left. Down below, the 13th-century pulpit may be a Romanesque masterpiece by Radovan (he of Trogir fame), but to my eye it's too big for the space it's in. The Baroque 17th-century chapel is the one housing the Domnius relics; the other two chapels are 15th-century Gothic. Finally, the choir itself may be 17th-century, but the stalls are around the same age as the cathedral doors, and are a fine example of early Dalmatian wood-carving.

Take the time to climb up inside the campanile for an excellent view over the palace and out to sea – this version dates from 1908, following the collapse of the original, which was built in stages from the 13th to 17th centuries.

Underneath the cathedral is the spooky circular crypt, dedicated to St Lucy, patron saint of the blind (legend has it that Diocletian put her eyes out). The function of this chamber in antiquity isn't known – it's unlikely that it would have been a prison, being under a mausoleum, but large numbers of human bones were found here, and it is the kind of damp, gloomy, airless place you could imagine being used as a dungeon. Ask in the cathedral if you want to see the crypt – it's not always open.

The basement halls (podrum) Don't miss the chance to see the huge semi-underground chambers that provided the foundations for the imperial quarters above. The only whole rooms remaining from the original palace, they give some idea of the sheer scale and size of Diocletian's ego. Remarkably, these chambers only survive because of sewage – during the Dark Ages, people simply threw their slops down holes in the floor, and it accumulated here, protecting the rooms from future squatters.

After World War II, the western rooms were cleared out and opened to the public, while the eastern wing wasn't excavated until 1997 – at various points you can see the original waste chutes coming in from above, along with the foundations of medieval houses. The halls are now used for temporary exhibitions, but look out for a few original curiosities, including some mosaics that clearly pre-date the palace – they run underneath Diocletian's walls – and a marble *mensa*, a Roman table with raised edges for resting your forearm on.

Beyond the palace Just outside the Golden Gate you can hardly fail to spot Meštrović's monumental 1928 statue of Grgur Ninski. Originally standing in the peristyle (which looked pretty wild – there's a photo in the first edition of Rebecca West's *Black Lamb and Grey Falcon*), the statue commemorates the 10th-century Bishop Gregorius of Nin, who tried (but failed) to introduce Croatian instead of Latin into the liturgy. According to local tradition, touch his big toe and your wish will come true – which explains why it's been worn golden.

Walk west a block and head down Marulićeva Bosanska, the narrow street separating the palace from the rest of the old town. This is the least well-preserved wall of the palace, with an unbroken row of houses built into the original fortifications. On the left-hand side, unmarked, is Split's first synagogue – Europe's third, after Prague and Dubrovnik.

Halfway down the street is the palace's Iron Gate, which leads out into the old town's main square, Narodni Trg (also known as Pjaca, pronounced piazza). Palazzi from different periods surround the square, with a Venetian Gothic town hall now housing the interesting **ethnographic museum**, and an Austrian Secessionist palace dominating the square's west end. The next square to the south, just off Riva, has an excellent statue of **Marko Marulić**, the father of Croatian literature, who died in 1524 but is still widely celebrated, and indeed read. Yes, you guessed – it's by Meštrović.

The old town's western boundary is the elegant shopping thoroughfare of Marmontova, named after Napoleon's Marshal Marmont, the captain of his Illyrian Provinces, and the man responsible for both the Riva – Narodni Trg had got too small to function as a collective town square – and Trg Republike, now used for summer concerts.

West of the town you'll find the popular old quarter of **Veli Varoš**, which leads up the slopes of the 182m **Marjan peninsula**, Split's own city park, featuring woods, picnic areas and beaches – a great place to get away from the crowds, though very popular with the locals at weekends. Stop in at **Vidilicia Café** for a cooling drink with a view over Split under a relaxed terrace, as the city unfolds below and the islands beckon in the distance.

Museums and galleries Split has four museums and galleries of particular note, two about a 15-minute walk north (head up Zrinko Frankopanska, from the top of Marmontova), and two a 20-minute walk west onto the Marjan peninsula – or a short hop on local bus #12 from Trg Republike.

Archaeological Museum (*Arheološki Muzej; Frankopanska 25;* ✆ *021 329 340;* ⊕ *09.00–13.00 & 17.00–20.00 Tue–Fri, 09.00–13.00 Sat–Sun; 20kn*) Heading north the secessionist Archaeological Museum houses Croatia's biggest collection of remains from antiquity, and especially strong (unsurprisingly) on artefacts from Salona (see box on page 289). The Roman findings include excellent glass, jewellery, ceramics and statues, including some extraordinarily rich sarcophagi. There's also an extensive collection from very early Christianity.

Split Art Gallery (*Lorevtska 11;* ⊕ *09.00–12.00 & 17.00–19.00 Mon–Sat; 10kn*) Has a terrific collection of paintings from the 14th century on. Unless you're an expert on Croatian art you won't recognise many of the names, but make the effort to come here and you'll find a rich tradition of painting which is especially strong on late 19th- and early 20th-century works, including a couple of masterpieces by Vlaho Bukovac (see box on page 343).

Museum of Croatian Archaeological Monuments (*Muzej Hrvatskih Arheoloških Spomenika; Šetalište Ivana Meštrovića;* ⊕ *10.00–16.00 Mon–Fri, 10.00–13.00 Sat; free*) Heading west from the old town, a 15-minute walk will get you to this unusual collection of Croatian artefacts from the 7th century on, housed in a wonderfully airy modern building. Around 5,000 items are on display (from a collection of more than 20,000 in total), running from old jewellery and stone inscriptions to a unique series of monuments from early Croatian churches, including gables, friezes, altar canopies and baptismal fonts. The captions, sadly, are only in Croatian; buy the English guide for full information.

Meštrović Gallery (*Galerija Ivana Meštrovića; Šetalište Ivana Meštrovića 46;* ✆ *021 340 800; www.mdc.hr/mestrovic;* ⊕ *summer 09.00–21.00 Tue–Sun, winter 09.00–16.00 Tue–Sat & 09.00–15.00 Sun; 30kn*) Five minutes west of the Museum of Croatian

If you know your archaeology, a trip out to Salona (now called Solin) might interest you – though be warned that anything which could be carried off has been carried off (some of the best pieces are in the Split Archaeological Museum), meaning you'll need to rely heavily on your imagination if you're going to people the dusty fields here with temples, houses, markets and an amphitheatre capable of seating nearly 20,000 people.

Salona is 5km north from the centre of Split, and is best reached on the #1 bus, which drops you off at the Caffe Bar Salona, at the entrance to the site. There's a small archaeological museum here (an offshoot of the one in town), called Tusculum, where you can pick up a local map – after which you're on your own to wander across the worn grass and traces of the extensive ruins of the city, home to around 60,000 people in the 1st century AD.

The amphitheatre is the most impressive ruin, though there's very little left beyond the foundations. The Venetians carted off most of the stone in the 17th century, and used it for local building works and fortifications, claiming the dismantlement was only to prevent the Turks from using the amphitheatre as a hideout.

If you've come this far, the quickest way back to Split is on the #37 city bus. Cross the new highway using the underpass, and walk towards Solin centre until you get to the bus stop.

Archaeological Monuments is this vast mansion built by the sculptor between 1931 and 1939, and intended both as a museum and as his retirement home – instead, he emigrated to the USA, dying there in 1962. If you're even remotely interested in Meštrović – and you should be – then this comprehensive collection is the best anywhere. Outside is the sculpture garden; indoors, the full range of the sculptor's work can be seen, from family portraits to religious tableaux, to allegorical works.

Kaštelet The same entry ticket for the Meštrović Gallery is also valid here, just down the road at number 39, which Meštrović bought to house one of his most important works, a series of large wooden friezes dedicated to the life of Christ, and which (pre)occupied the sculptor on and off from around 1916 until its completion in 1950.

Klis Just 9km north of Split, on the road to Sinj, are the magnificent monumental ruins of the fortress at Klis (Tvrđava Klis), situated along the length of a 340m hill. It was captured by the Turks in 1537 and remained in their hands for just over a century until the Venetians got their own back in 1648. Today there's not a great deal to see, but the ruins are highly atmospheric and make for a superb picnic spot. Look out also for the trio of informal restaurants that dish up first-rate local lamb simply served with crusty bread. You can reach Klis either by taking the #34 or #36 bus to Klis–Megdan (where you'll find the fortress entrance), or by taking the Sinj bus to Klis–Varoš, and hiking up the hill from there. By car, take the old road from Solin (rather than the new road from Split to Sinj), and turn left at the Tvrđava sign.

Sinj Thirty kilometres out of Split is the town of Sinj, famous mainly as the scene for the annual Sinjska Alka, a festival celebrating the 1715 victory over numerically superior Turks. Taking place on the Sunday before the Feast of the Assumption (15 August), the main feature is a contest in which metal rings suspended on a wire have to be speared at full gallop by chaps in traditional costume. It's all very noisy and

Central Dalmatia SPLIT

8

colourful, and one of only two places where the time-honoured Tilting at the Ring still takes place (the other is in the village of Barban, in Istria – see page 204).

Half-hourly buses from Split will bring you to Sinj in under an hour.

MAKARSKA/BIOKOVO

The 100km or so of coast south of Split, to **Drvenik**, is a long string of pebbly beaches, broken only by the **Cetina Gorge** which cuts through the mountains to emerge at **Omiš**, once home to audacious pirates but now a rather half-hearted resort, given over as much to industry as to tourism. Rafting trips are also possible in the gorge, ask at Omiš tourist information (*Trg Kneza Mislava;* ℅ *021 861 350; www.tz-omis.hr*) for details.

Twenty kilometres beyond Omiš, **Brela** marks the start of the 60km-long **Makarska Riviera**, a series of cheerfully touristy villages and beaches sheltered by the solid mass of **Biokovo** to the northeast. At the heart of it all is Makarska itself, a small but busy town, tastefully restored in stone after the devastating 1962 earthquake. With a lovely palm-studded front and a 2km beach across the Sveti Petar headland, it's a perfect sunny stop if you're travel-weary and footsore. If you don't have sore feet, then Makarska's also the gateway to some of the most spectacular hiking in Croatia, on the Biokovo massif, home to four rare species of eagle (golden, imperial, grey and snake) and culminating in one of the country's highest peaks, Sveti Jure, at 1,762m.

GETTING THERE AND AWAY Without your own wheels, you'll be arriving in Makarska either by bus or ferry. Ferries come in from Sumartin, on the eastern end of Brač, twice a day in winter and five times in summer, while ten daily buses stop in on their way from Split to Dubrovnik, and vice versa. There are direct buses to both Rijeka and Zagreb, twice daily.

WHERE TO STAY AND EAT From the bus station, on Ante Starčevića, the main road running above the town, it's a five-minute walk downhill to the front, where you'll find everything you need. The tourist office (*Kralja Tomislava 16;* ℅ *021 612 002;* f *021 616 288; www.makarska-info.hr*) has maps and information and can put you in touch with any number of agencies handling rooms and excursions – including SB Tours next door (*Kralja Tomislava 15a;* ℅ *021 611 005;* f *021 611 955*) and the Turist Biro (*Kralja Tomislava 2;* ℅ *021 611 688;* f *021 615 352; www.turistbiro-makarska.com*). Private rooms (doubles) go for € 15–30 depending on level of comfort and location, with the usual 30% surcharge for three nights or fewer. The nearest campsite is at **Baško Polje** (℅ *021 612 329*), nearly 10km back up the coast towards Split. Most of the big hotels in Makarska are on the town's long pebble beach, across the headland to the northeast of town.

☖ **Biokovka** (250 rooms) Put Cvitačke 9; ℅ 021 602 287; f 021 612 493; www.biokovka.hr. A little further up the beach from the Meteor is this 3-star, less overtly swanky & quite a bit cheaper. *Dbl* €72–105.
☖ **Biokovo** (55 rooms) Kralja Tomislava; ℅ 021 615 244; f 021 615 081; www.hotelbiokovo.hr. Right on the waterfront in the middle of town. With any number of busy late-night terraces on the Riva below it, you may be glad of the AC & double-glazing. *Dbl* €80–140.

☖ **Meteor** (270 rooms) Kralja Petra Kresimira IV; ℅ 021 602 600; f 021 611 419; www.hoteli-makarska.hr. The triangular front gives most rooms a generous sunny balcony, & the hotel has a good pool. *Dbl* €100–185.
☖ **Porin** (7 rooms) Marineta 2; ℅ 021 613 744; f 021 613 688; www.hotel-porin.hr. Lovely 19th-century building, once the local library, renovated & converted into a hotel in 2002. *Dbl* €75–105.

Makarska has no shortage of eateries along the front, where terraces spill out across the pavement, and slightly cheaper places a block or two back from the sea. There's also an excellent daily market, if you're looking for picnic food, just up from the town's only old square, Kačićev Trg.

WHAT TO SEE AND DO Makarska isn't a place you come to for culture – it's a town with a great beach and even better hiking up in the mountains – so the sights can be comfortably counted off on the fingers of one hand. On Kačićev Trg there's the 18th-century **St Mark's Church** (usually closed), while at the eastern end of town you'll find Croatia's finest **malacological museum** – that's seashells, to you – housed in the cellars of the Franciscan Monastery. The collection of more than 3,000 shells from around the world was put together by one of the Franciscan monks, Jure Radić, and opened in 1963. Radić also founded the botanical gardens in Kotišina (see below).

A couple of kilometres along the coast to the north there's a curious shrine at the **Vepric Cave**. Inaugurated in 1908, on the 50th anniversary of the apparitions in Lourdes, the sanctuary was founded by Bishop Carić (who was buried here on his death in 1921) and dedicated to Our Lady of Lourdes. It is popular with pilgrims, and is especially busy on 11 February, 25 March, 15 August and 7–8 September.

Finally, if you're here in May, don't miss Makarska's spectacular rowing regatta, which proves the town hasn't entirely forgotten its Venetian legacy.

BIOKOVO The Biokovo massif rises up steeply above the Makarska Riviera in three ever more spectacular shelves, providing hiking at all levels and fabulous views, but if you're coming here to head up into the mountains don't underestimate them, and start out as early in the day as you can. The weather can change very quickly, there's no water or food to be had once you're out, and the karst limestone is hard on even the toughest hiking boots. It's highly inadvisable to go out far if you're alone. If you run into trouble, it's unlikely anyone would find you, and – without wishing to sound alarmist – you should remember there are still wolves in the wild up here.

The two main summits reachable from Makarska are **Vošac** (1,420m or thereabouts, and a 3½-hour hike one way) and **Sveti Jure** (1,762m; allow a good 5 hours up and 4 hours back).

There are two paths up out of town leading to Vošac and on to Sveti Jure, one going via the village of **Makar**, and the other via the village of Kotišina. Once you get to either village the trail is well signed with red and white flashes, but pick up a map from the tourist office before you head out.

In either case, start off from Kačićev Trg, pass the church and market, and cross the main road, continuing up **Put Makra** until you reach the next main road, Dubravačka. For the Makar route you should then stay on the continuation of Put Makra until you reach the village. For Kotišina turn right after 200m up Put Mlinica, which leads to the village of **Mlinice**, from which you'll see signs for the path to Kotišina. Both Makar and Kotišina are at around 200m above sea-level and take around 45 minutes to reach on foot from the seafront.

The village of Kotišina was definitively abandoned after the 1962 earthquake, but locals still keep weekenders up here. It's well worth a visit, not just because of the interesting **fortress** built right into the rock here, but also because of the **Botanički Vrt**, the botanical gardens founded by Jure Radić. Radić knew more than anyone about the flora of Biokovo and built the gardens here – more an oversized rockery – as a plant haven. Sadly, since his death in 1990, it has all fallen somewhat into disrepair.

From Makar or Kotišina it's a tough hike to the summit of Vošac, but the views once you get there are absolutely stupendous, way out across the sea and islands. There's a refuge, **Dom Vošac**, at 1,370m, on the way up – five minutes or so off the marked path – but it has been closed for some time; ask at the tourist office for more information. Above the refuge, it's another steep hike to **Sveti Jure**, the highest point on the massif. At the top, there's a little church completely dwarfed by a TV transmitter.

If hiking's not for you, Sveti Jure isn't necessarily out of the question. There's a narrow road that goes up to the summit from Makarska, making for a 30km white-

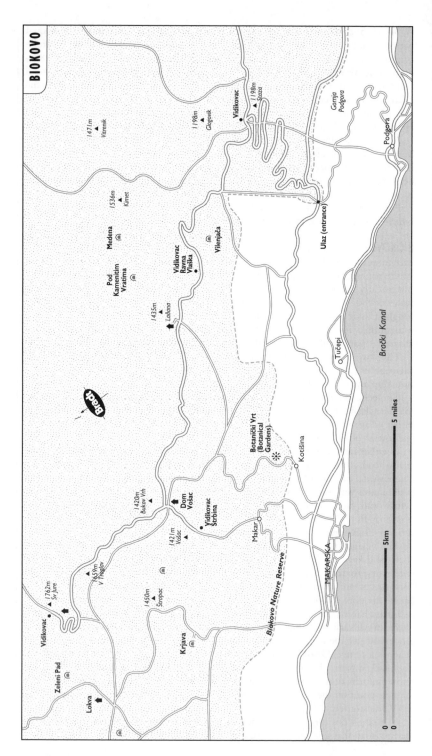

BIOKOVO

Vidikovac

1198m
Staza

Gornja
Podgora

Podgora

1471m
Vitrenik

1198m
Glogovik

1536m
Kimet

Medena

Pod
Kamenitim
Vratima

Vidikovac
Ravna
Vlaška

Vilenjača

Ulaz (entrance)

1435m
Lokva

Tučepi

Brač

Brački Kanal

Botanički Vrt
(Botanical
Gardens)

Kotišina

1420m
Bukov Vrh

Dom
Vošac

Vidikovac
Štrbina

1421m
Vošac

Makar

Biokovo Nature Reserve

MAKARSKA

1762m
Sv Jure

Vidikovac

1659m
V Troglav

1450m
Štropac

Krjava

Zeleni Pad

Lokva

5km

5 miles

0

0

knuckle ride, best performed by jeep and with someone else at the wheel. The road is the highest in Croatia, positively vertiginous, and has no safety barriers.

From Vošac and the road to Sveti Jure, a marked trail heads northwest along Biokovo to **Sveti Ilija** (1,642m), with more wonderful views – but this is further than you'll be able to get in a single day.

For more information on hiking or jeeping up the mountain contact the tourist office or Biokovo Active Holidays (*Gundulićeva 4;* \ *021 679 655;* f *021 679 657;* m *098 225 852; www.biokovo.net*) – especially if you're travelling alone and would like the security of some company on the trail – or see Rudolf Abraham's *Walking in Croatia*.

On the far side of the Biokovo mountains, tucked into the border with Bosnia & Herzegovina, and near **Imotski**, which is on the way to absolutely nowhere (a back road to Mostar or Sarajevo, conceivably), are two typically strange karstic phenomena, the so-called **Crveno Jezero** and **Modro Jezero** (the Red and Blue Lakes).

Each of the lakes was formed by the roof collapsing above a vast cave, and even though they're more than 20km from the sea as the crow flies, and on the wrong side of a major mountain range, the lakes are deep indeed – the bottom of Crveno Jezero is a mere 19m above sea-level, with the lake depth itself varying between 280m and 320m. Modro Jezero, for its part, really is blue. With less steep sides than Crveno Jezero, it's used by local boys for swimming – when there's water in it at all – or as a football pitch when it's dried up.

ŠOLTA

The island of Šolta, easily accessible from Split and right next to the much larger Brač, is something of a mystery. It's pretty, it's wooded, it has old stone hamlets (it even has a couple of prehistoric and Roman ruins, and a sprinkling of medieval monuments), it has appealing coves, beaches and bays, and yet it's somehow off the main tourist map – it sees only around a tenth of the visitors of Brač or Hvar, and most of those check in at the increasingly large apartment complex at Nečujam. Come and stay in one of the 120 or so private rooms on the island and you'll never believe Split's under half an hour away on the catamaran.

Šolta is 20km long but less than 5km wide, and has a local population of under 1,500, mainly in a handful of settlements along the north coast and in the interior. The south coast, a crenulated maze of inlets, coves and tiny bays, is almost entirely uninhabited. Olives, figs, wine production and fishing still drive the part of the economy that isn't fuelled by tourism.

Five ferries a day make the 1-hour crossing to Šolta's port, **Rogač**, all year round. In summer, the frequency more than doubles (depending on demand), and there's also a catamaran service which crosses to Rogač in just 25 minutes. More irregular crossings (aimed mainly at weekenders) are made by both ferry and catamaran in summer to Stomorska, and – by catamaran only – to Nečujam, the two main tourist centres.

Regular ferries and catamarans are met by the bus which connects all the main settlements – if you miss the bus or want to get around the island at other times your options are limited to walking or calling one of the island's two taxi drivers – Dušan Lisičić (\ *099 477 852*) drives a white van; Vladimir Vlak (\ *091 360 3388*) has a white Fiat. You can also get from port to port by local water taxi.

If you are walking, make sure you have plenty of water – it's a hot, dry place. It's around 2km up the hill from Rogač to the administrative centre, **Grohote**, which has a shop and pizzeria, as well as a regular market. From here it's the best part of 8km west, passing by the hamlets of **Srednje Selo** and **Donje Selo**, to the sheltered harbour and beaches at **Maslinica**.

Heading east from Grohote, it's around 7km to the once-upon-a-time village of **Nečujam**, now unashamedly a tourist resort.

ŠOLTA

Stipanska

Polebrnjak

Balkun

Maslinica

Brda
195m ▲

Donje Selo

Sv Mihovil ✝
212m ▲

Srednje Selo

Donja Krušica

Grohote

Rogač

Nečujam

Ferry to
Split

Catamaran to Split

Catamaran to Split

Stomorska

Vela Straža
237m ▲
Gornje Selo

Šolta

5km
3 miles
0
0

Bradt

Also 7km from Grohote, at the foot of the island's high point (Vela Straža, 237m), is the old stone village of **Gornje Selo**, itself 150m above sea-level. There's a paved path from the village to the top of the mountain, where you'll find great views and a large plain concrete crucifix. There are also footpaths down to the south coast, though stock up at the bakery or shop before you head off, as there's nothing on the coast itself.

From Grohote it's a downhill 3km to **Stomorska**, Šolta's other main tourist centre. Stomorska sits at the head of a lovely narrow bay, and although it can get busy (noisy, even) on summer weekends, a short walk along the coastal path in either direction will get you to some lovely little rocky beaches.

WHERE TO STAY There are no campsites on Šolta, so if you're staying here – you could also do a day trip from Split – accommodation is limited to the apartments in the Nečujam Centar, the luxurious new Martinis Marchi, or the much more affordable Villa Šolta.

The **Nečujam apartments** (☎ 021 650 149; f 021 650 153; www.soltaht.hr) are open from May to September, and go for around € 50 (two-person, with terrace) or € 70 (four-person, with balcony) a night at the top of the season – prices halve for May or September. The much more homely **Villa Šolta** in Rogač (☎ 021 654 540; f 021 654 396; www.villa-solta.com) consists of eight rooms and spacious apartments, with doubles going for € 40–50, and a good restaurant.

The island's private rooms can be sourced via the **tourist office** (☎ 021 654 151; f 021 654 130; www.solta.hr), or Šolta Tours (☎/f 021 338 244; www.soltatours.com). You could also try your luck on the spot at the tourist offices in Rogač, Nečujam, Stomorska or Maslinica, but you'd be far more sensible to try and book ahead, especially if you're planning on staying on the island in high summer. Private rooms come in at around € 30 a night for doubles.

BRAČ

Like Šolta, Brač is attractive, hot and sunny, and an easy boat trip from Split – but that's where the similarity ends. Brač is far larger (the third biggest island in the Adriatic, after Krk and Cres) and vastly more popular with tourists. Famous for its white marble – used in Diocletian's palace in Split in antiquity, and more recently in Washington's White House and Berlin's Reichstag – the island today depends mainly on tourism.

Away from the two main centres of Supetar in the north and Bol in the south, however, it's still often deserted, particularly in the mountainous interior, where whole villages have been abandoned to time, but also on the large sections of coast not developed or easily accessible by road.

Twelve car ferries a day run from Split to Supetar, rising to 14 a day in summer, and supplemented in season by catamarans direct to Bol on the southern shore, and catamarans from Split via Milna, on the western end of the island, to Hvar. Car ferries also run four times a day (five in summer) from Makarska to Sumartin, on the eastern tip of Brač. If you're already in Bol, and want to go on to Hvar, there are privately run services across to Jelsa in summer.

Brač also has a small airport, which is used mainly for charter arrivals but receives daily Croatia Airlines flights from Zagreb in summer as well. There's usually (but not always) a shuttle to Bol that meets flights. If you're heading onward to Supetar you'll either have to take a bus from Bol or a taxi direct from the airport.

Supetar is the bus hub, with most destinations served at least three times a day – once in the morning, once around lunchtime, and once in the late afternoon – and with about ten buses a day to Bol. This makes getting anywhere easy from Supetar, but can be a problem if you arrive in Milna or Sumartin and want to move on straight away. The afternoon ferry from Makarska, in particular, doesn't connect with onward transport until the following day. Fortunately people in Sumartin are friendly and will help to find you a room if you need one. Buses from Supetar to Bol run six times a day.

If you haven't got your own wheels and want to give yourself vastly more freedom to explore Brač, then renting transport is the way to go. In Supetar you'll find cycles, scooters and cars for hire, and even motorboats. Hire isn't cheap (though less expensive in Supetar than Bol), but gives you the run of the island, and is the only real way of getting away from the crowds in summer. Ultimately, a cycle or scooter is the best way of getting around, though if you're relying on pedal-power don't underestimate the summer heat or overestimate your fitness – it's a hilly 40km ride from Supetar to Bol.

SUPETAR The chances are you'll arrive in Supetar. A pleasant cluster of stone houses spreads round the harbour, where you'll find everything you need – the tourist office (*Porat 1;* ✆f *021 630 551; www.supetar.hr*), the bus station, and a couple of travel agencies. Atlas (✆ *021 631 105;* f *021 631 088; www.atlas-croatia.com*) or Maestral (✆ *021 631 258;* f *021 631 461; www.travel.maestral.hr*) should be able to fix you up with a private room, arrange excursions, or rent you transport. If you want a car, rather than a cycle or a scooter, it's pretty much essential to call ahead.

The main beaches are west of the town, and being shallow these are good for (and popular with) families. Most of the accommodation here is at the **Waterman Resort** complex (*Put Vele Luke 4;* ✆ *021 640 155;* f *021 631 130; www.watermanresorts.com*), which includes the smaller **Olea** & **Salvia**. Expect to pay around € 160 for sea-view doubles. A very pleasant alternative is the **Villa Britanida** (*Hrvatskih Velikana 26;* ✆ *021 631 038;* f *021 630 017; www.supetar.hr/britanida*), which is 300m east of the port, and features a fine restaurant. Book well ahead as it only has around 20 rooms (€ 58–66 for doubles), and only a few of these face the sea.

An interesting side trip can be made to **Škrip**, the island's oldest settlement and home to the **Museum of Brač**. The hilltop village is inland 3km from **Splitska**, itself 6km east of Supetar, and the museum, housed in a fortified old stone building, gives an interesting glance into the toughness of island life in the past; many of the original residents fled to the USA long ago. The usual three buses a day come up here, and it's a pleasant half- or three-quarter-hour walk back to Splitska if you fancy a swim afterwards. It's a further 4km east along the coast from Splitska to **Lovrečina**, the only sandy beach on Brač. It's no secret, believe me.

On Brač's southwestern corner is the sheltered little port of Milna, around 20km from Supetar on a thrice-daily bus. On your way you might want to come via **Sutivan**, the last settlement on the north coast, which is a charming stone village with access to some good pebble beaches. Private rooms are available through the tourist office (*Blato bb;* ✆ *021 638 357;* f *021 638 134; www.sutivan.hr*).

Milna – the birthplace of 2001 Wimbledon winner Goran Ivanišević – is at the head of a narrow inlet, and one of the nicest places in Brač, within easy reach of beaches that are never too busy. It comes as no surprise to find this once sleepy village now emerging as a favourite with the well-heeled international yachting community. There's the **Illyrian Resort** (✆ *021 636 566;* f *021 636 533; www.illyrian-resort.hr*), which has apartments from € 75–125, and the small **Hotel Milna** (✆ *021 636 116;* f *021 636 550*), which has 25 rooms at around € 100 for doubles, or you can get private rooms through the **tourist office** (✆ *021 636 233;* f *021 636 505; www.milna.hr*).

BOL Brač's biggest draw by far is Bol – or more accurately the extraordinary spit of fine shingle called **Zlatni Rat**, the Golden Cape. Featuring in every Croatian tourist promo, the tip of the south-facing 500m triangular spit shifts west or east depending on the season, and the beach attracts around 50,000 visitors a year. It's not the only place to swim near Bol – the town, sheltered by the mass of **Vidova Gora** behind it, is at the heart of a 15km stretch of beaches – but it's certainly the most popular.

BRAČ

Šumartin

Makarska

Povlja

Selca

Pučišća

Lovrečina

Praznice

Postira

Splitska

Škrip

Nerežišća

SUPETAR

Split

Sutivan

Bobovišća

Milna

Catamaran to Split

Dragon's Cave

Blaca Monastery

Murvica

778m
Vidova Gora ▲

Vidova Gora

Bol

Zlatni Rat

Catamaran to Jelsa

Catamaran from
Split to Jelsa via
Milna and Bol

Bradt

0   5km
0   3 miles

Zlatni Rat is a pleasant half-hour stroll west of Bol, which is a pretty little fishing harbour surrounded by old stone houses. New developments spread up the hill, but the centre itself is compact and charming. It's far too small to accommodate all the people who want to see it, however, so be warned ahead if you're crowd-phobic.

The tourist office (✆ *021 635 638;* f *021 635 972; www.bol.hr*) has a good supply of maps, which you'll find useful if you're planning on hiking up Vidova Gora or west to the Dragon's Cave or Blaca (see below).

Where to stay Accommodation mainly consists of the Bonaca, Borak and Elaphusa resort hotels near Zlatni Rat. There's not much to choose between them – they're all similarly priced (around € 150–170 for a double at the top of the season) and well located – though the Bonaca is popular with families and the Borak's a bit more upmarket than the others. All three can be centrally booked through the Bluesun Hotels company and offer a discount for online bookings (✆ *021 635 210;* f *021 635 150; www.bluesunhotels.com*). There are also a couple of smallish hotels in Bol itself:

Hotel Ivan David 11a; ✆ 021 640 888; f 021 640 846; www.hotel-ivan.com. A lovely stone hotel with a swimming pool & small fitness centre. *Dbl* €120–140.

Kaštil f Radića; ✆ 021 635 995; f 021 635 997; www.kastil.hr. Right on the fishing port, with sea-view rooms. *Dbl* €126 *in season,* €62 *off-season.*

For one of the town's 3,000 beds in private rooms, you'll need to go through an agency – Adria Tours (*Vladimira Nazora 28;* ✆ *021 635 966;* f *021 635 977; www.adria-bol.hr*), More (✆ *021 642 050;* f *021 642 049; www.more-bol.com*) and Bol Tours (✆ *021 635 693;* f *021 635 695; www.boltours.com*) are all in the middle of town (and can also organise the usual excursions and hire). Expect to pay € 40–50 for a double in season, and a surcharge of 20% for three nights or fewer.

What to see and do Once you've had your fill of beach life, one of the best side trips you can make is to head to the top of Vidova Gora. At 778m it's not just the highest point on Brač, but the highest point on any Adriatic island, and the views are terrific – down onto Zlatni Rat far below, and across to the island of Hvar, to the south, and back to the grey karst mountains on the mainland to the north. The easy way up is by road, either with your own wheels or on an excursion, but the most satisfying way to the summit is by hiking up from Bol. It's a good 2½ hours of steady trekking, but it's well worth it – walking boots are recommended. At the top there's a *konoba* that usually opens to coincide with the arrival of excursions.

Another interesting side trip you can make is to the **Dragon's Cave** (Zmajeva Spilja), above the little village of Murvica, to the west of Bol. It's a bit of a mystery as to who carved the wild beasts and mythological creatures here, but they're likely to date back to the 15th century at least. The cave itself is mostly closed – although there's nothing to stop you hiking up and peeking through the bars of the gate – check with the tourist office in Bol before setting off.

Finally, there's the extraordinary **Blaca Monastery**. This is most easily visited on an excursion, though you can get there on your own (but check the opening times at Bol's tourist office) if you have wheels and fancy a hike. There are two routes; either drive to the village of Murvica and walk from there (it's a 6-hour round trip) or get there from the Vidova Gora road – turn right down a gravel track marked Blaca, and leave your car at the start of the marked footpath around 4km further along (this route's a 3-hour round trip).

Set high up under a cliff, the imposing monastery served as a refuge from the 16th century on, and was still inhabited until the last monk, Niko Milčević, died here in 1963. It now houses a curious collection of astronomical instruments, old weapons and watches, and an exceptional library.

HVAR

Smooth, sultry and sexy, Hvar is the undisputed jewel in Croatia's Adriatic crown as far as Europe's cognoscenti and the local smart set are concerned. And indeed, the island, lying south of Brač and stretching finger-like towards the southern end of the Makarska Riviera, is one of the most pleasant in the Adriatic. It has an elegant 16th-century Venetian capital, plenty of beaches and great weather – it boasts 2,700 hours of annual sunshine and averages only eight snowy days a decade. In winter you'll find hotels offering 50% off your room rate for any day on which it rains for more than three daylight hours, and free board and lodging if it goes below freezing during the day.

Not surprisingly, the island is one of the Adriatic's worst-kept secrets – book well ahead if you want to stay in any of the island's hotels at the height of the season when the island is quite literally full. Or simply follow the example of Riccardo Mazzuchelli, the wealthy Italian businessman (and former husband of Ivana Trump, though at Bradt we wouldn't normally stoop to such tabloid gossip), who's bought himself a fabulous villa and grounds on the island. It's also worth looking at the Hvar website, at www.hvar.hr, where you can get advance details on much of the private accommodation across the island.

Hvar town sits at the sheltered south western tip of Hvar, separated from the other main settlements of Stari Grad, Vrboska and Jelsa by the 600m bulk of **Sveti Nikola**, which runs down the spine of the island. Hvar stretches nearly 70km from west to east, but almost everything that happens here happens in the western third, Sućuraj (on the eastern tip) serving only as an arrival point for car traffic on its way in from the Drvenik ferry.

The island's main crop – it won't take you long to work this out from the number of places it's on sale in Hvar – is lavender, which is cultivated in great swathes, and makes a spring break here a real treat. There's also a fair amount of wine made, and the usual crops of figs and olives.

GETTING THERE AND AROUND Arrival on the island is inevitably by ferry or catamaran. The most frequent crossing is also the shortest – it's only 5km (20 minutes) from Drvenik to Sućuraj, and the ferry runs five times a day in winter (up to 11 a day in summer). Count on doing this only if you have your own wheels, however, as the bus heading up the island leaves Sućuraj before 06.00, and only runs three times a week.

Contact the Sućuraj tourist office (*Sućuraj bb;* \f *021 717 288; www.tz.sucuraj.com*) for a smattering of private rooms if you get stuck here – and there are many worse places to spend a day or so, with nice beaches only a short walk from the tiny harbour, and a handful of cheerful cafés, restaurants and shops on hand. It's an option for arrival, with onward travel off the other end of the island. Much more on Sućuraj, including accommodation options, can be found on the cheery local website, www.sucuraj.com.

From Split there's a car ferry two or three times a day, all year round, direct to Stari Grad (actually a few kilometres out of town, but buses to Stari Grad, Jelsa and Hvar meet the ferry), with the frequency increasing substantially in summer. The journey takes a couple of hours. Reserve well ahead in summer on this route if you're coming by car.

The daily catamaran from Split to Vela Luka (on Korčula) and Ubli (on Lastovo) also stops in at Hvar town, and it's only a 50-minute journey from the mainland. The daily car ferry on the same route also stops by (taking 1½ hours from Split), but only twice a week in winter. These services offer you a good onward option for your journey, as both Korčula and Lastovo are compelling destinations in their own right. Note that although the ferry carries cars, you can't disembark at car-free Hvar town – come in through Sućuraj or Stari Grad if you're driving.

In summer there's also a daily catamaran that runs from Split to Jelsa via Bol, on Brač.

HVAR ISLAND

Pelješac

Drvenik

Sučuraj

Zaglav

Bogomolje

Grudac

Catamaran

Poljica

Grapčeva Špilja

Jelsa

Humac

Zečevo

Pitve

Šćedro

Korčula

Vela Luka

Brač

Bol

Glavica
Peninsula

Vrboska

STARI GRAD

Dol

Sv Nikola
628m

Sv Nedilja

Zavala

Catamaran
to Split

Brusje

Milna

HVAR

Rijeka
via Split

Catamaran to
Pescara

Catamaran
to Split

Pescara

Pakleni Islands

Catamaran to Vela Luka

Brodt

10km

6 miles

0

0

Finally, if you are here with your car, especially at the height of the season, plan your departure carefully, as the queues to get off the island can be pretty intimidating.

Public transport is limited to a handful of buses a day between Hvar, Stari Grad, Vrboska and Jelsa, though all incoming ferries are met (and outgoing ferries fed) by the bus network – with the exception of Sućuraj.

HVAR TOWN

Hvar town is Croatia's St Tropez, and one of Dalmatia's most attractive places, rivalling Dubrovnik or Korčula with its Venetian Renaissance charm – though it can get oppressively busy in summer. The heart of the town is the main square, Trg Sveti Stjepana, billed as Dalmatia's largest piazza, which runs east–west from the cathedral to the harbour. To the north of the square is the swanky old quarter, with the palaces of **Grad** sheltering under the 13th-century city walls and overlooked by the fortress on the hill. To the south is the old residential town of **Burg**.

In the early 15th century, Hvar became the wealthiest town in Dalmatia, under Venice, as all ships to and from the republic stopped in here. What you see today, however (barring the mostly original city walls), is uniformly late 16th century, as the Turks razed the town to the ground in 1571.

Where to stay If you're planning to stay in a hotel in Hvar, be prepared to pay the price, which is pretty high in the package hotels spread along the coast (most are within 10–15 minutes on foot), and even higher at one of the four hotels right in town. Count on € 130 a night for a decent double room with a view out of town, and anything from € 200 to € 450 a night in town. Almost every accommodation option in Hvar is owned by (and reserved through) Sunčani Hvar (021 750 750; f 021 750 751; www.suncanihvar.com) – for a summer visit, book as far ahead as you possibly can. Prices for these hotels follow match the examples above.

Adriana (62 rooms) Fabrika; 021 750 200; f 021 750 201; www.suncanihvar.com. The former Adriatic, right on the waterfront, has had a major makeover, including a huge spa, & the rooms have all the facilities you'd expect, including free Wi-Fi/LAN access.

Amfora Majerovica; 021 750 300; f 021 750 301; www.suncanihvar.com. This big, new complex round the shore from the old town has a cascading pool area & Bonj les Bains, an attractive private beach & shore colonnade with facilities including private massage tent, lounge & terrace bar, & sun bed & umbrella hire.

Palace (62 rooms) 021 741 966; f 021 742 420; www.suncanihvar.com. Sitting in a prime location right across from the Arsenal, the appropriately named Palace – actually the converted town hall – has been welcoming guests since 1903. The reception area is built into the original 16th-century loggia, while upstairs there's a fabulous open terrace giving onto the harbour & main square.

Park (15 rooms) Bankete; 021 718 337; f 021 718 355; www.hotelparkhvar.com. One of the few alternatives to the Sunčani hotels is this nice boutique place in the centre of town. Dbl €100–380.

Riva (54 rooms) Riva; 021 750 100; f 021 750 101; www.suncanihvar.com. Near to where the ferry docks, the former Slavija hotel has been done up big time, & if you remember the original then prepare to be blown away by the stunning refurbishment. Croatia's first (& so far only) member of Small Luxury Hotels of the World oozes understated style, & is justifiably proud of its Exclusive Roots restaurant & bar/club.

If the hotel prices have taken your breath away, then you'll probably be looking for a private room. These are handled by the **Pelegrini** and **Mengola** agencies – Pelegrini (021 742 743; f 021 742 250; www.pelegrini-hvar.hr) is close to where the ferry docks; Mengola (/f 021 742 099) is on the little harbour, across the water from the Arsenal and **tourist office** (/f 021 741 059; www.tzhvar.hr). Expect to pay at least € 60 for a one-night stay in a double room during the season; out of season you should be able to do a great deal better than this.

✖ Where to eat and drink What and where you end up eating and drinking in Hvar will depend a great deal on what time of year you're here. In high summer there are dozens of restaurants and even more bars and cafés, and you can pick and choose to some extent – though the fare mostly sticks to the traditional seafood/pasta/pizza variety; hardly surprising, given Hvar's enduring popularity with Italians. Out of season it's a different matter altogether, and when I was here at Easter – notwithstanding the religious festivities going on – there were only two restaurants open in the whole town, and a mere handful of bars. In recent years, some exciting new restaurants have opened for business, and others have upped the ante.

✖ Bounty Pjaca; ✆ 021 742 565. Full marks to this place on the old harbour, which served up the best fish soup I ate in Croatia on that trip, & offered the local Hvar house white wine at an all too reasonable 40kn a litre. In summer of course it's packed out & quite a bit more expensive; but well worth it all the same.

♀ Carpe Diem Hvar Riva; ✆ 021 742 369; www.carpe-diem-hvar.com. Offers one of Croatia's hottest party scenes in summer, with a number of bars to choose from, but the action always inevitably focuses on Carpe Diem, the legendary lounge bar on the waterfront. This is where Zagreb's movers & shakers come to pose & a certain Russian billionaire, popular in the west of London, is said to have been spotted here. Mere mortals can just come along &

enjoy a siesta on the sumptuous outdoor sofas before partying the night away.

✖ Luna Petra Hektorovića; ✆ 021 741 400. More affordable & inventive than Macondo (below), Luna serves up Adriatic dishes. Highlights include the seafood risotto, which bursts with shellfish & first-rate fish soup. The roof terrace can be atmospheric at night, but doesn't have a view.

✖ Macondo Petra Hektorovića; ✆ 021 742 850. Although a firm favourite with the locals, the service can be a bit hit & miss. Generally the seafood is excellent, but very pricey.

✖ Yakša Petra Hektorovića; ✆ 021 717 202. New funky addition to the Hvar restaurant scene using fresh Croatian ingredients with some interesting twists.

What to see and do The main sights are on or near the main square. The **cathedral** (actually a church, but let's not be pedantic) with its Renaissance trefoil façade is attractive enough (and the campanile, with its increasing number of windows on each storey, is lovely), but nothing particularly special inside, barring a fine 13th-century Madonna and Child, in striking contrast to the morbidly graphic Baroque paintings on the other altars. Check out the modern main doors, the work of the sculptor Kuzma Kovačić, the man also behind the design on Croatia's kuna and lipa coins. (If you're around on Maundy Thursday, just before Easter, don't miss the religious processions around the island, maintaining a 500-year-old tradition. The festivities reach a climax on Easter Monday, when the six big crosses from the island's main settlements are paraded around town.)

Also on the main square is the great hulk of the **Arsenal** – unusual indeed amongst naval buildings in having a theatre upstairs, and especially so in this case, as it was one of the first in the western world open to all comers. The **theatre** was built in 1612, as you can see by the inscription outside saying '*Anno Secundo Pacis MDCXII*' – the peace referred to here was the ending of the century-long spat between commoners and nobs throughout the 16th century, following the 1510 uprising by Matija Ivanić, when 19 men were hanged from galley masts here.

Access to the theatre is through an adjoining **art gallery**, which has highly variable temporary exhibitions from Croatian artists. The theatre itself is charming, with just 86 seats and 28 pint-sized boxes, and is finally benefiting from long-awaited restoration.

On the other side of the square, dominating the main town gate, you'll find the so-called **Hektorović Palace**, an ornate but unfinished Venetian Gothic building, unroofed and overgrown since the 15th century. The so-called palace pre-dates the famous poet, in fact – and a more fitting memorial can be seen at his actual palace in Stari Grad.

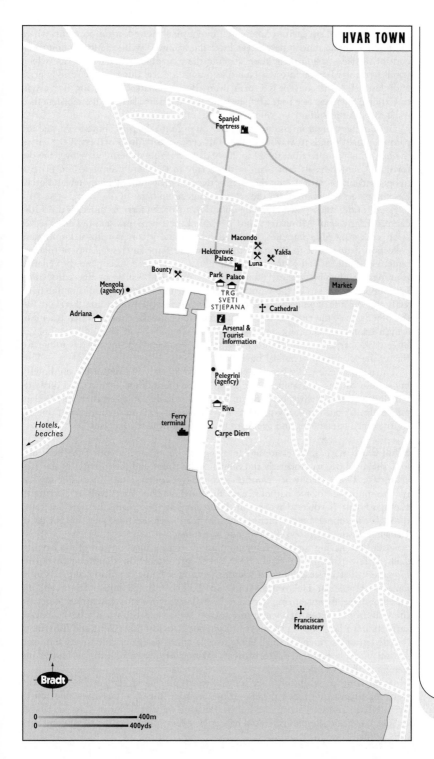

HVAR TOWN

Španjol Fortress

Macondo

Hektorović Palace

Yakša

Luna

Bounty

Park Palace

Mengola (agency)

TRG SVETI STJEPANA

Cathedral

Adriana

Market

Arsenal & Tourist information

Pelegrini (agency)

Riva

Hotels, beaches

Ferry terminal

Carpe Diem

Franciscan Monastery

Bradt

0   400m
0   400yds

303

Up the stepped street from here you'll find a small **Benedictine convent**, where the few remaining nuns – they never leave the hallowed walls, and are bound to an oath of silence – spend their hours making the extraordinarily intricate lace which you'll find for sale around town (you'll know it's the real thing by the serious price tags). Just below the convent is a small, plain church, remarkable only for the portrait of Cardinal Stjepinac (see page 109), bearing an even more alarming resemblance than usual to Vladimir Putin.

Continuing straight up the street brings you out into the park above town, and the path eventually winds its way up to the 16th-century **Španjol Fortress** at the top of the hill, which is open from 09.00 to 20.00 daily. With a wonderful view over the old town and across the Pakleni islands – especially in the early evening – the place is understandably popular. Inside the fortress there's a collection of amphorae and other bits and pieces fished out from the sea and dragged up here.

South of the town (just follow the quay down past the ferry terminal) is the 15th-century **Franciscan Monastery**. Just two monks live here now, and the place serves as an endearing little museum, with old oil jars and a comprehensive numismatic collection dating back to Roman times. There are some interesting bits of modern sculpture (some of it by one of the monks) and a collection of mostly Venetian paintings. The biggest of these, taking up most of an end wall, is an especially rowdy Last Supper. It's said to be the work of a Venetian painter who was in quarantine here, with only a cat for company – the cat's on the left and the painter's on the right. On the other side of the cloisters is a curious and rather spooky church, which is a bit of a mish-mash architecturally, but has good 16th-century choir stalls and a couple of huge dark altarpieces by Leandro Bassano. Look out amongst the various tombs for that of the local writer Hanibal Lučić (1485–1553).

There are several rocky beaches close to town (notably in front of the big hotels), but serious bathers will want to take a trip out to the **Pakleni Islands**, just offshore, which is where all the best beaches can be found (you'll be told that the name Pakleni means 'devils', but it actually refers to the pine resin). Pick up information from the tourist office (see above), and get there by taxi-boat from the harbour.

STARI GRAD Stari Grad, set around an elongated horseshoe harbour at the head of a long sheltered bay, was formerly the capital of the island, and the location of the 4th-century BC Greek colony of Pharos (the name Hvar comes from Pharos). The town is on the south side of the harbour, with the northern shore occupied by a string of package hotels. If you're driving from Hvar there are two roads, the new fast route through the tunnel, or the picturesque old road over the hills, past the village of **Brusje**. Take the high road if you're not in a rush.

With little having survived from antiquity (barring a small section of the original walls, a few paving slabs, and some Greek gravestones in the museum at the monastery), head instead for the **Tvrdalj**, the summer house of one of Dalmatia's most famous poets, Petar Hektorović (1487–1572). The fortified house has undergone numerous facelifts since being started in 1520, but features interesting inscriptions on the walls from Hektorović's work, in Croatian, Italian and Latin, and a heavy cloister surrounding a fishpond – a memorial to the poet's love of fish, fishing and fishermen.

The rest of the town is a small but agreeable hodge-podge of little streets and small squares, though there is a **Dominican Monastery** to visit, with an interesting museum off the cloisters.

If you want to get out of town, it's well worth picking up the good local booklet from the tourist office that details various walks in the area, including ones up to Svete Nikola and to Glavica, the hill overlooking the town. You can also rent bikes in Stari Grad, and the cycling round here is excellent, with quite flat terrain and very little traffic.

Where to stay and eat Tourist information (*Nova Riva 2;* \f *021 765 763; www.stari-grad-faros.hr*) is on the harbour, while private rooms can be arranged through **Mistral Tours** (\ *021 765 281;* f *021 395 851*), right where the bus stops. One recommendation is Karla (*Lučićeva 13;* \ *091 517 9126*), right in the old town, with doubles at € 20–30 and a nice roof terrace overlooking the town.

Hotel accommodation is across the bay in package hotels, including the **Lavanda**, the **Arkada** and the **Helios** (*for all,* \ *021 765 866;* f *021 765 128; www.heliosfaros.hr*), which do reasonable doubles with views for around € 110. There are plenty of places to eat and drink, but **Bar Antique**, in the old town comes highly recommended – for breakfast, lunch or dinner.

JELSA AND SURROUNDINGS

The small town of **Jelsa** – mostly modestly 19th-century, sitting on a pretty port – is today somewhat dwarfed by the hotel complexes on either side. Nonetheless it's an attractive place in itself, surrounded by pine forests and giving easy access to a number of beaches, including by taxi-boat to the best ones on the Glavica peninsula, and across to the naturist island of **Zečevo**. Some of Hvar's cool crowd are increasingly looking towards Jelsa, which has an ever-improving range of bars and restaurants.

Jelsa also offers one of the very few routes across the island to the south coast. You'll need wheels, as the route winds 4km up to the old village of **Pitve** before entering the **Vratnik** gorge, and a long tunnel, which comes out above the village of Zavala (around 7km from Pitve).

Zavala itself is a tiny fishing village, but it does have an excellent place to stay, the **Villa Stella Mare** (\ *021 767 128;* f *021 718 133; www.stellamare.hr*). A total of seven apartments go for around € 80 apiece per night in season, and the friendly staff can even rent you a bike, a scooter or a boat if you want to explore the deserted coves and beaches along Hvar's south coast.

Three kilometres offshore is the island of **Šćedro**. Protected since 1972, the island doesn't see many visitors (the occasional sailing boat and motor cruiser), and has a resident population of just one. It makes for a lovely day trip from Zavala (or Jelsa), with its dense woods, sheltered inlets, and the remains of a 15th-century monastery.

From Jelsa it's only a 45-minute walk west along the coast path (or a short taxi-boat ride away) to **Vrboska**, a charming old village set along both sides of an inlet. Stone bridges connect the two halves, which are dominated by the fortified 16th-century **Church of St Mary**, built after the Turks destroyed the place in 1571. You can climb up to the battlements for a nice view over the village.

East of Jelsa, Hvar becomes very empty indeed, and although there's plenty to explore if you have your own wheels, it's pretty much impossible otherwise. You can, however, get yourself on an organised tour from Jelsa to **Grapčeva Spilja**, an ancient cave complex with excellent stalactites and stalagmites, just south of the semi-abandoned hamlet of Humac. Ask at the Jelsa **tourist office** (\f *021 761 017; www.tzjelsa.hr*).

Practicalities Hotel accommodation in Jelsa is almost exclusively at the resort complexes which include the **Fontana**, the **Jadran** and the **Pinus** (*for all,* \f *021 761 810; www.hoteli-jelsa.hr*), with doubles at around € 80. Private rooms, however, are in good supply and considerably cheaper here than in Hvar town, and can be booked through Atlas (\f *021 761 605*), just up from the tourist information office. There is also the nice little family run **Pansion Murvica** (*Sv Roka;* \f *021 761 405; www.murvica.net*), near the bus station, with doubles for € 36–48. There are also some private rooms available in Vrboska – contact the Vrboska **tourist office** (\ *021 774 137;* f *021 717 255; www.vrboska.info*) for more details.

VIS

The lovely hilly island of Vis is Croatia's farthest flung possession, and also its oldest recorded settlement, having been colonised by the Greeks (from Syracuse, on Sicily) at the beginning of the 4th century BC. The colony of Issa then went on to found its own colonies (notably at Trogir and Salona) before succumbing to Roman rule, and following much the same historical fate as most of the rest of Dalmatia – Venetians, Austrians, the French, Austrians again, and then Yugoslavia – with the notable exception that Vis was also a British possession, from 1811 to 1814.

The British came back here in 1944, when the island was briefly Tito's headquarters – after the war, when Vis was Yugoslavia's naval staff headquarters, the only foreigners allowed on the island for decades were British veterans, who came back every September for their annual reunion.

Since 1989, Vis has been open for business, and tourism, while still relatively low-key, is growing by around 30% annually. Today the island is often seen simply as the jumping-off point for trips to the famous **Modra Špilja** ('Blue Cave') on nearby **Biševo**, but it's well worth visiting in its own right.

Vis has no freshwater sources, apart from a few springs near Komiža – water has to be brought in during the summer months by ship and stored in cisterns – so don't expect to be able to fill up here if you're sailing; head instead for Hvar and Korčula. The lack of water, however, doesn't stop the locals making excellent wine in great quantities, notably the red Plavac, and the dry (but sweet-scented) white Vugava.

The capital, Vis town, is in a sheltered inlet on the spectacular north side of the island (the cliffs at Gradac, nearby, rise 100m out of the sea), while Komiža, in a large bay facing west, is the other main settlement, closer to the island of Biševo.

Ferry schedules make Vis an unlikely day trip, unless you take an all-in excursion from the coast or one of the other nearby islands, and you should be warned that outside the summer months the 2½-hour ferry journey from Split can be a truly stomach-churning one. On the other hand if the weather's fine and the sea's calm, this is one journey where you're quite likely to see dolphins alongside the boat.

Two or three ferries a day come from Split all year round, stopping twice a week in Hvar, while in summer there's also a daily hydrofoil, which takes around 1½ hours from Split. Twice-weekly trans-Adriatic ferries from Ancona stop here in summer, along with twice-weekly hydrofoils from Pescara. Don't even think about trying to bring your car here in summer – rent a scooter or mountain bike on the island.

Public transport on Vis consists of the bus that meets the ferry and goes over to Komiža, a fairly spectacular half-hour (18km) ride. There's also a 10km track connecting the two towns, making for a pleasant 2½-hour walk, or a great hour on a mountain bike.

VIS TOWN Ferries arrive in Vis town, the diminutive capital, which consists of Luka to the west and Kut to the east, though the whole place is a ten-minute walk end-to-end, leading to the famous local quip, 'Vis town ain't big enough for the both of us'. The **tourist office** (❍ *021 717 017;* f *021 717 018; www.tz-vis.hr*) has some local information and maps, while Ionios (❍f *021 711 532*) is the place to go to rent bikes and scooters – a wonderful way of seeing the island.

There's not much to see in the way of Greek and Roman heritage, though the **Issa Museum** has a few treasures on show, including the famous 4th-century BC bronze head of a Greek goddess. They also have a useful leaflet detailing the sites of local ruins, though there isn't that much to see on the ground – the remains of the Greek cemetery and walls are really just vestiges, while what was once the Roman theatre has been firmly overbuilt by a Franciscan Monastery.

More immediately evocative – especially to students of English history – are the remains of the imperial forts. Head past the Hotel Issa and up the headland to the

VIS

ruins of the **Wellington Fort**, and on further to the even more dilapidated **King George III Fort**.

🏠 **Where to stay and eat** The **Issa** (*Apolonija Zanelle 5;* ☎ *021 711 124;* f *021 711 740*) and the **Tamaris** (*Obala Sv. Jurja 30;* ☎ *021 711 350;* f *021 711 349*) hotels are priced identically, with high-season doubles at around € 60, and while the 27 rooms at the older Tamaris, in the middle of town, are considerably nicer than the 130-odd at the newer Issa, the latter does have the advantage of being right on the beach. Both hotels are closed from the end of October to the beginning of May; in the shoulder months, off-season, the price of doubles plummets to a very reasonable € 35 – about the same as you'd expect to pay for a private room in town (available through the Ionios agency). An alternative is the ten-room **San Giorgio** (*Hektorovića 2;* ☎ *021 711 362;* f *021 717 501; www.hotelsangiorgiovis.com*), a small boutique hotel, originally the Paula, but newly renovated and rebranded. Doubles here go for € 150–240.

The town's best restaurant is unquestionably the rather swanky **Villa Kaliopa** (*Vladimira Nazora 32;* ☎ *021 711 855*), situated in the gardens of the fine 16th-century Renaissance Garibaldi Palace – it's pricey, but excellent, and increasingly popular with well-heeled Italians. They don't take credit cards.

Plainer and more inexpensive fare is available at half a dozen other restaurants and pizzerias.

KOMIŽA AND BIŠEVO Komiža, at the other end of the island, is a strong rival for Vis. Set under the bulk of Hum Mountain (587m), the town stretches in a lovely palm-studded sweep round the bay, and has plenty of appealingly run-down 16th- and 17th-century houses, as well as a fine 16th-century Venetian fortress, dominating one end of the harbour.

Behind the town, up the hill, is the austere fortified Benedictine **Monastery of St Nicholas**. On the saint's feast day, 6 December, the local fishermen drag a fishing boat up here and then set fire to it, in a display that certainly has nothing whatsoever to do with pagan rites.

Komiža's **tourist office** (*Riva Sv Mikule 2;* ✆/f *021 713 455; www.tz-komiza.hr*) can fill you in on local sights, while Srebrna Tours (*Ribarska 6;* ✆ *021 713 668;* f *021 717 840; www.srebrnatours.hr*) and Darlić & Darlić (*Riva Sv Mikule 13;* ✆ *021 713 760;* f *021 713 206; www.darlic-travel.hr*) have private rooms for around € 35. The town's only hotel, the **Biševo** (✆ *021 713 297;* f *021 713 098; www.hotel-bisevo.com*), has a handful of pleasant rooms overlooking a pebble beach, and is open all year round. High-season doubles go for around € 90, but from October to May you pay not much more than half this.

Eating and drinking go on around Komiža's attractive main square, Škor, which is home to a handful of bars, cafés and restaurants.

Modra Špilja
No trip to Vis seems to be complete without the obligatory visit to Modra Špilja cave, on the island of Biševo, 5km southwest of Vis (the island is now uninhabited, though families still tend the vines here, travelling back and forth by boat). And indeed, if you get there at the right time of day (between 11.00 and midday), and you have a moment in the cave to yourself, then it is surely one of the most beautiful sights on the planet. Sunlight filters down through the water and reflects off the pale sea-floor, giving a vibrant blue and turquoise shimmer to the cave. It's an absolutely incredible place to swim, especially if you've brought along a snorkel and mask.

Unfortunately, that's not the experience most people have. Out of season, access to the cave is often made impossible by choppy seas, while in July and August, on calm days, the cave gets almost as crowded as its namesake on Capri, and you'll be briskly ferried out to make room for the next boatload coming in.

The cave was discovered – and the entrance enlarged to allow boats in and out – in the 1880s. You can access the cave most easily via an excursion from either Vis or Komiža, though you can also easily charter your own boat. If you go, make sure you're wearing swimmers, and have a snorkel and mask if at all possible – even if your time in the cave is short you should have time for a quick dip. Excursions usually then take you on to one of Biševo's many coves and beaches, and often feature the obligatory fish picnic.

Finally, spare a thought while you're here for the terribly endangered Mediterranean monk seal, the world's rarest pinniped; the islet of Brusnik, off to the west, near Svetac, is one of the very few places where it's recently been sighted. Brusnik is also home to a charming endemic species of black lizard, *Podarcis melisellensis melisellensis*.

9

Southern Dalmatia

Telephone code 020 (+385 20 from abroad)

The biggest draw in southern Dalmatia is the extraordinary walled city of Dubrovnik, but the area is unusually rich in other sights as well, and – in spite of the Adriatic's cleanest waters – there are fewer resorts and package destinations here than further north. The islands range from the quiet Elaphites (Koločep, Lopud and Šipan) and the near-perfection of Mljet (most of which is a national park), to popular Korčula, remote Lastovo, and Dubrovnik's own back garden, Lokrum. Onshore there's the long, straggly wine-growing peninsula of Pelješac, with oyster-rich Ston at its base, while against the Bosnian border you'll find the wetlands of the Neretva Delta.

DUBROVNIK

Dubrovnik is an extraordinary place. Vast walls, up to 25m tall, come complete with fortresses, towers, crenellations and an ancient footpath along the entire 2km extent. The walls encircle an incredible stone-built red-roofed city, which juts out into the clearest, cleanest blue-green waters of the Adriatic. The streets are paved with time-polished pale marble, with the town's harmony owing as much to the 17th-century rebuilding programme following the Great Earthquake in 1667 as it does to Dubrovnik's remarkable history, stretching back well over 1,000 years.

Of course Byron's 'Pearl of the Adriatic' is no secret, with nearly half a million people a year staying at least one night, and even more coming in for the day on 440-odd foreign cruise ships every year. Nevertheless the city copes admirably with the influxes, and you'll find a place full of cheerful cafés, bars and restaurants, wonderful

---

A NOTE ON CROSSING BOSNIA & HERZEGOVINA

Southern Dalmatia is cut off from the rest of Croatia by Bosnia's land corridor to the sea, and while for most visitors (see page 30 for visa requirements) this isn't a problem, for some nationals it will mean getting a Bosnian visa – which is a serious hassle if this is all you need it for (it's not unknown for your passport to be sent to Sarajevo). If you're travelling by bus and don't plan on stopping in Bosnia, then you don't really need a visa as you can plead your transit case with the guards who board the bus – in the worst case you'll have to go around, via Pelješac (see page 355), but I've never known the guards to insist on this.

If you're driving yourself, however, you do in theory need a visa (I have met people who've winged it successfully, but it's not recommended). Safer by far, and completely legitimate, is to get round the Bosnian section of road altogether by taking a ferry from Ploče to Trpanj (on Pelješac) and continuing south from there – though it does add at least a couple of hours to your journey. When the motorway is open this particular hassle will be a thing of the past.

SOUTHERN DALMATIA

MONTENEGRO

BOSNIA & HERZEGOVINA

Adriatic Sea
(Italian waters)

Bari

New Motorway 2008/9

Neretva
Delta

Metković

Drvenik

Sućuraj

Hvar

Stari Grad

Ščedro

Ploče

Duba
Trpanj
Orebić

Lovište

Korčula

Čara

Blato

Vela Luka

Proizd

Korčula

Lumbarda

Pelješac

Summer only

Trstenik

Ston

Neum
(Bosnia)

Elaphites
ferry

Catamaran

Sobra

Polače

Pomena

Mljet

Lastovo

Ubli

Lastovo

Catamaran & ferry

Slano

Šipanska Luka

Sudurad

Šipan

Lopud

Lopud

Koloćep

Koloćep

New Bridge

DUBROVNIK

Lokrum

Cavtat

Čilipi

20km
10 miles

0
0

Bradt

architecture, intriguing museums, atmospheric churches and a world-famous summer festival. The entire old city is a UNESCO World Heritage Site.

As if that weren't enough, Dubrovnik is blessed with an especially kind climate. Winter daily maximums rarely fall below 12°C, the sun shines reliably right through the summer, and there are plenty of beaches, with swimming popular from May to October. The city even has its own perfect forested island, Lokrum, just a few hundred metres offshore.

HISTORY Although some Roman, Illyrian and early Christian remains have been found in Dubrovnik, it was only at the beginning of the 7th century that the area was permanently settled. Survivors from the Roman colony at Salona (near Split), which had been taken over by avaricious Avars, teamed up with the remnants of the colony at Epidaurus (now Cavtat), which had been ravaged by Slavs, and settled on the rocky outcrop which is now the part of the old town south of Stradun. Doubtless scarred by their recent experiences, they started building fortifications right away – and kept on doing so until the 16th century. They called their town Ragusa, which first shows up in print in the year 667.

Slavs, meanwhile, settled on the lower slopes of Mount Srđ, across the marshy channel that would become Stradun. Over the centuries the populations mixed, the channel was filled in, and the city walls grew to encompass both parts of the settlement. But even today there's a clear distinction between the steep narrow streets leading uphill from Stradun to the north and the palaces and churches and open squares that characterise the rest of the city to the south. To their dying day (which we'll get to in a little while) Ragusan patricians insisted they could trace their lineage back to Roman rather than Slav ancestors.

After switching between Byzantium and Venice and back again, and even throwing in its lot with the Normans on a couple of occasions at the end of the 11th century, Ragusa finally recognised that Venice was top dog in the Adriatic in 1205, and remained under Venetian sovereignty until 1358. It nonetheless kept its own currency and continued to develop its own institutions and culture.

Ragusa was also becoming a trading state of increasing importance, capitalising on its fortunate position between north and south and east and west. By the early 13th century favourable trading agreements were in place with many of the Italian city

WHAT'S IN A NAME?

For most of its extensive history – right from the 7th century through to 1918, in fact – Dubrovnik was known as Ragusa. The name was changed to Dubrovnik (according to Rebecca West, at least) only because Ragusa sounded too Italian by half.

The truth, as usual, is somewhat more complicated. Dubrovnik was originally not one place but two, divided by what's now the main street, Stradun. On the seaward side, which was originally almost an island, was Ragusa, which was populated by people of Roman origin. On the landward side, populated by Slavs, was Dubrovnik. Given that the nobles all came (or claimed to come) from Roman stock, Ragusa was the name which stuck – until the city was incorporated into the newly founded Kingdom of Serbs, Croats and Slovenes after World War I.

The name Ragusa is thought to be a corruption of the Greek word *lausa*, meaning rock, while the name Dubrovnik comes from the Croatian word for oak woods, *dubrava* – which were once plentiful on the hills above the town before being cut down and used to build Dubrovnik's impressive fleet of ships. (A fleet of ships that gave us another word, incidentally – argosy, a variant on the name Ragusa.)

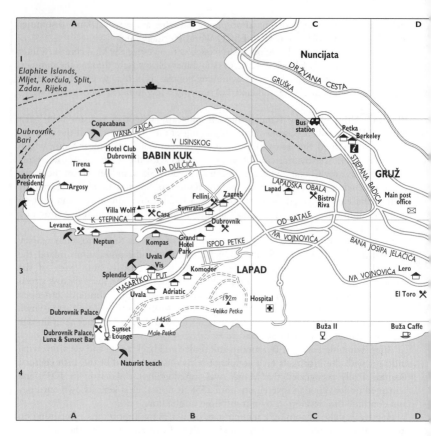

states and far inland into the Balkans. Over the years it developed a strong seafaring tradition, with trade routes eventually established all the way to Spain, Portugal and England. Dubrovnik sailors were even on board Columbus's ships when they discovered the West Indies in 1492.

Back at home the early 14th century saw a number of important developments. After a huge fire destroyed most of the city in 1296, a new urban plan was developed. Dominicans and Franciscans were allowed inside the city walls for the first time, on condition that they defended the two main land gates at either end of Stradun – where you'll still find their respective monasteries and churches today.

The city's first hospital was inaugurated in 1347, but all too quickly followed in 1348 by a seriously nasty dose of the plague, which reduced the population by 8,000. Soon, however, Dubrovnik was ready for its 'Golden Age', which began when it escaped Venice's grasp in 1358 by formally becoming part of the Hungarian–Croatian kingdom. In exchange for paying Hungary 500 ducats a year, however, and providing armed forces when called upon to do so, the republic was allowed to do pretty much whatever it liked.

The first thing it liked to do, it seemed, was to frogmarch the Venetian rector, Marco Saranzo, off on to his state galley, thereby kicking off the best part of 500 years of tension between the two republics – a situation only resolved when Napoleon dissolved La Serenissima in 1797.

In 1365, just seven years after sorting things out with Hungary, Dubrovnik signed a treaty with Sultan Murat I – again with a 500-ducat-per-year price tag – which allowed the republic free-trading status across the whole of the occupied territories of the

Ottoman Empire. By monopolising large chunks of the trade to and from the interior, Dubrovnik became hugely wealthy. Dubrovnik had freedom, liberty and independence – but it was Libertas (the republic's long-standing motto) bought with gold.

With money came territory, and during the Golden Age Dubrovnik's lands stretched from the town of Neum to the north (now in Bosnia) all the way to Sutorina, on the Bay of Kotor, to the south (now in Montenegro), a distance of around 120km. It included the Elaphite Islands (Koločep, Lopud and Šipan), the islands of Mljet and Lastovo, and the Pelješac peninsula.

At the beginning of the 15th century the remaining wooden houses in the town were demolished and rebuilt in stone. This was not so much for aesthetic reasons as to prevent fires from spreading. With many potential enemies, Dubrovnik had large stockpiles of munitions, and they had an unfortunate habit of going off – the Rector's Palace was destroyed by fire and explosions twice within a generation, in 1435 and then again in 1463.

The 15th century also saw Dubrovnik flourishing as a haven of liberalism. It offered asylum to refugees, including Jews, at times when many other cities turned them away at the gate. In 1416 slavery was definitively abolished, over 400 years ahead of Britain (1833) and America (1863). Many slaves subsequently had their freedom bought for them by Ragusan nobles. A public health service was in place as early as 1432, while the principle of education for all was established three years later, along with one of Europe's first orphanages and a free retirement home for the poor and elderly (it's still running, but no longer free).

The republic's wealth was also put to good use in a major building programme. The city walls were reinforced and defensive fortresses and towers constructed along their length. Onofrio della Cava, a bright engineer and architect from Naples, spent the six years to 1444 putting in place a sophisticated water supply (including an 8km aqueduct) which still works today and powers the two Onofrio Fountains on Stradun. In 1468 Stradun itself was repaved with marble, and in 1516 work began on the Customs House (formerly called the Divona and now known as the Sponza Palace).

Unfortunately an earthquake destroyed most of the city in 1520, and the plague returned in force in 1528, leaving 20,000 dead.

By the end of the 1520s, the Turks had pretty much defeated Hungary, and Dubrovnik was quick to change its allegiance from the Hungarian king to the Turkish sultan – now agreeing to pay an annual tribute of 12,500 ducats to keep the peace (that's inflation for you). The money was taken to the Sublime Porte every two years by envoys who then had to spend the next two years waiting there as effective hostages until they were relieved by the next cash-laden delegation.

In 1588 Dubrovnik joined the Spanish in their 'Invincible Armada' and lost a dozen of its finest ships. As a result, trade with Britain was interrupted for the best part of two centuries. The battle neatly marks the beginning of the long, slow decline of the republic. New trade routes across the Atlantic made Britain, Spain and Portugal into wealthy nations, and Mediterranean shipping was never to regain its former importance.

Real disaster didn't strike, however, until 08.00 on 6 April 1667, the Saturday before Easter, when a massive earthquake destroyed Dubrovnik. More than 5,000 people – including the rector, the entire Minor Council and more than half the Great Council – were killed. Only the Sponza Palace, the two monasteries, the bottom half of the Rector's Palace and the Revelin Fortress were left standing.

Seizing his opportunity, the Turkish sultan asked for a vast ransom to be paid if Dubrovnik wanted its freedom to continue as before. A delegation was sent in 1673 to the Porte to… well, 'talk turkey' with the Turks. Among the party were Nikola Bono and Marojica Koboga. Bono was to die in prison, but after the Turks were defeated at Vienna in 1683, Koboga came home to a hero's welcome. Dubrovnik had got away without paying the ransom, and was still free. It consolidated its position in 1699 by letting the Turks have chunks of land at either end of its territories – which is why today Neum is in Bosnia not Croatia, and Sutorina is in Montenegro. This meant that potential attacks from Venice could now only come from the sea and not overland.

Although Dubrovnik would never regain its former glories, the massive programme of rebuilding which went on through the early 18th century was to deliver the harmonious city you see today. Things started to look up for the republic, and by the end of the 18th century it had regained a considerable amount of its wealth and standing, and even boasted some 80 consulates in various cities across the continent.

Unfortunately, however, Napoleon was on the horizon, and on 26 May 1806 – as the only way to break a month-long siege by Russian and Montenegrin forces – the republic allowed a French garrison to enter the town. (Even now, clocks in the city's museums are often set to 17.45, the hour at which the troops entered the city.) Once installed, the French didn't leave, and on 31 January 1808 the republic was finally abolished. The following year it was absorbed into the newly created French 'Illyrian Provinces', which stretched all the way up the Adriatic coast to Trieste.

When Napoleon was defeated, Austria sent troops south and took control of Dubrovnik in 1814. Dubrovnik's noble families, in a terminal huff, took a vow of celibacy and swiftly died out. A century later Dubrovnik became part of Yugoslavia, but when Yugoslavia fell apart the city came under siege (see box on page 316).

GETTING THERE AND AWAY With no train line, you'll most likely be arriving by plane, boat or bus, or in your own car.

Ragusa's political system was a variant on that of its rival Venice, though it was somewhat more subtle and complex. The main governing body was the Great Council, which consisted of all the male nobles over the age of 20; their main function was to elect the head of state, the rector, and supervise the Senate. The Senate comprised 45 nobles over the age of 40, though it had a purely consultative mandate. From the Senate, five men over the age of 50 were given a one-year term by the Great Council as Proveditores, keepers of the legal statutes and the constitution.

Executive power was wielded by the Minor Council, which consisted of 11 nobles appointed by the rector, with the youngest taking on the role of Foreign Minister. The rector had a term of office of just one month, during which he lived alone in the Rector's Palace, separated from his family and the rest of society. He was only allowed to leave the palace on state business or to attend church, and couldn't be re-elected within two years. In spite of all these restrictions he was merely a figurehead, wielding no power.

The political system was designed to concentrate power into the hands of a trusted few – in the 15th century there were only 33 noble families – but to avoid any one person or family being able to dominate, and for centuries it worked remarkably effectively.

The class system was rigidly enforced. Inter-marriage between classes was forbidden and social relations between them strongly discouraged – though that doesn't seem to have been necessary, given the divisions even within classes. The nobles defined themselves as Salamancans or Sorbonnais, named after the respective Spanish and French universities, with the former sympathetic to Spanish Absolutism and the latter with a liberal Francophile outlook. Apparently hostility was such that members of the two factions couldn't even bring themselves to greet one another in the street.

Čilipi Airport is about 20km/half an hour south of town, and there's an airport shuttle that coincides with arriving flights. It returns to the airport from the Dubrovnik bus station 1½ hours before Croatia Airlines and Austrian Airlines departures, 2 hours before other regular flights, and costs 35kn. Taxis (✆ 20 970; www.taxi-dubrovnik.hr) cost around 200–250kn – if the meter's off make sure you've agreed and understood the fare with the driver before you set off.

All ferries come in to the city's port, Gruž, which is about 500m north of the bus station, itself just over 2km north of the old town (catch a local bus). There are also an increasing number of cruises featuring Dubrovnik; these too will bring you into Gruž harbour.

Long-distance buses come straight to the bus station (*Put Republike 19;* ✆ *060 305 070 or 020 357 020*), past the port. If you're coming from the north you'll have driven over the fabulous, spanking-new suspension bridge over the Dubrovačka Rijeka inlet, which cuts a welcome 15km off the journey. From one side you'll notice it labelled as the Tuđman Bridge, while from the other it's the Dubrovnik Bridge – telling you something useful about local politics. There's one direct bus a day from Frankfurt and Trieste, two from Sarajevo, eight buses a day from Zagreb, and 15 from Split. The bus station has Dubrovnik's only left-luggage facility, open from 04.30 to 21.00 daily.

If you're coming in by car, be warned that parking in Dubrovnik can be both a problem and expensive. Hotel car parks tend to be overflowing, while street parking, especially in summer, is a non-starter. There are two main car parks for the old town, one at the Pile Gate (10kn an hour) and the other alongside the north wall (5kn an hour), though both fill up fast. There's a larger car park at Gruž harbour (5kn an hour), which also offers a long-term rate of 25kn a day, and the huge new 24-hour car park at Ilijina Glavica (Zagrebačka ulica); there's a bus from there to the Pile Gate.

If you park illegally you can definitely expect your car to be towed away by the ruthlessly efficient 'Sanitat Dubrovnik' tow away service. The number to call when this happens is ☏ 020 331 016, 24 hours a day, and the pound, where your car will have been taken, is on Lichtensteineov put, in Lapad. The nearest bus route is the #9; take it to the terminus (the hospital) and walk round to the left to find the top end of Lichtensteineov put.

THE SIEGE OF DUBROVNIK

In October 1991, with the war in full flow, the Yugoslav army laid siege to Dubrovnik, shutting off the water and electricity supplies, and raining shells down into the heart of the old town from air, land and sea.

The quick capitulation the Serbs expected never happened, mainly because of determined resistance, but at least in part because Onofrio's fountains – supplied by 15th-century plumbing – continued to function throughout the siege. Nevertheless, for three months there was no water for anything other than drinking, and no electricity or telephone service at all.

More than 100 civilians lost their lives in Dubrovnik, either when their houses were bombed or by snipers up in the hills, looking straight down Stradun – people simply didn't believe they were going to be shot in the sunny streets of Dubrovnik's old town. On one day alone (6 December 1991) the Serbs shelled the city from 05.00 to 16.10 with only a 15-minute break. In all the siege lasted from October 1991 to August 1992, though a ceasefire of sorts was in force at the beginning of 1992.

The material damage caused was enormous, with 70% of the old town's 800 houses sustaining direct hits, and more than 50 shells landing on Stradun alone. Many churches and monuments were targeted in spite of being clearly marked with UNESCO flags.

Dubrovnik's newly refurbished airport was completely destroyed, with the brand-new equipment being looted and taken back to Montenegro and on to Belgrade. Many people moved out, and not all have moved back – the old town's population, at 4,000, is still around 20% less than it was in 1990.

The damage sustained to Dubrovnik's reputation as a holiday destination was incomparably worse, and it took a full decade to bring back just half the visitors.

Yet Dubrovnik has made a truly heroic recovery from the war. Today, beyond a few pockmarked buildings, and acres of new tiles on the roofs, you'd never know there had been a terrible siege just a decade ago. (Ironically, some of the old tiles pulled off roofs during renovations were sent to villages further north to repair war damage there – only to be caught in the 1996 earthquake which destroyed much of Slano and Ston, at the base of the Pelješac peninsula.)

The only real reminder that the war happened at all – beyond the psychological scars – are the multi-lingual signs at each entrance to the old town, showing the 'City Map of Damages caused by the aggression on Dubrovnik by the Yugoslav Army, Serbs and Montenegrins, 1991–1992'.

Some justice has been done – in March 2004 a retired Yugoslav navy admiral, Miodrag Jokić, was sentenced to seven years in prison at The Hague for his part in shelling Dubrovnik. Most of the perpetrators, however, will never be brought to trial.

GETTING AROUND Flat-fare Libertas buses cover the whole of Dubrovnik and most run from 05.00 to midnight. Tickets can be bought in advance from newspaper kiosks at 8kn apiece, or on the bus for 10kn – and you'll be expected to have the right money (except on the Cavtat bus).

The main bus routes used by visitors are:

#1A and #1B From Pile to the bus station & on to Gruž; about every half hour.

#3 From Pile to Gruž; about once an hour.

#4 From Pile to Lapad, passing many of the main hotels & terminating at the Dubrovnik Palace; 2 to 3 times an hour.

#5 From Pile to the Lapad post office & on to the Hotel Neptun on Babin Kuk; about once an hour. The return route goes round the one-way system, arriving at the Ploče Gate & then going round behind the old town walls to Pile.

#6 From Pile to the bus station, then up to the Lapad post office, terminating at the Dubrovnik President Hotel on Babin Kuk; about 4 times an hour.

#7B From Gruž to the bus station & then up towards Lapad, passing the Hotel Bellevue & the Lapad post office before terminating at the Dubrovnik President Hotel on Babin Kuk; about once an hour.

#8 From Pile to the bus station, then on to Gruž where it goes into a one-way system, which ends by coming down the hill past the Ploče hotels to the Ploče Gate, & round behind the old town walls to Pile; 2 to 3 times an hour, but less frequently at w/ends.

#9 From the bus station up to the Lapad post office & on to the hospital before taking a shorter return route to the bus station; about once an hour.

#10 From the bus station to Cavtat; about once an hour. The fare to Cavtat is 12kn & you pay on the bus.

Notwithstanding the excellent local buses, Dubrovnik also has plenty of taxis. There are taxi stands at Pile, Ploče, Gruž, the bus station and Lapad (on Kralja Tomislava, just before the Lapad post office). You can also call taxis from any of the main hotels.

TOURIST INFORMATION The main official tourist office is on Stradun [318–19 C/D3] (❯ *020 323 587; e ured.grad@ tzdubrovnik.hr; www.tzdubrovnik.hr;* ⏲ *09.00–21.00 daily*). They dish out maps and various leaflets and can help you with booking concert tickets etc, and the office handily cohabits with an internet café. There are also offices just outside the Pile gate (*Ante Starčićeva;* ❯ *020 427 591*) and at Gruž (*Gruška obala bb;* ❯ *020 417 983;* ⏲ *08.00–20.00 daily*), next door to the Jadrolinija ticket office.

You can also usually pick up maps and flyers from the various local tourist operators and agencies, though of late – particularly when a cruise ship arrives – they've taken to charging a token fee for maps.

WHERE TO STAY Dubrovnik's long been popular with visitors, with the first proper accommodation for them opening in 1347, and private rooms coming on-stream in the second half of the 14th century. The Grand Hotel Imperial, with 70 rooms just up from the Pile Gate, opened for business in 1897, but it was gutted by fire during the war in 1991. It reopened in 2005, as the Hilton Imperial, symbolic of a city once again ready for business.

During the siege of Dubrovnik (see box opposite) the city lost around half of its total hotel stock, with damage being caused first by bombs and then by refugees

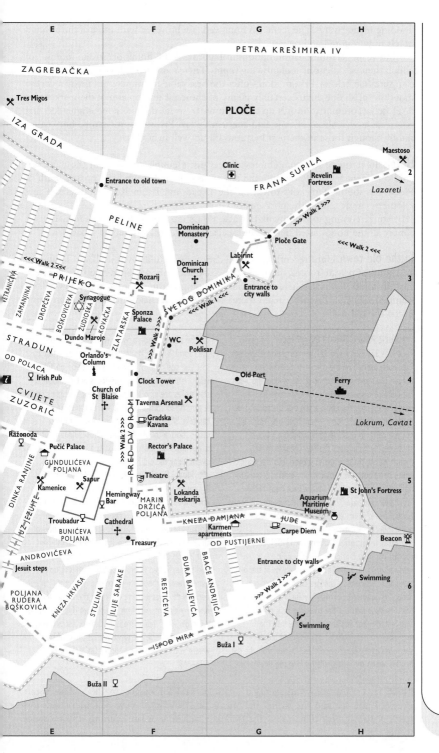

flooding in afterwards. The scene has improved fast, however, with most of the affected hotels now restored and reopened.

Your main accommodation options in Dubrovnik are hotels or private rooms – of which there is a plentiful and growing supply. There's also a youth hostel and a solitary campsite (see below). Private rooms offer the best value for money, but if you're in the mood to splash out there's certainly plenty of choice at the top end of the market too.

Hotel accommodation fills up fast in summer, so it's definitely recommended that you reserve well ahead of time, and confirm by fax. Private rooms can be booked on the fly, though those in the best locations fill up well in advance.

Hotels In terms of location, Dubrovnik has just a couple of hotels in the old town (and one right by the Pile Gate); the rest are distributed around the smart suburb of Ploče just south of the old town, on the Lapad and Babin Kuk peninsulas, a few kilometres away, and in the port area of Gruž.

If you're coming to Dubrovnik out of season, shop around for serious reductions at almost all the hotels listed here – but especially those in Lapad and on Babin Kuk.

In the old town Until recently, accommodation in the old town itself was limited to a handful of private rooms, but in 2003 two boutique hotels opened up for business. Bear in mind if you stay here that it can be stifling hot in summer, and views will be minimal – but on the other hand there's atmosphere in spades to be had from being inside the old walls.

⌂ **Pučić Palace** [318–19 E5] (17 rooms, 2 suites) Od Puća 1; ☎ 326 222; f 326 323; www.thepucicpalace.com. Fabulously located on the corner of Gundulićeva poljana, the heart of the action in the old city, the 5-star Pučić Palace is situated in a noble's luxuriously refurbished home. You could argue that the rooms – & particularly the bathrooms – have been over-restored, but you certainly couldn't complain about a lack of opulence. My favourite is the Ivan Gundulić room – though it's not the quietest, as it overlooks the square, which hosts both the early-morning market & the late-night revelry spilling out from the back door of the Troubadur (see page 328). As you'd expect it's not cheap. *Dbl €326–442 in winter, €442–568 in the shoulder season and €568–684 in summer.*

⌂ **Hilton Imperial Dubrovnik** [318–19 A2] (147 rooms) Marijana Blažića 2; ☎/f 320 220; www.hilton.com. It may not technically be in the old town, but it is right by the Pile Gate & offers jaw-dropping views of Dubrovnik's voluminous walls, the shimmering Adriatic & the towering hulk of Lovrijenac. The 5-star Hilton has thrown money into the impressive redevelopment of this grand old dame & she looks every bit as good, if not better, than she did in 1991 when she was shelled during the siege of the

city. Be sure to book a room with a sea view; some of the rooms & suites on the higher floors have balconies that you could throw a wedding reception on. Old-school grumpy Dalmatian service is out & smooth 5-star smiles are in, & facilities include a swimming pool & gym. An executive room is worth the extra as you can take b/fast & enjoy complimentary snacks & drinks, both alcoholic & non-alcoholic, throughout the day, in the lounge that also boasts a terrace overlooking the old city. *Dbl €205–270 in season.*

⌂ **Hotel Stari Grad** [318–19 D3] (8 rooms) Od Sigurate 4; ☎ 321 373, 322 244; f 321 256; www.hotelstarigrad.com. The newest hotel in the old town is the 3-star Stari Grad (meaning 'old town'), situated between Stradun & Prijeko, only a couple of alleys in from the Pile Gate. It's a tiny establishment, with 4 dbls & 4 sgls in an ancient renovated house. Old stone, flagged floors & tasteful furniture don't quite override the vague sense of unwelcome – or perhaps that was just the day I was there. You won't have any kind of view from your room (Od Sigurate is a narrow alley), but there is a 5th-floor terrace, with wicker furniture & fine views across the rooftops, where you can b/fast in summer. *Dbl €128–221, sgl €91–165.*

Ploče If you can afford it, there's a lot to be said for staying in Ploče. The hotels overlook the sea and the island of Lokrum and have that view of Dubrovnik's old town walls and port. Seen in the light of early morning or late evening, it's a prospect to die for.

🏠 **Hotel Argentina** [312–13 G3] (162 rooms) Frana Supila 14; ☎ 440 555; 📠 432 524; www.gva.hr. In a very similar mould to the Excelsior, the Argentina consists of a 1920s stone-built hotel with a modern annexe grafted on. It was entirely renovated in 2002, & offers everything you'd expect from a 5-star hotel, including a small swimming pool & fitness centre. There are lovely gardens running down to the sea, & almost 2km of private beach. It's also well worth trying the Caravelle restaurant, which specialises in Croatian cuisine. *Dbl from €180 in winter, around €300 summer.*

🏠 **Hotel Excelsior** [312–13 G3] (nearly 200 rooms) Frana Supila 12; ☎ 353 353; 📠 353 555; www.hotel-excelsior.hr. For years after 1991 the 5-star Excelsior enjoyed an uninterrupted reign as Dubrovnik's finest hotel. It may now have a string of competitors, but it has managed to raise its game, with more renovations planned, & no one can beat its views of the old town. Just 5mins walk uphill from the Ploče Gate, the Excelsior consists of a stone 1920s building & a largish glass & concrete annexe. It's unashamedly luxurious, with a private beach, a fitness centre, a great big indoor swimming pool with two jacuzzis, & wonderful terraces where you can sip cocktails & admire the views. The main restaurant, the Zagreb – which also serves as the b/fast room – is a bit too big for comfort, but the Taverna Rustica, set apart from the hotel up its own private path, has great atmosphere on its waterfront terrace & good regional cuisine. Some rooms have spectacular views. If you really want to splash out, try one of the lavish suites – the St Jacques suite, room 231a, has magnificent views of the old town through mirrored glass in the bathroom – as well as from the generous balcony. Great city breaks for €282 pp in winter & €457 in summer, comprising 3 nights in a room with a sea view, a dinner at the Taverna Rustica & airport transfers. *Dbl with views €122 in winter, €239 in summer, dbl with balcony €279 in summer.*

🏠 **Villa Dubrovnik** [312–13 G3] (48 rooms) Vlaha Bukovca 6; ☎ 422 933; 📠 423 465; www.villa-dubrovnik.hr. Another 600m along the coast beyond the Argentina (turn off the main road just after the Villa Scheherazade) is the Villa Dubrovnik – undergoing renovation in 2009, and due to reopen in 2010. Walk down about 60 steps to get to reception, & you'll find the rest of the hotel below in terraces, dropping down to the rocky shoreline. The public areas are tastefully modern, light & airy, with white linen furnishings & rattan furniture, & the dining room & bar (& all the rooms) have gorgeous views back to the old town. In general, the amenities are excellent (all rooms have sea views & balconies), and it has its own rocky beaches & a boat to take you into the old town, as well as a lovely outdoor area called the Bistro Giardino, which is a perfect place for a pre-dinner drink. *Dbl €190 in winter, €280 in summer; suites €290 in winter & €470 in summer (prices pre-renovation).*

🏠 **Hotel Villa Orsula** [312–13 G3] (12 rooms) Frana Supila 14; ☎ 440 555; 📠 432 524; www.gva.hr. Just 150m up the road from the Excelsior is the lovely 5-star Villa Orsula, under the same management (& connected to) the Argentina next door. The beautifully restored 1920s villa is somewhat dwarfed by the 2 big hotels on either side of it, but the rooms are delightful. All facilities are shared with the Argentina (see above). *Dbl with sea view €250 in winter, €330 in summer, balconies €20 extra.*

🏠 **Villa Scheherazade** [312–13 G3] (5 rooms) Frana Supila 14; ☎ 440 555; 📠 432 524; www.gva.hr. Further up the hill from the Argentina is the Villa Scheherazade. This Moorish-looking palace is a further luxury wing of the hotel. It certainly has plenty of atmosphere – it was formerly one of Tito's many residences, where (according to my trusty 1967 guide) the Marshal 'entertained Anthony Eden & many other world political figures'. *Rates similar to Villa Orsula.*

Lapad, Babin Kuk and Gruž

Most of Dubrovnik's accommodation is spread out around the Lapad and Babin Kuk peninsulas, and mainly caters to package tours. It has the advantage of being away from the bustle, and most of the hotels have access to a beach, but you may find yourself further away from the old town than you wish to be. That said, it's only a matter of 5km from the furthest point on Lapad to the old town, and there are regular buses (see page 317). By taxi you're looking at a 10–20-minute ride, depending on the hotel location and traffic density.

🏠 **Hotel Dubrovnik Palace** [312–13 A3/4] (308 rooms) Masarykov put 20; ☎ 430 300; 📠 430 100; www.dubrovnikpalace.hr. This 1st-rate hotel just can't seem to stop winning awards. Situated right at the end of the Lapad headland, Dubrovnik's biggest hotel reopened in 2004 after years of restoration & rebuilding. The 10-floor, 30,000m² complex boasts 3 outdoor swimming pools, rocky beaches & a diving centre, along with 2 indoor pools, 4 restaurants, 11 bars & a jazz club. Every room has a balcony & a sea view looking out towards the Elaphite Islands, & behind the hotel are lovely paths up into the woods leading to stone belvederes with views out to sea. The hotel is also home to a lavish health spa with signature hot stone massages, although many guests choose to while away hours in the pools & jacuzzi. Bus #4, which leaves from just outside the Pile Gate, takes you to the hotel; plans have also been mooted for a shuttle bus. *Dbl from €200.*

🏠 **Hotel Dubrovnik President** [312–13 A2] (180 rooms) Iva Dulčića 39; ☎ 448 266; 🖷 435 622; www.valamar.com. In a similar vein to the Dubrovnik Palace is the 4-star Dubrovnik President, which dominates the Babin Kuk headland. All rooms have a balcony & a view out across the sea to the Elaphite Islands, & there's a fairly large beach area. It's unashamed upmarket package-tour territory, but the location is excellent & the atmosphere cheerful. ☉ Mar–Dec. *Dbl €160–320.*

🏠 **Hotel Argosy** [312–13 A2] (308 rooms) Iva Dulčića 41; ☎ 448 267; 🖷 448 444; www.valamar.com. Behind the President is the Argosy, also owned by Valamar – a large hotel that is a step down in both facilities & price, though it still has access to the beach & tennis courts etc, & boasts a decent-sized outdoor swimming pool. ☉ Mar–Nov. *Dbl with sea view €80 low season, €195 in peak season.*

🏠 **Hotel Club Dubrovnik** [312–13 A2] (338 rooms) Iva Dulčića 18; ☎ 448 249; 🖷 448 444; www.valamar.com. Formerly the Minčeta, further into the Babin Kuk headland, & facing the islet of Daksa . Good family choice, within reach of one of Dubrovnik's most popular beaches, the Copacabana, where you can indulge your taste for 'water polo, water skiing, scuba diving, wind surfing, & banana rides'… it says here. ☉ Apr–Nov. *Dbl €76–115 in winter, €116–248, family room (4 people) €186–364 in summer.*

🏠 **Hotel Tirena** [312–13 A2] (208 rooms) Iva Dulčića 22; ☎ 448 237; 🖷 448 444; www.valamar.com. Last of the 4 hotels in the complex is the Tirena, which is located between the Argosy & the Club Dubrovnik, & therefore also within reach of Copacabana beach, although only 28 of the rooms offer sea views. Its main advantage over the others is in being attached to the little local shopping centre. ☉ Apr–Oct. *Dbl with balcony €64–92 in winter, €116–202 in summer.*

🏠 **Hotel Neptun** [312–13 A3] (150 rooms) Kardinala Stepinca 31; ☎ 440 100; 🖷 440 200; www.importanneresort.com. In a great location on Babin Kuk, facing south & with rocky beaches & a couple of nice swimming pools, is the 10-storey 3-star Hotel Neptun. Its rooms are bright, airy & most have sea views. *Dbl from €180.*

🏠 **Hotel Kompas** [312–13 B3] (115 rooms) Šetalište Kralja Zvonimira 56; ☎ 352 000; 🖷 435 877; www.hotel-kompas.hr. Right down by the attractive Uvala Bay beach, which marks the meeting point of the

Lapad & Babin Kuk peninsulas, is the 3-star Kompas. Its rooms mostly have sea views, & it has its own indoor pool, but the hotel has seen better days. It's now under the same management as the Excelsior & Dubrovnik Palace hotels, & there are plans to upgrade it to 4-star. *Dbl from €90.*

🏠 **Hotel Villa Wolff** [312–13 B2] (6 rooms) Nika i Meda Pučića 1; ☎/🖷 438 710; www.villa-wolff.hr. Right next door to the Kompas is the 4-star Hotel Villa Wolff, which opened in 2003. You wouldn't know it walking up the short flight of steep steps from the coastal path (next door to the Casa Bar), but above you is a charming little boutique hotel, with just 3 dbls; 1 junior suite, 2 suites with balconies & sea views). It has its own terrace & Mediterranean garden, complete with rosemary bushes, palms, cypresses & ancient olive trees, with a great view across the bay. *Dbl €144–182, suite with balcony €224.*

🏠 **Hotel Komodor** [312–13 B3] (63 rooms) Masarykov put 5; ☎ 433 500; 🖷 433 510; www.hotelimaestral.com. Across the bay from the Kompas, & firmly back on Lapad, is one of the peninsula's oldest hotels, the 3-star Komodor – the 1st in a line of 5 establishments along Masarykov put run by the Maestral hotel chain. The Komodor was refurbished in 1999, & has an outdoor swimming pool. *Dbl with sea view & balcony. €88 in winter, €180 in summer.*

🏠 **Hotel Adriatic** [312–13 B3] (158 rooms) Masarykov put 9; ☎ 433 520; 🖷 433 530; www.hotelimaestral.com. Just up the road is one of Dubrovnik's last-remaining 2-star hotels, the Adriatic. The beach is just across the street & it's a bargain (& almost invariably fully booked). But we have received negative reports from readers who have written in to say it's noisy, unwelcoming & that rooms aren't always up to standard. *Dbl with sea view €68 in winter, €148 summer.*

🏠 **Hotel Uvala** [312–13 B3] (51 rooms) Masarykov put 6; ☎ 433 580; 🖷 433 590; www.hotelimaestral.com. Almost next door is the newest addition to the group, the brand-new 4-star Uvala 'health & wellness centre', which promises to pamper the guests in its rooms, most of which have sea views. *Dbl with sea view from €150 in winter, €270 in summer.*

🏠 **Hotel Vis** [312–13 B3] (152 rooms) Masarykov put 4; ☎ 433 555; 🖷 433 550; www.hotelimaestral.com. Next up, but over on the seaward side of the street, is the 3-star Hotel Vis, whose main attraction is being right on its own decent-sized beach. Like the Adriatic, it's very often full up. *Dbl with sea view €82 in winter €182 in summer.*

🏠 **Hotel Splendid** [312–13 A/B3] (59 rooms) Masarykov put 10; ☎ 437 304; 🖷 437 404; www.hotelimaestral.com. Last of the bunch is the 2-star Splendid, which like the Vis is right on the beach. *Dbl with sea views & balcony €90 in winter, €238 in summer.*

⌂ **Grand Hotel Park** [312–13 B3] (248 rooms) Šetalište Kralja Zvonimira 39; ☎ 434 444; f 434 885; www.grandhotel-park.hr. Situated between the Kompas & the Komodor, & set back from the Uvala beach, is the boxy 3-star Grand Hotel Park. It has pretty good indoor & outdoor sea-water swimming pools, but make sure you go for a refurbished room; the older ones are really pretty tatty, making the sea-view dbl-room price tag (apparently all year round, but you can negotiate in winter) look a bit steep. *Dbl with sea view €188–214.*

⌂ **Hotel Dubrovnik** [312–13 B3] (22 rooms) Šetalište Kralja Zvonimira bb; ☎ 435 030; f 435 999; www.hoteldubrovnik.hr. A nicer option is the 3-star Hotel Dubrovnik (not to be confused with the Villa Dubrovnik, the Dubrovnik Palace or the Dubrovnik President), all of 100m away, which may have neither indoor nor outdoor pools, but does have clean, well-appointed rooms including 4 suites at reasonable rates, & a welcoming staff. *Dbl €68 in winter, €168 in summer.*

⌂ **Hotel Sumratin** [312–13 B2] (40 rooms) Šetalište Kralja Zvonimira 31; ☎ 438 930; f 436 006. Further inland still is the 2-star Sumratin, which has neither sea views nor a swimming pool, but is simple, clean & great value for money. Dubrovnik's most affordable hotel. *Dbl €50 in winter, €120 from Jul to mid-Sep.*

⌂ **Hotel Zagreb** [312–13 B2] (22 rooms) Šetalište Kralja Zvonimira 27; ☎ 438 930; f 436 006. Almost next door to the Sumratin – & under the same management – is one of my favourites, the 2-star Zagreb. It offers clean dbls at knock-down prices in a lovely refurbished old building. *Dbl €77 in winter, €110 in summer.*

⌂ **Hotel Lapad** [312–13 C2] (157 rooms) Lapadska obala 37; ☎ 432 922; f 417 230; www.hotel-lapad.hr. Situated down on the shore of Babin Kuk, facing Gruž harbour, is the Lapad, which is based around a renovated old building with a modern annexe. There's a small swimming pool, & the nearest beach is about 600m up the shore. If you're here in Jul or Aug, make sure you ask for one of the rooms with AC. Finally, if

you're vegetarian, & on HB, you can expect to eat omelette seven days a week. *Dbl €112–170.*

⌂ **Hotel Petka** (104 rooms) Obala Stjepana Radića 38; ☎ 410 500; f 410 127; www.hotelpetka.hr. Situated right next to the main ferry-landing in Gruž, the 3-star Petka features AC in all rooms, 64 of which have balconies giving views over the picturesque port. It's nothing fancy, but gives easy access to the islands, & is only a short bus ride away from the old town. The prices offer good value by Dubrovnik standards. *Dbl with sea views & balcony €125–155.*

⌂ **Hotel Lero** (160 rooms) Iva Vojnovića 14; ☎ 341 333; f 332 133; www.hotel-lero.hr. Although entirely renovated in 1998, the 3-star Lero still retains something of its 1971 feel – & its location on a busy main road may put some people off. But it's only a 15 or 20min walk from the Pile Gate, on a bus route, 200m from the nearest beach, & half of the rooms have sea views. It's pretty good value – & the HB supplement is a veritable snip at €6 pp per day. *Dbl €70–150.*

⌂ **Hotel Bellevue** (93 rooms) Pera Čingrije 7; ☎ 330 000; f 330 100; www.hotel-bellevue.hr. The 5-star Bellevue has long enjoyed one of the best locations in Dubrovnik, just 15mins from Pile Gate on a cliff top overlooking its own beach &, fully refurbished in 2008, is now one of the city's finest hotels. Renata Štrok (the wife of the man behind the Adriatic Luxury Hotels group, Goran), herself a successful businesswoman with an eye for fashion, has personally overseen the creation of a unique hotel bathed in natural light that makes good use of local stone, wood & fabrics. As well as 2 bars & 2 restaurants the hotel boasts a presidential suite. To give you an idea of the clientele they're aiming at, there's a car lift that has been built to take 'Lamborghinis & Ferraris'. *Dbl from €200.*

⌂ **Berkeley Hotel** (24 rooms and suites) Andrije Hebranga 116a; ☎ 494 160; f 494 170; www.berkeleyhotel.hr. Nice new aparthotel in Gruž. *Dbl €75–120, suite €80–240.*

Private rooms/apartments Dubrovnik has a huge supply of private rooms available, and although they're more expensive here than most places in Croatia, they're still a good deal cheaper than the hotels, with most private double rooms going for under €60 a night, even in summer.

The obvious way of finding a private room is through one of Dubrovnik's ubiquitous travel agencies, who will generally welcome your business. There are also a number of online resources if you want to book/look ahead – over a hundred properties are listed at each of www.dubrovnik-apartments.com and www.dubrovnik-online.com/english/private_accommodation.php, for example.

If you come in by ferry or bus, you're likely to be assailed on arrival by offers of private rooms. These may work out cheaper than anything you can get through travel agents, and unless the season's especially busy you can haggle – but check both the location and total price very carefully before accepting an offer.

Karmen apartments [318–19 G5] Bandureva 1; 323 433; m 098 619 282; e – the best way of reserving, for once – marc.van-bloemen@du.t-com.hr; www.karmendu.com. Of the places I've stayed at, the outstanding recommendation has to go to this place. The apartments are situated in an ancient stone building in a stunning location right on the old port. They're not cheap – but they're great value & perfectly located. *Apartments €70–110 per night in winter, €90–145 per night in summer. 20% surcharge for stays of under 3 nights.*

Nevena Abjanić (4 apartments) Ilije Sarake 8; 323 690; m 091 528 0091; www.abjanic.com. Another great recommendation goes to Nevena Abjanić, which has apartments just within the walls of the old town, all tastefully decorated & all with terraces. *Apartments €70–90 in winter, €100–130 in season.*

Villa Branko (4 rooms) Put Petra Kresimira IV 33; 423 412; m 091 883 6521; e info@villabranko-dubrovnik.com; www.villabranko-dubrovnik.com. Also highly recommended is Kathy Ljubojević's family-run

villa. The house is high up in Ploče with a staggering view down on to the old town & across to Lokrum. The rooms are clean & tidy; the front 2 have balconies & stupendous views; ideal ideal for small groups or families. *Whole villa €400 per night in summer; €250 in winter.*

Ivo Gugić (3 rooms) Hvarska 46; 417 354; m 091 517 0693; www.dubrovnik-online.com/rooms_ivo; e ivo.gugic1@du.t-com.hr. Finally, if you're on a tight budget, it's well worth contacting Ivo, who has rooms just round the corner from the Pile Gate, outside the city walls. They're functional, but now have AC, & are a bargain. Pre-book, & mention this guide, & he'll probably do you a deal. *Rooms around €30 pp in summer.*

Apartments Falkuša, Bracera & Galijan Ferićeva 1; m 098 455 847; www.dubrovnik4you.com.hr. 3 pleasant apartment for 2 or 4 people in the old town, just a short walk from the Pile Gate & Onofrio's Fountain. *Prices from 390–660 for 3 nights in season.*

Youth hostel/campsite Dubrovnik's youth hostel (*Vinka Sagrestana 3;* 423 241; f 412 592; *www.hfhs.hr*) is in a pretty good location, about 15 minutes uphill from the bus station, just off Bana Jelačića, and for single people on a budget it's as cheap as you'll find in Dubrovnik, at € 13–17 per person. That said, as you can imagine it's very hard to secure one of the 80-odd places, especially in summer, and for two or more people travelling together private accommodation can be not only more convenient – no daytime lockout, for example – but also competitive on price and location.

Dubrovnik also has a solitary campsite, on the Babin Kuk peninsula (managed by Valamar), but unless you're absolutely desperate to get under canvas, I can't really recommend it as an accommodation option for a short break. Having said that, if you are coming here with your tent, the Auto-Camp Solitudo (*Iva Dulčića 39;* 448 686; f 448 688; *www.valamar.com*) offers 166 pitches, newly refurbished bathrooms and laundry areas, and charges roughly € 7–10 per pitch, € 3.20–5.40 per person and a one-off fee of € 20 per reservation. It's also close to various beaches.

WHERE TO EAT AND DRINK As you'd expect, Dubrovnik is brimming with places to eat, though with a few exceptions there's often surprisingly little to distinguish one place from another. Food in the old town tends universally towards grilled fish, meat and shellfish at the upper end of the spectrum, and pizza and pasta dishes in the mid-tier establishments.

Inside the walls Dubrovnik's busiest restaurant district is along Prijeko, the street running parallel to Stradun on the landward side for its entire length. Unfortunately, it's managed to get itself something of a bad reputation over the years, which hasn't been helped by the touts along Stradun trying to entice passing trade. While there's no doubt good food to be had, there's a level of unscrupulousness here that probably comes from knowing the chances are you won't be coming back, and tales of poor-quality food and routine overcharging are legion. It's a pity, as the location is perfect and the atmosphere ought to be first-rate. One exception to the Prijeko rule seems to be Rozarij, right at the eastern end of the street – though, even there, readers have reported offhand service. It's also worth noting that in general, prices at restaurants and cafés on Stradun itself are usually significantly highter than elsewhere.

Expensive

✗ **Labirint** [318–19 G3] Svetog Dominika 2; ☎ 322 222. After more than a decade of renovation, the upmarket Labirint is finally open again. Set into the city walls near the Dominican Monastery, it offers a top-notch restaurant as well as various bars, terraces & a discreet nightclub. The fish soup is excellent, while pasta dishes come in at around 90kn. Mussels are comparatively expensive, with mouth-watering scallops a much better deal. Expect meat dishes to cost upwards of 150kn & wine to set you back around 200kn or more a bottle. Booking essential in season & w/ends.

✗ **Proto** [318–19 D3] Široka 1; ☎ 323 234; www.esculap-teo.hr. Proto is one of Dubrovnik's most famous landmarks & makes a big deal about having been in business since 1886 & having had Edward VIII & Wallis Simpson to dinner in the 1930s. In spite of the hype there's still a lot to be said for both the fish & meat dishes here, which are probably as good as anywhere in town – & the upstairs terrace is always packed in summer. Worth reserving ahead.

Mid-range

✗ **Domino** [318–19 C5] Od Domina 3; ☎ 323 103. At the top end of Od Domina, not far from the inside of the sea wall, Domino prides itself on its great steaks, but also has decent fish & seafood specialities, including a particularly good grilled squid. The outside terrace is enduringly popular. Check out its sister restaurant, Bistro Riva, on Lapad (see page 327).

✗ **Dundo Maroje** [318–19 E3] Kovačka; ☎ 321 021. On one of the tiny alleys connecting Stradun with Prijeko, Konoba Dundo Maroje comes highly recommended for its excellent & reasonably priced seafood dishes, & outsized plates of squid. No views whatsoever but great atmosphere.

✗ **Sapur** [318–19 E5] Gundulićeva poljana 2; ☎ 324 572. A welcome addition to one of the old town's most attractive squares, Sapur brings Adriatic cuisine with

French & Italian touches at very reasonable prices. On our visit oysters were a bargain 8kn apiece & the beef fillet came in at 90kn. Other highlights include lobster soup, scampi kebabs & 4 types of olive oil – a chilli-flavoured one, & oils from Šipan, Korčula & Mljet.

✗ **Taverna Arsenal** [318–19 F4] Pred Dvorom 1; ☎ 321 065; www.mea-culpa.hr. One of the city's newest dining places brings a cavernous deep red dining space to the old port, with wooden beams supposed to be evocative of an old Dubrovnik ship. During the day the interior is geared towards large groups, with other diners soaking up the old harbour views from the outdoor terrace. Veal kebabs are the standout amongst solid Dalmatian fare. At night the restaurant is transformed into a late-opening lounge bar, which stays open until 04.00.

Budget

✗ **Baracuda** [318–19 D4] Nikole Božidarevićeva 10; ☎ 323 160. One of the smallest yet cheeriest restaurants in town, serving up tasty pizzas & very little else (there really isn't room). Situated just off Od Puča, near the Serbian Orthodox church.

✗ **Jadran** [318–19 B3] Paska Milečevića 1; ☎ 323 405. The Jadran has a perfect location inside the old cloisters of the former Convent of St Clare (go through the alley to the right just after you come through the Pile Gate, past a sports shop on the right & a souvenir shop on the left). Dating originally from the 13th century, the convent became the republic's orphanage in 1432, & an open-air cinema after World War II. The gorgeous setting is a triumph over the somewhat average fare, but it's a lovely place to sit & while away an hour or two – especially if it's windy, as it's a well-sheltered spot.

✗ **Kamenice** [318–19 E5] Gundulićeva poljana 8; ☎ 323 685. Kamenice – literally small stones, but here meaning oysters – is a great place in a great location. It specialises in seafood, & in particular oysters. The menu is short but excellent, with the *frittura* (whitebait) & the

squid particularly good, & the house wine an affordable 70kn a litre. The service can be a little surly, but perhaps that's all part of the charm.

✗ **Lokanda Peskarija** [318–19 F5] Na Ponti; ☎ 324 750; www.mea-culpa.hr. Absolutely my favourite place in Dubrovnik out of season, even if it does have one of the world's shortest menus – or perhaps because of it. Situated right on the old port, the establishment is tiny, with a bar downstairs & a handful of tables upstairs, though in fine weather it quickly spreads out across the quayside. The fried squid here can be outstanding, but standards tend to fall off somewhat during high season. The restaurant's homemade fish pâté or the marinated anchovy fillets are good choices.

✗ **Mea Culpa** [318–19 B4] Za Rokom 3; ☎ 323 430; www.mea-culpa.hr. Owned by the same people as Lokanda Peskarija (see above), Mea Culpa is an unpretentious place at the other end of town, serving up large pizzas & simple seasonal salads. Tables spill out on to the street, & it's a popular place with locals & visitors alike, with draught Guinness on tap. Sadly it doesn't serve any Croatian beer, though, & the quality of the food can be a bit hit & miss.

✗ **Nishta** [318–19 D3] Prijeko 30; ▥ 098 186 7440; www.nishtarestaurant.com. New vegetarian option on Prijeko.

✗ **Poklisar** [318–19 F4] Ribarnica 1; ↘ 322 176. Poklisar has a great location right on the old port, next to the fish market (*riba* means fish). It has a lovely twin terrace & serves up the usual range of fish dishes as you'd expect, as well as reasonable pizzas – though you could argue that you're paying as much for the setting as for the food here. Claims to be open from 07.00 to midnight – & in high season that may well be true.

✗ **Rozarij** [318–19 F3] Zlatarska 4; ↘ 321 257. On the corner of Prijeko but with an address on Zlatarska, Rozarij manages to break the Prijeko mould (see the introductory section, above), serving up unpretentious

local Croatian fare in a nice setting near the Dominican Monastery.

✗ **Taj Mahal** [318–19 D5] Nikole Gučetica 2; ↘ 098 674 141. Just up the street from the mosque, this small newly opened restaurant serves up – in spite of the misleading name – excellent Bosnian food, including 1st-rate *ćevapčići* & spicy pies.

✗ **Toni** [318–19 C5] Nikole Božidarevićeva 14; ↘ 323 134. Just a couple of doors up from the Baracuda (see above) is the Spaghetteria Toni, which serves up some of the best pasta in town (though 1 reader certainly didn't agree). Check out the vast homemade lasagne or the various pasta dishes with seafood sauces. Toni feels like an Italian trattoria, only this one serves thick Turkish coffee; it's cheerful, informal & highly popular with locals – last time I ate there the director of the Museum of Modern Art was having dinner with friends at the next table.

Snack bars and ice cream If you're on a tight budget – or just don't fancy sitting down for a meal – there are plenty of snack bars and sandwich joints in town. Two of the best are near each other, towards the Pile end of Stradun. The first is the **Buffet Škola** [318–19 D3], which is on Antuninska, on the left-hand side heading up towards Prijeko. Here you can get terrific homemade sandwiches filled with cheese or *pršut* for 20–30kn. Across Stradun, in Široka, right by Proto (see above), is the **Fish Sandwich Bar** [318–19 C3], which sells wonderful… well, fish sandwiches. Fillings include fried fish or mussels and prices range from 15–35kn. Both places are open – broadly speaking – from about 10.00 to 14.00 and 18.00 to 21.00. But be warned that drinks can set you back as much as the food.

Dubrovnik's also great for ice cream. There's a flurry of establishments in the old town, with the best being **Dolce Vita** [318–19 D3], on Nalješkovićeva, one of the streets between Stradun and Prijeko, which serves quite the tastiest and freshest ice cream (and frozen yoghurt) in town. Also highly recommended is **Niko** [318–19 D4], on Od Puca, near the Serbian Orthodox Church.

Outside the old town walls
Expensive

✗ **Levanat** Nika i Meda Pučića 15; ↘ 435 352; www.dubrovnik-online.com/levanat. With an unbeatable waterfront location on Babin Kuk, Levanat is secluded, upmarket & pricey. It's easy to get to by walking along the footpath that starts at Casa (see below) for about 10mins, or from the Babin Kuk or Neptun hotels; otherwise you might want to consider getting a taxi, as it's quite a schlep from the old town. The menu focuses on excellent – & by Croatian standards – original fish dishes. You can also come here just for a drink. Reservations recommended (not least to check it's open).

✗ **Luna** Masarykov put 20; ↘ 430 000; www.dubrovnikpalace.hr. Fine dining with great views out towards the Elaphite Islands – & service as smooth & food as mouthwatering as you'd expect from the Dubrovnik Palace Hotel. The creative menu fuses international & Mediterranean cuisines.

✗ **Nautika** [318–19 A3] Brsalje 3; ↘ 442 526; www.esculap-teo.hr. For years the ritziest place in town, the Nautika trades heavily on having had Pope John Paul II to lunch on 6 June 2003, though it's hard to imagine the late pontiff scoffing his way through the 5-course menu on display. These days I'd personally rather eat at Labirint or Levanat if spending that kind of money, though Nautika does have an excellent location, on the water, right outside the Pile Gate, & a gorgeous pair of terraces, as well as smart dining rooms indoors. The food is excellent, as you'd expect for the price, & the service impeccable – but check your bill carefully as mistakes have been reported. Nautika also offers a 'Light Lunch' on the terrace outside, though I wasn't all that impressed. Reservations recommended.

✗ **Porat** Marijana Blažića 2; ↘ 320 320; www.hilton.com. The signature restaurant at the Hilton Imperial is a welcome addition to the dining scene, marrying as-good-as-it-gets Croatian food with international treats. Highlights on an ever-changing menu include the huge

starter of lobster spaghetti & a great cheese board from Pag. You can't go wrong with the steak, or traditional Adriatic cuisine. Reservations recommended.

Mid-range

✗ **Fellini** Mata Vodopića; ☎ 437 099. Engaging trattoria with a good atmosphere over in Lapad (between the Sumratin & Zagreb hotels) serving tasty Italian dishes including great pasta & classic meat dishes. Recommended.

✗ **Maestoso** [318–19 H2] Put od Bosanke 4; ☎ 420 986; www.restaurantmaestoso.hr. Well-known & popular restaurant just outside the Ploče Gate with a view across to the old town harbour. The fare is the traditional grilled meat & fish, but the place is (in this author's opinion) somewhat over-rated.

✗ **Orhan** Od Tabakarije 1; ☎ 411 918; www.restaurant-orhan.com. Orhan serves up the same

sturdy Adriatic staples – squid risotto, mussels & fish platters for 240kn – that you find all over Dubrovnik, with the tempting addition of a self-service salad bar for just 15kn a bowl. The real reason to come here though is the stunning views over the city walls from the terrace, right underneath the Lovrijenac Fortress. They also have a few private rooms available.

✗ **Shanghai** (or Šangaj, if you want the local spelling) Ante Starčićeva 25; ☎ 425 754. About 400m up from the Pile Gate, on the left-hand side, you'll find one of Dubrovnik's few Chinese restaurants. The food is everything you'd expect, though not comparable, sadly, to what you can get in the UK.

Budget

✗ **Bistro Riva** Lapadska Obala 20. Situated on Gruž harbour, but opposite the port (just before the Hotel Lapad), is the Bistro Riva. Simpler & less expensive than its sister restaurant, Domino, in the old town (see page 325), it serves up a wide range of tasty dishes including good pizzas. The only pity is that the courtyard is closed in, blocking off what would be great views across the water.

✗ **Casa** Nika i Meda Pučića 1; m 091 438 7105; www.villa-wolff.hr. Billed as 'Bar & Ristorante', Casa has a great location right on the waterfront at Uvala Bay, just where the Babin Kuk & Lapad peninsulas meet. It's right under the Hotel Villa Wolff & next door to the Hotel Kompas, & marks the start of the path that goes clockwise around Babin Kuk. It only actually serves food in summer, & then more of the snack variety than the full meal, but it's an excellent place to sit, with the light bouncing off the water.

✗ **El Toro** Ivo Vojnovića 5; ☎ 332 818. Just up the road from the Hotel Bellevue, with a nice leafy high-up terrace, you'll find the Café Pizzeria El Toro, which is cheap & cheerful & serves up reasonable pizzas at a good price.

✗ **Posat** [318–19 B2] Uz Posat 1; ☎ 421 194; www.restaurantposat.hr. Well located outside the Pile Gate (just up and to the right) is the Konoba Posat, which has a large & leafy terrace. It's as good a place as any for grilled meats.

✗ **Tres Miyos** [318–19 E1] Hvarska 6; ☎ 424 445. On the road running behind the old town (usually marked on maps as Iza Grada) you'll find a minute but friendly Mexican restaurant. It's a brave effort serving tortillas & chilli beans in a place where everyone's come for the fish, but it can make a pleasant change if you're here for a week.

Cafés and bars
With great weather and lots of visitors, there's no shortage of places to sit and have a drink in Dubrovnik, though fashions change quickly, and today's groovy hangout can all too rapidly become tomorrow's leftover.

In the old town

⬛ **Carpe Diem** [318–19 G5] Kneza Damjana Jude 4. Situated on the narrow street running down to the aquarium, & billing itself as an 'Art Caffe', Carpe Diem does a light b/fast in the morning & exotic cocktails in the evening. It's long, narrow, smartly decorated & popular late into the evening.

⬛ **D'Vino** [318–19 D3] Palmotićeva 4a; ☎ 321 223; www.columis.net/dvino. Largest selection of wines by the glass in Dubrovnik. ⊕ 17.00–24.00.

⬛ **Festival Café** [318–19 C3] Stradun. Benefiting from a perfect location on Stradun, the rather pricey Festival Café is especially popular through the day & in the early evenings, when it's a great place to see & be seen. Pull up a director's chair & watch the action unfold.

⬛ **Gradska Kavana** [318–19 F4] Pred Dvorom 1; www.mea-culpa.hr. In arguably the best location in town, next door to the Rector's Palace and opposite St

Blaise's Church, the newly renovated Gradska Kavana (literally 'town café') has a spacious interior & a raised terrace, which is perfect for people-watching.

♀ **Hemingway Bar** [318–19 E5] Pred Dvorom. Right opposite the Rector's Palace & next door to the cathedral is the relatively new & popular Hemingway Bar, which attracts the cocktail-drinking set. It's impossible to imagine what the old man of the sea himself would have thought. Surprisingly small inside, the lounge chairs outside are the main draw.

♀ **Irish Pub** [318–19 E4] Od Polača 5. Just 1 street back from Stradun you'll find the Irish Pub, which, although it's not a pub as you or I would know it, still serves a good range of beers, & is popular with local students, the growing expat community & tourists. The bar opposite has recently metamorphosed into a rival Irish bar. Happy hour 15.00–18.00.

♀ **Ražonoda** [318–19 E5] Od Puča; www.thepucicpalace.com. Next door to the Pučić Palace hotel & under the same management, Ražanoda is a swanky, upmarket wine bar with a good list of the best Croatian wines – & price tags to match. It's just a shame they don't sell wine by the glass.

⟁ **Smuuti** [318–19 D3] Palmotićeva 5; www.nishtarestaurant.com. Freshly squeezed juices and smoothies, breakfasts and cakes. Near to and owned by Nishta restaurant (see page 325).

♀ **Troubadur** [318–19 E5] Bunićeva poljana. Properly known as the Hard Jazz Café Troubadur, this is an excellent bar with a pub-like atmosphere & live music most evenings. The front door is on Bunićeva poljana & the back door on Gundulićeva poljana. The tables outside are made from old sewing machines, which is an unusual touch. The ambience has been somewhat ruined by the recent addition of a bright neon advertising sign right behind where the bands play. You can always choose to sit at one of a sprinkling of other bars with outdoor tables, & listen to the music from there.

Outside the old town walls Needless to say, Dubrovnik has its own life beyond that aimed at tourists, and there are a couple of areas where this goes on, notably on Bana Jelačića, running up into Lapad, and on Iva Vojnovića, in the heart of Lapad. A new scene has sprung up here in just the last few years, with a clutch of eight trendy new bars which are hugely popular with the locals and rarely visited by foreigners. Other than this, there are a handful of places worth noting:

⟁ **Buža I** [318–19 G7] Situated on the rocks outside the western (seaward) walls of the city, Buža is the place to come if you want to watch the sun go down. The only sounds are the sea & the gulls, and it's gloriously informal. The entrance is pretty well hidden & unsigned – so just look out for the 'no nudists' graffiti scrawled on the wall. To get there, go up behind the Jesuit Church & out of the square on the opposite corner, & then turn left under the walls along Od Margarite. After a short while you come to a hole in the wall on your right (*buža* means 'hole') that leads out on to the rocks – & there you are. Seats are set out on the rocks that spill down to the Adriatic. This is a great place for taking a dip, too, so don't forget your togs. Only open – you'll see why – when the weather's fine.

♀ **Buža II** [312–13 C4] Another hole-in-the-wall establishment, with a slightly different outlook over Lokrum & a slightly more formal set-up, with more chairs, tables & parasols in a main bar area. Again the bar isn't permanent, so no hot drinks, & of course no draught beers. Follow the directions for Buža I (above) but turn right under the walls along Od Margarite, instead of left. Again, you'll quickly come to a hole in the wall, but this time it will be on your left.

♀ **Casa** Nika i Meda Pučića 1; m 091 438 7105; www.villa-wolff.hr. Casa has a great location right on the waterfront at Uvala Bay, under the Villa Wolff, & although the drinks are pricier than you might be used to (20kn for a beer), the situation alone makes it worth the visit.

♀ **Kavana Dubravka** [318–19 A3] 1836 Brsalje; ☎ 426 319. Occupying prime real estate right outside the Pile Gate, opposite Nautika, the Kavana Dubravka has a lovely terrace set overlooking the little bay between the Bokar & Lovrijenac fortresses. Inside, it's worth having a look at the photos on the walls of the old trams that used to ply their way up the hill from here. For a well-invested 5kn you can use the toilets – which are a whole lot nicer than the public ones over on the other side of the Pile Gate.

♀ **Sunset Lounge** [312–13 A4] Masarykov put 20; ☎ 430 000; www.dubrovnikpalace.hr. It may only have been open for a couple of years, but the stylish Sunset Lounge at the Dubrovnik Palace Hotel is firmly established as the place to watch sunset in Dubrovnik, through floor-to-ceiling windows that provide spectacular views over the Elaphite Islands & the Adriatic as the day draws to a close. Prices are high (50–60kn for a cocktail), but worth it. Bus #4, which leaves from just outside the Pile Gate, will take you to the hotel.

Self-catering If you're looking for picnic food, you'll probably be reliant on the Konzum supermarket – there's a branch on Gundulićeva Poljana, and one outside each of the two main gates. There's also a huge new one down at Gruž, just past the ferry terminal.

NIGHTLIFE Though there's plenty of late-evening café activity and drinking going on in the old town, actual nightlife is decidedly thin on the ground in Dubrovnik, with most places closing up by 01.00. The newest addition to the nightlife scene is the wine/lounge bar at **Taverna Arsenal** [318–19 F4] (see page 325), however, which does stay open until 04.00 year round, and during the season the cocktail bar at the **Eastwest Beach Club**, located on the Branje beach just beyond the Ploče Gate, keeps going until 03.00.

In summer there are more chances to dance, but not a whole lot more. The best place is arguably the last of the **Lazareti** (↘ *324 871*), out past the Ploče Gate on Supila, which features DJs and probably the hippest music you'll find in the area – but Ibiza it ain't. Just outside the Pile Gate, on Brsalje, there's also the **Latino Club Fuego** [318–19 A3] (↘ *312 870; www.dubrovniknightclub.com*), which is open every night from 23.00 to 06.00 from May to October, and from 23.00 to 06.00 Thursday to Saturday for the rest of the year. It's one of the few dance places open that late and therefore quite popular with the over-served backpacker set. Otherwise there's Labirint's tiny nightclub in the town walls (part of the same establishment as the swanky restaurant, see page 324), which is also open until 04.00.

BEACHES The other way of entertaining yourself, of course, is with a trip to the beach. The nicest ones are out on the island of Lokrum, and it's well worth getting out there if you possibly can (see page 341) – it's also the nearest naturist beach to the old town.

If you simply fancy cooling off after a hot walk around the city walls, walk just round the corner at the old port and there's a swimming area off the rocks, by the jetty.

The city's main public beach is at Banje, just outside the Ploče Gate, facing the old port. It's recently been refurbished and you can now rent parasols and deckchairs here, and order yourself cocktails at the summer bar. In spite of being right next to the old port the water is beautifully clear.

Another option is the tiny beach underneath the Hotel Bellevue, half of which is public (the other half belongs to the revamped hotel). It's on a gorgeous little cove facing southeast, and hosts Dubrovnik's annual water-polo championships – each little beach and cove around the city has its own team.

For pure hedonistic beach-games and watersports you can't do better than the Copacabana beach on Babin Kuk, though in high season it does get mighty crowded with the package tours from the Babin Kuk hotel complex taking up most of the space. Finally, the Uvala Bay beach, on Lapad, is the locals' beach of choice, and offers lovely swimming out to sea between Babin Kuk and Lapad.

WHAT TO SEE AND DO The main sight of course is Dubrovnik itself, and the best way of seeing it is from the city walls, which are among the best preserved and most picturesque in the world. There's a promenade along their entire length, and you should make every effort to circum-perambulate at least once, as it really gives you the best possible perspective (physical and historical) of just what Dubrovnik really means. Another wonderful view can be had from the top of Mount Srđ (412m), the mountain looming above the city. Time was, you could take a cable car all the way up – and it's to be hoped that the war damage is repaired soon and it's pressed back into service, as the walk up the barren hillside can be a punishing one (see page 340).

Once you've seen Dubrovnik from above, choose your time of day for the city itself with care; after 11.00 there's a predictable tendency towards more visitors and less atmosphere – though early evening is a lovely time, regardless of the crowds, with soft light treating old stone kindly.

There's a lot to see in the old city, but don't be too obsessive – not all of the 48 churches within the walls need a visit (or indeed are open), and the museums are mostly fairly low key.

The city is great for walking around – if you want to tap into the knowledge of a local guide then consider booking a place on one of the guided walks organised by **Dubrovnik Walking Tours** (85–120kn per person). All tours leave from Onofrio's Great Fountain; ask at the tourist office for more detailed information.

The city walls The walls surround the entire old town and run for a whisper under 2km. At their highest they're 25m tall, and at their fattest 12m wide. There are five fortresses and around 20 towers. Work started on the walls in the 8th century and continued more or less continuously until the 16th, though much more than you might imagine is also late 20th-century restoration – even before the Serb shells pounded the city in 1991–92. Indeed, when I was here in the 1980s, the promenade around the walls wasn't actually complete. Since the war, huge amounts of restoration have been done throughout the old city, including the complete repaving of Stradun – not that you'd know – and the replacing of most of the houses' roof-tiles.

There are three places where you can get up onto the walls – on Stradun, right next to the Pile Gate (the busiest of the three); on Svetog Dominika, the road leading up to the Dominican Monastery; and on Kneza Damjana Jude, near the Aquarium. The walls are open from 09.00 to 19.00 in summer, with slightly shorter hours in winter, and the entrance fee is a fairly steep 50kn – up from 30kn just two years ago. The earlier you get up onto the walls the less crowded you'll find them.

If you stop to take pictures (and you will), the whole circuit takes a leisurely hour or so.

Inside the walls The main sights are all close to one another – the main street, Stradun, is all of 300m long. The following itinerary starts at the Pile Gate and works its way back and forth across the old city, before ending at the Church of St Blaise. At a leisurely pace – and without stopping for any length of time to admire the attractions or visit museums and churches – it would take about 1½ –2 hours. If you dip into a handful of the main sights you should count on a good half day; if you want a detailed visit to everything on the itinerary you'll need a couple of full days at least. If you do nothing else, visit the Rector's Palace, the two monasteries and the cathedral treasury.

RUĐER BOŠKOVIĆ – MATHEMATICAL GENIUS AND LATIN POET

Pictures of Ruđer Bošković (Ruggero Boscovich in Italian) – a brilliant mathematician and physicist born in Ragusa in 1711 – show a man with a slightly pudgy face and the permanently slightly exasperated look of the over-intelligent.

He was educated in Ragusa by the Jesuits and then went on at the age of 14 to study at the Jesuit Collegium Romanum in Rome – so successfully that he was appointed professor of mathematics and physics there at the tender age of 29. As one of Europe's brightest scientists, Bošković was a member of London's Royal Society and wrote around 70 papers on astronomy, gravitation, meteorology, optics and trigonometry. His most famous work is *A Theory of Natural Philosophy* – or *Philosophiae naturalis theoria redacta ad unicam legem virium in Natura existentium*, as it's more correctly known.

Bošković was also something of a Latin poet and was capable of describing his complex astronomical ideas in elegant metered verse. He died in Milan in 1787.

The **Pile Gate** [318–19 B3], dating back to 1471, is approached across a wooden drawbridge which used to be pulled up every night. Set into a niche here is the first of many statues you'll see of St Blaise (Sveti Vlaho), the city's patron saint. Indeed, as you enter the gate you'll immediately see another – this time by Ivan Meštrović, Croatia's most famous sculptor.

Once inside the gate you come straight on to Dubrovnik's famous main street, Stradun, which is paved in marble (be careful when it's wet; it can be lethally slippery). This was originally the marshy channel which separated the Roman settlement of Ragusa on one side from the Slavic settlement of Dubrovnik on the other.

On the square inside the Pile Gate stands **Onofrio's Great Fountain** [318–19 B3], which was completed in 1444 by the Neapolitan architect Onofrio della Cava as part of the city's smart new plumbing. Unfortunately all the fancy ornamental work from the upper part of the fountain was lost in the Great Earthquake of 1667.

To your left as you come into the city is the tiny **Church of Our Saviour** (Sveti Spas) [318–19 B3]. It was completed in 1528 as a thank you from the survivors of the 1520 earthquake, and itself survived the far more dramatic quake of 1667 – a tribute to the building skills of the Andrijić brothers, from Korčula, who also worked on the Sponza Palace (see page 332). The simple Renaissance trefoil façade and rose window are quietly pleasing, and hide a Gothic interior which is mainly used these days as a venue for candlelit concerts.

The Franciscan Monastery and Pharmacy [318–19 C3] (*Placa 2;* ☏ *321 410;* ⊕ *09.00–17:00 daily; 10kn*) Next door to Our Saviour is the Franciscan Church and Monastery. The church is entered from Stradun itself, where you'll find the south door crowned by a wonderful *pietà* – evocatively described by Rebecca West in 1937 as 'definite and sensible. The Madonna looks as if, had it been in her hands, she would have stopped the whole affair.'

The *pietà* survived the Great Earthquake, but the church itself was entirely gutted by fire and countless treasures were lost for ever. What you see today dates from the 18th century onwards, which explains the Baroque nature of it all. The church is famous locally as the final resting place of Ivan Gundulić (see page 117), though he's actually interred in a part of the church that is closed to the public – you can still pay your respects at a plaque on the north wall, however.

The rest of the monastery is accessed down a narrow passage next to Our Saviour. At the entrance you'll find the famous pharmacy, self-billed as the oldest in the world. Whether it is or not, it probably was one of the earliest to be open to the public, and it's still operating today, though from a 1901 refurbishment. The original pharmacy was established in 1317, and in the museum off the cloisters you can see an interesting collection of jars and poisons from the 15th century on, along with ancient pharmacopoeias. The museum also contains various religious artefacts, as well as a testy portrait of Ruđer Bošković, Dubrovnik's mathematical genius (see box opposite), painted in 1760 in London. Most interesting of all, however, is a canvas showing the old town before the earthquake – note how much greater Onofrio's Great Fountain was before 1667.

The cloisters themselves are truly exceptional, consisting of rows of double octagonal columns with individualised capitals. They are the work of Mihoje Brakov, a sculptor from Bar (in what's now Montenegro), who died here of the plague in 1348. One of the capitals near the entrance, depicting a medieval man with terrible toothache, is said to be a self-portrait of the sculptor. Inside the courtyard are palm trees and well-trimmed box hedges, and it's a great place to get away from the heat in high summer.

Stradun and Luža Square Stradun itself (also known as Placa – pronounced platsa) continues in a widening straight line all the way to the Clock Tower at the far end. As you'll notice, the houses along the street are nearly identical; a result of the careful

post-earthquake planning at the end of the 17th century. Note the distinctive '*na koljeno*' single-arched frame that combines the entrance door and window to provide a counter over which goods could be served to customers.

In Luža Square, at the far end of Stradun, you'll find **Orlando's Column** [318–19 E4], a statue of Roland symbolising the city's desire for freedom (*libertas*) and which has marked the centre of town since its erection in 1418. For centuries Roland's forearm was Ragusa's standard measure of length (the *lakat*, since you ask), a convenient 512mm long – you can see the reference groove at the base of the statue. All state declarations were read from a platform above the column in the days of the republic, and condemned criminals were executed at its base.

Behind Orlando's Column you can't miss the **Clock Tower** [318–19 F4], originally built in 1444, which features a complex astronomical clock, and a pair of green men (the *zelenci*) who strike the hour. The tower was rebuilt in 1929 (which is presumably when the digital clock was added), so the only thing that's really original now is the bell, dating from 1506, which weighs over two tonnes. The original clock mechanism and green men are in the Sponza Palace (see below). Next to the clock tower is **Onofrio's Small Fountain**, dating from 1441.

The Sponza Palace [318–19 F3/4] (*Luža;* ✎ *321 032*) On the left-hand side of Luža square is the Sponza Palace, which functioned variously as a cistern, the customs house and the state mint. Today it houses the Memorial Room of the Dubrovnik Defenders, the original innards of the city clock, and the State Archives. It's one of the most charming buildings in Dubrovnik, boldly mixing pure Venetian Gothic and late Renaissance into a harmonious whole. It was built in 1522 to plans by the local architect Pasko Miličević, and features work by the Andrijić brothers, the master sculptors who were also responsible for much of Korčula Cathedral – as well as the Church of Our Saviour at the other end of Stradun. The Sponza was one of the few buildings to survive the Great Earthquake of 1667.

The entrance is through a wide-arched Renaissance portico, above which there's a lovely Venetian-Gothic first storey, topped with a row of four late-Renaissance windows and a statue of St Blaise in a niche. Inside there's a courtyard with a double cloister.

The name Sponza comes from the Latin word *spongia*, meaning sponge, as there was originally a cistern on this site. The Sponza's main purpose, however, was to serve as the republic's customs house (which is why it's also sometimes referred to as the Divona or Dogana). On the ground floor here goods were measured for duty, under the inscription '*Fallere Nostra Vetant et Falli Pondera Meque Pondero cum Merces Ponderat ipse Deus*' – which translates roughly as 'the scales we use to weigh your goods are the same scales used by God to weigh us'.

The ground-floor rooms originally served as warehouse space, while those on the first floor were used for literary and scientific meetings. Up on the second floor was the state mint, which issued Dubrovnik's currency (*perperae, grossi* and *ducats*) from 1337 until 1803.

After World War II, the Sponza housed the **Museum of the Socialist Revolution**, though of course that's disappeared following the more recent war. Instead you'll find the original 16th-century mechanism for the city clock here, along with the two green men, Maro and Baro, who struck the bell until 1928. The space is used for concerts during the Summer Festival.

The **Memorial Room of the Dubrovnik Defenders** (⊕ *08.00–14.00 daily*), on the ground floor, is a commemoration of the tragic events here from 1 October 1991 to 26 October 1992, when more than 200 defenders and 100 civilians were killed. It's a terribly sobering place, with the remnants of the flag from the Imperial Fort on Srđ and the pictures and dates of all the young lives that were snuffed out during the siege. Many of the photos are the work of local photographer Pavo Urban, who was tragically cut down in his prime (aged just 23) by shrapnel just yards from the memorial room in December 1991.

The building also houses the **State Archives** (✆ *020 321 032;* e *arhiv-dubrovnik@ dad.hr*), which are among the most complete in the world, chronicling pretty much everything that happened during the 1,000-year history of the republic. Altogether there are some 8,000m of shelved documents, ranging from the 13th-century city statutes to Marshal Marmont's orders dissolving the republic in 1808. The archives are open to researchers daily – you should call ahead or email in advance if you want to visit.

The Dominican Monastery [318–19 F3] (*Sv Domina 4;* ✆ *321 423;* ⊕ *09.00–17.00 daily; 15kn*) The winding street Svetog Dominika leads up to the Ploče Gate. On the way you can't miss the Dominican Monastery. Notice the way the steps on the way up are walled in, up to a height of about two feet to protect the modesty of travellers and save the monks from impure ankle-related thoughts.

The monastery was used by the occupying French troops from 1808 – you can see from the outside where windows were sealed up to make a Napoleonic prison, and the church itself was used as stables. In the cloisters you can still see the horse troughs which were hacked into the retaining walls by the cavalrymen.

The original church here was completed in 1315, but had to be rebuilt after the Great Earthquake of 1667. It was then paved with the coats of arms of all the noble families, but unfortunately was repaved in 1910 with plain marble. Today it's a vast, boxy place, and most of the best art has been moved to the museum – though not the greatest treasure of all, a terrific 5m-by-4m crucifixion by Paolo Veneziano, which was installed here in 1358. There's also an interesting painting of St Dominic by local boy Vlaho Bukovac, though it's not, frankly, the artist's best work – you can see some of this at the Museum of Modern Art (see page 339) in Dubrovnik, and even more in the painter's home town, Cavtat (see page 342).

The cloisters are a late-Gothic masterpiece, built to a design by the Florentine architect Maso di Bartolomeo, but with extra flourishes added by local stonemasons. In the courtyard oranges and lemons grow, and – like the Franciscan cloisters – it's a wonderfully cool, shady place on a hot day.

The monastery also houses an interesting museum and an extraordinary library; with over 16,000 works and 240 incunabula, it was one of the greatest European libraries of the Renaissance. In the museum you'll find a rare 11th-century bible, along with a much-reproduced triptych featuring St Blaise with a model of pre-earthquake Ragusa in his right hand – still recognisable as Dubrovnik today, though both the Franciscan and Dominican monasteries sported bigger spires back then. Also of note is a marvellous altarpiece by Titian featuring Mary Magdalene with St Blaise and the Archangel Raphael – the chap on his knees is the member of the Pučić family who commissioned the work.

Up a couple of stairs there's a room full of votive gold – a fraction of what was here originally, as most of it was sold off after World War II to support the faculty of theology, unfunded in communist times. There's an interesting Flemish diptych here – with Jesus on the left while on the right there's a reversible panel, with love on one side and death on the other, usefully adaptable according to your moods and whims.

The synagogue [318–19 E3] (*Žudioska 5;* ✆ *412 219;* ⊕ *10.00–13.00 Mon–Fri; 10kn*) As you leave the monastery, turn right and you'll find yourself at the eastern end of Prijeko, which is best visited early in the day, before the eager restaurateurs can get their teeth into you, so to speak (see page 324). Take a detour down Žudioska, and you'll find one of Europe's oldest (and smallest) synagogues. It's Europe's second oldest

(after Prague) and in spite of restrictions placed on Jews here during World War II, it was the only European synagogue to function all the way through the war.

The synagogue – with original 17th-century furnishings – is on the second floor, while below it, on the first floor, there's a fascinating two-room museum, where you can see richly decorated Torah Scrolls and binders, and ancient Ark Curtains, as well as a copy of the letter signed by Marshal Marmont granting the Jewish community full emancipation from 1808. There's also a chilling selection of documents from 1941, issued by the fascist NDH (see page 15), restricting the movement of Jews and ordering them to wear yellow ribbons and badges.

War Photo Limited [318–19 D3] (*Antuninska 6;* ✆ *322 166; www.warphotoltd.com;* ☉ *Jun–Sep 09.00–21.00 daily; May & Oct 09.00–15.00 Tue–Sat, 10.00–14.00 Sun; closed Nov–Apr; 30kn*) Continue down Prijeko for most of its length – or if it's already approaching lunchtime consider avoiding the touts by walking along the old city's uppermost street, Peline, which gives great views down the steep-stepped streets crossing Prijeko – and then turn left down Antuninska, where you'll find the extraordinary War Photo Limited.

It's one of Dubrovnik's newest and most emotionally charged galleries, and I can't recommend a visit too highly. Specialising in first-rate temporary exhibitions by the world's greatest modern-war photographers, the gallery aims, as the New Zealand-born director, Wade Goddard, says: 'to strip away the Hollywood image of war, to replace the glamour, the heroic bravura, the "only the bad guys suffer" image of war, with the raw and undeniable evidence that war inflicts injustices on all who experience it'.

It would require a heart of stone to come away unmoved by the extraordinary (and often painful) images. In the summer of 2004, Ron Haviv's breathtaking Blood and Honey collection was on show – 'bal' being Turkish for 'honey' and 'kan' being Turkish for 'blood'. Haviv won the 'World Press Photo' award for his iconic pictures of the fall of Vukovar in 1991, and is one of the co-founders of agency vii (*see www.viiphoto.com*). The collection is nothing if not eclectic, taking in the troubled African continent in 2006 and Colombia in 2009.

To the Orthodox Church and Icon Museum On the other side of Stradun, a short walk along Garište brings you to Za Rokom, where you'll find the little Church of St Roc. Round on the right-hand wall of the church is a fine piece of carved graffiti dated 1597 and reading '*Pax vobis memento mori qui ludetis pilla*' – which translates roughly as 'Peace be with you, but remember that you must die, you who play ball here', clearly the work of an irate adult, keen to warn off noisy, football-mad kids.

Continue along Za Rokom until you get to the end of the street, then turn left into Široka. On the right-hand side you'll find the house where Marin Držić (see page 338) once lived – although unless you're a serious fan of the playwright's work, you won't get a great deal out of a visit. Equally, unless you have a lot of time on your hands you probably needn't visit the **Rupe Ethnographic Museum** [318–19 B5] (*od Rupa 2;* ☎ *323 018;* ⊕ *summer 09.00–18.00 daily, winter 09.00–14.00; 10kn*), a block away – though the former granary building itself is interesting, as you can see some of the vast chambers which were dug into the rock to store grain back in the 16th century, keeping the food dry and cool.

Turning on to Od Puča, you'll find the Orthodox Church on your left, and (two doors down) the Icon Museum (see below). This part of town is where most of the small remaining Serbian community lives and works. Just down Miha Pracata, on the left-hand side, you'll also find Dubrovnik's **mosque** [318–19 D4/5], which is open 10.00–13.00 daily – though there's really nothing special to see there.

The **Serb Orthodox Church** [318–19 D4] of the Holy Annunciation (*Od Puča;* ☎ *426 260;* ⊕ *09.00–16.00 daily*) is one of Dubrovnik's most recent, only being completed in 1877. A plain exterior shelters a rather spare interior, with a traditional iconostasis (with icons from the 15th to 19th centuries) separating the clergy from the congregation. The church was one of the last buildings in the old town – perhaps unsurprisingly – on which restoration work got underway after the end of the siege in 1992, but happily is now receiving both attention and funds; hopefully it will be fully restored in the near future.

Two doors down is the rarely visited **Icon Museum** [318–19 D4] (*Od Puča;* ☎ *323 283;* ⊕ *09.00–13.00 Mon–Sat; 10kn*), upstairs, on the second floor (past a sign in Cyrillic saying **СРПСКА** – Srpska, or Serbian). It's a pity as the two-room collection brings together a wide range of icons from the 18th and 19th centuries, as well as some earlier ones from the 15th and 16th centuries. They come from all across the Balkans and Russia and the differences between the various schools are fascinating – the Russian icons featuring long noses; the ones from the Bay of Kotor having deep, dark shadows. In the second room there are also half a dozen dark, dark portraits of local 19th-century Serb notables by Vlaho Bukovac (see box on page 343), quite unlike anything else you'll see by the famous local painter.

To Gundulićeva poljana Continuing down Od Puča brings you past the Pučić Palace hotel and out on to Gundulićeva poljana – literally Gundulić's little field. In the centre of the square stands a statue of Ivan Gundulić himself (see box opposite), which dates back to 1893. There's a marvellous allegorical vignette at the base of the statue; a bethroned Dubrovnik has both Turkey and Venice at her feet – with Turkey represented as the dragon on the left and Venice as the winged lion on the right. A certain irony, therefore, that the city's most expensive hotel, the Pučić Palace, overlooking the very same square, should today be Turkish-owned.

The Jesuit Church [318–19 D6] (*Properly the Church of St Ignatius of Loyola, or Ignacija Lojolskog;* ⊕ *08.00–19.00 daily*) Turn right out of Gundulićeva poljana and head up the great flight of steps – said to be modelled on the Spanish Steps in Rome – leading to the Jesuit Church, a massive structure clearly intended to make a point. It was built to plans by the Jesuit artist Andrea Pozzo, who had already done great works in Rome and would go on to design the cathedral in Ljubljana.

Completed in 1725, the church features a dramatic double-storeyed set of Corinthian columns lifting the façade skywards, and the church behind it is enormous, covering a surface of over 600m². Inside it feels very big and gloomy, as

Ask anyone about Dubrovnik's cathedral and it won't be long before Richard the Lionheart's name comes up. According to local legend, the English king ran into a terrible storm near here on his return home from the crusades at the end of 1192, and vowed that if he survived he would build a church on the spot. Miraculously, he was saved, and washed up on Lokrum.

On hearing the news of the arrival of such an important – and apparently loaded – visitor, Dubrovnik sent over a welcoming party, who persuaded King Richard that his money would be better spent on building a cathedral in Dubrovnik. In exchange, the Ragusan nobles would build a votive church on Lokrum at their own expense. Richard agreed, and handed over 100,000 ducats, before continuing on his journey to Italy and – eventually – England.

In all probability, however, the Lokrum part of this charming tale is a Benedictine fabrication. The monks on Lokrum had good cause for inventing – or at the very least embellishing – such a story. Because of it, they enjoyed various privileges in Dubrovnik's cathedral, including the abbot of Lokrum being allowed to hold the Candlemas pontifical mass, which is celebrated on 2 February, the day before St Blaise's feast day. This mass apparently enraged successive bishops of Dubrovnik, who demanded the privilege be rescinded. In the end, in the 1590s, the Ragusan government had to resort to writing letters to the pope, who finally decided in favour of Lokrum's Benedictines – thereby legitimising the Lionheart story.

you'd expect, with the interior modelled on the Gesù Church in Rome and featuring lots of fabulous *trompe l'oeil*, Pozzi's speciality – he was the author of a seminal work on perspective, *Prospettiva de' pittori et architect*, which revolutionised painting in the 18th century and is still used today. The main attraction is the inside of the apse, which features spectacular scenes from the life of Ignatius, the founder of the Jesuit order, by the Sicilian painter Gaetano Garcia.

Altogether less spiritually uplifting – though popular enough with local devotees, it seems – is the 'Grotto of Lourdes', which was added in 1885.

To the Maritime Museum and Aquarium (*Damjana Jude 2; Maritime Museum:* ℄ *323 904;* ⊕ *09.00–18.00 Tue–Sun; shorter hours in winter; 40kn; Aquarium:* ℄ *427 937;* ⊕ *summer 09.00–21.00 daily, winter 10.00–13.00 daily (except Mon); 20kn).* You can leave the rather tatty square in front of the Jesuit church by the far corner and wind your way all the way along Ispod mira, the alley leading along the inside of the city walls. This is perhaps the quietest and shabbiest part of the town, with lots of buildings still unrestored after being badly damaged in an earthquake in 1979.

At the end of the line, so to speak, you'll find **St John's Fortress** [318–19 H5], which houses the Maritime Museum upstairs and the aquarium on the ground floor. Spread out over two floors, the **Maritime Museum** covers the entire history of seafaring in the area, from the Golden Age of the republic through to the arrival of steam-powered ships. It's well worth a visit if you're into ships and sailing, with lots of maps, evocative old photos and models of various types of ship, along with bits of rigging and ship's supplies and cargoes.

Downstairs, you'll find Dubrovnik's dismal seawater **Aquarium**. Mostly it amounts to large Mediterranean fish (groupers, eels and the like) swimming listlessly round in tanks that don't seem big enough. The whole bleak experience is epitomised by the solitary giant turtle which paddles its way to and fro miserably in a pond-sized pool, while school groups shower the benighted beast with small change.

The cathedral and treasury [318–19 F5/6] (*Poljana Marina Držića; usually* ☉ *08.00–12.00 & 15.00–17.00 Mon–Sat, 11.00–13.00 & 15.00–17.00 Sun; treasury 7kn*) Heading back into the heart of the city, the first thing you come to is the cathedral. The former Romanesque number – said to have been bankrolled by a shipwrecked Richard the Lionheart (see box opposite) – was demolished by the Great Earthquake in 1667, so what you get today is the Baroque replacement, completed in 1713 to plans by the Italian architect Andrea Buffalini. The statues of the saints along the eaves are rather fine, though notice that St Mark has been relegated to an inferior position – perhaps a none-too-subtle snub to Venice.

Surprisingly, for Baroque, the cathedral is a rather spartan affair inside, with a chunky modern altar and acres of whitewash – and it's curious in having a west-facing altar. The compelling attraction is the treasury, though if you're here it's nonetheless worth having a look at the impressive (school of) Titian altarpiece.

Altogether, there are well over 100 priceless relics in the **treasury**, many of which are carried around the town in a grand procession on 3 February, the feast day of Dubrovnik's patron saint. The most important of these is the Head of St Blaise himself, which was bought from Byzantium (along with the saint's arms and a leg) in 1026. The head is housed in a fine casing decorated with 24 Byzantine enamel plaques from the 12th century, featuring austere, intense portraits of the saints.

The treasury also includes one of John the Baptist's hands, a bit of the True Cross incorporated into a crucifix, one of Christ's nappies in a silver box, and a dark wooden lectern which once belonged to England's Henry VIII – after the Reformation, treasures from the dissolved monasteries went up for sale, and a small selection ended up in the hands of enterprising sailors from Lopud (see page 346).

Over on the right-hand side is an extraordinary painting by Raphael, the Madonna della Seggiola (Sedia), which is almost identical to the 1514 version in the Palazzo Pitti in Florence. Why there's a copy here – painted on what looks like the bottom of a barrel – is a mystery, but the painting itself is a pure wonder.

Last but not least is an extraordinary pitcher and ewer from the 15th century, prominently on display, which is an allegory of Dubrovnik's flora and fauna. Featuring snakes and tortoises, eels and lizards, and some pre-Dalí lobsters, along with alarming amounts of vegetation, it looks like it would be the very devil to clean. It's thought to have been made as a gift for the Hungarian king of the day, Matthias Corvinus the Just, but ended up here as the king died before he could receive the tribute.

It's always aroused a certain amount of passion. In 1929, Count Voynovitch, author of a handy little guide to the city, said 'The basin is delightfully finished'. Just eight years later, however, (the ever-opinionated) Rebecca West was writing: 'Nothing could be more offensive to the eye, to the touch, or to common sense... it has the infinite elaborateness of eczema, and to add to the last touch of unpleasantness these animals are loosely fixed so that they may wobble and give an illusion of movement. Though Dubrovnik is beautiful, and this object was indescribably ugly, my dislike of the second explained to me why I felt doubtful in my appreciation of the first. The town regarded this horror as a masterpiece.'

And it's true; it does.

The Rector's Palace (Knežev Dvor) [318–19 F5] (*Pred Dvorom 3;* ☏ *321 437;* ☉ *09.00–18.00 daily, closes earlier in winter; 25kn*) Diagonally opposite the cathedral is the Rector's Palace, with the municipal theatre next door. If you get the chance, pop inside and admire the charming, miniature version of the grand Austro-Hungarian opera houses and theatres – complete with gilded boxes and velvet seating, which dates back to 1869.

The **Rector's Palace** was the seat of Ragusa's government. It would once have looked more like a castle than a palace, but after the original was accidentally blown up in 1435 (always a mistake keeping your gunpowder next to your government) it was rebuilt in the Venetian-Gothic style by Onofrio della Cava – he of the fountains' fame.

It wasn't to last, as the gunpowder went off again in 1463. This time the palace was restored by Michelozzo Michelozzi, who also did lots of work on the city's defensive fortresses, and Juraj Dalmatinac, who added various Renaissance touches.

You enter through a fine loggia topped with superb carved capitals on pillars of Korčula marble; the outer pairs are the original Gothic while the middle three are Renaissance. Most interesting of all is the rightmost capital, thought to portray Asclepius, the Greek god of healing, who was born in Epidaurus (now Cavtat). The main door leads into an atrium which is the (surprisingly small) venue for summer recitals. In here you'll find the only statue ever raised to an individual in Ragusa's long history. On dying in 1607, Miho Pracat (see page 346), a remarkable ship owner and adventurer from Lopud, left 1,000 shares in the Bank of St George in Genoa to the city. The city was suitably grateful – back then those shares were worth around 100 lira apiece, at a time when gold was fetching three and a half lira an ounce. The interest on the capital was used by the city to free slaves, and Pracat got his statue.

The ground floor of the palace was formerly a prison, handy for the courtroom off to the right, with a curious marble barrier and wooden bench being about all you can see today. Upstairs are the state offices and rector's chambers – from the day they were elected, rectors were effectively prisoners here, only allowed to leave with the senate's permission. Fortunately each only served a one-month term.

The main staircase was only used for the rector's inaugural procession on the first of the month, taking him upstairs to his confinement. Nobody ever came down the stairs unless the rector died in office – the hidden staircase behind was the way out. On your way up the main stairs notice the handrails, supported by realistic (if not entirely tasteful) carved hands.

At the top of the stairs, over the door which originally led into the Grand Council chamber, there's an inscription reading '*Obliti Privatorum Publica Curate*' – a quote from Pericles, reminding councillors to forget their private concerns and think of public affairs instead.

The upstairs rooms are a curious collection – mainly because the palace was plundered, first by the French in the early 19th century, and then again by Yugoslavia's King Aleksandar after World War I, for the Royal Palace in Belgrade. As a result they're for the most part furnished with private donations. You'll find an odd mix of

Venetian repro, Louis XV copies, painted wood, Neapolitan ebony and marble veneer, along with an unusual collection of canvases featuring local bigwigs. Note also the keys to the city – the gates were locked every night and the keys were kept in the rector's office – and the candlelit clock.

The Church of St Blaise [318–19 F4] (*Sveti Vlaho; usually* ☉ *08.00–20.00 daily*) The original church on this site was built in the 14th century, and although it (mostly) survived the Great Earthquake in 1667, it was subsequently consumed by fire. Miraculously, the 15th-century gold and silver statue of St Blaise escaped unharmed.

The new Baroque Church of St Blaise was completed in 1717 to plans by the Venetian architect Marino Grapelli, who based the interior design on the Church of San Maurizio in his home town. It's even more unusual than the cathedral in its orientation, in having a south-facing altar.

The church is an elegant tribute to the city's patron saint, with a classic Baroque façade. Inside it's not as austere as the cathedral but not too over the top either. The main attraction is the altar, where you can admire the famous statue of St Blaise holding the city – which shows you what it looked like in about 1485.

Also worth your attention is the painting across the organ loft representing the Martyrdom of St Blaise, which was painted by local boy Petar Matejević in the early 18th century. Spare a moment too for the stained-glass windows, which depict Sts Peter and Paul and Sts Cyril and Methodius, the creators of the Glagolitic alphabet (a later variant of which, Cyrillic, is named after St Cyril). These are the work of Ivo Dulčić, one of Dubrovnik's most famous modern artists, who died in 1975.

Ploče and the Museum of Modern Art The Ploče Gate leads out from the old town into the expensive suburb of Ploče. The gate is a complex structure actually comprising several gates and bridges which were built in the 15th century – though the current design dates from 1628. There's the familiar statue of St Blaise, and a drawbridge leading out into what used to be a market square.

The main road leads up to the **Lazareti**, Dubrovnik's quarantine houses. Dubrovnik was one of the first ports in Europe to introduce quarantine restrictions, and if you wanted to visit you had to spend 40 days here first before being allowed in. These days the houses and courtyards are used as artists' studios and performance spaces.

A little further up the hill, on the left-hand side, is Dubrovnik's excellent **Museum of Modern Art** (*Put Frana Supila 23;* ✆ *426 590;* ☉ *10.00–13.00 & 17.00–21.00 Tue–Sun; 20kn*) Even if there were no art to see, the building itself is magnificent and well worth a visit. Built in 1939 as the summer villa for a wealthy ship-owner, Božo Banac, it was designed in a Renaissance style reminiscent of the Rector's Palace and you wouldn't know it wasn't ancient. Since 1950 it has housed the museum's ever-expanding (and excellent) collection.

The permanent collection includes paintings and sculpture from Croatia's greatest artists as well as focusing on the burgeoning local scene. The works are rotated and there are usually temporary exhibitions, so what's on show at any one time varies. Look out for sculpture from two of Croatia's most representative and best-known sculptors, Ivan Meštrović and Frano Kršnić, as well as landscapes by Mato Celestin Medović and interiors and still lifes from Emanuel Vidović. The show is stolen, naturally, by Vlaho Bukovac (see box on page 343), and the gallery holds some of his very best work, including a number of gorgeous, complex portraits – though they're not always all on show.

Culture and the Dubrovnik Summer Festival Dubrovnik has a richly vibrant cultural scene, with its own symphony orchestra, theatre group and dance ensemble. Most performances take place during the season – broadly speaking from May to October

– when there's usually something on every night, but most important of all is the annual **Dubrovnik Summer Festival**.

The festival is big, prestigious and serious, with every conceivable space in the old town – indoors and out – being turned into a performance-stage. The 45-day festival kicks off on 10 July with the performers being given the keys to the city and closes on 25 August with a fabulous firework display.

During the festival you can find everything from opera and classical concerts to chamber music and soloists, while theatre performances tend to concentrate on Shakespeare and local boy Marin Držić (see box on page 338). A festival standard is the traditional performance of Hamlet in the Lovrijenac Fortress, which is a wonderfully atmospheric setting for the play.

Tickets for the main events sell out well in advance, so if you're serious about attending check out the website (*www.dubrovnik-festival.hr*) or contact the organisers (☎ *020 326 100;* ℻ *020 326 116*) as soon as the programme becomes available (usually in April) – and make sure you get your accommodation sorted out way ahead of time, too. If you haven't got tickets in advance there are usually places available for the lower-key performances on site – you can buy these from the festival kiosks on Stradun and at the Pile Gate.

Even outside the festival there are plenty of opportunities to listen to classical music, largely thanks to the tireless **Dubrovnik Symphony Orchestra** (*www.dso.hr*), which puts on an astonishing range of concerts, all year round. The two most common venues – outside festival time – are the Revelin Fortress, just outside the Ploče Gate, and the Church of Our Saviour (Sveti Spas), just inside the Pile Gate, where there are regular candlelit performances.

Dubrovnik also has one of the country's most famous folk dancing troupes in the form of the 300-strong Linđo ensemble. They're a regular mainstay of the festival, and also perform twice a week from May to October at the Lazareti, the old quarantine houses just up from the Ploče Gate. It makes for an amazing and authentic spectacle. Linđo's office is at Marojice Kaboge 12, two streets back from Gundulićeva poljana.

Mount Srđ Looming large above Dubrovnik, and visible from all over the city, is the mountain of Srđ. Up until 1991 there was a cable car that whisked visitors up to the top for the incredible view over the city and the islands, but it became one of the first victims of the war, dramatically destroyed by a Serb air raid.

The cable car hasn't been put back into service since then – apparently because of a long-running dispute, with the top and bottom stations owned by different companies. It's a great pity, as the only way up now is on foot – unless you happen to have access to a vehicle, in which case you can take the road up to the village of Bosanka, before turning left on to the road to the summit.

If you do decide to walk up, bear in mind that the path is long, steep, and entirely without shade for the last two-thirds. At first it's through pine trees, with butterflies and cicadas – magic and very cool. There's no water to be had, either on the way up or at the top, so take plenty with you. And although the path is perfectly safe, and the hillside is said to be clear of unexploded ordnance, you should stick to the main track just in case. Locals tend to hunt with shotguns here too, so be careful where you walk.

The path climbs up from the main road running above Dubrovnik – referred to variously as Državna Cesta or Jadranska Cesta (and formerly Put Jugoslavenske Narodne Armije). Starting at the Pile Gate, turn right just after the bus stop and work your way up Zrinsko-Frankopanska. Cross over Zagrebačka and then Gornji Kono, then take the next right and follow this slip road under Jadranska Cesta. After this the footpath starts off to your left, from the highway. From the Pile Gate it will take you anything between 1 and 2 hours to the top of Mount Srđ, depending on how fit you are.

At the top you'll find the Imperial Fort, which was built by the French in 1810. In the 1970s it became a popular discotheque (rumours that your author was once seen strutting his stuff there many years ago are clearly without foundation). Today, the fort is still badly damaged and can't be visited (it's fenced off), so the only reason to climb up this far is for the magnificent views – and of course the exercise. What you won't miss is the huge cross at the top, which now dominates the Old Town, especially when it's illuminated at night. As you climb up in the heat, spare a thought for the mothers of those killed in the war who follow the route as a pilgrimage for their sons, walking barefoot to the top and stopping to pray at each of the 13 crosses placed at corners along the way.

LOKRUM When you're in Dubrovnik, keep at least half a day free for a trip to sub-tropical Lokrum, the town's own offshore nature reserve. Said to have been visited unwillingly by Richard the Lionheart in 1192 (see box on page 336) the island is today just a 15-minute boat-ride away from the old town quay.

Lokrum remains undeveloped, and makes for a wonderful break from the crowds onshore. Even when the boats are arriving full, every half hour, the 2km-long island can easily absorb all comers, leaving an impression – away from a small central part – of calm and tranquillity, punctuated only by the cries of birds and the fluttering of butterflies.

A network of footpaths criss-crosses the island and provides access to the sea and into the dense woods. There are several rock beaches, and these are cleaner, fresher and less crowded than Dubrovnik's, as well as a warm saltwater lake (Mrtvo More, the Dead Sea), on the other side of the island from where the boat arrives. This has a 10m cliff which encourages the local lads to dive off it, apparently without harm. There's a naturist beach on Lokrum, too, on the south eastern end of the island, away from prying eyes – follow the FKK signs.

Lokrum's main attraction lies in its enormous variety of vegetation, which is all the more astonishing when you realise there's no fresh water supply – hence the absolute ban on making fires of any kind or even on smoking. When you're wandering the paths look out for numerous species of birds (including peacocks) and butterflies. On a visit here in June I saw white admirals, several sorts of fritillary and some skittish large yellows.

In the middle of the island, there's an old botanical garden, most of which seems like a series of wonderfully unmaintained secret gardens. Amongst slightly dilapidated walls you'll find palms with soft furry trunks, trellises of twisted vines and crippled trees supported on crutches, while broken cloches sprout thyme and basil and lettuce run to seed.

In the heavy silence and deep shade there's an agreeable air of mystery – which is shattered fairly unceremoniously when you round a corner and discover the restaurant and bar, and a small natural history museum, all within the structure of what was once a large Benedictine monastery.

On the summit of the island – a steepish 20-minute hike – there's a ruined fort. Built by the French in 1808, it gives great views out over Dubrovnik, and the nearby coast and the islands. Be careful here though – it's in a parlous state, and the steps leading inside and up to the lookout are on the point of collapse.

It was from the northern tip of Lokrum that I finally realised what it was I'd found vaguely make-believe about Dubrovnik all along: it's a film set. So many movies have plundered that fortified look – the big walls, the red-roofed houses nestled between them dominated by a smattering of palaces and churches – that it doesn't seem real. It looks like it's meant to be looked at, but could never really have been lived in.

To get to Lokrum, take the half-hourly boat (every day in season, otherwise only on weekends) from the old harbour, and make sure you know what time the last one is coming back. Tickets cost around 30kn return. If you're here on a weekday out of

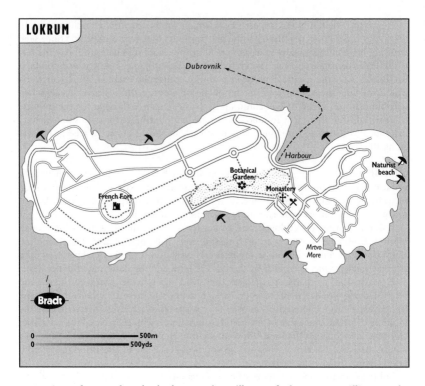

LOKRUM

Dubrovnik

Harbour

Botanical
Garden

Monastery

French Fort

Naturist
beach

Mrtvo
More

Bradt

0 ————— 500m
0 ————— 500yds

season just ask around at the harbour and you'll soon find someone willing to take you across. Expect to pay up to 100kn a head, and make sure the skipper knows what time you want to be picked up.

SOUTH OF DUBROVNIK

From Dubrovnik, it's 40km south to the Montenegrin border. On the way there's a string of resorts (Kupari, Srebreno, Mlini, Soline and Plat) collectively known as the Župa Dubrovačka, which lead to the town of Cavtat (pronounced *tsavtat*), after which there's just Čilipi Airport and the ruggedly beautiful Konavle region (the latter just opening up to tourists) before you reach the border.

CAVTAT Situated just 16km south, the small, pleasant seaside town of Cavtat makes an excellent and easy excursion from Dubrovnik – and can even be considered as an alternative place to stay, with regular buses and ferries between the two and accommodation both cheaper and easier to find here. If you're visiting the area by car, Cavtat makes an ideal base, with nothing like the parking hassles you'll find in Dubrovnik itself.

Cavtat was originally the Greek and then Roman colony of Epidaurus, though there's nothing left at all from that era barring a few classical fragments built into houses – fishermen, in Rebecca West's nicely turned phrase, having 'taken what they would of sculptures and bas-reliefs to build up their cottage walls, where they can be seen today, flowers in the buttonhole of poverty'.

Getting there The #10 Libertas bus runs about once an hour from 06.00 to midnight, and costs 12kn each way (pay on the bus) while the standard ferry runs until 18.00 and costs around 60kn return (40kn single) – and docks conveniently in Dubrovnik's old town harbour. If their hours don't suit, other ferry companies run to a different timetable, including one with a last return trip at 23.45. Rates are the same for all operators.

Where to stay If you want to stay in Cavtat, there are lots of private rooms available (just ask around – or contact the tourist office on ☏ *020 479 025;* f *020 478 025; www.tzcavtat-konavle.hr*). There are also a number of hotels, including one of Croatia's largest, the 5-star Hotel Croatia.

⌂ **Hotel Croatia** (482 rooms) Frankopanska 10; ☏ 020 475 555; f 020 475 793; www.hoteli-croatia.hr. This stunning multi-tiered, 5-star hotel does sea-view dbls. The hotel is happily sheltered from view by the headland, & has its own beaches (both standard & naturist). It's also home to the Feral restaurant, which has live music every evening. *Dbls €250 in season, €150 in winter.*

⌂ **Hotel Supetar** (28 rooms) A Starčićeva 27; ☏ 020 479 833; f 020 479 858; www.hoteli-croatia.hr/supetar. Run by the same management as the Croatia, this place is rather more endearing, if very traditional. The Supetar is stone-built with 3-star rooms right on the Cavtat quayside. *Dbl €134 in summer, €78 in winter, sea view supplemet €7.50.*

Where to eat One of the best of the town's many restaurants is **Leut** (*Trumbićev Put;* ☏ *020 478 477*), at the southern end of the town, right on the water. It's been in the Bobić family since 1971, and the food is excellent, as you'd expect for the price – though even an advance reservation won't necessarily guarantee they'll hold on to your waterside table here. If you lose your table at Leut, head over to the **Taverna Galjia** (*Vulčevića;* ☏ *020 478 566*), which also serves first-rate seafood.

What to see and do Cavtat (the name seems likely to be derived from the Latin word *civitas*) occupies a peninsula between two bays, and has a charming palm-studded front lined with cafés and restaurants. There's not a whole lot to do, though the Franciscan Monastery, at the end of the quay, hides a pair of lovely Renaissance paintings, and the Rector's Palace, at the other end of the waterfront, houses the town museum (☉ *09.00–13.00 Mon–Fri; 10kn*) – notable in particular for a selection of excellent works by the local painter Vlaho Bukovac (see box below).

VLAHO BUKOVAC – VIRTUOSO PAINTER

Vlaho Bukovac was born in Cavtat in 1855, and showed prodigious talent from an early age. In 1877, he went to the Beaux Arts in Paris to complete his studies and a year later became the first Croatian painter to be accepted into the prestigious Paris Salon. Travelling widely around Europe, Bukovac nonetheless played a vital part in the development of Croatian art – not just by being enormously prolific himself (he left over 2,000 works), but by supporting younger artists as well.

In his forties, Bukovac spent five years living in Cavtat before accepting the post of Professor of Fine Arts in Prague, though he returned to his childhood home regularly until shortly before his death in 1922.

At their best, Bukovac's paintings are simply marvellous, combining an almost photographic realism with impressionistic touches, and some of his portraits are truly stunning. As a virtuoso painter, he seems to have had a penchant for technically difficult or daring compositions, and there's a wonderful picture of a woman coming in (or going out?) through a doorway, which is in the Museum of Modern Art in Dubrovnik, along with a brilliant portrait of his daughter.

Southern Dalmatia SOUTH OF DUBROVNIK

9

Many more Bukovac paintings can be found at the artist's house, which is now the **Galerija Bukovac** (*Bukovčeva 5;* ✆ *020 478 646; www.kuca-bukovac.hr;* ⊕ *May–Oct 09.00–13.00 & 16.00–20.00 Tue–Sat, 16.00–20.00 Sun; Nov–Apr 09.00–13.00 & 14.00–17.00 Tue–Sat, 14.00–17.00 Sun; 20kn).* More than 80 of the artist's oils, spanning his entire career, are on show here.

Right at the end of the peninsula, in a gorgeous hilltop location overlooking the sea and surrounded by cypresses, is the town cemetery. Here you'll find one of Cavtat's most important treasures, the **Račić Mausoleum** (✆ *020 478 646;* ⊕ *10.00–12.00 & 18.00–20.00 Mon–Sat, 10.00–12.00 Sun; 5kn).* Its commissioning by a daughter of the ship-owning Račić family seems to have been their downfall. No sooner was the building underway than she, her father and her brother died in quick succession, and just as soon as the mausoleum was completed her mother followed them into it.

The mausoleum is one of the most important works by Croatia's most famous sculptor, Ivan Meštrović, with the white-marble Byzantine sepulchre dating from 1922. Topped with a cupola and featuring sculpted angels, dogs and eagles, along with the four Račić sarcophagi, it's a quite extraordinary work. It excited mixed feelings in Rebecca West when she was here in 1937: 'There are some terrible errors, such as four boy musician angels, who recall the horrid Japaneseries of Aubrey Beardsley… but there are moments in the chapel which exquisitely illustrate the theory that the goodness of God stretches under human destiny, like the net below trapeze acts at the circus.'

If you're after something a little less esoteric, there's a pleasant walk around the headland, with plenty of places where you can swim off the rocks, and regular trips across the bay for around 50kn to the tiny, almost barren island of **Supetar**, which boasts a simple restaurant.

Rather more strenuous are a couple of local **hikes**. The shorter of these leads from Cavtat to Močiči and Čilipi, taking around 1½ hours. The other involves a three- to four-hour trek up the 'Ronald Brown Pathway' (Pjesačka Staza Ronald Brown) that starts from the main road above the town and leads up into the mountains to the cross commemorating the delegation led by the American Minister of Trade in 1996.

SOUTH TO THE MONTENEGRIN BORDER

Past the airport of the same name you'll find the pretty village of **Čilipi**. After Sunday mass the locals put on a show of folk music and dancing in the main square here, so it's not surprising that it's become something of a Sunday-morning excursion from Dubrovnik and the nearby resort hotels.

Three buses a day run from Dubrovnik to Čilipi and on to **Molunat**, a sleepy resort which has sprung up around a tiny fishing village in a lovely cove right at the very end of Croatia. With just a handful of private rooms, and no hotels nearby, it's within an hour of Dubrovnik, and an utterly charming place to stay. To be honest, however, given the bus times and the minuteness of the place, you'd need to be in Dubrovnik on an extended visit to make the excursion worthwhile.

If you've got your own transport then it's also worth checking out the frontline trenches, bunkers and anti-aircraft gun emplacements at **Đurinići**; not to mention the remains of an old Illyrian hill fort. There's an English language information board, but this is well off the tourist trail, so keep your eyes peeled for the tatty Croatian flag flying above a small cattle shed.

Finally, the **Prevlaka Adventure Park** (✆ *020 791 555; www.prevlaka.hr*) – located at the southernmost tip of the Croatian coast in a former army base – features charming coves, a climbing wall, paintball, bike trails, an animal farm, a labyrinth of underground tunnels, a lighthouse, and a tourist train to take visitors around the park.

Where to eat

✖ **Konoba Konavle** Vojski Do, Šilješki; m 098 674 363; www.dubrovnik-online.com/konoba_konavle. Welcoming family restaurant housed in a stone building that used to be a railway station. Dine on homemade cheese, *pršut* & grilled meats from the station platform (*peka*-cooked dishes need to be ordered a day in advance) & soak up the views of Čilipi & the Konavle from this elevated position. The restaurant is signposted from the main Dubrovnik to Čilipi road, from where the road snakes up the mountainside, so keep your eyes peeled.

THE ELAPHITE ISLANDS (KOLOČEP, LOPUD, ŠIPAN)

The Elaphite Islands lie in a string north of Dubrovnik. These once-quiet islands have seen tourism well and truly arrive, with a new ferry company, Nova International, rivalling Jadrolinija, and an ever-growing number of day trip operators allowing much easier access to the islands.

From June through to the end of September, Nova International (☎ 020 313 599; *www.nova-dubrovnik.hr*) operates a shuttle service to the Elaphites from both the Old City harbour and Gruž. A day ticket (150kn) allows you to visit all three inhabited islands in the same day, though you won't get that much time ashore. The Jadrolinija ferry runs up and down the Elaphites from Dubrovnik three times daily all year round – if you're clever with the Jadrolinija timetables you can also use these ferries to combine the islands with a trip to Mljet.

Even with more tourism than there used to be, the Elaphites still make for a great excursion, getting you away from the crowds and into nature; there are no cars on Koločep and Lopud, and barely a handful on Šipan. If you're interested in staying in private rooms or apartments it's well worth contacting Elaphiti Travel (☎/f 456 345 *www.elaphiti.hr*), which specialises in accommodation on the islands.

KOLOČEP The first inhabited island in the Elaphites is Koločep, just 7km and 25 minutes away from Dubrovnik on the ferry, making it a very easy day trip. The ferry – which costs just 12kn – docks at Donje Čelo, and although there's another settlement on the other side of the island, it's here that you'll find the main infrastructure.

Outside the tourist season Koločep has an official population of just 148, and the doctor only comes once a week. Indeed, if you come here before May, you'll find only a single shop and a post office open in the mornings, and nowhere on the island to eat or drink at all – so bring a picnic, and make sure you know what time the last ferry leaves.

Donje Čelo is spread around a gentle bay, and has a biggish and reasonably sandy beach. A concrete path heads up from the ferry landing and winds across the island, leading through lovely woods and dry-stone-walled fields to the settlement of Gornje Čelo on Koločep's southeastern shore – where you'll find a couple of bars in summer and nothing whatsoever in winter. Smaller paths head on into the scented woods, and the island's sufficiently large for you to lose sight of anyone else, but small enough for most people to avoid getting lost.

Where to stay and eat If you want to stay (from May to October), there's a single hotel in Donje Čelo, across the bay from the ferry landing, called the **Hotel Villas Koločep** (☎ 020 757 025; f 020 757 027; *www.hotel-kolocep.hr*). At the height of the season, expect to pay €150 a night for doubles, in one of the eight buildings comprising the 150-room 3-star hotel. In May and October the rate drops to €80 a night. When the hotel's open there are also three restaurants on the island, two near the ferry terminal and the other one beyond the hotel. There are also a handful of private rooms available – just ask on arrival if you haven't made prior arrangements.

LOPUD Half an hour – and a mere 10kn more on the ferry – beyond Koločep is the larger island of Lopud. Important in Ragusan times, it once had a population of 4,000 and harboured nearly 100 ships, as well as being home to Miho Pracat, the man whose bust sits in the Rector's Palace in Dubrovnik (see box on page 337).

Today the 4.5km-long island has a population of just 348 (though locals put the figure even lower, at barely half that). Everyone lives in one settlement, the eponymous Lopud, on a curved bay with a decent beach facing the village of Suđurađ on the next-door island of Šipan. There's no traffic, no pollution and no crime – and out of season nothing much open beyond a bar and a couple of shops. In summer, however, Lopud really comes into its own, and the village positively hums; it's a great place to come for the day or even for a holiday in its own right.

Where to stay and eat If you want to stay on Lopud, there are quite a few private rooms and apartments for rent (ask on arrival, or contact Elaphiti Travel – see page 345). Pretty much everything, including all the hotels and most of the island's restaurants, close from November to April.

Glavović (12 rooms, 2 apartments) Iva Kuljevana; ☎ 020 759 359; f 020 759 358; www.hotel-glavovic.hr. The 3-star Glavović was the island's 1st hotel. It opened in 1927 & was renovated in 2004. Even if it's comfortable enough, the accommodation is still fairly basic – though the sandy beach just outside is a bonus. *Dbl €120 in season, €80 in May & Oct.*

Lafodia (200 rooms) Iva Kuljevana; ☎ 020 759 022; f 020 759 026; www.lafodiahotel.com. Located at the far end of the bay from the ferry terminal & harbour, the 2-star Lafodia is Lopud's main package tour hotel. Currently under refurbishment, due to reopen 2011. *Dbl €100 in summer, €60 in May & Oct.*

Villa Vilina Iva Kuljevana 5; ☎ 020 759 333; f 020 759 060; www.villa-vilina.hr. A restored mansion that's been in the Vilina family since 1792 now houses Lopud's most upmarket accommodation option (4-star), with nicely furnished sea-view dbls & a lovely suite with its own balcony at €306 a night in season. *Dbl €120–196.*

There are restaurants and bars all along the front, but it's also worth climbing up the street near the harbour to **Terrasse Peggy**, which does a great grill in summer and boasts breezy views out across the sea to the island of Šipan. Try their versions of *limoncello* and a curiously potent, nameless local drink made from honey and herbs.

What to see and do There's not a huge amount to see or do, but if you're here (and it's open) check out the church above the harbour, which has some fine 16th-century

MIHO PRACAT AND THE KING'S SHAVING GOWN

Born into a wealthy family on Lopud in 1528, Miho Pracat sought fame and fortune at sea but twice returned home penniless and in tatters. On the third try, however, he succeeded, and came back to Lopud a fabulously wealthy man – having saved Spain, it's said, from starvation after a bad harvest by using his ships to supply grain (no doubt at a healthy premium).

At an audience with a grateful King Charles V, Pracat was offered gold and a post as a colonial governor, but being wealthy and a patriotic Ragusan to boot he refused both. Instead, he asked for the king's shaving gown – which is why it's in Lopud's Town Museum today.

Pracat's only problem, it seems, was fertility – neither of his two wives produced an heir for him. When he finally died, in 1607, Pracat left his enormous fortune to the republic, mostly in the form of trusts. He was rewarded with the only statue ever raised to one of its own citizens – you can see it today in the Rector's Palace in Dubrovnik.

Venetian paintings and lovely 15th-century carved choir stalls. The church – one of 33 on the island – forms part of the Franciscan Monastery, which was dissolved by the French in 1808.

Also of interest is the small **town museum and treasury**, which are just off the quay opposite the end of the harbour, on Zlatarska. If they're closed – and they usually seem to be – pop through the gap between the two into a walled courtyard and seek out Lopud's priest, Don Ivan Vlašić, who holds the keys.

The treasury houses an assortment of ancient icons, vestments and sacred remnants, and a handful of very battered 9th-, 11th- and 12th-century frescoes. In the museum you'll find an extraordinary assembly of stuff ranging from Roman amphorae to 500-year-old pudding bowls to 19th-century English pottery. There's a nasty-looking French bayonet from 1806, a couple of pulleys from Miho Pracat's ship, and a cloak from the Giorgis, one of Dubrovnik's last noble families. Most curious of all is a shaving gown that belonged to King Charles V of Spain, which was a gift to Miho Pracat (see box opposite).

Behind the museum you can see the crumbling ruins of the Dubrovnik **Rector's summer palace**, testimony to the fact that even now there are far more houses on Lopud than there are people. Walk further along the quayside, and there's a lovely park featuring tall pines and palms – each one planted, it's said, by grateful sailors who'd avoided shipwreck.

Just beyond the park, before the former Grand Hotel, there's a path leading up to the left which crosses the island and comes out half an hour later at **Šunj**, one of the loveliest beaches on the Adriatic. On the crest of the hill, on the left, there's a concrete monument to Viktor Dyk, the Czech poet, author and political journalist, who died unexpectedly of a heart attack while on holiday here in May 1931, aged only 53.

The sandy beach at Šunj has a lovely shallow descent into the water and a temporary bar/restaurant open in season. It's an ill-kept secret, however, with sizeable crowds of locals coming over from the mainland during summer weekends.

The name Šunj provides the clue to Lopud's apparently mysterious use of a snake swallowing a child on its coat of arms – something you're more likely to have seen as the right half of the Alfa Romeo logo. According to the legend, Otto Visconti was shipwrecked here in 1098, on his way back from the crusades, and so grateful was he to survive that he had a votive church built on the hill above the bay. This was decorated with a copy of a shield which had been used by one of the defeated Saracens – featuring the snake and the child – and which subsequently became the Visconti crest. Over time the locale became known as *biscione*, the Italian for 'big snake', which was later abbreviated to Šunj.

The present church of **Our Lady of Šunj** (Gospa od Šunja) above the bay – turn left just after the Dyk memorial, if you're coming from Lopud – dates from the end of the 15th century. If it's open (which sadly is not all that often) it's well worth looking in to see the marvellous carved wooden altarpiece featuring Mary and the apostles. This, oddly enough, is English, from the 16th century. Lopud sailors – arguably among the best in the world at the time – heard that Henry VIII was in conflict with the pope and busily dissolving the monasteries, so off they went to go and buy bargain relics and religious treasures. The background to the altarpiece shows the Lopud ship which brought the Madonna here.

There's a direct path leading back from the church into the town; off to the right of this, heading away from Šunj, there's a track leading up to a great ruined **fortress**. Built originally in the 16th century, it was reinforced and expanded by the French from 1808 to 1813. Today it's soulful and dilapidated, and there's nothing special to see – though the views across to the island of Šipan are fabulous.

ŠIPAN Furthest away, largest and least-visited of the Elaphites, Šipan is lovely. Known as the 'Golden Island', it once had 300,000 olive trees and a sizeable population, but centuries of emigration have left it with fewer than 500 inhabitants and – like Lopud – with many more houses than people. During Dubrovnik's Golden Age, it was fashionable for wealthy nobles to spend the summer season on Šipan, and you'll come across their (mostly dilapidated) summer residences all over the island – along with a smattering of Roman ruins and a score of churches from the 11th century onwards, but the main reason to come here is very much to get away from it all.

It takes the best part of 2 hours to get to Šipan from Dubrovnik (and costs a princely 14kn), with the ferry stopping at both the south western and north eastern ends. The main centres – and the only places where you'll find anything at all to eat or drink – are the ferry terminals: **Šipanska Luka**, to the northwest, at the end of a deep inlet, and **Suđurađ** to the southeast, opposite Lopud. The two settlements are about 7km apart, and connected by an irregular minibus service run by Libertas. There's also a handful of other hamlets across the island.

🏠 **Where to stay** Everything on the island is pretty much closed from November to April. In season, there are a few private rooms available at either end of the island, and you may find people touting these as you get off the boat – otherwise just ask around. There are also two hotels, one at each end of Šipan:

🏠 **Šipan** (84 rooms) Šipanska Luka; ☎ 020 754 900; f 020 754 910; www.hotel-sipan.com. Enjoying a great location on Šipanska Luka's harbour, this hotel has fairly functional rooms. *Dbl with sea view €170–196 high season, €144–160 May & Oct.*

🏠 **Hotel Božica** (26 rooms) Suđurađ; ☎ 020 325 400; f 020 325 401; m 098 936 5735; www.hotel-bozica.hr. A good value 4-star hotel with a good restaurant offering stunning views back from Suđurađ towards the Croatian mainland. *Dbl €135–185 in season, €120–172 shoulder season.*

What to see and do An excellent excursion is to take the ferry to one end of the island and then walk across to the other end and catch the return ferry home from there. It takes a leisurely 2 hours by the most direct route, on Šipan's only paved road. The interior of the island is a fertile valley where you'll see grapes, figs and olives being grown, and there are plenty of places to stop and have a picnic and a bottle of wine.

You can also wander up any of the many tracks on the island (though stay well away from any remaining uncleared ordnance – well-marked signs mark the spots), which lead up to the island's two limestone ridges. Here you'll find abandoned olive groves surrounded by crumbling dry-stone walls, though above Šipanska Luka itself work is progressing apace on bringing some of the olive trees back into production. You may also come across the rooting-marks made by wild boar here. They're a recent arrival on the island, and something of a nuisance to the olive farmers, having swum across from the mainland after a forest fire at the end of the 1990s.

As you traverse the island, look out for the ruined Napoleonic fortress on the southern ridge, along with a hospital and barracks dating from the same era. There are also secretive military tunnels which dive into the hillside nearby, though for the time being these are off limits to the public.

If you're walking from Šipanska Luka to Suđurađ you'll pass a great fortress of a church dating from the 16th century, dedicated to **Sveti Duh** (the Holy Spirit), as you climb up out of the central valley. Just after this the road forks – if you go right it passes the local clinic and loops down to the port; if you go straight on it goes directly through Suđurađ itself before emerging at the harbour.

The dominating feature of Suđurađ is the summer residence of Vice Stjepović-Skočibuha, which is the only one of Šipan's 42 original mansions to be entirely preserved. It was built in 1563, with the tower being added in 1577, and is today used for conferences and functions. It houses an excellent restaurant and bar, **Na Taraci**.

Other places to eat at this end of the island include an informal bar-restaurant on the waterfront and **Karmelo Cvjetković**, where Tomaš and his dad serve up fish soup for 6kn, salad for 8kn, homemade wine at 40kn a litre and homemade cheese or *pršut* at a fraction of Dubrovnik prices. After lunch, you can enjoy a coffee on the floating terrace of **Café Moak**, soaking up the view and watching the fish swim beneath your feet.

If you want to explore further afield, you'll find boats down on the harbour whose owners are happy to take you out to the uninhabited Elaphite islands as well as to delightful unspoiled coves and beaches on Šipan itself – if there's nobody around ask at the little bar along the harbour front, which is where most of the fishermen and seafaring types hang out.

MLJET

Mljet is one of the most attractive islands in the whole Adriatic. Despite being unusually beautiful, and entirely unspoiled by deforestation (it was never ruled by Venice, hence also the lack of towns of any size), it has hitherto remained relatively unvisited – though with the fast connection from Dubrovnik more people are coming every year. Nonetheless, the island is easily big enough, at over 100km², to absorb many more visitors without getting overcrowded.

The entire western end of Mljet is a national park, and features two gorgeous salt-water lakes, the larger of which has an island with a ruined monastery on it. It's easy to visit on a day trip from Dubrovnik, but if you want to stay longer there's a hotel and some private rooms, and the island has great walking, cycling and canoeing, along with a nascent (if rather casual) diving school, and the opportunity of learning to sail.

HISTORY Legend has it that Ulysses stopped here for seven years on his Odyssey, and while there's absolutely no historical basis for the assertion, it makes a nice story. More credence can be given to the theory that on his way to martyrdom in Rome, St Paul was shipwrecked here, not on Malta. It's not just the name (Mljet used to be called Melita), but also the snakes – St Paul was bitten by one soon after arriving, which would be improbable (then as now) on Malta, whereas Mljet was notoriously snake-infested until the 19th century.

What's sure is the island's use by the Illyrians and the Romans – the remains of the Illyrian fort can still be seen on the summit of Mali Gradac, near **Babine Kuče**, while the settlement of **Polače** is named after the ruins of the 4th- or 5th-century Roman palace there.

The next significant development was in 1151, when Mljet was given to the Benedictines, who built the monastery on St Mary's Island. They stayed on even though Mljet itself was handed over to Dubrovnik in 1333, and lived a peaceful life until the arrival of Napoleon's troops in 1808, after which the monastery was abandoned.

The administrative centre of the island, **Babino Polje**, dates from the Middle Ages, but apart from the monastery, nothing on the western end of the island reaches back beyond the late 18th century, and the new port of **Pomena** wasn't established until after World War II.

WILDLIFE Mljet is famous for being the only place in Europe where you can find mongooses in the wild. The Indian grey mongoose was introduced to Mljet in 1910, by the Austrians, in an attempt to eradicate the infestation of venomous snakes. This had been a problem since time immemorial – and was probably the reason why the Benedictines built their monastery on the island in the first place ('Never mind the beauty and the isolation, Brother Jacob, let's get away from those blasted snakes!').

Seven male and four female mongooses were introduced, and they adapted well to the Mljet lifestyle, proliferating and practically eradicating the snake population over

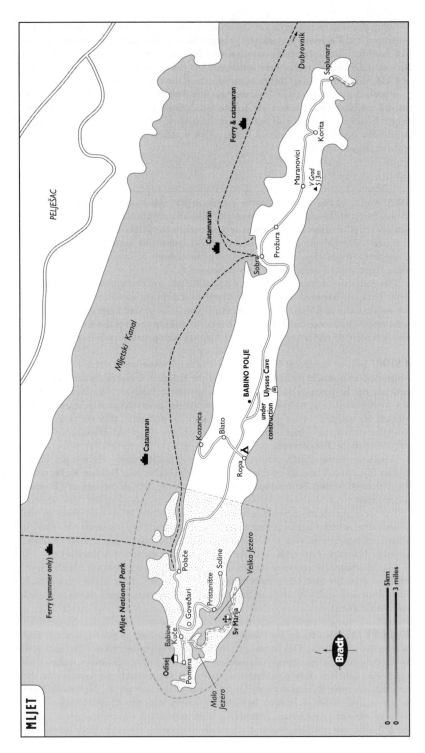

MLJET

PELJEŠAC

Mljetski Kanal

Dubrovnik

Saplunara

Korita

Maranovici

V Grad
▲ 513m

Prožura

Sobra

Ferry & catamaran

Catamaran

BABINO POLJE

Ulysses Cave
under
construction

Kozarica

Blato

Ropa

Catamaran

Mljet National Park

Polače

Goveđari

Pristanište

Soline

Veliko Jezero

Sv Marija

Babine
Kuče

Odisej

Pomena

Malo
Jezero

Ferry (summer only)

Bradt

5km
3 miles

0
0

the next 20 years. So successful were they, in fact, that they lost their statutory protection in 1949, and excessive numbers have proven difficult to curb. Small animals, as well as both resident and migratory birds, fall prey to the feral hunters, and they're not over-popular with the islanders, either.

Mljet's other fauna used to include the Mediterranean monk seal, though none has been spotted here since 1974. You may, however, see the Turkish gecko, the sharp-snouted lizard, or Dahl's whip snake (if the mongooses haven't got to him first), and there are now quite a few fallow deer in the forests – following their introduction in 1958.

GETTING THERE AND AWAY There's a daily Jadrolinija ferry from Dubrovnik, though as this arrives in Mljet in the late afternoon and returns at 06.30 in the morning it does mean an overnight stopover. The crossing takes around 4 hours. In summer, however, you can take the 1½-hour crossing on the fast catamaran *Nona Ana* (*www.gv-line.hr*), which comes out to Mljet in the morning and returns in the afternoon (before continuing to Korčula and Lastovo). The fare is around 100kn return. It is also possible to go direct from Bari to Mljet, as the Jadrolinija ferry to Dubrovnik stops at Sobra three times a week.

All ferries dock just east of **Sobra**, about a third of the way along Mljet's north shore, and are met by the local bus – but be warned that on busy days in summer there can be fewer buses than passengers, and if you're stranded your only realistic option is to rent a bike – at sellers' prices (and it's a long, hard, hot and hilly ride). To solve this problem the catamaran has taken to sailing on to **Polače**, and if you're on a day trip this is definitely the way to go. There's also a ferry linking Polače with Trstenik on the Pelješac peninsula between mid-July and mid-September.

The easiest way of seeing Mljet is by taking an all-inclusive package from Dubrovnik or Korčula (available from all the usual agencies – see page 361). These go for around 250–400kn, and include the ferry fare, the entry fee to the national park, a trip out to the island on the lake, and (sometimes) a guided tour, as well as the chance to swim. Bring a bottle of wine and a picnic, and it makes a wonderful day out.

GETTING AROUND Apart from the local buses that run between Sobra and Pomena to coincide with the Jadrolinija ferry arrivals and departures, there's no public transport.

If you want to cycle on the island the best place to rent bikes is at the Hotel Odisej (see below), in Pomena, or by the lakes themselves. Rates run from 20kn an hour to 110kn a day, and the paths around the lakes are absolutely perfect for cyclists. (There are several other places which rent out bikes too, if the stock at the Odisej's already out on loan, or if you haven't yet got as far as Pomena, including Sobra and Polače.) Even on the main roads, there's no traffic to speak of. You can rent buggies, cars or scooters outside the hotel, too, as well as at Sobra and Polače, with cars going from around 400kn a day, including fuel and 100km.

WHERE TO STAY AND EAT The monastery on St Mary's Island served from 1960 to 1988 as the lovely Hotel Melita, but since it was handed back to the Dubrovnik bishopric it's fallen into ruin. Although restoration commenced in 2004, nobody's sure what will become of it – there's no doubt it would make the most wonderful boutique hotel, but there are also plans to turn it into a research or information centre, or to leave it as a visitor attraction. At present, there's just a modest restaurant serving the numerous visitors to the island throughout the day.

For the time being, therefore, Mljet has only one hotel, the 3-star **Odisej** (\ *020 362 111; f 020 475 973; www.hotelodisej.hr*), in Pomena, which has 150 rooms spread across a number of buildings, with sea-view doubles with balconies going for around

€ 120–160 a night at the peak of the season, and € 64–110 outside July and August. The hotel is closed from November until just before Easter.

Mljet also has a reasonable (and steadily increasing) supply of **private rooms**, but it's a very good idea to book ahead. This can be arranged through tourist offices in Polače (✆ *020 744 086*), Babino Polje (✆/f *745 125*) and Goveđari (✆ *744 086; f 744 186;* e *tz-mjesta@du.htnet.hr*), or travel agents in Dubrovnik. Polače, a few kilometres away from the Hotel Odisej, but still within easy walking distance of the lakes, has excellent private rooms on the shore, and also has a bakery and a couple of cheerful restaurants. Pomena, too, has some good private accommodation, including the highly recommended Apartments Stražičić (✆/f *020 419 122;* e *lavica.strazicic@du.htnet.hr*), where a double apartment costs 450kn a night in July and August, or 340kn at other times. Half-a-dozen restaurants line the harbour, which is very popular with people from visiting yachts (as indeed is Polače), but food shopping is limited to the early morning bakery van, a couple of fruit stalls and the absolute basics.

There are two rather plain **campsites** on the island – one in Babino Polje, the other in Ropa. Other, more personal sites are run by private individuals – just ask around when you arrive at the port.

ACTIVITIES If you're here for more than a day trip, take advantage of the island's excellent **walking and hiking**. From the gentle paths around the lakes to the harder trails into the hills, Mljet's unspoiled beauty is overwhelming, and away from the lakes you'll pretty much have the place to yourself. Even on the lakeshore, you don't have to walk far to have almost total seclusion. There's a good marked trail from near Soline up Montokuč overlooking the lakes (the ascent takes around 40 minutes), with great views from the top. Rather than retrace your steps, you could return to Pristanište or continue to Polače or Goveđari. Within the park, trails lead to unexplored coves on the island's northwest tip, while even outside the park the ratio of nature to people is very high. If you're going to be walking or hiking here, or elsewhere in Croatia, it's well worth getting hold of *Walking in Croatia* by Rudolf Abraham or *Croatia: car tours and walks* by Sandra Bardwell, both of which do a great job of covering the country from a walker's perspective.

If it's watersports you're after, there's plenty of choice. Exploring by **kayak or canoe** makes for a great way of seeing the lakes at your own pace – they can be rented by the little bridge or at the hotel, with prices roughly the same as for bikes (see page 351). Windsurfers can be rented out from the hotel, too, and there's also a sailing school based here, though it's a pity they don't have dinghies on hand. For divers, the local diving centre (*book through the hotel or phone Mario on* m *098 479 916*) can take you out to a Roman wreck, complete with original amphorae, or to a defunct German U-boat. Expect to pay € 50 for a dive with a guide, including equipment – though if you're a novice you might want to take heed of reports of a certain laxity in this department. Visits to either of the wrecks cost an additional € 15.

WHAT TO SEE AND DO
Mljet National Park Mljet's main draw is the national park, and specifically the two saltwater lakes, Veliko Jezero (with St Mary's Island and the crumbling monastery) and Malo Jezero – literally 'Big Lake' and 'Small Lake'. If you're on a day trip you won't have time to see a great deal else.

As you'll probably guess – the saltwater's a bit of a giveaway – neither Malo nor Veliko Jezero is actually a lake. The sea feeds into the larger one, and that feeds into the smaller one. The tidal changes allowed the monks to run a useful watermill in the past, and although the mill's long gone you can still easily see which way the tide's headed from the bridge over the shallow channel between Malo and Veliko Jezero.

Unfortunately, the bridge originally spanning the seaward exit of Veliko Jezero was lost when the channel was widened and deepened in 1960 (under Tito's orders, so tourists could come in by ship straight to the former hotel), so you can't now do the full 12km circuit round the lake without getting wet. A word of warning: If you decide to swim the 13.6m wide and 2.6m deep channel, be very sure which way the current's going, and how fast it's moving – there's an awful lot of water coming in and out of here, and it's frighteningly easy to be swept out to sea.

The boat out to **St Mary's Island** (Sveti Marija) runs several times a day, and the fare is included in the national park entry fee (see below). On the island itself there's not been much to see in recent years, but the monastery is currently being restored and the church is now open for services at 11.30 on Sunday. You can visit the monks' gardens, complete with lemon trees, in the original cloisters (if they're open). The island also has a couple of restaurants, which are highly popular as the luncheon venues for excursions, as well as ice cream stopovers.

Take the ten-minute path around the little island and you'll see two other plain but evocative votive chapels dating from the 17th or 18th century. These were built by grateful sailors who'd survived shipwrecks or storms. If you're here in spring, you'll find lots of wild asparagus, while in summer you'll be overwhelmed by the noise of cicadas in the afternoon haze.

Established in 1960, the national park (☏ *020 744 041;* ☏ *020 744 043; www.np-mljet.hr*) is run from the settlement of **Goveđari**, roughly equidistant from both Pomena and Polače. Entry is 90kn, and the money goes to the upkeep of the park, so don't be tempted to try and avoid paying. Anyway, if you're caught without a ticket, you'll be charged – double. Detailed maps are available from the park office (on the shore of the main lake, at the locality called **Pristanište**) or from the kiosk selling tickets in Pomena, though the footpath network shown on these maps is none too accurate. There's another kiosk on the road in from Polače.

The national park is unusual among nature reserves in including the main villages, the hotel and the basic tourist infrastructure within its boundaries, but don't be lulled into a sense of false security. You're in an ecologically fragile area here, and it's important to follow the rules, especially relating to fire – in 1917 an accidental blaze destroyed much of the old forest and the restoration took decades. So don't light fires, don't smoke, don't camp – and do stay on the paths.

Beyond the national park Three-quarters of Mljet is forest-covered, meaning good shade in the summer heat (but take plenty of water with you; there are no supplies at all), while the few settlements are rarely visited, and you'll be made to feel welcome by the locals. This is especially true on the 15km stretch of the island east of Sobra, where the settlements of **Prožura**, **Maranovići** and **Korita** are practically never visited by foreigners. Right at the far eastern tip, at **Saplunara**, are two sandy beaches, the only ones on the island. You'll need a car (or a bike, and strong legs) to get here as no buses run beyond Sobra. The first is below the village itself; the other, round the next bay, has a shallow and very sheltered lagoon, and is almost deserted. Debris washed in on the tide is a problem in parts at present, but with the current promotion by the tourist board, this – and the seclusion – are likely to change.

The highest point on the island (Veli Grad, 513m) is just above Mljet's diminutive administrative capital, **Babino Polje**, again practically unvisited, and will likely be even less so once the new bypass is finished. Babino Polje sits on the side of the island's largest field system – the endless dry-stone walls here are the result of centuries of clearing stones from the fields. The main produce is olives and (surprisingly expensive but incredibly tasty) goat's cheese. Much of the island's very drinkable wine comes from the village of Blato, just outside the national park.

Directly south of Babino Polje is **Ulysses Cave** (Odisejeva spilja), a good half hour's tough walk across fields and down the cliff, but well worth the effort. It's not suitable for young children, however – if you're travelling with the family take the boat trip from the Odisej Hotel, as it's a magical cave to explore in calm seas.

TRSTENO

Just 18km up the coast from Dubrovnik is the little village of Trsteno, which would be entirely unremarkable were it not for the wonderful arboretum here. Originally created as the summer residence and gardens of Ivan Gučetić, a Dubrovnik noble, in 1502, and expanded over the centuries, the estate was nationalised by the communists in 1948 and re-branded as the Arboretum of the Yugoslav (now Croatian) Academy of Arts and Sciences. Inexplicably it was subject to Serb shelling during the 1991–92 war.

Anyway, the gardens here are delightful, and make a charming excursion out of Dubrovnik. The bus to Split, which goes every half hour or so, sets down and picks up in the middle of the village, where the first thing you'll see is a splendid pair of huge 500-year-old plane trees. Beyond these, heading towards the sea in a series of terraces, is the arboretum itself (❧ *751 019;* ☉ *daily summer 07.00–19.00, winter 08.00–15.00; 20kn*).

There's nothing special to do other than to wander round the gardens, which vary from the formality of the oldest part, beneath the villa, with geometrical box hedges enclosing different planted areas, to the wilder areas off to the sides. There's a lovely orchard with citrus fruits, avenues of palms and firs, and all manner of exotic semi-tropical plants, most of them usefully labelled. There's even a rather fanciful 18th-century grotto, where you'll find Neptune with his trident presiding over a water-lily-strewn fishpond and playful water-spouting fountains in the form of dolphins.

PLOČE AND THE NERETVA DELTA

Roughly halfway between Split and Dubrovnik lies the industrial port of **Ploče**. Known during the 1980s as Kardeljevo, after one of Tito's pals, it still handles most of Bosnia & Herzegovina's sea-bound freight (the coastal town of Neum, actually in Bosnia's land corridor, is a dreary little resort with no proper port) and acts as a transport hub.

The re-established rail link to Sarajevo (a spectacular journey) starts from here, and there are Jadrolinija car ferries across to Trpanj, on Pelješac – three a day in winter, seven in summer. Otherwise there's no reason to break your journey.

South of Ploče is the extraordinary **Neretva Delta**. Long a marshy, malarial swamp, the pancake-flat river delta is now a series of fertile agricultural wetlands, producing Croatia's best citrus fruits (you'll see delicious tangerines for sale along the roadside), and providing shelter to waterfowl and wading birds, as well as spawning grounds for many species of fish, including eels.

Deep in the delta are six hard-to-find dedicated ornithological reserves. You'll need time, patience and your own transport – in which case you should keep a weather-eye on the main road for flying customs squads, on the lookout for Bosnian contraband and speeding tourists.

A total of 299 species of bird have been recorded in the delta, with 92 nesting here, including the pigmy cormorant, coots, crakes, warblers and shrikes, several species of heron and egret, all five species of European grebe and almost every species of European duck. In 1999, a government proposal was initiated to proclaim the entire delta as a nature park, but obstacles include various development and road-improvement plans.

Easily the best way of visiting is to persuade one of the locals to take you around in a punt (the indigenous *trupica* or *lađa*), poling you along the reedy channels which separate the reclaimed market gardens, and giving you a chance to soak up the mysterious atmosphere. Far simpler, however, is to book yourself on a day-long excursion from Dubrovnik for around 300kn – this includes a comprehensively guided boat tour and is available from most local travel agencies. Take insect repellent with you – the mosquitoes here can be fearsome.

🏠 WHERE TO STAY AND EAT

🏠 **Hotel Restaurant Villa Neretva** Krvavac II, Metković; ☎ 672 200; f 671 199; www.restaurant-villa-neretva.hr. The main reason to stop off here is for the photo safaris that take you by boat to the hotel's sister property Neretva House, which can only be reached by water; Dalmatian cuisine dominates the menus at both restaurants. The photo safari costs 500kn per boat, so bring some friends. If you want to stay over, there are plain but clean rooms. *Dbl €50–65.*

PELJEŠAC PENINSULA

An island in all but name, the 65km Pelješac peninsula runs up from the isthmus at Ston to the island of Korčula. Never more than 7km wide, Pelješac is mountainous and rocky, an unlikely home to two of Croatia's best wines, the hearty Dingač and Postup reds.

Three buses a day travel up and down the main road from Dubrovnik to Ston and on to Orebić, the main departure point for Korčula, and buses also hook up with Trpanj, the arrival point for ferries from Ploče, on the mainland. But if you want to explore the dozens of small villages, or the myriad hidden bays and beaches, you'll definitely need your own wheels.

STON The land entrance to Pelješac is at Ston, which guards the isthmus with a series of remarkably well-preserved walls from the 14th century on. On the south coast is the village of **Veliki Ston**, while on the northern bay is **Mali Ston** – the two settlements are a 20-minute walk apart, should you get off the bus at the wrong stop.

The reason for a visit here is twofold – firstly to see (and clamber upon) the walls, which rival Dubrovnik's, and secondly to sample Croatia's best oysters and mussels, which are farmed here. The walls were built from the 14th century on, primarily to protect the salt-pans – the salt trade was one of the republic's biggest earners, and it's said that Napoleon was even more keen to get his hands on Ston than Dubrovnik. Today 20 of the original 40 towers and some 5km of walls are still standing, and if you climb high enough up – the public access is from Veliki Ston – there are great views across to the island of Mljet (see page 349).

The area was subjected to Serb shelling during the war and then badly hit by an earthquake in 1996, which destroyed many of the houses in both Veliki and Mali Ston, along with most of the town of Slano, further down the coast towards Dubrovnik – and even today many of the properties here remain boarded up. Nonetheless, Mali Ston's tourist infrastructure is thriving, and the village is increasingly popular with Croatian romantics on oyster-fuelled weekend breaks.

🏠 **Where to stay and eat** If you decide to stay over, there are two lovely small hotels in Mali Ston. Just outside the old walls is the attractive **Vila Koruna** (☎ *020 754 999;* f *754 642; www.vila-koruna.hr*), which has half a dozen simple doubles at € 90 a night all year round, and a great covered terrace of a dining room, right on the water. Oysters go for 10kn a pop, while a plate of mussels comes in at 45kn. The lobster (at an eye-watering 400kn a kilo) is superb. Just inside the walls is the somewhat more upmarket **Ostrea** (☎ *020 754 555;* f *754 575; www.ostrea.hr*), which has nine rooms at € 160 a night. The **tourist office** in Veliki Ston (*Pelješki put 1;* ☎/f *754 452; www.ston.hr*) can also point you in the direction of the few private rooms available locally. Finally, there are two great restaurants on the harbour in Mali Ston, Kapetanova Kuča and Taverna Bota.

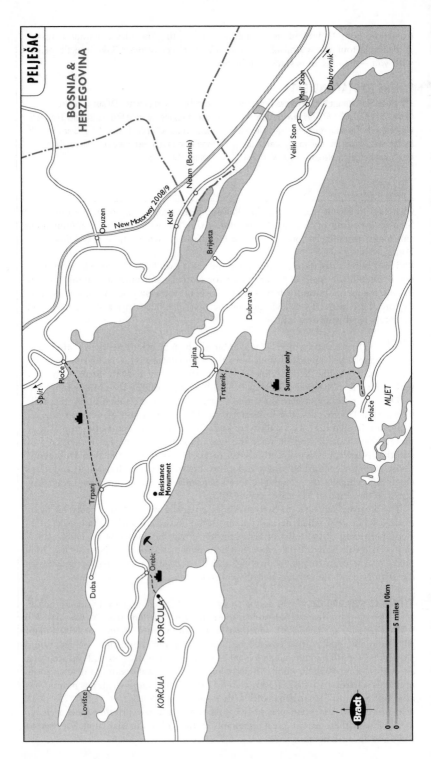

PELJEŠAC

BOSNIA & HERZEGOVINA

BOSNIA & HERCEGOVINA

Opuzen

New Motorway 2008/9

Klek

Neum (Bosnia)

Brijesta

Mali Ston

Veliki Ston

Dubrovnik

Dubrava

Janjina

Trstenik

Summer only

Polače

MLJET

Split

Ploče

Trpanj

Resistance Monument

Duba

Orebić

KORČULA

KORČULA

Lovište

Bradt

0   10km

0   5 miles

NORTH OF STON Between Ston and Trstenik there's a flat, tree-shaded campsite at **Prapratno**, set back from a wide, secluded beach. Directly above, on the side of the road, the **Bella Vista** is a good stopover for coffee and cakes, or indeed something more substantial.

The small holiday village of **Trstenik** on Pelješac's southern coast is of note for the summer ferry linking the peninsula with Polače on Mljet, a pleasant hour or so's trip away, from mid-July to mid-September. There's a sheltered beach here, with diving available through Mario on Mljet (see page 352), and the nearby winery is open to visitors.

Resistance monument As you progress up the peninsula, about 40km from Ston, there's a huge monument to the resistance, right where the road crests a hill, near the locality of Pijavičino. If you're under your own steam, stop here by the abandoned restaurant, and take a moment to look at the stylised bronze frieze depicting scenes from World War II, showing brutal oppression, firing squads, the first signs of resistance and uprising, and finally the joy of freedom. On the back of the curved walls is the endless list of the local dead, while the whole is dominated by a pair of curved concrete pillars stretching about 30m into the sky.

TRPANJ In a sweeping bay on Pelješac's north coast is the small town of Trpanj, arrival point for the ferries from Ploče (three a day in winter, seven a day in summer, with an extra service to Drvenik, further up the mainland coast, in season). The cheerful little town has a couple of cafés and restaurants, and a charmingly tatty but helpful tourist office (*Zalo 7;* ☎ *020 743 433; www.tzo-trpanj.hr*) hidden behind the Flok pizzeria on the front, which can arrange private rooms. Opening hours in winter are sporadic to say the least.

Trpanj has one hotel, the **Faraon** (*Put Vila 1;* ☎ *020 743 408;* f *020 743 422; www.hoteli-jadran.hr*), with around 150 rooms, all with balcony and sea view, which go for around € 140 a night at the height of the season, including obligatory full board. It sits right on the large pebble beach to the west of the harbour, facing across to the Biokovo massif on the mainland.

Buses connect with the ferries here, and take you to Orebić, which leads on to Korčula or back to Ston and Dubrovnik.

OREBIĆ Pelješac's best-known resort, Orebić, is an unpretentious little town with an excellent climate – it's protected by the mountains from the *bura* wind, giving it mild winters, early springs and long-lasting summers. The town is right across the strait from Korčula, and in summer 18 ferries a day go in each direction (seven in winter). To get back to the mainland the easiest routes are to either take the direct bus to Dubrovnik (three a day) or to catch the ferry to Korčula and then go on the next ferry to Split from there. Alternatively, you can catch the bus to Trpanj, and the ferry from there across to Ploče (or Drvenik, in summer).

To the west of Orebić are a series of resort hotels, on a mixture of nice sandy and pebble beaches, while 500m to the east you'll find the **Trstenica** beach, which ought to be one of the nicest little stretches of the Adriatic coast – it's backed by cacti and palms, and home to a row of fine 18th- and 19th-century villas – but it has been known to be filthy in the early summer, strewn with litter and beer bottles, and badly in need of a clean-up.

The **tourist office** (*Trg Mimbelli;* ☎ *020 713 718; www.tz-orebic.com*) has walking maps (which used to be excellent, although recent reports imply they might be giving out a new, less accurate version) and access to a supply of private rooms. The nearest hotel to the centre is the 2-star **Bellevue** (*Obala pomoraca 36;* ☎f *020 713 148; www.orebic-htp.hr*), which has around 80 rooms and faces on to a rocky beach. Sea-view doubles go for around € 55.

9

From the Bellevue, it's an uphill hike westwards to the 15th-century **Franciscan Monastery** which houses the icon known as 'Our Lady of the Angels' – for centuries sailors came here with votive gifts after being saved from shipwreck, storms or pirates. The terrace of the monastery, at 150m above sea-level, looks down across the strait to Korčula town, a lovely view.

Even finer panoramas can be had from the 961m summit of Mount St Ilija. It's a steep hike, 4 hours up from Orebić including rests, and another 2 for the descent, but the simply wonderful views from the summit include the whole of the island of Korčula, Mljet to the south, and the gaunt karst mountains of the mainland to the north.

If you're hiking up here wear proper hiking boots (there are reported sightings of vipers), start very early (there's little or no shade), take plenty of water, and use common sense and the route markings rather than the map. Follow the path up to the monastery, and then continue to Bilopolje, after which the track bears off to the right, following red and white flashes to the summit. For further information see *Walking in Croatia* by Rudolf Abraham.

Some of Croatia's best red wine is produced not far from Orebić, in Pelješac's Dingač region, and some of the vineyards are open for **wine tours** – contact Orebić Tours (❧ *020 713 367*) in Orebić or Kantun Tours in Korčula (see page 360).

KORČULA

Like Hvar, Korčula has a lovely old town and lots of hard-to-reach coves and beaches. Like Hvar, too, Korčula's no secret, but it doesn't have nearly the visitor numbers of its northern neighbour (though Korčula's numbers are growing significantly faster, year on year).

The island is nestled up to the western end of Pelješac (less than 1.5km of sea separates them at the narrowest point) and stretches about 45km west into the Adriatic. On average it's about 6km across, from north to south, and has a mountainous spine rising to 568m just west of the village of Pupnat.

The main attraction on the island is the old town of Korčula itself, almost opposite Orebić (on Pelješac), though a close second has to be Korčula's powerful white wines, notably Pošip, Rukatac, and Lumbarda's Grk. Korčula also makes a pretty good base for exploring Pelješac, and offers easy excursions over to Mljet (see page 349).

HISTORY Korčula's history stretches back as far as anywhere in Croatia, with Neolithic settlements here followed by the arrival of Greek colonists in the 6th century BC. The Greeks co-existed peaceably with Illyrians on the island for several hundred years before the Romans barged in during the 1st century BC, enraged by the island's propensity for harbouring pirates. Most of the population was either killed, exiled or enslaved, setting something of a pattern until the late Middle Ages, when Korčula went through the usual southern Adriatic tussle between Venice, Dubrovnik and the Turks.

In 1298, just off Lumbarda, a total of more than 180 galleys from the rival Venetian and outnumbered Genoan fleets clashed in one of the biggest sea battles of the Middle Ages. Genoa won the day, and took 7,000 prisoners, including a certain Marco Polo (see box on page 364), who was back in the Adriatic after more than 20 years in Asia with his father and uncle, and was on that day at the helm of one of the Venetian battleships.

Today, Marco Polo is unquestionably Korčula's most famous son, though some scholars now think he may have been born in Šibenik, further up the Dalmatian coast. Whatever the truth, Korčula does much more for Marco Polo than anywhere else, and the setting of the old town here is suitably evocative as the kind of place he might have been brought up.

KORČULA ISLAND

PELJEŠAC
(see pages 347–350)

Trpanj

Ploče

Drvenik

Lovište

Orebić

Badija

Vrnik

Lumbarda

Dominče

KORČULA

88m
Rožnjić

Žrnovo

Pupnat

568m

Zavalatica

Čara

Smokvica

Brna

Blato

Vela Luka

Vela
Špilje

Ojjak

Proizd

Hvar,
Split

Lastovo

Šćedro

Bradt

NOTE
Source information from Branko Babić–Korčula

0   5 miles
0   10km

Recent history on Korčula has been dominated by tourism, though there's still a fish-processing factory in Vela Luka, at the western end of the island, and the wine business is increasingly important. Olive oil has also been a valuable source of revenue.

GETTING THERE AND AROUND Daily buses arrive on Korčula from Dubrovnik and Zagreb, rolling on to the car ferry from Orebić for the last couple of kilometres. The journey from Dubrovnik, up through the Pelješac peninsula, takes a little under 4 hours; from Zagreb it's a 12- or 13-hour overnighter.

From Vela Luka to Korčula town there are half a dozen buses a day, though fewer at weekends – the ferries always connect with a bus, however. In summer, there's also a service (one to three times a day) from Drvenik direct to Korčula.

Car ferries from Orebić (arrive early if you're bringing your car) come in at Dominče, 3km south of Korčula town, seven times a day in winter, 18 in summer. If you're not on the bus already you can avoid the hike into town by hopping onto one of the hourly buses from Lumbarda to Korčula, though don't rely on this service at weekends. As a foot passenger, you're better off taking the smaller boat which runs from Orebić directly to Korčula town's west harbour (seven a day in winter, ten in summer).

A daily ferry service runs from Split to Vela Luka, at the western end of Korčula (and on to Lastovo), taking around 3½ hours; the same journey can be done in under 2 hours on the daily catamaran.

There's a daily catamaran (*2³/₄ hours, www.krilo.hr*) from Split to Korčula town itself, departing Korčula early in the morning and returning from Split in the afternoon. The Rijeka–Dubrovnik ferry also calls in at Korčula town.

If you're reliant on public transport you'll be pretty much limited to Korčula town, the sandy beaches of Lumbarda, 6km southeast (hourly buses; flaky weekend service), a few buses to the village of Račišće along the north coast of the island, and the main road to Vela Luka – for access to Korčula's many hidden beaches and coves, which tend to be at the end of long gravelly roads, you'll definitely need your own wheels.

A great, liberating option is to rent a bike, which you can do from many of the tour agencies in town – try Kantun Tours (❧ *020 715 622;* f *020 716 072; www.kantun-tours.com*) or Korčula Travel (❧ *020 716 590*), which have mountain bikes from 80kn or 90kn day.

Pick up the superb maps of both the town and the island from the friendly **tourist office** (❧ *020 715 701;* f *020 715 866*), right next door to the Hotel Korčula.

If you don't have your own transport and can't face biking, you might consider taking an organised tour (from Korčula Travel or Kantun Tours in Korčula town) to get more of a feel for the island's hidden charms. On offer are anything from a fish picnic to an island tour, to boat trips round the local islands, to an excursion to Mljet or Dubrovnik. Kantun Tours (see above) also offer wine tours on Pelješać. Alternatively you can negotiate with one of the water taxis at the eastern harbour of Korčula town to take you to one of the local islands or remoter beaches, and pick you up a few hours later.

WHERE TO STAY

Bon Repos (370 rooms) Dubrovacka cesta 19; ❧ 020 726 880; f 020 726 699; www.korcula-hotels.com. Traditional tourist comfort in an enormous establishment 2km out of town on the road to Lumbarda, which is easiest reached by taxi-boat. *Dbl with sea view* €120.

Hotel Korčula (20 rooms) Obala Franje Tuđmana; ❧ 020 711 078; f 020 711 746; www.hotelkorcula.com. The rooms themselves aren't anything to write home about, but the location, right on the old town's western harbour, is perfection itself – so book ahead. This was a popular café in 1871, & became the town's first hotel (the Hotel de la Ville) in 1912. *Dbl* €130–150.

Lešić Dimitri Palace (13 rooms) Don Pavle Pose; ❧ 020 715 560; f 020 715 561; www.lesic-dimitri.com. Korčula's brand new, 5-star luxury option opened in 2009, occupying an 18th century bishop's palace & five medieval cottages. *Dbl* €595–995.

Liburna (83 rooms) Put od Luke; 020 726 006; f 020 726 272; www.korcula-hotels.com. Located a 20min walk east of the old town, this place offers a swimming pool, tennis courts, private car park & bike hire. More importantly some of its rooms have stunning views back over Korčula. *Dbl €100–176.*

One Love Hostel (65 beds in dorms) 020 716 755; www.korculabackpacker.com. Very much a 'party'-oriented hostel – for those who fit within its 18–35 age restriction. If, that is, you can find anyone on reception. Summer only. *Dorm beds from €14.*

If none of those appeal, or you're on a budget, there are plenty of good private rooms and apartments available – especially along the waterfront west of the town (*Put Sv Nikole*). Try Kantun Tours (020 715 622; f 020 716 072; *www.kantun-tours.com*), and expect to pay around € 40 for a double, with a 30% supplement for stays of three days or less. If you come in by boat or bus, you'll be met by people offering you rooms, and while these can be better value, check the agencies as well, especially if you're staying for four or more days. It's worth checking out the website at www.korcula.net/firme/indexp.html for private rooms and apartments online.

✗ WHERE TO EAT AND DRINK

✗ **Adio Mare** Svetog Roka 2; m 098 243 845. Korčula's best restaurant serves up delicious fish dishes in a nautically themed restaurant.

✗ **Konoba Gajeta** Šetalište Petra Kanavelića; 020 716 359 Very good, unpretentious restauarant serving a range of reasonably priced dishes, overlooking the water on the east side of town.

✗ **Massimo** Šetalište Petra Kanavelića; 020 715 073. The place to enjoy a sundowner atop a stone tower that was once part of the city's fortifications. Not for those with vertigo (or if you've had a few) as you have to climb up/down a ladder to get there. Seeing your drink hauled up on a pulley is all part of the fun.

✗ **Pizzeria Caenazzo** Trg Sv Marka; m 098 244 012 Excellent, well-priced pizzeria on the square in front of the cathedral.

WHAT TO SEE AND DO Korčula's top draw is the old town itself, set on a tiny peninsula jutting north into the Pelješac channel. The medieval walls have largely disappeared (Austria wouldn't pay for the upkeep), but there are still towers and buttresses here and there, and the old quarter is a harmonious mix of 15th-century Gothic with 16th-century Renaissance trimmings. The leaf-veined network of narrow streets was designed to keep the place cool in summer yet sheltered in winter – the roads to the west are straight, allowing in the summer sea breezes, while those to the east are curved, to minimise the effects of the nasty winter *bura*. The arched entrances to the old cellars were built that way to ease the passage of barrels, a reminder of Korčula's long-standing importance as a centre of wine production.

In various places around the town you'll see sculptures by Frano Kršnić, who was born in Lumbarda – they're softer and gentler than the works of Ivan Meštrović, with more than a passing nod to Rodin, and a tribute to Korčula's centuries-old tradition of stone-carving.

The obvious access to the old town is through the southern land gate and the 15th-century **Revelin Tower**, which has a small Moreška exhibition inside, and excellent views from the top. The sweep of stone steps leading up to the gate was only added in 1907, replacing the drawbridge. On the left-hand side as you come in through the gate there's a fine loggia (and a pleasant café). The main street then leads straight to **St Mark's Cathedral** (like Rab's and Hvar's, actually a church, since the island long ago lost its bishopric, but who's quibbling?). It's crammed into a space that's manifestly too small, and one of around 150 churches still used on the island.

Over the main door there's a throned statue of St Mark, flanked by a pair of fine Venetian lions on buttresses, the early 15th-century work of Bonino, the Italian sculptor. Supporting the lions are a wonderfully primitive, cowering Adam and Eve, while the blind pillars feature unusual carved clove-hitches half way up. Inside, at the

KORČULA TOWN

To Monastry and
Church of Sv Nikola

PUT SV NIKOLE

OBALA DR FRANJE

TRG
POMIRENJA

TRG
KORČULANSKIH
KLESARA I
KIPARA

One Love
Hostel

KNEŽEV PROLAZ

ŽITNICA

ULICA OD TEATRA

ULICA GIUNIO

ULICA ISMAELLI

ULICA DR DINKA MIROŠEVIĆA

ULICA RAFA ARNERIJA

Town Museum

TRG
SV MARKA

PLOKATA 19 TRAVNJA 1921

FOŠA

Loggia

TRG ANTUNA
I STJEPANA
RADIĆA

U KORČULANSKOG STATUTA 1214

Bishop's Palace-
Treasury

TRG
KRALJA
TOMISLAVA

Revelin
Tower

St Michael's

Korčula
Travel

ULICA DOBROETVORNOSTI

KAPOROVA ULICA

ULICA OPATA DON IVE MATIJACA

ULICA BANIČEVIĆA

ULICA MARKA ANDRIJIĆA

Kantun
Tours

OBALA KORČULANSKIH
BRODOGRADITELIJA

RAMPADA

All Saints'

Icon
Gallery

Konoba
Gajeta

ŠETALIŠTE PETRA KAN

OBALA VINKA PALETINA

Ferry Korcula – *Korcula – Rijeka/Dubrovnik,
catamaran Korčula – Hvar/Split*

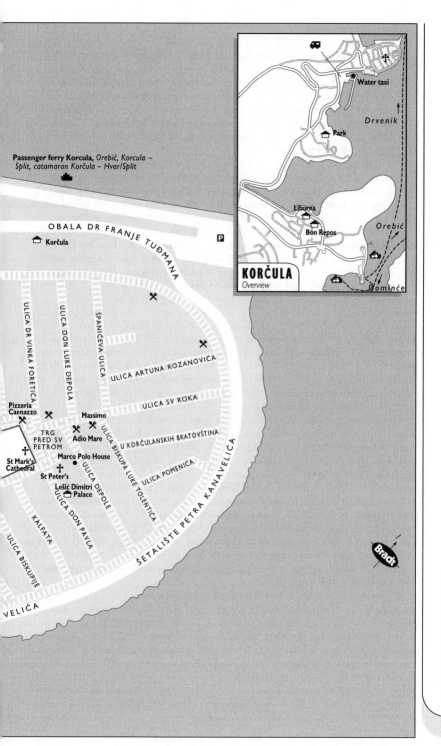

Passenger ferry Korcula, *Orebić, Korcula – Split, catamaran Korčula – Hvar/Split*

OBALA DR FRANJE TUĐMANA

Korčula

Water taxi

Drvenik

Park

Liburna

Bon Repos

Orebić

KORČULA
Overview

Domince

ULICA DR VINKA FORETIĆA

ULICA DON LUKE DEPOLA

ŠPANIĆEVA ULICA

ULICA ARTUNA ROZANOVIĆA

ULICA SV ROKA

Pizzeria Caenazzo

Massimo

Adio Mare

ULICA BISKUPA LUKE TOLENTIĆA

U KORČULANSKIH BRATOVŠTINA

TRG PRED SV PETROM

Marco Polo House

St Mark's Cathedral

St Peter's

Lešić Dimitri Palace

ULICA DEPOLE

ULICA POMENIĆA

ŠETALIŠTE PETRA KANAVELIĆA

KALEATA

ULICA DON PAVLA

ULICA BISKUPIJE

VELIČA

Brač

end of the curiously skewed nave (look at the ceiling), there's a famous but frankly rather heavyweight altar canopy from the late 15th century and a couple of paintings attributed to Tintoretto – the altarpiece featuring St Mark, and an Annunciation in the southern nave. Also inside you'll find halberds from a 1483 battle and cannonballs from the Battle of Lepanto in 1571. Near these is a rare and celebrated 14th-century icon which came from the monastery on Badija; it's due for return to the Franciscans there once restorations have been completed.

On the left-hand side of the church is the large chapel dedicated to Roc, the patron saint of the plague; here you'll find a convincing St Blaise by Meštrović and a dusty sculpture over the doorway of St Michael killing Lucifer. If you're in town on 29 July, you'll see the relics of the cathedral's co-patron, St Theodore, being carried in a procession around town.

Next door to the cathedral is the **Bishop's Palace**, which houses an impressive treasury, though it's really more of a museum. It's an extraordinary collection, covering everything from ancient kitchenware to contemporary art. There are collections of coins, church silver, relics from the Roman catacombs, medieval ballot boxes and a birth register from 1583. Strangest of all is a statue of Mary Queen of Scots, carved in ivory in the early 17th century – her skirts open to reveal a tiny triptych. The last room is lined with antique ecclesiastical robes, which get an airing on ecclesiastical shoulders during the Easter processions.

Opposite the treasury is the **Town Museum**, on several floors of a nice old building. It's in need of restoration, however, and the collection's a bit piecemeal to say the least – but there are some interesting bits of sculpture on the ground floor, where you'll also find the (reproduction – the original's in Zagreb) Greek tablet known as the Lumbarda stone, which lists the names of the families who lived on Korčula around 2,300 years ago. Upstairs there's a replica of an old-fashioned kitchen, a section on shipbuilding and a re-creation of an elegant 18th-century salon. Most evocative of all, however, are the black and white photos on the stairs, showing the arrival of the likes of Fitzroy Maclean during World War II, bringing British aid to the partisans (Maclean's widow, Veronica, still spends part of every year in Korčula).

Heading away from the centre of town you'll find the so-called **Marco Polo House**, which has been bought by the town council and will eventually become a Marco Polo Museum. There are great views from the top of the small tower upstairs. There are also plans to build a full-scale reproduction of the galley he used in the famous battle in 1298, and if you're here in May or September you'll definitely want to take part in the **Marco Polo Days**, when everyone dresses up to stage a minor re-creation of the battle in which Marco Polo was captured by the Genovese. The festivities culminate with the great 'local' explorer being given a triumphant welcome home.

In the southeastern corner of town there's an interesting **Icon Gallery** – and entry to this also gives you access to **All Saints' Church**, across the little bridge which is still used on special occasions by the local Brotherhood, or Guild. Indeed, the Guilds play an important part in Korčula life, with most people belonging to one or another – the Guild of All Saints was founded in 1301, that of St Roc in 1571, and that of St Michael in 1603. In the icon museum check out the huge candles which are paraded around on feast days, and a fine two-sided cross for use in processions, which dates back to 1430. The church itself was originally the town's cathedral, and features an altar canopy similar to the one in St Mark's, along with a fine carved wooden altarpiece.

Beyond the main sights it's really worth getting up at dawn and walking round the outside of the old town and through the narrow streets, when the place is practically deserted. The pale light of early morning does wonders for the old stone – most of which was quarried locally, on the island of **Vrnik**, just behind Badija. Vrnik also provided stone for the walls of Dubrovnik, for the Parliament in Vienna, and for Stockholm's Town Hall. To the west of town, just around the headland, are the attractive monastery and **Church of Sv Nikola**.

It's also well worth taking one of the regular taxi-boats from Korčula's eastern harbour to the island of **Badija**, just offshore, as it has the best (and closest) beaches to Korčula town, including one reserved for naturists. You have to wonder what the Franciscan monks – who've now been given back the monastery (now undergoing restoration) that was used as rather spartan tourist accommodation in the socialist era – think of the naturists. Or indeed vice versa.

MOORISH DANCES – THE MOREŠKA

For around 400 years the people of Korčula have been dressing up and performing the Moreška, a famous sword dance which continues a tradition once common across the whole of Europe. Few of the dances retain anything remotely Moorish about them (least of all Britain's Morris Dancers), but the name has stuck fast. Korčula is special, however, in still using real swords in what is effectively a war dance.

Originally an annual festival, the Moreška is now performed around twice a week (in a much condensed version – 40 minutes instead of the original 2 hours) in Korčula town in summer, and makes for a spectacular evening show. The plot's pretty simple – bad king runs off with good king's squeeze; good king's soldiers fight bad king's soldiers; squeeze is saved from bad king's embraces – but none the less enjoyable for all that. Mind the flying, broken swords in the front row....

In other villages on Korčula they perform a similar dance, the Kumpanija (the main difference being that it's sabres rather than swords which are used), particularly in Blato, towards the western end of the island. These are hard to get to without your own transport.

9

LUMBARDA The rest of Korčula doesn't entirely live up to the capital's promise, though it has any number of lovely holiday places if you have your own wheels. Even without your own transport, however, it's easy enough to get to Lumbarda – there are hourly buses in the week, and a restricted service at weekends. But assuming you're heading for the seaside, and not the unassuming village itself, you're much better off taking a taxi-boat, and negotiating to be dropped right at the beach.

Lumbarda sits on the north shore of Korčula's southeastern peninsula, and the sandy soil here makes not just for the excellent local Grk wines, but also for some of the island's best beaches, all around the Ražnjić headland.

Where to stay

Hotel Borik 020 712 215; f 020 712 433; www.hotelborik.hr. Clean, simple dbls with HB for €72–120 in season.

Villa Vesna f 020 712 183; www.bebic.hr. Just out of Lumbarda, this guesthouse & restaurant has dbls with HB for around €80.

Pansion Marinka-Bire f 020 712 007. Nice apartments with views down to the sea. They also have their own wine, & frequent tasting sessions.

VELA LUKA Right at the other end of the island is Korčula's largest town, Vela Luka. It's much maligned, and in the past was known only for its shipyard and fish-processing factory, but with a great situation, at the head of a well-sheltered bay, and industry slowing down, the town is increasingly a tourist destination in its own right. It has a cheerful heart, a handful of good places to stay, brilliant beaches on nearby offshore islands, and good transport connections. Direct buses come from Dubrovnik and Korčula town, and it's also on the main ferry and catamaran lines running from Split to Hvar to Vela Luka to Lastovo.

The **tourist office** (f 020 813 619; www.tzvelaluka.hr), on the front, can provide you with maps and local information.

Where to stay

Dalmacija f 020 812 022; www.humhotels.hr. Situated right on the waterfront, with clean if rather plain dbls at €80 in season.

Pension Hotel Jadran 020 812 022; www.humhotels.hr. Located near to the Dalmacija, it has dbls for €60 in season.

If you want a private room then the place to go is Mediterano Tourist Agency (Obala 3; 020 813 832; www.mediterano.hr), who will sort you out in a jiffy – expect to pay around €30 for a double room in summer.

What to see and do If you're here for any time, it's well worth making the effort to walk out of town to an impressive **Neolithic cave**, Vela Špilje – check with the tourist office for visiting times. There's also an **olive oil mill** (Oil Mill Zlokić; Ulica 6/13; m 098 92 95 073) just outside town, which has a display on traditional olive oil production.

If you're feeling more hedonistic, an attractive alternative to the Big Cave (Vela Špilje means 'Big Cave'; Vela Luka means 'Big Bay') is to take one of the thrice-daily boats to the lovely little island of **Proizd**, right off Korčula's northwestern tip. This has several pebble beaches and some of the clearest waters I've ever swum in. There's a cheerful restaurant operational between the first and last boats, and a couple of naturist beaches, if that's your thing. Otherwise just enjoy the sea and sunshine – there's absolutely nothing else to do here. You can also rent yourself a boat from the quayside in Vela Luka (at around 200kn a day, plus 30kn for fuel), and motor out to the even closer island, Ošjak, which is almost within Vela Luka's harbour – it has lovely beaches and is popular with romantic couples; hardly surprising as the name means 'island of love'.

LASTOVO

A dozen kilometres south of Korčula is the island of Lastovo, barely 10km long. Like Vis (see page 306), it was off-limits for half a century and only opened up in 1989. In 2006 Lastovo and its archipelago gained the status of a nature park. Tourists are still comparatively rare, though numbers are growing rapidly.

It's a low-key destination, with (as yet) only one large(ish) hotel – in Pasadur at the western end of the island – and nothing remotely like nightlife. But if you like lobster, fresh white wine, a chance to meet the local people, and peace and quiet, then Lastovo's your place – unless you come during the carnival, when it goes berserk in a small-town sort of way, especially on Poklad's Tuesday (see below).

GETTING THERE Lastovo is the last stop for the daily ferry and catamaran from Split to Vela Luka (on Korčula), with boats arriving at Ubli in the early evening and leaving at the crack of dawn (before 05.00), effectively meaning you can't 'do' the island in less than two nights. It takes over five hours for the ferry to come from Split (75 minutes from Vela Luka), but under three hours on the catamaran (45 minutes from Vela Luka).

A bus meets the incoming boats in Ubli, and takes you the 10km to the village of Lastovo, spread out on a steep hillside facing away from the sea and sheltered from the *bura*. The **tourist office** (\/f *020 801 018*), right where the bus stops, has sporadic hours, but always opens when the bus comes in.

WHERE TO STAY AND EAT The tourist office (see above) can furnish you with a basic map and fix you up with a private room. You can also try www.lastovo.net and www.lastovoapartments.com. Otherwise there's the **Hotel Solitudo** (*Uvala Pasadur;* \ *020 802-100; www.hotel-solitudo.com*), which has 73 rooms out at Pasadur. Doubles go for about € 112. **Konoba Augusta Insula** (\ *020 801 167; www.augustainsula.com*) serves up excellent dishes at Zaklopatica, in the north of the island.

WHAT TO SEE AND DO There's nothing much to see in town – a handful of small 15th- to 17th-century churches pretty much sums it up – but do make the hike up to the ruined French fort right at the top of the hill, dating from 1810. It's now a weather station, with fabulous views.

You can also walk to various other hamlets on the island – the total population is well under 1,000 – which give access to the few points from which swimming is really an option. More attractive by far is to persuade a local boat owner to take you out to one of the string of islands to the east (the Lastovo archipelago). Here you'll find old lighthouses, pebble and rock beaches, and very, very few other people.

Poklad Festival Lastovo's biggest annual festival is Shrove Tuesday (known here as Poklad Tuesday), which brings home expatriates from around the world to take part in the ritual humiliation and slaughter of Poklad.

Legend has it that Poklad was an unfortunate messenger sent by pirates to tell Lastovo to surrender, or else. The local people prayed hard and the pirate fleet was duly scuppered by a storm, leaving the luckless Poklad to be paraded round town on a donkey, run down a long rope, and then burned to death. Charming.

The festival pretty much follows the legend, though it's a luckless puppet rather than messenger which gets to play the lead. First off the puppet is paraded round town on the donkey, after which it's slid down a 300m-long rope from the top of town to the bottom, complete with firecrackers going off from its feet. On arrival it's met by uniformed men brandishing drawn swords, before being hauled back up the hill for another two descents. The whole thing ends with Poklad being put back on the donkey before being speared and burned à la Guy Fawkes – though you won't see the Lastovo sword dances on bonfire nights in Britain. It's an extraordinary spectacle.

Appendix I

LANGUAGE

The official language is Croatian, written using a Latin alphabet. For 98.5% of the population, this is their mother tongue. Croatian is a tough language to learn, but words are nothing like as difficult to pronounce as you'd think, since every letter always has a unique pronunciation – albeit often not the same as in English. Although you're unlikely to have time to learn much Croatian, grab at least a handful of words and phrases to take with you – the effort will be richly rewarded.

The language comes from the group usually described by linguists as Serbo-Croat, meaning that Serbs, Croats and Bosnians can readily understand each other – not that you'd necessarily know this, judging by the strife of the past 20 (or even 200) years. Within Croatia itself, there are also regional variations and dialects, with the one you'll most likely notice being the three different ways Croats have of saying 'what?'. The official version – used in the media – is the Slavonian '*Što?*', but in the Zagreb you'll hear '*kaj?*' and along the coast it's invariably '*ča?*'.

The use of the Latin alphabet is largely to do with religion, and the east–west division of the Roman empire – it was in Croatia in the 9th century that Sts Cyril and Methodius invented the Glagolitic alphabet (see Glagolitic Alley, in Istria), which was converted by St Clement, in Ohrid (now in the Former Yugoslav Republic of Macedonia), into the Cyrillic alphabet, variants of which are now used throughout the Orthodox world. You won't see Cyrillic – unless you happen into an Orthodox or Greek Catholic church, or you're travelling on into neighbouring Serbia, Bosnia or Montenegro.

Most people – especially in the capital and along the coast – speak at least one foreign language, with German very widely spoken, and English being increasingly taught and popular among the young. Italian is understood by many on the coast and islands.

PRONUNCIATION Croatian words aren't anything like as hard to pronounce as you might expect them to be – just concentrate on pronouncing each letter the same way every time, and you won't go far wrong.

A	as in **pa**rty
B	as in **bed**
C	as in fa**ts**, ba**ts**
Č, č	as in nur**tu**re, cul**tu**re
Ć, ć	as in **ch**ew, **ch**ump
D	as in **d**ote
Đ, đ	as in **G**eorge, **j**am (sometimes written Dj, dj, to help non-natives)
E	as in **pe**t
F	as in **f**ree
G	as in **g**oat
H	as in **h**at
I	as in f**ee**t, p**i**zza
J	as in **y**et
K	as in **k**ept

L	as in **l**eg
M	as in **m**other
N	as in **n**o
O	as in h**o**t
P	as in **p**ie
R	as in **air**
S	as in **s**and
Š, š	as in **sh**ovel, **ch**ampagne
T	as in **t**oo
U	as l**oo**k
V	as in **v**ery
Z	as in **z**oo
Ž, ž	as in trea**su**re

WORDS AND PHRASES
Courtesies

hello/bye (informal)	*bok* (only used in Zagreb – even more familiar is *bok bok* – in other areas *bog*)
cheers!	*živjeli!* [**zhi**-vel-ee]
good morning	*dobro jutro* [**dob**-ro you-tro]
good day	*dobar dan* [**dob**ber dan]
good evening	*dobra večer* [**dob**-ro vetch-air]
good night (on leaving)	*laku noć* [**la**koo notch]
good luck (as a salutation)	*sretno* (old miners' greeting) [**sret**-no]
how are you?	*kako ste?* [ka-ko stay]
I'm fine, thank you	*dobro, hvala* [**dob**-ro, hfar-la]
please/thank you	*molim/hvala* [mo-**leem**/hfar-la]
thank you very much	*hvala lijepo* [hfar-la lee-**ye**po]
excuse me	*oprostite/sori* [o-pros-ti-te/sorry]
goodbye	*doviđenja* [**doe**-vee **jen**-ya]

Basic words

yes/no	*da/ne* [dar/**nay**] (nema = emphatic no) [nay-ma]
that's right	*tako je* [ta-ko yay]
OK	*OK* [okay]
Maybe	*možda* [mozh-da]
large/small	*veliko/malo* [veli-ko/mar-lo] (*velika/mala* are feminine forms)
more/less	*više/manje* [vee-sh/man-ye]
good/bad	*dobro/loše* [**dob**-ro/lo-sh]
hot/cold	*toplo/hladno* [top-lo/hlad-no]
toilet	*zahod* [zar-hod] (also *toalet* [toe-a-let], *WC* [vay-say])
men/women	*muški/ženski* [moosh-kee/zhen-skee]

Numbers

zero	*nula* [**noo**-la]	nine	*devet* [**dev**-et]
one	*jedan* [**yeh**-dan]	ten	*deset* [**deh**-set]
two	*dva* [dvar]	twelve	*dvanaest* [**dvar**-na-est]
three	*tri* [tree]	fifteen	*petnaest* [**pet**-na-est]
four	*četiri* [**tchet**-ree]	twenty	*dvadeset* [**dvar**-deh-set]
five	*pet* [pet]	fifty	*pedeset* [**ped**-deh-set]
six	*šest* [shest]	one hundred	*sto* [**sto**]
seven	*sedam* [**seh**-dam]	one thousand	*tisuću* [ti-su-chu]
eight	*osam* [**o**-sam]		

370

Questions

how?	*kako?* [ka-ko]
how much?	*koliko?* [ko-lee-ko]
what's your name?	*kako se zovete?* [ka-ko say zov-et-e]
when?	*kada?* [ka-da]
where?	*gdje?* [gud-ee-ya]
who?	*tko?* [teko]
why?	*zašto?* [**za**-shto]
do you speak English?	*govorite li engleski?* [gov-**or**-itay lee en-gleski]
how do you say in Croatian?	*kako se to kaže na hrvatskom?*
	[ka-ko say toe ka-zhay na hair-vat-skom]
can you tell me the way to…?	*možete mi reći put do…?*
	[mo-**zhet**-e mee retchi put doe]
how do I get to…?	*kako mogu doći do…?*
	[ka-ko moe-goo **do**-tchi doe]
is this the right way to…?	*je li ovo pravi put do…?*
	[yay lee ovo **prar**-vee put doe]
is it far to walk?	*je li daleko pješice…?*
	[yay lee dal-ecko **pyay**-shee-tzay]
can you show me on the map?	*možete mi pokazati na karti?*
	[mo-zhet-ay mee pocka-zarti na **kar**-tee]

Getting around

bus/bus station	*autobus/autobusni kolodvor*
	[out-o-**boos**/out-o-**boosnee** kolo-dvor]
train/express train	*vlak/brzi vlak* [vlack/berzee vlack]
main train station/railway station	*glavni kolodvor/željeznički kolodvor*
	[glav-nee kolo-dvor/zhel-**yez**-neetchki kolo-dvor]
plane/airport	*avion/zračna luka* or *aerodrom*
	[av-ion/zratch-na **loo**-ka or air-o-drom]
car/taxi	*auto/taxi* [out-o/taksi]
petrol/petrol station	*benzin/benzinska stanica*
	[ben-zin/ben-zinska **stan**-itza]
entrance/exit	*ulaz/izlaz* [oo-laz/iz-laz]
arrival/departure	*dolazak/odlazak* [do-laz-ak/odd-laz-ak]
open/closed	*otvoreno/zatvoreno* [otvo-ren-o/zatvo-ren-o]
here/there	*ovdje/tamo* [ov-**dee**-ye/**tar**-mo]
near/far	*blizu/daleko* [bleezu/dal-ecko]
left/right	*lijevo/desno* [lee-**yeh**-vo/des-no]
straight on	*ravno* [rav-no]
ahead/behind	*naprijed/iza* [nap-ree-**yed**/eeza]
up/down	*gore/dolje* [go-reh/dol-yeh]
under/over	*ispod/preko* [iz-pod/precko]
north/south	*sjever/jug* [syeh-vair/yoog]
east/west	*istok/zapad* [iz-tok/zap-ad]
road/bridge	*cesta/most* [tzesta/most]
hill/mountain	*brežuljak/planina* [breh-**zhul**-yak/plan-**eena**]
village/town	*selo/grad* [**seh**-lo/grad]
waterfall	*slap* [slap]

Accommodation

reservation	*rezervacija* [rez-air-vatz-eeya]
passport	*putovnica* [put-ov-nitza]

bed	*krevet* [krev-et]
room	*soba* [**so**-ba]
key	*ključ* [kl-youtch]
shower/bath	*tuš/kada* [toosh/ka-da]
hot water/cold water	*topla voda/hladna voda*
	[top-la **vo**-da/hlad-na **vo**-da]

Miscellaneous

tourist office	*turistički ured* [tooris-**titch**-kee u-red]
consulate	*konzularni ured* [kon-zoo-larnee u-red]
doctor	*liječnik/doktor* [lee-**yetch**-nik / doktor]
dentist	*zubar* [**zoo**-bar]
hospital/clinic	*bolnica/klinika* [bol-**nitza**/klin-icka]
police	*policija* [**pol**-itz-ee-yah]

Time

hour/minute	*sat/minuta* [sat/min-**oota**]
week/day	*tjedan/dan* [**tjeh**-dan/dan]
year/month	*godina/mjesec* [god-eena/mee-**yeh**-setz]
now/soon	*sada/uskoro* [sa-da/oos-koro]
today/tomorrow	*danas/sutra* [da-nas/**soo**-tra]
yesterday	*jučer* [**you**-tchair]
this week/next week	*ovaj tjedan/slijedeći tjedan*
	[ov-eye **tyeh**-dan/sli-**yeh**-detchi tyeh-dan]
morning/afternoon	*jutro/poslije podne* [**you**-tro/poz-**lee**-yeh pod-nay]
evening/night	*večer/noć* [**vetch**-air/notch]

Monday	*ponedjeljak* [pon-ed-**yeh**-lee-yak]
Tuesday	*utorak* [**oot**-or-ak]
Wednesday	*srijeda* [sree-**yeh**-da]
Thursday	*četvrtak* [**tchet**-ver-tak]
Friday	*petak* [**pet**-ak]
Saturday	*subota* [**soo**-bo-ta]
Sunday	*nedjela* [ned-yeh-la]

January	*siječanj* [**si**-yeh-tchan-yeh]
February	*veljača* [**vel**-ya-tcha]
March	*ožujak* [o-zhu-yak]
April	*travanj* [trav-anya]
May	*svibanj* [svee-banya]
June	*lipanj* [lip-anya]
July	*srpanj* [ser-panya]
August	*kolovoz* [kolo-voz]
September	*rujan* [**roo**-yan]
October	*listopad* [lis-toe-pad]
November	*studeni* [**stoo**-den-ee]
December	*prosinac* [pro-seen-atz]

spring	*proljeće* [pro-**lyeh**-tcheh]
summer	*ljeto* [lyeh-toe]
autumn	*jesen* [yeh-sen]
winter	*zima* [zeema]

Food and drink

bon appetit!   *dobar tek!* [**dob**-bar-tek]

Essentials

breakfast	*doručak* [do**roo**-tchak]
lunch	*ručak* [roo-tchak]
dinner	*večera* [**vetch**-air-a]
water	*voda* [**vo**-da]
beer	*pivo* [**pee**-vo]
draught beer	*točeno pivo* [totch-**ay**-no **pee**-vo]
wine	*vino* [**vee**-no]
white wine	*bijelo vino* [bee-**yello vee**-no]
white wine and soda	*špricer* (1dl)/*gemišt* (2dl) [spritzer/gem-**isht**]
red wine	*crno vino* [**tzair**-noe **vee**-noe]
rosé wine	*roze vino* [rozay **vee**-no]
house wine	*domaće vino* [dom-**atch**-ay **vee**-no]
spirit (generic)	*rakija* [**rak**-ee-ya]
spirit (from herbs)	*travarica* [trav-**are**-itza]
brandy	*lozovača* [lozov-atch-ka]
pear spirit	*kruškovača* [kroosh-kov-atch-a]
cold	*hladno* [**hlad**-no]
hot	*vruće* [**vroo**-tchay]
bread/bakery	*kruh/pekarnica* [kroo/pek-**are**-nitza]
jam	*džem* [d-zhem] (some say *pekmez* [**peck**-mez])
coffee	*kava* [ka-va]
tea	*čaj* [tchai – rhymes with 'try']
tea with milk	*crni čaj s mlijekom* [tzair-nee tchai soo mil-yeh-kom] (ask for black, otherwise you get fruit tea with milk…)
tea with lemon	*čaj s limunom* [tchai soo lee-**moon**-om]
sugar	*šećer* [**shetch**-air]
salt	*slan* [slun]
cheese	*sir* [seer]
soup	*juha* [**you**-ha]
thick soup/bean soup	*ragu/grah* [ra-**goo**/grar] (not a vegetarian dish!)
egg (eggs)	*jaje (jaja)* [**ya**-yay/(ya-ya)]
ham	*šunka* [**shoon**ka]
air-dried ham	*pršut* [per-**shoot**]
fish	*riba* [**ree**ba]
chips	*pomfrit* [pom-**freet**]
meat	*meso* [**may**-so]
vegetables	*povrće* [pov-air-tchay]
fruits	*voće* [**vo**-tchay]
homemade	*domaće* [dom-**a**-tchay]
grilled	*sa roštilja* [sar rosh-til-ya]
baked	*pečeno* [petch-**ay**no]
fried	*prženo* [per-**zay**no]
boiled	*kuhano* [**koo**-hano]
stuffed	*punjeno* [**poon**-yayno]

Fish

sardines	*sardina* [sar-**dee**na]
mackerel	*skuša* [skoo-sha]

AI

bass	*lubin/brancin* [loo-ben/bran-tsin]
grey mullet	*cipal* [tzi-pal]
red mullet	*barbun* [bar-boon]
bream	*zubatac* [zoo-ba-tatz]
tuna	*tuna* [toona]
trout	*pastrva* [pas-ter-va]
salmon	*losos* [loss-oss]
perch	*grgeč* [gerg-etch]
zander/pike-perch	*smuđ* [smoodge]
catfish	*som* [som]
pike	*štuka* [shtooka]
squid	*lignje* [lig-nyeh]
mussels	*dagnje/školjka* [dag-nyeh/shkol-yeka]
	(in general – there are other variants)
oysters	*oštrige/kamenice* [osh-trig-eh/kam-en-itz-eh]
prawns/crayfish	*škampi* [shkampi]
crab	*rak* [rak]
lobster	*jastog* [yah-stog]
spicy fish stew	*fiš paprikaš* [fish pap-rik-ash]

Meat

beef	*govedina* [goved-**eena**]
pork	*svinjetina* [svin-yet-**eena**]
lamb	*janjetina* [yan-yet-**eena**]
mutton	*ovčetina* [ov-tchet-**eena**]
veal	*teletina* [tel-et-**eena**]
chicken	*piletina* [pil-et-**eena**]
spicy smoked sausage	*kulen* [**kool**-en]
goulash	*gulaš* [**gool**-ash]
wild boar	*divlja svinja* [div-**lee**-yah **svin**-yah]
moussaka	*musaka* [**b**-sarka]
meat stews	
pepper and tomato	*sataraš* [**sat**-a-rash]
rice and tomato	*đuveč* [**joo**-vetch]
beef with dumplings	*pašticada* [pash-titz-arda]
stuffed vine leaves	*sarma* [sar-ma]

Vegetables and side-dishes

potatoes	*krumpir* [krum-**peer**]
rice	*riža* [**ree**-zha]
green peppers	*paprika* [pap-**reeka**]
onion	*luk* [look]
garlic	*češnjak* [tchesh-nyak]
asparagus	*šparoge* [shpar-o-gay]

Salads

salad	*salata* [sal-ata]
green salad	*zelena salata* [**zel**-ena sal-ata]
cucumber	*krastavac* [krasta-vatz]
cabbage	*kupus* [koo-poos]
tomato	*rajčica* [rai-tch-itza]
	(*paradajz* [para-dize] is sometimes used)
mixed	*miješana* [me-**yeh**-sha-na]

with chillies and cheese	*grčka* [**gertch**-ka]
with tomatoes and cheese	*šopska* [**shop**-ska] (many also use name *grčka*)

Fruit

orange	*narandža* [na-**rand**-zha]
	(or *naranča* [na-rand-tcha])
lemon/s	*limun* [lee-**moon**]
plums	*šljive* [sh**lyee**-vay]
melon	*dinja* [din-ya]
pears	*kruške* [kroosh-kay]
peaches	*breskve* [**bresk**-vay]
cherries	*trešnje* [tresh-nee-yeh]
strawberries	*jagode* [yag-o-deh]
apples	*jabuke* [ya-**boo**-keh]
bananas	*banane* [ba-na-neh]

Appendix 2

FURTHER INFORMATION

BOOKS Many of the books listed here are long out of print, but most can be found secondhand – either by trawling through old bookshops, or online at places like Abe Books (*www.abebooks.com*).

History/politics

Glenny, Misha *The Fall of Yugoslavia* Penguin, 1996, 3rd edition. Former BBC correspondent's account of how it all fell apart – compelling, if depressing, reading.

Goldstein, Ivo *Croatia: A History* C Hurst & Co, 1999, 2nd edition. Well-balanced Croat historian's view of Croatian history from Roman times to the present day. Hard to find, however, in spite of its relatively recent publication.

Harris, Robin *Dubrovnik – A History* Saqi, 2003. Solid doorstop of a hardback with a wealth of fascinating insight and wonderful illustrations – but quite a dent in the wallet at 25 quid.

Hawkesworth, Celia *Zagreb: A Cultural and Literary History* Signal Books, 2007

Macan, Trpimir, and Šentija, Josip *The Bridge – A Short History of Croatia* Journal of Croatian Literature, Zagreb, 1992. Notwithstanding the rather fanatical introduction by Yale professor Ivo Banac, this is an excellent history of Croatia in two sections, the first up to 1941, and the second from 1941 to 1991, with semi-official status. Hard to find, however.

Margaritoni, Marko *Dubrovnik, Between History and Legend* Dubrovnik State Archives, 2001. Lots of wonderful tales and legends by a local author. Order the book for 200kn from the man himself, at marko.margaritoni@du.htnet.hr.

Rheubottom, David *Age, Marriage and Politics in 15th-century Ragusa* Oxford University Press, 2000. Intriguing – if at times weighty – insights into the inter-relationships between politics, kinship and marriage in the republic. Expensive, however, even secondhand.

Silber, Laura et al *The Death of Yugoslavia* Penguin, 1996. Tie-in with the BBC series, and while it's not wholly successful without having seen the programmes it's still a frightening blow-by-blow account of the events of the war.

Tanner, Marcus *Croatia: A Nation Forged in War* Yale University Press, 1997. An excellent and detailed history of Croatia, by the Independent's correspondent during the conflict – probably the best book currently available.

Travel and travel literature

Abraham, Rudolf *Walking in Croatia* Cicerone, 2010, 2nd edition. Detailed guide to hiking in Croatia, covering the main ranges (Velebit, Gorski kotar etc) as well as well as islands and areas further inland.

Abraham, Rudolf *The Mountains of Montenegro* Cicerone, 2007. Detailed guide to hiking in Montenegro.

Bardwell, Sandra *Croatia: car tours and walks* Sunflower, 2006. Excellent guide aimed at walkers and hikers, and covering the coast and islands as well as the Plitvice Lakes.

Bridge, Ann *Illyrian Spring* Chatto & Windus, 1935. Rather fey (very 1930s) novel about a lady painter working her way down the Adriatic coast in search of inspiration and love – but great descriptions of Pula, Split, Dubrovnik etc.

Clancy, Tim *Bosnia & Herzegovina: The Bradt Travel Guide* Bradt, 2004. Comprehensive guide to this newly accessible Croatian neighbour.

Coyler, William *Dubrovnik and the Southern Adriatic Coast from Split to Kotor* Ward Lock & Co, 1967. Delightfully dated mini hardback with lots of black and white photos.

Cuddon, J A *The Companion Guide to Jugoslavia*. Collins, 1986, 3rd edition.

Delalle, Ivan *Guide to Trogir* Trogir Tourist Board, 1963. Brilliant black-and-white pocket guide to the city first published in 1936; full of words like 'historiography'.

Goldring, Patrick *Yugoslavia* Collins Holiday Guides, 1967. Marvellous pocket guide featuring mainly Croatia – worth buying just for the splendid peasant smoking a roll-up on the cover.

Kaplan, Robert *Balkan Ghosts* Picador, 1994. The author uses his 1990 odyssey through the Balkans to explain the conflictual politics across the region in depth. Relatively easily available secondhand.

Kastrapeli et al *Dubrovnik Tourist Guide* Minčeta, 1967. Classic 1960s mini guide – gushing prose, black and white photos.

Letcher, Piers *Dubrovnik: The Bradt City Guide* Bradt, 2007, 2nd edition. Just the guide you need if you're doing Dubrovnik in detail – or venturing across the border into nearby Bosnia & Herzegovina or Montenegro.

Letcher, Piers and Parkes, Sarah *Zagreb: The Bradt City Guide* Bradt, 2007. The perfect guide if you're doing Zagreb in-depth.

McKelvie, Robin and McKelvie, Jenny *Slovenia: The Bradt Travel Guide* Bradt, 2005. The essential companion if you're going on to Slovenia.

Murphy, Dervla *Through the Embers of Chaos – Balkan Journeys* John Murray, 2002. Brilliant account of a long cycle tour through the Balkans, including Dubrovnik, Split, Zagreb etc. Truly a wonderful, inspirational book.

Phillips, Adrian and Scotchmer, Jo *Hungary: The Bradt Travel Guide* Bradt, 2005. You couldn't look for a better guide if you're heading on to Hungary.

Rellie, Annalisa *Montenegro: The Bradt Travel Guide* Bradt, 2005, 2nd edition. Essential reading if you're digging deeper into Montenegro.

Voynovitch, Count Louis *A Historical Saunter through Dubrovnik (Ragusa)* Jadran, 1929. Nearly impossible to find, but marvellous short guide to the city from a 1929 perspective. It's amazing how little has changed in spite of both a world and a local war.

West, Rebecca *Black Lamb and Grey Falcon* Canongate Books, 1993. Without question the most comprehensive (1,200pp) and best-written account of Yugoslavia in the 1930s. Rebecca West travelled widely in Croatia (and the other republics of the former Yugoslavia) in 1936 and 1937, and spent five years researching and writing this book. Fatally flawed in places, and terribly naïve in its conclusion, it's nonetheless by turns funny, passionate and tragic – and always brilliantly opinionated. If you come across the original two-volume hardback from the 1940s, go for it; there are excellent black-and-white photographs.

Natural history

Gorman, Gerard *Central and Eastern European Wildlife* Bradt, 2008. Excellent all-round introduction, well illustrated.

Mitchell-Jones, A J et al *The Atlas of European Mammals* Academic Press, 1999. Heavyweight guide to nearly 200 species, with distribution maps and a real wealth of detail.

Polunin, Oleg *Flowers of Greece and the Balkans* Oxford, 1980. The definitive guide to the flora of southeast Europe.

Still, John *Butterflies and Moths of Britain and Europe* Collins, 1996. Handy guide for lepidopterists.

Svensson Lars *Collins Bird Guide* Collins, 2001, new edition. Simply excellent guide to European birds, with truly wonderful illustrations. The many Collins field guides (trees, flowers etc) are also highly recommended.

Art and culture

Beretić, Dubravka *Art Treasures of Dubrovnik* Jugoslavija Guides, 1968. Obscure guide dating back to the communist heyday – still remarkably accurate, however.

Crnković, Vladimir *The Art of the Hlebine School* Croatian Museum of Naïve Art, 2005. Definitive snapshot of Croatia's naïve art scene and the people and places behind it, by the curator of the museum in Zagreb himself.

Pavičic, Liliana and Pirker-Mosher, Gordana *The Best of Croatian Cooking* Hippocrene Books, 2000. You're back home and missing those Croatian dishes? This is the book for you.

Radovčić, Jakov *Gorjanović-Kramberger and Krapina Early Man* Školska Knjiga Zagreb, 1988. Fascinating biography of the man who discovered and created the Krapina Man collection, by the current curator and the man responsible for the new museum opening in Krapina.

Susnjar, Ante *Croatian-English/English-Croatian Dictionary and Phrasebook* Hippocrene, 2000. Good, helpful reference guide to the language.

WEBSITES There's a mountain of information and a wealth of resources concerning Croatia on the web. Here's a selection:

General

www.croatia.hr The National Tourist Board's exemplary website, with a huge amount of practical information and the phone number of most hotels, travel agencies and campsites across the country.

www.tportal.hr/imenik Croatia's online phone directory (including an English-language option). Just what you need when it turns out the phone number listed in this guide has already changed.

www.dalmacija.net Dalmatia's own tourist information site, with online hotel bookings etc. See below for the sailing section.

www.zagreb-touristinfo.hr The official site of the Zagreb Tourist Board. Excellent, detailed information about just about everything you'd want to know.

www.hr The so-called 'Croatian Homepage', an English-language site featuring 7,500 links in hundreds of categories, all about Croatia. You can spend many hours here.

www.hr/wwwhr/useful.en.html In the same site, features especially useful categorised links.

www.uhpa.hr Association of Croatian Travel Agencies. A good way of finding out what can be organised for you.

meteo.hr (and mirror site at www.dhmz.htnet.hr) Croatian Meteorological Service. Click on the flag for English and find out everything you ever wanted to know about Croatia's weather, including forecasts.

www.hfhs.hr Croatian Youth Hostel Association. Gives the latest situation concerning youth hostels across the country, and works as a central reservation office, though make sure you have your confirmation with you when you actually show up at the hostels.

www.diving-hrs.hr Croatian Diving Federation. Small (the English part, anyway) but useful site listing the rules and regs for scuba diving.

www.eudict.com Excellent English-Croatian and Croatian-English dictionaries, though you need to have some idea of context as the responses are provided without separate definitions (the word 'set' gives you 41 different responses, for example).

www.mdc.hr Muzejski dokumentacijski centar, with details of most museums in Croatia.

Transport

www.adriatica.it, www.jadrolinija.hr, www.blueline-ferries.com The three main ferry companies plying the Adriatic.

www.akz.hr Zagreb bus station, mostly in Croatian. Nonetheless excellent site with all arrivals and departures, including costs – go to Vozni red (timetable) from the homepage.

www.hznet.hr National Railway. Even in Croatian you'll be able to find your way round the timetables, and the standard fares are displayed when the times come up – online booking is a bit trickier.

www.ina.hr The state-owned oil company. Complete with fuel prices and the locations and opening hours of every petrol station in the country.

www.hak.hr Hrvatski Autoklub (Croatian Automobile Club). In Croatian only, though it does have an interactive traffic snarl-up area in English.

Government and media

www.mvp.hr Ministry of Foreign Affairs. Everything you need to know about visa requirements etc.

www.dzs.hr Croatian Bureau of Statistics. Everything you ever wanted to know.

www.mint.hr Ministry of Tourism. More statistics and all the forms you'll need if you're planning on starting a business in the Croatian tourist industry.

www.hrt.hr Croatian national TV and radio (in Croatian).

www.tportal.hr Big customisable portal in Croatian from the main telecoms provider, with daily news bulletins, weather, traffic, entertainment etc.

www.hic.hr/english/index.htm Another news portal (also available in Croatian and Spanish).

Hiking

http://en.plsavez.hr/hr Hrvatski planinarski savez (Croatian Mountaineering Association)

Sailing

www.aci-club.hr Adriatic Croatia International Club homepage, with full details of everything ACI offers.

www.dalmacija.net An excellent section on sailing is included on the Split & Dalmatia County Tourist Information Service, with lots of information on marinas, regulations for foreign boats, where to get charts, weather, safety etc.

www.planetadria.com Lots of good sailing resources, including rentals, hire, etc.

www.itinerances-dalmates.com Excellent French site with lots of rentals and good information on sailing, winds, guides etc. In French, of course.

www.portfocus.com/croatia Site providing links to harbours and ports in Croatia, as well as weather and satellite photos.

Bradt Travel Guides

www.bradtguides.com

Africa

Access Africa: Safaris for People with Limited Mobility	£16.99
Africa Overland	£16.99
Algeria	£15.99
Angola	£17.99
Botswana	£16.99
Cameroon	£15.99
Cape Verde Islands	£14.99
Congo	£15.99
Eritrea	£15.99
Ethiopia	£16.99
Gambia, The	£13.99
Ghana	£15.99
Johannesburg	£6.99
Madagascar	£15.99
Malawi	£15.99
Mali	£14.99
Mauritius, Rodrigues & Réunion	£15.99
Mozambique	£13.99
Namibia	£15.99
Niger	£14.99
Nigeria	£17.99
North Africa: Roman Coast	£15.99
Rwanda	£14.99
São Tomé & Principe	£14.99
Seychelles	£14.99
Sierra Leone	£16.99
Sudan	£15.99
Tanzania, Northern	£14.99
Tanzania	£17.99
Uganda	£16.99
Zambia	£17.99
Zanzibar	£14.99
Zimbabwe	£15.99

Britain

Britain from the Rails	£14.99
Go Slow: Devon & Exmoor	£14.99
Go Slow: Norfolk & Suffolk	£14.99
Go Slow: North Yorkshire: Moors, Dales & more	£14.99

Europe

Abruzzo	£14.99
Albania	£15.99
Armenia	£14.99
Azores	£13.99
Baltic Cities	£14.99
Belarus	£14.99
Bosnia & Herzegovina	£14.99
Bratislava	£9.99
Budapest	£9.99
Bulgaria	£13.99
Cork	£6.99
Croatia	£13.99

Cyprus see North Cyprus	
Czech Republic	£13.99
Dresden	£7.99
Dubrovnik	£6.99
Estonia	£14.99
Faroe Islands	£15.99
Georgia	£14.99
Greece: The Peloponnese	£14.99
Helsinki	£7.99
Hungary	£15.99
Iceland	£14.99
Kosovo	£14.99
Lapland	£13.99
Latvia	£13.99
Lille	£9.99
Lithuania	£14.99
Ljubljana	£7.99
Luxembourg	£13.99
Macedonia	£15.99
Malta	£12.99
Montenegro	£14.99
North Cyprus	£12.99
Riga	£6.99
Serbia	£14.99
Slovakia	£14.99
Slovenia	£13.99
Spitsbergen	£16.99
Switzerland Without a Car	£14.99
Tallinn	£6.99
Transylvania	£14.99
Ukraine	£15.99
Vilnius	£6.99
Zagreb	£6.99

Middle East, Asia and Australasia

Bangladesh	£15.99
Borneo	£17.99
China: Yunnan Province	£13.99
Great Wall of China	£13.99
Iran	£15.99
Iraq: Then & Now	£15.99
Israel	£15.99
Kazakhstan	£15.99
Kyrgyzstan	£15.99
Lake Baikal	£15.99
Maldives	£15.99
Mongolia	£16.99
North Korea	£14.99
Oman	£13.99
Shangri-La: A Travel Guide to the Himalayan Dream	£14.99
Sri Lanka	£15.99
Syria	£15.99
Tibet	£13.99
Yemen	£14.99

The Americas and the Caribbean

Amazon, The	£14.99
Argentina	£15.99
Bolivia	£14.99
Cayman Islands	£14.99
Chile	£16.95
Colombia	£16.99
Costa Rica	£13.99
Dominica	£14.99
Grenada, Carriacou & Petite Martinique	£14.99
Guyana	£14.99
Nova Scotia	£14.99
Panama	£14.99
Paraguay	£14.99
St Helena	£14.99
Turks & Caicos Islands	£14.99
Uruguay	£14.99
USA by Rail	£14.99
Yukon	£14.99

Wildlife

100 Animals to See Before They Die	£16.99
Antarctica: Guide to the Wildlife	£15.99
Arctic: Guide to the Wildlife	£15.99
Central & Eastern European Wildlife	£15.99
Chinese Wildlife	£16.99
East African Wildlife	£19.99
Galápagos Wildlife	£15.99
Madagascar Wildlife	£16.99
New Zealand Wildlife	£14.99
North Atlantic Wildlife	£16.99
Pantanal Wildlife	£16.99
Peruvian Wildlife	£15.99
Southern African Wildlife	£18.95
Sri Lankan Wildlife	£15.99
Wildlife and Conservation Volunteering: The Complete Guide	£13.99

Eccentric Guides

Eccentric Australia	£12.99
Eccentric Britain	£13.99
Eccentric Cambridge	£6.99
Eccentric London	£13.99

Others

Something Different for the Weekend	£9.99
Weird World	£14.99
Your Child Abroad: A Travel Health Guide	£10.95

WIN £100 CASH!
READER QUESTIONNAIRE

**Send in your completed questionnaire for the chance to win
£100 cash in our regular draw**

All respondents may order a Bradt guide at half the UK retail price – please
complete the order form overleaf.
(Entries may be posted or faxed to us, or scanned and emailed.)

We are interested in getting feedback from our readers to help us plan future Bradt
guides. Please answer ALL the questions below and return the form to us in order
to qualify for an entry in our regular draw.

Have you used any other Bradt guides? If so, which titles? . . . .
. . . .
What other publishers' travel guides do you use regularly? . . . .
. . . .
Where did you buy this guidebook? . . . .
What was the main purpose of your trip to Croatia (or for what other reason did
you read our guide)? eg: holiday/business/charity etc.. . . . .
. . . .
What other destinations would you like to see covered by a Bradt guide?
. . . .
Would you like to receive our catalogue/newsletters?
YES / NO (If yes, please complete details on reverse)
If yes – by post or email? . . . .
Age (circle relevant category) 16–25   26–45   46–60   60+
Male/Female (delete as appropriate)
Home country . . . .
Please send us any comments about our guide to Croatia or other Bradt Travel
Guides. . . . .
. . . .
. . . .
. . . .

Bradt Travel Guides
23 High Street, Chalfont St Peter, Bucks SL9 9QE, UK
☏ +44 (0)1753 893444 **f** +44 (0)1753 892333
e info@bradtguides.com
www.bradtguides.com

CLAIM YOUR HALF-PRICE BRADT GUIDE!

Order Form

To order your half-price copy of a Bradt guide, and to enter our prize draw to win £100 (see overleaf), please fill in the order form below, complete the questionnaire overleaf, and send it to Bradt Travel Guides by post, fax or email.

Please send me one copy of the following guide at half the UK retail price

Title	Retail price	Half price
...	....	....

Please send the following additional guides at full UK retail price

No	Title	Retail price	Total
...	......	....	....
...	......	....	....
...	......	....	....

Sub total	....
Post & packing	....
(£2 per book UK; £4 per book Europe; £6 per book rest of world)	
Total	....

Name ....

Address..

Tel .... Email ....

☐ I enclose a cheque for £........ made payable to Bradt Travel Guides Ltd

☐ I would like to pay by credit card. Number: ....

Expiry date: ... / ...   3-digit security code (on reverse of card) .....

Issue no (debit cards only) .....

☐ Please add my name to your catalogue mailing list.

☐ I would be happy for you to use my name and comments in Bradt marketing material.

Send your order on this form, with the completed questionnaire, to:

Bradt Travel Guides CRO4
23 High Street, Chalfont St Peter, Bucks SL9 9QE
☏ +44 (0)1753 893444   f +44 (0)1753 892333
e info@bradtguides.com   www.bradtguides.com

NOTES

NOTES

Index

Entries in **bold** indicate main entries; those in *italics* indicate maps